POKéMON
10th Anniversary Pokédex

Eric 'ECM' Mylonas

Prima Games
A Division of Random House, Inc.
3000 Lava Ridge Court
Roseville, CA 95661
1-800-733-3000
www.primagames.com

Product Manager: Mario De Govia
Project Editor: Alaina Yee
Design: Keating Design
Layout: Jamie Knight and Melissa Smith

ISBN: 0-7615-5377-0
Library of Congress Catalog Card Number: 2006903653
Printed in the United States of America

06 07 08 09 LL 10 9 8 7 6 5 4 3 2 1

Contents

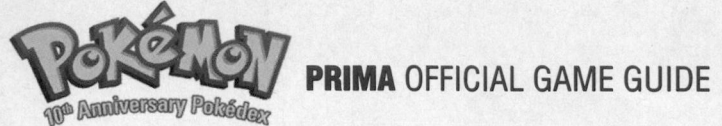

Exclusive Artwork by Ken Sugimori

SNORLAX™

VENUSAUR™

CHARIZARD™

MEWTWO™

FireRed & LeafGreen Soundtrack Released in Japan on April 26, 2004
"GBA Pokémon *FireRed & LeafGreen* Music Super Complete"
by Ken Sugimori

"Pokémon Gallery: Encounter with Shiny Pokémon" by Ken Sugimori

The Bare Essentials

Calling All Poké Maniacs!

Welcome to Prima's Official Guide for the ever-expanding world of *Pokémon*! Here you'll find information on every Pokémon discovered thus far.

That's right, this book is the definitive source for info on every Pokémon from Bulbasaur (001) up to and including the most recently discovered Pokémon, Deoxys (386), and every one in between. It also provides their locations throughout the three most recent *Pokémon* titles as well as stats, moves, and types.

In addition to the Pokémon entries, we also give you a very solid primer for getting started in the world of *Pokémon*, from how to "catch 'em all" to tips on battling and breeding. If you need Pokémon info, we've got you covered!

So, without further ado, start flipping those pages and immerse yourself in the world of *Pokémon* and the creatures that inhabit Kanto, Hoenn, and Orre and have taken your world—and your play time—by storm!

note Though you'll also find ample strategy and abridged walkthroughs for the most recent Pokémon titles (*Ruby/Sapphire*, *FireRed/LeafGreen*, and *Colosseum*), this book's primary purpose is to serve as a complete Pokémon encyclopedia. If you're after specific game information, you should seek out *Prima's Official Game Guides* for the respective titles for all the information you could possibly want about every last nook and cranny of those games.

The Essentials

FIRE [AND ICE AND WATER AND...] IT UP!

Pokémon Types

Normal	Grass	Fighting	Flying	Rock	Dark
Fire	Electric	Poison	Psychic	Ghost	Steel
Water	Ice	Ground	Bug	Dragon	

 VS.

Electric meets Water: Water takes it on the chin

There are seventeen different types of Pokémon, with many actually being dual-types: Bulbasaur, for example, is both Grass- and Poison-type. These different types determine the best matches. Check out the Damage Multiplier table to determine which types work best against one another.

The most effective way to play the game is with a well-balanced party made of six of the seventeen Pokémon types (many Pokémon actually belong to two types). This way, you are always equipped, in some fashion, to take advantage of *Pokémon*'s Rock, Paper, Scissors-style gameplay.

Essentially, each type of Pokémon has strengths and weaknesses versus other types, with damage multipliers applied accordingly. For example, while a Fire-type Pokémon may be super effective against a Grass type, Water has the same damage multiplier effect against Fire. Thus, succeeding in battle really comes down to effectively matching Pokémon type-for-type. A well-balanced party has enough Pokémon straddling each category so that you almost always have the right team to devastate your opponent.

The following tables show how the various matches shake out. Damage can go as high as 4x if a Pokémon is comprised of two classes that would each normally take 2x damage from a specific type. For example, a Pokémon that is both Steel- and Electric-type would be *very* vulnerable to Ground-type attacks and, if the attacking Pokémon's level is within 5 levels of the defending Pokémon's level, it means an instant KO.

Damage Multiplier Table

Condition	Multiplier
Move is the same type as Pokémon	1.5x
Move is effective against opponent's type	2–4x
Move scores a Critical Hit!	2x
Pokémon has an item that raises the move's Strength	1.1x
Rain Dance or Sunny Day effects (depending on move)	1.5x or .5x

Pokémon Move Compatibility

	NORMAL	FIRE	WATER	GRASS	ELECTRIC	ICE	FIGHTING	POISON	GROUND	FLYING	PSYCHIC	BUG	ROCK	GHOST	DRAGON	DARK	STEEL
NORMAL													▲	■			▲
FIRE		▲	▲	●		●						●	▲		▲		●
WATER		●	▲	▲					●				●		▲		
GRASS		▲	●	▲				▲	●	▲		▲	●		▲		▲
ELECTRIC			●	▲	▲				■	●					▲		
ICE		▲	▲	●		▲			●	●					●		▲
FIGHTING	●					●		▲		▲	▲	▲	●	■		●	●
POISON				●				▲	▲				▲	▲			■
GROUND		●		▲	●			●		■		▲	●				●
FLYING				●	▲		●					●	▲				▲
PSYCHIC							●	●			▲					■	▲
BUG		▲		●			▲	▲		▲	●			▲		●	▲
ROCK		●				●	▲		▲	●		●					▲
GHOST	■										●			●		▲	▲
DRAGON															●		▲
DARK							▲				●			●		▲	▲
STEEL		▲	▲		▲	●							●				▲

● = 2x damage   ▲ = 1/2 damage   ■ = It has no effect

Move Tutor Stats

You'll find lists of all the moves a Pokémon can perform at the end of their entries in the Pokédex. To find the stats for each of those moves refer back to this table.

MOVE TUTOR

Name	Type	Power	ACC	PP	Name	Type	Power	ACC	PP	Name	Type	Power	ACC	PP
Body Slam*†	Normal	85	100	15	Ice Punch**†	Ice	75	100	15	Seismic Toss*†	Fighting	—	100	20
Counter*†	Fighting	—	100	20	Icy Wind**†	Ice	55	95	15	Sleep Talk**	Normal	—	—	10
Defense Curl**†	Normal	—	—	40	Mega Kick*†	Normal	120	85	5	Snore**†	Normal	40	100	15
Double-Edge*	Normal	120	100	15	Mega Punch*†	Normal	80	75	20	Softboiled**				
Dream Eater*†	Psychic	100	100	15	Metronome**	Normal	—	100	10	Substitute*	Normal	—	—	10
Dynamicpunch**	Fighting	100	50	5	Mimic*	Normal	—	100	10	Swagger**	Normal	—	90	15
Endure**†	Normal	—	—	10	Mud-Slap**†	Ground	20	100	10	Swift**†	Normal	60	—	20
Explosion*	Normal	250	100	5	Psych Up**†	Normal	—	—	10	Swords Dance*†	Normal	—	—	30
Fire Punch**†	Fire	75	100	15	Rock Slide*†	Rock	75	90	10	Thunderpunch**†	Electric	75	100	15
Fury Cutter**	Bug	10	95	20	Rollout**	Rock	30	90	20	Thunder Wave*†	Electric	—	100	20

* FireRed/LeafGreen and Emerald Only   ** Emerald Only   † Battle Frontier tutor move (Emerald)

Catch 'Em All!

Catching Them All: On One Cartridge

You may have noticed at the outset of *Ruby, Sapphire, FireRed, LeafGreen,* and *Emerald* that your Pokédex simply doesn't have enough space to view 386 Pokémon. The key to collecting them all is to obtain the National Pokédex— sort of an über-Pokédex, that has enough memory to contain a massive number of Pokémon. Here's how to get it:

FireRed and LeafGreen

Defeat the Elite Four, then make sure you have 60 Pokémon captured (not just viewed!) and speak to Professor Oak in Pallet Town.

Ruby and Sapphire

Trade any Pokémon to *FireRed* and *LeafGreen* (via the Game Link Cable).

This goes for any of the four cartridges, so if your friend happens to have earned the National Pokédex in *FireRed* and *LeafGreen*, simply trade a Pokémon to him and, voilà, you'll have it, too, on your *Ruby* and *Sapphire* cartridge.

If you want to fill your Pokédex, you're going to have to catch a lot of Pokémon. Bear in mind that each edition of *Pokémon* has its own unique roster and you have to trade with the other versions (either your own or a friend's) to fill out the National Pokédex.

The following sections detail exactly how to collect the vast majority of the Pokémon in the games.

TALL GRASS

If you've played the game(s) before, you know that the best source of Pokémon is tall grass. Simply wading into these vast fields of foliage, lilting in the breeze, sends Pokémon running—hopefully into you. Contact here is entirely random and, once you find a Pokémon, a battle begins. From there, your goal is to wear it down and use the various Poké Balls at your disposal to capture it and add it to the Pokédex.

Tools of the Trade: Poké Balls

There's only one way to catch a wild Pokémon, and that's via the Trainer's tool of choice: the Ball! Poké Balls come in various types, each with specific traits.

The shops scattered about each of the continents sell three types of Balls: standard Poké Balls, Great Balls and Ultra Balls. Each is slightly more expensive than the previous one and each is successively more efficient.

That being said, luck does play a very large part in how effective Poké Ball can be in a given situation. While you might guess that Ultra Balls are the best in every situation, it isn't always so.

Your best bet is to learn through experimentation which works best for you. After all, there's no need to lay down the big bucks for Ultra Balls if a regular Poké Ball does the trick.

Bear in mind that *Ruby, Sapphire,* and *Emerald* have a great many more Poké Balls than *FireRed* and *LeafGreen* including a whole host of specialty Balls. These are *not* transferable.

FISHING

While running through the tall grass is a great way to catch lots of Pokémon, you may need to head to a pond, bay, or sea to obtain those elusive Water-type Pokémon. To do this, however, you need to locate the various fishing rods (Old, Good, and Super) scattered throughout the games. Once equipped, you simply need to move to a body of water and use the rod to fish. If you get a bite, a battle ensues with the Pokémon you hooked. Poké Balls determine whether you walk away empty-handed.

SURFING

First off, before even attempting to Surf, you need to track down HM03 Surf and teach it to a compatible Pokémon. From there, approach a body of water and hit Ⓐ to take to the sea astride your Pokémon. Simply swim about until a Pokémon throws itself at you. From there, you know the drill: Weaken the invader and then cap things off with a handy Poké Ball.

EVOLVING

LV18   LV36

Pidgey's Evolutionary path

After you've caught a Pokémon, there's every chance that, at some point, you'll want to evolve it into another form. This is a good idea for a number of reasons:

- Every time a Pokémon evolves, that new form is added to your Pokédex as another Pokémon, so that's one less Pokémon you'll have to trade or catch. This is the easiest way to add Pokémon to your Pokédex—especially if you have access to a Day Care Center (more on those in the breeding section).

- An evolved Pokémon, generally, ends up more powerful than its forebear, giving you a decided edge in combat. For example, a Level 55 Venusaur is stronger than a Level 55 Bulbasaur (Venusaur's initial form).

Clearly there's value in seeing your Pokémon attain newer levels of development, but that naturally begs the question of how to do it. . . .

Evolve Via Experience

LV16   LV36

Charmander's Evolutionary path

The most straightforward way to evolve a Pokémon is simply by having your Pokémon fight, and defeat, other Pokémon throughout your adventure. This way they gain experience which, once you reach a certain level, automatically triggers the change into that particular Pokémon's next form. Of course, the Pokémon you want to evolve in this manner *must* battle and cannot simply sit on the sideline, as it won't gain any experience that way.

 Experience is shared if you use multiple Pokémon in the course of a single battle.

Evolution Canceling

You may occasionally not want a Pokémon to evolve. The transformation begins when the Pokémon reaches the minimum number of experience points required to trigger it. At that point, during the animation sequence, quickly press Ⓡ to cancel the Evolution, keeping the Pokémon in its current state.

Why would you want to prevent the Evolution? Sometimes a Pokémon learns better moves by staying in a less-evolved state until reaching a predetermined level.

Sandshrew

For example, Sandshrew automatically evolves into Sandslash when it reaches Level 22. However, if you'd like to earn the move Swift a bit sooner, you would do well to cancel the Evolution. Normally Sandslash would get Swift at Level 33, but Sandshrew earns it at Level 30, thus you get that move three levels earlier.

caution Unless you have an Everstone, every time your Pokémon reaches another level (and you want it to stay in its current form), you'll need to hit Ⓑ to cancel the Evolution. Otherwise, let it go to automatically transition to its next state.

Trade 'Em All!

One of the most fun (and only) ways to collect a large quantity of Pokémon is via trading with other players. Whether it's trading via the Game Link Cable or the wireless adapter, meet your friends in the Union Room located above each and every Pokémon Center in the games.

Evolve via Trade

Pokémon in this category include Kadabra and its next evolutionary state, Alakazam. You must trade it to a friend to induce this Evolution and no amount of leveling up will do Kadabra any good after it evolves from Abra.

EVOLVE VIA TRADE

Evolution via Trade with Item

Pokémon in this group include the evolved form of Onix, Steelix. It won't go on to its final Evolution without being traded with a Metal Coat attached. Needless to say, once your friend has hold of a Pokémon who's fairly tricky to acquire, you may have some trouble getting it back!

TRADE WITH METAL COAT

Via Evolution Stones

The final special Evolution category includes those Pokémon such as Vulpix and Pikachu who won't evolve into their final forms (Ninetales and Raichu) without the use of a specific stone.

THUNDER STONE

To trigger these transitions, simply select the Item in question from your bag and use it on the Pokémon you want to evolve. From there, nature will take its course.

 See the Pokédex section for exactly when a given Pokémon will evolve to its next stage and how.

Via Friendship

On rare occasions, a few Pokémon (basically all those that fall into the pre-evolutionary category) will only evolve when their Friendship level is maxed out. How do you know when you're on the right track? Well, in *Ruby*, *Sapphire*, and *Emerald*, you need to visit the Friendship Rater in Verdanturf Town and in *FireRed* and *LeafGreen* you need to visit your Rival's sister in Pallet Town *after* you conquer the Elite Four.

FRIENDSHIP

 A Pokémon's Friendship level is determined by how well you treat it: Letting it faint too much, letting negative Status Effects linger, and feeding it bitter-tasting berries and potions all have a negative effect on your Pokémon's Friendship.

Pokémon Breeding 101

 **note** For starters, in order to even consider breeding, you need access to a Day Care Center.

THE BASICS

When you drop off two of your Pokémon at Day Care, there's a chance that they'll end up producing an Egg. Of course, there is a whole host of rules involved for those two Pokémon to begin down the path of parenthood and we cover these rules in levels, starting here with the most basic.

First, you need a male and a female Pokémon, as two of the same gender cannot reproduce. You also cannot breed relatives, for example, mother with son or father with daughter. You can, however, check their compatibility with the Day Care attendant, though the tables that follow tell you all you need to know in that area.

Also, certain Pokémon are not capable of being bred at all. Typically this involves the very powerful or very rare Pokémon, so don't think you're going to have Groudon and Mewtwo produce any earth-shattering offspring.

note The offspring of two Pokémon will be the base form of the mother; for example, breeding a female Fearow with a male Togepi will yield a Level 5 Spearow. Gender, however, is determined at random.

So why breed Pokémon when you can simply catch them in the vast majority of cases? Simply put, you get much more powerful Pokémon by breeding than you could ever catch in the wild, as well as moves that are only obtainable via breeding (Egg Moves are listed in the Pokédex).

Inheriting Stats

The entire inheritance process, while semi-scientific, also features pitfalls because of the random nature of gender-assignment. Because a female baby inherits her stats from her father and a male baby inherits his stats from his mother, it can take several tries to get the desired effect. Patience, in these cases, is a virtue.

Inheriting Moves

Your efforts at customizing a Pokémon show in the moves with which your new Pokémon is born. These moves come in three types: Learned Moves, Inherited Moves, and Hereditary Moves.

Learned Moves are the ones that your Pokémon would start with if caught in the wild at Level 5.

Inherited Moves cover any move or TM your Pokémon would normally learn, although not at Level 5. These Moves are inherited from the male Pokémon used in the breeding.

Hereditary Moves (also known as "Egg Moves") are also inherited from the father, but they are special. Egg Moves are ones the newly hatched Pokémon would not normally be able to learn. Of the Pokémon you can obtain through breeding, most of them can inherit up to eight moves through breeding that they would not normally learn.

Here's how it works: When a baby Pokémon hatches from its Egg, it starts with the moves that a wild Pokémon of the same level would know. So, for example, a newly hatched Bagon will know one move, Rage, while a newly hatched Pichu will know two, Thundershock and Charm. The remaining spaces, not filled with Learned Moves, can be filled with other types of Inherited Moves.

Don't worry if your bred Pokémon starts with too many naturally Learned Moves. Inherited and Egg Moves take precedence over Learned Moves, so if your target Pokémon starts with three moves and stands the chance to inherit two more moves, the first move on the list of Learned Moves is erased and replaced by one of the two Inherited Moves.

Next, if both the male and female Pokémon used in breeding know a move that the baby Pokémon would learn later in life (after Level 5), then the baby Pokémon hatches with this move. For example, if you breed two Pokémon who currently know Defense Curl, then the baby Pokémon starts with that move too. This works well when you want your baby Pokémon to start with a high-powered move that it would otherwise learn later in life.

Similarly, if the male Pokémon knows an attack that the offspring can learn in the form of a Technical Machine, the baby Pokémon will inherit that move. This lets you "reuse" your TMs by breeding the attacks they contain into other Pokémon.

BREEDING FOR HEREDITARY MOVES

To breed for Egg Moves, find a compatible male Pokémon who can learn the desired Hereditary Move, then mate it with a female version of the target Pokémon.

Sometimes, the Pokémon who learn the desired Egg Move are not compatible with the target Pokémon. In this case, you need to find another compatible Pokémon to act as an intermediate. Breed the two Pokémon, and if the baby born is male (and you should continue breeding those two Pokémon until they produce a male Pokémon), then you can breed it with the target female Pokémon.

CRACK 'EM ALL!

Hatching the Eggs is a pretty straightforward process: After you collect the Egg (remember an Egg takes up one slot in your roster) you simply have to carry it around with you till it hatches. And, to make things more interesting, there isn't a universal number of steps required to hatch an Egg, so some take longer than others to yield a bouncing baby Pokémon.

To speed up the process a bit, you can do two things:

- Breed two of the same Pokémon, for example, two Doduo (unfortunately this isn't terribly practical or very useful).

- Transfer Pokémon from a different version of the game as they have different ID numbers, which speeds up the process—this is fairly easy if you have a Pokémon in *Ruby/Sapphire* and transfer it to *FireRed/LeafGreen* or *Emerald* or vice versa.

Pokémon Compatibility

The following charts provide all the info you need to determine whether Pokémon are compatible with one another. This way, you know what to expect. And, as is usually the case, there are a couple of rules:

- Pokémon belonging to Group X cannot produce Eggs, period.

- In order to breed, the two Pokémon in question, in addition to the aforementioned rules, can only produce Eggs with members of the same group.

With that in mind, check out the following charts and see what kind of super-Pokémon you can come up with!

Group X: Cannot Breed

Articuno	Metang
Azurill	Metagross
Baltoy	Nidoking
Beldum	Nidoqueen
Claydol	Rayquaza
Cleffa	Regice
Elekid	Regirock
Electrode	Registeel
Igglybuff	Shedinja
Groudon	Smoochum
Kyogre	Solrock
Latias	Starmie
Latios	Staryu
Lunatone	Tangela
Mew	Togepi
Mewtwo	Tyrogue
Moltres	Unown
Pichu	Voltorb
Magby	Wynaut
Magnemite	Zapdos
Magneton	

Group 1: Plant-Group Pokémon

Bayleef	Nuzleaf
Bellossom	Oddish
Bellsprout	Paras
Breloom	Parasect
Bulbasaur	Roselia
Cacnea	Seedot
Cacturne	Shiftry
Chikorita	Shroomish
Exeggcute	Skiploom
Exeggutor	Sunflora
Gloom	Sunkern
Hoppip	Tropius
Ivysaur	Venusaur
Jumpluff	Victreebel
Lombre	Vileplume
Lotad	Weepinbell
Ludicolo	
Meganium	

Group 2: Bug-Group Pokémon

Ariados	Paras
Beautifly	Parasect
Beedrill	Pineco
Butterfree	Pinsir
Cascoon	Scizor
Caterpie	Scyther
Dustox	Shuckle
Flygon	Silcoon
Forretress	Spinarak
Gligar	Surskit
Heracross	Trapinch
Illumise	Venomoth
Kakuna	Venonat
Ledian	Vibrava
Ledyba	Volbeat
Masquerain	Weedle
Metapod	Wurmple
Nincada	Yanma
Ninjask	

Group 3: Flying-Group Pokémon

Aerodactyl	Pidgey
Altaria	Pidgeot
Crobat	Pidgeotto
Dodrio	Skarmory
Doduo	Spearow
Farfetch'd	Swablu
Fearow	Swellow
Golbat	Taillow
Hoothoot	Togetic
Murkrow	Wingull
Natu	Xatu
Noctowl	Zubat
Pelipper	

Group 4: Humanshape-Group Pokémon

Abra	Kadabra
Alakazam	Machamp
Cacnea	Machoke
Cacturne	Machop
Drowzee	Magmar
Electabuzz	Makuhita
Hariyama	Medicham
Hitmonchan	Meditite
Hitmonlee	Mr. Mime
Hitmontop	Sableye
Hypno	Spinda
Illumise	Volbeat
Jynx	

Group 5: Mineral-Group Pokémon

Geodude	Porygon
Glalie	Porygon2
Golem	Snorunt
Graveler	Steelix
Nosepass	Sudowoodo
Onix	

Group 6: Indeterminate-Group Pokémon

Banette	Kirlia
Castform	Koffing
Chimecho	Magcargo
Dusclops	Misdreavus
Duskull	Muk
Gardevoir	Ralts
Gastly	Shuppet
Gengar	Slugma
Grimer	Swalot
Gulpin	Weezing
Haunter	Wobbuffet

Group 7: Ground-Group Pokémon

Absol	Phanpy
Aipom	Pikachu
Ampharos	Piloswine
Arbok	Ponyta
Arcanine	Poochyena
Blaziken	Primeape
Camerupt	Psyduck
Combusken	Quagsire
Cyndaquil	Quilava
Delcatty	Raichu
Delibird	Rapidash
Dewgong	Rattata
Diglett	Raticate
Donphan	Rhydon
Dugtrio	Rhyhorn
Dunsparce	Sandshrew
Ekans	Sandslash
Electrike	Sealeo
Eevee	Seedot
Espeon	Seel
Exploud	Sentret
Flaaffy	Seviper
Flareon	Shiftry
Furret	Skitty
Girafarig	Slaking
Golduck	Slakoth
Granbull	Smeargle
Growlithe	Sneasel
Grumpig	Snubbull
Houndoom	Spheal
Houndour	Spinda
Jolteon	Spoink
Kecleon	Swinub
Linoone	Tauros
Loudred	Teddiursa
Manectric	Torkoal
Mankey	Torchic
Mareep	Typhlosion
Mawile	Umbreon
Meowth	Ursaring
Mightyena	Vaporeon
Miltank	Vigoroth
Nidoran ♀	Vulpix
Nidoran ♂	Wailmer
Nidorina	Wailord
Nidorino	Walrein
Ninetales	Whismur
Numel	Wooper
Nuzleaf	Zangoose
Persian	Zigzagoon

Group 8: Water 1-Group Pokémon

Azumarill	Masquerain
Blastoise	Milotic
Clamperl	Mudkip
Corphish	Omanyte
Corsola	Omastar
Crawdaunt	Pelipper
Croconaw	Politoed
Dewgong	Poliwag
Dragonair	Poliwhirl
Dragonite	Poliwrath
Dratini	Psyduck
Feebas	Quagsire
Feraligatr	Seaking
Golduck	Sealeo
Gorebyss	Seel
Horsea	Slowbro
Huntail	Slowking
Kabuto	Slowpoke
Kabutops	Spheal
Kingdra	Squirtle
Lapras	Surskit
Lombre	Swampert
Lotad	Totodile
Ludicolo	Walrein
Mantine	Wartortle
Marill	Wingull
Marshtomp	Wooper

Group 9: Water 2-Group Pokémon

Barboach	Relicanth
Carvanha	Seaking
Chinchou	Sharpedo
Goldeen	Quilfish
Gyarados	Remoraid
Lanturn	Wailmer
Luvdisc	Wailord
Magikarp	Whiscash
Octillery	

Group 10: Water 3-Group Pokémon

Anorith	Kingler
Armaldo	Krabby
Cloyster	Lileep
Corphish	Omanyte
Corsola	Omastar
Cradily	Shellder
Crawdaunt	Staryu
Kabuto	Tentacool
Kabutops	Tentacruel

Group 11: Monster-Group Pokémon

Aggron	Marowak
Ampharos	Marshtomp
Aron	Mudkip
Bayleef	Nidoran ♀
Blastoise	Nidoran ♂
Bulbasaur	Nidorina
Charizard	Nidorino
Charmander	Pupitar
Charmeleon	Rhydon
Chikorita	Rhyhorn
Croconaw	Sceptile
Cubone	Slowbro
Exploud	Slowking
Feraligatr	Slowpoke
Flaaffy	Snorlax
Grovyle	Squirtle
Ivysaur	Swampert
Kangaskhan	Totodile
Lairon	Treecko
Lapras	Tropius
Larvitar	Tyranitar
Lickitung	Venusaur
Loudred	Wartortle
Meganium	Whismur
Mareep	

Group 12: Fairy-Group Pokémon

Azumarill	Mawile
Blissey	Minun
Breloom	Pikachu
Castform	Plusle
Chansey	Raichu
Clefable	Roselia
Clefairy	Shroomish
Delcatty	Skiploom
Glalie	Skitty
Granbull	Snorunt
Hoppip	Snubbull
Jigglypuff	Togetic
Jumpluff	Wigglytuff
Marill	

Group 13: Dragon-Group Pokémon

Altaria	Gyarados
Arbok	Horsea
Bagon	Kingdra
Charizard	Magikarp
Charmander	Milotic
Charmeleon	Salamence
Dragonair	Sceptile
Dragonite	Seadra
Dratini	Seviper
Ekans	Shelgon
Feebas	Swablu
Grovyle	Treecko

Version Exclusives

This section details the Pokémon exclusive to each of the principal games: *Ruby*, *Sapphire*, *FireRed*, *LeafGreen*, and *Colosseum*. It is *impossible* to collect all 386 Pokémon without having access to *all* of these games.

 The following lists are organized by the Pokémon's Evolutionary hierarchy.

FireRed

Oddish	Arcanine
Gloom	Scyther
Vileplume	Scizor
Bellossom	Shellder
Elekid	Cloyster
Electabuzz	Wooper
Psyduck	Quagsire
Golduck	Murkrow
Ekans	Skarmory
Arbok	Quilfish
Growlithe	Delibird

Ruby

Seedot	Zangoose
Nuzleaf	Solrock
Shiftry	Groudon
Mawile	Latios

LeafGreen

Bellsprout	Pinsir
Weepinbell	Staryu
Victreebel	Starmie
Magby	Azurill
Magmar	Marill
Slowpoke	Azumarill
Slowbro	Misdreavus
Slowking	Sneasel
Sandshrew	Remoraid
Sandslash	Octillery
Vulpix	Mantine
Ninetales	

Sapphire

Kyogre	Seviper
Lotad	Lunatone
Lombre	Latias

Colosseum

Chikorita	Hoothoot
Bayleef	Noctowl
Meganium	Sudowoodo
Cyndaquil	Sunkern
Quilava	Sunflora
Typhlosion	Gligar
Totodile	Snubbull
Croconaw	Granbull
Feraligatr	Miltank

 Even if you don't have all the games (and all versions), you can still get certain Pokémon because there is some overlap between versions. See the Pokédex entries for more info.

Unique Pokémon

The following Pokémon are known as Unique Pokémon and are, generally, very tough to catch. In many cases you get only *one* shot at collecting them. Finally, be aware that catching some of them (for example, Entei, Raikou, and Suicune) depend on which Pokémon you start the game with. So, in other words, you have to play *FireRed/LeafGreen* through three times each (picking a different starter Pokémon each time) to nab these Unique Pokémon after completing the main quest.

FireRed/LeafGreen

Articuno	Mewtwo
Deoxys	Moltres
Entei	Raikou
Ho-Oh (also catchable in *Colosseum*)	Suicune
	Zapdos
Lugia	

Emerald

Groudon	Latias
Kyorgre	Latios

Ruby/Sapphire

Groudon (*Sapphire* only)	Registeel
Kyogre (*Ruby* only)	Latias (*Sapphire* only)
Regirock	Latios (*Ruby* only)
Regice	Rayquaza

XD

Articuno	Moltres
Lugia	Zapdos

Pokédex

Pokédex Alphabetical Listing

001 Bulbasaur™

GRASS   POISON

GENERAL INFO
SPECIES: Seed Pokémon
HEIGHT: 2'04"
WEIGHT: 15 lbs.
ABILITY: Overgrow
Bulbasaur's Grass-type attack power multiplies by 1.5 when its HPs get low.

STATS
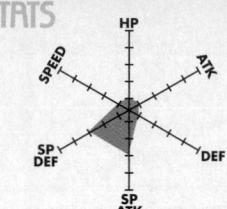

EVOLUTIONS

LV16   LV32

LOCATION(S):

RUBY Rarity: **None**
Trade from *FireRed/LeafGreen*

SAPPHIRE Rarity: **None**
Trade from *FireRed/LeafGreen*

FIRERED Rarity: **Only One**
Starter Pokémon from Professor Oak in Pallet Town

LEAFGREEN Rarity: **Only One**
Starter Pokémon from Professor Oak in Pallet Town

COLOSSEUM Rarity: **None**
Trade from *FireRed/LeafGreen*

EMERALD Rarity: **None**
Trade from *FireRed/LeafGreen*

XD Rarity: **None**
Trade from *FireRed/LeafGreen*

MOVES

Level	Attack	Type	Power	ACC	PP
—	Tackle	Normal	35	95	35
4	Growl	Normal	—	100	40
7	Leech Seed	Grass	—	90	10
10	Vine Whip	Grass	35	100	10
15	Poisonpowder	Grass	—	75	15
15	Sleep Powder	Grass	—	75	15
20	Razor Leaf	Grass	55	95	25
25	Sweet Scent	Normal	—	100	20
32	Growth	Normal	—	—	40
39	Synthesis	Grass	—	—	5
46	Solarbeam	Grass	120	100	10

TM/HM

TM/HM#	Name	Type	Power	ACC	PP
TM06	Toxic	Poison	—	85	10
TM09	Bullet Seed	Grass	10	100	30
TM10	Hidden Power	Normal	—	100	15
TM11	Sunny Day	Fire	—	—	5
TM17	Protect	Normal	—	—	10
TM19	Giga Drain	Grass	60	100	5
TM21	Frustration	Normal	—	100	20
TM22	Solarbeam	Grass	120	100	10
TM27	Return	Normal	—	100	20
TM32	Double Team	Normal	—	—	15
TM36	Sludge Bomb	Poison	90	100	10
TM42	Facade	Normal	70	100	20
TM43	Secret Power	Normal	70	100	20
TM44	Rest	Psychic	—	—	10
TM45	Attract	Normal	—	100	15
HM01	Cut	Normal	50	95	30
HM04	Strength	Normal	80	100	20
HM05	Flash	Normal	—	70	20
HM06	Rock Smash	Fighting	20	100	15

EGG MOVES*

Name	Type	Power	ACC	PP
Charm	Normal	—	100	20
Curse	—	—	—	10
Grasswhistle	Grass	—	55	15
Light Screen	Psychic	—	—	30
Magical Leaf	Grass	60	—	20
Petal Dance	Grass	70	100	20
Safeguard	Normal	—	—	25
Skull Bash	Normal	100	100	15

*Learned Via Breeding

MOVE TUTOR
FireRed/LeafGreen and *Emerald* Only

Body Slam*	Double-Edge	Mimic
Substitute	Swords Dance*	

*Battle Frontier tutor move (*Emerald*)

002 Ivysaur™

GRASS   POISON

GENERAL INFO
SPECIES: Seed Pokémon
HEIGHT: 3'03"
WEIGHT: 29 lbs.
ABILITY: Overgrow
Ivysaur's Grass-type attack power multiplies by 1.5 when its HPs get low.

STATS

EVOLUTIONS

LV16   LV32

LOCATION(S):

RUBY Rarity: **None**
Trade from *FireRed/LeafGreen*

SAPPHIRE Rarity: **None**
Trade from *FireRed/LeafGreen*

FIRERED Rarity: **Evolve**
Evolve Bulbasaur

LEAFGREEN Rarity: **Evolve**
Evolve Bulbasaur

COLOSSEUM Rarity: **None**
Trade from *FireRed/LeafGreen*

EMERALD Rarity: **None**
Trade from *FireRed/LeafGreen*

XD Rarity: **None**
Trade from *FireRed/LeafGreen*

MOVES

Level	Attack	Type	Power	ACC	PP
—	Tackle	Normal	35	95	35
—	Growl	Normal	—	100	40
—	Leech Seed	Grass	—	90	10
10	Vine Whip	Grass	35	100	10
15	Poisonpowder	Grass	—	75	15
15	Sleep Powder	Grass	—	75	15
22	Razor Leaf	Grass	55	95	25
29	Sweet Scent	Normal	—	100	20
38	Growth	Normal	—	—	40
47	Synthesis	Grass	—	—	5
56	Solarbeam	Grass	120	100	10

TM/HM

TM/HM#	Name	Type	Power	ACC	PP
TM06	Toxic	Poison	—	85	10
TM09	Bullet Seed	Grass	10	100	30
TM10	Hidden Power	Normal	—	100	15
TM11	Sunny Day	Fire	—	—	5
TM17	Protect	Normal	—	—	10
TM19	Giga Drain	Grass	60	100	5
TM21	Frustration	Normal	—	100	20
TM22	Solarbeam	Grass	120	100	10
TM27	Return	Normal	—	100	20
TM32	Double Team	Normal	—	—	15
TM36	Sludge Bomb	Poison	90	100	10
TM42	Facade	Normal	70	100	20
TM43	Secret Power	Normal	70	100	20
TM44	Rest	Psychic	—	—	10
TM45	Attract	Normal	—	100	15
HM01	Cut	Normal	50	95	30
HM04	Strength	Normal	80	100	20
HM05	Flash	Normal	—	70	20
HM06	Rock Smash	Fighting	20	100	15

MOVE TUTOR
FireRed/LeafGreen and *Emerald* Only

Body Slam*	Double-Edge	Mimic
Substitute	Swords Dance*	

*Battle Frontier tutor move (*Emerald*)

003 Venusaur™

GRASS | POISON

GENERAL INFO
SPECIES: Seed Pokémon
HEIGHT: 6'07"
WEIGHT: 221 lbs.
ABILITY: Overgrow

Venusaur's Grass-type attack power multiplies by 1.5 when its HPs get low.

STATS

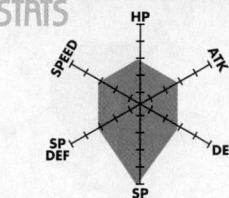

EVOLUTIONS

LV16   LV32

LOCATION(S):

RUBY	**Rarity:**	**None**
Trade from *FireRed/LeafGreen*		
SAPPHIRE	**Rarity:**	**None**
Trade from *FireRed/LeafGreen*		
FIRERED	**Rarity:**	**Evolve**
Evolve Ivysaur		
LEAFGREEN	**Rarity:**	**Evolve**
Evolve Ivysaur		
COLOSSEUM	**Rarity:**	**None**
Trade from *FireRed/LeafGreen*		
EMERALD	**Rarity:**	**None**
Trade from *FireRed/LeafGreen*		
XD	**Rarity:**	**None**
Trade from *FireRed/LeafGreen*		

MOVES

Level	Attack	Type	Power	ACC	PP	Level	Attack	Type	Power	ACC	PP
—	Tackle	Normal	35	95	35	22	Razor Leaf	Grass	55	95	25
—	Growl	Normal	—	100	40	29	Sweet Scent	Normal	—	100	20
—	Leech Seed	Grass	—	90	10	41	Growth	Normal	—	—	40
—	Vine Whip	Grass	35	100	10	53	Synthesis	Grass	—	—	5
15	Poisonpowder	Grass	—	75	15	65	Solarbeam	Grass	120	100	10
15	Sleep Powder	Grass	—	75	15						

TM/HM

TM/HM#	Name	Type	Power	ACC	PP	TM/HM#	Name	Type	Power	ACC	PP
TM05	Roar	Normal	—	100	20	TM27	Return	Normal	—	100	20
TM06	Toxic	Poison	—	85	10	TM32	Double Team	Normal	—	—	15
TM09	Bullet Seed	Grass	10	100	30	TM36	Sludge Bomb	Poison	90	100	10
TM10	Hidden Power	Normal	—	100	15	TM42	Facade	Normal	70	100	20
TM11	Sunny Day	Fire	—	—	5	TM43	Secret Power	Normal	70	100	20
TM15	Hyper Beam	Normal	150	90	5	TM44	Rest	Psychic	—	—	10
TM17	Protect	Normal	—	—	10	TM45	Attract	Normal	—	100	15
TM19	Giga Drain	Grass	60	100	5	HM01	Cut	Normal	50	95	30
TM21	Frustration	Normal	—	100	20	HM04	Strength	Normal	80	100	15
TM22	Solarbeam	Grass	120	100	10	HM05	Flash	Normal	—	70	20
TM26	Earthquake	Ground	100	100	10	HM06	Rock Smash	Fighting	20	100	15

MOVE TUTOR
FireRed/LeafGreen and *Emerald* Only

Body Slam*	Double-Edge	Frenzy Plant
Mimic	Substitute	Swords Dance*

*Battle Frontier tutor move (*Emerald*)

---

004 Charmander™

FIRE

GENERAL INFO
SPECIES: Lizard Pokémon
HEIGHT: 2'00"
WEIGHT: 19 lbs.
ABILITY: Blaze

Charmander's Fire-type attack power multiplies by 1.5 when its HPs get low.

STATS

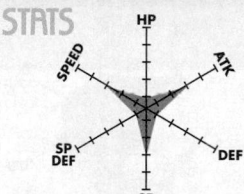

EVOLUTIONS

LV16   LV36

LOCATION(S):

RUBY	**Rarity:**	**None**
Trade from *FireRed/LeafGreen*		
SAPPHIRE	**Rarity:**	**None**
Trade from *FireRed/LeafGreen*		
FIRERED	**Rarity:**	**Only One**
Starter Pokémon from Professor Oak in Pallet Town		
LEAFGREEN	**Rarity:**	**Only One**
Starter Pokémon from Professor Oak in Pallet Town		
COLOSSEUM	**Rarity:**	**None**
Trade from *FireRed/LeafGreen*		
EMERALD	**Rarity:**	**None**
Trade from *FireRed/LeafGreen*		
XD	**Rarity:**	**None**
Trade from *FireRed/LeafGreen*		

MOVES

Level	Attack	Type	Power	ACC	PP	Level	Attack	Type	Power	ACC	PP
—	Scratch	Normal	40	100	35	25	Scary Face	Normal	—	90	10
—	Growl	Normal	—	100	40	31	Flamethrower	Fire	95	100	15
7	Ember	Fire	40	100	25	37	Slash	Normal	70	100	20
13	Metal Claw	Steel	50	95	35	43	Dragon Rage	Dragon	—	100	10
19	Smokescreen	Normal	—	100	20	49	Fire Spin	Fire	15	70	15

TM/HM

TM/HM#	Name	Type	Power	ACC	PP	TM/HM#	Name	Type	Power	ACC	PP
TM01	Focus Punch	Fighting	150	100	20	TM35	Flamethrower	Fire	95	100	15
TM02	Dragon Claw	Dragon	80	100	15	TM38	Fire Blast	Fire	120	85	5
TM06	Toxic	Poison	—	85	10	TM40	Aerial Ace	Flying	60	—	20
TM10	Hidden Power	Normal	—	100	15	TM42	Facade	Normal	70	100	20
TM11	Sunny Day	Fire	—	—	5	TM43	Secret Power	Normal	70	100	20
TM17	Protect	Normal	—	—	10	TM44	Rest	Psychic	—	—	10
TM21	Frustration	Normal	—	100	20	TM45	Attract	Normal	—	100	15
TM23	Iron Tail	Steel	75	75	15	TM50	Overheat	Fire	140	90	5
TM27	Return	Normal	—	100	20	HM01	Cut	Normal	50	95	30
TM28	Dig	Ground	60	100	10	HM04	Strength	Normal	80	100	15
TM31	Brick Break	Fighting	75	100	15	HM06	Rock Smash	Fighting	20	100	15
TM32	Double Team	Normal	—	—	15						

EGG MOVES*

Name	Type	Power	ACC	PP
Ancientpower	Rock	60	100	5
Beat Up	Dark	10	100	10
Belly Drum	Normal	—	—	10
Bite	Dark	60	100	25
Dragon Dance	Dragon	—	—	20
Outrage	Dragon	90	100	15
Rock Slide	Rock	75	90	10
Swords Dance	Normal	—	—	30

*Learned Via Breeding

MOVE TUTOR
FireRed/LeafGreen and *Emerald* Only

Body Slam*	Counter*	Double-Edge
Mega Kick*	Mega Punch*	Mimic
Rock Slide*	Seismic Toss*	Substitute
Swords Dance*		

*Battle Frontier tutor move (*Emerald*)

009 Blastoise™

GENERAL INFO
SPECIES: Shellfish Pokémon
HEIGHT: 5'03"
WEIGHT: 189 lbs.
ABILITY: Torrent

Blastoise's Water-type attack power multiplies by 1.5 when its HPs get low.

STATS
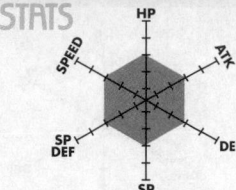

EVOLUTIONS

LV16   LV36

LOCATION[S]:

RUBY   **Rarity: None**
Trade from *FireRed/LeafGreen*

SAPPHIRE   **Rarity: None**
Trade from *FireRed/LeafGreen*

FIRERED   **Rarity: Evolve**
Evolve Wartortle

LEAFGREEN   **Rarity: Evolve**
Evolve Wartortle

COLOSSEUM   **Rarity: None**
Trade from *FireRed/LeafGreen*

EMERALD   **Rarity: None**
Trade from *FireRed/LeafGreen*

XD   **Rarity: None**
Trade from *FireRed/LeafGreen*

MOVES

Level	Attack	Type	Power	ACC	PP
—	Tackle	Normal	35	95	35
—	Tail Whip	Normal	—	100	30
—	Bubble	Water	20	100	30
—	Withdraw	Normal	—	—	40
13	Water Gun	Water	40	100	25
19	Bite	Dark	60	100	25
25	Rapid Spin	Normal	20	100	40
31	Protect	Normal	—	—	10
42	Rain Dance	Water	—	—	5
55	Skull Bash	Normal	100	100	15
68	Hydro Pump	Water	120	80	5

TM/HM

TM/HM#	Name	Type	Power	ACC	PP
TM01	Focus Punch	Fighting	150	100	20
TM03	Water Pulse	Water	60	95	20
TM05	Roar	Normal	—	100	20
TM06	Toxic	Poison	—	85	10
TM07	Hail	Ice	—	—	10
TM10	Hidden Power	Normal	—	100	15
TM13	Ice Beam	Ice	95	100	10
TM14	Blizzard	Ice	120	70	5
TM15	Hyper Beam	Normal	150	90	5
TM17	Protect	Normal	—	—	10
TM18	Rain Dance	Water	—	—	5
TM21	Frustration	Normal	—	100	20
TM23	Iron Tail	Steel	75	75	15
TM26	Earthquake	Ground	100	100	10
TM27	Return	Normal	—	100	20
TM28	Dig	Ground	60	100	10
TM31	Brick Break	Fighting	75	100	15
TM32	Double Team	Normal	—	—	15
TM42	Facade	Normal	70	100	20
TM43	Secret Power	Normal	70	100	20
TM44	Rest	Psychic	—	—	10
TM45	Attract	Normal	—	100	15
HM03	Surf	Water	95	100	15
HM04	Strength	Normal	80	100	15
HM06	Rock Smash	Fighting	20	100	15
HM07	Waterfall	Water	80	100	15
HM08	Dive	Water	60	100	10

MOVE TUTOR
FireRed/LeafGreen and *Emerald* Only

Body Slam*	Counter*	Double-Edge
Hydro Cannon	Mega Kick*	Mega Punch*
Mimic	Seismic Toss*	Substitute

*Battle Frontier tutor move (*Emerald*)

010 Caterpie™

GENERAL INFO
SPECIES: Worm Pokémon
HEIGHT: 1'00"
WEIGHT: 6 lbs.
ABILITY: Shield Dust

Protects Caterpie from being hit by any additional move effects.

STATS
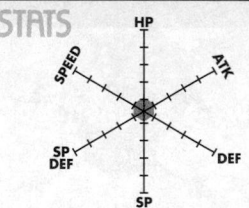

EVOLUTIONS
 LV7  LV10

LOCATION[S]:

RUBY   **Rarity: None**
Trade from *FireRed/LeafGreen*

SAPPHIRE   **Rarity: None**
Trade from *FireRed/LeafGreen*

FIRERED   **Rarity: Common**
Viridian Forest, Six Island, Route 25

LEAFGREEN   **Rarity: Common**
Viridian Forest, Six Island, Route 25

COLOSSEUM   **Rarity: None**
Trade from *FireRed/LeafGreen*

EMERALD   **Rarity: None**
Trade from *FireRed/LeafGreen*

XD   **Rarity: None**
Trade from *FireRed/LeafGreen*

MOVES

Level	Attack	Type	Power	ACC	PP
—	Tackle	Normal	35	95	35
—	String Shot	Bug	—	95	40

TM/HM

TM/HM#	Name	Type	Power	ACC	PP
None					

EGG MOVES*

Name	Type	Power	ACC	PP
None				

*Learned Via Breeding

MOVE TUTOR
FireRed/LeafGreen and *Emerald* Only
None

011 Metapod™

BUG

GENERAL INFO

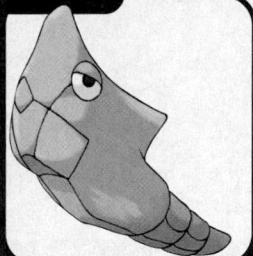

SPECIES: Cocoon Pokémon
HEIGHT: 2'04"
WEIGHT: 22 lbs.
ABILITY: Shed Skin

Enables Metapod to only have a status effect for one turn. Has a 30% chance of success.

STATS

EVOLUTIONS

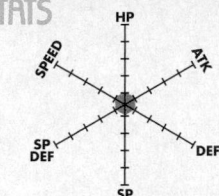 LV7  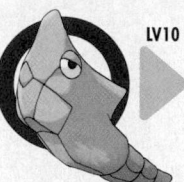 LV10

LOCATION(S):

RUBY	Rarity: **None**	**COLOSSEUM**	Rarity: **None**
Trade from *FireRed/LeafGreen*		Trade from *FireRed/LeafGreen*	
SAPPHIRE	Rarity: **None**	**EMERALD**	Rarity: **None**
Trade from *FireRed/LeafGreen*		Trade from *FireRed/LeafGreen*	
FIRERED	Rarity: **Common**	**XD**	Rarity: **None**
Evolve Caterpie, Viridian Forest, Six Island, Route 25		Trade from *FireRed/LeafGreen*	
LEAFGREEN	Rarity: **Common**		
Evolve Caterpie, Viridian Forest, Six Island, Route 25			

MOVES

Level	Attack	Type	Power	ACC	PP
—	Harden	Normal	—	—	30

TM/HM

TM/HM#	Name	Type	Power	ACC	PP
None					

EGG MOVES*

Name	Type	Power	ACC	PP
None				

*Learned Via Breeding

MOVE TUTOR

FireRed/LeafGreen and *Emerald* Only

None

---

012 Butterfree™

BUG   FLYING

GENERAL INFO

SPECIES: Butterfly Pokémon
HEIGHT: 3'07"
WEIGHT: 71 lbs.
ABILITY: Compoundeyes

Raises Butterfree's Accuracy by 30%.

STATS

EVOLUTIONS

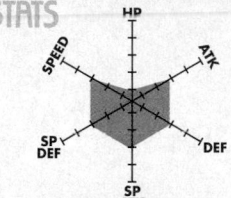 LV7 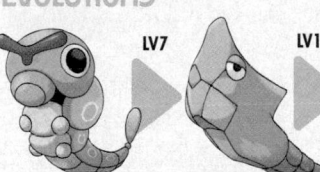 LV10

LOCATION(S):

RUBY	Rarity: **None**
Trade from *FireRed/LeafGreen*	
SAPPHIRE	Rarity: **None**
Trade from *FireRed/LeafGreen*	
FIRERED	Rarity: **Common**
Evolve Metapod	
LEAFGREEN	Rarity: **Common**
Evolve Metapod	
COLOSSEUM	Rarity: **None**
Trade from *FireRed/LeafGreen*	
EMERALD	Rarity: **None**
Trade from *FireRed/LeafGreen*	
XD	Rarity: **Only One**
Cipher Key Lair (Capture from Cipher Peon Targ)	

MOVES

Level	Attack	Type	Power	ACC	PP	Level	Attack	Type	Power	ACC	PP
—	Confusion	Psychic	50	100	25	23	Whirlwind	Normal	—	100	20
13	Poisonpowder	Poison	—	75	35	28	Gust	Flying	40	100	35
14	Stun Spore	Grass	—	75	30	34	Psybeam	Psychic	65	100	20
15	Sleep Powder	Grass	—	75	15	40	Safeguard	Normal	—	—	25
18	Supersonic	Normal	—	55	20	47	Silver Wind	Bug	60	100	5

TM/HM

TM/HM#	Name	Type	Power	ACC	PP	TM/HM#	Name	Type	Power	ACC	PP
TM06	Toxic	Poison	—	85	10	TM29	Psychic	Psychic	90	100	10
TM10	Hidden Power	Normal	—	100	15	TM30	Shadow Ball	Ghost	80	100	15
TM11	Sunny Day	Fire	—	—	5	TM32	Double Team	Normal	—	—	15
TM15	Hyper Beam	Normal	150	90	5	TM40	Aerial Ace	Flying	60	—	20
TM17	Protect	Normal	—	—	10	TM42	Facade	Normal	70	100	20
TM18	Rain Dance	Water	—	—	5	TM43	Secret Power	Normal	70	100	20
TM19	Giga Drain	Grass	60	100	5	TM44	Rest	Psychic	—	—	10
TM20	Safeguard	Normal	—	—	25	TM45	Attract	Normal	—	100	15
TM21	Frustration	Normal	—	100	20	TM46	Thief	Dark	40	100	10
TM22	Solarbeam	Grass	120	100	10	TM48	Skill Swap	Psychic	—	100	10
TM27	Return	Normal	—	100	20	HM05	Flash	Normal	—	70	20

MOVE TUTOR

FireRed/LeafGreen and *Emerald* Only

Double-Edge	Dream Eater*	Mimic
Substitute		

*Battle Frontier tutor move (*Emerald*)

013 Weedle™

BUG POISON

GENERAL INFO
SPECIES: Hairy Bug Pokémon
HEIGHT: 1'00"
WEIGHT: 7 lbs.
ABILITY: Shield Dust
Protects Weedle from being hit by any additional move effects.

STATS
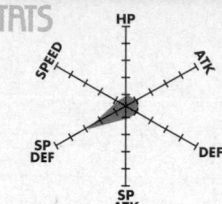

EVOLUTIONS
 LV7  LV10

LOCATION(S):

RUBY Rarity: **None**
Trade from *FireRed/LeafGreen*

SAPPHIRE Rarity: **None**
Trade from *FireRed/LeafGreen*

FIRERED Rarity: **Common**
Viridian Forest, Six Island, Route 25

LEAFGREEN Rarity: **Common**
Viridian Forest, Six Island, Route 25

COLOSSEUM Rarity: **None**
Trade from *FireRed/LeafGreen*

EMERALD Rarity: **None**
Trade from *FireRed/LeafGreen*

XD Rarity: **None**
Trade from *FireRed/LeafGreen*

MOVES

Level	Attack	Type	Power	ACC	PP
—	Poison Sting	Poison	15	100	35
—	String Shot	Bug	—	95	40

TM/HM

TM/HM#	Name	Type	Power	ACC	PP
None					

EGG MOVES*

Name	Type	Power	ACC	PP
None				

*Learned Via Breeding

MOVE TUTOR
FireRed/LeafGreen and *Emerald* Only

None

014 Kakuna™

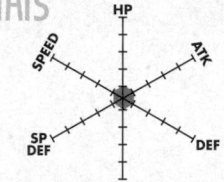

BUG POISON

GENERAL INFO
SPECIES: Cocoon Pokémon
HEIGHT: 2'00"
WEIGHT: 22 lbs.
ABILITY: Shed Skin
Enables Kakuna to only have a status effect for one turn. Has a 30% chance of success.

STATS

EVOLUTIONS
 LV7  LV10

LOCATION(S):

RUBY Rarity: **None**
Trade from *FireRed/LeafGreen*

SAPPHIRE Rarity: **None**
Trade from *FireRed/LeafGreen*

FIRERED Rarity: **Rare**
Evolve Weedle, Viridian Forest, Six Island, Route 25

LEAFGREEN Rarity: **Rare**
Evolve Weedle, Viridian Forest, Six Island, Route 25

COLOSSEUM Rarity: **None**
Trade from *FireRed/LeafGreen*

EMERALD Rarity: **None**
Trade from *FireRed/LeafGreen*

XD Rarity: **None**
Trade from *FireRed/LeafGreen*

MOVES

Level	Attack	Type	Power	ACC	PP
—	Harden	Normal	—	—	30

TM/HM

TM/HM#	Name	Type	Power	ACC	PP
None					

EGG MOVES*

Name	Type	Power	ACC	PP
None				

*Learned Via Breeding

MOVE TUTOR
FireRed/LeafGreen and *Emerald* Only

None

015 Beedrill™

BUG | POISON

GENERAL INFO

SPECIES: Poison Bee Pokémon
HEIGHT: 3'03"
WEIGHT: 65 lbs.
ABILITY: Swarm

Beedrill's Bug-type attacks multiply by 1.5 when its HPs get low.

STATS

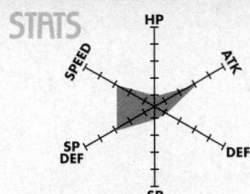

EVOLUTIONS

 LV7  LV10

LOCATION[S]:

RUBY — Rarity: **None**
Trade from *FireRed/LeafGreen*

SAPPHIRE — Rarity: **None**
Trade from *FireRed/LeafGreen*

FIRERED — Rarity: **None**
Evolve Kakuna

LEAFGREEN — Rarity: **None**
Evolve Kakuna

COLOSSEUM — Rarity: **None**
Trade from *FireRed/LeafGreen*

EMERALD — Rarity: **None**
Trade from *FireRed/LeafGreen*

XD — Rarity: **Only One**
Cipher Key Lair (Capture from Cipher Peon Lok)

MOVES

Level	Attack	Type	Power	ACC	PP
10	Fury Attack	Normal	15	85	20
15	Focus Energy	Normal	—	—	30
20	Twineedle	Bug	25	100	20
25	Rage	Normal	20	100	20
30	Pursuit	Dark	40	100	20
35	Pin Missile	Bug	14	85	20
40	Agility	Psychic	—	—	30
45	Endeavor	Normal	—	100	5

TM/HM

TM/HM#	Name	Type	Power	ACC	PP
TM06	Toxic	Poison	—	85	10
TM10	Hidden Power	Normal	—	100	15
TM11	Sunny Day	Fire	—	—	5
TM15	Hyper Beam	Normal	150	90	5
TM17	Protect	Normal	—	—	10
TM19	Giga Drain	Grass	60	100	5
TM21	Frustration	Normal	—	100	20
TM22	Solarbeam	Grass	120	100	10
TM27	Return	Normal	—	100	20
TM31	Brick Break	Fighting	75	100	15
TM32	Double Team	Normal	—	—	15
TM36	Sludge Bomb	Poison	90	100	10
TM40	Aerial Ace	Flying	60	—	20
TM42	Facade	Normal	70	100	20
TM43	Secret Power	Normal	70	100	20
TM44	Rest	Psychic	—	—	10
TM45	Attract	Normal	—	100	15
TM46	Thief	Dark	40	100	10
HM01	Cut	Normal	50	95	30
HM06	Rock Smash	Fighting	20	100	15

EGG MOVES*

Name	Type	Power	ACC	PP
None				

*Learned Via Breeding

MOVE TUTOR

FireRed/LeafGreen and *Emerald* Only

Double-Edge	Mimic	Substitute
Sword Dance*		

*Battle Frontier tutor move (*Emerald*)

016 Pidgey™

NORMAL | FLYING

GENERAL INFO

SPECIES: Tiny Bird Pokémon
HEIGHT: 1'00"
WEIGHT: 4 lbs.
ABILITY: Keen Eye

Protects Pidgey from having its Accuracy lowered.

STATS

EVOLUTIONS

LV18 LV36

LOCATION[S]:

RUBY — Rarity: **None**
Trade from *FireRed/LeafGreen*

SAPPHIRE — Rarity: **None**
Trade from *FireRed/LeafGreen*

FIRERED — Rarity: **Common**
Routes 1, 2, 3, 5, 6, 7, 8, 12, 13, 14, 15, 25

LEAFGREEN — Rarity: **Common**
Routes 1, 2, 3, 5, 6, 7, 8, 12, 13, 14, 15, 25

COLOSSEUM — Rarity: **None**
Trade from *FireRed/LeafGreen*

EMERALD — Rarity: **None**
Trade from *FireRed/LeafGreen*

XD — Rarity: **None**
Trade from *FireRed/LeafGreen*

MOVES

Level	Attack	Type	Power	ACC	PP
—	Tackle	Normal	35	95	35
5	Sand-Attack	Ground	—	100	15
9	Gust	Flying	40	100	35
13	Quick Attack	Normal	40	100	30
19	Whirlwind	Normal	—	100	20
25	Wing Attack	Flying	60	100	35
31	Featherdance	Flying	—	100	15
39	Agility	Psychic	—	—	30
47	Mirror Move	Flying	—	—	20

TM/HM

TM/HM#	Name	Type	Power	ACC	PP
TM06	Toxic	Poison	—	85	10
TM10	Hidden Power	Normal	—	100	15
TM11	Sunny Day	Fire	—	—	5
TM17	Protect	Normal	—	—	10
TM18	Rain Dance	Water	—	—	5
TM21	Frustration	Normal	—	100	20
TM27	Return	Normal	—	100	20
TM32	Double Team	Normal	—	—	15
TM40	Aerial Ace	Flying	60	—	20
TM42	Facade	Normal	70	100	20
TM43	Secret Power	Normal	70	100	20
TM44	Rest	Psychic	—	—	10
TM45	Attract	Normal	—	100	15
TM46	Thief	Dark	40	100	10
TM47	Steel Wing	Steel	70	90	25
HM02	Fly	Flying	70	95	15

EGG MOVES*

Name	Type	Power	ACC	PP
Air Cutter	Flying	55	95	25
Faint Attack	Dark	60	—	20
Foresight	Normal	—	100	40
Pursuit	Dark	40	100	20
Steel Wing	Steel	70	90	25

*Learned Via Breeding

MOVE TUTOR

FireRed/LeafGreen and *Emerald* Only

Double-Edge	Mimic	Substitute

017 Pidgeotto™

NORMAL | FLYING

GENERAL INFO

SPECIES: Bird Pokémon
HEIGHT: 3'07"
WEIGHT: 66 lbs.
ABILITY: Keen Eye
Protects Pidgeotto from having its Accuracy lowered.

STATS

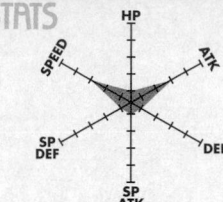

EVOLUTIONS

LV18 | LV36

LOCATION[S]:

RUBY   Rarity: **None**
Trade from *FireRed/LeafGreen*

SAPPHIRE   Rarity: **None**
Trade from *FireRed/LeafGreen*

FIRERED   Rarity: **Rare**
Evolve Pidgey, Route 13, Route 14, Route 15, Three Island, Five Island

LEAFGREEN   Rarity: **Rare**
Evolve Pidgey, Route 13, Route 14, Route 15, Three Island, Five Island

COLOSSEUM   Rarity: **None**
Trade from *FireRed/LeafGreen*

EMERALD   Rarity: **None**
Trade from *FireRed/LeafGreen*

XD   Rarity: **Only One**
Cipher Key Lair (Capture from Cipher Peon Lok)

MOVES

Level	Attack	Type	Power	ACC	PP	Level	Attack	Type	Power	ACC	PP
—	Tackle	Normal	35	95	35	20	Whirlwind	Normal	—	100	20
—	Sand-Attack	Ground	—	100	15	27	Wing Attack	Flying	60	100	35
—	Gust	Flying	40	100	35	34	Featherdance	Flying	—	100	15
13	Quick Attack	Normal	40	100	30	43	Agility	Psychic	—	—	30
						52	Mirror Move	Flying	—	—	20

TM/HM

TM/HM#	Name	Type	Power	ACC	PP	TM/HM#	Name	Type	Power	ACC	PP
TM06	Toxic	Poison	—	85	10	TM40	Aerial Ace	Flying	60	—	20
TM10	Hidden Power	Normal	—	100	15	TM42	Facade	Normal	70	100	20
TM11	Sunny Day	Fire	—	—	5	TM43	Secret Power	Normal	70	100	20
TM17	Protect	Normal	—	—	10	TM44	Rest	Psychic	—	—	10
TM18	Rain Dance	Water	—	—	5	TM45	Attract	Normal	—	100	15
TM21	Frustration	Normal	—	100	20	TM46	Thief	Dark	40	100	10
TM27	Return	Normal	—	100	20	TM47	Steel Wing	Steel	70	90	25
TM32	Double Team	Normal	—	—	15	HM02	Fly	Flying	70	95	15

MOVE TUTOR

FireRed/LeafGreen and *Emerald* Only

Double-Edge	Mimic	Substitute

018 Pidgeot™

NORMAL | FLYING

GENERAL INFO

SPECIES: Bird Pokémon
HEIGHT: 4'11"
WEIGHT: 87 lbs.
ABILITY: Keen Eye
Protects Pidgeot from having its Accuracy lowered.

STATS

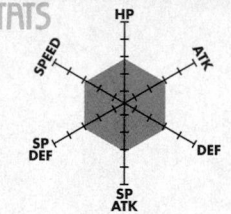

EVOLUTIONS

LV18 | LV36

LOCATION[S]:

RUBY   Rarity: **None**
Trade from *FireRed/LeafGreen*

SAPPHIRE   Rarity: **None**
Trade from *FireRed/LeafGreen*

FIRERED   Rarity: **Evolve**
Evolve Pidgeotto

LEAFGREEN   Rarity: **Evolve**
Evolve Pidgeotto

COLOSSEUM   Rarity: **None**
Trade from *FireRed/LeafGreen*

EMERALD   Rarity: **None**
Trade from *FireRed/LeafGreen*

XD   Rarity: **Evolve**
Evolve Pidgeotto

MOVES

Level	Attack	Type	Power	ACC	PP	Level	Attack	Type	Power	ACC	PP
—	Tackle	Normal	35	95	35	20	Whirlwind	Normal	—	100	20
—	Sand-Attack	Ground	—	100	15	27	Wing Attack	Flying	60	100	35
—	Gust	Flying	40	100	35	34	Featherdance	Flying	—	100	15
—	Quick Attack	Normal	40	100	30	48	Agility	Psychic	—	—	30
						62	Mirror Move	Flying	—	—	20

TM/HM

TM/HM#	Name	Type	Power	ACC	PP	TM/HM#	Name	Type	Power	ACC	PP
TM06	Toxic	Poison	—	85	10	TM40	Aerial Ace	Flying	60	—	20
TM10	Hidden Power	Normal	—	100	15	TM42	Facade	Normal	70	100	20
TM11	Sunny Day	Fire	—	—	5	TM43	Secret Power	Normal	70	100	20
TM15	Hyper Beam	Normal	150	90	5	TM44	Rest	Psychic	—	—	10
TM17	Protect	Normal	—	—	10	TM45	Attract	Normal	—	100	15
TM18	Rain Dance	Water	—	—	5	TM46	Thief	Dark	40	100	10
TM21	Frustration	Normal	—	100	20	TM47	Steel Wing	Steel	70	90	25
TM27	Return	Normal	—	100	20	HM02	Fly	Flying	70	95	15
TM32	Double Team	Normal	—	—	15						

MOVE TUTOR

FireRed/LeafGreen and *Emerald* Only

Double-Edge	Mimic	Substitute

019 Rattata™

NORMAL

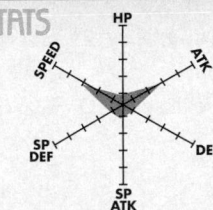

GENERAL INFO

SPECIES: Mouse Pokémon
HEIGHT: 1'00"
WEIGHT: 8 lbs.
ABILITY 1: Run Away
Allows Rattata to run away from wild Pokémon.

ABILITY 2: Guts
When Rattata has a status condition, its attack power multiplies by 1.5.

STATS

EVOLUTIONS

LV20

LOCATION(S):

RUBY   **Rarity: None**
Trade from *FireRed/LeafGreen*

SAPPHIRE   **Rarity: None**
Trade from *FireRed/LeafGreen*

FIRERED   **Rarity: None**
Routes 1, 2, 4, 9, 17, 18, 22, Pokémon Mansion

LEAFGREEN   **Rarity: None**
Routes 1, 2, 4, 9, 17, 18, 22, Pokémon Mansion

COLOSSEUM   **Rarity: None**
Trade from *FireRed/LeafGreen*

EMERALD   **Rarity: None**
Trade from *FireRed/LeafGreen*

XD   **Rarity: None**
Trade from *FireRed/LeafGreen*

MOVES

Level	Attack	Type	Power	ACC	PP	Level	Attack	Type	Power	ACC	PP
—	Tackle	Normal	35	95	35	20	Focus Energy	Normal	—	—	30
—	Tail Whip	Normal	—	100	30	27	Pursuit	Dark	40	100	20
7	Quick Attack	Normal	40	100	30	34	Super Fang	Normal	—	90	10
13	Hyper Fang	Normal	80	90	15	41	Endeavor	Normal	—	100	5

TM/HM

TM/HM#	Name	Type	Power	ACC	PP	TM/HM#	Name	Type	Power	ACC	PP
TM06	Toxic	Poison	—	85	10	TM27	Return	Normal	—	100	20
TM10	Hidden Power	Normal	—	100	15	TM28	Dig	Ground	60	100	10
TM11	Sunny Day	Fire	—	—	5	TM30	Shadow Ball	Ghost	80	100	15
TM12	Taunt	Dark	—	100	20	TM32	Double Team	Normal	—	—	15
TM13	Ice Beam	Ice	95	100	10	TM34	Shock Wave	Electric	60	—	20
TM14	Blizzard	Ice	120	70	5	TM42	Facade	Normal	70	100	20
TM17	Protect	Normal	—	—	10	TM43	Secret Power	Normal	70	100	20
TM18	Rain Dance	Water	—	—	5	TM44	Rest	Psychic	—	—	10
TM21	Frustration	Normal	—	100	20	TM45	Attract	Normal	—	100	15
TM23	Iron Tail	Steel	75	75	15	TM46	Thief	Dark	40	100	10
TM24	Thunderbolt	Electric	95	100	15	HM01	Cut	Normal	50	95	30
TM25	Thunder	Electric	120	70	10	HM06	Rock Smash	Fighting	20	100	15

EGG MOVES*

Name	Type	Power	ACC	PP
Bite	Dark	60	100	25
Counter	Fighting	—	100	20
Flame Wheel	Fire	60	100	25
Fury Swipes	Normal	18	80	15
Reversal	Fighting	—	100	15
Screech	Normal	—	85	40
Swagger	Normal	—	90	15
Uproar	Normal	50	100	10

*Learned Via Breeding

MOVE TUTOR

FireRed/LeafGreen and *Emerald* Only

Body Slam*	Counter*	Double-Edge
Mimic	Substitute	Thunder Wave*

*Battle Frontier tutor move (*Emerald*)

---

020 Raticate™

NORMAL

GENERAL INFO

SPECIES: Mouse Pokémon
HEIGHT: 2'04"
WEIGHT: 41 lbs.
ABILITY 1: Run Away
Allows Raticate to run away from wild Pokémon.

ABILITY 2: Guts
When Raticate' has a status condition, its attack power multiplies by 1.5.

STATS

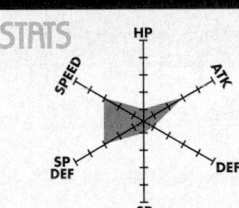

EVOLUTIONS

LV20

LOCATION(S):

RUBY   **Rarity: None**
Trade from *FireRed/LeafGreen*

SAPPHIRE   **Rarity: None**
Trade from *FireRed/LeafGreen*

FIRERED   **Rarity: Rare**
Route 17, Route 18, Pokémon Mansion

LEAFGREEN   **Rarity: Rare**
Route 17, Route 18, Pokémon Mansion

COLOSSEUM   **Rarity: None**
Trade from *FireRed/LeafGreen*

EMERALD   **Rarity: None**
Trade from *FireRed/LeafGreen*

XD   **Rarity: Only One**
Citadark Island (Capture from Furgy)

MOVES

Level	Attack	Type	Power	ACC	PP	Level	Attack	Type	Power	ACC	PP
—	Tackle	Normal	35	95	35	20	Scary Face	Normal	—	90	10
—	Tail Whip	Normal	—	100	30	30	Pursuit	Dark	40	100	20
—	Quick Attack	Normal	40	100	30	40	Super Fang	Normal	—	90	10
13	Hyper Fang	Normal	80	90	15	50	Endeavor	Normal	—	100	5

TM/HM

TM/HM#	Name	Type	Power	ACC	PP	TM/HM#	Name	Type	Power	ACC	PP
TM05	Roar	Normal	—	100	20	TM27	Return	Normal	—	100	20
TM06	Toxic	Poison	—	85	10	TM28	Dig	Ground	60	100	10
TM10	Hidden Power	Normal	—	100	15	TM30	Shadow Ball	Ghost	80	100	15
TM11	Sunny Day	Fire	—	—	5	TM32	Double Team	Normal	—	—	15
TM12	Taunt	Dark	—	100	20	TM34	Shock Wave	Electric	60	—	20
TM13	Ice Beam	Ice	95	100	10	TM42	Facade	Normal	70	100	20
TM14	Blizzard	Ice	120	70	5	TM43	Secret Power	Normal	70	100	20
TM15	Hyper Beam	Normal	150	90	5	TM44	Rest	Psychic	—	—	10
TM17	Protect	Normal	—	—	10	TM45	Attract	Normal	—	100	15
TM18	Rain Dance	Water	—	—	5	TM46	Thief	Dark	40	100	10
TM21	Frustration	Normal	—	100	20	HM01	Cut	Normal	50	95	30
TM23	Iron Tail	Steel	75	75	15	HM04	Strength	Normal	80	100	15
TM24	Thunderbolt	Electric	95	100	15	HM06	Rock Smash	Fighting	20	100	15
TM25	Thunder	Electric	120	70	10						

MOVE TUTOR

FireRed/LeafGreen and *Emerald* Only

Body Slam*	Counter*	Double-Edge
Mimic	Substitute	Thunder Wave*

*Battle Frontier tutor move (*Emerald*)

021 Spearow™

NORMAL | FLYING

GENERAL INFO
SPECIES: Tiny Bird Pokémon
HEIGHT: 1'00"
WEIGHT: 4 lbs.
ABILITY: Keen Eye
Protects Spearow from having its Accuracy lowered.

STATS
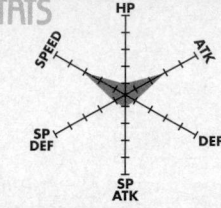

EVOLUTIONS

LV20

LOCATION[S]:

RUBY   Rarity: **None**
Trade from *FireRed/LeafGreen*

SAPPHIRE   Rarity: **None**
Trade from *FireRed/LeafGreen*

FIRERED   Rarity: **Common**
Routes 3, 4, 9, 10, 11, 17, 22, 23, One Island, Two Island, Six Island, Seven Island

LEAFGREEN   Rarity: **Common**
Routes 3, 4, 9, 10, 11, 17, 22, 23, One Island, Two Island, Six Island, Seven Island

COLOSSEUM   Rarity: **None**
Trade from *FireRed/LeafGreen*

EMERALD   Rarity: **None**
Trade from *FireRed/LeafGreen*

XD   Rarity: **Only One**
Phenac City (Capture from Cipher Peon Ezin)

MOVES

Level	Attack	Type	Power	ACC	PP	Level	Attack	Type	Power	ACC	PP
—	Peck	Flying	35	100	35	19	Pursuit	Dark	40	100	20
—	Growl	Normal	—	100	40	25	Aerial Ace	Flying	60	—	20
7	Leer	Normal	—	100	30	31	Mirror Move	Flying	—	—	20
13	Fury Attack	Normal	15	85	20	37	Drill Peck	Flying	80	100	20
						43	Agility	Psychic	—	—	30

TM/HM

TM/HM#	Name	Type	Power	ACC	PP	TM/HM#	Name	Type	Power	ACC	PP
TM06	Toxic	Poison	—	85	10	TM40	Aerial Ace	Flying	60	—	20
TM10	Hidden Power	Normal	—	100	15	TM42	Facade	Normal	70	100	20
TM11	Sunny Day	Fire	—	—	5	TM43	Secret Power	Normal	70	100	20
TM17	Protect	Normal	—	—	10	TM44	Rest	Psychic	—	—	10
TM18	Rain Dance	Water	—	—	5	TM45	Attract	Normal	—	100	15
TM21	Frustration	Normal	—	100	20	TM46	Thief	Dark	40	100	10
TM27	Return	Normal	—	100	20	TM47	Steel Wing	Steel	70	90	25
TM32	Double Team	Normal	—	—	15	HM02	Fly	Flying	70	95	15

EGG MOVES*

Name	Type	Power	ACC	PP
Astonish	Ghost	30	100	15
Faint Attack	Dark	60	—	20
False Swipe	Normal	40	100	40
Quick Attack	Normal	40	100	30
Scary Face	Normal	—	90	10
Sky Attack	Flying	140	90	5
Tri Attack	Normal	80	100	10

*Learned Via Breeding

MOVE TUTOR
FireRed/LeafGreen and *Emerald* Only

Double-Edge	Mimic	Substitute

---

022 Fearow™

NORMAL | FLYING

GENERAL INFO
SPECIES: Beak Pokémon
HEIGHT: 3'11"
WEIGHT: 84 lbs.
ABILITY: Keen Eye
Protects Fearow from having its Accuracy lowered.

STATS
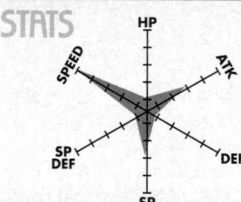

EVOLUTIONS

LV20

LOCATION[S]:

RUBY   Rarity: **None**
Trade from *FireRed/LeafGreen*

SAPPHIRE   Rarity: **None**
Trade from *FireRed/LeafGreen*

FIRERED   Rarity: **Rare**
Evolve Spearow, One Island, Two Island, Six Island, Seven Island, Routes 17, 18, 23

LEAFGREEN   Rarity: **Rare**
Evolve Spearow, One Island, Two Island, Six Island, Seven Island, Routes 17, 18, 23

COLOSSEUM   Rarity: **None**
Trade from *FireRed/LeafGreen*

EMERALD   Rarity: **None**
Trade from *FireRed/LeafGreen*

XD   Rarity: **Evolve**
Evolve Spearow

MOVES

Level	Attack	Type	Power	ACC	PP	Level	Attack	Type	Power	ACC	PP
—	Peck	Flying	35	100	35	26	Pursuit	Dark	40	100	20
—	Growl	Normal	—	100	40	32	Mirror Move	Flying	—	—	20
—	Leer	Normal	—	100	30	40	Drill Peck	Flying	80	100	20
—	Fury Attack	Normal	15	85	20	47	Agility	Psychic	—	—	30

TM/HM

TM/HM#	Name	Type	Power	ACC	PP	TM/HM#	Name	Type	Power	ACC	PP
TM06	Toxic	Poison	—	85	10	TM40	Aerial Ace	Flying	60	—	20
TM10	Hidden Power	Normal	—	100	15	TM42	Facade	Normal	70	100	20
TM11	Sunny Day	Fire	—	—	5	TM43	Secret Power	Normal	70	100	20
TM15	Hyper Beam	Normal	150	90	5	TM44	Rest	Psychic	—	—	10
TM17	Protect	Normal	—	—	10	TM45	Attract	Normal	—	100	15
TM18	Rain Dance	Water	—	—	5	TM46	Thief	Dark	40	100	10
TM21	Frustration	Normal	—	100	20	TM47	Steel Wing	Steel	70	90	25
TM27	Return	Normal	—	100	20	HM02	Fly	Flying	70	95	15
TM32	Double Team	Normal	—	—	15						

MOVE TUTOR
FireRed/LeafGreen and *Emerald* Only

Double-Edge	Mimic	Substitute

023 Ekans™

POISON

GENERAL INFO
SPECIES: Snake Pokémon
HEIGHT: 6'07"
WEIGHT: 15 lbs.
ABILITY 1: Shed Skin
Ekans only has status effects for one turn. Has a 30% chance of success.

ABILITY 2: Intimidate
Lowers an opponent's Attack when Ekans is brought into battle.

STATS

EVOLUTIONS

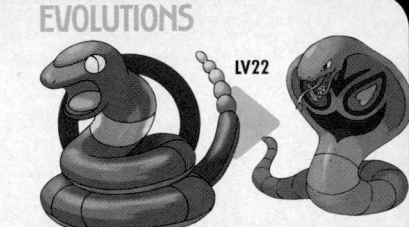
LV22

LOCATION[S]:

RUBY — Rarity: **None**
Trade from *FireRed/LeafGreen*

SAPPHIRE — Rarity: **None**
Trade from *FireRed/LeafGreen*

FIRERED — Rarity: **Common**
Routes 4, 8, 9, 10, 11, 23

LEAFGREEN — Rarity: **None**
Trade from *FireRed/LeafGreen*

COLOSSEUM — Rarity: **None**
Trade from *FireRed/LeafGreen*

EMERALD — Rarity: **None**
Trade from *FireRed/LeafGreen*

XD — Rarity: **None**
Trade from *FireRed/LeafGreen*

MOVES

Level	Attack	Type	Power	ACC	PP	Level	Attack	Type	Power	ACC	PP
—	Wrap	Normal	15	85	20	25	Screech	Normal	—	85	40
—	Leer	Normal	—	100	30	32	Acid	Poison	40	100	30
8	Poison Sting	Poison	15	100	35	37	Stockpile	Normal	—	—	10
13	Bite	Dark	60	100	25	37	Swallow	Normal	—	—	10
20	Glare	Normal	—	75	30	37	Spit Up	Normal	100	100	10
						44	Haze	Ice	—	—	30

TM/HM

TM/HM#	Name	Type	Power	ACC	PP	TM/HM#	Name	Type	Power	ACC	PP
TM06	Toxic	Poison	—	85	10	TM32	Double Team	Normal	—	—	15
TM10	Hidden Power	Normal	—	100	15	TM36	Sludge Bomb	Poison	90	100	10
TM11	Sunny Day	Fire	—	—	5	TM41	Torment	Dark	—	100	15
TM17	Protect	Normal	—	—	10	TM42	Facade	Normal	70	100	20
TM18	Rain Dance	Water	—	—	5	TM43	Secret Power	Normal	70	100	20
TM19	Giga Drain	Grass	60	100	5	TM44	Rest	Psychic	—	—	10
TM21	Frustration	Normal	—	100	20	TM45	Attract	Normal	—	100	15
TM23	Iron Tail	Steel	75	75	15	TM46	Thief	Dark	40	100	10
TM26	Earthquake	Ground	100	100	10	TM49	Snatch	Dark	—	100	10
TM27	Return	Normal	—	100	20	HM04	Strength	Normal	80	100	15
TM28	Dig	Ground	60	100	10						

EGG MOVES*

Name	Type	Power	ACC	PP
Beat Up	Dark	10	100	10
Poison Fang	Poison	50	100	15
Pursuit	Dark	40	100	20
Slam	Normal	80	75	20
Spite	Ghost	—	100	10

*Learned Via Breeding

MOVE TUTOR
FireRed/LeafGreen and Emerald Only

Body Slam*	Double-Edge	Mimic
Rock Slide*	Substitute	

*Battle Frontier tutor move (*Emerald*)

024 Arbok™

POISON

GENERAL INFO
SPECIES: Cobra Pokémon
HEIGHT: 11'06"
WEIGHT: 143 lbs.
ABILITY 1: Shed Skin
Arbok only has status effects for one turn. Has a 30% chance of success.

ABILITY 2: Intimidate
Lowers an opponent's Attack when Arbok is brought into battle.

STATS
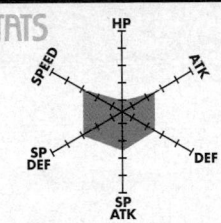

EVOLUTIONS

LV22

LOCATION[S]:

RUBY — Rarity: **None**
Trade from *FireRed/LeafGreen*

SAPPHIRE — Rarity: **None**
Trade from *FireRed/LeafGreen*

FIRERED — Rarity: **Common**
Evolve Ekans, Route 23, Victory Road

LEAFGREEN — Rarity: **None**
Trade from *FireRed*

COLOSSEUM — Rarity: **None**
Trade from *FireRed/LeafGreen*

EMERALD — Rarity: **None**
Trade from *FireRed/LeafGreen*

XD — Rarity: **Only One**
Cipher Key Lair (Capture from Cipher Peon Smarton)

MOVES

Level	Attack	Type	Power	ACC	PP	Level	Attack	Type	Power	ACC	PP
—	Wrap	Normal	15	85	20	28	Screech	Normal	—	85	40
—	Leer	Normal	—	100	30	38	Acid	Poison	40	100	30
—	Poison Sting	Poison	15	100	35	46	Stockpile	Normal	—	—	10
—	Bite	Dark	60	100	25	46	Swallow	Normal	—	—	10
20	Glare	Normal	—	75	30	46	Spit Up	Normal	100	100	10
						56	Haze	Ice	—	—	30

TM/HM

TM/HM#	Name	Type	Power	ACC	PP	TM/HM#	Name	Type	Power	ACC	PP
TM06	Toxic	Poison	—	85	10	TM28	Dig	Ground	60	100	10
TM10	Hidden Power	Normal	—	100	15	TM32	Double Team	Normal	—	—	15
TM11	Sunny Day	Fire	—	—	5	TM36	Sludge Bomb	Poison	90	100	10
TM15	Hyper Beam	Normal	150	90	5	TM41	Torment	Dark	—	100	15
TM17	Protect	Normal	—	—	10	TM42	Facade	Normal	70	100	20
TM18	Rain Dance	Water	—	—	5	TM43	Secret Power	Normal	70	100	20
TM19	Giga Drain	Grass	60	100	5	TM44	Rest	Psychic	—	—	10
TM21	Frustration	Normal	—	100	20	TM45	Attract	Normal	—	100	15
TM23	Iron Tail	Steel	75	75	15	TM46	Thief	Dark	40	100	10
TM26	Earthquake	Ground	100	100	10	TM49	Snatch	Dark	—	100	10
TM27	Return	Normal	—	100	20	HM04	Strength	Normal	80	100	20

MOVE TUTOR
FireRed/LeafGreen and Emerald Only

Body Slam*	Double-Edge	Mimic
Rock Slide*	Substitute	

*Battle Frontier tutor move (*Emerald*)

025 Pikachu™

ELECTRIC

GENERAL INFO
SPECIES: Mouse Pokémon
HEIGHT: 1'04"
WEIGHT: 13 lbs.
ABILITY: Static

An opponent has a 30% chance of being paralyzed if it strikes Pikachu.

STATS

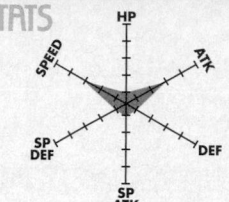

EVOLUTIONS

FRIENDSHIP — THUNDER STONE

LOCATION(S):

RUBY	Rarity: **Rare**
Safari Zone	
SAPPHIRE	Rarity: **Rare**
Safari Zone	
FIRERED	Rarity: **Rare**
Viridian Forest, Power Plant	
LEAFGREEN	Rarity: **Rare**
Viridian Forest, Power Plant	
COLOSSEUM	Rarity: **None**
Trade from *Ruby/Sapphire/FireRed/LeafGreen*	
EMERALD	Rarity: **Rare**
Safari Zone	
XD	Rarity: **None**
Trade from *Ruby/Sapphire/FireRed/LeafGreen*	

MOVES

Level	Attack	Type	Power	ACC	PP	Level	Attack	Type	Power	ACC	PP
—	Thundershock	Electric	40	100	30	15	Double Team	Normal	—	—	15
—	Growl	Normal	—	100	40	20	Slam	Normal	80	75	20
6	Tail Whip	Normal	—	100	30	26	Thunderbolt	Electric	95	100	15
8	Thunder Wave	Electric	—	100	20	33	Agility	Psychic	—	—	30
11	Quick Attack	Normal	40	100	30	41	Thunder	Electric	120	70	10
						50	Light Screen	Psychic	—	—	30

TM/HM

TM/HM#	Name	Type	Power	ACC	PP	TM/HM#	Name	Type	Power	ACC	PP
TM01	Focus Punch	Fighting	150	100	20	TM28	Dig	Ground	60	100	10
TM06	Toxic	Poison	—	85	10	TM31	Brick Break	Fighting	75	100	15
TM10	Hidden Power	Normal	—	100	15	TM32	Double Team	Normal	—	—	15
TM16	Light Screen	Psychic	—	—	30	TM34	Shock Wave	Electric	60	—	20
TM17	Protect	Normal	—	—	10	TM42	Facade	Normal	70	100	20
TM18	Rain Dance	Water	—	—	5	TM43	Secret Power	Normal	70	100	20
TM21	Frustration	Normal	—	100	20	TM44	Rest	Psychic	—	—	10
TM23	Iron Tail	Steel	75	75	15	TM45	Attract	Normal	—	100	15
TM24	Thunderbolt	Electric	95	100	15	HM04	Strength	Normal	80	100	20
TM25	Thunder	Electric	120	70	10	HM05	Flash	Normal	—	70	20
TM27	Return	Normal	—	100	20	HM06	Rock Smash	Fighting	20	100	15

MOVE TUTOR
FireRed/LeafGreen and *Emerald* Only

Body Slam*	Counter*	Double-Edge
Mega Kick*	Mega Punch*	Mimic
Seismic Toss*	Substitute	Thunder Wave*

***Emerald* Only**

Defense Curl*	Dynamicpunch*	Endure*
Mud-Slap*	Rollout	Sleep Talk
Snore*	Swagger	Swift*
Thunderpunch*		

*Battle Frontier tutor move (*Emerald*)

---

026 Raichu™

ELECTRIC

GENERAL INFO
SPECIES: Mouse Pokémon
HEIGHT: 2'07"
WEIGHT: 66 lbs.
ABILITY: Static

An opponent has a 30% chance of being paralyzed if it strikes Raichu.

STATS

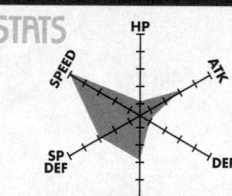

EVOLUTIONS

FRIENDSHIP — THUNDER STONE

LOCATION(S):

RUBY	Rarity: **Rare**
Evolve Pikachu	
SAPPHIRE	Rarity: **Evolve**
Evolve Pikachu	
FIRERED	Rarity: **Evolve**
Evolve Pikachu	
LEAFGREEN	Rarity: **Evolve**
Evolve Pikachu	
COLOSSEUM	Rarity: **None**
Evolve Pikachu	
EMERALD	Rarity: **Rare**
Evolve Pikachu	
XD	Rarity: **None**
Evolve Pikachu	

MOVES

Level	Attack	Type	Power	ACC	PP	Level	Attack	Type	Power	ACC	PP
—	Thundershock	Electric	40	100	30	—	Quick Attack	Normal	40	100	30
—	Tail Whip	Normal	—	100	30	—	Thunderbolt	Electric	95	100	15

TM/HM

TM/HM#	Name	Type	Power	ACC	PP	TM/HM#	Name	Type	Power	ACC	PP
TM01	Focus Punch	Fighting	150	100	20	TM28	Dig	Ground	60	100	10
TM06	Toxic	Poison	—	85	10	TM31	Brick Break	Fighting	75	100	15
TM10	Hidden Power	Normal	—	100	15	TM32	Double Team	Normal	—	—	15
TM15	Hyper Beam	Normal	150	90	5	TM34	Shock Wave	Electric	60	—	20
TM16	Light Screen	Psychic	—	—	30	TM42	Facade	Normal	70	100	20
TM17	Protect	Normal	—	—	10	TM43	Secret Power	Normal	70	100	20
TM18	Rain Dance	Water	—	—	5	TM44	Rest	Psychic	—	—	10
TM21	Frustration	Normal	—	100	20	TM45	Attract	Normal	—	100	15
TM23	Iron Tail	Steel	75	75	15	TM46	Thief	Dark	40	100	10
TM24	Thunderbolt	Electric	95	100	15	HM04	Strength	Normal	80	100	20
TM25	Thunder	Electric	120	70	10	HM05	Flash	Normal	—	70	20
TM27	Return	Normal	—	100	20	HM06	Rock Smash	Fighting	20	100	15

MOVE TUTOR
FireRed/LeafGreen and *Emerald* Only

Body Slam*	Counter*	Double-Edge
Mega Kick*	Mega Punch*	Mimic
Seismic Toss*	Substitute	Thunder Wave*

***Emerald* Only**

Defense Curl*	Dynamicpunch*	Endure*
Mud-Slap*	Rollout	Sleep Talk
Snore*	Swagger	Swift*
Thunderpunch*		

*Battle Frontier tutor move (*Emerald*)

027 Sandshrew™

GROUND

GENERAL INFO

SPECIES: Mouse Pokémon
HEIGHT: 2'00"
WEIGHT: 26 lbs.
ABILITY: Sand Veil

During a sandstorm, Sandshrew gains the ability to evade more moves.

STATS

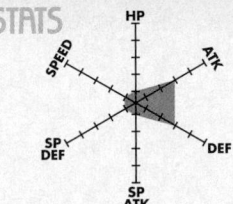

EVOLUTIONS

LV22

LOCATION[S]:

RUBY — Rarity: **Common**
Route 111

SAPPHIRE — Rarity: **Common**
Route 111

FIRERED — Rarity: **None**
Trade from *Ruby/Sapphire/LeafGreen*

LEAFGREEN — Rarity: **Rare**
Routes 4, 8, 9, 10, 11, 23

COLOSSEUM — Rarity: **None**
Trade from *Ruby/Sapphire/LeafGreen*

EMERALD — Rarity: **Common**
Route 111, Mirage Tower

XD — Rarity: **Common**
Rock Poké Spot

MOVES

Level	Attack	Type	Power	ACC	PP
—	Scratch	Normal	40	100	35
6	Defense Curl	Normal	—	—	40
11	Sand-Attack	Ground	—	100	15
17	Poison Sting	Poison	15	100	35

Level	Attack	Type	Power	ACC	PP
23	Slash	Normal	70	100	20
30	Swift	Normal	60	—	20
37	Fury Swipes	Normal	18	80	15
45	Sand Tomb	Ground	15	70	15
53	Sandstorm	Rock	—	—	10

TM/HM

TM/HM#	Name	Type	Power	ACC	PP
TM01	Focus Punch	Fighting	150	100	20
TM06	Toxic	Poison	—	85	10
TM10	Hidden Power	Normal	—	100	15
TM11	Sunny Day	Fire	—	—	5
TM17	Protect	Normal	—	—	10
TM21	Frustration	Normal	—	100	20
TM23	Iron Tail	Steel	75	75	15
TM26	Earthquake	Ground	100	100	10
TM27	Return	Normal	—	100	20
TM28	Dig	Ground	60	100	10
TM31	Brick Break	Fighting	75	100	15

TM/HM#	Name	Type	Power	ACC	PP
TM32	Double Team	Normal	—	—	15
TM37	Sandstorm	Ground	—	—	10
TM39	Rock Tomb	Rock	50	80	10
TM40	Aerial Ace	Flying	60	—	20
TM42	Facade	Normal	70	100	20
TM43	Secret Power	Normal	70	100	20
TM44	Rest	Psychic	—	—	10
TM45	Attract	Normal	—	100	15
TM46	Thief	Dark	40	100	10
HM01	Cut	Normal	50	95	30
HM04	Strength	Normal	80	100	20
HM06	Rock Smash	Fighting	20	100	15

EGG MOVES*

Name	Type	Power	ACC	PP
Counter	Fighting	—	100	20
Crush Claw	Normal	75	95	10
Flail	Normal	—	100	15
Rapid Spin	Normal	20	100	40
Rock Slide	Rock	75	90	10
Safeguard	Normal	—	—	25
Swords Dance	Normal	—	—	30
Metal Claw	Steel	50	95	35

*Learned Via Breeding

MOVE TUTOR

FireRed/LeafGreen and *Emerald* Only

Body Slam*	Counter*	Double-Edge
Mimic	Rock Slide*	Seismic Toss*
Substitute	Swords Dance*	

Emerald Only

Defense Curl*	Dynamicpunch*	Endure*
Fury Cutter	Mud-Slap*	Rollout
Sleep Talk	Snore*	Swagger
Swift*		

*Battle Frontier tutor move (*Emerald*)

---

028 Sandslash™

GROUND

GENERAL INFO

SPECIES: Mouse Pokémon
HEIGHT: 3'03"
WEIGHT: 65 lbs.
ABILITY: Sand Veil

During a sandstorm, Sandslash gains the ability to evade more moves.

STATS

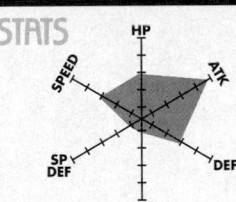

EVOLUTIONS

LV22

LOCATION[S]:

RUBY — Rarity: **Evolve**
Evolve Sandshrew

SAPPHIRE — Rarity: **Evolve**
Evolve Sandshrew

FIRERED — Rarity: **None**
Trade from *Ruby/Sapphire/LeafGreen*

LEAFGREEN — Rarity: **Rare**
Route 23, Victory Road

COLOSSEUM — Rarity: **None**
Trade from *Ruby/Sapphire/LeafGreen*

EMERALD — Rarity: **Evolve**
Evolve Sandshrew

XD — Rarity: **Evolve**
Evolve Sandshrew

MOVES

Level	Attack	Type	Power	ACC	PP
—	Scratch	Normal	40	100	35
—	Defense Curl	Normal	—	—	40
—	Sand Attack	Ground	—	100	15
17	Poison Sting	Poison	15	100	35

Level	Attack	Type	Power	ACC	PP
24	Slash	Normal	70	100	20
33	Swift	Normal	60	—	20
42	Fury Swipes	Normal	18	80	15
52	Sand Tomb	Ground	15	70	15
62	Sandstorm	Rock	—	—	10

TM/HM

TM/HM#	Name	Type	Power	ACC	PP
TM01	Focus Punch	Fighting	150	100	20
TM06	Toxic	Poison	—	85	10
TM10	Hidden Power	Normal	—	100	15
TM11	Sunny Day	Fire	—	—	5
TM15	Hyper Beam	Normal	150	90	5
TM17	Protect	Normal	—	—	10
TM21	Frustration	Normal	—	100	20
TM23	Iron Tail	Steel	75	75	15
TM26	Earthquake	Ground	100	100	10
TM27	Return	Normal	—	100	20
TM28	Dig	Ground	60	100	10
TM31	Brick Break	Fighting	75	100	15

TM/HM#	Name	Type	Power	ACC	PP
TM32	Double Team	Normal	—	—	15
TM37	Sandstorm	Ground	—	—	10
TM39	Rock Tomb	Rock	50	80	10
TM40	Aerial Ace	Flying	60	—	20
TM42	Facade	Normal	70	100	20
TM43	Secret Power	Normal	70	100	20
TM44	Rest	Psychic	—	—	10
TM45	Attract	Normal	—	100	15
TM46	Thief	Dark	40	100	10
HM01	Cut	Normal	50	95	30
HM04	Strength	Normal	80	100	20
HM06	Rock Smash	Fighting	20	100	15

MOVE TUTOR

FireRed/LeafGreen and *Emerald* Only

Body Slam*	Counter*	Double-Edge
Mimic	Rock Slide*	Seismic Toss*
Substitute	Swords Dance*	

Emerald Only

Defense Curl*	Dynamicpunch*	Endure*
Fury Cutter	Mud-Slap*	Rollout
Sleep Talk	Snore*	Swagger
Swift*		

*Battle Frontier tutor move (*Emerald*)

029 Nidoran♀™

POISON

GENERAL INFO
SPECIES: Poison Pin Pokémon
HEIGHT: 1'04"
WEIGHT: 15 lbs.
ABILITY: Poison Point
If an opponent is striking Nidoran♀, it has a 30% chance of being poisoned.

STATS
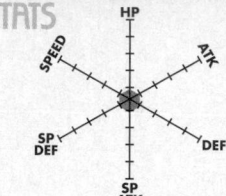

EVOLUTIONS

LV16 — MOON STONE

LOCATION(S):

RUBY — Rarity: **None**
Trade from *FireRed/LeafGreen*

SAPPHIRE — Rarity: **None**
Trade from *FireRed/LeafGreen*

FIRERED — Rarity: **Common**
Route 3, Safari Zone

LEAFGREEN — Rarity: **Common**
Route 3, Safari Zone

COLOSSEUM — Rarity: **None**
Trade from *FireRed/LeafGreen*

EMERALD — Rarity: **None**
Trade from *FireRed/LeafGreen*

XD — Rarity: **None**
Trade from *FireRed/LeafGreen*

MOVES

Level	Attack	Type	Power	ACC	PP	Level	Attack	Type	Power	ACC	PP
—	Scratch	Normal	40	100	35	20	Bite	Dark	60	100	25
—	Growl	Normal	—	100	40	23	Helping Hand	Normal	—	100	20
8	Tail Whip	Normal	—	100	30	30	Fury Swipes	Normal	18	80	15
12	Double Kick	Fighting	30	100	30	38	Flatter	Dark	—	100	15
17	Poison Sting	Poison	15	100	35	47	Crunch	Dark	80	100	15

TM/HM

TM/HM#	Name	Type	Power	ACC	PP	TM/HM#	Name	Type	Power	ACC	PP
TM03	Water Pulse	Water	60	95	20	TM28	Dig	Ground	60	100	10
TM06	Toxic	Poison	—	85	10	TM32	Double Team	Normal	—	—	15
TM10	Hidden Power	Normal	—	100	15	TM34	Shock Wave	Electric	60	—	20
TM11	Sunny Day	Fire	—	—	5	TM36	Sludge Bomb	Poison	90	100	10
TM13	Ice Beam	Ice	95	100	10	TM40	Aerial Ace	Flying	60	—	20
TM14	Blizzard	Ice	120	70	5	TM42	Facade	Normal	70	100	20
TM17	Protect	Normal	—	—	10	TM43	Secret Power	Normal	70	100	20
TM18	Rain Dance	Water	—	—	5	TM44	Rest	Psychic	—	—	10
TM21	Frustration	Normal	—	100	20	TM45	Attract	Normal	—	100	15
TM23	Iron Tail	Steel	75	75	15	TM46	Thief	Dark	40	100	10
TM24	Thunderbolt	Electric	95	100	15	HM01	Cut	Normal	50	95	30
TM25	Thunder	Electric	120	70	10	HM04	Strength	Normal	80	100	20
TM27	Return	Normal	—	100	20	HM06	Rock Smash	Fighting	20	100	15

EGG MOVES*

Name	Type	Power	ACC	PP
Beat Up	Dark	10	100	10
Charm	Normal	—	100	20
Counter	Fighting	—	100	20
Disable	Normal	—	55	20
Focus Energy	Normal	—	—	30
Supersonic	Normal	—	55	20
Take Down	Normal	90	85	20

*Learned Via Breeding

MOVE TUTOR
FireRed/LeafGreen and *Emerald* Only

Body Slam*	Counter*	Double-Edge
Mimic	Rock Slide*	Substitute

*Battle Frontier tutor move (*Emerald*)

---

030 Nidorina™

POISON

GENERAL INFO
SPECIES: Poison Pin Pokémon
HEIGHT: 2'07"
WEIGHT: 44 lbs.
ABILITY: Poison Point
If an opponent is striking Nidorina, it has a 30% chance of being poisoned.

STATS
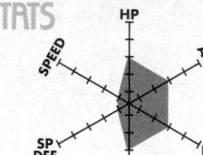

EVOLUTIONS
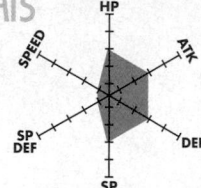
LV16 — MOON STONE

LOCATION(S):

RUBY — Rarity: **None**
Trade from *FireRed/LeafGreen*

SAPPHIRE — Rarity: **None**
Trade from *FireRed/LeafGreen*

FIRERED — Rarity: **Rare**
Safari Zone

LEAFGREEN — Rarity: **Rare**
Safari Zone

COLOSSEUM — Rarity: **None**
Trade from *FireRed/LeafGreen*

EMERALD — Rarity: **None**
Trade from *FireRed/LeafGreen*

XD — Rarity: **None**
Trade from *FireRed/LeafGreen*

MOVES

Level	Attack	Type	Power	ACC	PP	Level	Attack	Type	Power	ACC	PP
—	Scratch	Normal	40	100	35	22	Bite	Dark	60	100	25
—	Growl	Normal	—	100	40	26	Helping Hand	Normal	—	100	20
8	Tail Whip	Normal	—	100	30	34	Fury Swipes	Normal	18	80	15
12	Double Kick	Fighting	30	100	30	43	Flatter	Dark	—	100	15
18	Poison Sting	Poison	15	100	35	53	Crunch	Dark	80	100	15

TM/HM

TM/HM#	Name	Type	Power	ACC	PP	TM/HM#	Name	Type	Power	ACC	PP
TM03	Water Pulse	Water	60	95	20	TM28	Dig	Ground	60	100	10
TM06	Toxic	Poison	—	85	10	TM32	Double Team	Normal	—	—	15
TM10	Hidden Power	Normal	—	100	15	TM34	Shock Wave	Electric	60	—	20
TM11	Sunny Day	Fire	—	—	5	TM36	Sludge Bomb	Poison	90	100	10
TM13	Ice Beam	Ice	95	100	10	TM40	Aerial Ace	Flying	60	—	20
TM14	Blizzard	Ice	120	70	5	TM42	Facade	Normal	70	100	20
TM17	Protect	Normal	—	—	10	TM43	Secret Power	Normal	70	100	20
TM18	Rain Dance	Water	—	—	5	TM44	Rest	Psychic	—	—	10
TM21	Frustration	Normal	—	100	20	TM45	Attract	Normal	—	100	15
TM23	Iron Tail	Steel	75	75	15	TM46	Thief	Dark	40	100	10
TM24	Thunderbolt	Electric	95	100	15	HM01	Cut	Normal	50	95	30
TM25	Thunder	Electric	120	70	10	HM04	Strength	Normal	80	100	20
TM27	Return	Normal	—	100	20	HM06	Rock Smash	Fighting	20	100	15

MOVE TUTOR
FireRed/LeafGreen and *Emerald* Only

Body Slam*	Counter*	Double-Edge
Mimic	Substitute	

*Battle Frontier tutor move (*Emerald*)

031 Nidoqueen™

POISON | **GROUND**

GENERAL INFO
SPECIES: Drill Pokémon
HEIGHT: 4'03"
WEIGHT: 132 lbs.
ABILITY: Poison Point
If an opponent is striking Nidoqueen, it has a 30% chance of being poisoned.

STATS
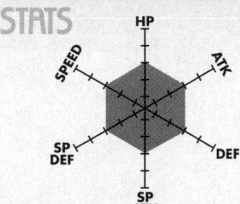

EVOLUTIONS
 LV16  MOON STONE

LOCATION(S):

RUBY — Rarity: **None**
Trade from *FireRed/LeafGreen*

SAPPHIRE — Rarity: **None**
Trade from *FireRed/LeafGreen*

FIRERED — Rarity: **Evolve**
Evolve Nidorina

LEAFGREEN — Rarity: **Evolve**
Evolve Nidorina

COLOSSEUM — Rarity: **None**
Trade from *FireRed/LeafGreen*

EMERALD — Rarity: **None**
Trade from *FireRed/LeafGreen*

XD — Rarity: **None**
Trade from *FireRed/LeafGreen*

MOVES

Level	Attack	Type	Power	ACC	PP	Level	Attack	Type	Power	ACC	PP
—	Scratch	Normal	40	100	35	—	Poison Sting	Poison	15	100	35
—	Tail Whip	Normal	—	100	30	22	Body Slam	Normal	85	100	15
—	Double Kick	Fighting	30	100	30	43	Superpower	Fighting	120	100	5

TM/HM

TM/HM#	Name	Type	Power	ACC	PP	TM/HM#	Name	Type	Power	ACC	PP
TM01	Focus Punch	Fighting	150	100	20	TM31	Brick Break	Fighting	75	100	15
TM03	Water Pulse	Water	60	95	20	TM32	Double Team	Normal	—	—	15
TM05	Roar	Normal	—	100	20	TM34	Shock Wave	Electric	60	—	20
TM06	Toxic	Poison	—	85	10	TM35	Flamethrower	Fire	95	100	15
TM10	Hidden Power	Normal	—	100	15	TM36	Sludge Bomb	Poison	90	100	10
TM11	Sunny Day	Fire	—	—	5	TM37	Sandstorm	Ground	—	—	10
TM12	Taunt	Dark	—	100	20	TM38	Fire Blast	Fire	120	85	5
TM13	Ice Beam	Ice	95	100	10	TM39	Rock Tomb	Rock	50	80	10
TM14	Blizzard	Ice	120	70	5	TM40	Aerial Ace	Flying	60	—	20
TM15	Hyper Beam	Normal	150	90	5	TM41	Torment	Dark	—	100	15
TM17	Protect	Normal	—	—	10	TM42	Facade	Normal	70	100	20
TM18	Rain Dance	Water	—	—	5	TM43	Secret Power	Normal	70	100	20
TM21	Frustration	Normal	—	100	20	TM44	Rest	Psychic	—	—	10
TM23	Iron Tail	Steel	75	75	15	TM45	Attract	Normal	—	100	15
TM24	Thunderbolt	Electric	95	100	15	TM46	Thief	Dark	40	100	10
TM25	Thunder	Electric	120	70	10	HM01	Cut	Normal	50	95	30
TM26	Earthquake	Ground	100	100	10	HM03	Surf	Water	95	100	15
TM27	Return	Normal	—	100	20	HM04	Strength	Normal	80	100	20
TM28	Dig	Ground	60	100	10	HM06	Rock Smash	Fighting	20	100	15
TM30	Shadow Ball	Ghost	80	100	15						

MOVE TUTOR
FireRed/LeafGreen and *Emerald* Only

Body Slam*	Counter*	Double-Edge
Mega Kick*	Mega Punch*	Mimic
Rock Slide*	Seismic Toss*	Substitute

*Battle Frontier tutor move (*Emerald*)

---

032 Nidoran♂™

POISON

GENERAL INFO
SPECIES: Poison Pin Pokémon
HEIGHT: 1'08"
WEIGHT: 20 lbs.
ABILITY: Poison Point
If an opponent is striking Nidoran♂, it has a 30% chance of being poisoned.

STATS
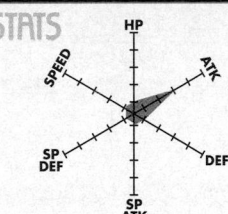

EVOLUTIONS

 LV16 MOON STONE

LOCATION(S):

RUBY — Rarity: **None**
Trade from *FireRed/LeafGreen*

SAPPHIRE — Rarity: **None**
Trade from *FireRed/LeafGreen*

FIRERED — Rarity: **Common**
Route 3, Safari Zone

LEAFGREEN — Rarity: **Rare**
Route 3, Safari Zone

COLOSSEUM — Rarity: **None**
Trade from *FireRed/LeafGreen*

EMERALD — Rarity: **None**
Trade from *FireRed/LeafGreen*

XD — Rarity: **None**
Trade from *FireRed/LeafGreen*

MOVES

Level	Attack	Type	Power	ACC	PP	Level	Attack	Type	Power	ACC	PP
—	Leer	Normal	—	100	30	20	Horn Attack	Normal	65	100	25
—	Peck	Flying	35	100	35	23	Helping Hand	Normal	—	100	20
8	Focus Energy	Normal	—	—	30	30	Fury Attack	Normal	15	85	20
12	Double Kick	Fighting	30	100	30	38	Flatter	Dark	—	100	15
17	Poison Sting	Poison	15	100	35	47	Horn Drill	Normal	—	30	5

TM/HM

TM/HM#	Name	Type	Power	ACC	PP	TM/HM#	Name	Type	Power	ACC	PP
TM03	Water Pulse	Water	60	95	20	TM27	Return	Normal	—	100	20
TM06	Toxic	Poison	—	85	10	TM28	Dig	Ground	60	100	10
TM10	Hidden Power	Normal	—	100	15	TM32	Double Team	Normal	—	—	15
TM11	Sunny Day	Fire	—	—	5	TM34	Shock Wave	Electric	60	—	20
TM13	Ice Beam	Ice	95	100	10	TM36	Sludge Bomb	Poison	90	100	10
TM14	Blizzard	Ice	120	70	5	TM42	Facade	Normal	70	100	20
TM17	Protect	Normal	—	—	10	TM43	Secret Power	Normal	70	100	20
TM18	Rain Dance	Water	—	—	5	TM44	Rest	Psychic	—	—	10
TM21	Frustration	Normal	—	100	20	TM45	Attract	Normal	—	100	15
TM23	Iron Tail	Steel	75	75	15	TM46	Thief	Dark	40	100	10
TM24	Thunderbolt	Electric	95	100	15	HM01	Cut	Normal	50	95	30
TM25	Thunder	Electric	120	70	10	HM04	Strength	Normal	80	100	20
						HM06	Rock Smash	Fighting	20	100	15

EGG MOVES*

Name	Type	Power	ACC	PP
Beat Up	Dark	10	100	10
Counter	Fighting	—	100	20
Disable	Normal	—	55	20
Focus Energy	Normal	—	—	30
Supersonic	Normal	—	55	20
Take Down	Normal	90	85	20
Amnesia	Psychic	—	—	20
Confusion	Psychic	50	100	25

*Learned Via Breeding

MOVE TUTOR
FireRed/LeafGreen and *Emerald* Only

Body Slam*	Counter*	Double-Edge
Mimic	Substitute	

*Battle Frontier tutor move (*Emerald*)

033 Nidorino™

POISON

GENERAL INFO

SPECIES: Poison Pin Pokémon
HEIGHT: 2'11"
WEIGHT: 43 lbs.
ABILITY: Poison Point

If an opponent is striking Nidorino, it has a 30% chance of being poisoned.

STATS

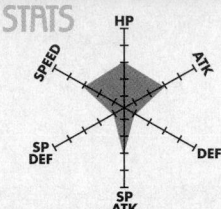

EVOLUTIONS

LV16 — MOON STONE

LOCATION[S]:

RUBY   Rarity: **None**
Trade from *FireRed/LeafGreen*

SAPPHIRE   Rarity: **None**
Trade from *FireRed/LeafGreen*

FIRERED   Rarity: **Rare**
Safari Zone

LEAFGREEN   Rarity: **Rare**
Safari Zone

COLOSSEUM   Rarity: **None**
Trade from *FireRed/LeafGreen*

EMERALD   Rarity: **None**
Trade from *FireRed/LeafGreen*

XD   Rarity: **None**
Trade from *FireRed/LeafGreen*

MOVES

Level	Attack	Type	Power	ACC	PP	Level	Attack	Type	Power	ACC	PP
—	Leer	Normal	—	100	30	22	Horn Attack	Normal	65	100	25
—	Peck	Flying	35	100	35	26	Helping Hand	Normal	—	100	20
8	Focus Energy	Normal	—	—	30	34	Fury Attack	Normal	15	85	20
12	Double Kick	Fighting	30	100	30	43	Flatter	Dark	—	100	15
18	Poison Sting	Poison	15	100	35	53	Horn Drill	Normal	—	30	5

TM/HM

TM/HM#	Name	Type	Power	ACC	PP	TM/HM#	Name	Type	Power	ACC	PP
TM03	Water Pulse	Water	60	95	20	TM27	Return	Normal	—	100	20
TM06	Toxic	Poison	—	85	10	TM28	Dig	Ground	60	100	10
TM10	Hidden Power	Normal	—	100	15	TM32	Double Team	Normal	—	—	15
TM11	Sunny Day	Fire	—	—	5	TM34	Shock Wave	Electric	60	—	20
TM13	Ice Beam	Ice	95	100	10	TM36	Sludge Bomb	Poison	90	100	10
TM14	Blizzard	Ice	120	70	5	TM42	Facade	Normal	70	100	20
TM17	Protect	Normal	—	—	10	TM43	Secret Power	Normal	70	100	20
TM18	Rain Dance	Water	—	—	5	TM44	Rest	Psychic	—	—	10
TM21	Frustration	Normal	—	100	20	TM45	Attract	Normal	—	100	15
TM23	Iron Tail	Steel	75	75	15	TM46	Thief	Dark	40	100	10
TM24	Thunderbolt	Electric	95	100	15	HM01	Cut	Normal	50	95	30
TM25	Thunder	Electric	120	70	10	HM04	Strength	Normal	80	100	15
						HM06	Rock Smash	Fighting	20	100	15

MOVE TUTOR

FireRed/LeafGreen and *Emerald* Only

Body Slam*	Counter*	Double-Edge
Mimic	Substitute	

*Battle Frontier tutor move (*Emerald*)

---

034 Nidoking™

POISON   GROUND

GENERAL INFO

SPECIES: Drill Pokémon
HEIGHT: 4'07"
WEIGHT: 137 lbs.
ABILITY: Poison Point

If an opponent is striking Nidoking, it has a 30% chance of being poisoned.

STATS

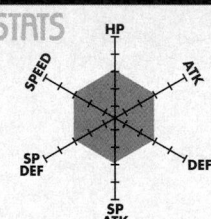

EVOLUTIONS

LV16 — MOON STONE

LOCATION[S]:

RUBY   Rarity: **None**
Trade from *FireRed/LeafGreen*

SAPPHIRE   Rarity: **None**
Trade from *FireRed/LeafGreen*

FIRERED   Rarity: **Evolve**
Evolve Nidorino

LEAFGREEN   Rarity: **Evolve**
Evolve Nidorino

COLOSSEUM   Rarity: **None**
Trade from *FireRed/LeafGreen*

EMERALD   Rarity: **None**
Trade from *FireRed/LeafGreen*

XD   Rarity: **None**
Trade from *FireRed/LeafGreen*

MOVES

Level	Attack	Type	Power	ACC	PP	Level	Attack	Type	Power	ACC	PP
—	Poison Sting	Poison	15	100	35	—	Focus Energy	Normal	—	—	30
—	Double Kick	Fighting	30	100	30	22	Thrash	Normal	90	100	20
—	Peck	Flying	35	100	35	43	Megahorn	Bug	120	85	10

TM/HM

TM/HM#	Name	Type	Power	ACC	PP	TM/HM#	Name	Type	Power	ACC	PP
TM01	Focus Punch	Fighting	150	100	20	TM30	Shadow Ball	Ghost	80	100	15
TM03	Water Pulse	Water	60	95	20	TM31	Brick Break	Fighting	75	100	15
TM05	Roar	Normal	—	100	20	TM32	Double Team	Normal	—	—	15
TM06	Toxic	Poison	—	85	10	TM34	Shock Wave	Electric	60	—	20
TM10	Hidden Power	Normal	—	100	15	TM35	Flamethrower	Fire	95	100	15
TM11	Sunny Day	Fire	—	—	5	TM36	Sludge Bomb	Poison	90	100	10
TM12	Taunt	Dark	—	100	20	TM37	Sandstorm	Ground	—	—	10
TM13	Ice Beam	Ice	95	100	10	TM38	Fire Blast	Fire	120	85	5
TM14	Blizzard	Ice	120	70	5	TM39	Rock Tomb	Rock	50	80	10
TM15	Hyper Beam	Normal	150	90	5	TM41	Torment	Dark	—	100	15
TM17	Protect	Normal	—	—	10	TM42	Facade	Normal	70	100	20
TM18	Rain Dance	Water	—	—	5	TM43	Secret Power	Normal	70	100	20
TM21	Frustration	Normal	—	100	20	TM44	Rest	Psychic	—	—	10
TM23	Iron Tail	Steel	75	75	15	TM45	Attract	Normal	—	100	15
TM24	Thunderbolt	Electric	95	100	15	TM46	Thief	Dark	40	100	10
TM25	Thunder	Electric	120	70	10	HM01	Cut	Normal	50	95	30
TM26	Earthquake	Ground	100	100	10	HM03	Surf	Water	95	100	15
TM27	Return	Normal	—	100	20	HM04	Strength	Normal	80	100	15
TM28	Dig	Ground	60	100	10	HM06	Rock Smash	Fighting	20	100	15

MOVE TUTOR

FireRed/LeafGreen and *Emerald* Only

Body Slam*	Counter*	Double-Edge
Mega Kick*	Mega Punch*	Mimic
Rock Slide*	Seismic Toss*	Substitute

*Battle Frontier tutor move (*Emerald*)

035 Clefairy™

NORMAL

GENERAL INFO

SPECIES: Fairy Pokémon
HEIGHT: 2'00"
WEIGHT: 17 lbs.
ABILITY: Cute Charm

If an opponent is striking Clefairy, it has a 30% chance of being attracted.

STATS

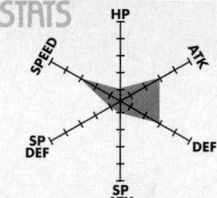

EVOLUTIONS

FRIENDSHIP   MOON STONE

LOCATION[S]:

RUBY   Rarity: **None**
Trade from *FireRed/LeafGreen*

SAPPHIRE   Rarity: **None**
Trade from *FireRed/LeafGreen*

FIRERED   Rarity: **Rare**
Mt. Moon

LEAFGREEN Rarity: **Rare**
Mt. Moon

COLOSSEUM Rarity: **None**
Trade from *FireRed/LeafGreen*

EMERALD   Rarity: **None**
Trade from *FireRed/LeafGreen*

XD   Rarity: **None**
Trade from *FireRed/LeafGreen*

MOVES

Level	Attack	Type	Power	ACC	PP	Level	Attack	Type	Power	ACC	PP
—	Pound	Normal	40	100	35	21	Minimize	Normal	—	—	20
—	Growl	Normal	—	100	40	25	Defense Curl	Normal	—	—	40
5	Encore	Normal	—	100	5	29	Metronome	Normal	—	—	10
9	Sing	Normal	—	55	15	33	Cosmic Power	Normal	—	—	20
13	Doubleslap	Normal	15	85	10	37	Moonlight	Normal	—	—	5
17	Follow Me	Normal	—	100	20	41	Light Screen	Psychic	—	—	30
						45	Meteor Mash	Steel	100	85	10

TM/HM

TM/HM#	Name	Type	Power	ACC	PP	TM/HM#	Name	Type	Power	ACC	PP
TM01	Focus Punch	Fighting	150	100	20	TM27	Return	Normal	—	100	20
TM03	Water Pulse	Water	60	95	20	TM28	Dig	Ground	60	100	10
TM04	Calm Mind	Psychic	—	—	20	TM29	Psychic	Psychic	90	100	10
TM06	Toxic	Poison	—	85	10	TM30	Shadow Ball	Ghost	80	100	15
TM10	Hidden Power	Normal	—	100	15	TM31	Brick Break	Fighting	75	100	15
TM11	Sunny Day	Fire	—	—	5	TM32	Double Team	Normal	—	—	15
TM13	Ice Beam	Ice	95	100	10	TM33	Reflect	Normal	—	—	20
TM14	Blizzard	Ice	120	70	5	TM34	Shock Wave	Electric	60	—	20
TM16	Light Screen	Psychic	—	—	30	TM35	Flamethrower	Fire	95	100	15
TM17	Protect	Normal	—	—	10	TM38	Fire Blast	Fire	120	85	5
TM18	Rain Dance	Water	—	—	5	TM42	Facade	Normal	70	100	20
TM20	Safeguard	Normal	—	—	25	TM43	Secret Power	Normal	70	100	20
TM21	Frustration	Normal	—	100	20	TM44	Rest	Psychic	—	—	10
TM22	Solarbeam	Grass	120	100	10	TM45	Attract	Normal	—	100	15
TM23	Iron Tail	Steel	75	75	15	TM49	Snatch	Dark	—	100	10
TM24	Thunderbolt	Electric	95	100	15	HM04	Strength	Normal	80	100	20
TM25	Thunder	Electric	120	70	10	HM05	Flash	Normal	—	70	20

MOVE TUTOR

FireRed/LeafGreen and Emerald Only

Body Slam*	Counter*	Double-Edge
Dream Eater*	Mega Kick*	Mega Punch*
Metronome	Mimic	Seismic Toss*
Softboiled	Substitute	Thunder Wave*

*Battle Frontier tutor move (*Emerald*)

---

036 Clefable™

NORMAL

GENERAL INFO

SPECIES: Fairy Pokémon
HEIGHT: 4'03"
WEIGHT: 88 lbs.
ABILITY: Cute Charm

If an opponent is striking Clefable, it has a 30% chance of being attracted.

STATS

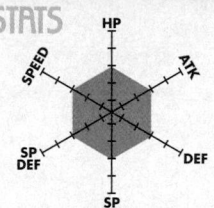

EVOLUTIONS

FRIENDSHIP   MOON STONE

LOCATION[S]:

RUBY   Rarity: **None**
Trade from *FireRed/LeafGreen*

SAPPHIRE   Rarity: **None**
Trade from *FireRed/LeafGreen*

FIRERED   Rarity: **Rare**
Evolve Clefairy

LEAFGREEN Rarity: **Rare**
Evolve Clefairy

COLOSSEUM Rarity: **None**
Trade from *FireRed/LeafGreen*

EMERALD   Rarity: **None**
Trade from *FireRed/LeafGreen*

XD   Rarity: **None**
Trade from *FireRed/LeafGreen*

MOVES

Level	Attack	Type	Power	ACC	PP	Level	Attack	Type	Power	ACC	PP
—	Sing	Normal	—	55	15	—	Minimize	Normal	—	—	20
—	Doubleslap	Normal	15	85	10	—	Metronome	Normal	—	—	10

TM/HM

TM/HM#	Name	Type	Power	ACC	PP	TM/HM#	Name	Type	Power	ACC	PP
TM01	Focus Punch	Fighting	150	100	20	TM27	Return	Normal	—	100	20
TM03	Water Pulse	Water	60	95	20	TM28	Dig	Ground	60	100	10
TM04	Calm Mind	Psychic	—	—	20	TM29	Psychic	Psychic	90	100	10
TM06	Toxic	Poison	—	85	10	TM30	Shadow Ball	Ghost	80	100	15
TM10	Hidden Power	Normal	—	100	15	TM31	Brick Break	Fighting	75	100	15
TM11	Sunny Day	Fire	—	—	5	TM32	Double Team	Normal	—	—	15
TM13	Ice Beam	Ice	95	100	10	TM33	Reflect	Normal	—	—	20
TM14	Blizzard	Ice	120	70	5	TM34	Shock Wave	Electric	60	—	20
TM15	Hyper Beam	Normal	150	90	5	TM35	Flamethrower	Fire	95	100	15
TM16	Light Screen	Psychic	—	—	30	TM38	Fire Blast	Fire	120	85	5
TM17	Protect	Normal	—	—	10	TM42	Facade	Normal	70	100	20
TM18	Rain Dance	Water	—	—	5	TM43	Secret Power	Normal	70	100	20
TM20	Safeguard	Normal	—	—	25	TM44	Rest	Psychic	—	—	10
TM21	Frustration	Normal	—	100	20	TM45	Attract	Normal	—	100	15
TM22	Solarbeam	Grass	120	100	10	TM49	Snatch	Dark	—	100	10
TM23	Iron Tail	Steel	75	75	15	HM04	Strength	Normal	80	100	20
TM24	Thunderbolt	Electric	95	100	15	HM05	Flash	Normal	—	70	20
TM25	Thunder	Electric	120	70	10						

MOVE TUTOR

FireRed/LeafGreen and Emerald Only

Body Slam*	Counter*	Double-Edge
Dream Eater*	Mega Kick*	Mega Punch*
Metronome	Mimic	Seismic Toss*
Softboiled	Substitute	Thunder Wave*

*Battle Frontier tutor move (*Emerald*)

037 Vulpix™

FIRE

GENERAL INFO
SPECIES: Fox Pokémon
HEIGHT: 2'00"
WEIGHT: 22 lbs.
ABILITY: Flash Fire
Enhances its Fire-type moves and protects Vulpix from being damaged by Fire-type moves.

STATS
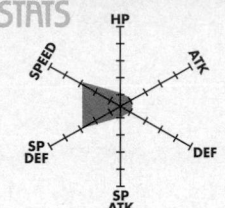

EVOLUTIONS
 FIRE STONE

LOCATION[S]:

RUBY **Rarity: Common**
Mt. Pyre

SAPPHIRE **Rarity: Common**
Mt. Pyre

FIRERED **Rarity: None**
Trade from *Ruby/Sapphire/LeafGreen*

LEAFGREEN **Rarity: Common**
Pokémon Mansion, Route 7, Route 8

COLOSSEUM **Rarity: None**
Trade from *Ruby/Sapphire/LeafGreen*

EMERALD **Rarity: Common**
Mt. Pyre

XD **Rarity: Only One**
Pyrite Town (Capture from Cipher Peon Mesin)

MOVES

Level	Attack	Type	Power	ACC	PP	Level	Attack	Type	Power	ACC	PP
—	Ember	Fire	40	100	25	21	Confuse Ray	Ghost	—	100	10
5	Tail Whip	Normal	—	100	30	25	Imprison	Psychic	—	100	15
9	Roar	Normal	—	100	20	29	Flamethrower	Fire	95	100	15
13	Quick Attack	Normal	40	100	30	33	Safeguard	Normal	—	—	25
17	Will-O-Wisp	Fire	—	75	15	37	Grudge	Ghost	—	100	5
						41	Fire Spin	Fire	15	70	15

TM/HM

TM/HM#	Name	Type	Power	ACC	PP	TM/HM#	Name	Type	Power	ACC	PP
TM05	Roar	Normal	—	100	20	TM28	Dig	Ground	60	100	10
TM06	Toxic	Poison	—	85	10	TM32	Double Team	Normal	—	—	15
TM10	Hidden Power	Normal	—	100	15	TM35	Flamethrower	Fire	95	100	15
TM11	Sunny Day	Fire	—	—	5	TM38	Fire Blast	Fire	120	85	5
TM17	Protect	Normal	—	—	10	TM42	Facade	Normal	70	100	20
TM20	Safeguard	Normal	—	—	25	TM43	Secret Power	Normal	70	100	20
TM21	Frustration	Normal	—	100	20	TM44	Rest	Psychic	—	—	10
TM23	Iron Tail	Steel	75	75	15	TM45	Attract	Normal	—	100	15
TM27	Return	Normal	—	100	20	TM50	Overheat	Fire	140	90	5

EGG MOVES*

Name	Type	Power	ACC	PP
Faint Attack	Dark	60	—	20
Hypnosis	Psychic	—	60	20
Flail	Normal	—	100	15
Disable	Normal	—	55	20
Howl	Normal	—	—	40
Psych Up	Normal	—	—	10
Heat Wave	Fire	100	90	10
Spite	Ghost	—	100	10

*Learned Via Breeding

MOVE TUTOR
FireRed/LeafGreen and *Emerald* Only

Body Slam*	Double-Edge	Mimic
Substitute		

Emerald Only

Endure*	Sleep Talk	Snore
Swagger	Swift*	

*Battle Frontier tutor move (*Emerald*)

---

038 Ninetales™

FIRE

GENERAL INFO
SPECIES: Fox Pokémon
HEIGHT: 3'07"
WEIGHT: 44 lbs.
ABILITY: Flash Fire
Enhances its Fire-type moves and protects Ninetales from being damaged by Fire-type moves.

STATS
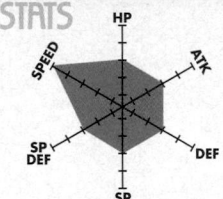

EVOLUTIONS
 FIRE STONE

LOCATION[S]:

RUBY **Rarity: Evolve**
Evolve Vulpix

SAPPHIRE **Rarity: Evolve**
Evolve Vulpix

FIRERED **Rarity: None**
Trade from *Ruby/Sapphire/LeafGreen*

LEAFGREEN **Rarity: Evolve**
Evolve Vulpix

COLOSSEUM **Rarity: None**
Trade from *Ruby/Sapphire/LeafGreen*

EMERALD **Rarity: Evolve**
Evolve Vulpix

XD **Rarity: Evolve**
Evolve Vulpix

MOVES

Level	Attack	Type	Power	ACC	PP	Level	Attack	Type	Power	ACC	PP
—	Ember	Fire	40	100	25	—	Confuse Ray	Ghost	—	100	10
—	Quick Attack	Normal	40	100	30	—	Safeguard	Normal	—	—	25
						45	Fire Spin	Fire	15	70	15

TM/HM

TM/HM#	Name	Type	Power	ACC	PP	TM/HM#	Name	Type	Power	ACC	PP
TM05	Roar	Normal	—	100	20	TM28	Dig	Ground	60	100	10
TM06	Toxic	Poison	—	85	10	TM32	Double Team	Normal	—	—	15
TM10	Hidden Power	Normal	—	100	15	TM35	Flamethrower	Fire	95	100	15
TM11	Sunny Day	Fire	—	—	5	TM38	Fire Blast	Fire	120	85	5
TM15	Hyper Beam	Normal	150	90	5	TM42	Facade	Normal	70	100	20
TM17	Protect	Normal	—	—	10	TM43	Secret Power	Normal	70	100	20
TM20	Safeguard	Normal	—	—	25	TM44	Rest	Psychic	—	—	10
TM21	Frustration	Normal	—	100	20	TM45	Attract	Normal	—	100	15
TM23	Iron Tail	Steel	75	75	15	TM50	Overheat	Fire	140	90	5
TM27	Return	Normal	—	100	20						

MOVE TUTOR
FireRed/LeafGreen and *Emerald* Only

Body Slam*	Double-Edge	Mimic
Substitute		

Emerald Only

Endure*	Sleep Talk	Snore
Swagger	Swift*	

*Battle Frontier tutor move (*Emerald*)

039 Jigglypuff™

NORMAL

GENERAL INFO
SPECIES: **Balloon Pokémon**
HEIGHT: **1'08"**
WEIGHT: **12 lbs.**
ABILITY: **Cute Charm**
If an opponent is striking Jigglypuff, it has a 30% chance of being attracted.

STATS
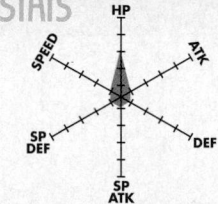

EVOLUTIONS

FRIENDSHIP   MOON STONE

LOCATION(S):

RUBY Rarity: **Common**
Route 115

SAPPHIRE Rarity: **Common**
Route 115

FIRERED Rarity: **Rare**
Route 3

LEAFGREEN Rarity: **Rare**
Route 3

COLOSSEUM Rarity: **None**
Trade from *Ruby/Sapphire/FireRed/LeafGreen*

EMERALD Rarity: **Common**
Route 115

XD Rarity: **None**
Trade from *Ruby/Sapphire/FireRed/LeafGreen*

MOVES

Level	Attack	Type	Power	ACC	PP
—	Sing	Normal	—	55	15
4	Defense Curl	Normal	—	—	40
9	Pound	Normal	40	100	35
14	Disable	Normal	—	55	20
19	Rollout	Rock	30	90	20
24	Doubleslap	Normal	15	85	10
29	Rest	Psychic	—	—	10
34	Body Slam	Normal	85	100	15
39	Mimic	Normal	—	100	10
44	Hyper Voice	Normal	90	100	10
49	Double-Edge	Normal	120	100	15

TM/HM

TM/HM#	Name	Type	Power	ACC	PP
TM01	Focus Punch	Fighting	150	100	20
TM03	Water Pulse	Water	60	95	20
TM06	Toxic	Poison	—	85	10
TM10	Hidden Power	Normal	—	100	15
TM11	Sunny Day	Fire	—	—	5
TM13	Ice Beam	Ice	95	100	10
TM14	Blizzard	Ice	120	70	5
TM16	Light Screen	Psychic	—	—	30
TM17	Protect	Normal	—	—	10
TM18	Rain Dance	Water	—	—	5
TM20	Safeguard	Normal	—	—	25
TM21	Frustration	Normal	—	100	20
TM22	Solarbeam	Grass	120	100	10
TM24	Thunderbolt	Electric	95	100	15
TM25	Thunder	Electric	120	70	10
TM27	Return	Normal	—	100	20
TM28	Dig	Ground	60	100	10
TM29	Psychic	Psychic	90	100	10
TM30	Shadow Ball	Ghost	80	100	15
TM31	Brick Break	Fighting	75	100	15
TM32	Double Team	Normal	—	—	15
TM33	Reflect	Normal	—	—	20
TM34	Shock Wave	Electric	60	—	20
TM35	Flamethrower	Fire	95	100	15
TM38	Fire Blast	Fire	120	85	5
TM42	Facade	Normal	70	100	20
TM43	Secret Power	Normal	70	100	20
TM44	Rest	Psychic	—	—	10
TM45	Attract	Normal	—	100	15
TM49	Snatch	Dark	—	100	10
HM04	Strength	Normal	80	100	20
HM05	Flash	Normal	—	70	20

MOVE TUTOR
FireRed/LeafGreen and Emerald Only

Body Slam* • Counter* • Double-Edge
Dream Eater* • Mega Kick* • Mega Punch*
Mimic • Seismic Toss* • Substitute
Thunder Wave*

Emerald Only
Defense Curl* • Dynamicpunch* • Endure*
Fire Punch* • Ice Punch* • Metronome
Mud-Slap* • Psych Up* • Rollout
Sleep Talk • Snore* • Swagger
Thunderpunch*
*Battle Frontier tutor move (*Emerald*)

---

040 Wigglytuff™

NORMAL

GENERAL INFO
SPECIES: **Balloon Pokémon**
HEIGHT: **3'03"**
WEIGHT: **26 lbs.**
ABILITY: **Cute Charm**
If an opponent is striking Wigglytuff, it has a 30% chance of being attracted.

STATS
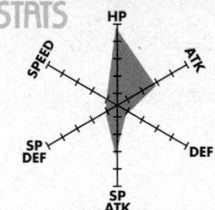

EVOLUTIONS

FRIENDSHIP   MOON STONE

LOCATION(S):

RUBY Rarity: **Evolve**
Evolve Jigglypuff

SAPPHIRE Rarity: **Evolve**
Evolve Jigglypuff

FIRERED Rarity: **Evolve**
Evolve Jigglypuff

LEAFGREEN Rarity: **Evolve**
Evolve Jigglypuff

COLOSSEUM Rarity: **None**
Trade from *Ruby/Sapphire/FireRed/LeafGreen*

EMERALD Rarity: **Evolve**
Evolve Jigglypuff

XD Rarity: **None**
Trade from *Ruby/Sapphire/FireRed/LeafGreen*

MOVES

Level	Attack	Type	Power	ACC	PP
—	Sing	Normal	—	55	15
—	Defense Curl	Normal	—	—	40
—	Disable	Normal	—	55	20
—	Doubleslap	Normal	15	85	10

TM/HM

TM/HM#	Name	Type	Power	ACC	PP
TM01	Focus Punch	Fighting	150	100	20
TM03	Water Pulse	Water	60	95	20
TM06	Toxic	Poison	—	85	10
TM10	Hidden Power	Normal	—	100	15
TM11	Sunny Day	Fire	—	—	5
TM13	Ice Beam	Ice	95	100	10
TM14	Blizzard	Ice	120	70	5
TM15	Hyper Beam	Normal	150	90	5
TM16	Light Screen	Psychic	—	—	30
TM17	Protect	Normal	—	—	10
TM18	Rain Dance	Water	—	—	5
TM20	Safeguard	Normal	—	—	25
TM21	Frustration	Normal	—	100	20
TM22	Solarbeam	Grass	120	100	10
TM24	Thunderbolt	Electric	95	100	15
TM25	Thunder	Electric	120	70	10
TM27	Return	Normal	—	100	20
TM28	Dig	Ground	60	100	10
TM29	Psychic	Psychic	90	100	10
TM30	Shadow Ball	Ghost	80	100	15
TM31	Brick Break	Fighting	75	100	15
TM32	Double Team	Normal	—	—	15
TM33	Reflect	Normal	—	—	20
TM34	Shock Wave	Electric	60	—	20
TM35	Flamethrower	Fire	95	100	15
TM38	Fire Blast	Fire	120	85	5
TM42	Facade	Normal	70	100	20
TM43	Secret Power	Normal	70	100	20
TM44	Rest	Psychic	—	—	10
TM45	Attract	Normal	—	100	15
TM49	Snatch	Dark	—	100	10
HM04	Strength	Normal	80	100	20
HM05	Flash	Normal	—	70	20

MOVE TUTOR
FireRed/LeafGreen and Emerald Only

Body Slam* • Counter* • Double-Edge
Dream Eater* • Mega Kick* • Mega Punch*
Mimic • Seismic Toss* • Substitute
Thunder Wave*

Emerald Only
Defense Curl* • Dynamicpunch* • Endure*
Fire Punch* • Ice Punch* • Metronome
Mud-Slap* • Psych Up* • Rollout
Sleep Talk • Snore* • Swagger
Thunderpunch*
*Battle Frontier tutor move (*Emerald*)

041 Zubat™

POISON | FLYING

GENERAL INFO
SPECIES: Bat Pokémon
HEIGHT: 2'07"
WEIGHT: 17 lbs.
ABILITY: Inner Focus
Zubat no longer flinches.

STATS
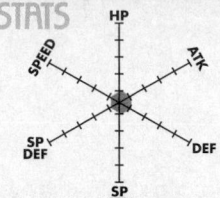

EVOLUTIONS

LV22 | FRIENDSHIP

LOCATION[S]:

RUBY   Rarity: **Common**
Cave of Origin, Granite Cave, Shoal Cave, Seafloor Cavern, Victory Road, Meteor Falls

SAPPHIRE   Rarity: **Common**
Cave of Origin, Granite Cave, Shoal Cave, Seafloor Cavern, Victory Road, Meteor Falls

FIRERED   Rarity: **Common**
Five Island, Mt. Moon, Rock Tunnel, Victory Road

LEAFGREEN   Rarity: **Common**
Five Island, Mt. Moon, Rock Tunnel, Victory Road

COLOSSEUM   Rarity: **None**
Trade from *Ruby/Sapphire/FireRed/LeafGreen*

EMERALD   Rarity: **Common**
Altering Cave, Cave of Origin, Granite Cave, Shoal Cave, Seafloor Cavern, Meteor Falls

XD   Rarity: **Common**
Cave Poké Spot

MOVES

Level	Attack	Type	Power	ACC	PP	Level	Attack	Type	Power	ACC	PP
—	Leech Life	Bug	20	100	15	26	Confuse Ray	Ghost	—	100	10
6	Astonish	Ghost	30	100	15	31	Air Cutter	Flying	55	95	25
11	Supersonic	Normal	—	55	20	36	Mean Look	Normal	—	100	5
16	Bite	Dark	60	100	25	41	Poison Fang	Poison	50	100	15
21	Wing Attack	Flying	60	100	35	46	Haze	Ice	—	—	30

TM/HM

TM/HM#	Name	Type	Power	ACC	PP	TM/HM#	Name	Type	Power	ACC	PP
TM06	Toxic	Poison	—	85	10	TM36	Sludge Bomb	Poison	90	100	10
TM10	Hidden Power	Normal	—	100	15	TM40	Aerial Ace	Flying	60	—	20
TM11	Sunny Day	Fire	—	—	5	TM41	Torment	Dark	—	100	15
TM12	Taunt	Dark	—	100	20	TM42	Facade	Normal	70	100	20
TM17	Protect	Normal	—	—	10	TM43	Secret Power	Normal	70	100	20
TM18	Rain Dance	Water	—	—	5	TM44	Rest	Psychic	—	—	10
TM19	Giga Drain	Grass	60	100	5	TM45	Attract	Normal	—	100	15
TM21	Frustration	Normal	—	100	20	TM46	Thief	Dark	40	100	10
TM27	Return	Normal	—	100	20	TM47	Steel Wing	Steel	70	90	25
TM30	Shadow Ball	Ghost	80	100	15	TM49	Snatch	Dark	—	100	10
TM32	Double Team	Normal	—	—	15						

EGG MOVES*

Name	Type	Power	ACC	PP
Quick Attack	Normal	40	100	30
Pursuit	Dark	40	100	20
Faint Attack	Dark	60	—	20
Whirlwind	Normal	—	100	20
Curse	Normal	—	—	—

*Learned Via Breeding

MOVE TUTOR
FireRed/LeafGreen and *Emerald* Only

Double-Edge	Mimic	Substitute

Emerald Only

Endure*	Sleep Talk	Snore*
Swagger	Swift*	

*Battle Frontier tutor move (*Emerald*)

---

042 Golbat™

POISON | FLYING

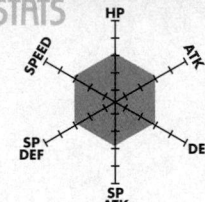

GENERAL INFO
SPECIES: Bat Pokémon
HEIGHT: 5'03"
WEIGHT: 121 lbs.
ABILITY: Inner Focus
Golbat no longer flinches.

STATS

EVOLUTIONS

LV22 | FRIENDSHIP

LOCATION[S]:

RUBY   Rarity: **Common**
Evolve Zubat, Cave of Origin, Granite Cave, Shoal Cave, Seafloor Cavern, Victory Road, Meteor Falls

SAPPHIRE   Rarity: **Common**
Evolve Zubat, Cave of Origin, Granite Cave, Shoal Cave, Seafloor Cavern, Victory Road, Meteor Falls

FIRERED   Rarity: **Rare**
Evolve Zubat, Five Island, Seafoam Islands, Victory Road

LEAFGREEN   Rarity: **Rare**
Evolve Zubat, Five Island, Seafoam Islands, Victory Road

COLOSSEUM   Rarity: **None**
Trade from *Ruby/Sapphire/FireRed/LeafGreen*

EMERALD   Rarity: **Common**
Evolve Zubat, Cave of Origin, Granite Cave, Shoal Cave, Seafloor Cavern, Victory Road, Meteor Falls, Sky Pillar

XD   Rarity: **Evolve**
Evolve Zubat

MOVES

Level	Attack	Type	Power	ACC	PP	Level	Attack	Type	Power	ACC	PP
—	Leech Life	Bug	20	100	15	21	Wing Attack	Flying	60	100	35
—	Screech	Normal	—	85	40	28	Confuse Ray	Ghost	—	100	10
—/6	Astonish	Ghost	30	100	15	35	Air Cutter	Flying	55	95	25
—/11	Supersonic	Normal	—	55	20	42	Mean Look	Normal	—	100	5
16	Bite	Dark	60	100	25	49	Poison Fang	Poison	50	100	15
						56	Haze	Ice	—	—	30

TM/HM

TM/HM#	Name	Type	Power	ACC	PP	TM/HM#	Name	Type	Power	ACC	PP
TM06	Toxic	Poison	—	85	10	TM32	Double Team	Normal	—	—	15
TM10	Hidden Power	Normal	—	100	15	TM36	Sludge Bomb	Poison	90	100	10
TM11	Sunny Day	Fire	—	—	5	TM40	Aerial Ace	Flying	60	—	20
TM12	Taunt	Dark	—	100	20	TM41	Torment	Dark	—	100	15
TM15	Hyper Beam	Normal	150	90	5	TM42	Facade	Normal	70	100	20
TM17	Protect	Normal	—	—	10	TM43	Secret Power	Normal	70	100	20
TM18	Rain Dance	Water	—	—	5	TM44	Rest	Psychic	—	—	10
TM19	Giga Drain	Grass	60	100	5	TM45	Attract	Normal	—	100	15
TM21	Frustration	Normal	—	100	20	TM46	Thief	Dark	40	100	10
TM27	Return	Normal	—	100	20	TM47	Steel Wing	Steel	70	90	25
TM30	Shadow Ball	Ghost	80	100	15	TM49	Snatch	Dark	—	100	10

= Emerald Only

MOVE TUTOR
FireRed/LeafGreen and *Emerald* Only

Double-Edge	Mimic	Substitute

Emerald Only

Endure*	Sleep Talk	Snore*
Swagger	Swift*	

*Battle Frontier tutor move (*Emerald*)

043 Oddish™

GRASS | POISON

GENERAL INFO
SPECIES: Weed Pokémon
HEIGHT: 1'08"
WEIGHT: 12 lbs.
ABILITY: Chlorophyll
Oddish's Speed is doubled when the sunlight is strong.

STATS
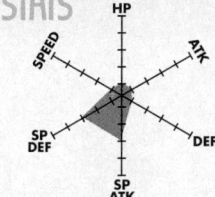

EVOLUTIONS

LEAF STONE

LV21

SUN STONE

LOCATION(s):

RUBY   Rarity: **Rare**
Routes 110, 117, 119, 120, 121, 123, Safari Zone

SAPPHIRE   Rarity: **Rare**
Routes 110, 117, 119, 120, 121, 123, Safari Zone

FIRERED   Rarity: **Rare**
Two Island, Three Island, Six Island, Routes 5, 6, 7, 12, 13, 14, 15, 24, 25

LEAFGREEN   Rarity: **None**
Trade from *Ruby/Sapphire/FireRed*

COLOSSEUM   Rarity: **None**
Trade from *Ruby/Sapphire/FireRed/LeafGreen*

EMERALD   Rarity: **Common**
Routes 110, 117, 119, 120, 121, 123, Safari Zone

XD   Rarity: **None**
Trade from *Ruby/Sapphire/FireRed*

MOVES

Level	Attack	Type	Power	ACC	PP	Level	Attack	Type	Power	ACC	PP
—	Absorb	Grass	20	100	20	18	Sleep Powder	Grass	—	75	15
7	Sweet Scent	Normal	—	100	20	23	Acid	Poison	40	100	30
14	Poisonpowder	Poison	—	75	35	32	Moonlight	Normal	—	—	5
16	Stun Spore	Grass	—	75	30	39	Petal Dance	Grass	70	100	20

TM/HM

TM/HM#	Name	Type	Power	ACC	PP	TM/HM#	Name	Type	Power	ACC	PP
TM06	Toxic	Poison	—	85	10	TM32	Double Team	Normal	—	—	15
TM09	Bullet Seed	Grass	10	100	30	TM36	Sludge Bomb	Poison	90	100	10
TM10	Hidden Power	Normal	—	100	15	TM42	Facade	Normal	70	100	20
TM11	Sunny Day	Fire	—	—	5	TM43	Secret Power	Normal	70	100	20
TM17	Protect	Normal	—	—	10	TM44	Rest	Psychic	—	—	10
TM19	Giga Drain	Grass	60	100	5	TM45	Attract	Normal	—	100	15
TM21	Frustration	Normal	—	100	20	HM01	Cut	Normal	50	95	30
TM22	Solarbeam	Grass	120	100	10	HM05	Flash	Normal	—	70	20
TM27	Return	Normal	—	100	20						

EGG MOVES*

Name	Type	Power	ACC	PP
Charm	Normal	—	100	20
Flail	Normal	—	100	15
Ingrain	Grass	—	100	20
Razor Leaf	Grass	55	95	25
Synthesis	Grass	—	—	5
Swords Dance	Normal	—	—	30

*Learned Via Breeding

MOVE TUTOR
FireRed/LeafGreen and *Emerald* Only

Double-Edge	Mimic	Substitute
Swords Dance*		

Emerald Only

Endure*	Sleep Talk	Snore*
Swagger		

*Battle Frontier tutor move (*Emerald*)

---

044 Gloom™

GRASS | POISON

GENERAL INFO
SPECIES: Weed Pokémon
HEIGHT: 2'07"
WEIGHT: 19 lbs.
ABILITY: Chlorophyll
Gloom's Speed is doubled when the sunlight is strong.

STATS
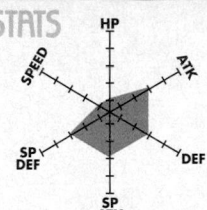
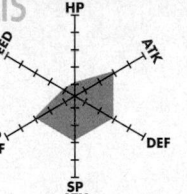

EVOLUTIONS

LEAF STONE

LV21

SUN STONE

LOCATION(s):

RUBY   Rarity: **Rare**
Evolve Oddish, Route 121, Route 123, Safari Zone

SAPPHIRE   Rarity: **Rare**
Evolve Oddish, Route 121, Route 123, Safari Zone

FIRERED   Rarity: **Rare**
Evolve Oddish, Two Island, Three Island, Six Island, Routes 12, 13, 14, 15

LEAFGREEN   Rarity: **None**
Evolve Oddish, Trade from *Ruby/Sapphire/FireRed*

COLOSSEUM   Rarity: **None**
Trade from *Ruby/Sapphire*

EMERALD   Rarity: **Rare**
Evolve Oddish, Route 121, Route 123, Safari Zone

XD   Rarity: **None**
Trade from *Ruby/Sapphire/FireRed*

MOVES

Level	Attack	Type	Power	ACC	PP	Level	Attack	Type	Power	ACC	PP
—	Absorb	Grass	20	100	20	18	Sleep Powder	Grass	—	75	15
—	Sweet Scent	Normal	—	100	20	24	Acid	Poison	40	100	30
—	Poisonpowder	Poison	—	75	35	35	Moonlight	Normal	—	—	5
16	Stun Spore	Grass	—	75	30	44	Petal Dance	Grass	70	100	20

TM/HM

TM/HM#	Name	Type	Power	ACC	PP	TM/HM#	Name	Type	Power	ACC	PP
TM06	Toxic	Poison	—	85	10	TM32	Double Team	Normal	—	—	15
TM09	Bullet Seed	Grass	10	100	30	TM36	Sludge Bomb	Poison	90	100	10
TM10	Hidden Power	Normal	—	100	15	TM42	Facade	Normal	70	100	20
TM11	Sunny Day	Fire	—	—	5	TM43	Secret Power	Normal	70	100	20
TM17	Protect	Normal	—	—	10	TM44	Rest	Psychic	—	—	10
TM19	Giga Drain	Grass	60	100	5	TM45	Attract	Normal	—	100	15
TM21	Frustration	Normal	—	100	20	HM01	Cut	Normal	50	95	30
TM22	Solarbeam	Grass	120	100	10	HM05	Flash	Normal	—	70	20
TM27	Return	Normal	—	100	20						

MOVE TUTOR
FireRed/LeafGreen and *Emerald* Only

Double-Edge	Mimic	Substitute
Swords Dance*		

Emerald Only

Endure*	Sleep Talk	Snore*
Swagger		

*Battle Frontier tutor move (*Emerald*)

045 Vileplume™

GRASS | **POISON**

GENERAL INFO
SPECIES: Flower Pokémon
HEIGHT: 3'11"
WEIGHT: 41 lbs.
ABILITY: Chlorophyll
Vileplume's Speed is doubled when the sunlight is strong.

STATS
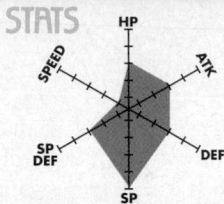

EVOLUTIONS
Oddish → Gloom **LV21** → Vileplume **LEAF STONE**

LOCATION[S]:

RUBY — Rarity: **Evolve**
Evolve Gloom

SAPPHIRE — Rarity: **Evolve**
Evolve Gloom

FIRERED — Rarity: **Evolve**
Evolve Gloom

LEAFGREEN — Rarity: **Evolve**
Evolve Gloom, Trade from *Ruby/Sapphire/FireRed*

COLOSSEUM — Rarity: **None**
Trade from *Ruby/Sapphire/FireRed*

EMERALD — Rarity: **Evolve**
Evolve Gloom

XD — Rarity: **None**
Trade from *Ruby/Sapphire/FireRed*

MOVES

Level	Attack	Type	Power	ACC	PP	Level	Attack	Type	Power	ACC	PP
—	Absorb	Grass	20	100	20	—	Stun Spore	Grass	—	75	30
—	Aromatherapy	Grass	—	—	5	—	Mega Drain	Grass	40	100	10
						44	Petal Dance	Grass	70	100	20

TM/HM

TM/HM#	Name	Type	Power	ACC	PP	TM/HM#	Name	Type	Power	ACC	PP
TM06	Toxic	Poison	—	85	10	TM27	Return	Normal	—	100	20
TM09	Bullet Seed	Grass	10	100	30	TM32	Double Team	Normal	—	—	15
TM10	Hidden Power	Normal	—	100	15	TM36	Sludge Bomb	Poison	90	100	10
TM11	Sunny Day	Fire	—	—	5	TM42	Facade	Normal	70	100	20
TM15	Hyper Beam	Normal	150	90	5	TM43	Secret Power	Normal	70	100	20
TM17	Protect	Normal	—	—	10	TM44	Rest	Psychic	—	—	10
TM19	Giga Drain	Grass	60	100	5	TM45	Attract	Normal	—	100	15
TM21	Frustration	Normal	—	100	20	HM01	Cut	Normal	50	95	30
TM22	Solarbeam	Grass	120	100	10	HM05	Flash	Normal	—	70	20

MOVE TUTOR
FireRed/LeafGreen and *Emerald* Only

Body Slam*	Double-Edge	Mimic
Substitute	Swords Dance*	

Emerald Only

Endure*	Sleep Talk	Snore*
Swagger		

*Battle Frontier tutor move (*Emerald*)

---

046 Paras™

BUG | **GRASS**

GENERAL INFO
SPECIES: Mushroom Pokémon
HEIGHT: 1'00"
WEIGHT: 12 lbs.
ABILITY: Effect Spore
An opponent has a 10% chance of being paralyzed, poisoned, or put to sleep if it hits Paras.

STATS
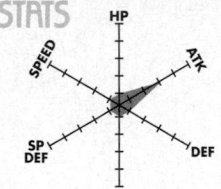

EVOLUTIONS
 Parasect **LV24**

LOCATION[S]:

RUBY — Rarity: **None**
Trade from *FireRed/LeafGreen*

SAPPHIRE — Rarity: **None**
Trade from *FireRed/LeafGreen*

FIRERED — Rarity: **Common**
Mt. Moon, Safari Zone

LEAFGREEN — Rarity: **Common**
Mt. Moon, Safari Zone

COLOSSEUM — Rarity: **None**
Trade from *FireRed/LeafGreen*

EMERALD — Rarity: **None**
Trade from *FireRed/LeafGreen*

XD — Rarity: **Only One**
Cipher Key Lair (Capture from Cipher Peon Humah)

MOVES

Level	Attack	Type	Power	ACC	PP	Level	Attack	Type	Power	ACC	PP
—	Scratch	Normal	40	100	35	25	Spore	Grass	—	100	15
7	Stun Spore	Grass	—	75	30	31	Slash	Normal	70	100	20
13	Poisonpowder	Poison	—	75	35	37	Growth	Normal	—	—	40
19	Leech Life	Bug	20	100	15	43	Giga Drain	Grass	60	100	5
						49	Aromatherapy	Grass	—	—	5

TM/HM

TM/HM#	Name	Type	Power	ACC	PP	TM/HM#	Name	Type	Power	ACC	PP
TM06	Toxic	Poison	—	85	10	TM36	Sludge Bomb	Poison	90	100	10
TM09	Bullet Seed	Grass	10	100	30	TM40	Aerial Ace	Flying	60	—	20
TM10	Hidden Power	Normal	—	100	15	TM42	Facade	Normal	70	100	20
TM11	Sunny Day	Fire	—	—	5	TM43	Secret Power	Normal	70	100	20
TM17	Protect	Normal	—	—	10	TM44	Rest	Psychic	—	—	10
TM19	Giga Drain	Grass	60	100	5	TM45	Attract	Normal	—	100	15
TM21	Frustration	Normal	—	100	20	TM46	Thief	Dark	40	100	10
TM22	Solarbeam	Grass	120	100	10	HM01	Cut	Normal	50	95	30
TM27	Return	Normal	—	100	20	HM05	Flash	Normal	—	70	20
TM28	Dig	Ground	60	100	10	HM06	Rock Smash	Fighting	20	100	15
TM32	Double Team	Normal	—	—	15						

EGG MOVES*

Name	Type	Power	ACC	PP
Counter	Fighting	—	100	20
False Swipe	Normal	40	100	40
Flail	Normal	—	100	15
Light Screen	Psychic	—	—	30
Psybeam	Psychic	65	100	20
Pursuit	Dark	40	100	20
Screech	Normal	—	85	40
Sweet Scent	Normal	—	100	20

*Learned Via Breeding

MOVE TUTOR
FireRed/LeafGreen and *Emerald* Only

Body Slam*	Counter*	Double-Edge
Mimic	Substitute	Swords Dance*

*Battle Frontier tutor move (*Emerald*)

047 Parasect™

BUG | GRASS

GENERAL INFO
SPECIES: Mushroom Pokémon
HEIGHT: 3'03"
WEIGHT: 65 lbs.
ABILITY: Effect Spore
An opponent has a 10% chance of being paralyzed, poisoned, or put to sleep if it hits Parasect.

STATS
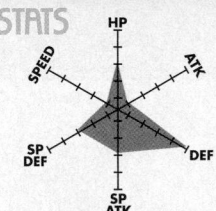

EVOLUTIONS

LV24

LOCATION(S):

RUBY	Rarity: **None**
Trade from *FireRed/LeafGreen*

SAPPHIRE	Rarity: **None**
Trade from *FireRed/LeafGreen*

FIRERED	Rarity: **Rare**
Evolve Paras, Safari Zone

LEAFGREEN	Rarity: **Rare**
Evolve Paras, Safari Zone

COLOSSEUM	Rarity: **None**
Trade from *FireRed/LeafGreen*

EMERALD	Rarity: **None**
Trade from *FireRed/LeafGreen*

XD	Rarity: **Evolve**
Evolve Paras

MOVES

Level	Attack	Type	Power	ACC	PP	Level	Attack	Type	Power	ACC	PP
—	Scratch	Normal	40	100	35	27	Spore	Grass	—	100	15
—	Stun Spore	Grass	—	75	30	35	Slash	Normal	70	100	20
—	Poisonpowder	Poison	—	75	35	43	Growth	Normal	—	—	40
19	Leech Life	Bug	20	100	15	51	Giga Drain	Grass	60	100	5
						59	Aromatherapy	Grass	—	—	5

TM/HM

TM/HM#	Name	Type	Power	ACC	PP	TM/HM#	Name	Type	Power	ACC	PP
TM06	Toxic	Poison	—	85	10	TM32	Double Team	Normal	—	—	15
TM09	Bullet Seed	Grass	10	100	30	TM36	Sludge Bomb	Poison	90	100	10
TM10	Hidden Power	Normal	—	100	15	TM40	Aerial Ace	Flying	60	—	20
TM11	Sunny Day	Fire	—	—	5	TM42	Facade	Normal	70	100	20
TM15	Hyper Beam	Normal	150	90	5	TM43	Secret Power	Normal	70	100	20
TM17	Protect	Normal	—	—	10	TM44	Rest	Psychic	—	—	10
TM19	Giga Drain	Grass	60	100	5	TM45	Attract	Normal	—	100	15
TM21	Frustration	Normal	—	100	20	TM46	Thief	Dark	40	100	10
TM22	Solarbeam	Grass	120	100	10	HM01	Cut	Normal	50	95	30
TM27	Return	Normal	—	100	20	HM05	Flash	Normal	—	70	20
TM28	Dig	Ground	60	100	10	HM06	Rock Smash	Fighting	20	100	15

MOVE TUTOR
FireRed/LeafGreen and *Emerald* Only

Body Slam*	Counter*	Double-Edge
Mimic	Substitute	Swords Dance*

*Battle Frontier tutor move (*Emerald*)

---

048 Venonat™

BUG | POISON

GENERAL INFO
SPECIES: Insect Pokémon
HEIGHT: 3'03"
WEIGHT: 33 lbs.
ABILITY: Compoundeyes
Raises Venonat's Accuracy by 30%.

STATS
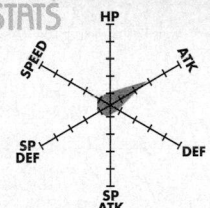

EVOLUTIONS

LV31

LOCATION(S):

RUBY	Rarity: **None**
Trade from *FireRed/LeafGreen*

SAPPHIRE	Rarity: **None**
Trade from *FireRed/LeafGreen*

FIRERED	Rarity: **Common**
Three Island, Routes 12, 13, 14, 15, Safari Zone

LEAFGREEN	Rarity: **Common**
Three Island, Routes 12, 13, 14, 15, Safari Zone

COLOSSEUM	Rarity: **None**
Trade from *FireRed/LeafGreen*

EMERALD	Rarity: **None**
Trade from *FireRed/LeafGreen*

XD	Rarity: **None**
Trade from *FireRed/LeafGreen*

MOVES

Level	Attack	Type	Power	ACC	PP	Level	Attack	Type	Power	ACC	PP
—	Tackle	Normal	35	95	35	20	Poisonpowder	Poison	—	75	35
—	Disable	Normal	—	55	20	25	Leech Life	Bug	20	100	15
—	Foresight	Normal	—	100	40	28	Stun Spore	Grass	—	75	30
9	Supersonic	Normal	—	55	20	33	Psybeam	Psychic	65	100	20
17	Confusion	Psychic	50	100	25	36	Sleep Powder	Grass	—	75	15
						41	Psychic	Psychic	90	100	10

TM/HM

TM/HM#	Name	Type	Power	ACC	PP	TM/HM#	Name	Type	Power	ACC	PP
TM06	Toxic	Poison	—	85	10	TM32	Double Team	Normal	—	—	15
TM10	Hidden Power	Normal	—	100	15	TM36	Sludge Bomb	Poison	90	100	10
TM11	Sunny Day	Fire	—	—	5	TM42	Facade	Normal	70	100	20
TM17	Protect	Normal	—	—	10	TM43	Secret Power	Normal	70	100	20
TM19	Giga Drain	Grass	60	100	5	TM44	Rest	Psychic	—	—	10
TM21	Frustration	Normal	—	100	20	TM45	Attract	Normal	—	100	15
TM22	Solarbeam	Grass	120	100	10	TM46	Thief	Dark	40	100	10
TM27	Return	Normal	—	100	20	TM48	Skill Swap	Psychic	—	100	10
TM29	Psychic	Psychic	90	100	10	HM05	Flash	Normal	—	70	20

EGG MOVES*

Name	Type	Power	ACC	PP
Baton Pass	Normal	—	—	40
Giga Drain	Grass	60	100	5
Screech	Normal	—	85	40
Signal Beam	Bug	75	100	15

*Learned Via Breeding

MOVE TUTOR
FireRed/LeafGreen and *Emerald* Only

Double-Edge	Mimic	Substitute

049 Venomoth

BUG | POISON

GENERAL INFO
SPECIES: Poison Moth Pokémon
HEIGHT: 4'11"
WEIGHT: 28 lbs.
ABILITY: Shield Dust
Protects Venomoth from being struck by extra effects of moves.

STATS
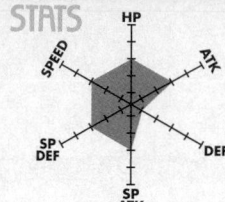

EVOLUTIONS
 LV31

LOCATION[S]:

RUBY	**Rarity: None**
Trade from *FireRed/LeafGreen*	
SAPPHIRE	**Rarity: None**
Trade from *FireRed/LeafGreen*	
FIRERED	**Rarity: Rare**
Three Island, Safari Zone	
LEAFGREEN	**Rarity: Rare**
Three Island, Safari Zone	
COLOSSEUM	**Rarity: None**
Trade from *FireRed/LeafGreen*	
EMERALD	**Rarity: None**
Trade from *FireRed/LeafGreen*	
XD	**Rarity: Only One**
Cipher Key Lair (Capture from Cipher Peon Angic)	

MOVES

Level	Attack	Type	Power	ACC	PP	Level	Attack	Type	Power	ACC	PP
—	Tackle	Normal	35	95	35	20	Poison Powder	Poison	—	75	35
—	Disable	Normal	—	55	20	25	Leech Life	Bug	20	100	15
—	Foresight	Normal	—	100	40	28	Stun Spore	Grass	—	75	30
—	Silver Wind	Bug	60	100	5	31	Gust	Flying	40	100	35
—	Supersonic	Normal	—	55	20	36	Psybeam	Psychic	65	100	10
17	Confusion	Psychic	50	100	25	42	Sleep Powder	Grass	—	75	15
						52	Psychic	Psychic	90	100	10

TM/HM

TM/HM#	Name	Type	Power	ACC	PP	TM/HM#	Name	Type	Power	ACC	PP
TM06	Toxic	Poison	—	85	10	TM32	Double Team	Normal	—	—	15
TM10	Hidden Power	Normal	—	100	15	TM36	Sludge Bomb	Poison	90	100	10
TM11	Sunny Day	Fire	—	—	5	TM40	Aerial Ace	Flying	60	—	20
TM15	Hyper Beam	Normal	150	90	5	TM42	Facade	Normal	70	100	20
TM17	Protect	Normal	—	—	10	TM43	Secret Power	Normal	70	100	20
TM19	Giga Drain	Grass	60	100	5	TM44	Rest	Psychic	—	—	10
TM21	Frustration	Normal	—	100	20	TM45	Attract	Normal	—	100	15
TM22	Solarbeam	Grass	120	100	10	TM46	Thief	Dark	40	100	10
TM27	Return	Normal	—	100	20	TM48	Skill Swap	Psychic	—	100	10
TM29	Psychic	Psychic	90	100	10	HM05	Flash	Normal	—	70	20

MOVE TUTOR
FireRed/LeafGreen and *Emerald* Only

Double-Edge	Mimic	Substitute

---

050 Diglett

GROUND

GENERAL INFO
SPECIES: Mole Pokémon
HEIGHT: 0'08"
WEIGHT: 2 lbs.
ABILITY 1: Sand Veil
During a sandstorm, Diglett is able to evade more moves.

ABILITY 2: Arena Trap
Opponent cannot escape battle.

STATS
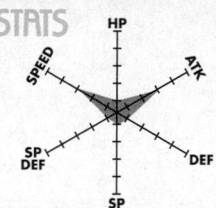

EVOLUTIONS
 LV26

LOCATION[S]:

RUBY	**Rarity: None**
Trade from *FireRed/LeafGreen*	
SAPPHIRE	**Rarity: None**
Trade from *FireRed/LeafGreen*	
FIRERED	**Rarity: Common**
Diglett's Cave	
LEAFGREEN	**Rarity: Common**
Diglett's Cave	
COLOSSEUM	**Rarity: None**
Trade from *FireRed/LeafGreen*	
EMERALD	**Rarity: None**
Trade from *FireRed/LeafGreen*	
XD	**Rarity: None**
Trade from *FireRed/LeafGreen*	

MOVES

Level	Attack	Type	Power	ACC	PP	Level	Attack	Type	Power	ACC	PP
—	Scratch	Normal	40	100	35	21	Fury Swipes	Normal	18	80	15
—	Sand-Attack	Ground	—	100	15	25	Mud-Slap	Ground	20	100	10
5	Growl	Normal	—	100	40	33	Slash	Normal	70	100	20
9	Magnitude	Ground	—	100	30	41	Earthquake	Ground	100	100	10
17	Dig	Ground	60	100	10	49	Fissure	Ground	—	30	5

TM/HM

TM/HM#	Name	Type	Power	ACC	PP	TM/HM#	Name	Type	Power	ACC	PP
TM06	Toxic	Poison	—	85	10	TM39	Rock Tomb	Rock	50	80	10
TM10	Hidden Power	Normal	—	100	15	TM40	Aerial Ace	Flying	60	—	20
TM11	Sunny Day	Fire	—	—	5	TM42	Facade	Normal	70	100	20
TM17	Protect	Normal	—	—	10	TM43	Secret Power	Normal	70	100	20
TM21	Frustration	Normal	—	100	20	TM44	Rest	Psychic	—	—	10
TM26	Earthquake	Ground	100	100	10	TM45	Attract	Normal	—	100	15
TM27	Return	Normal	—	100	20	TM46	Thief	Dark	40	100	10
TM28	Dig	Ground	60	100	10	HM01	Cut	Normal	50	95	30
TM32	Double Team	Normal	—	—	15	HM06	Rock Smash	Fighting	20	100	15
TM36	Sludge Bomb	Poison	90	100	10						

EGG MOVES*

Name	Type	Power	ACC	PP
Ancientpower	Rock	60	100	5
Beat Up	Dark	10	100	10
Faint Attack	Dark	60	—	20
Pursuit	Dark	40	100	20
Rock Slide	Rock	75	90	10
Screech	Normal	—	85	40
Uproar	Normal	50	100	10

*Learned Via Breeding

MOVE TUTOR
FireRed/LeafGreen and *Emerald* Only

Body Slam*	Double-Edge	Mimic
Rock Slide*	Substitute	

*Battle Frontier tutor move (*Emerald*)

051 Dugtrio™

GENERAL INFO
SPECIES: Mole Pokémon
HEIGHT: 2'04"
WEIGHT: 73 lbs.
ABILITY 1: Sand Veil   **ABILITY 2:** Arena Trap
During a sandstorm, Dugtrio is able to evade more moves.   *Prevents an opponent from escaping during battle.*

STATS

EVOLUTIONS

LV26

LOCATION[S]:

RUBY   Rarity: **None**
Trade from *FireRed/LeafGreen*

SAPPHIRE   Rarity: **None**
Trade from *FireRed/LeafGreen*

FIRERED   Rarity: **Rare**
Diglett's Cave

LEAFGREEN   Rarity: **Rare**
Diglett's Cave

COLOSSEUM   Rarity: **None**
Trade from *FireRed/LeafGreen*

EMERALD   Rarity: **None**
Trade from *FireRed/LeafGreen*

XD   Rarity: **Only One**
Citadark Island (Capture from Cipher Admin Kolax)

MOVES

Level	Attack	Type	Power	ACC	PP	Level	Attack	Type	Power	ACC	PP
—	Scratch	Normal	40	100	35	21	Fury Swipes	Normal	18	80	15
—	Sand-Attack	Ground	—	100	15	25	Mud-Slap	Ground	20	100	10
—	Tri Attack	Normal	80	100	10	26	Sand Tomb	Ground	15	70	15
—	Growl	Normal	—	100	40	38	Slash	Normal	70	100	20
9	Magnitude	Ground	—	100	30	51	Earthquake	Ground	100	100	10
17	Dig	Ground	60	100	10	64	Fissure	Ground	—	30	5

TM/HM

TM/HM#	Name	Type	Power	ACC	PP	TM/HM#	Name	Type	Power	ACC	PP
TM06	Toxic	Poison	—	85	10	TM36	Sludge Bomb	Poison	90	100	10
TM10	Hidden Power	Normal	—	100	15	TM39	Rock Tomb	Rock	50	80	10
TM11	Sunny Day	Fire	—	—	5	TM40	Aerial Ace	Flying	60	—	20
TM15	Hyper Beam	Normal	150	90	5	TM42	Facade	Normal	70	100	20
TM17	Protect	Normal	—	—	10	TM43	Secret Power	Normal	70	100	20
TM21	Frustration	Normal	—	100	20	TM44	Rest	Psychic	—	—	10
TM26	Earthquake	Ground	100	100	10	TM45	Attract	Normal	—	100	15
TM27	Return	Normal	—	100	20	TM46	Thief	Dark	40	100	10
TM28	Dig	Ground	60	100	10	HM01	Cut	Normal	50	95	30
TM32	Double Team	Normal	—	—	15	HM06	Rock Smash	Fighting	20	100	15

MOVE TUTOR
FireRed/LeafGreen and *Emerald* Only

Body Slam*	Double-Edge	Mimic
Rock Slide*	Substitute	

*Battle Frontier tutor move (*Emerald*)

---

052 Meowth™

GENERAL INFO
SPECIES: Scratch Cat Pokémon
HEIGHT: 1'04"
WEIGHT: 9 lbs.
ABILITY: Pickup
Allows Meowth to take items from opponent, and while walking in the wild.

STATS

EVOLUTIONS

LV28

LOCATION[S]:

RUBY   Rarity: **None**
Trade from *FireRed/LeafGreen*

SAPPHIRE   Rarity: **None**
Trade from *FireRed/LeafGreen*

FIRERED   Rarity: **Common**
Routes 5–8, Islands One, Two, Three, Five, Six, Seven

LEAFGREEN   Rarity: **Common**
Routes 5–8, Islands One, Two, Three, Five, Six, Seven

COLOSSEUM   Rarity: **None**
Trade from *FireRed/LeafGreen*

EMERALD   Rarity: **Only One**
Battle Frontier

XD   Rarity: **Only One**
Phenac City (Capture from Cipher Peon Fostin)

MOVES

Level	Attack	Type	Power	ACC	PP	Level	Attack	Type	Power	ACC	PP
—	Scratch	Normal	40	100	35	31	Screech	Normal	—	85	40
—	Growl	Normal	—	100	40	36	Fury Swipes	Normal	18	80	15
10	Bite	Dark	60	100	25	40	Slash	Normal	70	100	20
18	Pay Day	Normal	40	100	20	43	Fake Out	Normal	40	100	10
25	Faint Attack	Dark	60	—	20	45	Swagger	Normal	—	90	15

TM/HM

TM/HM#	Name	Type	Power	ACC	PP	TM/HM#	Name	Type	Power	ACC	PP
TM03	Water Pulse	Water	60	95	20	TM30	Shadow Ball	Ghost	80	100	15
TM06	Toxic	Poison	—	85	10	TM32	Double Team	Normal	—	—	15
TM10	Hidden Power	Normal	—	100	15	TM34	Shock Wave	Electric	60	—	20
TM11	Sunny Day	Fire	—	—	5	TM40	Aerial Ace	Flying	60	—	20
TM12	Taunt	Dark	—	100	20	TM41	Torment	Dark	—	100	15
TM17	Protect	Normal	—	—	10	TM42	Facade	Normal	70	100	20
TM18	Rain Dance	Water	—	—	5	TM43	Secret Power	Normal	70	100	20
TM21	Frustration	Normal	—	100	20	TM44	Rest	Psychic	—	—	10
TM23	Iron Tail	Steel	75	75	15	TM45	Attract	Normal	—	100	15
TM24	Thunderbolt	Electric	95	100	15	TM46	Thief	Dark	40	100	10
TM25	Thunder	Electric	120	70	10	TM49	Snatch	Dark	—	100	10
TM27	Return	Normal	—	100	20	HM01	Cut	Normal	50	95	30
TM28	Dig	Ground	60	100	10	HM05	Flash	Normal	—	70	20

EGG MOVES*

Name	Type	Power	ACC	PP
Amnesia	Psychic	—	—	20
Assist	Normal	—	100	20
Charm	Normal	—	100	20
Hypnosis	Psychic	—	60	20
Psych Up	Normal	—	—	10
Spite	Ghost	—	100	10

*Learned Via Breeding

MOVE TUTOR
FireRed/LeafGreen and *Emerald* Only

Body Slam*	Double-Edge	Dream Eater*
Mimic	Substitute	

*Battle Frontier tutor move (*Emerald*)

053 Persian™

NORMAL

GENERAL INFO
SPECIES: Classy Cat Pokémon
HEIGHT: 3'03"
WEIGHT: 71 lbs.
ABILITY: Limber
Prevents Persian from being paralyzed.

STATS
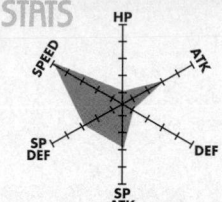

EVOLUTIONS

LV28

LOCATION(S):

RUBY   Rarity: **None**
Trade from *FireRed/LeafGreen*

SAPPHIRE   Rarity: **None**
Trade from *FireRed/LeafGreen*

FIRERED   Rarity: **Rare**
Evolve Meowth, Islands One, Two, Three, Five, Six, Seven

LEAFGREEN   Rarity: **Rare**
Evolve Meowth, Islands One, Two, Three, Five, Six, Seven

COLOSSEUM   Rarity: **None**
Trade from *FireRed/LeafGreen*

EMERALD   Rarity: **None**
Trade from *FireRed/LeafGreen*

XD   Rarity: **Evolve**
Evolve Meowth

MOVES

Level	Attack	Type	Power	ACC	PP	Level	Attack	Type	Power	ACC	PP
—	Scratch	Normal	40	100	35	34	Screech	Normal	—	85	40
—	Growl	Normal	—	100	40	42	Fury Swipes	Normal	18	80	15
—	Bite	Dark	60	100	25	49	Slash	Normal	70	100	20
18	Pay Day	Normal	40	100	20	55	Fake Out	Normal	40	100	10
25	Faint Attack	Dark	60	—	20	61	Swagger	Normal	—	90	15

TM/HM

TM/HM#	Name	Type	Power	ACC	PP	TM/HM#	Name	Type	Power	ACC	PP
TM03	Water Pulse	Water	60	95	20	TM28	Dig	Ground	60	100	10
TM05	Roar	Normal	—	100	20	TM30	Shadow Ball	Ghost	80	100	15
TM06	Toxic	Poison	—	85	10	TM32	Double Team	Normal	—	—	15
TM10	Hidden Power	Normal	—	100	15	TM34	Shock Wave	Electric	60	—	20
TM11	Sunny Day	Fire	—	—	5	TM40	Aerial Ace	Flying	60	—	20
TM12	Taunt	Dark	—	100	20	TM41	Torment	Dark	—	100	15
TM15	Hyper Beam	Normal	150	90	5	TM42	Facade	Normal	70	100	20
TM17	Protect	Normal	—	—	10	TM43	Secret Power	Normal	70	100	20
TM18	Rain Dance	Water	—	—	5	TM44	Rest	Psychic	—	—	10
TM21	Frustration	Normal	—	100	20	TM45	Attract	Normal	—	100	15
TM23	Iron Tail	Steel	75	75	15	TM46	Thief	Dark	40	100	10
TM24	Thunderbolt	Electric	95	100	15	TM49	Snatch	Dark	—	100	10
TM25	Thunder	Electric	120	70	10	HM01	Cut	Normal	50	95	30
TM27	Return	Normal	—	100	20	HM05	Flash	Normal	—	70	20

MOVE TUTOR
FireRed/LeafGreen and *Emerald* Only

Body Slam*	Double-Edge*	Dream Eater*
Mimic	Substitute	

*Battle Frontier tutor move (*Emerald*)

---

054 Psyduck™

WATER

GENERAL INFO
SPECIES: Duck Pokémon
HEIGHT: 2'07"
WEIGHT: 43 lbs.
ABILITY 1: Damp
Prevents the opponent from using Selfdestruct or Explosion when Psyduck is in battle.

ABILITY 2: Cloud Nine
Prevents weather effects on all Pokémon while Psyduck is in that battle.

STATS
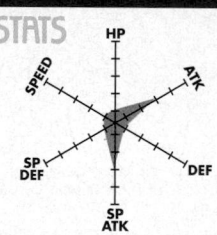

EVOLUTIONS

LV33

LOCATION(S):

RUBY   Rarity: **Common**
Safari Zone

SAPPHIRE   Rarity: **Common**
Safari Zone

FIRERED   Rarity: **Common**
Routes 4, 6, 10, 11, 13, 19, 21, 24, Seafoam Islands, Safari Zone, Fuchsia City, Islands One, Two, Three, Five, Six, Seven

LEAFGREEN   Rarity: **None**
Trade from *Ruby/Sapphire/FireRed*

COLOSSEUM   Rarity: **None**
Trade from *Ruby/Sapphire/FireRed*

EMERALD   Rarity: **Common**
Safari Zone

XD   Rarity: **None**
Trade from *Ruby/Sapphire/FireRed*

MOVES

Level	Attack	Type	Power	ACC	PP	Level	Attack	Type	Power	ACC	PP
—	Water Sport	Water	—	100	15	16	Confusion	Psychic	50	100	25
—	Scratch	Normal	40	100	35	23	Screech	Normal	—	85	40
5	Tail Whip	Normal	—	100	30	31	Psych Up	Normal	—	—	10
10	Disable	Normal	—	55	20	40	Fury Swipes	Normal	18	80	15
						50	Hydro Pump	Water	120	80	5

TM/HM

TM/HM#	Name	Type	Power	ACC	PP	TM/HM#	Name	Type	Power	ACC	PP
TM01	Focus Punch	Fighting	150	100	20	TM31	Brick Break	Fighting	75	100	15
TM03	Water Pulse	Water	60	95	20	TM32	Double Team	Normal	—	—	15
TM04	Calm Mind	Psychic	—	—	20	TM40	Aerial Ace	Flying	60	—	20
TM06	Toxic	Poison	—	85	10	TM42	Facade	Normal	70	100	20
TM07	Hail	Ice	—	—	10	TM43	Secret Power	Normal	70	100	20
TM10	Hidden Power	Normal	—	100	15	TM44	Rest	Psychic	—	—	10
TM13	Ice Beam	Ice	95	100	10	TM45	Attract	Normal	—	100	15
TM14	Blizzard	Ice	120	70	5	HM03	Surf	Water	95	100	15
TM17	Protect	Normal	—	—	10	HM04	Strength	Normal	80	100	20
TM18	Rain Dance	Water	—	—	5	HM05	Flash	Normal	—	70	20
TM21	Frustration	Normal	—	100	20	HM06	Rock Smash	Fighting	20	100	15
TM23	Iron Tail	Steel	75	75	15	HM07	Waterfall	Water	80	100	15
TM27	Return	Normal	—	100	20	HM08	Dive	Water	60	100	10
TM28	Dig	Ground	60	100	10						

EGG MOVES*

Name	Type	Power	ACC	PP
Hypnosis	Psychic	—	60	20
Psybeam	Psychic	65	100	20
Foresight	Normal	—	100	40
Light Screen	Psychic	—	—	30
Future Sight	Psychic	80	90	15
Psychic	Psychic	90	100	10
Refresh	Normal	—	100	20
Cross Chop	Fighting	100	80	5

*Learned Via Breeding

MOVE TUTOR
FireRed/LeafGreen and *Emerald* Only

Body Slam*	Counter*	Double-Edge
Mega Kick*	Mega Punch*	Mimic
Seismic Toss*	Substitute	

Emerald Only

Dynamicpunch	Endure*	Ice Punch*
Icy Wind*	Mud-Slap*	Psych Up*
Sleep Talk	Snore*	Swagger
Swift*		

*Battle Frontier tutor move (*Emerald*)

055 Golduck™

WATER

GENERAL INFO

SPECIES: Duck Pokémon
HEIGHT: 5'07"
WEIGHT: 169 lbs.
ABILITY 1: Damp
Prevents the opponent from using Selfdestruct or Explosion when Golduck is in battle.

ABILITY 2: Cloud Nine
Prevents weather effects on all Pokémon while Golduck is in that battle.

STATS

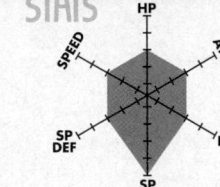

EVOLUTIONS

LV33

LOCATION[S]:

RUBY Rarity: **Rare**
Safari Zone

SAPPHIRE Rarity: **Rare**
Safari Zone

FIRERED Rarity: **Rare**
Two Island, Three Island, Seafoam Island

LEAFGREEN Rarity: **None**
Trade from Ruby/Sapphire/FireRed

COLOSSEUM Rarity: **None**
Trade from Ruby/Sapphire/FireRed

EMERALD Rarity: **Rare**
Safari Zone

XD Rarity: **Only One**
Citadark Island (Capture from Navigator Abson)

MOVES

Level	Attack	Type	Power	ACC	PP	Level	Attack	Type	Power	ACC	PP
—	Water Sport	Water	—	100	15	16	Confusion	Psychic	50	100	25
—	Scratch	Normal	40	100	35	23	Screech	Normal	—	85	40
5	Tail Whip	Normal	—	100	30	31	Psych Up	Normal	—	—	10
10	Disable	Normal	—	55	20	44	Fury Swipes	Normal	18	80	15
						58	Hydro Pump	Water	120	80	5

TM/HM

TM/HM#	Name	Type	Power	ACC	PP	TM/HM#	Name	Type	Power	ACC	PP
TM01	Focus Punch	Fighting	150	100	20	TM28	Dig	Ground	60	100	10
TM03	Water Pulse	Water	60	95	20	TM31	Brick Break	Fighting	75	100	15
TM04	Calm Mind	Psychic	—	—	20	TM32	Double Team	Normal	—	—	15
TM06	Toxic	Poison	—	85	10	TM40	Aerial Ace	Flying	60	—	20
TM07	Hail	Ice	—	—	10	TM42	Facade	Normal	70	100	20
TM10	Hidden Power	Normal	—	100	15	TM43	Secret Power	Normal	70	100	20
TM13	Ice Beam	Ice	95	100	10	TM44	Rest	Psychic	—	—	10
TM14	Blizzard	Ice	120	70	5	TM45	Attract	Normal	—	100	15
TM15	Hyper Beam	Normal	150	90	5	HM03	Surf	Water	95	100	15
TM17	Protect	Normal	—	—	10	HM04	Strength	Normal	80	100	20
TM18	Rain Dance	Water	—	—	5	HM05	Flash	Normal	—	70	20
TM21	Frustration	Normal	—	100	20	HM06	Rock Smash	Fighting	20	100	15
TM23	Iron Tail	Steel	75	75	15	HM07	Waterfall	Water	80	100	15
TM27	Return	Normal	—	100	20	HM08	Dive	Water	60	100	10

MOVE TUTOR

FireRed/LeafGreen and *Emerald* Only

Body Slam*	Counter*	Double-Edge
Mega Kick*	Mega Punch*	Mimic
Seismic Toss*	Substitute	

Emerald Only

Dynamicpunch	Endure*	Fury Cutter
Ice Punch*	Icy Wind*	Mud-Slap*
Psych Up*	Sleep Talk*	Snore*
Swagger	Swift*	

*Battle Frontier tutor move (*Emerald*)

---

056 Mankey™

FIGHTING

GENERAL INFO

SPECIES: Pig Monkey Pokémon
HEIGHT: 1'08"
WEIGHT: 62 lbs.
ABILITY: Vital Spirit
Protects Mankey from being put to sleep.

STATS

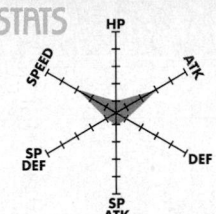

EVOLUTIONS

LV28

LOCATION[S]:

RUBY Rarity: **None**
Trade from FireRed/LeafGreen

SAPPHIRE Rarity: **None**
Trade from FireRed/LeafGreen

FIRERED Rarity: **Common**
Routes 3, 4, 22, 23, Rock Tunnel

LEAFGREEN Rarity: **Common**
Routes 3, 4, 22, 23, Rock Tunnel

COLOSSEUM Rarity: **None**
Trade from FireRed/LeafGreen

EMERALD Rarity: **None**
Trade from FireRed/LeafGreen

XD Rarity: **None**
Trade from FireRed/LeafGreen

MOVES

Level	Attack	Type	Power	ACC	PP	Level	Attack	Type	Power	ACC	PP
—	Scratch	Normal	40	100	35	21	Focus Energy	Normal	—	—	30
—	Leer	Normal	—	100	30	26	Seismic Toss	Fighting	—	100	20
6	Low Kick	Fighting	—	100	20	31	Cross Chop	Fighting	100	80	5
11	Karate Chop	Fighting	50	100	25	36	Swagger	Normal	—	90	15
16	Fury Swipes	Normal	18	80	15	41	Screech	Normal	—	85	40
						46	Thrash	Normal	90	100	20

TM/HM

TM/HM#	Name	Type	Power	ACC	PP	TM/HM#	Name	Type	Power	ACC	PP
TM01	Focus Punch	Fighting	150	100	20	TM28	Dig	Ground	60	100	10
TM06	Toxic	Poison	—	85	10	TM31	Brick Break	Fighting	75	100	15
TM08	Bulk Up	Fighting	—	—	20	TM32	Double Team	Normal	—	—	15
TM10	Hidden Power	Normal	—	100	15	TM39	Rock Tomb	Rock	50	80	10
TM11	Sunny Day	Fire	—	—	5	TM40	Aerial Ace	Flying	60	—	20
TM12	Taunt	Dark	—	100	20	TM42	Facade	Normal	70	100	20
TM17	Protect	Normal	—	—	10	TM43	Secret Power	Normal	70	100	20
TM18	Rain Dance	Water	—	—	5	TM44	Rest	Psychic	—	—	10
TM21	Frustration	Normal	—	100	20	TM45	Attract	Normal	—	100	15
TM23	Iron Tail	Steel	75	75	15	TM46	Thief	Dark	40	100	10
TM24	Thunderbolt	Electric	95	100	15	TM50	Overheat	Fire	140	90	5
TM25	Thunder	Electric	120	70	10	HM04	Strength	Normal	80	100	20
TM26	Earthquake	Ground	100	100	10	HM06	Rock Smash	Fighting	20	100	15
TM27	Return	Normal	—	100	20						

EGG MOVES*

Name	Type	Power	ACC	PP
Beat Up	Dark	10	100	10
Foresight	Normal	—	100	40
Counter	Fighting	—	100	20
Meditate	Psychic	—	—	40
Revenge	Fighting	60	100	10
Reversal	Fighting	—	100	15
Rock Slide	Rock	75	90	10
Smellingsalt	Normal	60	100	10

*Learned Via Breeding

MOVE TUTOR

FireRed/LeafGreen and *Emerald* Only

Body Slam*	Counter*	Double-Edge
Mega Kick*	Mega Punch*	Metronome
Mimic	Rock Slide*	Seismic Toss*
Substitute		

*Battle Frontier tutor move (*Emerald*)

057 Primeape™

FIGHTING

GENERAL INFO
SPECIES: Pig Monkey Pokémon
HEIGHT: 3'03"
WEIGHT: 71 lbs.
ABILITY: Vital Spirit
Protects Primeape from being put to sleep.

STATS
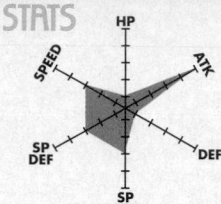

EVOLUTIONS

LV28

LOCATION[S]:

RUBY — Rarity: **None**
Trade from *FireRed/LeafGreen*

SAPPHIRE — Rarity: **None**
Trade from *FireRed/LeafGreen*

FIRERED — Rarity: **Common**
Route 23, Victory Road

LEAFGREEN — Rarity: **Common**
Route 23, Victory Road

COLOSSEUM — Rarity: **None**
Trade from *FireRed/LeafGreen*

EMERALD — Rarity: **None**
Trade from *FireRed/LeafGreen*

XD — Rarity: **Only One**
Cipher Key Lair (Capture from Cipher Admin Gorigan)

MOVES

Level	Attack	Type	Power	ACC	PP	Level	Attack	Type	Power	ACC	PP
—	Scratch	Normal	40	100	35	21	Focus Energy	Normal	—	—	30
—	Leer	Normal	—	100	30	26	Seismic Toss	Fighting	—	100	20
—	Low Kick	Fighting	—	100	20	28	Rage	Normal	20	100	20
—	Rage	Normal	20	100	20	35	Cross Chop	Fighting	100	80	5
11	Karate Chop	Fighting	50	100	25	44	Swagger	Normal	—	90	15
16	Fury Swipes	Normal	18	80	15	53	Screech	Normal	—	85	40
						62	Thrash	Normal	90	100	20

TM/HM

TM/HM#	Name	Type	Power	ACC	PP	TM/HM#	Name	Type	Power	ACC	PP
TM01	Focus Punch	Fighting	150	100	20	TM27	Return	Normal	—	100	20
TM06	Toxic	Poison	—	85	10	TM28	Dig	Ground	60	100	10
TM08	Bulk Up	Fighting	—	—	20	TM31	Brick Break	Fighting	75	100	15
TM10	Hidden Power	Normal	—	100	15	TM32	Double Team	Normal	—	—	15
TM11	Sunny Day	Fire	—	—	5	TM39	Rock Tomb	Rock	50	80	10
TM12	Taunt	Dark	—	100	20	TM40	Aerial Ace	Flying	60	—	20
TM15	Hyper Beam	Normal	150	90	5	TM42	Facade	Normal	70	100	20
TM17	Protect	Normal	—	—	10	TM43	Secret Power	Normal	70	100	20
TM18	Rain Dance	Water	—	—	5	TM44	Rest	Psychic	—	—	10
TM21	Frustration	Normal	—	100	20	TM45	Attract	Normal	—	100	15
TM23	Iron Tail	Steel	75	75	15	TM46	Thief	Dark	40	100	10
TM24	Thunderbolt	Electric	95	100	15	TM50	Overheat	Fire	140	90	5
TM25	Thunder	Electric	120	70	10	HM04	Strength	Normal	80	100	20
TM26	Earthquake	Ground	100	100	10	HM06	Rock Smash	Fighting	20	100	15

MOVE TUTOR
FireRed/LeafGreen and *Emerald* Only

Body Slam* · Counter* · Double-Edge
Mega Kick* · Mega Punch* · Metronome
Mimic · Rock Slide* · Seismic Toss*
Substitute

*Battle Frontier tutor move (*Emerald*)

---

058 Growlithe™

FIRE

GENERAL INFO
SPECIES: Puppy Pokémon
HEIGHT: 2'04"
WEIGHT: 42 lbs.
ABILITY 1: Flash Fire
Raises the power of Growlithe's Fire-type attacks and prevents it from being damaged by Fire-type attacks.

ABILITY 2: Intimidate
The opponent's attack power lowers when Growlithe goes into battle.

STATS
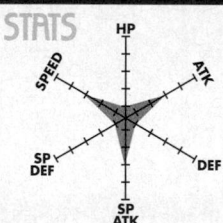

EVOLUTIONS

FIRE STONE

LOCATION[S]:

RUBY — Rarity: **None**
Trade from *FireRed*

SAPPHIRE — Rarity: **None**
Trade from *FireRed*

FIRERED — Rarity: **Rare**
Route 7, Route 8, Pokémon Mansion

LEAFGREEN — Rarity: **None**
Trade from *FireRed*

COLOSSEUM — Rarity: **None**
Trade from *FireRed*

EMERALD — Rarity: **None**
Trade from *FireRed*

XD — Rarity: **Only One**
Cipher Key Lair (Capture from Cipher Peon Humah)

MOVES

Level	Attack	Type	Power	ACC	PP	Level	Attack	Type	Power	ACC	PP
—	Bite	Dark	60	100	25	25	Take Down	Normal	90	85	20
—	Roar	Normal	—	100	20	31	Flame Wheel	Fire	60	100	25
7	Ember	Fire	40	100	25	37	Helping Hand	Normal	—	100	20
13	Leer	Normal	—	100	30	43	Agility	Psychic	—	—	30
19	Odor Sleuth	Normal	—	100	40	49	Flamethrower	Fire	95	100	15

TM/HM

TM/HM#	Name	Type	Power	ACC	PP	TM/HM#	Name	Type	Power	ACC	PP
TM05	Roar	Normal	—	100	20	TM38	Fire Blast	Fire	120	85	5
TM06	Toxic	Poison	—	85	10	TM40	Aerial Ace	Flying	60	—	20
TM10	Hidden Power	Normal	—	100	15	TM42	Facade	Normal	70	100	20
TM11	Sunny Day	Fire	—	—	5	TM43	Secret Power	Normal	70	100	20
TM17	Protect	Normal	—	—	10	TM44	Rest	Psychic	—	—	10
TM21	Frustration	Normal	—	100	20	TM45	Attract	Normal	—	100	15
TM23	Iron Tail	Steel	75	75	15	TM46	Thief	Dark	40	100	10
TM27	Return	Normal	—	100	20	TM50	Overheat	Fire	140	90	5
TM28	Dig	Ground	60	100	10	HM04	Strength	Normal	80	100	20
TM32	Double Team	Normal	—	—	15	HM06	Rock Smash	Fighting	20	100	15
TM35	Flamethrower	Fire	95	100	15						

EGG MOVES*

Name	Type	Power	ACC	PP
Body Slam	Normal	85	100	15
Crunch	Dark	80	100	15
Fire Spin	Fire	15	70	15
Heat Wave	Fire	100	90	10
Howl	Normal	—	—	40
Safeguard	Normal	—	—	25
Thrash	Normal	90	100	20

*Learned Via Breeding

MOVE TUTOR
FireRed/LeafGreen and *Emerald* Only

Body Slam* · Double-Edge · Mimic
Substitute

*Battle Frontier tutor move (*Emerald*)

059 Arcanine™

FIRE

GENERAL INFO
SPECIES: **Legendary Pokémon**
HEIGHT: **6'03"**
WEIGHT: **342 lbs.**
ABILITY 1: **Flash Fire**
Raises the power of Growlithe's Fire-type Attacks and prevents it from being damaged by Fire-type attacks.
ABILITY 2: **Intimidate**
The opponent's attack power lowers when Growlithe goes into battle.

STATS

EVOLUTIONS

FIRE STONE

LOCATION(S):

RUBY — Rarity: **None**
Trade from *FireRed*

SAPPHIRE — Rarity: **None**
Trade from *FireRed*

FIRERED — Rarity: **Evolve**
Evolve Growlithe

LEAFGREEN — Rarity: **None**
Trade from *FireRed*

COLOSSEUM — Rarity: **None**
Trade from *FireRed*

EMERALD — Rarity: **None**
Trade from *FireRed*

XD — Rarity: **Evolve**
Evolve Growlithe

MOVES

Level	Attack	Type	Power	ACC	PP
—	Bite	Dark	60	100	25
—	Roar	Normal	—	100	20

Level	Attack	Type	Power	ACC	PP
—	Ember	Fire	40	100	25
—	Odor Sleuth	Normal	—	100	40
49	Extremespeed	Normal	80	100	5

TM/HM

TM/HM#	Name	Type	Power	ACC	PP
TM05	Roar	Normal	—	100	20
TM06	Toxic	Poison	—	85	10
TM10	Hidden Power	Normal	—	100	15
TM11	Sunny Day	Fire	—	—	5
TM15	Hyper Beam	Normal	150	90	5
TM17	Protect	Normal	—	—	10
TM21	Frustration	Normal	—	100	20
TM23	Iron Tail	Steel	75	75	15
TM27	Return	Normal	—	100	20
TM28	Dig	Ground	60	100	10
TM32	Double Team	Normal	—	—	15

TM/HM#	Name	Type	Power	ACC	PP
TM35	Flamethrower	Fire	95	100	15
TM38	Fire Blast	Fire	120	85	5
TM40	Aerial Ace	Flying	60	—	20
TM42	Facade	Normal	70	100	20
TM43	Secret Power	Normal	70	100	20
TM44	Rest	Psychic	—	—	10
TM45	Attract	Normal	—	100	15
TM46	Thief	Dark	40	100	10
TM50	Overheat	Fire	140	90	5
HM04	Strength	Normal	80	100	20
HM06	Rock Smash	Fighting	20	100	15

MOVE TUTOR
FireRed/LeafGreen and *Emerald* Only
Body Slam* — Double-Edge — Mimic — Substitute
*Battle Frontier tutor move (*Emerald*)

---

060 Poliwag™

WATER

GENERAL INFO
SPECIES: **Tadpole Pokémon**
HEIGHT: **2'00"**
WEIGHT: **27 lbs.**
ABILITY 1: **Damp**
No one can use Selfdestruct or Explosion while Poliwag is in battle.
ABILITY 2: **Water Absorb**
When a Water-type attack hits Poliwag, it gains 1/4 of its HPs back.

STATS

EVOLUTIONS

WATER STONE
LV25
TRADE WITH KING'S ROCK

LOCATION(S):

RUBY — Rarity: **None**
Trade from *FireRed/LeafGreen*

SAPPHIRE — Rarity: **None**
Trade from *FireRed/LeafGreen*

FIRERED — Rarity: **Common**
Two Island, Four Island, Six Island, Viridian City, Safari Zone

LEAFGREEN — Rarity: **Common**
Two Island, Four Island, Six Island, Viridian City, Safari Zone

COLOSSEUM — Rarity: **None**
Trade from *FireRed/LeafGreen*

EMERALD — Rarity: **None**
Trade from *FireRed/LeafGreen*

XD — Rarity: **None**
Trade from *FireRed/LeafGreen*

MOVES

Level	Attack	Type	Power	ACC	PP
—	Bubble	Water	20	100	30
7	Hypnosis	Psychic	—	60	20
13	Water Gun	Water	40	100	25
19	Doubleslap	Normal	15	85	10

Level	Attack	Type	Power	ACC	PP
25	Rain Dance	Water	—	—	5
31	Body Slam	Normal	85	100	15
37	Belly Drum	Normal	—	—	10
43	Hydro Pump	Water	120	80	5

TM/HM

TM/HM#	Name	Type	Power	ACC	PP
TM03	Water Pulse	Water	60	95	20
TM06	Toxic	Poison	—	85	10
TM07	Hail	Ice	—	—	10
TM10	Hidden Power	Normal	—	100	15
TM13	Ice Beam	Ice	95	100	10
TM14	Blizzard	Ice	120	70	5
TM17	Protect	Normal	—	—	10
TM18	Rain Dance	Water	—	—	5
TM21	Frustration	Normal	—	100	20
TM27	Return	Normal	—	100	20
TM28	Dig	Ground	60	100	10

TM/HM#	Name	Type	Power	ACC	PP
TM29	Psychic	Psychic	90	100	10
TM32	Double Team	Normal	—	—	15
TM42	Facade	Normal	70	100	20
TM43	Secret Power	Normal	70	100	20
TM44	Rest	Psychic	—	—	10
TM45	Attract	Normal	—	100	15
TM46	Thief	Dark	40	100	10
HM03	Surf	Water	95	100	15
HM07	Waterfall	Water	80	100	15
HM08	Dive	Water	60	100	10

EGG MOVES*

Name	Type	Power	ACC	PP
Bubblebeam	Water	65	100	20
Haze	Ice	—	—	30
Ice Ball	Ice	30	90	20
Mind Reader	Normal	—	100	5
Mist	Ice	—	—	30
Water Sport	Water	—	100	15
Bounce	Flying	85	85	5

*Learned Via Breeding

MOVE TUTOR
FireRed/LeafGreen and *Emerald* Only
Body Slam* — Double-Edge — Mimic — Substitute
*Battle Frontier tutor move (*Emerald*)

Pokémon

10th Anniversary Pokédex

PRIMA **OFFICIAL** GAME GUIDE

061 Poliwhirl™

WATER

GENERAL INFO
SPECIES: Tadpole Pokémon
HEIGHT: 3'03"
WEIGHT: 44 lbs.
ABILITY 1: Damp
No one can use Selfdestruct or Explosion while Poliwhirl is in battle.

ABILITY 2: Water Absorb
When a Water attack hits Poliwhirl, it gains 1/4 of its HPs back.

STATS

EVOLUTIONS

WATER STONE
LV25
KING'S ROCK

LOCATION(S):

RUBY	**Rarity: None**
Trade from *FireRed/LeafGreen*	
SAPPHIRE	**Rarity: None**
Trade from *FireRed/LeafGreen*	
FIRERED	**Rarity: Rare**
Two Island, Six Island	
LEAFGREEN	**Rarity: Rare**
Two Island, Six Island	
COLOSSEUM	**Rarity: None**
Trade from *FireRed/LeafGreen*	
EMERALD	**Rarity: None**
Trade from *FireRed/LeafGreen*	
XD	**Rarity: None**
Trade from *FireRed/LeafGreen*	

MOVES

Level	Attack	Type	Power	ACC	PP	Level	Attack	Type	Power	ACC	PP
—	Bubble	Water	20	100	30	27	Rain Dance	Water	—	—	5
—	Hypnosis	Psychic	—	60	20	35	Body Slam	Normal	85	100	15
—	Water Gun	Water	40	100	25	43	Belly Drum	Normal	—	—	10
19	Doubleslap	Normal	15	85	10	51	Hydro Pump	Water	120	80	5

TM/HM

TM/HM#	Name	Type	Power	ACC	PP	TM/HM#	Name	Type	Power	ACC	PP
TM01	Focus Punch	Fighting	150	100	20	TM29	Psychic	Psychic	90	100	10
TM03	Water Pulse	Water	60	95	20	TM31	Brick Break	Fighting	75	100	15
TM06	Toxic	Poison	—	85	10	TM32	Double Team	Normal	—	—	15
TM07	Hail	Ice	—	—	10	TM42	Facade	Normal	70	100	20
TM10	Hidden Power	Normal	—	100	15	TM43	Secret Power	Normal	70	100	20
TM13	Ice Beam	Ice	95	100	10	TM44	Rest	Psychic	—	—	10
TM14	Blizzard	Ice	120	70	5	TM45	Attract	Normal	—	100	15
TM17	Protect	Normal	—	—	10	TM46	Thief	Dark	40	100	10
TM18	Rain Dance	Water	—	—	5	HM03	Surf	Water	95	100	15
TM21	Frustration	Normal	—	100	20	HM04	Strength	Normal	80	100	15
TM26	Earthquake	Ground	100	100	10	HM06	Rock Smash	Fighting	20	100	15
TM27	Return	Normal	—	100	20	HM07	Waterfall	Water	80	100	15
TM28	Dig	Ground	60	100	10	HM08	Dive	Water	60	100	10

MOVE TUTOR
FireRed/LeafGreen and Emerald Only

Body Slam*	Counter*	Double-Edge
Mega Kick*	Mega Punch*	Metronome
Mimic	Seismic Toss*	Substitute

*Battle Frontier tutor move (*Emerald*)

---

062 Poliwrath™

WATER | FIGHTING

GENERAL INFO
SPECIES: Tadpole Pokémon
HEIGHT: 4'03"
WEIGHT: 119 lbs.
ABILITY 1: Damp
No one can use Selfdestruct or Explosion while Poliwrath is in battle.

ABILITY 2: Water Absorb
When a Water attack hits Poliwrath, it gains 1/4 of its HPs back.

STATS

EVOLUTIONS

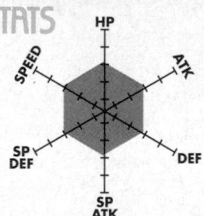  

LV25
WATER STONE

LOCATION(S):

RUBY	**Rarity: None**
Trade from *FireRed/LeafGreen*	
SAPPHIRE	**Rarity: None**
Trade from *FireRed/LeafGreen*	
FIRERED	**Rarity: Evolve**
Evolve Poliwhirl	
LEAFGREEN	**Rarity: Evolve**
Evolve Poliwhirl	
COLOSSEUM	**Rarity: None**
Trade from *FireRed/LeafGreen*	
EMERALD	**Rarity: None**
Trade from *FireRed/LeafGreen*	
XD	**Rarity: Only One**
Citadark Island (Capture from Cipher Admin Gorigan)	

MOVES

Level	Attack	Type	Power	ACC	PP	Level	Attack	Type	Power	ACC	PP
—	Hypnosis	Psychic	—	60	20	—	Doubleslap	Normal	15	85	10
—	Water Gun	Water	40	100	25	—	Submission	Fighting	80	80	25
						51	Mind Reader	Normal	—	100	5

TM/HM

TM/HM#	Name	Type	Power	ACC	PP	TM/HM#	Name	Type	Power	ACC	PP
TM01	Focus Punch	Fighting	150	100	20	TM29	Psychic	Psychic	90	100	10
TM03	Water Pulse	Water	60	95	20	TM31	Brick Break	Fighting	75	100	15
TM06	Toxic	Poison	—	85	10	TM32	Double Team	Normal	—	—	15
TM07	Hail	Ice	—	—	10	TM39	Rock Tomb	Rock	50	80	10
TM08	Bulk Up	Fighting	—	—	20	TM42	Facade	Normal	70	100	20
TM10	Hidden Power	Normal	—	100	15	TM43	Secret Power	Normal	70	100	20
TM13	Ice Beam	Ice	95	100	10	TM44	Rest	Psychic	—	—	10
TM14	Blizzard	Ice	120	70	5	TM45	Attract	Normal	—	100	15
TM15	Hyper Beam	Normal	150	90	5	TM46	Thief	Dark	40	100	10
TM17	Protect	Normal	—	—	10	HM03	Surf	Water	95	100	15
TM18	Rain Dance	Water	—	—	5	HM04	Strength	Normal	80	100	15
TM21	Frustration	Normal	—	100	20	HM06	Rock Smash	Fighting	20	100	15
TM26	Earthquake	Ground	100	100	10	HM07	Waterfall	Water	80	100	15
TM27	Return	Normal	—	100	20	HM08	Dive	Water	60	100	10
TM28	Dig	Ground	60	100	10						

MOVE TUTOR
FireRed/LeafGreen and Emerald Only

Body Slam*	Counter*	Double-Edge
Mega Kick*	Mega Punch*	Metronome
Mimic	Seismic Toss*	Substitute

*Battle Frontier tutor move (*Emerald*)

063 Abra™

PSYCHIC

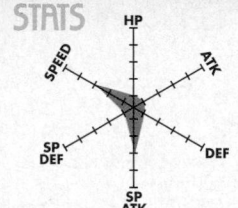

GENERAL INFO

SPECIES: Psi Pokémon
HEIGHT: 2'11"
WEIGHT: 43 lbs.
ABILITY1: Synchronize
When an opponent inflicts a Poison, Paralyze, or Burn condition on Abra, it receives the same status ailment.

ABILITY2: Inner Focus
Prevents Abra from flinching.

STATS

EVOLUTIONS

LV16   EVOLVE VIA TRADING

LOCATION[S]:

RUBY Rarity: **Common**
Granite Cave

SAPPHIRE Rarity: **Common**
Granite Cave

FIRERED Rarity: **Rare**
Route 24, Route 25

LEAFGREEN Rarity: **Rare**
Route 24, Route 25

COLOSSEUM Rarity: **None**
Trade from *Ruby/Sapphire/FireRed/LeafGreen*

EMERALD Rarity: **Common**
Granite Cave, Route 116

XD Rarity: **None**
Trade from *Ruby/Sapphire/FireRed/LeafGreen*

MOVES

Level	Attack	Type	Power	ACC	PP
—	Teleport	Psychic	—	—	20

TM/HM

TM/HM#	Name	Type	Power	ACC	PP	TM/HM#	Name	Type	Power	ACC	PP
TM01	Focus Punch	Fighting	150	100	20	TM30	Shadow Ball	Ghost	80	100	15
TM04	Calm Mind	Psychic	—	—	20	TM32	Double Team	Normal	—	—	15
TM06	Toxic	Poison	—	85	10	TM33	Reflect	Normal	—	—	20
TM10	Hidden Power	Normal	—	100	15	TM34	Shock Wave	Electric	60	—	20
TM11	Sunny Day	Fire	—	—	5	TM41	Torment	Dark	—	100	15
TM12	Taunt	Dark	—	100	20	TM42	Facade	Normal	70	100	20
TM16	Light Screen	Psychic	—	—	30	TM43	Secret Power	Normal	70	100	20
TM17	Protect	Normal	—	—	10	TM44	Rest	Psychic	—	—	10
TM18	Rain Dance	Water	—	—	5	TM45	Attract	Normal	—	100	15
TM20	Safeguard	Normal	—	—	25	TM46	Thief	Dark	40	100	10
TM21	Frustration	Normal	—	100	20	TM48	Skill Swap	Psychic	—	100	10
TM23	Iron Tail	Steel	75	75	15	TM49	Snatch	Dark	—	100	10
TM27	Return	Normal	—	100	20	HM05	Flash	Normal	—	70	20
TM29	Psychic	Psychic	90	100	10						

EGG MOVES*

Name	Type	Power	ACC	PP
Encore	Normal	—	100	5
Knock Off	Dark	20	100	20
Fire Punch	Fire	75	100	15
Thunderpunch	Electric	75	100	15
Ice Punch	Ice	75	100	15
Barrier	Psychic	—	—	30

*Learned Via Breeding

MOVE TUTOR

FireRed/LeafGreen and Emerald Only

Body Slam*	Counter*	Double-Edge
Dream Eater*	Mega Kick*	Mega Punch*
Mimic	Seismic Toss*	Substitute
Thunder Wave*		

Emerald Only

Dynamicpunch	Endure*	Fire Punch*
Ice Punch*	Metronome	Psych Up*
Sleep Talk	Snore*	Swagger
Thunderpunch*		

*Battle Frontier tutor move (*Emerald*)

064 Kadabra™

PSYCHIC

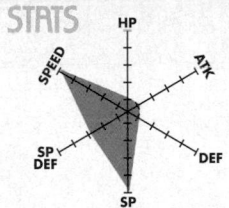

GENERAL INFO

SPECIES: Psi Pokémon
HEIGHT: 4'03"
WEIGHT: 125 lbs.

ABILITY1: Synchronize
When an opponent inflicts a Poison, Paralyze, or Burn condition on Kadabra, it receives the same status ailment.

ABILITY2: Inner Focus
Prevents Kadabra from flinching.

STATS

EVOLUTIONS

LV16   EVOLVE VIA TRADING

LOCATION[S]:

RUBY Rarity: **Evolve**
Evolve Abra

SAPPHIRE Rarity: **Evolve**
Evolve Abra

FIRERED Rarity: **Rare**
Cerulean Cave

LEAFGREEN Rarity: **Rare**
Cerulean Cave

COLOSSEUM Rarity: **None**
Trade from *Ruby/Sapphire/FireRed/LeafGreen*

EMERALD Rarity: **Evolve**
Evolve Abra

XD Rarity: **None**
Trade from *Ruby/Sapphire/FireRed/LeafGreen*

MOVES

Level	Attack	Type	Power	ACC	PP	Level	Attack	Type	Power	ACC	PP
—	Teleport	Psychic	—	—	20	25	Recover	Normal	—	—	20
—	Kinesis	Psychic	—	80	15	30	Future Sight	Psychic	80	90	15
—/16	Confusion	Psychic	50	100	25	33	Role Play	Psychic	—	100	10
18	Disable	Normal	—	55	20	36	Psychic	Psychic	90	100	10
21	Psybeam	Psychic	65	100	20	43	Trick	Psychic	—	100	10
23	Reflect	Psychic	—	—	20						

TM/HM

TM/HM#	Name	Type	Power	ACC	PP	TM/HM#	Name	Type	Power	ACC	PP
TM01	Focus Punch	Fighting	150	100	20	TM30	Shadow Ball	Ghost	80	100	15
TM04	Calm Mind	Psychic	—	—	20	TM32	Double Team	Normal	—	—	15
TM06	Toxic	Poison	—	85	10	TM33	Reflect	Normal	—	—	20
TM10	Hidden Power	Normal	—	100	15	TM34	Shock Wave	Electric	60	—	20
TM11	Sunny Day	Fire	—	—	5	TM41	Torment	Dark	—	100	15
TM12	Taunt	Dark	—	100	20	TM42	Facade	Normal	70	100	20
TM16	Light Screen	Psychic	—	—	30	TM43	Secret Power	Normal	70	100	20
TM17	Protect	Normal	—	—	10	TM44	Rest	Psychic	—	—	10
TM18	Rain Dance	Water	—	—	5	TM45	Attract	Normal	—	100	15
TM20	Safeguard	Normal	—	—	25	TM46	Thief	Dark	40	100	10
TM21	Frustration	Normal	—	100	20	TM48	Skill Swap	Psychic	—	100	10
TM23	Iron Tail	Steel	75	75	15	TM49	Snatch	Dark	—	100	10
TM27	Return	Normal	—	100	20	HM05	Flash	Normal	—	70	20
TM29	Psychic	Psychic	90	100	10						

= Emerald Only

MOVE TUTOR

FireRed/LeafGreen and Emerald Only

Body Slam*	Counter*	Double-Edge
Dream Eater*	Mega Kick*	Mega Punch*
Mimic	Seismic Toss*	Substitute
Thunder Wave*		

Emerald Only

Dynamicpunch	Endure*	Fire Punch*
Ice Punch*	Metronome	Psych Up*
Sleep Talk	Snore*	Swagger
Thunderpunch*		

*Battle Frontier tutor move (*Emerald*)

065 Alakazam™

PSYCHIC

GENERAL INFO
SPECIES: Psi Pokémon
HEIGHT: 4'11"
WEIGHT: 106 lbs.

ABILITY 1: Synchronize
When an opponent inflicts a Poison, Paralyze, or Burn condition on Alakazam, it receives the same status ailment.

ABILITY 2: Inner Focus
Prevents Alakazam from flinching.

STATS
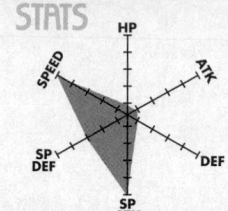

EVOLUTIONS
LV16   EVOLVE VIA TRADING

LOCATION[S]:

RUBY	**Rarity: Evolve**
Evolve Kadabra	
SAPPHIRE	**Rarity: Evolve**
Evolve Kadabra	
FIRERED	**Rarity: Evolve**
Evolve Kadabra	
LEAFGREEN	**Rarity: Evolve**
Evolve Kadabra	
COLOSSEUM	**Rarity: None**
Trade from *Ruby/Sapphire/FireRed/LeafGreen*	
EMERALD	**Rarity: Evolve**
Evolve Kadabra	
XD	**Rarity: None**
Trade from *Ruby/Sapphire/FireRed/LeafGreen*	

MOVES

Level	Attack	Type	Power	ACC	PP	Level	Attack	Type	Power	ACC	PP
—	Teleport	Psychic	—	—	20	23	Reflect	Psychic	—	—	20
—	Kinesis	Psychic	—	80	15	25	Recover	Normal	—	—	20
—/16	Confusion	Psychic	50	100	25	30	Future Sight	Psychic	80	90	15
18	Disable	Normal	—	55	20	33	Calm Mind	Psychic	—	—	20
21	Psybeam	Psychic	65	100	20	36	Psychic	Psychic	90	100	10
						43	Trick	Psychic	—	100	10

TM/HM

TM/HM#	Name	Type	Power	ACC	PP	TM/HM#	Name	Type	Power	ACC	PP
TM01	Focus Punch	Fighting	150	100	20	TM29	Psychic	Psychic	90	100	10
TM04	Calm Mind	Psychic	—	—	20	TM30	Shadow Ball	Ghost	80	100	15
TM06	Toxic	Poison	—	85	10	TM32	Double Team	Normal	—	—	15
TM10	Hidden Power	Normal	—	100	15	TM33	Reflect	Normal	—	—	20
TM11	Sunny Day	Fire	—	—	5	TM34	Shock Wave	Electric	60	—	20
TM12	Taunt	Dark	—	100	20	TM41	Torment	Dark	—	100	15
TM15	Hyper Beam	Normal	150	90	5	TM42	Facade	Normal	70	100	20
TM16	Light Screen	Psychic	—	—	30	TM43	Secret Power	Normal	70	100	20
TM17	Protect	Normal	—	—	10	TM44	Rest	Psychic	—	—	10
TM18	Rain Dance	Water	—	—	5	TM45	Attract	Normal	—	100	15
TM20	Safeguard	Normal	—	—	25	TM46	Thief	Dark	40	100	10
TM21	Frustration	Normal	—	100	20	TM48	Skill Swap	Psychic	—	100	10
TM23	Iron Tail	Steel	75	75	15	TM49	Snatch	Dark	—	100	10
TM27	Return	Normal	—	100	20	HM05	Flash	Normal	—	70	20

 # = Emerald Only

MOVE TUTOR
FireRed/LeafGreen and *Emerald* Only

Body Slam*	Counter*	Double-Edge
Dream Eater*	Mega Kick*	Mega Punch*
Mimic	Seismic Toss*	Substitute
Thunder Wave*		

Emerald Only

Dynamicpunch	Endure*	Fire Punch*
Ice Punch*	Metronome	Psych Up*
Sleep Talk	Snore*	Swagger
Thunderpunch*		

*Battle Frontier tutor move (Emerald)

066 Machop™

FIGHTING

GENERAL INFO
SPECIES: Superpower Pokémon
HEIGHT: 2'07"
WEIGHT: 43 lbs.
ABILITY: Guts
When Machop has a status condition, its attack power multiplies by 1.5.

STATS
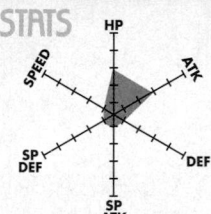

EVOLUTIONS

LV28   EVOLVE VIA TRADING

LOCATION[S]:

RUBY	**Rarity: Common**
Route 112, Jagged Pass, Fiery Path	
SAPPHIRE	**Rarity: Common**
Route 112, Jagged Pass, Fiery Path	
FIRERED	**Rarity: Common**
One Island, Rock Tunnel, Victory Road	
LEAFGREEN	**Rarity: Common**
One Island, Rock Tunnel, Victory Road	
COLOSSEUM	**Rarity: None**
Trade from *Ruby/Sapphire/FireRed/LeafGreen*	
EMERALD	**Rarity: Rare**
Jagged Pass, Fiery Path	
XD	**Rarity: None**
Trade from *Ruby/Sapphire/FireRed/LeafGreen*	

MOVES

Level	Attack	Type	Power	ACC	PP	Level	Attack	Type	Power	ACC	PP
—	Low Kick	Fighting	—	100	20	25	Revenge	Fighting	60	100	10
—	Leer	Normal	—	100	30	31	Vital Throw	Fighting	70	100	10
7	Focus Energy	Normal	—	—	30	37	Submission	Fighting	80	80	25
13	Karate Chop	Fighting	50	100	25	40	Cross Chop	Fighting	100	80	5
19	Seismic Toss	Fighting	—	100	20	43	Scary Face	Normal	—	90	10
22	Foresight	Normal	—	100	40	49	Dynamicpunch	Fighting	100	50	5

TM/HM

TM/HM#	Name	Type	Power	ACC	PP	TM/HM#	Name	Type	Power	ACC	PP
TM01	Focus Punch	Fighting	150	100	20	TM32	Double Team	Normal	—	—	15
TM06	Toxic	Poison	—	85	10	TM35	Flamethrower	Fire	95	100	15
TM08	Bulk Up	Fighting	—	—	20	TM38	Fire Blast	Fire	120	85	5
TM10	Hidden Power	Normal	—	100	15	TM39	Rock Tomb	Rock	50	80	10
TM11	Sunny Day	Fire	—	—	5	TM42	Facade	Normal	70	100	20
TM17	Protect	Normal	—	—	10	TM43	Secret Power	Normal	70	100	20
TM18	Rain Dance	Water	—	—	5	TM44	Rest	Psychic	—	—	10
TM21	Frustration	Normal	—	100	20	TM45	Attract	Normal	—	100	15
TM26	Earthquake	Ground	100	100	10	TM46	Thief	Dark	40	100	10
TM27	Return	Normal	—	100	20	HM04	Strength	Normal	80	100	15
TM28	Dig	Ground	60	100	10	HM06	Rock Smash	Fighting	20	100	15
TM31	Brick Break	Fighting	75	100	15						

EGG MOVES*

Name	Type	Power	ACC	PP
Light Screen	Psychic	—	—	30
Meditate	Psychic	—	—	40
Encore	Normal	—	100	5
Smellingsalt	Normal	60	100	10
Counter	Fighting	—	100	20
Rock Slide	Rock	75	90	10
Rolling Kick	Fighting	60	85	10

*Learned Via Breeding

MOVE TUTOR
FireRed/LeafGreen and *Emerald* Only

Body Slam*	Counter*	Double-Edge
Mega Kick*	Mega Punch*	Mimic
Seismic Toss*	Substitute	Thunder Wave*

Emerald Only

Defense Curl*	Dynamicpunch	Endure*
Fire Punch*	Ice Punch*	Metronome
Mud-Slap*	Sleep Talk	Snore*
Swagger	Thunderpunch*	

*Battle Frontier tutor move (Emerald)

067 Machoke™

FIGHTING

GENERAL INFO
SPECIES: Superpower Pokémon
HEIGHT: 4'01"
WEIGHT: 155 lbs.
ABILITY: Guts
When Machoke has a status condition, its attack power multiplies by 1.5.

STATS
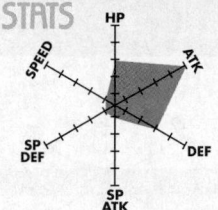
HP, ATK, DEF, SP ATK, SP DEF, SPEED

EVOLUTIONS

LV28 — EVOLVE VIA TRADING

LOCATION[S]:

RUBY — Rarity: **Evolve**
Evolve Machop

SAPPHIRE — Rarity: **Evolve**
Evolve Machop

FIRERED — Rarity: **Rare**
Cerulean Cave, Victory Road, One Island

LEAFGREEN — Rarity: **Rare**
Cerulean Cave, Victory Road, One Island

COLOSSEUM — Rarity: **None**
Trade from Ruby/Sapphire/FireRed/LeafGreen

EMERALD — Rarity: **Evolve**
Evolve Machop

XD — Rarity: **None**
Trade from Ruby/Sapphire/FireRed/LeafGreen

MOVES

Level	Attack	Type	Power	ACC	PP	Level	Attack	Type	Power	ACC	PP
—	Low Kick	Fighting	—	100	20	25	Revenge	Fighting	60	100	10
—	Leer	Normal	—	100	30	33	Vital Throw	Fighting	70	100	10
—/7	Focus Energy	Normal	—	—	30	41	Submission	Fighting	80	80	25
13	Karate Chop	Fighting	50	100	25	46	Cross Chop	Fighting	100	80	5
19	Seismic Toss	Fighting	—	100	20	51	Scary Face	Normal	—	90	10
22	Foresight	Normal	—	100	40	59	Dynamicpunch	Fighting	100	50	5

= Emerald Only

TM/HM

TM/HM#	Name	Type	Power	ACC	PP	TM/HM#	Name	Type	Power	ACC	PP
TM01	Focus Punch	Fighting	150	100	20	TM32	Double Team	Normal	—	—	15
TM06	Toxic	Poison	—	85	10	TM35	Flamethrower	Fire	95	100	15
TM08	Bulk Up	Fighting	—	—	20	TM38	Fire Blast	Fire	120	85	5
TM10	Hidden Power	Normal	—	100	15	TM39	Rock Tomb	Rock	50	80	10
TM11	Sunny Day	Fire	—	—	5	TM42	Facade	Normal	70	100	20
TM17	Protect	Normal	—	—	10	TM43	Secret Power	Normal	70	100	20
TM18	Rain Dance	Water	—	—	5	TM44	Rest	Psychic	—	—	10
TM21	Frustration	Normal	—	100	20	TM45	Attract	Normal	—	100	15
TM26	Earthquake	Ground	100	100	10	TM46	Thief	Dark	40	100	10
TM27	Return	Normal	—	100	20	HM04	Strength	Normal	80	100	20
TM28	Dig	Ground	60	100	10	HM06	Rock Smash	Fighting	20	100	15
TM31	Brick Break	Fighting	75	100	15						

MOVE TUTOR
***FireRed/LeafGreen* and *Emerald* Only**

Body Slam*	Counter*	Double-Edge
Mega Kick*	Mega Punch*	Mimic
Rock Slide*	Seismic Toss*	Substitute

***Emerald* Only**

Dynamicpunch	Endure*	Fire Punch*
Ice Punch*	Metronome	Mud-Slap*
Sleep Talk	Snore*	Swagger
Thunderpunch*		

*Battle Frontier tutor move (*Emerald*)

---

068 Machamp™

FIGHTING

GENERAL INFO
SPECIES: Superpower Pokémon
HEIGHT: 5'03"
WEIGHT: 287 lbs.
ABILITY: Guts
When Machamp has a status condition, its attack power multiplies by 1.5.

STATS
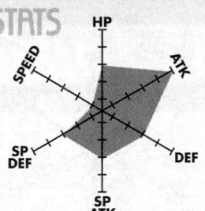
HP, ATK, DEF, SP ATK, SP DEF, SPEED

EVOLUTIONS

LV28 — EVOLVE VIA TRADING

LOCATION[S]:

RUBY — Rarity: **Evolve**
Evolve Machoke

SAPPHIRE — Rarity: **Evolve**
Evolve Machoke

FIRERED — Rarity: **Evolve**
Evolve Machoke

LEAFGREEN — Rarity: **Evolve**
Evolve Machoke

COLOSSEUM — Rarity: **None**
Trade from Ruby/Sapphire/FireRed/LeafGreen

EMERALD — Rarity: **Evolve**
Evolve Machoke

XD — Rarity: **None**
Trade from Ruby/Sapphire/FireRed/LeafGreen

MOVES

Level	Attack	Type	Power	ACC	PP	Level	Attack	Type	Power	ACC	PP
—	Low Kick	Fighting	—	100	20	25	Revenge	Fighting	60	100	10
—	Leer	Normal	—	100	30	33	Vital Throw	Fighting	70	100	10
—/7	Focus Energy	Normal	—	—	30	41	Submission	Fighting	80	80	25
13	Karate Chop	Fighting	50	100	25	46	Cross Chop	Fighting	100	80	5
19	Seismic Toss	Fighting	—	100	20	51	Scary Face	Normal	—	90	10
22	Foresight	Normal	—	100	40	59	Dynamicpunch	Fighting	100	50	5

= Emerald Only

TM/HM

TM/HM#	Name	Type	Power	ACC	PP	TM/HM#	Name	Type	Power	ACC	PP
TM01	Focus Punch	Fighting	150	100	20	TM31	Brick Break	Fighting	75	100	15
TM06	Toxic	Poison	—	85	10	TM32	Double Team	Normal	—	—	15
TM08	Bulk Up	Fighting	—	—	20	TM35	Flamethrower	Fire	95	100	15
TM10	Hidden Power	Normal	—	100	15	TM38	Fire Blast	Fire	120	85	5
TM11	Sunny Day	Fire	—	—	5	TM39	Rock Tomb	Rock	50	80	10
TM15	Hyper Beam	Normal	150	90	5	TM42	Facade	Normal	70	100	20
TM17	Protect	Normal	—	—	10	TM43	Secret Power	Normal	70	100	20
TM18	Rain Dance	Water	—	—	5	TM44	Rest	Psychic	—	—	10
TM21	Frustration	Normal	—	100	20	TM45	Attract	Normal	—	100	15
TM26	Earthquake	Ground	100	100	10	TM46	Thief	Dark	40	100	10
TM27	Return	Normal	—	100	20	HM04	Strength	Normal	80	100	20
TM28	Dig	Ground	60	100	10	HM06	Rock Smash	Fighting	20	100	15

EGG MOVES*

Name	Type	Power	ACC	PP
Light Screen	Psychic	—	—	30
Mediate	Psychic	—	—	40
Encore	Normal	—	100	5
Smellingsalt	Normal	60	100	10
Counter	Fighting	—	100	20
Rock Slide	Rock	75	90	10

*Learned Via Breeding

MOVE TUTOR
***FireRed/LeafGreen* and *Emerald* Only**

Body Slam*	Counter*	Double-Edge
Mega Kick*	Mega Punch*	Mimic
Rock Slide*	Seismic Toss*	Substitute

***Emerald* Only**

Dynamicpunch	Endure*	Fire Punch*
Ice Punch*	Metronome	Mud-Slap*
Sleep Talk	Snore*	Swagger
Thunderpunch*		

*Battle Frontier tutor move (*Emerald*)

073 Tentacruel™

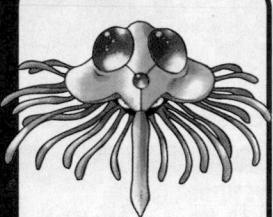

WATER | POISON

GENERAL INFO

SPECIES: **Jellyfish Pokémon**
HEIGHT: **5'03"**
WEIGHT: **121 lbs.**
ABILITY 1: **Clear Body**
Protects Tentacruel from having its stats lowered.
ABILITY 2: **Liquid Ooze**
Damages opponents when they absorb HPs from Tentacruel.

STATS

EVOLUTIONS

LV30

LOCATION[S]:

RUBY — Rarity: **Rare**
Abandoned Ship

SAPPHIRE — Rarity: **Rare**
Abandoned Ship

FIRERED — Rarity: **Rare**
Evolve Tentacool, Islands One, Three, Five, Six, Seven

LEAFGREEN — Rarity: **Common**
Evolve Tentacool, Islands One, Three, Five, Six, Seven

COLOSSEUM — Rarity: **None**
Trade from *Ruby/Sapphire/FireRed/LeafGreen*

EMERALD — Rarity: **Rare**
Evolve Tentacool, Abandoned Ship

XD — Rarity: **None**
Trade from *Ruby/Sapphire/FireRed/LeafGreen*

MOVES

Level	Attack	Type	Power	ACC	PP
—	Poison Sting	Poison	15	100	35
—/6	Supersonic	Normal	—	55	20
—/12	Constrict	Normal	10	100	35
19	Acid	Poison	40	100	30
25	Bubblebeam	Water	65	100	20
30	Wrap	Normal	15	85	20
38	Barrier	Psychic	—	—	30
47	Screech	Normal	—	85	40
55	Hydro Pump	Water	120	80	5

= Emerald Only

TM/HM

TM/HM#	Name	Type	Power	ACC	PP
TM03	Water Pulse	Water	60	95	20
TM06	Toxic	Poison	—	85	10
TM07	Hail	Ice	—	—	10
TM10	Hidden Power	Normal	—	100	15
TM13	Ice Beam	Ice	95	100	10
TM14	Blizzard	Ice	120	70	5
TM15	Hyper Beam	Normal	150	90	5
TM17	Protect	Normal	—	—	10
TM18	Rain Dance	Water	—	—	5
TM19	Giga Drain	Grass	60	100	5
TM21	Frustration	Normal	—	100	20
TM27	Return	Normal	—	100	20
TM32	Double Team	Normal	—	—	15
TM36	Sludge Bomb	Poison	90	100	10
TM42	Facade	Normal	70	100	10
TM43	Secret Power	Normal	70	100	20
TM44	Rest	Psychic	—	—	10
TM45	Attract	Normal	—	100	15
TM46	Thief	Dark	40	100	10
HM01	Cut	Normal	50	95	30
HM03	Surf	Water	95	100	15
HM07	Waterfall	Water	80	100	15
HM08	Dive	Water	60	100	10

MOVE TUTOR

FireRed/LeafGreen and *Emerald* **Only**

Double-Edge	Mimic	Substitute
Sword Dance*		

Emerald **Only**

Endure*	Icy Wind*	Sleep Talk
Snore*	Swagger	

*Battle Frontier tutor move (*Emerald*)

074 Geodude™

ROCK | GROUND

GENERAL INFO

SPECIES: **Rock Pokémon**
HEIGHT: **1'04"**
WEIGHT: **44 lbs.**
ABILITY 1: **Rock Head**
Protects Geodude from receiving recoil damage from Submission, Take Down, and Double-Edge.
ABILITY 2: **Sturdy**
Prevents Geodude from receiving a one hit KO.

STATS

EVOLUTIONS

LV25 | EVOLVE VIA TRADE

LOCATION[S]:

RUBY — Rarity: **Common**
Route 111, Route 114, Victory Road, Safari Zone, Granite Cave

SAPPHIRE — Rarity: **Common**
Route 111, Route 114, Victory Road, Safari Zone, Granite Cave

FIRERED — Rarity: **Common**
One Island, Seven Island, Victory Road, Mt. Moon, Rock Tunnel

LEAFGREEN — Rarity: **Common**
One Island, Seven Island, Victory Road, Mt. Moon, Rock Tunnel

COLOSSEUM — Rarity: **None**
Trade from *Ruby/Sapphire/FireRed/LeafGreen*

EMERALD — Rarity: **Common**
Route 111, Route 114, Granite Cave, Magma Hideout, Victory Road, Safari Zone, Cerulean Cave, One Island, Seven Island

XD — Rarity: **None**
Trade from *Ruby/Sapphire/FireRed/LeafGreen*

MOVES

Level	Attack	Type	Power	ACC	PP
—	Tackle	Normal	35	95	35
—	Defense Curl	Normal	—	—	40
6	Mud Sport	Ground	—	100	15
11	Rock Throw	Rock	50	90	15
16	Magnitude	Ground	—	100	30
21	Selfdestruct	Normal	200	100	5
26	Rollout	Rock	30	90	20
31	Rock Blast	Rock	25	80	10
36	Earthquake	Ground	100	100	10
41	Explosion	Normal	250	100	5
46	Double-Edge	Normal	120	100	15

TM/HM

TM/HM#	Name	Type	Power	ACC	PP
TM01	Focus Punch	Fighting	150	100	20
TM06	Toxic	Poison	—	85	10
TM10	Hidden Power	Normal	—	100	15
TM11	Sunny Day	Fire	—	—	5
TM17	Protect	Normal	—	—	10
TM21	Frustration	Normal	—	100	20
TM26	Earthquake	Ground	100	100	10
TM27	Return	Normal	—	100	20
TM28	Dig	Ground	60	100	10
TM31	Brick Break	Fighting	75	100	15
TM32	Double Team	Normal	—	—	15
TM35	Flamethrower	Fire	95	100	15
TM37	Sandstorm	Ground	—	—	10
TM38	Fire Blast	Fire	120	85	5
TM39	Rock Tomb	Rock	50	80	10
TM42	Facade	Normal	70	100	10
TM43	Secret Power	Normal	70	100	20
TM44	Rest	Psychic	—	—	10
TM45	Attract	Normal	—	100	15
HM04	Strength	Normal	80	100	15
HM06	Rock Smash	Fighting	20	100	15

EGG MOVES*

Name	Type	Power	ACC	PP
Rock Slide	Rock	75	90	10
Block	Normal	—	100	5
Mega Punch	Normal	80	85	20

*Learned Via Breeding

MOVE TUTOR

FireRed/LeafGreen and *Emerald* **Only**

Body Slam*	Counter*	Double-Edge
Explosion	Mega Punch*	Mimic
Rock Slide*	Seismic Toss*	Substitute

Emerald **Only**

Defense Curl*	Dynamicpunch*	Endure*
Fire Punch*	Metronome	Mud-Slap*
Rollout	Sleep Talk	Snore*
Swagger		

*Battle Frontier tutor move (*Emerald*)

075 Graveler™

ROCK | GROUND

GENERAL INFO

SPECIES: Rock Pokémon
HEIGHT: 3'03"
WEIGHT: 232 lbs.
ABILITY 1: Rock Head
Protects Graveler from receiving recoil damage from Submission, Take Down, and Double-Edge.

ABILITY 2: Sturdy
Prevents Graveler from receiving a one hit KO.

STATS

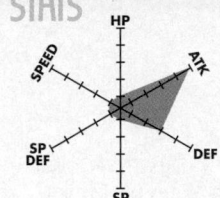

EVOLUTIONS

LV25 | EVOLVE VIA TRADE

LOCATION(S):

RUBY	Rarity: **Common**
Victory Road	
SAPPHIRE	Rarity: **Common**
Victory Road	
FIRERED	Rarity: **Rare**
Cerulean Cave	
LEAFGREEN	Rarity: **Rare**
Cerulean Cave	
COLOSSEUM	Rarity: **None**
Trade from *Ruby/Sapphire/FireRed/LeafGreen*	
EMERALD	Rarity: **Common**
Evolve Geodude, Magma Hideout, Victory Road	
XD	Rarity: **None**
Trade from *Ruby/Sapphire/FireRed/LeafGreen*	

MOVES

Level	Attack	Type	Power	ACC	PP		Level	Attack	Type	Power	ACC	PP
—	Tackle	Normal	35	95	35		21	Selfdestruct	Normal	200	100	5
—	Defense Curl	Normal	—	—	40		29	Rollout	Rock	30	90	20
—/6	Mud Sport	Ground	—	100	15		37	Rock Blast	Rock	25	80	10
—/11	Rock Throw	Rock	50	90	15		45	Earthquake	Ground	100	100	10
16	Magnitude	Ground	—	100	30		53	Explosion	Normal	250	100	5
							62	Double-Edge	Normal	120	100	5

TM/HM

TM/HM#	Name	Type	Power	ACC	PP		TM/HM#	Name	Type	Power	ACC	PP
TM01	Focus Punch	Fighting	150	100	20		TM35	Flamethrower	Fire	95	100	15
TM06	Toxic	Poison	—	85	10		TM37	Sandstorm	Ground	—	—	10
TM10	Hidden Power	Normal	—	100	15		TM38	Fire Blast	Fire	120	85	5
TM11	Sunny Day	Fire	—	—	5		TM39	Rock Tomb	Rock	50	80	10
TM17	Protect	Normal	—	—	10		TM42	Facade	Normal	70	100	20
TM21	Frustration	Normal	—	100	20		TM43	Secret Power	Normal	70	100	20
TM26	Earthquake	Ground	100	100	10		TM44	Rest	Psychic	—	—	10
TM27	Return	Normal	—	100	20		TM45	Attract	Normal	—	100	15
TM28	Dig	Ground	60	100	10		HM04	Strength	Normal	80	100	20
TM31	Brick Break	Fighting	75	100	15		HM06	Rock Smash	Fighting	20	100	15
TM32	Double Team	Normal	—	—	15							

= Emerald Only

MOVE TUTOR

FireRed/LeafGreen and *Emerald* Only

Body Slam*	Counter*	Double-Edge
Explosion	Mega Punch*	Mimic
Rock Slide*	Seismic Toss*	Substitute

Emerald Only

Defense Curl*	Dynamicpunch	Endure*
Fire Punch*	Metronome	Mud-Slap*
Rollout	Sleep Talk	Snore*
Swagger		

*Battle Frontier tutor move (*Emerald*)

---

076 Golem™

ROCK | GROUND

GENERAL INFO

SPECIES: Megaton Pokémon
HEIGHT: 4'07"
WEIGHT: 662 lbs.
ABILITY 1: Rock Head
Protects Golem from receiving recoil damage from Submission, Take Down, and Double-Edge.

ABILITY 2: Sturdy
Prevents Golem from receiving a one hit KO.

STATS

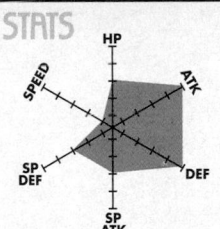

EVOLUTIONS

LV25 | EVOLVE VIA TRADE

LOCATION(S):

RUBY	Rarity: **Trade**
Evolve Graveler	
SAPPHIRE	Rarity: **Trade**
Evolve Graveler	
FIRERED	Rarity: **Evolve**
Evolve Graveler	
LEAFGREEN	Rarity: **Evolve**
Evolve Graveler	
COLOSSEUM	Rarity: **None**
Trade from *Ruby/Sapphire/FireRed/LeafGreen*	
EMERALD	Rarity: **Evolve**
Evolve Graveler	
XD	Rarity: **None**
Trade from *Ruby/Sapphire/FireRed/LeafGreen*	

MOVES

Level	Attack	Type	Power	ACC	PP		Level	Attack	Type	Power	ACC	PP
—	Tackle	Normal	35	95	35		21	Selfdestruct	Normal	200	100	5
—	Defense Curl	Normal	—	—	40		29	Rollout	Rock	30	90	20
—/6	Mud Sport	Ground	—	100	15		37	Rock Blast	Rock	25	80	10
—/11	Rock Throw	Rock	50	90	15		45	Earthquake	Ground	100	100	10
16	Magnitude	Ground	—	100	30		53	Explosion	Normal	250	100	5
							62	Double-Edge	Normal	120	100	15

TM/HM

TM/HM#	Name	Type	Power	ACC	PP		TM/HM#	Name	Type	Power	ACC	PP
TM01	Focus Punch	Fighting	150	100	20		TM32	Double Team	Normal	—	—	15
TM05	Roar	Normal	—	100	20		TM35	Flamethrower	Fire	95	100	15
TM06	Toxic	Poison	—	85	10		TM37	Sandstorm	Ground	—	—	10
TM10	Hidden Power	Normal	—	100	15		TM38	Fire Blast	Fire	120	85	5
TM11	Sunny Day	Fire	—	—	5		TM39	Rock Tomb	Rock	50	80	10
TM15	Hyper Beam	Normal	150	90	5		TM42	Facade	Normal	70	100	20
TM17	Protect	Normal	—	—	10		TM43	Secret Power	Normal	70	100	20
TM21	Frustration	Normal	—	100	20		TM44	Rest	Psychic	—	—	10
TM26	Earthquake	Ground	100	100	10		TM45	Attract	Normal	—	100	15
TM27	Return	Normal	—	100	20		HM04	Strength	Normal	80	100	20
TM28	Dig	Ground	60	100	10		HM06	Rock Smash	Fighting	20	100	15
TM31	Brick Break	Fighting	75	100	15							

= Emerald Only

MOVE TUTOR

FireRed/LeafGreen and *Emerald* Only

Body Slam*	Counter*	Double-Edge
Explosion	Mega Kick*	Mega Punch*
Mimic	Rock Slide*	Seismic Toss*
Substitute		

Emerald Only

Defense Curl*	Dynamicpunch	Endure*
Fire Punch*	Fury Cutter	Metronome
Mud-Slap*	Rollout	Sleep Talk
Snore*	Swagger	

*Battle Frontier tutor move (*Emerald*)

077 Ponyta™

FIRE

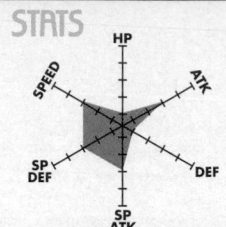

GENERAL INFO
SPECIES: Fire Horse Pokémon
HEIGHT: 3'03"
WEIGHT: 66 lbs.
ABILITY 1: Flash Fire
Raises Ponyta's Fire-type attacks; prevents Fire-type Attacks from damaging Ponyta.

ABILITY 2: Run Away
Allows Ponyta to escape from wild Pokémon.

STATS

EVOLUTIONS

LV40

LOCATION[S]:

RUBY   Rarity: **None**
Trade from *FireRed/LeafGreen*

SAPPHIRE   Rarity: **None**
Trade from *FireRed/LeafGreen*

FIRERED   Rarity: **Common**
One Island

LEAFGREEN   Rarity: **Common**
One Island

COLOSSEUM   Rarity: **None**
Trade from *Ruby/Sapphire/FireRed/LeafGreen*

EMERALD   Rarity: **None**
Trade from *FireRed/LeafGreen*

XD   Rarity: **None**
Trade from *Ruby/Sapphire/FireRed/LeafGreen*

MOVES

Level	Attack	Type	Power	ACC	PP	Level	Attack	Type	Power	ACC	PP
—	Quick Attack	Normal	40	100	30	25	Fire Spin	Fire	15	70	15
5	Growl	Normal	—	100	40	31	Take Down	Normal	90	85	20
9	Tail Whip	Normal	—	100	30	38	Agility	Psychic	—	—	30
14	Ember	Fire	40	100	25	45	Bounce	Flying	85	85	5
19	Stomp	Normal	65	100	20	53	Fire Blast	Fire	120	85	5

TM/HM

TM/HM#	Name	Type	Power	ACC	PP	TM/HM#	Name	Type	Power	ACC	PP
TM06	Toxic	Poison	—	85	10	TM35	Flamethrower	Fire	95	100	15
TM10	Hidden Power	Normal	—	100	15	TM38	Fire Blast	Fire	120	85	5
TM11	Sunny Day	Fire	—	—	5	TM42	Facade	Normal	70	100	20
TM17	Protect	Normal	—	—	10	TM43	Secret Power	Normal	70	100	20
TM21	Frustration	Normal	—	100	20	TM44	Rest	Psychic	—	—	10
TM22	Solarbeam	Grass	120	100	10	TM45	Attract	Normal	—	100	15
TM23	Iron Tail	Steel	75	75	15	TM50	Overheat	Fire	140	90	5
TM27	Return	Normal	—	100	20	HM04	Strength	Normal	80	100	20
TM32	Double Team	Normal	—	—	15						

EGG MOVES*

Name	Type	Power	ACC	PP
Charm	Normal	—	100	20
Double Kick	Fighting	30	100	30
Double-Edge	Normal	120	100	15
Flame Wheel	Fire	60	100	25
Hypnosis	Psychic	—	60	20
Thrash	Normal	90	100	20

*Learned Via Breeding

MOVE TUTOR
FireRed/LeafGreen and *Emerald* **Only**

Body Slam*	Double-Edge	Mimic
Substitute		

*Battle Frontier tutor move (*Emerald*)

078 Rapidash™

FIRE

GENERAL INFO
SPECIES: Fire Horse Pokémon
HEIGHT: 5'07"
WEIGHT: 209 lbs.
ABILITY 1: Flash Fire
Raises Rapidash's Fire-type attacks; prevents Fire-type Attacks from damaging Rapidash.

ABILITY 2: Run Away
Allows Rapidash to escape from wild Pokémon.

STATS

EVOLUTIONS
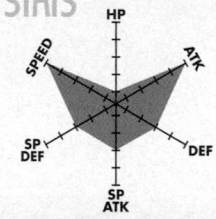
LV40

LOCATION[S]:

RUBY   Rarity: **None**
Trade Ponyta

SAPPHIRE   Rarity: **None**
Trade Ponyta

FIRERED   Rarity: **Rare**
Evolve Ponyta, One Island

LEAFGREEN   Rarity: **Rare**
Evolve Ponyta, One Island

COLOSSEUM   Rarity: **None**
Trade from *FireRed/LeafGreen*

EMERALD   Rarity: **None**
Trade from *FireRed/LeafGreen*

XD   Rarity: **Only One**
Citadark Island (Capture from Cipher Peon Kolest)

MOVES

Level	Attack	Type	Power	ACC	PP	Level	Attack	Type	Power	ACC	PP
—	Quick Attack	Normal	40	100	30	25	Fire Spin	Fire	15	70	15
—	Growl	Normal	—	100	40	31	Take Down	Normal	90	85	20
—	Tail Whip	Normal	—	100	30	38	Agility	Psychic	—	—	30
—	Ember	Fire	40	100	25	40	Fury Attack	Normal	15	85	20
19	Stomp	Normal	65	100	20	50	Bounce	Flying	85	85	5
						63	Fire Blast	Fire	120	85	5

TM/HM

TM/HM#	Name	Type	Power	ACC	PP	TM/HM#	Name	Type	Power	ACC	PP
TM06	Toxic	Poison	—	85	10	TM32	Double Team	Normal	—	—	15
TM10	Hidden Power	Normal	—	100	15	TM35	Flamethrower	Fire	95	100	15
TM11	Sunny Day	Fire	—	—	5	TM38	Fire Blast	Fire	120	85	5
TM15	Hyper Beam	Normal	150	90	5	TM42	Facade	Normal	70	100	20
TM17	Protect	Normal	—	—	10	TM43	Secret Power	Normal	70	100	20
TM21	Frustration	Normal	—	100	20	TM44	Rest	Psychic	—	—	10
TM22	Solarbeam	Grass	120	100	10	TM45	Attract	Normal	—	100	15
TM23	Iron Tail	Steel	75	75	15	TM50	Overheat	Fire	140	90	5
TM27	Return	Normal	—	100	20	HM04	Strength	Normal	80	100	20

MOVE TUTOR
FireRed/LeafGreen and *Emerald* **Only**

Body Slam*	Double-Edge	Mimic
Substitute		

*Battle Frontier tutor move (*Emerald*)

079 Slowpoke™

WATER | PSYCHIC

GENERAL INFO

SPECIES: Dopey Pokémon
HEIGHT: 3'11"
WEIGHT: 79 lbs.

ABILITY 1: Oblivious
Prevents Slowpoke from being attracted.

ABILITY 2: Own Tempo
Prevents Slowpoke from being confused.

STATS

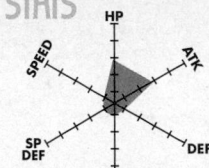

EVOLUTIONS

LV37

KING'S ROCK

LOCATION(S):

RUBY Rarity: **None**
Trade from *LeafGreen*

SAPPHIRE Rarity: **None**
Trade from *LeafGreen*

FIRERED Rarity: **None**
Trade from *LeafGreen*

LEAFGREEN Rarity: **Common**
Islands One, Two, Three, Four, Five, Six, Seven, Routes 4, 10, 11, 12, 13, 14, 19, 20, 21, 24, 25, Fuchsia City, Vermilion City, Viridian City, Safari Zone

COLOSSEUM Rarity: **None**
Trade from *LeafGreen*

EMERALD Rarity: **None**
Trade from *LeafGreen*

XD Rarity: **None**
Trade from *LeafGreen*

MOVES

Level	Attack	Type	Power	ACC	PP
—	Curse	—	—	—	10
—	Tackle	Normal	35	95	35
—	Yawn	Normal	—	100	10
6	Growl	Normal	—	100	40
13	Water Gun	Water	40	100	25
17	Confusion	Psychic	50	100	25
24	Disable	Normal	—	55	20
29	Headbutt	Normal	70	100	15
36	Amnesia	Psychic	—	—	20
40	Psychic	Psychic	90	100	10
47	Psych Up	Normal	—	—	10

TM/HM

TM/HM#	Name	Type	Power	ACC	PP
TM03	Water Pulse	Water	60	95	20
TM04	Calm Mind	Psychic	—	—	20
TM06	Toxic	Poison	—	85	10
TM07	Hail	Ice	—	—	10
TM10	Hidden Power	Normal	—	100	15
TM11	Sunny Day	Fire	—	—	5
TM13	Ice Beam	Ice	95	100	10
TM14	Blizzard	Ice	120	70	5
TM17	Protect	Normal	—	—	10
TM18	Rain Dance	Water	—	—	5
TM20	Safeguard	Normal	—	—	25
TM21	Frustration	Normal	—	100	20
TM23	Iron Tail	Steel	75	75	15
TM26	Earthquake	Ground	100	100	10
TM27	Return	Normal	—	100	20
TM28	Dig	Ground	60	100	10
TM29	Psychic	Psychic	90	100	10
TM30	Shadow Ball	Ghost	80	100	15
TM32	Double Team	Normal	—	—	15
TM35	Flamethrower	Fire	95	100	15
TM38	Fire Blast	Fire	120	85	5
TM42	Facade	Normal	70	100	20
TM43	Secret Power	Normal	70	100	20
TM44	Rest	Psychic	—	—	10
TM45	Attract	Normal	—	100	15
TM48	Skill Swap	Psychic	—	100	10
HM03	Surf	Water	95	100	15
HM04	Strength	Normal	80	100	20
HM05	Flash	Normal	—	70	20
HM08	Dive	Water	60	100	10

EGG MOVES*

Name	Type	Power	ACC	PP
Belly Drum	Normal	—	—	10
Future Sight	Psychic	80	90	15
Mud Sport	Ground	—	100	15
Safeguard	Normal	—	—	25
Sleep Talk	Normal	—	—	10
Snore	Normal	40	100	15
Stomp	Normal	65	100	20

*Learned Via Breeding

MOVE TUTOR

FireRed/LeafGreen and *Emerald* Only

Body Slam*	Double-Edge	Dream Eater*
Mimic	Substitute	Thunder Wave*

*Battle Frontier tutor move (*Emerald*)

---

080 Slowbro™

WATER | PSYCHIC

GENERAL INFO

SPECIES: Hermit Crab Pokémon
HEIGHT: 5'03"
WEIGHT: 173 lbs.

ABILITY 1: Oblivious
Prevents Slowbro from being attracted.

ABILITY 2: Own Tempo
Prevents Slowbro from being confused.

STATS

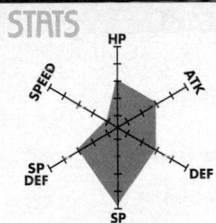

EVOLUTIONS

L37

LOCATION(S):

RUBY Rarity: **None**
Trade from *LeafGreen*

SAPPHIRE Rarity: **None**
Trade from *LeafGreen*

FIRERED Rarity: **None**
Trade from *LeafGreen*

LEAFGREEN Rarity: **Rare**
Two Island, Three Island, Seafoam Islands

COLOSSEUM Rarity: **None**
Trade from *LeafGreen*

EMERALD Rarity: **None**
Trade from *LeafGreen*

XD Rarity: **None**
Trade from *LeafGreen*

MOVES

Level	Attack	Type	Power	ACC	PP
—	Curse	—	—	—	10
—	Tackle	Normal	35	95	35
—	Yawn	Normal	—	100	10
—	Growl	Normal	—	100	40
13	Water Gun	Water	40	100	25
17	Confusion	Psychic	50	100	25
24	Disable	Normal	—	55	20
29	Headbutt	Normal	70	100	15
36	Amnesia	Psychic	—	—	20
37	Withdraw	Normal	—	—	40
44	Psychic	Psychic	90	100	10
55	Psych Up	Normal	—	—	10

TM/HM

TM/HM#	Name	Type	Power	ACC	PP
TM01	Focus Punch	Fighting	150	100	20
TM03	Water Pulse	Water	60	95	20
TM04	Calm Mind	Psychic	—	—	20
TM06	Toxic	Poison	—	85	10
TM07	Hail	Ice	—	—	10
TM10	Hidden Power	Normal	—	100	15
TM11	Sunny Day	Fire	—	—	5
TM13	Ice Beam	Ice	95	100	10
TM14	Blizzard	Ice	120	70	5
TM15	Hyper Beam	Normal	150	90	5
TM17	Protect	Normal	—	—	10
TM18	Rain Dance	Water	—	—	5
TM20	Safeguard	Normal	—	—	25
TM21	Frustration	Normal	—	100	20
TM23	Iron Tail	Steel	75	75	15
TM26	Earthquake	Ground	100	100	10
TM27	Return	Normal	—	100	20
TM28	Dig	Ground	60	100	10
TM29	Psychic	Psychic	90	100	10
TM30	Shadow Ball	Ghost	80	100	15
TM31	Brick Break	Fighting	75	100	15
TM32	Double Team	Normal	—	—	15
TM35	Flamethrower	Fire	95	100	15
TM38	Fire Blast	Fire	120	85	5
TM42	Facade	Normal	70	100	20
TM43	Secret Power	Normal	70	100	20
TM44	Rest	Psychic	—	—	10
TM45	Attract	Normal	—	100	15
TM48	Skill Swap	Psychic	—	100	10
HM03	Surf	Water	95	100	15
HM04	Strength	Normal	80	100	20
HM05	Flash	Normal	—	70	20
HM06	Rock Smash	Fighting	20	100	15
HM08	Dive	Water	60	100	10

MOVE TUTOR

FireRed/LeafGreen and *Emerald* Only

Body Slam*	Counter*	Double-Edge
Dream Eater*	Mega Kick*	Mega Punch*
Mimic	Seismic Toss*	Substitute
Thunder Wave*		

*Battle Frontier tutor move (*Emerald*)

081 Magnemite™

ELECTRIC STEEL

GENERAL INFO
SPECIES: Magnet Pokémon
HEIGHT: 1'00"
WEIGHT: 13 lbs.
ABILITY 1: Magnet Pull
Other Steel-types cannot escape while Magnemite is in battle.
ABILITY 2: Sturdy
A one hit KO cannot hit Magnemite.

STATS

EVOLUTIONS
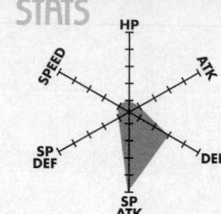
LV30

LOCATION(S):

RUBY Rarity: **Common**
New Mauville

SAPPHIRE Rarity: **Common**
New Mauville

FIRERED Rarity: **Common**
Power Plant

LEAFGREEN Rarity: **Common**
Power Plant

COLOSSEUM Rarity: **None**
Trade from *Ruby/Sapphire/FireRed/LeafGreen*

EMERALD Rarity: **Common**
New Mauville

XD Rarity: **None**
Trade from *Ruby/Sapphire/FireRed/LeafGreen*

MOVES

Level	Attack	Type	Power	ACC	PP	Level	Attack	Type	Power	ACC	PP
—	Metal Sound	Steel	—	85	40	21	Thunder Wave	Electric	—	100	20
—	Tackle	Normal	35	95	35	26	Spark	Electric	65	100	20
6	Thundershock	Electric	40	100	30	32	Lock-on	Normal	—	100	5
11	Supersonic	Normal	—	55	20	38	Swift	Normal	60	—	20
16	Sonicboom	Normal	—	90	20	44	Screech	Normal	—	85	40
						50	Zap Cannon	Electric	100	50	5

TM/HM

TM/HM#	Name	Type	Power	ACC	PP	TM/HM#	Name	Type	Power	ACC	PP
TM06	Toxic	Poison	—	85	10	TM27	Return	Normal	—	100	20
TM10	Hidden Power	Normal	—	100	15	TM32	Double Team	Normal	—	—	15
TM11	Sunny Day	Fire	—	—	5	TM33	Reflect	Normal	—	—	20
TM17	Protect	Normal	—	—	10	TM34	Shock Wave	Electric	60	—	20
TM18	Rain Dance	Water	—	—	5	TM42	Facade	Normal	70	100	20
TM21	Frustration	Normal	—	100	20	TM43	Secret Power	Normal	70	100	20
TM24	Thunderbolt	Electric	95	100	15	TM44	Rest	Psychic	—	—	10
TM25	Thunder	Electric	120	70	10	HM05	Flash	Normal	—	70	20

MOVE TUTOR
FireRed/LeafGreen and *Emerald* Only

Double-Edge	Mimic	Substitute
Thunder Wave*		

Emerald Only

Endure*	Rollout	Sleep Talk
Snore*	Swagger	Swift*

*Battle Frontier tutor move (*Emerald*)

---

082 Magneton™

ELECTRIC STEEL

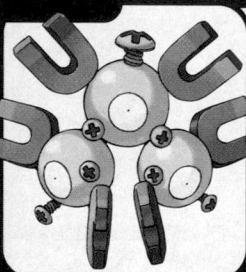

GENERAL INFO
SPECIES: Magnet Pokémon
HEIGHT: 3'03"
WEIGHT: 132 lbs.
ABILITY 1: Magnet Pull
Other Steel-types cannot escape while Magneton is in battle.
ABILITY 2: Sturdy
A one hit KO cannot hit Magneton.

STATS

EVOLUTIONS
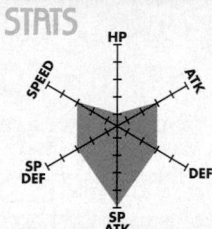
LV30

LOCATION(S):

RUBY Rarity: **Rare**
Evolve from Magnemite, New Mauville

SAPPHIRE Rarity: **Rare**
Evolve from Magnemite, New Mauville

FIRERED Rarity: **Common**
Evolve from Magnemite, Power Plant, Cerulean Cave

LEAFGREEN Rarity: **Common**
Evolve from Magnemite, Power Plant, Cerulean Cave

COLOSSEUM Rarity: **None**
Trade from *Ruby/Sapphire/FireRed/LeafGreen*

EMERALD Rarity: **Rare**
Evolve from Magnemite, New Mauville

XD Rarity: **Only One**
Cipher Key Lair (Capture from Snidle)

MOVES

Level	Attack	Type	Power	ACC	PP	Level	Attack	Type	Power	ACC	PP
—	Metal Sound	Steel	—	85	40	21	Thunder Wave	Electric	—	100	20
—	Tackle	Normal	35	95	35	26	Spark	Electric	65	100	20
—/6	Thundershock	Electric	40	100	30	35	Lock-on	Normal	—	100	5
—/11	Supersonic	Normal	—	55	20	44	Tri Attack	Normal	80	100	10
16	Sonicboom	Normal	—	90	20	53	Screech	Normal	—	85	40
						62	Zap Cannon	Electric	100	50	5

TM/HM

TM/HM#	Name	Type	Power	ACC	PP	TM/HM#	Name	Type	Power	ACC	PP
TM06	Toxic	Poison	—	85	10	TM27	Return	Normal	—	100	20
TM10	Hidden Power	Normal	—	100	15	TM32	Double Team	Normal	—	—	15
TM11	Sunny Day	Fire	—	—	5	TM33	Reflect	Normal	—	—	20
TM15	Hyper Beam	Normal	150	90	5	TM34	Shock Wave	Electric	60	—	20
TM17	Protect	Normal	—	—	10	TM42	Facade	Normal	70	100	20
TM18	Rain Dance	Water	—	—	5	TM43	Secret Power	Normal	70	100	20
TM21	Frustration	Normal	—	100	20	TM44	Rest	Psychic	—	—	10
TM24	Thunderbolt	Electric	95	100	15	HM05	Flash	Normal	—	70	20
TM25	Thunder	Electric	120	70	10	# = *Emerald* Only					

MOVE TUTOR
FireRed/LeafGreen and *Emerald* Only

Double-Edge	Mimic	Substitute
Thunder Wave*		

Emerald Only

Endure*	Rollout	Sleep Talk
Snore*	Swagger	Swift*

*Battle Frontier tutor move (*Emerald*)

083 Farfetch'd™

`NORMAL` `FLYING`

GENERAL INFO

SPECIES: Wild Duck Pokémon
HEIGHT: 2'07"
WEIGHT: 33 lbs.
ABILITY 1: Keen Eye
Prevents Farfetch'd from having its accuracy lowered.

ABILITY 2: Inner Focus
Prevents Farfetch'd from flinching.

STATS

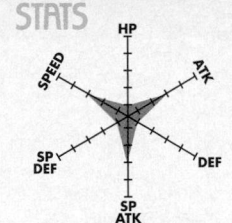

EVOLUTIONS

DOES NOT EVOLVE

LOCATION(S):

RUBY Rarity: **None**
Trade from *FireRed/LeafGreen*

SAPPHIRE Rarity: **None**
Trade from *FireRed/LeafGreen*

FIRERED Rarity: **Only One**
Trade for Spearow in Vermilion City

LEAFGREEN Rarity: **Only One**
Trade for Spearow in Vermilion City

COLOSSEUM Rarity: **None**
Trade from *Ruby/Sapphire/FireRed/LeafGreen*

EMERALD Rarity: **None**
Trade from *FireRed/LeafGreen*

XD Rarity: **Only One**
Citadark Island (Capture from Cipher Admin Lovrina)

MOVES

Level	Attack	Type	Power	ACC	PP	Level	Attack	Type	Power	ACC	PP
—	Peck	Flying	35	100	35	26	Fury Cutter	Bug	10	95	20
6	Sand-Attack	Ground	—	100	15	31	Swords Dance	Normal	—	—	30
11	Leer	Normal	—	100	30	36	Agility	Psychic	—	—	30
16	Fury Attack	Normal	15	85	20	41	Slash	Normal	70	100	20
21	Knock Off	Dark	20	100	20	46	False Swipe	Normal	40	100	40

TM/HM

TM/HM#	Name	Type	Power	ACC	PP	TM/HM#	Name	Type	Power	ACC	PP
TM06	Toxic	Poison	—	85	10	TM42	Facade	Normal	70	100	20
TM10	Hidden Power	Normal	—	100	15	TM43	Secret Power	Normal	70	100	20
TM11	Sunny Day	Fire	—	—	5	TM44	Rest	Psychic	—	—	10
TM17	Protect	Normal	—	—	10	TM45	Attract	Normal	—	100	15
TM21	Frustration	Normal	—	100	20	TM46	Thief	Dark	40	100	10
TM23	Iron Tail	Steel	75	75	15	TM47	Steel Wing	Steel	70	90	25
TM27	Return	Normal	—	100	20	HM01	Cut	Normal	50	95	30
TM32	Double Team	Normal	—	—	15	HM02	Fly	Flying	70	95	15
TM40	Aerial Ace	Flying	60	—	20						

EGG MOVES*

Name	Type	Power	ACC	PP
Curse	—	—	—	10
Featherdance	Flying	—	100	15
Flail	Normal	—	100	15
Foresight	Normal	—	100	40
Mirror Move	Flying	—	—	20
Quick Attack	Normal	40	100	30
Steel Wing	Steel	70	90	25
Whirlwind	Normal	—	100	20

*Learned Via Breeding

MOVE TUTOR

FireRed/LeafGreen and *Emerald* Only

Body Slam*	Double-Edge	Mimic
Substitute	Swords Dance*	

*Battle Frontier tutor move (*Emerald*)

---

084 Doduo™

`NORMAL` `FLYING`

GENERAL INFO

SPECIES: Twin Bird Pokémon
HEIGHT: 4'07"
WEIGHT: 86 lbs.
ABILITY 1: Run Away
Allows Doduo to escape from wild Pokémon.

ABILITY 2: Early Bird
Allows Doduo to wake up earlier when put to sleep.

STATS

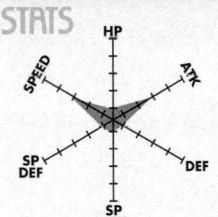

EVOLUTIONS

LV31

LOCATION(S):

RUBY Rarity: **Common**
Safari Zone

SAPPHIRE Rarity: **Common**
Safari Zone

FIRERED Rarity: **Common**
Route 16, Route 17, Route 18, Safari Zone

LEAFGREEN Rarity: **Common**
Route 16, Route 17, Route 18, Safari Zone

COLOSSEUM Rarity: **None**
Trade from *Ruby/Sapphire/FireRed/LeafGreen*

EMERALD Rarity: **Common**
Safari Zone

XD Rarity: **None**
Trade from *Ruby/Sapphire/FireRed/LeafGreen*

MOVES

Level	Attack	Type	Power	ACC	PP	Level	Attack	Type	Power	ACC	PP
—	Peck	Flying	35	100	35	21	Tri Attack	Normal	80	100	10
—	Growl	Normal	—	100	40	25	Rage	Normal	20	100	20
9	Pursuit	Dark	40	100	20	33	Uproar	Normal	50	100	10
13	Fury Attack	Normal	15	85	20	37	Drill Peck	Flying	80	100	20
						45	Agility	Psychic	—	—	30

TM/HM

TM/HM#	Name	Type	Power	ACC	PP	TM/HM#	Name	Type	Power	ACC	PP
TM06	Toxic	Poison	—	85	10	TM42	Facade	Normal	70	100	20
TM10	Hidden Power	Normal	—	100	15	TM43	Secret Power	Normal	70	100	20
TM11	Sunny Day	Fire	—	—	5	TM44	Rest	Psychic	—	—	10
TM17	Protect	Normal	—	—	10	TM45	Attract	Normal	—	100	15
TM21	Frustration	Normal	—	100	20	TM46	Thief	Dark	40	100	10
TM27	Return	Normal	—	100	20	TM47	Steel Wing	Steel	70	90	25
TM32	Double Team	Normal	—	—	15	HM02	Fly	Flying	70	95	15
TM40	Aerial Ace	Flying	60	—	20						

EGG MOVES*

Name	Type	Power	ACC	PP
Quick Attack	Normal	40	100	30
Supersonic	Normal	—	55	20
Haze	Ice	—	—	30
Endeavor	Normal	—	100	5
Faint Attack	Dark	60	—	20
Flail	Normal	—	100	15

*Learned Via Breeding

MOVE TUTOR

FireRed/LeafGreen and *Emerald* Only

Body Slam*	Double-Edge	Mimic
Substitute		

Emerald Only

Endure*	Mud-Slap*	Sleep Talk
Snore*	Swagger	Swift

*Battle Frontier tutor move (*Emerald*)

085 Dodrio™

NORMAL · FLYING

GENERAL INFO
SPECIES: Triple Bird Pokémon
HEIGHT: 5'11"
WEIGHT: 188 lbs.
ABILITY 1: Run Away
Allows Dodrio to escape from wild Pokémon.
ABILITY 2: Early Bird
Allows Dodrio to wake up earlier when put to sleep.

STATS
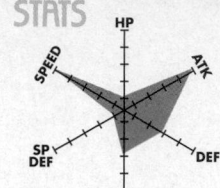

EVOLUTIONS
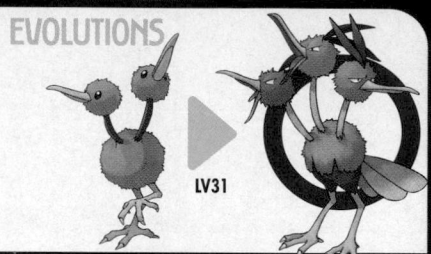
LV31

LOCATION[S]:

RUBY — Rarity: **Rare**
Evolve Doduo, Safari Zone

SAPPHIRE — Rarity: **Rare**
Evolve Doduo, Safari Zone

FIRERED — Rarity: **Evolve**
Evolve Doduo

LEAFGREEN — Rarity: **Evolve**
Evolve Doduo

COLOSSEUM — Rarity: **None**
Trade from Ruby/Sapphire/FireRed/LeafGreen

EMERALD — Rarity: **Rare**
Evolve Doduo, Safari Zone

XD — Rarity: **Only One**
Citadark Island (Capture from Cipher Peon Furgy)

MOVES

Level	Attack	Type	Power	ACC	PP
—	Peck	Flying	35	100	35
—	Growl	Normal	—	100	40
—	Pursuit	Dark	40	100	20
—	Fury Attack	Normal	15	85	20
21	Tri Attack	Normal	80	100	10
25	Rage	Normal	20	100	20
38	Uproar	Normal	50	100	10
47	Drill Peck	Flying	80	100	20
50/60	Agility	Psychic	—	—	30

TM/HM

TM/HM#	Name	Type	Power	ACC	PP
TM06	Toxic	Poison	—	85	10
TM10	Hidden Power	Normal	—	100	15
TM11	Sunny Day	Fire	—	—	5
TM12	Taunt	Dark	—	100	20
TM15	Hyper Beam	Normal	150	90	5
TM17	Protect	Normal	—	—	10
TM21	Frustration	Normal	—	100	20
TM27	Return	Normal	—	100	20
TM32	Double Team	Normal	—	—	15
TM40	Aerial Ace	Flying	60	—	20
TM41	Torment	Dark	—	100	15
TM42	Facade	Normal	70	100	20
TM43	Secret Power	Normal	70	100	20
TM44	Rest	Psychic	—	—	10
TM45	Attract	Normal	—	100	15
TM46	Thief	Dark	40	100	10
TM47	Steel Wing	Steel	70	90	25
HM02	Fly	Flying	70	95	15

= Emerald Only

MOVE TUTOR
FireRed/LeafGreen and Emerald Only

Body Slam	Double-Edge	Mimic
Substitute		

Emerald Only

Endure*	Mud-Slap*	Sleep Talk
Snore*	Swagger	Swift*

*Battle Frontier tutor move (Emerald)

086 Seel™

WATER

GENERAL INFO
SPECIES: Sea Lion Pokémon
HEIGHT: 3'07"
WEIGHT: 198 lbs.
ABILITY: Thick Fat
Effects of an opponent's Ice- and Fire-type moves used on Seel are halved.

STATS
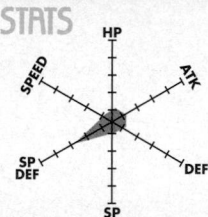

EVOLUTIONS

LV34

LOCATION[S]:

RUBY — Rarity: **None**
Trade from FireRed/LeafGreen

SAPPHIRE — Rarity: **None**
Trade from FireRed/LeafGreen

FIRERED — Rarity: **Common**
Seafoam Islands

LEAFGREEN — Rarity: **Common**
Seafoam Islands

COLOSSEUM — Rarity: **None**
Trade from FireRed/LeafGreen

EMERALD — Rarity: **None**
Trade from FireRed/LeafGreen

XD — Rarity: **Only One**
Phenac City (Capture from Cipher Peon Egrog)

MOVES

Level	Attack	Type	Power	ACC	PP
—	Headbutt	Normal	70	100	15
9	Growl	Normal	—	100	40
17	Icy Wind	Ice	55	95	15
21	Aurora Beam	Ice	65	100	20
29	Rest	Psychic	—	—	10
37	Take Down	Normal	90	85	20
41	Ice Beam	Ice	95	100	10
49	Safeguard	Normal	—	—	25

TM/HM

TM/HM#	Name	Type	Power	ACC	PP
TM03	Water Pulse	Water	60	95	20
TM06	Toxic	Poison	—	85	10
TM07	Hail	Ice	—	—	10
TM10	Hidden Power	Normal	—	100	15
TM13	Ice Beam	Ice	95	100	10
TM14	Blizzard	Ice	120	70	5
TM17	Protect	Normal	—	—	10
TM18	Rain Dance	Water	—	—	5
TM20	Safeguard	Normal	—	—	25
TM21	Frustration	Normal	—	100	20
TM27	Return	Normal	—	100	20
TM32	Double Team	Normal	—	—	15
TM42	Facade	Normal	70	100	20
TM43	Secret Power	Normal	70	100	20
TM44	Rest	Psychic	—	—	10
TM45	Attract	Normal	—	100	15
TM46	Thief	Dark	40	100	10
HM03	Surf	Water	95	100	15
HM07	Waterfall	Water	80	100	15
HM08	Dive	Water	60	100	10

EGG MOVES*

Name	Type	Power	ACC	PP
Disable	Normal	—	55	20
Encore	Normal	—	100	5
Fake Out	Normal	40	100	10
Horn Drill	Normal	—	30	5
Icicle Spear	Ice	10	100	30
Lick	Ghost	20	100	30
Perish Song	Normal	—	—	5
Slam	Normal	80	75	20

*Learned Via Breeding

MOVE TUTOR
FireRed/LeafGreen and Emerald Only

Body Slam*	Double-Edge	Mimic
Substitute		

*Battle Frontier tutor move (Emerald)

087 Dewgong™

WATER | ICE

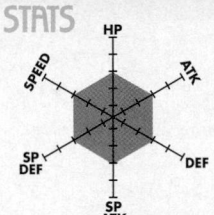

GENERAL INFO
SPECIES: Sea Lion Pokémon
HEIGHT: 5'07"
WEIGHT: 265 lbs.
ABILITY: Thick Fat

Effects of an opponent's Ice- and Fire-type moves used on Dewgong are halved.

STATS
HP / ATK / DEF / SP ATK / SP DEF / SPEED

EVOLUTIONS
LV34

LOCATION(S):

RUBY — Rarity: **None**
Trade from *FireRed/LeafGreen*

SAPPHIRE — Rarity: **None**
Trade from *FireRed/LeafGreen*

FIRERED — Rarity: **Rare**
Evolve Seel, Seafoam Islands

LEAFGREEN — Rarity: **Rare**
Evolve Seel, Seafoam Islands

COLOSSEUM — Rarity: **None**
Trade from *FireRed/LeafGreen*

EMERALD — Rarity: **None**
Trade from *FireRed/LeafGreen*

XD — Rarity: **Evolve**
Evolve Seel

MOVES

Level	Attack	Type	Power	ACC	PP
—	Signal Beam	Bug	75	100	15
—	Headbutt	Normal	70	100	15
—	Growl	Normal	—	100	40
—	Icy Wind	Ice	55	95	15
—	Aurora Beam	Ice	65	100	20
29	Rest	Psychic	—	—	10
34	Sheer Cold	Ice	—	30	5
42	Take Down	Normal	90	85	20
51	Ice Beam	Ice	95	100	10
64	Safeguard	Normal	—	—	25

TM/HM

TM/HM#	Name	Type	Power	ACC	PP
TM03	Water Pulse	Water	60	95	20
TM06	Toxic	Poison	—	85	10
TM07	Hail	Ice	—	—	10
TM10	Hidden Power	Normal	—	100	15
TM13	Ice Beam	Ice	95	100	10
TM14	Blizzard	Ice	120	70	5
TM15	Hyper Beam	Normal	150	90	5
TM17	Protect	Normal	—	—	10
TM18	Rain Dance	Water	—	—	5
TM20	Safeguard	Normal	—	—	25
TM21	Frustration	Normal	—	100	20
TM27	Return	Normal	—	100	20
TM32	Double Team	Normal	—	—	15
TM42	Facade	Normal	70	100	20
TM43	Secret Power	Normal	70	100	20
TM44	Rest	Psychic	—	—	10
TM45	Attract	Normal	—	100	15
TM46	Thief	Dark	40	100	10
HM03	Surf	Water	95	100	15
HM07	Waterfall	Water	80	100	15
HM08	Dive	Water	60	100	10

MOVE TUTOR
FireRed/LeafGreen and Emerald Only
Body Slam* | Double-Edge | Mimic | Substitute

*Battle Frontier tutor move (*Emerald*)

---

088 Grimer™

POISON

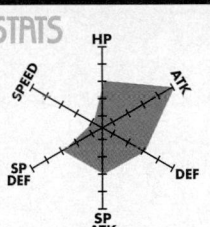

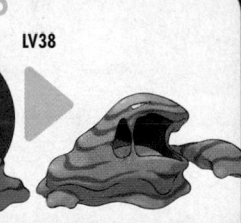

GENERAL INFO
SPECIES: Sludge Pokémon
HEIGHT: 2'11"
WEIGHT: 66 lbs.

ABILITY 1: Stench
When Grimer is in the first slot, the chances of running into a wild Pokémon decrease.

ABILITY 2: Sticky Hold
Prevents an opponent from stealing a Held Item Grimer may have.

STATS
HP / ATK / DEF / SP ATK / SP DEF / SPEED

EVOLUTIONS
LV38

LOCATION(S):

RUBY — Rarity: **Rare**
Fiery Path

SAPPHIRE — Rarity: **Rare**
Fiery Path

FIRERED — Rarity: **Common**
Pokémon Mansion

LEAFGREEN — Rarity: **Common**
Pokémon Mansion

COLOSSEUM — Rarity: **None**
Trade from *Ruby/Sapphire/FireRed/LeafGreen*

EMERALD — Rarity: **Rare**
Fiery Path

XD — Rarity: **Only One**
Phenac City (Capture from Cipher Peon Faltly)

MOVES

Level	Attack	Type	Power	ACC	PP
—	Poison Gas	Poison	—	55	40
—	Pound	Normal	40	100	35
4	Harden	Normal	—	—	30
8	Disable	Normal	—	55	20
13	Sludge	Poison	65	100	20
19	Minimize	Normal	—	—	20
26	Screech	Normal	—	85	40
34	Acid Armor	Poison	—	—	40
43	Sludge Bomb	Poison	90	100	10
53	Memento	Dark	—	100	10

TM/HM

TM/HM#	Name	Type	Power	ACC	PP
TM06	Toxic	Poison	—	85	10
TM10	Hidden Power	Normal	—	100	15
TM11	Sunny Day	Fire	—	—	5
TM12	Taunt	Dark	—	100	20
TM17	Protect	Normal	—	—	10
TM18	Rain Dance	Water	—	—	5
TM19	Giga Drain	Grass	60	100	5
TM21	Frustration	Normal	—	100	20
TM24	Thunderbolt	Electric	95	100	15
TM25	Thunder	Electric	120	70	10
TM27	Return	Normal	—	100	20
TM28	Dig	Ground	60	100	10
TM32	Double Team	Normal	—	—	15
TM34	Shock Wave	Electric	60	—	20
TM35	Flamethrower	Fire	95	100	15
TM36	Sludge Bomb	Poison	90	100	10
TM38	Fire Blast	Fire	120	85	5
TM39	Rock Tomb	Rock	50	80	10
TM41	Torment	Dark	—	100	15
TM42	Facade	Normal	70	100	20
TM43	Secret Power	Normal	70	100	20
TM44	Rest	Psychic	—	—	10
TM45	Attract	Normal	—	100	15
TM46	Thief	Dark	40	100	10

EGG MOVES*

Name	Type	Power	ACC	PP
Haze	Ice	—	—	30
Mean Look	Normal	—	100	5
Imprison	Psychic	—	100	15
Curse	—	—	—	10
Shadow Punch	Ghost	60	—	20
Explosion	Normal	250	100	5
Lick	Ghost	20	100	30

*Learned Via Breeding

MOVE TUTOR
FireRed/LeafGreen and Emerald Only
Body Slam* | Explosion | Mimic | Substitute

Emerald Only
Dynamicpunch | Endure* | Fire Punch* | Ice Punch* | Mud-Slap* | Snore* | Swagger | Sleep Talk

*Battle Frontier tutor move (*Emerald*)

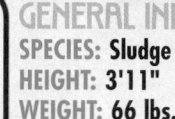

089 Muk™

POISON

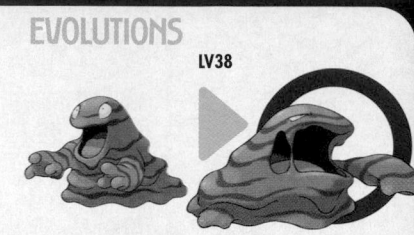

GENERAL INFO
SPECIES: Sludge Pokémon
HEIGHT: 3'11"
WEIGHT: 66 lbs.

ABILITY 1: Stench
When Muk is in the first slot, the chances of running into a wild Pokémon decrease.

ABILITY 2: Sticky Hold
Prevents an opponent from stealing a Held Item Muk may have.

STATS

EVOLUTIONS
LV38

LOCATION[S]:

RUBY — Rarity: **Evolve**
Evolve Grimer

SAPPHIRE — Rarity: **Evolve**
Evolve Grimer

FIRERED — Rarity: **Evolve**
Evolve Grimer

LEAFGREEN — Rarity: **Rare**
Evolve Grimer, Pokémon Mansion

COLOSSEUM — Rarity: **None**
Trade from *Ruby/Sapphire/FireRed/LeafGreen*

EMERALD — Rarity: **Evolve**
Evolve Grimer

XD — Rarity: **Evolve**
Evolve Grimer

MOVES

Level	Attack	Type	Power	ACC	PP
—	Poison Gas	Poison	—	55	40
—	Pound	Normal	40	100	35
—	Harden	Normal	—	—	30
8	Disable	Normal	—	55	20
13	Sludge	Poison	65	100	20
19	Minimize	Normal	—	—	20
26	Screech	Normal	—	85	40
34	Acid Armor	Poison	—	—	40
47	Sludge Bomb	Poison	90	100	10
61	Memento	Dark	—	100	10

TM/HM

TM/HM#	Name	Type	Power	ACC	PP
TM01	Focus Punch	Fighting	150	100	20
TM06	Toxic	Poison	—	85	10
TM10	Hidden Power	Normal	—	100	15
TM11	Sunny Day	Fire	—	—	5
TM12	Taunt	Dark	—	100	20
TM15	Hyper Beam	Normal	150	90	5
TM17	Protect	Normal	—	—	10
TM18	Rain Dance	Water	—	—	5
TM19	Giga Drain	Grass	60	100	5
TM21	Frustration	Normal	—	100	20
TM24	Thunderbolt	Electric	95	100	15
TM25	Thunder	Electric	120	70	10
TM27	Return	Normal	—	100	20
TM28	Dig	Ground	60	100	10
TM31	Brick Break	Fighting	75	100	15
TM32	Double Team	Normal	—	—	15
TM34	Shock Wave	Electric	60	—	20
TM35	Flamethrower	Fire	95	100	15
TM36	Sludge Bomb	Poison	90	100	10
TM38	Fire Blast	Fire	120	85	5
TM39	Rock Tomb	Rock	50	80	10
TM41	Torment	Dark	—	100	15
TM42	Facade	Normal	70	100	20
TM43	Secret Power	Normal	70	100	20
TM44	Rest	Psychic	—	—	10
TM45	Attract	Normal	—	100	15
TM46	Thief	Dark	40	100	10
HM04	Strength	Normal	80	100	20
HM06	Rock Smash	Fighting	20	100	15

MOVE TUTOR
FireRed/LeafGreen and Emerald Only

Body Slam*	Explosion	Mimic
Substitute		

Emerald Only

Dynamicpunch	Endure*	Fire Punch*
Ice Punch*	Mud-Slap*	Sleep Talk
Snore*	Swagger	Thunderpunch*

*Battle Frontier tutor move (*Emerald*)

---

090 Shellder™

WATER

GENERAL INFO
SPECIES: Bivalve Pokémon
HEIGHT: 1'00"
WEIGHT: 9 lbs.
ABILITY: Shell Armor
Protects Shellder from being struck by critical hits.

STATS

EVOLUTIONS

EVOLVE WITH WATER STONE

LOCATION[S]:

RUBY — Rarity: **None**
Trade from *FireRed*

SAPPHIRE — Rarity: **None**
Trade from *FireRed*

FIRERED — Rarity: **Common**
One Island, Five Island, Vermilion City

LEAFGREEN — Rarity: **None**
Trade from *FireRed*

COLOSSEUM — Rarity: **None**
Trade from *FireRed*

EMERALD — Rarity: **None**
Trade from *FireRed*

XD — Rarity: **Only One**
Cipher Key Lair (Capture from Cipher Peon Gorog)

MOVES

Level	Attack	Type	Power	ACC	PP
—	Tackle	Normal	35	95	35
—	Withdraw	Normal	—	—	40
8	Icicle Spear	Ice	10	100	30
15	Supersonic	Normal	—	55	20
22	Aurora Beam	Ice	65	100	20
29	Protect	Normal	—	—	10
36	Leer	Normal	—	100	30
43	Clamp	Water	35	75	10
50	Ice Beam	Ice	95	100	10

TM/HM

TM/HM#	Name	Type	Power	ACC	PP
TM03	Water Pulse	Water	60	95	20
TM06	Toxic	Poison	—	85	10
TM07	Hail	Ice	—	—	10
TM10	Hidden Power	Normal	—	100	15
TM13	Ice Beam	Ice	95	100	10
TM14	Blizzard	Ice	120	70	5
TM17	Protect	Normal	—	—	10
TM18	Rain Dance	Water	—	—	5
TM21	Frustration	Normal	—	100	20
TM27	Return	Normal	—	100	20
TM32	Double Team	Normal	—	—	15
TM42	Facade	Normal	70	100	20
TM43	Secret Power	Normal	70	100	20
TM44	Rest	Psychic	—	—	10
TM45	Attract	Normal	—	100	15
HM03	Surf	Water	95	100	15
HM08	Dive	Water	60	100	10

EGG MOVES*

Name	Type	Power	ACC	PP
Barrier	Psychic	—	—	30
Bubblebeam	Water	65	100	20
Icicle Spear	Ice	10	100	30
Rapid Spin	Normal	20	100	40
Screech	Normal	—	85	40

*Learned Via Breeding

MOVE TUTOR
FireRed/LeafGreen and Emerald Only

Double-Edge	Explosion	Mimic
Substitute		

091 Cloyster™

WATER | ICE

GENERAL INFO
SPECIES: Bivalve Pokémon
HEIGHT: 4'11"
WEIGHT: 292 lbs.
ABILITY: Shell Armor
Protects Cloyster from being struck by critical hits.

STATS
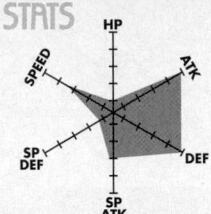

EVOLUTIONS

WATER STONE

LOCATION[S]:

RUBY   Rarity: **None**
Trade from *FireRed*

SAPPHIRE   Rarity: **None**
Trade from *FireRed*

FIRERED   Rarity: **Evolve**
Evolve Shellder

LEAFGREEN   Rarity: **None**
Trade from *FireRed*

COLOSSEUM   Rarity: **None**
Trade from *FireRed*

EMERALD   Rarity: **None**
Trade from *FireRed*

XD   Rarity: **Evolve**
Evolve Shellder

MOVES

Level	Attack	Type	Power	ACC	PP
—	Withdraw	Normal	—	—	40
—	Supersonic	Normal	—	55	20
—	Aurora Beam	Ice	65	100	20
—	Protect	Normal	—	—	10
36	Spikes	Ground	—	—	20
43	Spike Cannon	Normal	20	100	15

TM/HM

TM/HM#	Name	Type	Power	ACC	PP
TM03	Water Pulse	Water	60	95	20
TM06	Toxic	Poison	—	85	10
TM07	Hail	Ice	—	—	10
TM10	Hidden Power	Normal	—	100	15
TM13	Ice Beam	Ice	95	100	10
TM14	Blizzard	Ice	120	70	5
TM15	Hyper Beam	Normal	150	90	5
TM17	Protect	Normal	—	—	10
TM18	Rain Dance	Water	—	—	5
TM21	Frustration	Normal	—	100	20
TM27	Return	Normal	—	100	20
TM32	Double Team	Normal	—	—	15
TM41	Torment	Dark	—	100	15
TM42	Facade	Normal	70	100	20
TM43	Secret Power	Normal	70	100	20
TM44	Rest	Psychic	—	—	10
TM45	Attract	Normal	—	100	15
HM03	Surf	Water	95	100	15
HM08	Dive	Water	60	100	10

MOVE TUTOR
FireRed/LeafGreen and *Emerald* Only

Double-Edge | Explosion | Mimic
Substitute

092 Gastly™

GHOST | POISON

GENERAL INFO
SPECIES: Gas Pokémon
HEIGHT: 4'03"
WEIGHT: .02 lbs.
ABILITY: Levitate
Protects Gastly from Ground-type attacks.

STATS
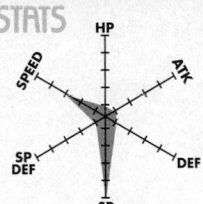

EVOLUTIONS

LV25   **EVOLVE VIA TRADE**

LOCATION[S]:

RUBY   Rarity: **None**
Trade from *FireRed/LeafGreen*

SAPPHIRE   Rarity: **None**
Trade from *FireRed/LeafGreen*

FIRERED   Rarity: **Common**
Pokémon Tower

LEAFGREEN   Rarity: **Common**
Pokémon Tower

COLOSSEUM   Rarity: **None**
Trade from *FireRed/LeafGreen*

EMERALD   Rarity: **None**
Trade from *FireRed/LeafGreen*

XD   Rarity: **None**
Trade from *FireRed/LeafGreen*

MOVES

Level	Attack	Type	Power	ACC	PP
—	Lick	Ghost	20	100	30
—	Hypnosis	Psychic	—	60	20
8	Spite	Ghost	—	100	10
13	Curse	—	—	—	10
16	Night Shade	Ghost	—	100	15
21	Confuse Ray	Ghost	—	100	10
28	Dream Eater	Psychic	100	100	15
33	Destiny Bond	Ghost	—	—	5
36	Shadow Ball	Ghost	80	100	15
41	Nightmare	Ghost	—	100	15
48	Mean Look	Normal	—	100	5

TM/HM

TM/HM#	Name	Type	Power	ACC	PP
TM06	Toxic	Poison	—	85	10
TM10	Hidden Power	Normal	—	100	15
TM11	Sunny Day	Fire	—	—	5
TM12	Taunt	Dark	—	100	20
TM17	Protect	Normal	—	—	10
TM18	Rain Dance	Water	—	—	5
TM19	Giga Drain	Grass	60	100	5
TM21	Frustration	Normal	—	100	20
TM24	Thunderbolt	Electric	95	100	15
TM27	Return	Normal	—	100	20
TM29	Psychic	Psychic	90	100	10
TM30	Shadow Ball	Ghost	80	100	15
TM32	Double Team	Normal	—	—	15
TM36	Sludge Bomb	Poison	90	100	10
TM41	Torment	Dark	—	100	15
TM42	Facade	Normal	70	100	20
TM43	Secret Power	Normal	70	100	20
TM44	Rest	Psychic	—	—	10
TM45	Attract	Normal	—	100	15
TM46	Thief	Dark	40	100	10
TM48	Skill Swap	Psychic	—	—	10
TM49	Snatch	Dark	—	100	10

EGG MOVES*

Name	Type	Power	ACC	PP
Astonish	Ghost	30	100	15
Explosion	Normal	250	100	5
Grudge	Ghost	—	100	5
Haze	Ice	—	—	30
Perish Song	Normal	—	—	5
Psywave	Psychic	—	80	15
Will-O-Wisp	Fire	—	75	15

*Learned Via Breeding

MOVE TUTOR
FireRed/LeafGreen and *Emerald* Only

Dream Eater* | Explosion | Mimic
Substitute

*Battle Frontier tutor move (*Emerald*)

093 Haunter™

GHOST	POISON

GENERAL INFO
SPECIES: Gas Pokémon
HEIGHT: 5'03"
WEIGHT: .02 lbs.
ABILITY: Levitate
Protects Haunter from Ground-type attacks.

STATS
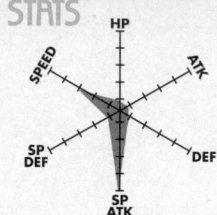

EVOLUTIONS

LV25   EVOLVE VIA TRADE

LOCATION[S]:

RUBY — Rarity: **None**
Trade from *FireRed/LeafGreen*

SAPPHIRE — Rarity: **None**
Trade from *FireRed/LeafGreen*

FIRERED — Rarity: **Common**
Evolve Gastly, Five Island, Pokémon Tower

LEAFGREEN — Rarity: **Common**
Evolve Gastly, Five Island, Pokémon Tower

COLOSSEUM — Rarity: **None**
Trade from *FireRed/LeafGreen*

EMERALD — Rarity: **None**
Trade from *FireRed/LeafGreen*

XD — Rarity: **None**
Trade from *FireRed/LeafGreen*

MOVES

Level	Attack	Type	Power	ACC	PP
—	Lick	Ghost	20	100	30
—	Hypnosis	Psychic	—	60	20
—	Spite	Ghost	—	100	10
13	Curse	—	—	—	10
16	Night Shade	Ghost	—	100	15
21	Confuse Ray	Ghost	—	100	10
25	Shadow Punch	Ghost	60	—	20
31	Dream Eater	Psychic	100	100	15
39	Destiny Bond	Ghost	—	—	5
45	Shadow Ball	Ghost	80	100	15
53	Nightmare	Ghost	—	100	15
64	Mean Look	Normal	—	100	5

TM/HM

TM/HM#	Name	Type	Power	ACC	PP
TM06	Toxic	Poison	—	85	10
TM10	Hidden Power	Normal	—	100	15
TM11	Sunny Day	Fire	—	—	5
TM12	Taunt	Dark	—	100	20
TM17	Protect	Normal	—	—	10
TM18	Rain Dance	Water	—	—	5
TM19	Giga Drain	Grass	60	100	5
TM21	Frustration	Normal	—	100	20
TM24	Thunderbolt	Electric	95	100	15
TM27	Return	Normal	—	100	20
TM29	Psychic	Psychic	90	100	10
TM30	Shadow Ball	Ghost	80	100	15
TM32	Double Team	Normal	—	—	15
TM36	Sludge Bomb	Poison	90	100	10
TM41	Torment	Dark	—	100	15
TM42	Facade	Normal	70	100	20
TM43	Secret Power	Normal	70	100	20
TM44	Rest	Psychic	—	—	10
TM45	Attract	Normal	—	100	15
TM46	Thief	Dark	40	100	10
TM48	Skill Swap	Psychic	—	100	10
TM49	Snatch	Dark	—	100	10

MOVE TUTOR
FireRed/LeafGreen and *Emerald* Only

Dream Eater*	Explosion	Mimic
Substitute		

*Battle Frontier tutor move (*Emerald*)

---

094 Gengar™

GHOST	POISON

GENERAL INFO
SPECIES: Shadow Pokémon
HEIGHT: 4'11"
WEIGHT: 89 lbs.
ABILITY: Levitate
Protects Gengar from Ground-type attacks.

STATS
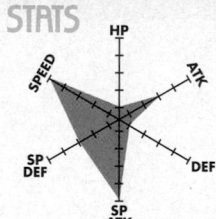

EVOLUTIONS

LV25   EVOLVE VIA TRADE

LOCATION[S]:

RUBY — Rarity: **None**
Trade from *FireRed/LeafGreen*

SAPPHIRE — Rarity: **None**
Trade from *FireRed/LeafGreen*

FIRERED — Rarity: **Evolve**
Evolve Haunter

LEAFGREEN — Rarity: **Evolve**
Evolve Haunter

COLOSSEUM — Rarity: **None**
Trade from *FireRed/LeafGreen*

EMERALD — Rarity: **None**
Trade from *FireRed/LeafGreen*

XD — Rarity: **None**
Trade from *FireRed/LeafGreen*

MOVES

Level	Attack	Type	Power	ACC	PP
—	Lick	Ghost	20	100	30
—	Hypnosis	Psychic	—	60	20
—	Spite	Ghost	—	100	10
13	Curse	—	—	—	10
16	Night Shade	Ghost	—	100	15
21	Confuse Ray	Ghost	—	100	10
25	Shadow Punch	Ghost	60	—	20
31	Dream Eater	Psychic	100	100	15
39	Destiny Bond	Ghost	—	—	5
45	Shadow Ball	Ghost	80	100	15
53	Nightmare	Ghost	—	100	15
64	Mean Look	Normal	—	100	5

TM/HM

TM/HM#	Name	Type	Power	ACC	PP
TM01	Focus Punch	Fighting	150	100	20
TM06	Toxic	Poison	—	85	10
TM10	Hidden Power	Normal	—	100	15
TM11	Sunny Day	Fire	—	—	5
TM12	Taunt	Dark	—	100	20
TM15	Hyper Beam	Normal	150	90	5
TM17	Protect	Normal	—	—	10
TM18	Rain Dance	Water	—	—	5
TM19	Giga Drain	Grass	60	100	5
TM21	Frustration	Normal	—	100	20
TM24	Thunderbolt	Electric	95	100	15
TM25	Thunder	Electric	120	70	10
TM27	Return	Normal	—	100	20
TM29	Psychic	Psychic	90	100	10
TM30	Shadow Ball	Ghost	80	100	15
TM31	Brick Break	Fighting	75	100	15
TM32	Double Team	Normal	—	—	15
TM36	Sludge Bomb	Poison	90	100	10
TM41	Torment	Dark	—	100	15
TM42	Facade	Normal	70	100	20
TM43	Secret Power	Normal	70	100	20
TM44	Rest	Psychic	—	—	10
TM45	Attract	Normal	—	100	15
TM46	Thief	Dark	40	100	10
TM48	Skill Swap	Psychic	—	100	10
TM49	Snatch	Dark	—	100	10
HM04	Strength	Normal	80	100	20
HM06	Rock Smash	Fighting	20	100	15

MOVE TUTOR
FireRed/LeafGreen and *Emerald* Only

Body Slam*	Counter*	Double-Edge*
Dream Eater*	Explosion	Mega Kick*
Mega Punch*	Metronome	Mimic
Seismic Toss*	Substitute	

*Battle Frontier tutor move (*Emerald*)

095 Onix™

ROCK | GROUND

GENERAL INFO
SPECIES: Rock Snake Pokémon
HEIGHT: 28'10"
WEIGHT: 463 lbs.
ABILITY 1: Sturdy
Prevents a one hit KO from hitting Onix.
ABILITY 2: Rock Head
Prevents Onix from receiving recoil damage.

STATS
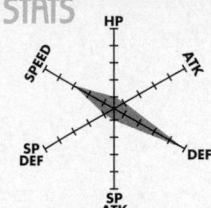

EVOLUTIONS
 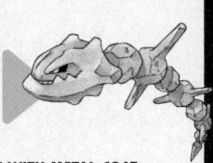
TRADE WITH METAL COAT

LOCATION[S]:

RUBY   Rarity: **None**
Trade from *FireRed/LeafGreen*

SAPPHIRE   Rarity: **None**
Trade from *FireRed/LeafGreen*

FIRERED   Rarity: **Common**
Victory Road, Rock Tunnel, Seven Island

LEAFGREEN   Rarity: **Common**
Victory Road, Rock Tunnel, Seven Island

COLOSSEUM   Rarity: **None**
Trade from *FireRed/LeafGreen*

EMERALD   Rarity: **None**
Trade from *FireRed/LeafGreen*

XD   Rarity: **None**
Trade from *FireRed/LeafGreen*

MOVES

Level	Attack	Type	Power	ACC	PP	Level	Attack	Type	Power	ACC	PP
—	Tackle	Normal	35	95	35	30	Dragonbreath	Dragon	60	100	20
—	Screech	Normal	—	85	40	34	Sandstorm	Rock	—	—	10
8	Bind	Normal	15	75	20	41	Slam	Normal	80	75	20
12	Rock Throw	Rock	50	90	15	45	Iron Tail	Steel	100	75	15
19	Harden	Normal	—	—	30	52	Sand Tomb	Ground	15	70	15
23	Rage	Normal	20	100	20	56	Double-Edge	Normal	120	100	15

TM/HM

TM/HM#	Name	Type	Power	ACC	PP	TM/HM#	Name	Type	Power	ACC	PP
TM05	Roar	Normal	—	100	20	TM32	Double Team	Normal	—	—	15
TM06	Toxic	Poison	—	85	10	TM37	Sandstorm	Ground	—	—	10
TM10	Hidden Power	Normal	—	100	15	TM39	Rock Tomb	Rock	50	80	10
TM11	Sunny Day	Fire	—	—	5	TM41	Torment	Dark	—	100	15
TM12	Taunt	Dark	—	100	20	TM42	Facade	Normal	70	100	20
TM17	Protect	Normal	—	—	10	TM43	Secret Power	Normal	70	100	20
TM21	Frustration	Normal	—	100	20	TM44	Rest	Psychic	—	—	10
TM23	Iron Tail	Steel	75	75	15	TM45	Attract	Normal	—	100	15
TM26	Earthquake	Ground	100	100	10	HM04	Strength	Normal	80	100	20
TM27	Return	Normal	—	100	20	HM06	Rock Smash	Fighting	20	100	15
TM28	Dig	Ground	60	100	10						

EGG MOVES*

Name	Type	Power	ACC	PP
Block	Normal	—	100	5
Explosion	Normal	250	100	5
Flail	Normal	—	100	15
Rock Slide	Rock	75	90	10

*Learned Via Breeding

MOVE TUTOR
FireRed/LeafGreen and *Emerald* Only

Body Slam*	Double-Edge	Explosion
Mimic	Rock Slide*	Substitute

*Battle Frontier tutor move (*Emerald*)

---

096 Drowzee™

PSYCHIC

GENERAL INFO
SPECIES: Hypnosis Pokémon
HEIGHT: 3'03"
WEIGHT: 71 lbs.
ABILITY 1: Insomnia
Protects Drowzee from an opponent's sleep attack.

STATS
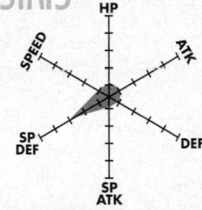

EVOLUTIONS

LV26

LOCATION[S]:

RUBY   Rarity: **None**
Trade from *FireRed/LeafGreen*

SAPPHIRE   Rarity: **None**
Trade from *FireRed/LeafGreen*

FIRERED   Rarity: **Common**
Three Island, Route 11

LEAFGREEN   Rarity: **Common**
Three Island, Route 11

COLOSSEUM   Rarity: **None**
Trade from *FireRed/LeafGreen*

EMERALD   Rarity: **None**
Trade from *FireRed/LeafGreen*

XD   Rarity: **None**
Trade from *FireRed/LeafGreen*

MOVES

Level	Attack	Type	Power	ACC	PP	Level	Attack	Type	Power	ACC	PP
—	Pound	Normal	40	100	35	21	Poison Gas	Poison	—	55	40
—	Hypnosis	Psychic	—	60	20	27	Mediate	Psychic	—	—	40
7	Disable	Normal	—	55	20	31	Psychic	Psychic	90	100	10
11	Confusion	Psychic	50	100	25	37	Psych Up	Normal	—	—	10
17	Headbutt	Normal	70	100	15	41	Swagger	Normal	—	90	15
						47	Future Sight	Psychic	80	90	15

TM/HM

TM/HM#	Name	Type	Power	ACC	PP	TM/HM#	Name	Type	Power	ACC	PP
TM01	Focus Punch	Fighting	150	100	20	TM30	Shadow Ball	Ghost	80	100	15
TM04	Calm Mind	Psychic	—	—	20	TM31	Brick Break	Fighting	75	100	15
TM06	Toxic	Poison	—	85	10	TM32	Double Team	Normal	—	—	15
TM10	Hidden Power	Normal	—	100	15	TM33	Reflect	Normal	—	—	20
TM11	Sunny Day	Fire	—	—	5	TM41	Torment	Dark	—	100	15
TM12	Taunt	Dark	—	100	20	TM42	Facade	Normal	70	100	20
TM16	Light Screen	Psychic	—	—	30	TM43	Secret Power	Normal	70	100	20
TM17	Protect	Normal	—	—	10	TM44	Rest	Psychic	—	—	10
TM18	Rain Dance	Water	—	—	5	TM45	Attract	Normal	—	100	15
TM20	Safeguard	Normal	—	—	25	TM46	Thief	Dark	40	100	10
TM21	Frustration	Normal	—	100	20	TM48	Skill Swap	Psychic	—	100	10
TM27	Return	Normal	—	100	20	TM49	Snatch	Dark	—	100	10
TM29	Psychic	Psychic	90	100	10	HM05	Flash	Normal	—	70	20

EGG MOVES*

Name	Type	Power	ACC	PP
Assist	Normal	—	100	20
Barrier	Psychic	—	—	30
Fire Punch	Fire	75	100	15
Thunderpunch	Electric	75	100	15
Ice Punch	Ice	75	100	15
Role Play	Psychic	—	100	10

*Learned Via Breeding

MOVE TUTOR
FireRed/LeafGreen and *Emerald* Only

Body Slam*	Counter*	Double-Edge
Dream Eater*	Mega Kick*	Mega Punch*
Metronome	Mimic	Seismic Toss*
Substitute	Thunder Wave*	

*Battle Frontier tutor move (*Emerald*)

097 Hypno™

PSYCHIC

GENERAL INFO
SPECIES: Hypnosis Pokémon
HEIGHT: 5'03"
WEIGHT: 167 lbs.
ABILITY: Insomnia
Protects Hypno from an opponent's sleep attack.

STATS
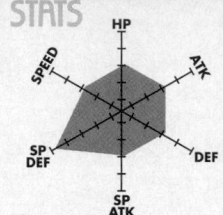

EVOLUTIONS
 ▶
LV26

LOCATION(S):

RUBY — Rarity: **None**
Trade from *FireRed/LeafGreen*

SAPPHIRE — Rarity: **None**
Trade from *FireRed/LeafGreen*

FIRERED — Rarity: **Common**
Three Island

LEAFGREEN — Rarity: **Common**
Three Island

COLOSSEUM — Rarity: **None**
Trade from *FireRed/LeafGreen*

EMERALD — Rarity: **None**
Trade from *FireRed/LeafGreen*

XD — Rarity: **Only One**
Cipher Key Lair (Capture from Cipher Admin Gorigan)

MOVES

Level	Attack	Type	Power	ACC	PP	Level	Attack	Type	Power	ACC	PP
—	Nightmare	Ghost	—	100	15	21	Poison Gas	Poison	—	55	40
—	Pound	Normal	40	100	35	29	Mediate	Psychic	—	—	40
—	Hypnosis	Psychic	—	60	20	35	Psychic	Psychic	90	100	10
—	Disable	Normal	—	55	20	43	Psych Up	Normal	—	—	10
—	Confusion	Psychic	50	100	25	49	Swagger	Normal	—	90	15
17	Headbutt	Normal	70	100	15	57	Future Sight	Psychic	80	90	15

TM/HM

TM/HM#	Name	Type	Power	ACC	PP	TM/HM#	Name	Type	Power	ACC	PP
TM01	Focus Punch	Fighting	150	100	20	TM30	Shadow Ball	Ghost	80	100	15
TM04	Calm Mind	Psychic	—	—	20	TM31	Brick Break	Fighting	75	100	15
TM06	Toxic	Poison	—	85	10	TM32	Double Team	Normal	—	—	15
TM10	Hidden Power	Normal	—	100	15	TM33	Reflect	Normal	—	—	20
TM11	Sunny Day	Fire	—	—	5	TM41	Torment	Dark	—	100	15
TM12	Taunt	Dark	—	100	20	TM42	Facade	Normal	70	100	20
TM15	Hyper Beam	Normal	150	90	5	TM43	Secret Power	Normal	70	100	20
TM16	Light Screen	Psychic	—	—	30	TM44	Rest	Psychic	—	—	10
TM17	Protect	Normal	—	—	10	TM45	Attract	Normal	—	100	15
TM18	Rain Dance	Water	—	—	5	TM46	Thief	Dark	40	100	10
TM20	Safeguard	Normal	—	—	25	TM48	Skill Swap	Psychic	—	100	10
TM21	Frustration	Normal	—	100	20	TM49	Snatch	Dark	—	100	10
TM27	Return	Normal	—	100	20	HM05	Flash	Normal	—	70	20
TM29	Psychic	Psychic	90	100	10						

MOVE TUTOR
FireRed/LeafGreen and *Emerald* Only

Body Slam*	Counter*	Double-Edge
Dream Eater*	Mega Kick*	Mega Punch*
Mimic	Seismic Toss*	Substitute
Thunder Wave*		

*Battle Frontier tutor move (*Emerald*)

098 Krabby™

WATER

GENERAL INFO
SPECIES: River Crab Pokémon
HEIGHT: 1'04"
WEIGHT: 14 lbs.
ABILITY 1: Shell Armor
Protects Krabby from critical hits.
ABILITY 2: Hyper Cutter
Prevents effects that reduce the Pokémon's attack power.

STATS
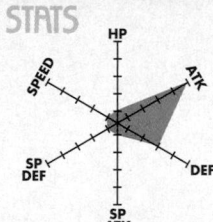

EVOLUTIONS

LV28

LOCATION(S):

RUBY — Rarity: **None**
Trade from *FireRed/LeafGreen*

SAPPHIRE — Rarity: **None**
Trade from *FireRed/LeafGreen*

FIRERED — Rarity: **Common**
Islands One, Three, Four, Five, Six, Seven, Routes 4, 10, 11, 12, 13, 19, 20, 21, 24, Cerulean City, Vermilion City

LEAFGREEN — Rarity: **Common**
Islands One, Three, Four, Five, Six, Seven, Routes 4, 10, 11, 12, 13, 19, 20, 21, 24, Cerulean City, Vermilion City

COLOSSEUM — Rarity: **None**
Trade from *FireRed/LeafGreen*

EMERALD — Rarity: **None**
Trade from *FireRed/LeafGreen*

XD — Rarity: **None**
Trade from *FireRed/LeafGreen*

MOVES

Level	Attack	Type	Power	ACC	PP	Level	Attack	Type	Power	ACC	PP
—	Bubble	Water	20	100	30	27	Stomp	Normal	65	100	20
5	Leer	Normal	—	100	30	34	Guillotine	Normal	—	30	5
12	Vicegrip	Normal	55	100	30	38	Protect	Normal	—	—	10
16	Harden	Normal	—	—	30	45	Crabhammer	Water	90	85	10
23	Mud Shot	Ground	55	95	15	49	Flail	Normal	—	100	15

TM/HM

TM/HM#	Name	Type	Power	ACC	PP	TM/HM#	Name	Type	Power	ACC	PP
TM03	Water Pulse	Water	60	95	20	TM39	Rock Tomb	Rock	50	80	10
TM06	Toxic	Poison	—	85	10	TM42	Facade	Normal	70	100	20
TM07	Hail	Ice	—	—	10	TM43	Secret Power	Normal	70	100	20
TM10	Hidden Power	Normal	—	100	15	TM44	Rest	Psychic	—	—	10
TM13	Ice Beam	Ice	95	100	10	TM45	Attract	Normal	—	100	15
TM14	Blizzard	Ice	120	70	5	TM46	Thief	Dark	40	100	10
TM17	Protect	Normal	—	—	10	HM01	Cut	Normal	50	95	30
TM18	Rain Dance	Water	—	—	5	HM03	Surf	Water	95	100	15
TM21	Frustration	Normal	—	100	20	HM04	Strength	Normal	80	100	15
TM27	Return	Normal	—	100	20	HM06	Rock Smash	Fighting	20	100	15
TM28	Dig	Ground	60	100	10	HM08	Dive	Water	60	100	10
TM32	Double Team	Normal	—	—	15						

EGG MOVES*

Name	Type	Power	ACC	PP
Amnesia	Psychic	—	—	20
Dig	Ground	60	100	10
Flail	Normal	—	100	15
Haze	Ice	—	—	30
Knock Off	Dark	20	100	20
Slam	Normal	80	75	10
Swords Dance	Normal	—	—	30

*Learned Via Breeding

MOVE TUTOR
FireRed/LeafGreen and *Emerald* Only

Body Slam*	Double-Edge	Mimic
Substitute	Swords Dance*	

*Battle Frontier tutor move (*Emerald*)

099 Kingler™

WATER

GENERAL INFO

SPECIES: Pincer Pokémon
HEIGHT: 4'03"
WEIGHT: 132 lbs.
ABILITY 1: Shell Armor
Protects Kingler from critical hits.
ABILITY 2: Hyper Cutter
Prevents effects that reduce the Pokémon's attack power.

STATS

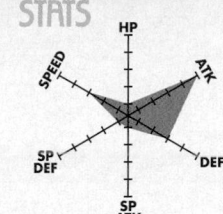

EVOLUTIONS

LV28

LOCATION(S):

RUBY — Rarity: **None**
Trade from *FireRed/LeafGreen*

SAPPHIRE — Rarity: **None**
Trade from *FireRed/LeafGreen*

FIRERED — Rarity: **Rare**
Evolve Krabby

LEAFGREEN — Rarity: **Rare**
Evolve Krabby, Islands One, Three, Five, Six, Seven, Routes 19–21

COLOSSEUM — Rarity: **None**
Trade from *FireRed/LeafGreen*

EMERALD — Rarity: **None**
Trade from *FireRed/LeafGreen*

XD — Rarity: **None**
Trade from *FireRed/LeafGreen*

MOVES

Level	Attack	Type	Power	ACC	PP	Level	Attack	Type	Power	ACC	PP
—	Metal Claw	Steel	50	95	35	23	Mud Shot	Ground	55	95	15
—	Bubble	Water	20	100	30	27	Stomp	Normal	65	100	20
—	Leer	Normal	—	100	30	38	Guillotine	Normal	—	30	5
—	Vicegrip	Normal	55	100	30	42	Protect	Normal	—	—	10
—	Harden	Normal	—	—	30	57	Crabhammer	Water	90	85	10
						65	Flail	Normal	—	100	15

TM/HM

TM/HM#	Name	Type	Power	ACC	PP	TM/HM#	Name	Type	Power	ACC	PP
TM03	Water Pulse	Water	60	95	20	TM32	Double Team	Normal	—	—	15
TM06	Toxic	Poison	—	85	10	TM39	Rock Tomb	Rock	50	80	10
TM07	Hail	Ice	—	—	10	TM42	Facade	Normal	70	100	20
TM10	Hidden Power	Normal	—	100	15	TM43	Secret Power	Normal	70	100	20
TM13	Ice Beam	Ice	95	100	10	TM44	Rest	Psychic	—	—	10
TM14	Blizzard	Ice	120	70	5	TM45	Attract	Normal	—	100	15
TM15	Hyper Beam	Normal	150	90	5	TM46	Thief	Dark	40	100	10
TM17	Protect	Normal	—	—	10	HM01	Cut	Normal	50	95	30
TM18	Rain Dance	Water	—	—	5	HM03	Surf	Water	95	100	15
TM21	Frustration	Normal	—	100	20	HM04	Strength	Normal	80	100	20
TM27	Return	Normal	—	100	20	HM06	Rock Smash	Fighting	20	100	15
TM28	Dig	Ground	60	100	10	HM08	Dive	Water	60	100	10

MOVE TUTOR

FireRed/LeafGreen and *Emerald* Only

Body Slam*	Double-Edge	Mimic
Substitute	Swords Dance*	

*Battle Frontier tutor move (*Emerald*)

100 Voltorb™

ELECTRIC

GENERAL INFO

SPECIES: Ball Pokémon
HEIGHT: 1'08"
WEIGHT: 23 lbs.
ABILITY 1: Soundproof
Prevents Grasswhistle, Growl, Heal Bell, Hyper Voice, Metal Sound, Perish Song, Roar, Screech, Sing, Snore, Supersonic, and Uproar from hitting Voltorb.
ABILITY 2: Static
The opponent has a 30% chance of being paralyzed if a physical attack hits Voltorb.

STATS

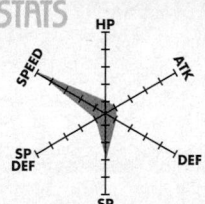

EVOLUTIONS

LV30

LOCATION(S):

RUBY — Rarity: **Common**
New Mauville

SAPPHIRE — Rarity: **Common**
New Mauville

FIRERED — Rarity: **Common**
Power Plant, Route 10

LEAFGREEN — Rarity: **Common**
Power Plant, Route 10

COLOSSEUM — Rarity: **None**
Trade from *Ruby/Sapphire*

EMERALD — Rarity: **Common**
New Mauville

XD — Rarity: **Only One**
Cave Poké Spot (Capture from Miror B.)

MOVES

Level	Attack	Type	Power	ACC	PP	Level	Attack	Type	Power	ACC	PP
—	Charge	Electric	—	100	20	27	Selfdestruct	Normal	200	100	5
—	Tackle	Normal	35	95	35	32	Rollout	Rock	30	90	20
8	Screech	Normal	—	85	40	37	Light Screen	Psychic	—	—	30
15	Sonicboom	Normal	—	90	20	42	Swift	Normal	60	—	20
21	Spark	Electric	65	100	20	46	Explosion	Normal	250	100	5
						49	Mirror Coat	Psychic	—	100	20

TM/HM

TM/HM#	Name	Type	Power	ACC	PP	TM/HM#	Name	Type	Power	ACC	PP
TM06	Toxic	Poison	—	85	10	TM27	Return	Normal	—	100	20
TM10	Hidden Power	Normal	—	100	15	TM32	Double Team	Normal	—	—	15
TM12	Taunt	Dark	—	100	20	TM34	Shock Wave	Electric	60	—	20
TM16	Light Screen	Psychic	—	—	30	TM41	Torment	Dark	—	100	15
TM17	Protect	Normal	—	—	10	TM42	Facade	Normal	70	100	20
TM18	Rain Dance	Water	—	—	5	TM43	Secret Power	Normal	70	100	20
TM21	Frustration	Normal	—	100	20	TM44	Rest	Psychic	—	—	10
TM24	Thunderbolt	Electric	95	100	15	TM46	Thief	Dark	40	100	10
TM25	Thunder	Electric	120	70	10	HM05	Flash	Normal	—	70	20

MOVE TUTOR

FireRed/LeafGreen and *Emerald* Only

Explosion	Mimic	Substitute
Thunder Wave*		

Emerald Only

Endure*	Rollout	Sleep Talk
Snore*	Swagger	Swift*

*Battle Frontier tutor move (*Emerald*)

101 Electrode™

ELECTRIC

GENERAL INFO
SPECIES: Ball Pokémon
HEIGHT: 3'11"
WEIGHT: 147 lbs.
ABILITY 1: Soundproof
Prevents Electrode from being hit by Grasswhistle, Growl, Heal Bell, Hyper Voice, Metal Sound, Perish Song, Roar, Screech, Sing, Snore, Supersonic, and Uproar.

ABILITY 2: Static
The opponent has a 30% chance of being paralyzed if a physical attack hits Electrode.

STATS

EVOLUTIONS

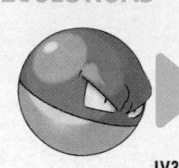 

LV30

LOCATION[S]:

RUBY   Rarity: **Rare**
New Mauville (Fake Poké Ball), Team Aqua/Team Magma Base

SAPPHIRE   Rarity: **Rare**
New Mauville (Fake Poké Ball), Team Aqua/Team Magma Base (Fake Poké Ball)

FIRERED   Rarity: **Rare**
Cerulean Cave

LEAFGREEN   Rarity: **Rare**
Cerulean Cave

COLOSSEUM   Rarity: **None**
Trade from *Ruby/Sapphire/FireRed/LeafGreen*

EMERALD   Rarity: **Rare**
Aqua Hideout, New Mauville

XD   Rarity: **Evolve**
Evolve Voltorb

MOVES

Level	Attack	Type	Power	ACC	PP
—	Charge	Electric	—	100	20
—	Tackle	Normal	35	95	35
—/8	Screech	Normal	—	85	40
—/15	Sonicboom	Normal	—	90	20
21	Spark	Electric	65	100	20
27	Selfdestruct	Normal	200	100	5
34	Rollout	Rock	30	90	20
41	Light Screen	Psychic	—	—	30
48	Swift	Normal	60	—	20
54	Explosion	Normal	250	100	5
59	Mirror Coat	Psychic	—	100	20

TM/HM

TM/HM#	Name	Type	Power	ACC	PP
TM06	Toxic	Poison	—	85	10
TM10	Hidden Power	Normal	—	100	15
TM12	Taunt	Dark	—	100	20
TM15	Hyper Beam	Normal	150	90	5
TM16	Light Screen	Psychic	—	—	30
TM17	Protect	Normal	—	—	10
TM18	Rain Dance	Water	—	—	5
TM21	Frustration	Normal	—	100	20
TM24	Thunderbolt	Electric	95	100	15
TM25	Thunder	Electric	120	70	10
TM27	Return	Normal	—	100	20
TM32	Double Team	Normal	—	—	15
TM34	Shock Wave	Electric	60	—	20
TM41	Torment	Dark	—	100	15
TM42	Facade	Normal	70	100	20
TM43	Secret Power	Normal	70	100	20
TM44	Rest	Psychic	—	—	10
TM46	Thief	Dark	40	100	10
HM05	Flash	Normal	—	70	20

= Emerald Only

MOVE TUTOR
FireRed/LeafGreen and Emerald Only

Explosion	Mimic	Substitute
Thunder Wave*		

Emerald Only

Endure*	Rollout	Sleep Talk
Snore*	Swagger	Swift*

*Battle Frontier tutor move (*Emerald*)

---

102 Exeggcute™

GRASS   PSYCHIC

GENERAL INFO
SPECIES: Egg Pokémon
HEIGHT: 1'04"
WEIGHT: 6 lbs.
ABILITY: Chlorophyll
When the sunlight is strong, Exeggcute's Speed doubles.

STATS

EVOLUTIONS

EVOLVE WITH LEAF STONE

LOCATION[S]:

RUBY   Rarity: **None**
Trade from *FireRed/LeafGreen*

SAPPHIRE   Rarity: **None**
Trade from *FireRed/LeafGreen*

FIRERED   Rarity: **Common**
Safari Zone

LEAFGREEN   Rarity: **Common**
Safari Zone

COLOSSEUM   Rarity: **None**
Trade from *FireRed/LeafGreen*

EMERALD   Rarity: **None**
Trade from *FireRed/LeafGreen*

XD   Rarity: **None**
Trade from *FireRed/LeafGreen*

MOVES

Level	Attack	Type	Power	ACC	PP
—	Barrage	Normal	12	85	20
—	Hypnosis	Psychic	—	60	20
—	Uproar	Normal	50	100	10
7	Reflect	Psychic	—	—	20
13	Leech Seed	Grass	—	90	10
19	Confusion	Psychic	50	100	25
25	Stun Spore	Grass	—	75	30
31	Poisonpowder	Poison	—	75	35
37	Sleep Powder	Grass	—	75	15
43	Solarbeam	Grass	120	100	10

TM/HM

TM/HM#	Name	Type	Power	ACC	PP
TM06	Toxic	Poison	—	85	10
TM09	Bullet Seed	Grass	10	100	30
TM10	Hidden Power	Normal	—	100	15
TM11	Sunny Day	Fire	—	—	5
TM16	Light Screen	Psychic	—	—	30
TM17	Protect	Normal	—	—	10
TM19	Giga Drain	Grass	60	100	5
TM21	Frustration	Normal	—	100	20
TM22	Solarbeam	Grass	120	100	10
TM27	Return	Normal	—	100	20
TM29	Psychic	Psychic	90	100	10
TM32	Double Team	Normal	—	—	15
TM33	Reflect	Normal	—	—	20
TM36	Sludge Bomb	Poison	90	100	10
TM42	Facade	Normal	70	100	20
TM43	Secret Power	Normal	70	100	20
TM44	Rest	Psychic	—	—	10
TM45	Attract	Normal	—	100	15
TM46	Thief	Dark	40	100	10
TM48	Skill Swap	Psychic	—	100	10
HM04	Strength	Normal	80	100	15
HM05	Flash	Normal	—	70	20

EGG MOVES*

Name	Type	Power	ACC	PP
Ancientpower	Rock	60	100	5
Curse	—	—	—	10
Ingrain	Grass	—	100	20
Moonlight	Normal	—	—	5
Psych Up	Normal	—	—	10
Reflect	Psychic	—	—	20
Synthesis	Grass	—	—	5

*Learned Via Breeding

MOVE TUTOR
FireRed/LeafGreen and Emerald Only

Double-Edge	Dream Eater*	Explosion
Mimic	Substitute	

*Battle Frontier tutor move (*Emerald*)

103 Exeggutor™

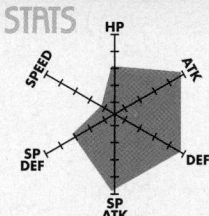

GRASS | PSYCHIC

GENERAL INFO

SPECIES: Coconut Pokémon
HEIGHT: 6'07"
WEIGHT: 265 lbs.
ABILITY: Chlorophyll

When the sunlight is strong, Exeggutor's Speed doubles.

STATS

EVOLUTIONS

EVOLVE WITH LEAF STONE

LOCATION(S):

RUBY Rarity: **None**
Trade from *FireRed/LeafGreen*

SAPPHIRE Rarity: **None**
Trade from *FireRed/LeafGreen*

FIRERED Rarity: **Evolve**
Evolve Exeggcute

LEAFGREEN Rarity: **Evolve**
Evolve Exeggcute

COLOSSEUM Rarity: **None**
Trade from *FireRed/LeafGreen*

EMERALD Rarity: **None**
Trade from *FireRed/LeafGreen*

XD Rarity: **Only One**
Citadark Island (Capture from Master Greevil)

MOVES

Level	Attack	Type	Power	ACC	PP	Level	Attack	Type	Power	ACC	PP
—	Barrage	Normal	12	85	20	—	Confusion	Psychic	50	100	25
—	Hypnosis	Psychic	—	60	20	19	Stomp	Normal	65	100	20
						31	Egg Bomb	Normal	100	75	10

TM/HM

TM/HM#	Name	Type	Power	ACC	PP	TM/HM#	Name	Type	Power	ACC	PP
TM06	Toxic	Poison	—	85	10	TM32	Double Team	Normal	—	—	15
TM09	Bullet Seed	Grass	10	100	30	TM33	Reflect	Normal	—	—	20
TM10	Hidden Power	Normal	—	100	15	TM36	Sludge Bomb	Poison	90	100	10
TM11	Sunny Day	Fire	—	—	5	TM42	Facade	Normal	70	100	20
TM15	Hyper Beam	Normal	150	90	5	TM43	Secret Power	Normal	70	100	20
TM16	Light Screen	Psychic	—	—	30	TM44	Rest	Psychic	—	—	10
TM17	Protect	Normal	—	—	10	TM45	Attract	Normal	—	100	15
TM19	Giga Drain	Grass	60	100	10	TM46	Thief	Dark	40	100	10
TM21	Frustration	Normal	—	100	20	TM48	Skill Swap	Psychic	—	100	10
TM22	Solarbeam	Grass	120	100	10	HM04	Strength	Normal	80	100	20
TM27	Return	Normal	—	100	20	HM05	Flash	Normal	—	70	20
TM29	Psychic	Psychic	90	100	10						

MOVE TUTOR

FireRed/LeafGreen and *Emerald* Only

Double-Edge | Dream Eater* | Explosion
Mimic | Substitute |

*Battle Frontier tutor move (*Emerald*)

---

104 Cubone™

GROUND

GENERAL INFO

SPECIES: Lonely Pokémon
HEIGHT: 1'04"
WEIGHT: 14 lbs.
ABILITY 1: Lightningrod

All Electric-type attacks go toward Cubone during a 2-on-2 battle.

ABILITY 2: Rock Head

Protects Cubone from recoil damage.

STATS

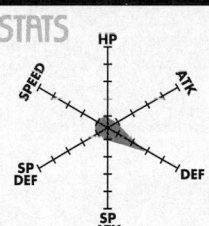

EVOLUTIONS

LV28

LOCATION(S):

RUBY Rarity: **None**
Trade from *FireRed/LeafGreen*

SAPPHIRE Rarity: **None**
Trade from *FireRed/LeafGreen*

FIRERED Rarity: **Rare**
Pokémon Tower, Seven Island

LEAFGREEN Rarity: **Rare**
Pokémon Tower, Seven Island

COLOSSEUM Rarity: **None**
Trade from *FireRed/LeafGreen*

EMERALD Rarity: **None**
Trade from *FireRed/LeafGreen*

XD Rarity: **None**
Trade from *FireRed/LeafGreen*

MOVES

Level	Attack	Type	Power	ACC	PP	Level	Attack	Type	Power	ACC	PP
—	Growl	Normal	—	100	40	25	Bonemerang	Ground	50	90	10
5	Tail Whip	Normal	—	100	30	29	Rage	Normal	20	100	20
9	Bone Club	Ground	65	85	20	33	False Swipe	Normal	40	100	40
13	Headbutt	Normal	70	100	15	37	Thrash	Normal	90	100	20
17	Leer	Normal	—	100	30	41	Bone Rush	Ground	25	80	10
21	Focus Energy	Normal	—	—	30	45	Double-Edge	Normal	120	100	15

TM/HM

TM/HM#	Name	Type	Power	ACC	PP	TM/HM#	Name	Type	Power	ACC	PP
TM01	Focus Punch	Fighting	150	100	20	TM32	Double Team	Normal	—	—	15
TM06	Toxic	Poison	—	85	10	TM35	Flamethrower	Fire	95	100	15
TM10	Hidden Power	Normal	—	100	15	TM37	Sandstorm	Ground	—	—	10
TM11	Sunny Day	Fire	—	—	5	TM38	Fire Blast	Fire	120	85	5
TM13	Ice Beam	Ice	95	100	10	TM39	Rock Tomb	Rock	50	80	10
TM14	Blizzard	Ice	120	70	5	TM40	Aerial Ace	Flying	60	—	20
TM17	Protect	Normal	—	—	10	TM42	Facade	Normal	70	100	20
TM21	Frustration	Normal	—	100	20	TM43	Secret Power	Normal	70	100	20
TM23	Iron Tail	Steel	75	75	15	TM44	Rest	Psychic	—	—	10
TM26	Earthquake	Ground	100	100	10	TM45	Attract	Normal	—	100	15
TM27	Return	Normal	—	100	20	TM46	Thief	Dark	40	100	10
TM28	Dig	Ground	60	100	10	HM04	Strength	Normal	80	100	20
TM31	Brick Break	Fighting	75	100	15	HM06	Rock Smash	Fighting	20	100	15

EGG MOVES*

Name	Type	Power	ACC	PP
Ancientpower	Rock	60	100	5
Belly Drum	Normal	—	—	10
Perish Song	Normal	—	—	5
Rock Slide	Rock	75	90	10
Screech	Normal	—	85	40
Skull Bash	Normal	100	100	15
Swords Dance	Normal	—	—	30

*Learned Via Breeding

MOVE TUTOR

FireRed/LeafGreen and *Emerald* Only

Body Slam* | Counter* | Double-Edge
Mega Kick* | Mega Punch* | Mimic
Rock Slide* | Seismic Toss* | Substitute
Swords Dance* | |

*Battle Frontier tutor move (*Emerald*)

105 Marowak™

GROUND

GENERAL INFO
SPECIES: Bone Keeper Pokémon
HEIGHT: 3'03"
WEIGHT: 99 lbs.
ABILITY 1: Lightningrod
All Electric-type attacks go toward Marowak during a 2-on-2 Battle.
ABILITY 2: Rock Head
Protects Marowak from recoil damage.

STATS

EVOLUTIONS

 LV28

LOCATION[S]:

RUBY — Rarity: **None**
Trade from *FireRed/LeafGreen*

SAPPHIRE — Rarity: **None**
Trade from *FireRed/LeafGreen*

FIRERED — Rarity: **Rare**
Victory Road, Seven Island

LEAFGREEN — Rarity: **Rare**
Victory Road, Seven Island

COLOSSEUM — Rarity: **None**
Trade from *FireRed/LeafGreen*

EMERALD — Rarity: **None**
Trade from *FireRed/LeafGreen*

XD — Rarity: **Only One**
Citadark Island (Capture from Cipher Admin Eldes)

MOVES

Level	Attack	Type	Power	ACC	PP	Level	Attack	Type	Power	ACC	PP
—	Growl	Normal	—	100	40	25	Bonemerang	Ground	50	90	10
—	Tail Whip	Normal	—	100	30	32	Rage	Normal	20	100	20
—	Bone Club	Ground	65	85	20	39	False Swipe	Normal	40	100	40
—	Headbutt	Normal	70	100	15	46	Thrash	Normal	90	100	20
17	Leer	Normal	—	100	30	53	Bone Rush	Ground	25	80	10
21	Focus Energy	Normal	—	—	30	61	Double-Edge	Normal	120	100	15

TM/HM

TM/HM#	Name	Type	Power	ACC	PP	TM/HM#	Name	Type	Power	ACC	PP
TM01	Focus Punch	Fighting	150	100	20	TM32	Double Team	Normal	—	—	15
TM06	Toxic	Poison	—	85	10	TM35	Flamethrower	Fire	95	100	15
TM10	Hidden Power	Normal	—	100	15	TM37	Sandstorm	Ground	—	—	10
TM11	Sunny Day	Fire	—	—	5	TM38	Fire Blast	Fire	120	85	5
TM13	Ice Beam	Ice	95	100	10	TM39	Rock Tomb	Rock	50	80	10
TM14	Blizzard	Ice	120	70	5	TM40	Aerial Ace	Flying	60	—	20
TM15	Hyper Beam	Normal	150	90	5	TM42	Facade	Normal	70	100	20
TM17	Protect	Normal	—	—	10	TM43	Secret Power	Normal	70	100	20
TM21	Frustration	Normal	—	100	20	TM44	Rest	Psychic	—	—	10
TM23	Iron Tail	Steel	75	75	15	TM45	Attract	Normal	—	100	15
TM26	Earthquake	Ground	100	100	10	TM46	Thief	Dark	40	100	10
TM27	Return	Normal	—	100	20	HM04	Strength	Normal	80	100	20
TM28	Dig	Ground	60	100	10	HM06	Rock Smash	Fighting	20	100	15
TM31	Brick Break	Fighting	75	100	15						

MOVE TUTOR
FireRed/LeafGreen and *Emerald* Only

Body Slam*	Counter*	Double-Edge
Mega Kick*	Mega Punch*	Mimic
Rock Slide*	Seismic Toss*	Substitute
Swords Dance*		

*Battle Frontier tutor move (*Emerald*)

---

106 Hitmonlee™

FIGHTING

GENERAL INFO
SPECIES: Kicking Pokémon
HEIGHT: 4'11"
WEIGHT: 110 lbs.
ABILITY: Limber
Protects Hitmonlee from being paralyzed.

STATS

EVOLUTIONS

 LV20 (ATTACK<DEFENSE)

LOCATION[S]:

RUBY — Rarity: **None**
Trade from *FireRed/LeafGreen*

SAPPHIRE — Rarity: **None**
Trade from *FireRed/LeafGreen*

FIRERED — Rarity: **Only One**
Fighting Gym in Saffron City

LEAFGREEN — Rarity: **Only One**
Fighting Gym in Saffron City

COLOSSEUM — Rarity: **None**
Trade from *FireRed/LeafGreen*

EMERALD — Rarity: **None**
Trade from *FireRed/LeafGreen*

XD — Rarity: **Only One**
Citadark Island (Capture from Cipher Peon Petro)

MOVES

Level	Attack	Type	Power	ACC	PP	Level	Attack	Type	Power	ACC	PP
—	Revenge	Fighting	60	100	10	21	Focus Energy	Normal	—	—	30
—	Double-Kick	Fighting	30	100	30	26	Hi Jump Kick	Fighting	85	90	20
6	Mediate	Psychic	—	—	40	31	Mind Reader	Normal	—	100	5
11	Rolling Kick	Fight	60	85	15	36	Foresight	Normal	—	100	40
16	Jump Kick	Fight	70	95	25	41	Endure	Normal	—	—	10
20	Brick Break	Fighting	75	100	15	46	Mega Kick	Normal	120	75	5
21	Focus Energy	Normal	—	—	30	51	Reversal	Fighting	—	100	15

TM/HM

TM/HM#	Name	Type	Power	ACC	PP	TM/HM#	Name	Type	Power	ACC	PP
TM01	Focus Punch	Fighting	150	100	20	TM31	Brick Break	Fighting	75	100	15
TM06	Toxic	Poison	—	85	10	TM32	Double Team	Normal	—	—	15
TM08	Bulk Up	Fighting	—	—	20	TM39	Rock Tomb	Rock	50	80	10
TM10	Hidden Power	Normal	—	100	15	TM42	Facade	Normal	70	100	20
TM11	Sunny Day	Fire	—	—	5	TM43	Secret Power	Normal	70	100	20
TM17	Protect	Normal	—	—	10	TM44	Rest	Psychic	—	—	10
TM18	Rain Dance	Water	—	—	5	TM45	Attract	Normal	—	100	15
TM21	Frustration	Normal	—	100	20	TM46	Thief	Dark	40	100	10
TM26	Earthquake	Ground	100	100	10	HM04	Strength	Normal	80	100	20
TM27	Return	Normal	—	100	20	HM06	Rock Smash	Fighting	20	100	15

MOVE TUTOR
FireRed/LeafGreen and *Emerald* Only

Body Slam*	Counter*	Double-Edge
Mega Kick*	Mega Punch*	Metronome
Mimic	Rock Slide*	Seismic Toss*
Substitute		

*Battle Frontier tutor move (*Emerald*)

107 Hitmonchan™

FIGHTING

GENERAL INFO

SPECIES: Punching Pokémon
HEIGHT: 4'7"
WEIGHT: 111 lbs.
ABILITY: Keen Eye
Prevents Hitmonchan from having its Accuracy lowered.

STATS

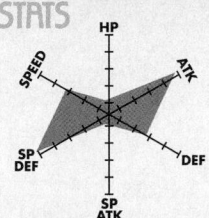

EVOLUTIONS

LV20
(ATTACK<DEFENSE)

LOCATION[S]:

RUBY — Rarity: **None**
Trade from *FireRed/LeafGreen*

SAPPHIRE — Rarity: **None**
Trade from *FireRed/LeafGreen*

FIRERED — Rarity: **Only One**
Fighting Gym in Saffron City

LEAFGREEN — Rarity: **Only One**
Fighting Gym in Saffron City

COLOSSEUM — Rarity: **None**
Trade from *FireRed/LeafGreen*

EMERALD — Rarity: **None**
Trade from *FireRed/LeafGreen*

XD — Rarity: **Only One**
Citadark Island (Capture from Cipher Peon Karbon)

MOVES

Level	Attack	Type	Power	ACC	PP	Level	Attack	Type	Power	ACC	PP
—	Comet Punch	Normal	18	85	15	26	Ice Punch	Ice	75	100	15
—	Revenge	Fighting	60	100	10	26	Thunderpunch	Electric	75	100	15
7	Agility	Psychic	—	—	30	32	Sky Uppercut	Fighting	85	90	15
13	Pursuit	Dark	40	100	20	38	Mega Punch	Normal	80	85	20
20	Mach Punch	Fighting	40	100	30	44	Detect	Fight	—	—	5
26	Fire Punch	Fire	75	100	15	50	Counter	Fighting	—	100	20

TM/HM

TM/HM#	Name	Type	Power	ACC	PP	TM/HM#	Name	Type	Power	ACC	PP
TM01	Focus Punch	Fighting	150	100	20	TM31	Brick Break	Fighting	75	100	15
TM06	Toxic	Poison	—	85	10	TM32	Double Team	Normal	—	—	15
TM08	Bulk Up	Fighting	—	—	20	TM39	Rock Tomb	Rock	50	80	10
TM10	Hidden Power	Normal	—	100	15	TM42	Facade	Normal	70	100	20
TM11	Sunny Day	Fire	—	—	5	TM43	Secret Power	Normal	70	100	20
TM17	Protect	Normal	—	—	10	TM44	Rest	Psychic	—	—	10
TM18	Rain Dance	Water	—	—	5	TM45	Attract	Normal	—	100	15
TM21	Frustration	Normal	—	100	20	TM46	Thief	Dark	40	100	10
TM26	Earthquake	Ground	100	100	10	HM04	Strength	Normal	80	100	15
TM27	Return	Normal	—	100	20	HM06	Rock Smash	Fighting	20	100	15

MOVE TUTOR

FireRed/LeafGreen and *Emerald* Only

Body Slam*	Counter*	Double-Edge
Mega Kick*	Mega Punch*	Metronome
Mimic	Rock Slide*	Seismic Toss*
Substitute		

*Battle Frontier tutor move (*Emerald*)

---

108 Lickitung™

NORMAL

GENERAL INFO

SPECIES: Licking Pokémon
HEIGHT: 3'11"
WEIGHT: 144 lbs.
ABILITY 1: Oblivious
Prevents Lickitung from being attracted.
ABILITY 2: Own Tempo
Prevents Lickitung from being confused.

STATS

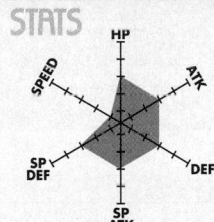

EVOLUTIONS

DOES NOT EVOLVE

LOCATION[S]:

RUBY — Rarity: **None**
Trade from *FireRed/LeafGreen*

SAPPHIRE — Rarity: **None**
Trade from *FireRed/LeafGreen*

FIRERED — Rarity: **Only One**
Trade for Golduck (Route 18)

LEAFGREEN — Rarity: **Only One**
Trade for Slowbro (Route 18)

COLOSSEUM — Rarity: **None**
Trade from *FireRed/LeafGreen*

EMERALD — Rarity: **None**
Trade from *FireRed/LeafGreen*

XD — Rarity: **Only One**
Citadark Island (Capture from Cipher Peon Geftal)

MOVES

Level	Attack	Type	Power	ACC	PP	Level	Attack	Type	Power	ACC	PP
—	Lick	Ghost	20	100	30	29	Wrap	Normal	15	85	20
7	Supersonic	Normal	—	55	20	34	Disable	Normal	—	55	20
12	Defense Curl	Normal	—	—	40	40	Slam	Normal	80	75	20
18	Knock Off	Dark	20	100	20	45	Screech	Normal	—	85	40
23	Stomp	Normal	65	100	20	51	Refresh	Normal	—	100	20

TM/HM

TM/HM#	Name	Type	Power	ACC	PP	TM/HM#	Name	Type	Power	ACC	PP
TM01	Focus Punch	Fighting	150	100	20	TM30	Shadow Ball	Ghost	80	100	15
TM03	Water Pulse	Water	60	95	20	TM31	Brick Break	Fighting	75	100	15
TM06	Toxic	Poison	—	85	10	TM32	Double Team	Normal	—	—	15
TM10	Hidden Power	Normal	—	100	15	TM34	Shock Wave	Electric	60	—	20
TM11	Sunny Day	Fire	—	—	5	TM35	Flamethrower	Fire	95	100	15
TM13	Ice Beam	Ice	95	100	10	TM37	Sandstorm	Ground	—	—	10
TM14	Blizzard	Ice	120	70	5	TM38	Fire Blast	Fire	120	85	5
TM15	Hyper Beam	Normal	150	90	5	TM39	Rock Tomb	Rock	50	80	10
TM17	Protect	Normal	—	—	10	TM42	Facade	Normal	70	100	20
TM18	Rain Dance	Water	—	—	5	TM43	Secret Power	Normal	70	100	20
TM21	Frustration	Normal	—	100	20	TM44	Rest	Psychic	—	—	10
TM22	Solarbeam	Grass	120	100	10	TM45	Attract	Normal	—	100	15
TM23	Iron Tail	Steel	75	75	15	TM46	Thief	Dark	40	100	10
TM24	Thunderbolt	Electric	95	100	15	HM01	Cut	Normal	50	95	30
TM25	Thunder	Electric	120	70	10	HM03	Surf	Water	95	100	15
TM26	Earthquake	Ground	100	100	10	HM04	Strength	Normal	80	100	15
TM27	Return	Normal	—	100	20	HM06	Rock Smash	Fighting	20	100	15
TM28	Dig	Ground	60	100	10						

EGG MOVES*

Name	Type	Power	ACC	PP
Belly Drum	Normal	—	—	10
Body Slam	Normal	85	100	15
Curse	—	—	—	10
Magnitude	Ground	—	100	30
Sleep Talk	Normal	—	—	10
Smellingsalt	Normal	60	100	10
Snore	Normal	40	100	15
Substitute	Normal	—	—	10

*Learned Via Breeding

MOVE TUTOR

FireRed/LeafGreen and *Emerald* Only

Body Slam*	Counter*	Double-Edge
Dream Eater*	Mega Kick*	Mega Punch*
Mimic	Rock Slide*	Seismic Toss*
Substitute	Swords Dance*	

*Battle Frontier tutor move (*Emerald*)

109 Koffing™

POISON

GENERAL INFO

SPECIES: Poison Gas Pokémon
HEIGHT: 2'00"
WEIGHT: 2 lbs.
ABILITY: Levitate
Protects Koffing from being hit by Ground-type attacks.

STATS

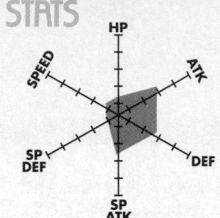

EVOLUTIONS

LV35

LOCATION[S]:

RUBY   Rarity: **Common**
Fiery Path

SAPPHIRE   Rarity: **Common**
Fiery Path

FIRERED   Rarity: **Common**
Pokémon Mansion

LEAFGREEN   Rarity: **Common**
Pokémon Mansion

COLOSSEUM   Rarity: **None**
Trade from *Ruby/Sapphire/FireRed/LeafGreen*

EMERALD   Rarity: **Common**
Fiery Path

XD   Rarity: **None**
Trade from *Ruby/Sapphire/FireRed/LeafGreen*

MOVES

Level	Attack	Type	Power	ACC	PP	Level	Attack	Type	Power	ACC	PP
—	Poison Gas	Poison	—	55	40	25	Smokescreen	Normal	—	100	20
—	Tackle	Normal	35	95	35	33	Haze	Ice	—	—	30
9	Smog	Poison	20	70	20	41	Explosion	Normal	250	100	5
17	Selfdestruct	Normal	200	100	5	45	Destiny Bond	Ghost	—	—	5
21	Sludge	Poison	65	100	20	49	Memento	Dark	—	100	10

TM/HM

TM/HM#	Name	Type	Power	ACC	PP	TM/HM#	Name	Type	Power	ACC	PP
TM06	Toxic	Poison	—	85	10	TM34	Shock Wave	Electric	60	—	20
TM10	Hidden Power	Normal	—	100	15	TM35	Flamethrower	Fire	95	100	15
TM11	Sunny Day	Fire	—	—	5	TM36	Sludge Bomb	Poison	90	100	10
TM12	Taunt	Dark	—	100	20	TM38	Fire Blast	Fire	120	85	5
TM17	Protect	Normal	—	—	10	TM41	Torment	Dark	—	100	15
TM18	Rain Dance	Water	—	—	5	TM42	Facade	Normal	70	100	20
TM21	Frustration	Normal	—	100	20	TM43	Secret Power	Normal	70	100	20
TM24	Thunderbolt	Electric	95	100	15	TM44	Rest	Psychic	—	—	10
TM25	Thunder	Electric	120	70	10	TM45	Attract	Normal	—	100	15
TM27	Return	Normal	—	100	20	TM46	Thief	Dark	40	100	10
TM30	Shadow Ball	Ghost	80	100	15	HM05	Flash	Normal	—	70	20
TM32	Double Team	Normal	—	—	15						

EGG MOVES*

Name	Type	Power	ACC	PP
Screech	Normal	—	85	40
Psywave	Psychic	—	80	15
Destiny Bond	Ghost	—	—	5
Will-O-Wisp	Fire	—	75	15
Psybeam	Psychic	65	100	20
Pain Split	Normal	—	100	10

*Learned Via Breeding

MOVE TUTOR

FireRed/LeafGreen and *Emerald* Only

Explosion	Mimic	Substitute

Emerald Only

Endure*	Rollout	Sleep Talk
Snore*	Swagger	

*Battle Frontier tutor move (*Emerald*)

---

110 Weezing™

POISON

GENERAL INFO

SPECIES: Poison Gas Pokémon
HEIGHT: 3'11"
WEIGHT: 21 lbs.
ABILITY: Levitate
Protects Weezing from being hit by Ground-type attacks.

STATS

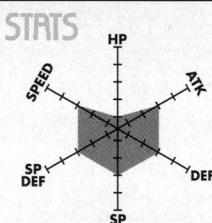

EVOLUTIONS

  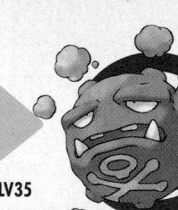

LV35

LOCATION[S]:

RUBY   Rarity: **Evolve**
Evolve Koffing

SAPPHIRE   Rarity: **Evolve**
Evolve Koffing

FIRERED   Rarity: **Rare**
Evolve Koffing, Pokémon Mansion

LEAFGREEN   Rarity: **Evolve**
Evolve Koffing

COLOSSEUM   Rarity: **None**
Trade from *Ruby/Sapphire/FireRed/LeafGreen*

EMERALD   Rarity: **Evolve**
Evolve Koffing

XD   Rarity: **None**
Trade from *Ruby/Sapphire/FireRed/LeafGreen*

MOVES

Level	Attack	Type	Power	ACC	PP	Level	Attack	Type	Power	ACC	PP
—	Poison Gas	Poison	—	55	40	25	Smokescreen	Normal	—	100	20
—	Tackle	Normal	35	95	35	33	Haze	Ice	—	—	30
—	Smog	Poison	20	70	20	44	Explosion	Normal	250	100	5
—	Selfdestruct	Normal	200	100	5	51	Destiny Bond	Ghost	—	—	5
21	Sludge	Poison	65	100	20	58	Memento	Dark	—	100	10

TM/HM

TM/HM#	Name	Type	Power	ACC	PP	TM/HM#	Name	Type	Power	ACC	PP
TM06	Toxic	Poison	—	85	10	TM32	Double Team	Normal	—	—	15
TM10	Hidden Power	Normal	—	100	15	TM34	Shock Wave	Electric	60	—	20
TM11	Sunny Day	Fire	—	—	5	TM35	Flamethrower	Fire	95	100	15
TM12	Taunt	Dark	—	100	20	TM36	Sludge Bomb	Poison	90	100	10
TM15	Hyper Beam	Normal	150	90	5	TM38	Fire Blast	Fire	120	85	5
TM17	Protect	Normal	—	—	10	TM41	Torment	Dark	—	100	15
TM18	Rain Dance	Water	—	—	5	TM42	Facade	Normal	70	100	20
TM21	Frustration	Normal	—	100	20	TM43	Secret Power	Normal	70	100	20
TM24	Thunderbolt	Electric	95	100	15	TM44	Rest	Psychic	—	—	10
TM25	Thunder	Electric	120	70	10	TM45	Attract	Normal	—	100	15
TM27	Return	Normal	—	100	20	TM46	Thief	Dark	40	100	10
TM30	Shadow Ball	Ghost	80	100	15	HM05	Flash	Normal	—	70	20

MOVE TUTOR

FireRed/LeafGreen and *Emerald* Only

Explosion	Mimic	Substitute

Emerald Only

Endure*	Rollout	Sleep Talk
Snore*	Swagger	

*Battle Frontier tutor move (*Emerald*)

111 Rhyhorn™

GROUND · ROCK

GENERAL INFO
SPECIES: Spikes Pokémon
HEIGHT: 3'03"
WEIGHT: 254 lbs.
ABILITY 1: Rock Head
Prevents Rhyhorn from taking recoil damage from Submission, Take Down, and Double-Edge.
ABILITY 2: Lightningrod
In a 2-on-2 battle, Electric-type moves attack Rhyhorn.

STATS
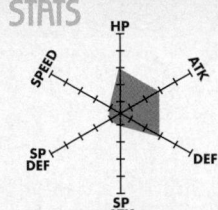

EVOLUTIONS

LV42

LOCATION(S):

RUBY	Rarity: **Common**	
Safari Zone		
SAPPHIRE	Rarity: **Common**	
Safari Zone		
FIRERED	Rarity: **Rare**	
Safari Zone		
LEAFGREEN	Rarity: **Rare**	
Safari Zone		
COLOSSEUM	Rarity: **None**	
Trade from *Ruby/Sapphire/FireRed/LeafGreen*		
EMERALD	Rarity: **Common**	
Safari Zone		
XD	Rarity: **None**	
Trade from *Ruby/Sapphire/FireRed/LeafGreen*		

MOVES

Level	Attack	Type	Power	ACC	PP	Level	Attack	Type	Power	ACC	PP
—	Horn Attack	Normal	65	100	25	29	Rock Blast	Rock	25	80	10
—	Tail Whip	Normal	—	100	30	38	Horn Drill	Normal	—	30	5
10	Stomp	Normal	65	100	20	43	Take Down	Normal	90	85	20
15	Fury Attack	Normal	15	85	20	52	Earthquake	Ground	100	100	10
24	Scary Face	Normal	—	90	10	57	Megahorn	Bug	120	85	10

TM/HM

TM/HM#	Name	Type	Power	ACC	PP	TM/HM#	Name	Type	Power	ACC	PP
TM05	Roar	Normal	—	100	20	TM28	Dig	Ground	60	100	10
TM06	Toxic	Poison	—	85	10	TM32	Double Team	Normal	—	—	15
TM10	Hidden Power	Normal	—	100	15	TM34	Shock Wave	Electric	60	—	20
TM11	Sunny Day	Fire	—	—	5	TM35	Flamethrower	Fire	95	100	15
TM13	Ice Beam	Ice	95	100	10	TM37	Sandstorm	Ground	—	—	10
TM14	Blizzard	Ice	120	70	5	TM38	Fire Blast	Fire	120	85	5
TM17	Protect	Normal	—	—	10	TM39	Rock Tomb	Rock	50	80	10
TM18	Rain Dance	Water	—	—	5	TM42	Facade	Normal	70	100	20
TM21	Frustration	Normal	—	100	20	TM43	Secret Power	Normal	70	100	20
TM23	Iron Tail	Steel	75	75	15	TM44	Rest	Psychic	—	—	10
TM24	Thunderbolt	Electric	95	100	15	TM45	Attract	Normal	—	100	15
TM25	Thunder	Electric	120	70	10	TM46	Thief	Dark	40	100	10
TM26	Earthquake	Ground	100	100	10	HM04	Strength	Normal	80	100	20
TM27	Return	Normal	—	100	20	HM06	Rock Smash	Fighting	20	100	15

EGG MOVES*

Name	Type	Power	ACC	PP
Crunch	Dark	80	100	15
Reversal	Fighting	—	100	15
Rock Slide	Rock	75	90	10
Counter	Fighting	—	100	20
Magnitude	Ground	—	100	30
Swords Dance	Normal	—	—	30
Curse	—	—	—	10
Crush Claw	Normal	75	95	10

*Learned Via Breeding

MOVE TUTOR
FireRed/LeafGreen and *Emerald* Only

Body Slam*	Counter*	Double-Edge
Mimic	Rock Slide*	Substitute
Swords Dance*		

Emerald Only

Endure*	Icy Wind*	Mud-Slap*
Rollout	Sleep Talk	Swagger

*Battle Frontier tutor move (*Emerald*)

---

112 Rhydon™

GROUND · ROCK

GENERAL INFO
SPECIES: Drill Pokémon
HEIGHT: 6'03"
WEIGHT: 265 lbs.
ABILITY 1: Rock Head
Prevents Rhydon from taking recoil damage from Submission, Take Down, and Double-Edge.
ABILITY 2: Lightningrod
In a 2-on-2 battle, Electric-type moves attack Rhydon.

STATS
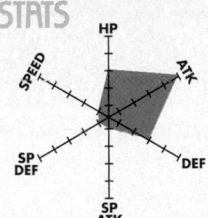

EVOLUTIONS

LV42

LOCATION(S):

RUBY	Rarity: **Evolve**	
Evolve Rhyhorn		
SAPPHIRE	Rarity: **Evolve**	
Evolve Rhyhorn		
FIRERED	Rarity: **Evolve**	
Evolve Rhyhorn		
LEAFGREEN	Rarity: **Evolve**	
Evolve Rhyhorn		
COLOSSEUM	Rarity: **None**	
Trade from *Ruby/Sapphire/FireRed/LeafGreen*		
EMERALD	Rarity: **Evolve**	
Evolve Rhyhorn		
XD	Rarity: **Only One**	
Citadark Island (Capture from Master Greevil)		

MOVES

Level	Attack	Type	Power	ACC	PP	Level	Attack	Type	Power	ACC	PP
—	Horn Attack	Normal	65	100	25	29	Rock Blast	Rock	25	80	10
—	Tail Whip	Normal	—	100	30	38	Horn Drill	Normal	—	30	5
—	Stomp	Normal	65	100	20	46	Take Down	Normal	90	85	20
—	Fury Attack	Normal	15	85	20	58	Earthquake	Ground	100	100	10
24	Scary Face	Normal	—	90	10	66	Megahorn	Bug	120	85	10

TM/HM

TM/HM#	Name	Type	Power	ACC	PP	TM/HM#	Name	Type	Power	ACC	PP
TM01	Focus Punch	Fighting	150	100	20	TM31	Brick Break	Fighting	75	100	15
TM05	Roar	Normal	—	100	20	TM32	Double Team	Normal	—	—	15
TM06	Toxic	Poison	—	85	10	TM34	Shock Wave	Electric	60	—	20
TM10	Hidden Power	Normal	—	100	15	TM35	Flamethrower	Fire	95	100	15
TM11	Sunny Day	Fire	—	—	5	TM37	Sandstorm	Ground	—	—	10
TM13	Ice Beam	Ice	95	100	10	TM38	Fire Blast	Fire	120	85	5
TM14	Blizzard	Ice	120	70	5	TM39	Rock Tomb	Rock	50	80	10
TM15	Hyper Beam	Normal	150	90	5	TM42	Facade	Normal	70	100	20
TM17	Protect	Normal	—	—	10	TM43	Secret Power	Normal	70	100	20
TM18	Rain Dance	Water	—	—	5	TM44	Rest	Psychic	—	—	10
TM21	Frustration	Normal	—	100	20	TM45	Attract	Normal	—	100	15
TM23	Iron Tail	Steel	75	75	15	TM46	Thief	Dark	40	100	10
TM24	Thunderbolt	Electric	95	100	15	HM01	Cut	Normal	50	95	30
TM25	Thunder	Electric	120	70	10	HM03	Surf	Water	95	100	15
TM26	Earthquake	Ground	100	100	10	HM04	Strength	Normal	80	100	20
TM27	Return	Normal	—	100	20	HM06	Rock Smash	Fighting	20	100	15
TM28	Dig	Ground	60	100	10						

MOVE TUTOR
FireRed/LeafGreen and *Emerald* Only

Body Slam*	Counter*	Double-Edge
Mega Kick*	Mega Punch*	Mimic
Rock Slide*	Seismic Toss*	Substitute
Swords Dance*		

Emerald Only

Dynamicpunch*	Endure*	Fire Punch*
Fury Cutter*	Icy Wind*	Mud-Slap*
Rollout	Sleep Talk	Snore*
Swagger	Thunderpunch*	

*Battle Frontier tutor move (*Emerald*)

113 Chansey™

NORMAL

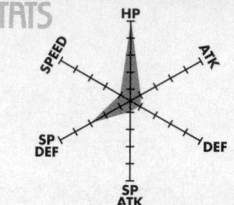

GENERAL INFO
SPECIES: Egg Pokémon
HEIGHT: 3'07"
WEIGHT: 76 lbs.
ABILITY 1: Natural Cure
Any status problem is cured when Chansey is switched out.
ABILITY 2: Serene Grace
When Chansey is in battle, the chances of extra effects occurring are doubled.

STATS

EVOLUTIONS

(FRIENDSHIP)

LOCATION[S]:

RUBY Rarity: **None**
Trade from *FireRed/LeafGreen*

SAPPHIRE Rarity: **None**
Trade from *FireRed/LeafGreen*

FIRERED Rarity: **Rare**
Safari Zone

LEAFGREEN Rarity: **Rare**
Safari Zone

COLOSSEUM Rarity: **None**
Trade from *FireRed/LeafGreen*

EMERALD Rarity: **None**
Trade from *FireRed/LeafGreen*

XD Rarity: **Only One**
Citadark Island (Capture from Cipher Peon Leden)

MOVES

Level	Attack	Type	Power	ACC	PP
—	Pound	Normal	40	100	35
—	Growl	Normal	—	100	40
5	Tail Whip	Normal	—	100	30
9	Refresh	Normal	—	100	20
13	Softboiled	Normal	—	100	10
17	Doubleslap	Normal	15	85	10
23	Minimize	Normal	—	—	20
29	Sing	Normal	—	55	15
35	Egg Bomb	Normal	100	75	10
41	Defense Curl	Normal	—	—	40
49	Light Screen	Psychic	—	—	30
57	Double-Edge	Normal	120	100	15

TM/HM

TM/HM#	Name	Type	Power	ACC	PP
TM01	Focus Punch	Fighting	150	100	20
TM03	Water Pulse	Water	60	95	20
TM04	Calm Mind	Psychic	—	—	20
TM06	Toxic	Poison	—	85	10
TM07	Hail	Ice	—	—	10
TM10	Hidden Power	Normal	—	100	15
TM11	Sunny Day	Fire	—	—	5
TM13	Ice Beam	Ice	95	100	10
TM14	Blizzard	Ice	120	70	5
TM15	Hyper Beam	Normal	150	90	5
TM16	Light Screen	Psychic	—	—	30
TM17	Protect	Normal	—	—	10
TM18	Rain Dance	Water	—	—	5
TM20	Safeguard	Normal	—	—	25
TM21	Frustration	Normal	—	100	20
TM22	Solarbeam	Grass	120	100	10
TM23	Iron Tail	Steel	75	75	15
TM24	Thunderbolt	Electric	95	100	15
TM25	Thunder	Electric	120	70	10
TM26	Earthquake	Ground	100	100	10
TM27	Return	Normal	—	100	20
TM29	Psychic	Psychic	90	100	10
TM30	Shadow Ball	Ghost	80	100	15
TM31	Brick Break	Fighting	75	100	15
TM32	Double Team	Normal	—	—	15
TM34	Shock Wave	Electric	60	—	20
TM35	Flamethrower	Fire	95	100	15
TM37	Sandstorm	Ground	—	—	10
TM38	Fire Blast	Fire	120	85	5
TM39	Rock Tomb	Rock	50	80	10
TM42	Facade	Normal	70	100	20
TM43	Secret Power	Normal	70	100	20
TM44	Rest	Psychic	—	—	10
TM45	Attract	Normal	—	100	15
TM48	Skill Swap	Psychic	—	100	10
TM49	Snatch	Dark	—	100	10
HM04	Strength	Normal	80	100	20
HM05	Flash	Normal	—	70	20
HM06	Rock Smash	Fighting	20	100	15

EGG MOVES*

Name	Type	Power	ACC	PP
Aromatherapy	Grass	—	—	5
Heal Bell	Normal	—	—	5
Metronome	Normal	—	—	10
Present	Normal	—	90	15
Substitute	Normal	—	—	10

*Learned Via Breeding

MOVE TUTOR
FireRed/LeafGreen and *Emerald* Only

Body Slam*	Counter*	Double-Edge
Dream Eater*	Mega Kick*	Mega Punch*
Metronome	Mimic	Seismic Toss*
Softboiled*	Substitute	Thunder Wave*

*Battle Frontier tutor move (*Emerald*)

114 Tangela™

GRASS

GENERAL INFO
SPECIES: Vine Pokémon
HEIGHT: 3'03"
WEIGHT: 77 lbs.
ABILITY: Chlorophyll
When the sunlight is strong, Tangela's Speed doubles.

STATS
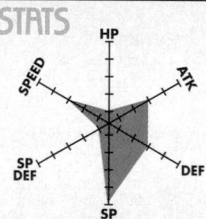

EVOLUTIONS

DOES NOT EVOLVE

LOCATION[S]:

RUBY Rarity: **None**
Trade from *FireRed/LeafGreen*

SAPPHIRE Rarity: **None**
Trade from *FireRed/LeafGreen*

FIRERED Rarity: **Rare**
Route 21, One Island

LEAFGREEN Rarity: **Rare**
Route 21, One Island

COLOSSEUM Rarity: **None**
Trade from *FireRed/LeafGreen*

EMERALD Rarity: **None**
Trade from *FireRed/LeafGreen*

XD Rarity: **Only One**
Cipher Key Lair (Capture from Cipher Peon Targ)

MOVES

Level	Attack	Type	Power	ACC	PP
—	Constrict	Normal	10	100	35
—	Ingrain	Grass	—	100	20
4	Sleep Powder	Grass	—	75	15
10	Absorb	Grass	20	100	25
13	Growth	Normal	—	—	40
19	Poisonpowder	Poison	—	75	35
22	Vine Whip	Grass	35	100	10
28	Bind	Normal	15	75	20
31	Mega Drain	Grass	40	100	10
37	Stun Spore	Grass	—	75	30
40	Slam	Normal	80	75	20
46	Tickle	Normal	—	100	20

TM/HM

TM/HM#	Name	Type	Power	ACC	PP
TM06	Toxic	Poison	—	85	10
TM09	Bullet Seed	Grass	10	100	30
TM10	Hidden Power	Normal	—	100	15
TM11	Sunny Day	Fire	—	—	5
TM15	Hyper Beam	Normal	150	90	5
TM17	Protect	Normal	—	—	10
TM19	Giga Drain	Grass	60	100	5
TM21	Frustration	Normal	—	100	20
TM22	Solarbeam	Grass	120	100	10
TM27	Return	Normal	—	100	20
TM32	Double Team	Normal	—	—	15
TM36	Sludge Bomb	Poison	90	100	10
TM42	Facade	Normal	70	100	20
TM43	Secret Power	Normal	70	100	20
TM44	Rest	Psychic	—	—	10
TM45	Attract	Normal	—	100	15
TM46	Thief	Dark	40	100	10
HM01	Cut	Normal	50	95	30
HM05	Flash	Normal	—	70	20
HM06	Rock Smash	Fighting	20	100	15

EGG MOVES*

Name	Type	Power	ACC	PP
Amnesia	Psychic	—	—	20
Confusion	Psychic	50	100	25
Flail	Normal	—	100	15
Leech Seed	Grass	—	90	10
Mega Drain	Grass	40	100	10
Nature Power	Normal	—	95	10
Reflect	Psychic	—	—	20

*Learned Via Breeding

MOVE TUTOR
FireRed/LeafGreen and *Emerald* Only

Body Slam*	Double-Edge	Mimic
Substitute	Swords Dance	

*Battle Frontier tutor move (*Emerald*)

115 Kangaskhan™

GENERAL INFO
SPECIES: Parent Pokémon
HEIGHT: 7'03"
WEIGHT: 176 lbs.
ABILITY: Early Bird
Allows Kangaskhan to wake up earlier when put to sleep.

STATS

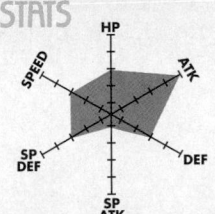

EVOLUTIONS

DOES NOT EVOLVE

LOCATION[S]:

RUBY Rarity: **None**
Trade from *FireRed/LeafGreen*

SAPPHIRE Rarity: **None**
Trade from *FireRed/LeafGreen*

FIRERED Rarity: **Rare**
Safari Zone

LEAFGREEN Rarity: **Rare**
Safari Zone

COLOSSEUM Rarity: **None**
Trade from *FireRed/LeafGreen*

EMERALD Rarity: **None**
Trade from *FireRed/LeafGreen*

XD Rarity: **Only One**
Citadark Island (Capture from Cipher Peon Leden)

MOVES

Level	Attack	Type	Power	ACC	PP
—	Comet Punch	Normal	18	85	15
—	Leer	Normal	—	100	30
7	Bite	Dark	60	100	25
13	Tail Whip	Normal	—	100	30
19	Fake Out	Normal	40	100	10

Level	Attack	Type	Power	ACC	PP
25	Mega Punch	Normal	80	85	20
31	Rage	Normal	20	100	20
37	Endure	Normal	—	—	10
43	Dizzy Punch	Normal	70	100	10
49	Reversal	Fighting	—	100	15

TM/HM#	Name	Type	Power	ACC	PP
TM01	Focus Punch	Fighting	150	100	20
TM03	Water Pulse	Water	60	95	20
TM05	Roar	Normal	—	100	20
TM06	Toxic	Poison	—	85	10
TM07	Hail	Ice	—	—	10
TM10	Hidden Power	Normal	—	100	15
TM11	Sunny Day	Fire	—	—	5
TM13	Ice Beam	Ice	95	100	10

TM/HM#	Name	Type	Power	ACC	PP
TM14	Blizzard	Ice	120	70	5
TM15	Hyper Beam	Normal	150	90	5
TM17	Protect	Normal	—	—	10
TM18	Rain Dance	Water	—	—	5
TM21	Frustration	Normal	—	100	20
TM22	Solarbeam	Grass	120	100	10
TM23	Iron Tail	Steel	75	75	15
TM24	Thunderbolt	Electric	95	100	15
TM25	Thunder	Electric	120	70	10
TM26	Earthquake	Ground	100	100	10
TM27	Return	Normal	—	100	20
TM28	Dig	Ground	60	100	10
TM30	Shadow Ball	Ghost	80	100	15
TM31	Brick Break	Fighting	75	100	15
TM32	Double Team	Normal	—	—	15

TM/HM#	Name	Type	Power	ACC	PP
TM34	Shock Wave	Electric	60	—	20
TM35	Flamethrower	Fire	95	100	15
TM37	Sandstorm	Ground	—	—	10
TM38	Fire Blast	Fire	120	85	5
TM39	Rock Tomb	Rock	50	80	10
TM40	Aerial Ace	Flying	60	—	20
TM42	Facade	Normal	70	100	20
TM43	Secret Power	Normal	70	100	20
TM44	Rest	Psychic	—	—	10
TM45	Attract	Normal	—	100	15
TM46	Thief	Dark	40	100	10
HM01	Cut	Normal	50	95	30
HM03	Surf	Water	95	100	15
HM04	Strength	Normal	80	100	15
HM06	Rock Smash	Fighting	20	100	15

EGG MOVES*

Name	Type	Power	ACC	PP
Counter	Fighting	—	100	20
Crush Claw	Normal	75	95	10
Disable	Normal	—	55	20
Focus Energy	Normal	—	—	30
Foresight	Normal	—	100	40
Safeguard	Normal	—	—	25
Stomp	Normal	65	100	20
Substitute	Normal	—	—	10

*Learned Via Breeding

MOVE TUTOR
FireRed/LeafGreen and *Emerald* Only

Body Slam*	Counter*	Double-Edge
Mega Kick*	Mega Punch*	Mimic
Rock Slide*	Seismic Toss*	Substitute

*Battle Frontier tutor move (*Emerald*)

---

116 Horsea™

GENERAL INFO
SPECIES: Dragon Pokémon
HEIGHT: 1'04"
WEIGHT: 18 lbs.
ABILITY: Swift Swim
Increases Horsea's Speed when it's raining.

STATS

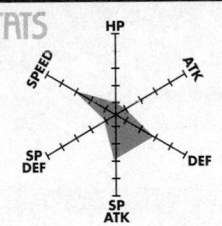

EVOLUTIONS

LV32   TRADE WITH DRAGON SCALE

LOCATION[S]:

RUBY Rarity: **Common**
Routes 132, 133, 134 (Super Rod)

SAPPHIRE Rarity: **Common**
Routes 132, 133, 134 (Super Rod)

FIRERED Rarity: **Common**
Routes 4, 10, 12, 13, 19, 20, 21, 24, Vermilion City

LEAFGREEN Rarity: **Common**
Routes 4, 10, 12, 13, 19, 20, 21, 24, Vermilion City

COLOSSEUM Rarity: **None**
Trade from *Ruby/Sapphire/FireRed/LeafGreen*

EMERALD Rarity: **Common**
Routes 132, 133, 134, Pacifidlog Town

XD Rarity: **None**
Trade from *Ruby/Sapphire/FireRed/LeafGreen*

MOVES

Level	Attack	Type	Power	ACC	PP
—	Bubble	Water	20	100	30
8	Smokescreen	Normal	—	100	20
15	Leer	Normal	—	100	30
22	Water Gun	Water	40	100	25

Level	Attack	Type	Power	ACC	PP
29	Twister	Dragon	40	100	20
36	Agility	Psychic	—	—	30
43	Hydro Pump	Water	120	80	5
50	Dragon Dance	Dragon	—	—	20

TM/HM

TM/HM#	Name	Type	Power	ACC	PP
TM03	Water Pulse	Water	60	95	20
TM06	Toxic	Poison	—	85	10
TM07	Hail	Ice	—	—	10
TM10	Hidden Power	Normal	—	100	15
TM13	Ice Beam	Ice	95	100	10
TM14	Blizzard	Ice	120	70	5
TM17	Protect	Normal	—	—	10
TM18	Rain Dance	Water	—	—	5
TM21	Frustration	Normal	—	100	20

TM/HM#	Name	Type	Power	ACC	PP
TM27	Return	Normal	—	100	20
TM32	Double Team	Normal	—	—	15
TM42	Facade	Normal	70	100	20
TM43	Secret Power	Normal	70	100	20
TM44	Rest	Psychic	—	—	10
TM45	Attract	Normal	—	100	15
HM03	Surf	Water	95	100	15
HM07	Waterfall	Water	80	100	15
HM08	Dive	Water	60	100	10

EGG MOVES*

Name	Type	Power	ACC	PP
Flail	Normal	—	100	15
Aurora Beam	Ice	65	100	20
Disable	Normal	—	55	20
Dragon Rage	Dragon	—	100	10
Dragonbreath	Dragon	60	100	20
Octazooka	Water	65	85	10
Bounce	Flying	85	85	5

*Learned Via Breeding

MOVE TUTOR
FireRed/LeafGreen and *Emerald* Only

Double-Edge	Mimic	Substitute

Emerald Only

Endure*	Icy Wind*	Sleep Talk
Snore*	Swagger*	Swift*

*Battle Frontier tutor move (*Emerald*)

117 Seadra™

WATER

GENERAL INFO

SPECIES: Dragon Pokémon
HEIGHT: 3'11"
WEIGHT: 55 lbs.
ABILITY: Poison Point

The opponent has a 30% chance of being poisoned if Seadra is directly hit.

STATS

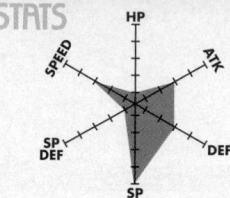

EVOLUTIONS

LV32   TRADE WITH DRAGON SCALE

LOCATION(S):

RUBY   Rarity: **Evolve**
Evolve Horsea

SAPPHIRE   Rarity: **Evolve**
Evolve Horsea

FIRERED   Rarity: **Rare**
Evolve Horsea, Islands One, Three, Five, Six, Seven, Routes 19–21

LEAFGREEN   Rarity: **Evolve**
Evolve Horsea

COLOSSEUM   Rarity: **None**
Trade from *Ruby/Sapphire/FireRed/LeafGreen*

EMERALD   Rarity: **Evolve**
Evolve Horsea

XD   Rarity: **None**
Trade from *Ruby/Sapphire/FireRed/LeafGreen*

MOVES

Level	Attack	Type	Power	ACC	PP	Level	Attack	Type	Power	ACC	PP
—	Bubble	Water	20	100	30	29	Twister	Dragon	40	100	20
—	Smokescreen	Normal	—	100	20	40	Agility	Psychic	—	—	30
—	Leer	Normal	—	100	30	51	Hydro Pump	Water	120	80	5
—	Water Gun	Water	40	100	25	62	Dragon Dance	Dragon	—	—	20

TM/HM

TM/HM#	Name	Type	Power	ACC	PP	TM/HM#	Name	Type	Power	ACC	PP
TM03	Water Pulse	Water	60	95	20	TM27	Return	Normal	—	100	20
TM06	Toxic	Poison	—	85	10	TM32	Double Team	Normal	—	—	15
TM07	Hail	Ice	—	—	10	TM42	Facade	Normal	70	100	20
TM10	Hidden Power	Normal	—	100	15	TM43	Secret Power	Normal	70	100	20
TM13	Ice Beam	Ice	95	100	10	TM44	Rest	Psychic	—	—	10
TM14	Blizzard	Ice	120	70	5	TM45	Attract	Normal	—	100	15
TM15	Hyper Beam	Normal	150	90	5	HM03	Surf	Water	95	100	15
TM17	Protect	Normal	—	—	10	HM07	Waterfall	Water	80	100	15
TM18	Rain Dance	Water	—	—	5	HM08	Dive	Water	60	100	10
TM21	Frustration	Normal	—	100	20						

MOVE TUTOR

FireRed/LeafGreen and *Emerald* Only

Double-Edge	Mimic	Substitute

Emerald Only

Endure*	Icy Wind*	Sleep Talk
Snore*	Swagger	Swift*

*Battle Frontier tutor move (*Emerald*)

---

118 Goldeen™

WATER

GENERAL INFO

SPECIES: Goldfish Pokémon
HEIGHT: 2'00"
WEIGHT: 33 lbs.
ABILITY 1: Swift Swim   **ABILITY 2:** Water Veil

Doubles Goldeen's Speed when it's raining.   *Protects Goldeen from being burned.*

STATS

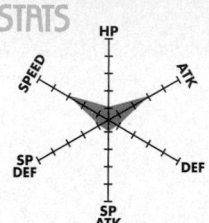

EVOLUTIONS

LV33

LOCATION(S):

RUBY   Rarity: **Common**
Routes 102, 111, 114, 117, 120, Petalburg City, Victory Road, Meteor Falls, Safari Zone

SAPPHIRE   Rarity: **Common**
Routes 102, 111, 114, 117, 120, Petalburg City, Victory Road, Meteor Falls, Safari Zone

FIRERED   Rarity: **Common**
Viridian City, Cerulean Cave, Islands Two, Three, Four, Six, Safari Zone

LEAFGREEN   Rarity: **Common**
Viridian City, Cerulean Cave, Islands Two, Three, Four, Six, Safari Zone

COLOSSEUM   Rarity: **None**
Trade from *Ruby/Sapphire/FireRed/LeafGreen*

EMERALD   Rarity: **Common**
Routes 102, 111, 114, 117, 120, Meteor Falls, Safari Zone, Victory Road

XD   Rarity: **None**
Trade from *Ruby/Sapphire/FireRed/LeafGreen*

MOVES

Level	Attack	Type	Power	ACC	PP	Level	Attack	Type	Power	ACC	PP
—	Peck	Flying	35	100	35	29	Fury Attack	Normal	15	85	20
—	Tail Whip	Normal	—	100	30	38	Waterfall	Water	80	100	15
—	Water Sport	Water	—	100	15	43	Horn Drill	Normal	—	30	5
10	Supersonic	Normal	—	55	20	52	Agility	Psychic	—	—	30
15	Horn Attack	Normal	65	100	25	57	Megahorn*	Bug	120	85	10
24	Flail	Normal	—	100	15						

* Not Available in *Emerald*

TM/HM

TM/HM#	Name	Type	Power	ACC	PP	TM/HM#	Name	Type	Power	ACC	PP
TM03	Water Pulse	Water	60	95	20	TM27	Return	Normal	—	100	20
TM06	Toxic	Poison	—	85	10	TM32	Double Team	Normal	—	—	15
TM07	Hail	Ice	—	—	10	TM42	Facade	Normal	70	100	20
TM10	Hidden Power	Normal	—	100	15	TM43	Secret Power	Normal	70	100	20
TM13	Ice Beam	Ice	95	100	10	TM44	Rest	Psychic	—	—	10
TM14	Blizzard	Ice	120	70	5	TM45	Attract	Normal	—	100	15
TM17	Protect	Normal	—	—	10	HM03	Surf	Water	95	100	15
TM18	Rain Dance	Water	—	—	5	HM07	Waterfall	Water	80	100	15
TM21	Frustration	Normal	—	100	20	HM08	Dive	Water	60	100	10

EGG MOVES*

Name	Type	Power	ACC	PP
Psybeam	Psychic	65	100	20
Hydro Pump	Water	120	80	5
Sleep Talk	Normal	—	—	10
Mud Sport	Ground	—	100	15
Haze	—	—	—	30

*Learned Via Breeding

MOVE TUTOR

FireRed/LeafGreen and *Emerald* Only

Double-Edge	Mimic	Substitute

Emerald Only

Endure*	Icy Wind*	Sleep Talk
Snore*	Swagger	Swift*

*Battle Frontier tutor move (*Emerald*)

119 Seaking™

WATER

GENERAL INFO
SPECIES: Goldfish Pokémon
HEIGHT: 4'03"
WEIGHT: 86 lbs.
ABILITY 1: Swift Swim
Increases Seaking's Speed when it's raining.
ABILITY 2: Water Veil
Protects Seaking from being burned.

STATS
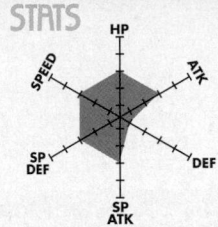

EVOLUTIONS

LV33

LOCATION(S):

RUBY Rarity: **Common**
Evolve Goldeen, Safari Zone

SAPPHIRE Rarity: **Common**
Evolve Goldeen, Safari Zone

FIRERED Rarity: **Rare**
Evolve Goldeen, Three Island, Safari Zone, Fuchsia City

LEAFGREEN Rarity: **Rare**
Evolve Goldeen, Three Island, Safari Zone, Fuchsia City

COLOSSEUM Rarity: **None**
Trade from *Ruby/Sapphire/FireRed/LeafGreen*

EMERALD Rarity: **Common**
Evolve Goldeen, Safari Zone

XD Rarity: **None**
Trade from *Ruby/Sapphire/FireRed/LeafGreen*

MOVES

Level	Attack	Type	Power	ACC	PP	Level	Attack	Type	Power	ACC	PP
—	Peck	Flying	35	100	35	29	Fury Attack	Normal	15	85	20
—	Tail Whip	Normal	—	100	30	41	Waterfall	Water	80	100	15
—	Water Sport	Water	—	100	15	49	Horn Drill	Normal	—	30	5
—/10	Supersonic	Normal	—	55	20	61	Agility	Psychic	—	—	30
15	Horn Attack	Normal	65	100	25	69	Megahorn*	Bug	120	85	10
24	Flail	Normal	—	100	15						

= Emerald Only   * Not Available in Emerald

TM/HM

TM/HM#	Name	Type	Power	ACC	PP	TM/HM#	Name	Type	Power	ACC	PP
TM03	Water Pulse	Water	60	95	20	TM27	Return	Normal	—	100	20
TM06	Toxic	Poison	—	85	10	TM32	Double Team	Normal	—	—	15
TM07	Hail	Ice	—	—	10	TM42	Facade	Normal	70	100	20
TM10	Hidden Power	Normal	—	100	15	TM43	Secret Power	Normal	70	100	20
TM13	Ice Beam	Ice	95	100	10	TM44	Rest	Psychic	—	—	10
TM14	Blizzard	Ice	120	70	5	TM45	Attract	Normal	—	100	15
TM15	Hyper Beam	Normal	150	90	5	HM03	Surf	Water	95	100	15
TM17	Protect	Normal	—	—	10	HM07	Waterfall	Water	80	100	15
TM18	Rain Dance	Water	—	—	5	HM08	Dive	Water	60	100	10
TM21	Frustration	Normal	—	100	20						

MOVE TUTOR
FireRed/LeafGreen and Emerald Only

Double-Edge	Mimic	Substitute

Emerald Only

Endure*	Icy Wind*	Sleep Talk
Snore*	Swagger	Swift*

*Battle Frontier tutor move (*Emerald*)

---

120 Staryu™

WATER

GENERAL INFO
SPECIES: Star Shape Pokémon
HEIGHT: 2'07"
WEIGHT: 76 lbs.
ABILITY 1: Illuminate
When Staryu is in the first slot, the chances of running into a wild Pokémon increase.
ABILITY 2: Natural Cure
When Staryu gets switched out, whatever status condition it had is cured.

STATS
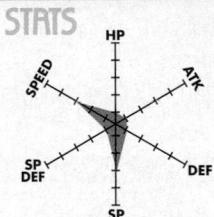

EVOLUTIONS
EVOLVE WITH WATER STONE

LOCATION(S):

RUBY Rarity: **Common**
Lilycove City (Super Rod)

SAPPHIRE Rarity: **Common**
Lilycove City (Super Rod)

FIRERED Rarity: **None**
Trade from *Ruby/Sapphire/LeafGreen*

LEAFGREEN Rarity: **Common**
One Island, Five Island, Pallet Town, Vermilion City (Fish)

COLOSSEUM Rarity: **None**
Trade from *Ruby/Sapphire/LeafGreen*

EMERALD Rarity: **Common**
Lilycove City (Super Rod)

XD Rarity: **None**
Trade from *Ruby/Sapphire/LeafGreen*

MOVES

Level	Attack	Type	Power	ACC	PP	Level	Attack	Type	Power	ACC	PP
—	Tackle	Normal	35	95	35	24	Swift	Normal	60	—	20
—	Harden	Normal	—	—	30	28	Bubblebeam	Water	65	100	20
6	Water Gun	Water	40	100	25	33	Minimize	Normal	—	—	20
10	Rapid Spin	Normal	20	100	40	37	Light Screen	Psychic	—	—	30
15	Recover	Normal	—	—	20	42	Cosmic Power	Normal	—	—	20
19	Camouflage	Normal	—	100	20	46	Hydro Pump	Water	120	80	5

TM/HM

TM/HM#	Name	Type	Power	ACC	PP	TM/HM#	Name	Type	Power	ACC	PP
TM03	Water Pulse	Water	60	95	20	TM27	Return	Normal	—	100	20
TM06	Toxic	Poison	—	85	10	TM29	Psychic	Psychic	90	100	10
TM07	Hail	Ice	—	—	10	TM32	Double Team	Normal	—	—	15
TM10	Hidden Power	Normal	—	100	15	TM33	Reflect	Normal	—	—	20
TM13	Ice Beam	Ice	95	100	10	TM42	Facade	Normal	70	100	20
TM14	Blizzard	Ice	120	70	5	TM43	Secret Power	Normal	70	100	20
TM16	Light Screen	Psychic	—	—	30	TM44	Rest	Psychic	—	—	10
TM17	Protect	Normal	—	—	10	HM03	Surf	Water	95	100	15
TM18	Rain Dance	Water	—	—	5	HM05	Flash	Normal	—	70	20
TM21	Frustration	Normal	—	100	20	HM07	Waterfall	Water	80	100	15
TM24	Thunderbolt	Electric	95	100	15	HM08	Dive	Water	60	100	10
TM25	Thunder	Electric	120	70	10						

MOVE TUTOR
FireRed/LeafGreen and Emerald Only

Double-Edge	Mimic	Substitute
Thunder Wave*		

Emerald Only

Endure*	Icy Wind*	Psych Up*
Sleep Talk	Snore*	Swagger
Swift*		

*Battle Frontier tutor move (*Emerald*)

121 Starmie™

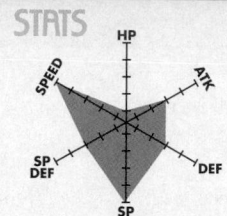

WATER	PSYCHIC

GENERAL INFO
SPECIES: Mysterious Pokémon
HEIGHT: 3'07"
WEIGHT: 176 lbs.
ABILITY 1: Illuminate
When Starmie is in the first slot, the chances of running into a wild Pokémon increase.

ABILITY 2: Natural Cure
When Starmie gets switched out, whatever status condition it had is cured.

STATS

EVOLUTIONS
EVOLVE WITH WATER STONE

LOCATION(S):

RUBY — Rarity: **Evolve**
Evolve Staryu

SAPPHIRE — Rarity: **Evolve**
Evolve Staryu

FIRERED — Rarity: **None**
Trade from *Ruby/Sapphire/LeafGreen*

LEAFGREEN — Rarity: **Evolve**
Evolve Staryu

COLOSSEUM — Rarity: **None**
Trade from *Ruby/Sapphire/LeafGreen*

EMERALD — Rarity: **Evolve**
Evolve Staryu

XD — Rarity: **Only One**
Citadark Island (Capture from Cipher Admin Snattle)

MOVES

Level	Attack	Type	Power	ACC	PP
—	Water Gun	Water	40	100	25
—	Rapid Spin	Normal	20	100	40

Level	Attack	Type	Power	ACC	PP
—	Recover	Normal	—	—	20
—	Swift	Normal	60	—	20
33	Confuse Ray	Ghost	—	100	10

TM/HM

TM/HM#	Name	Type	Power	ACC	PP
TM03	Water Pulse	Water	60	95	20
TM06	Toxic	Poison	—	85	10
TM07	Hail	Ice	—	—	10
TM10	Hidden Power	Normal	—	100	15
TM13	Ice Beam	Ice	95	100	10
TM14	Blizzard	Ice	120	70	5
TM15	Hyper Beam	Normal	150	90	5
TM16	Light Screen	Psychic	—	—	30
TM17	Protect	Normal	—	—	10
TM18	Rain Dance	Water	—	—	5
TM21	Frustration	Normal	—	100	20
TM24	Thunderbolt	Electric	95	100	15
TM25	Thunder	Electric	120	70	10

TM/HM#	Name	Type	Power	ACC	PP
TM27	Return	Normal	—	100	20
TM29	Psychic	Psychic	90	100	10
TM32	Double Team	Normal	—	—	15
TM33	Reflect	Normal	—	—	20
TM42	Facade	Normal	70	100	20
TM43	Secret Power	Normal	70	100	20
TM44	Rest	Psychic	—	—	10
TM48	Skill Swap	Psychic	—	100	10
HM03	Surf	Water	95	100	15
HM05	Flash	Normal	—	70	20
HM07	Waterfall	Water	80	100	15
HM08	Dive	Water	60	100	10

MOVE TUTOR
FireRed/LeafGreen and *Emerald* Only

Double-Edge	Dream Eater*	Mimic
Substitute	Thunder Wave*	

Emerald Only

Endure*	Icy Wind*	Psych Up*
Sleep Talk	Snore*	Swagger
Swift*		

*Battle Frontier tutor move (*Emerald*)

---

122 Mr. Mime™

PSYCHIC

GENERAL INFO
SPECIES: Barrier Pokémon
HEIGHT: 4'03"
WEIGHT: 123 lbs.
ABILITY: Soundproof
Prevents Mr. Mime from being hit by Grasswhistle, Growl, Heal Bell, Hyper Voice, Metal Sound, Perish Song, Roar, Screech, Sing, Snore, Supersonic, and Uproar.

STATS

EVOLUTIONS

DOES NOT EVOLVE

LOCATION(S):

RUBY — Rarity: **None**
Trade from *FireRed/LeafGreen*

SAPPHIRE — Rarity: **None**
Trade from *FireRed/LeafGreen*

FIRERED — Rarity: **Only One**
Trade for Abra on Route 2

LEAFGREEN — Rarity: **Only One**
Trade for Abra on Route 2

COLOSSEUM — Rarity: **None**
Trade from *FireRed/LeafGreen*

EMERALD — Rarity: **None**
Trade from *FireRed/LeafGreen*

XD — Rarity: **Only One**
Citadark Island (Capture from Cipher Admin Gorigan)

MOVES

Level	Attack	Type	Power	ACC	PP
—	Barrier	Psychic	—	—	30
5	Confusion	Psychic	50	100	25
8	Substitute	Normal	—	—	10
12	Mediate	Psychic	—	—	40
15	Doubleslap	Normal	15	85	10
19	Light Screen	Psychic	—	—	30
19	Reflect	Psychic	—	—	20
22	Magical Leaf	Grass	60	—	20

Level	Attack	Type	Power	ACC	PP
26	Encore	Normal	—	100	5
29	Psybeam	Psychic	65	100	20
33	Recycle	Normal	—	100	10
36	Trick	Psychic	—	100	10
40	Role Play	Psychic	—	—	10
43	Psychic	Psychic	90	100	10
47	Baton Pass	Normal	—	—	40
50	Safeguard	Normal	—	—	25

TM/HM

TM/HM#	Name	Type	Power	ACC	PP
TM01	Focus Punch	Fighting	150	100	20
TM04	Calm Mind	Psychic	—	—	20
TM06	Toxic	Poison	—	85	10
TM10	Hidden Power	Normal	—	100	15
TM11	Sunny Day	Fire	—	—	5
TM12	Taunt	Dark	—	100	20
TM15	Hyper Beam	Normal	150	90	5
TM16	Light Screen	Psychic	—	—	30
TM17	Protect	Normal	—	—	10
TM18	Rain Dance	Water	—	—	5
TM20	Safeguard	Normal	—	—	25
TM21	Frustration	Normal	—	100	20
TM22	Solarbeam	Grass	120	100	10
TM24	Thunderbolt	Electric	95	100	15
TM25	Thunder	Electric	120	70	10
TM27	Return	Normal	—	100	20

TM/HM#	Name	Type	Power	ACC	PP
TM29	Psychic	Psychic	90	100	10
TM30	Shadow Ball	Ghost	80	100	15
TM31	Brick Break	Fighting	75	100	15
TM32	Double Team	Normal	—	—	15
TM33	Reflect	Normal	—	—	20
TM34	Shock Wave	Electric	60	—	20
TM41	Torment	Dark	—	100	15
TM42	Facade	Normal	70	100	20
TM43	Secret Power	Normal	70	100	20
TM44	Rest	Psychic	—	—	10
TM45	Attract	Normal	—	100	15
TM46	Thief	Dark	40	100	10
TM48	Skill Swap	Psychic	—	100	10
TM49	Snatch	Dark	—	100	10
HM05	Flash	Normal	—	70	20

EGG MOVES*

Name	Type	Power	ACC	PP
Fake Out	Normal	40	100	10
Future Sight	Psychic	80	90	15
Hypnosis	Psychic	—	60	20
Mimic	Normal	—	—	10
Psych Up	Normal	—	—	10
Trick	Psychic	—	100	10

*Learned Via Breeding

MOVE TUTOR
FireRed/LeafGreen and *Emerald* Only

Body Slam*	Counter*	Double-Edge
Dream Eater*	Mega Kick*	Mega Punch*
Metronome	Mimic	Seismic Toss*
Substitute	Thunder Wave*	

*Battle Frontier tutor move (*Emerald*)

123 Scyther™

BUG | FLYING

GENERAL INFO
SPECIES: Mantis Pokémon
HEIGHT: 4'11"
WEIGHT: 124 lbs.
ABILITY: Swarm
Multiplies Scyther's Bug-type moves when HPs are low.

STATS
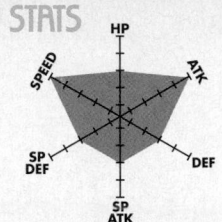

EVOLUTIONS
TRADE WITH METAL COAT

LOCATION[S]:

RUBY Rarity: **None**
Trade from *FireRed*

SAPPHIRE Rarity: **None**
Trade from *FireRed*

FIRERED Rarity: **Rare**
Safari Zone

LEAFGREEN Rarity: **None**
Trade from *FireRed*

COLOSSEUM Rarity: **None**
Trade from *FireRed*

EMERALD Rarity: **None**
Trade from *FireRed*

XD Rarity: **Only One**
Citadark Island (Capture from Cipher Peon Leden)

MOVES

Level	Attack	Type	Power	ACC	PP
—	Quick Attack	Normal	40	100	30
—	Leer	Normal	—	100	30
6	Focus Energy	Normal	—	—	30
11	Pursuit	Dark	40	100	20
16	False Swipe	Normal	40	100	40
21	Agility	Psychic	—	—	30
26	Wing Attack	Flying	60	100	35
31	Slash	Normal	70	100	20
36	Swords Dance	Normal	—	—	30
41	Double Team	Normal	—	—	15
46	Fury Cutter	Bug	10	95	20

TM/HM

TM/HM#	Name	Type	Power	ACC	PP
TM06	Toxic	Poison	—	85	10
TM10	Hidden Power	Normal	—	100	15
TM11	Sunny Day	Fire	—	—	5
TM15	Hyper Beam	Normal	150	90	5
TM17	Protect	Normal	—	—	10
TM18	Rain Dance	Water	—	—	5
TM21	Frustration	Normal	—	100	20
TM27	Return	Normal	—	100	20
TM32	Double Team	Normal	—	—	15
TM40	Aerial Ace	Flying	60	—	20
TM42	Facade	Normal	70	100	20
TM43	Secret Power	Normal	70	100	20
TM44	Rest	Psychic	—	—	10
TM45	Attract	Normal	—	100	15
TM46	Thief	Dark	40	100	10
TM47	Steel Wing	Steel	70	90	25
HM01	Cut	Normal	50	95	30
HM06	Rock Smash	Fighting	20	100	15

EGG MOVES*

Name	Type	Power	ACC	PP
Baton Pass	Normal	—	—	40
Counter	Fighting	—	100	20
Endure	Normal	—	—	10
Light Screen	Psychic	—	—	30
Reversal	Fighting	—	100	15
Safeguard	Normal	—	—	25
Silver Wind	Bug	60	100	5

*Learned Via Breeding

MOVE TUTOR
FireRed/LeafGreen and *Emerald* Only

Counter*	Double-Edge	Mimic
Substitute	Swords Dance*	

*Battle Frontier tutor move (*Emerald*)

---

124 Jynx™

ICE | PSYCHIC

GENERAL INFO
SPECIES: Human Shape Pokémon
HEIGHT: 4'07"
WEIGHT: 90 lbs.
ABILITY: Oblivious
Prevents Jynx from being attracted.

STATS
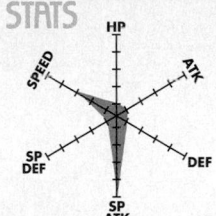

EVOLUTIONS

LV30

LOCATION[S]:

RUBY Rarity: **None**
Trade from *FireRed/LeafGreen*

SAPPHIRE Rarity: **None**
Trade from *FireRed/LeafGreen*

FIRERED Rarity: **Only One**
Trade for Poliwhirl in Cerulean City

LEAFGREEN Rarity: **Only One**
Trade for Poliwhirl in Cerulean City

COLOSSEUM Rarity: **None**
Trade from *FireRed/LeafGreen*

EMERALD Rarity: **None**
Trade from *FireRed/LeafGreen*

XD Rarity: **None**
Trade from *FireRed/LeafGreen*

MOVES

Level	Attack	Type	Power	ACC	PP
—	Pound	Normal	40	100	35
—	Lick	Ghost	20	100	30
—	Lovely Kiss	Normal	—	75	10
—	Powder Snow	Ice	40	100	25
21	Doubleslap	Normal	15	85	10
25	Ice Punch	Ice	75	100	15
35	Mean Look	Normal	—	—	5
41	Fake Tears	Dark	—	100	20
51	Body Slam	Normal	85	100	15
57	Perish Song	Normal	—	—	5
67	Blizzard	Ice	120	70	5

TM/HM

TM/HM#	Name	Type	Power	ACC	PP
TM01	Focus Punch	Fighting	150	100	20
TM03	Water Pulse	Water	60	95	20
TM04	Calm Mind	Psychic	—	—	20
TM06	Toxic	Poison	—	85	10
TM07	Hail	Ice	—	—	10
TM10	Hidden Power	Normal	40	100	15
TM12	Taunt	Dark	—	100	20
TM13	Ice Beam	Ice	95	100	10
TM14	Blizzard	Ice	120	70	5
TM15	Hyper Beam	Normal	150	90	5
TM16	Light Screen	Psychic	—	—	30
TM17	Protect	Normal	—	—	10
TM18	Rain Dance	Water	—	—	5
TM21	Frustration	Normal	—	100	20
TM27	Return	Normal	—	100	20
TM29	Psychic	Psychic	90	100	10
TM30	Shadow Ball	Ghost	80	100	15
TM31	Brick Break	Fighting	75	100	15
TM32	Double Team	Normal	—	—	15
TM33	Reflect	Normal	—	—	20
TM41	Torment	Dark	—	100	15
TM42	Facade	Normal	70	100	20
TM43	Secret Power	Normal	70	100	20
TM44	Rest	Psychic	—	—	10
TM45	Attract	Normal	—	100	15
TM46	Thief	Dark	40	100	10
TM48	Skill Swap	Psychic	—	100	10
HM05	Flash	Normal	—	70	20

MOVE TUTOR
FireRed/LeafGreen and *Emerald* Only

Body Slam*	Counter*	Double-Edge
Dream Eater*	Mega Kick*	Mega Punch*
Metronome	Mimic	Seismic Toss*
Substitute		

*Battle Frontier tutor move (*Emerald*)

125 Electabuzz™

GENERAL INFO
SPECIES: Electric Pokémon
HEIGHT: 3'07"
WEIGHT: 66 lbs.
ABILITY: Static

An opponent has a 30% chance of being paralyzed when it directly strikes Electabuzz.

STATS
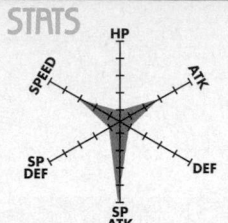

EVOLUTIONS
 LV30

LOCATION[S]:

RUBY	**Rarity: None**
Trade from *FireRed*	
SAPPHIRE	**Rarity: None**
Trade from *FireRed*	
FIRERED	**Rarity: Rare**
Power Plant	
LEAFGREEN	**Rarity: None**
Trade from *FireRed*	
COLOSSEUM	**Rarity: None**
Trade from *FireRed*	
EMERALD	**Rarity: None**
Trade from *FireRed*	
XD	**Rarity: Only One**
Citadark Island (Capture from Cipher Admin Ardos)	

MOVES

Level	Attack	Type	Power	ACC	PP	Level	Attack	Type	Power	ACC	PP
—	Quick Attack	Normal	40	100	30	25	Swift	Normal	60	—	20
—	Leer	Normal	—	100	30	36	Screech	Normal	—	85	40
—	Thunderpunch	Electric	75	100	15	47	Thunderbolt	Electric	95	100	15
17	Light Screen	Psychic	—	—	30	58	Thunder	Electric	120	70	10

TM/HM

TM/HM#	Name	Type	Power	ACC	PP	TM/HM#	Name	Type	Power	ACC	PP
TM01	Focus Punch	Fighting	150	100	20	TM29	Psychic	Psychic	90	100	10
TM06	Toxic	Poison	—	85	10	TM31	Brick Break	Fighting	75	100	15
TM10	Hidden Power	Normal	—	100	15	TM32	Double Team	Normal	—	—	15
TM15	Hyper Beam	Normal	150	90	5	TM34	Shock Wave	Electric	60	—	20
TM16	Light Screen	Psychic	—	—	30	TM42	Facade	Normal	70	100	20
TM17	Protect	Normal	—	—	10	TM43	Secret Power	Normal	70	100	20
TM18	Rain Dance	Water	—	—	5	TM44	Rest	Psychic	—	—	10
TM21	Frustration	Normal	—	100	20	TM45	Attract	Normal	—	100	15
TM23	Iron Tail	Steel	75	75	15	TM46	Thief	Dark	40	100	10
TM24	Thunderbolt	Electric	95	100	15	HM04	Strength	Normal	80	100	15
TM25	Thunder	Electric	120	70	10	HM05	Flash	Normal	—	70	20
TM27	Return	Normal	—	100	20	HM06	Rock Smash	Fighting	20	100	15

MOVE TUTOR
FireRed/LeafGreen and *Emerald* Only

Body Slam*	Counter*	Double-Edge
Mega Kick*	Mega Punch*	Mimic
Seismic Toss*	Substitute	Thunder Wave*

*Battle Frontier tutor move (*Emerald*)

126 Magmar™

GENERAL INFO
SPECIES: Spitfire Pokémon
HEIGHT: 4'03"
WEIGHT: 98 lbs.
ABILITY: Flame Body

If Magmar is struck directly, the opponent has a 30% chance of being burned.

STATS
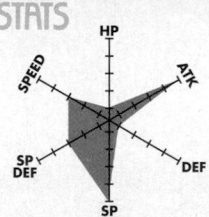

EVOLUTIONS
  LV30

LOCATION[S]:

RUBY	**Rarity: None**
Trade from *LeafGreen*	
SAPPHIRE	**Rarity: None**
Trade from *LeafGreen*	
FIRERED	**Rarity: None**
Trade from *LeafGreen*	
LEAFGREEN	**Rarity: Rare**
One Island	
COLOSSEUM	**Rarity: None**
Trade from *LeafGreen*	
EMERALD	**Rarity: None**
Trade from *LeafGreen*	
XD	**Rarity: Only One**
Citadark Island (Capture from Cipher Peon Grupel)	

MOVES

Level	Attack	Type	Power	ACC	PP	Level	Attack	Type	Power	ACC	PP
—	Ember	Fire	40	100	25	25	Smokescreen	Normal	—	100	20
—	Leer	Normal	—	100	30	33	Sunny Day	Fire	—	—	5
—	Smog	Poison	20	70	20	41	Flamethrower	Fire	95	100	15
—	Fire Punch	Fire	75	100	15	49	Confuse Ray	Ghost	—	100	10
						57	Fire Blast	Fire	120	85	5

TM/HM

TM/HM#	Name	Type	Power	ACC	PP	TM/HM#	Name	Type	Power	ACC	PP
TM01	Focus Punch	Fighting	150	100	20	TM32	Double Team	Normal	—	—	15
TM06	Toxic	Poison	—	85	10	TM35	Flamethrower	Fire	95	100	15
TM10	Hidden Power	Normal	—	100	15	TM38	Fire Blast	Fire	120	85	5
TM11	Sunny Day	Fire	—	—	5	TM42	Facade	Normal	70	100	20
TM15	Hyper Beam	Normal	150	90	5	TM43	Secret Power	Normal	70	100	20
TM17	Protect	Normal	—	—	10	TM44	Rest	Psychic	—	—	10
TM21	Frustration	Normal	—	100	20	TM45	Attract	Normal	—	100	15
TM23	Iron Tail	Steel	75	75	15	TM46	Thief	Dark	40	100	10
TM27	Return	Normal	—	100	20	HM04	Strength	Normal	80	100	20
TM29	Psychic	Psychic	90	100	10	HM06	Rock Smash	Fighting	20	100	15
TM31	Brick Break	Fighting	75	100	15						

MOVE TUTOR
FireRed/LeafGreen and *Emerald* Only

Body Slam*	Counter*	Double-Edge
Mega Kick*	Mega Punch*	Mimic
Seismic Toss*	Substitute	

*Battle Frontier tutor move (*Emerald*)

127 Pinsir™

BUG

GENERAL INFO

SPECIES: Stag Beetle Pokémon
HEIGHT: 4'11"
WEIGHT: 121 lbs.
ABILITY: Hyper Cutter

Pinsir's attack power cannot be decreased.

STATS

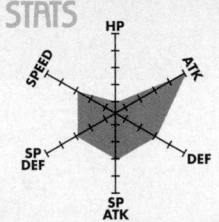

EVOLUTIONS

DOES NOT EVOLVE

LOCATION[S]:

RUBY — Rarity: **Rare**
Safari Zone

SAPPHIRE — Rarity: **Rare**
Safari Zone

FIRERED — Rarity: **None**
Trade from *Ruby/Sapphire/LeafGreen*

LEAFGREEN — Rarity: **Rare**
Safari Zone

COLOSSEUM — Rarity: **None**
Trade from *Ruby/Sapphire/LeafGreen*

EMERALD — Rarity: **Rare**
Safari Zone

XD — Rarity: **Only One**
Citadark Island (Capture from Cipher Peon Grupel)

MOVES

Level	Attack	Type	Power	ACC	PP	Level	Attack	Type	Power	ACC	PP
—	Vicegrip	Normal	55	100	30	25	Revenge	Fighting	60	100	10
—	Focus Energy	Normal	—	—	30	31	Brick Break	Fighting	75	100	15
7	Bind	Normal	15	75	20	37	Guillotine	Normal	—	30	5
13	Seismic Toss	Fighting	—	100	20	43	Submission	Fighting	80	80	25
19	Harden	Normal	—	—	30	49	Swords Dance	Normal	—	—	30

TM/HM

TM/HM#	Name	Type	Power	ACC	PP	TM/HM#	Name	Type	Power	ACC	PP
TM01	Focus Punch	Fighting	150	100	20	TM31	Brick Break	Fighting	75	100	15
TM06	Toxic	Poison	—	85	10	TM32	Double Team	Normal	—	—	15
TM08	Bulk Up	Fighting	—	—	20	TM39	Rock Tomb	Rock	50	80	10
TM10	Hidden Power	Normal	—	100	15	TM42	Facade	Normal	70	100	20
TM11	Sunny Day	Fire	—	—	5	TM43	Secret Power	Normal	70	100	20
TM15	Hyper Beam	Normal	150	90	5	TM44	Rest	Psychic	—	—	10
TM17	Protect	Normal	—	—	10	TM45	Attract	Normal	—	100	15
TM18	Rain Dance	Water	—	—	5	TM46	Thief	Dark	40	100	10
TM21	Frustration	Normal	—	100	20	HM01	Cut	Normal	50	95	30
TM26	Earthquake	Ground	100	100	10	HM04	Strength	Normal	80	100	15
TM27	Return	Normal	—	100	20	HM06	Rock Smash	Fighting	20	100	15
TM28	Dig	Ground	60	100	10						

EGG MOVES*

Name	Type	Power	ACC	PP
Fury Attack	Normal	15	85	20
False Swipe	Normal	40	100	40
Faint Attack	Dark	60	—	20
Flail	Normal	—	100	15

*Learned Via Breeding

MOVE TUTOR

FireRed/LeafGreen and Emerald Only

Body Slam*	Double-Edge	Mimic
Rock Slide*	Seismic Toss*	Substitute
Swords Dance*		

Emerald Only

Endure*	Fury Cutter	Sleep Talk
Snore*	Swagger	

*Battle Frontier tutor move (*Emerald*)

---

128 Tauros™

NORMAL

GENERAL INFO

SPECIES: Wild Bull Pokémon
HEIGHT: 4'07"
WEIGHT: 195 lbs.
ABILITY: Intimidate

An opponent's Attack decreases when Tauros is summoned into battle.

STATS

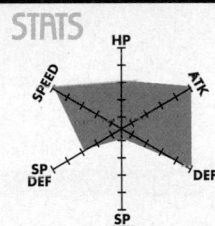

EVOLUTIONS

DOES NOT EVOLVE

LOCATION[S]:

RUBY — Rarity: **None**
Trade from *FireRed/LeafGreen*

SAPPHIRE — Rarity: **None**
Trade from *FireRed/LeafGreen*

FIRERED — Rarity: **Rare**
Safari Zone

LEAFGREEN — Rarity: **Rare**
Safari Zone

COLOSSEUM — Rarity: **None**
Trade from *FireRed/LeafGreen*

EMERALD — Rarity: **None**
Trade from *FireRed/LeafGreen*

XD — Rarity: **Only One**
Citadark Island (Capture from Master Greevil)

MOVES

Level	Attack	Type	Power	ACC	PP	Level	Attack	Type	Power	ACC	PP
—	Tackle	Normal	35	95	35	19	Pursuit	Dark	40	100	20
—	Tail Whip	Normal	—	100	30	26	Swagger	Normal	—	90	15
4	Rage	Normal	20	100	20	34	Rest	Psychic	—	—	10
8	Horn Attack	Normal	65	100	25	43	Thrash	Normal	90	100	20
13	Scary Face	Normal	—	90	10	53	Take Down	Normal	90	85	20

TM/HM

TM/HM#	Name	Type	Power	ACC	PP	TM/HM#	Name	Type	Power	ACC	PP
TM03	Water Pulse	Water	60	95	20	TM27	Return	Normal	—	100	20
TM06	Toxic	Poison	—	85	10	TM32	Double Team	Normal	—	—	15
TM10	Hidden Power	Normal	—	100	15	TM34	Shock Wave	Electric	60	—	20
TM11	Sunny Day	Fire	—	—	5	TM35	Flamethrower	Fire	95	100	15
TM13	Ice Beam	Ice	95	100	10	TM37	Sandstorm	Ground	—	—	10
TM14	Blizzard	Ice	120	70	5	TM38	Fire Blast	Fire	120	85	5
TM15	Hyper Beam	Normal	150	90	5	TM39	Rock Tomb	Rock	50	80	10
TM17	Protect	Normal	—	—	10	TM42	Facade	Normal	70	100	20
TM18	Rain Dance	Water	—	—	5	TM43	Secret Power	Normal	70	100	20
TM21	Frustration	Normal	—	100	20	TM44	Rest	Psychic	—	—	10
TM22	Solarbeam	Grass	120	100	10	TM45	Attract	Normal	—	100	15
TM23	Iron Tail	Steel	75	75	15	HM03	Surf	Water	95	100	15
TM24	Thunderbolt	Electric	95	100	15	HM04	Strength	Normal	80	100	15
TM25	Thunder	Electric	120	70	10	HM06	Rock Smash	Fighting	20	100	15
TM26	Earthquake	Ground	100	100	10						

MOVE TUTOR

FireRed/LeafGreen and Emerald Only

Body Slam*	Double-Edge	Mimic
Substitute		

*Battle Frontier tutor move (*Emerald*)

129 Magikarp™

WATER

GENERAL INFO
SPECIES: Fish Pokémon
HEIGHT: 2'11"
WEIGHT: 22 lbs.
ABILITY: Swift Swim

Increases Magikarp's Speed when it's raining.

STATS
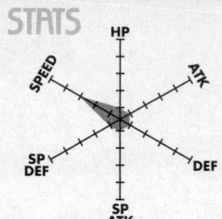

EVOLUTIONS

LV20

LOCATION[S]:

RUBY Rarity: **Common**
All Fishing Holes

SAPPHIRE Rarity: **Common**
All Fishing Holes

FIRERED Rarity: **Common**
All Fishing Holes

LEAFGREEN Rarity: **Common**
All Fishing Holes

COLOSSEUM Rarity: **None**
Trade from *Ruby/Sapphire/ FireRed/LeafGreen*

EMERALD Rarity: **Common**
All Fishing Holes

XD Rarity: **None**
Trade from *Ruby/Sapphire/ FireRed/LeafGreen*

MOVES
Level	Attack	Type	Power	ACC	PP
—	Splash	Normal	—	—	40
15	Tackle	Normal	35	95	35
30	Flail	Normal	—	100	15

TM/HM
TM/HM#	Name	Type	Power	ACC	PP
None					

EGG MOVES*
Name	Type	Power	ACC	PP
None				

*Learned Via Breeding

MOVE TUTOR
FireRed/LeafGreen and *Emerald* Only
None

130 Gyarados™

WATER   FLYING

GENERAL INFO
SPECIES: Atrocious Pokémon
HEIGHT: 21'04"
WEIGHT: 518 lbs.
ABILITY: Intimidate

When Gyarados enters battle, the opponent's Attack lowers.

STATS
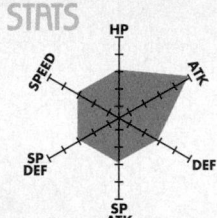

EVOLUTIONS

LV20

LOCATION[S]:

RUBY Rarity: **Common**
Sootopolis City

SAPPHIRE Rarity: **Common**
Sootopolis City

FIRERED Rarity: **Common**
All Fishing Holes

LEAFGREEN Rarity: **Common**
All Fishing Holes

COLOSSEUM Rarity: **None**
Trade from *Ruby/Sapphire/FireRed/LeafGreen*

EMERALD Rarity: **Rare**
Sootopolis City

XD Rarity: **None**
Trade from *Ruby/Sapphire/FireRed/LeafGreen*

MOVES
Level	Attack	Type	Power	ACC	PP		Level	Attack	Type	Power	ACC	PP
—	Thrash	Normal	90	100	20		35	Twister	Dragon	40	100	20
20	Bite	Dark	60	100	25		40	Hydro Pump	Water	120	80	5
25	Dragon Rage	Dragon	—	100	10		45	Rain Dance	Water	—	—	5
30	Leer	Normal	—	100	30		50	Dragon Dance	Dragon	—	—	20
							55	Hyper Beam	Normal	150	90	5

TM/HM
TM/HM#	Name	Type	Power	ACC	PP		TM/HM#	Name	Type	Power	ACC	PP
TM03	Water Pulse	Water	60	95	20		TM27	Return	Normal	—	100	20
TM05	Roar	Normal	—	100	20		TM32	Double Team	Normal	—	—	15
TM06	Toxic	Poison	—	85	10		TM35	Flamethrower	Fire	95	100	15
TM07	Hail	Ice	—	—	10		TM37	Sandstorm	Ground	—	—	10
TM10	Hidden Power	Normal	—	100	15		TM38	Fire Blast	Fire	120	85	5
TM12	Taunt	Dark	—	100	20		TM41	Torment	Dark	—	100	15
TM13	Ice Beam	Ice	95	100	10		TM42	Facade	Normal	70	100	20
TM14	Blizzard	Ice	120	70	5		TM43	Secret Power	Normal	70	100	20
TM15	Hyper Beam	Normal	150	90	5		TM44	Rest	Psychic	—	—	10
TM17	Protect	Normal	—	—	10		TM45	Attract	Normal	—	100	15
TM18	Rain Dance	Water	—	—	5		HM03	Surf	Water	95	100	15
TM21	Frustration	Normal	—	100	20		HM04	Strength	Normal	80	100	20
TM24	Thunderbolt	Electric	95	100	15		HM06	Rock Smash	Fighting	20	100	15
TM25	Thunder	Electric	120	70	10		HM07	Waterfall	Water	80	100	15
TM26	Earthquake	Ground	100	100	10		HM08	Dive	Water	60	100	10

MOVE TUTOR
FireRed/LeafGreen and *Emerald* Only
Body Slam*	Double-Edge	Mimic
Substitute	Thunder Wave*	

Emerald Only
Endure*	Icy Wind*	Sleep Talk
Snore*	Swagger	

*Battle Frontier tutor move (*Emerald*)

131 Lapras™

WATER | ICE

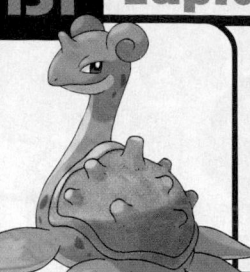

GENERAL INFO
SPECIES: Transport Pokémon
HEIGHT: 8'02"
WEIGHT: 485 lbs.
ABILITY 1: Water Absorb
Lapras gets 1/4 HPs back when a Water-type attack hits it.
ABILITY 2: Shell Armor
Protects Lapras from being hit by a critical hit.

STATS
HP, ATK, DEF, SP ATK, SP DEF, SPEED

EVOLUTIONS

DOES NOT EVOLVE

LOCATION(S):

RUBY Rarity: **None**
Trade from *FireRed/LeafGreen*

SAPPHIRE Rarity: **None**
Trade from *FireRed/LeafGreen*

FIRERED Rarity: **Rare**
Sylph Co., Four Island

LEAFGREEN Rarity: **Rare**
Sylph Co., Four Island

COLOSSEUM Rarity: **None**
Trade from *FireRed/LeafGreen*

EMERALD Rarity: **None**
Trade from *FireRed/LeafGreen*

XD Rarity: **Only One**
Citadark Island (Capture from Cipher Admin Eldes)

MOVES

Level	Attack	Type	Power	ACC	PP
—	Water Gun	Water	40	100	25
—	Growl	Normal	—	100	40
—	Sing	Normal	—	55	15
7	Mist	Ice	—	—	30
13	Body Slam	Normal	85	100	15
19	Confuse Ray	Ghost	—	100	10
25	Perish Song	Normal	—	—	5
31	Ice Beam	Ice	95	100	10
37	Rain Dance	Water	—	—	5
43	Safeguard	Normal	—	—	25
49	Hydro Pump	Water	120	80	5
55	Sheer Cold	Ice	—	30	5

TM/HM

TM/HM#	Name	Type	Power	ACC	PP
TM03	Water Pulse	Water	60	95	20
TM05	Roar	Normal	—	100	20
TM06	Toxic	Poison	—	85	10
TM07	Hail	Ice	—	—	10
TM10	Hidden Power	Normal	—	100	15
TM13	Ice Beam	Ice	95	100	10
TM14	Blizzard	Ice	120	70	5
TM15	Hyper Beam	Normal	150	90	5
TM17	Protect	Normal	—	—	10
TM18	Rain Dance	Water	—	—	5
TM20	Safeguard	Normal	—	—	25
TM21	Frustration	Normal	—	100	20
TM23	Iron Tail	Steel	75	75	15
TM24	Thunderbolt	Electric	95	100	15
TM25	Thunder	Electric	120	70	10
TM27	Return	Normal	—	100	20
TM29	Psychic	Psychic	90	100	10
TM32	Double Team	Normal	—	—	15
TM34	Shock Wave	Electric	60	—	20
TM42	Facade	Normal	70	100	20
TM43	Secret Power	Normal	70	100	20
TM44	Rest	Psychic	—	—	10
TM45	Attract	Normal	—	100	15
HM03	Surf	Water	95	100	15
HM04	Strength	Normal	80	100	20
HM06	Rock Smash	Fighting	20	100	15
HM07	Waterfall	Water	80	100	15
HM08	Dive	Water	60	100	10

EGG MOVES*

Name	Type	Power	ACC	PP
Curse	—	—	—	10
Dragon Dance	Dragon	—	—	20
Foresight	Normal	—	100	40
Horn Drill	Normal	—	30	5
Refresh	Normal	—	100	20
Sleep Talk	Normal	—	—	10
Substitute	Normal	—	—	10
Tickle	Normal	—	100	20

*Learned Via Breeding

MOVE TUTOR
FireRed/LeafGreen and *Emerald* Only

Body Slam* | Double-Edge | Dream Eater*
Mimic | Substitute

*Battle Frontier tutor move (*Emerald*)

---

132 Ditto™

NORMAL

GENERAL INFO
SPECIES: Transform Pokémon
HEIGHT: 1'00"
WEIGHT: 9 lbs.
ABILITY: Limber
Protects Ditto from being paralyzed.

STATS
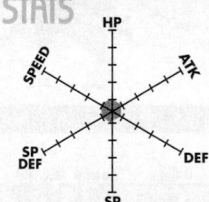
HP, ATK, DEF, SP ATK, SP DEF, SPEED

EVOLUTIONS

DOES NOT EVOLVE

LOCATION(S):

RUBY Rarity: **None**
Trade from *FireRed/LeafGreen*

SAPPHIRE Rarity: **None**
Trade from *FireRed/LeafGreen*

FIRERED Rarity: **Common**
Cerulean Cave, Pokémon Mansion, Route 13, Route 14

LEAFGREEN Rarity: **Common**
Cerulean Cave, Pokémon Mansion, Route 13, Route 14

COLOSSEUM Rarity: **None**
Trade from *FireRed/LeafGreen*

EMERALD Rarity: **None**
Trade from *FireRed/LeafGreen*

XD Rarity: **None**
Trade from *FireRed/LeafGreen*

MOVES

Level	Attack	Type	Power	ACC	PP
—	Transform	Normal	—	—	10

TM/HM

TM/HM# Name	Type	Power	ACC	PP
None				

EGG MOVES*

Name	Type	Power	ACC	PP
None				

*Learned Via Breeding

MOVE TUTOR
FireRed/LeafGreen and *Emerald* Only
None

137 Porygon™

NORMAL

GENERAL INFO
SPECIES: Virtual Pokémon
HEIGHT: 2'07"
WEIGHT: 80 lbs.
ABILITY: Trace
Allows Porygon to copy the opponent's ability.

STATS
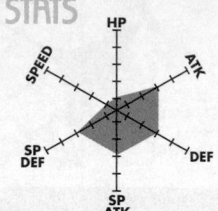

EVOLUTIONS
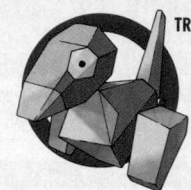

TRADE WITH UP-GRADE

LOCATION(S):

RUBY   Rarity: **None**
Trade from *FireRed/LeafGreen*

SAPPHIRE   Rarity: **None**
Trade from *FireRed/LeafGreen*

FIRERED   Rarity: **Common**
Game Corner: 9,999 Coins

LEAFGREEN   Rarity: **Common**
Game Corner: 6,500 Coins

COLOSSEUM   Rarity: **None**
Trade from *FireRed/LeafGreen*

EMERALD   Rarity: **None**
Trade from *FireRed/LeafGreen*

XD   Rarity: **None**
Trade from *FireRed/LeafGreen*

MOVES

Level	Attack	Type	Power	ACC	PP	Level	Attack	Type	Power	ACC	PP
—	Tackle	Normal	35	95	35	20	Recover	Normal	—	—	20
—	Conversion	Normal	—	—	30	24	Sharpen	Normal	—	—	30
—	Conversion 2	Normal	—	—	30	32	Lock-on	Normal	—	100	5
9	Agility	Psychic	—	—	30	36	Tri Attack	Normal	80	100	10
12	Psybeam	Psychic	65	100	20	44	Recycle	Normal	—	100	10
						48	Zap Cannon	Electric	100	50	5

TM/HM

TM/HM#	Name	Type	Power	ACC	PP	TM/HM#	Name	Type	Power	ACC	PP
TM06	Toxic	Poison	—	85	10	TM25	Thunder	Electric	120	70	10
TM10	Hidden Power	Normal	—	100	15	TM27	Return	Normal	—	100	20
TM11	Sunny Day	Fire	—	—	5	TM29	Psychic	Psychic	90	100	10
TM13	Ice Beam	Ice	95	100	10	TM30	Shadow Ball	Ghost	80	100	15
TM14	Blizzard	Ice	120	70	5	TM32	Double Team	Normal	—	—	15
TM15	Hyper Beam	Normal	150	90	5	TM34	Shock Wave	Electric	60	—	20
TM17	Protect	Normal	—	—	10	TM40	Aerial Ace	Flying	60	—	20
TM18	Rain Dance	Water	—	—	5	TM42	Facade	Normal	70	100	20
TM21	Frustration	Normal	—	100	20	TM43	Secret Power	Normal	70	100	20
TM22	Solarbeam	Grass	120	100	10	TM44	Rest	Psychic	—	—	10
TM23	Iron Tail	Steel	75	75	15	TM46	Thief	Dark	40	100	10
TM24	Thunderbolt	Electric	95	100	15	HM05	Flash	Normal	—	70	20

MOVE TUTOR
FireRed/LeafGreen and *Emerald* Only

Double-Edge	Dream Eater*	Mimic
Substitute	Thunder Wave*	

*Battle Frontier tutor move (Emerald)

---

138 Omanyte™

ROCK   WATER

GENERAL INFO
SPECIES: Spiral Pokémon
HEIGHT: 1'04"
WEIGHT: 17 lbs.
ABILITY 1: Swift Swim   **ABILITY 2:** Shell Armor
Increases Omanyte's Speed when it's raining.   *Prevents Omanyte from receiving critical hits.*

STATS
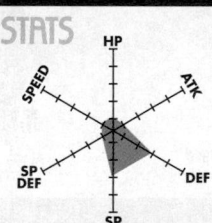

EVOLUTIONS

LV40

LOCATION(S):

RUBY   Rarity: **None**
Trade from *FireRed/LeafGreen*

SAPPHIRE   Rarity: **None**
Trade from *FireRed/LeafGreen*

FIRERED   Rarity: **Only One**
Revive from Helix Fossil

LEAFGREEN   Rarity: **Only One**
Revive from Helix Fossil

COLOSSEUM   Rarity: **None**
Trade from *FireRed/LeafGreen*

EMERALD   Rarity: **None**
Trade from *FireRed/LeafGreen*

XD   Rarity: **None**
Trade from *FireRed/LeafGreen*

MOVES

Level	Attack	Type	Power	ACC	PP	Level	Attack	Type	Power	ACC	PP
—	Withdraw	Normal	—	—	40	31	Leer	Normal	—	100	30
—	Constrict	Normal	10	100	35	37	Protect	Normal	—	—	10
13	Bite	Dark	60	100	25	43	Tickle	Normal	—	100	20
19	Water Gun	Water	40	100	25	49	Ancientpower	Rock	60	100	5
25	Mud Shot	Ground	55	95	15	55	Hydro Pump	Water	120	80	5

TM/HM

TM/HM#	Name	Type	Power	ACC	PP	TM/HM#	Name	Type	Power	ACC	PP
TM03	Water Pulse	Water	60	95	20	TM37	Sandstorm	Ground	—	—	10
TM06	Toxic	Poison	—	85	10	TM39	Rock Tomb	Rock	50	80	10
TM07	Hail	Ice	—	—	10	TM42	Facade	Normal	70	100	20
TM10	Hidden Power	Normal	—	100	15	TM43	Secret Power	Normal	70	100	20
TM13	Ice Beam	Ice	95	100	10	TM44	Rest	Psychic	—	—	10
TM14	Blizzard	Ice	120	70	5	TM45	Attract	Normal	—	100	15
TM17	Protect	Normal	—	—	10	TM46	Thief	Dark	40	100	10
TM18	Rain Dance	Water	—	—	5	HM03	Surf	Water	95	100	15
TM21	Frustration	Normal	—	100	20	HM06	Rock Smash	Fighting	20	100	15
TM27	Return	Normal	—	100	20	HM07	Waterfall	Water	80	100	15
TM32	Double Team	Normal	—	—	15	HM08	Dive	Water	60	100	10

EGG MOVES*

Name	Type	Power	ACC	PP
Aurora Beam	Ice	65	100	20
Bubblebeam	Water	65	100	20
Haze	Ice	—	—	30
Rock Slide	Rock	75	90	10
Slam	Normal	80	75	20
Spikes	Ground	—	—	20
Supersonic	Normal	—	55	20

*Learned Via Breeding

MOVE TUTOR
FireRed/LeafGreen and *Emerald* Only

Body Slam*	Double-Edge*	Mimic
Rock Slide*	Substitute	

*Battle Frontier tutor move (Emerald)

139 Omastar™

ROCK | WATER

GENERAL INFO
SPECIES: Spiral Pokémon
HEIGHT: 3'03"
WEIGHT: 77 lbs.
ABILITY 1: Swift Swim
Increases Omastar's Speed when it's raining.

ABILITY 2: Shell Armor
Prevents Omastar from receiving critical hits.

STATS
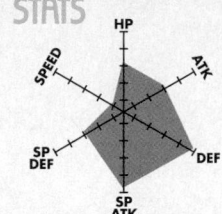

EVOLUTIONS

LV40

LOCATION[S]:

RUBY — Rarity: **None**
Trade from *FireRed/LeafGreen*

SAPPHIRE — Rarity: **None**
Trade from *FireRed/LeafGreen*

FIRERED — Rarity: **None**
Evolve Omanyte

LEAFGREEN — Rarity: **None**
Evolve Omanyte

COLOSSEUM — Rarity: **None**
Trade from *FireRed/LeafGreen*

EMERALD — Rarity: **None**
Trade from *FireRed/LeafGreen*

XD — Rarity: **None**
Trade from *FireRed/LeafGreen*

MOVES

Level	Attack	Type	Power	ACC	PP	Level	Attack	Type	Power	ACC	PP
—	Withdraw	Normal	—	—	40	31	Leer	Normal	—	100	30
—	Constrict	Normal	10	100	35	37	Protect	Normal	—	—	10
—	Bite	Dark	60	100	25	40	Spike Cannon	Normal	20	100	15
—	Water Gun	Water	40	100	25	46	Tickle	Normal	—	100	20
25	Mud Shot	Ground	55	95	15	55	Ancientpower	Rock	60	100	5
						65	Hydro Pump	Water	120	80	5

TM/HM

TM/HM#	Name	Type	Power	ACC	PP	TM/HM#	Name	Type	Power	ACC	PP
TM03	Water Pulse	Water	60	95	20	TM37	Sandstorm	Ground	—	—	10
TM06	Toxic	Poison	—	85	10	TM39	Rock Tomb	Rock	50	80	10
TM07	Hail	Ice	—	—	10	TM42	Facade	Normal	70	100	20
TM10	Hidden Power	Normal	—	100	15	TM43	Secret Power	Normal	70	100	20
TM13	Ice Beam	Ice	95	100	10	TM44	Rest	Psychic	—	—	10
TM14	Blizzard	Ice	120	70	5	TM45	Attract	Normal	—	100	15
TM15	Hyper Beam	Normal	150	90	5	TM46	Thief	Dark	40	100	10
TM17	Protect	Normal	—	—	10	HM03	Surf	Water	95	100	15
TM18	Rain Dance	Water	—	—	5	HM06	Rock Smash	Fighting	20	100	15
TM21	Frustration	Normal	—	100	20	HM07	Waterfall	Water	80	100	15
TM27	Return	Normal	—	100	20	HM08	Dive	Water	60	100	10
TM32	Double Team	Normal	—	—	15						

MOVE TUTOR
FireRed/LeafGreen and *Emerald* Only

Body Slam*	Double-Edge	Mimic
Rock Slide*	Seismic Toss*	Substitute

*Battle Frontier tutor move (*Emerald*)

---

140 Kabuto™

ROCK | WATER

GENERAL INFO
SPECIES: Shellfish Pokémon
HEIGHT: 1'08"
WEIGHT: 25 lbs.
ABILITY 1: Swift Swim
Increases Kabuto's Speed when it's raining.

ABILITY 2: Battle Armor
Prevents Kabuto from receiving critical hits.

STATS
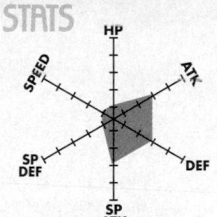

EVOLUTIONS

LV40

LOCATION[S]:

RUBY — Rarity: **None**
Trade from *FireRed/LeafGreen*

SAPPHIRE — Rarity: **None**
Trade from *FireRed/LeafGreen*

FIRERED — Rarity: **Only One**
Revive from Dome Fossil

LEAFGREEN — Rarity: **Only One**
Revive from Dome Fossil

COLOSSEUM — Rarity: **None**
Trade from *FireRed/LeafGreen*

EMERALD — Rarity: **None**
Trade from *FireRed/LeafGreen*

XD — Rarity: **None**
Trade from *FireRed/LeafGreen*

MOVES

Level	Attack	Type	Power	ACC	PP	Level	Attack	Type	Power	ACC	PP
—	Scratch	Normal	40	100	35	31	Sand-Attack	Ground	—	100	15
—	Harden	Normal	—	—	30	37	Endure	Normal	—	—	10
13	Absorb	Grass	20	100	25	43	Metal Sound	Steel	—	85	40
19	Leer	Normal	—	100	30	49	Mega Drain	Grass	40	100	10
25	Mud Shot	Ground	55	95	15	55	Ancientpower	Rock	60	100	5

TM/HM

TM/HM#	Name	Type	Power	ACC	PP	TM/HM#	Name	Type	Power	ACC	PP
TM03	Water Pulse	Water	60	95	20	TM32	Double Team	Normal	—	—	15
TM06	Toxic	Poison	—	85	10	TM37	Sandstorm	Ground	—	—	10
TM07	Hail	Ice	—	—	10	TM39	Rock Tomb	Rock	50	80	10
TM10	Hidden Power	Normal	—	100	15	TM40	Aerial Ace	Flying	60	—	20
TM13	Ice Beam	Ice	95	100	10	TM42	Facade	Normal	70	100	20
TM14	Blizzard	Ice	120	70	5	TM43	Secret Power	Normal	70	100	20
TM17	Protect	Normal	—	—	10	TM44	Rest	Psychic	—	—	10
TM18	Rain Dance	Water	—	—	5	TM45	Attract	Normal	—	100	15
TM19	Giga Drain	Grass	60	100	5	TM46	Thief	Dark	40	100	10
TM21	Frustration	Normal	—	100	20	HM03	Surf	Water	95	100	15
TM27	Return	Normal	—	100	20	HM06	Rock Smash	Fighting	20	100	15
TM28	Dig	Ground	60	100	10	HM07	Waterfall	Water	80	100	15

EGG MOVES*

Name	Type	Power	ACC	PP
Aurora Beam	Ice	65	100	20
Bubblebeam	Water	65	100	20
Confuse Ray	Ghost	—	100	10
Dig	Ground	60	100	10
Flail	Normal	—	100	15
Knock Off	Dark	20	100	20
Rapid Spin	Normal	20	100	40

*Learned Via Breeding

MOVE TUTOR
FireRed/LeafGreen and *Emerald* Only

Body Slam*	Double-Edge	Mimic
Rock Slide*	Substitute	

*Battle Frontier tutor move (*Emerald*)

141 Kabutops™

ROCK   WATER

GENERAL INFO
SPECIES: Shellfish Pokémon
HEIGHT: 4'03"
WEIGHT: 89 lbs.
ABILITY 1: Swift Swim
Increases Kabutops's Speed when it's raining.
ABILITY 2: Battle Armor
Prevents Kabutops from receiving critical hits.

STATS
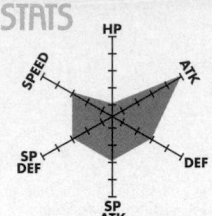

EVOLUTIONS

LV40

LOCATION[S]:

RUBY — **Rarity: None**
Trade from *FireRed/LeafGreen*

SAPPHIRE — **Rarity: None**
Trade from *FireRed/LeafGreen*

FIRERED — **Rarity: Evolve**
Evolve Kabuto

LEAFGREEN — **Rarity: Evolve**
Evolve Kabuto

COLOSSEUM — **Rarity: None**
Trade from *FireRed/LeafGreen*

EMERALD — **Rarity: None**
Trade from *FireRed/LeafGreen*

XD — **Rarity: None**
Trade from *FireRed/LeafGreen*

MOVES

Level	Attack	Type	Power	ACC	PP	Level	Attack	Type	Power	ACC	PP
—	Fury Cutter	Bug	10	95	20	31	Sand Attack	Ground	—	100	15
—	Scratch	Normal	40	100	35	37	Endure	Normal	—	—	10
—	Harden	Normal	—	—	30	40	Slash	Normal	70	100	20
—	Absorb	Grass	20	100	20	46	Metal Sound	Steel	—	85	40
—	Leer	Normal	—	100	30	55	Mega Drain	Grass	40	100	10
25	Mud Shot	Ground	55	95	15	65	Ancientpower	Rock	60	100	5

TM/HM

TM/HM#	Name	Type	Power	ACC	PP	TM/HM#	Name	Type	Power	ACC	PP
TM03	Water Pulse	Water	60	95	20	TM32	Double Team	Normal	—	—	15
TM06	Toxic	Poison	—	85	10	TM37	Sandstorm	Ground	—	—	10
TM07	Hail	Ice	—	—	10	TM39	Rock Tomb	Rock	50	80	10
TM10	Hidden Power	Normal	—	100	15	TM40	Aerial Ace	Flying	60	—	20
TM13	Ice Beam	Ice	95	100	10	TM42	Facade	Normal	70	100	20
TM14	Blizzard	Ice	120	70	5	TM43	Secret Power	Normal	70	100	20
TM15	Hyper Beam	Normal	150	90	5	TM44	Rest	Psychic	—	—	10
TM17	Protect	Normal	—	—	10	TM45	Attract	Normal	—	100	15
TM18	Rain Dance	Water	—	—	5	TM46	Thief	Dark	40	100	10
TM19	Giga Drain	Grass	60	100	5	HM01	Cut	Normal	50	95	30
TM21	Frustration	Normal	—	100	20	HM03	Surf	Water	95	100	15
TM27	Return	Normal	—	100	20	HM06	Rock Smash	Fighting	20	100	15
TM28	Dig	Ground	60	100	10	HM07	Waterfall	Water	80	100	15
TM31	Brick Break	Fighting	75	100	15	HM08	Dive	Water	60	100	10

MOVE TUTOR
FireRed/LeafGreen and *Emerald* Only

Body Slam*	Double-Edge	Mega Kick*
Mimic	Rock Slide*	Seismic Toss*
Substitute	Swords Dance*	

*Battle Frontier tutor move (Emerald)

---

142 Aerodactyl™

ROCK   FLYING

GENERAL INFO
SPECIES: Fossil Pokémon
HEIGHT: 5'11"
WEIGHT: 130 lbs.
ABILITY 1: Pressure
When an opponent damages Aerodactyl, it uses 2 PPs for that move.
ABILITY 2: Rock Head
Aerodactyl doesn't take recoil damage.

STATS
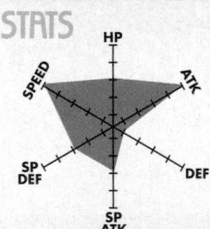

EVOLUTIONS

DOES NOT EVOLVE

LOCATION[S]:

RUBY — **Rarity: None**
Trade from *FireRed/LeafGreen*

SAPPHIRE — **Rarity: None**
Trade from *FireRed/LeafGreen*

FIRERED — **Rarity: Only One**
Revive the Old Amber (Found in Pewter Museum)

LEAFGREEN — **Rarity: Only One**
Revive the Old Amber (Found in Pewter Museum)

COLOSSEUM — **Rarity: None**
Trade from *FireRed/LeafGreen*

EMERALD — **Rarity: None**
Trade from *FireRed/LeafGreen*

XD — **Rarity: None**
Trade from *FireRed/LeafGreen*

MOVES

Level	Attack	Type	Power	ACC	PP	Level	Attack	Type	Power	ACC	PP
—	Wing Attack	Flying	60	100	35	29	Ancientpower	Rock	60	100	5
8	Agility	Psychic	—	—	30	36	Scary Face	Normal	—	90	10
15	Bite	Dark	60	100	25	43	Take Down	Normal	90	85	20
22	Supersonic	Normal	—	55	20	50	Hyper Beam	Normal	150	90	5

TM/HM

TM/HM#	Name	Type	Power	ACC	PP	TM/HM#	Name	Type	Power	ACC	PP
TM02	Dragon Claw	Dragon	80	100	15	TM37	Sandstorm	Ground	—	—	10
TM05	Roar	Normal	—	100	20	TM38	Fire Blast	Fire	120	85	5
TM06	Toxic	Poison	—	85	10	TM39	Rock Tomb	Rock	50	80	10
TM10	Hidden Power	Normal	—	100	15	TM40	Aerial Ace	Flying	60	—	20
TM11	Sunny Day	Fire	—	—	5	TM41	Torment	Dark	—	100	15
TM12	Taunt	Dark	—	100	20	TM42	Facade	Normal	70	100	20
TM15	Hyper Beam	Normal	150	90	5	TM43	Secret Power	Normal	70	100	20
TM17	Protect	Normal	—	—	10	TM44	Rest	Psychic	—	—	10
TM18	Rain Dance	Water	—	—	5	TM45	Attract	Normal	—	100	15
TM21	Frustration	Normal	—	100	20	TM46	Thief	Dark	40	100	10
TM23	Iron Tail	Steel	75	75	15	TM47	Steel Wing	Steel	70	90	25
TM26	Earthquake	Ground	100	100	10	HM02	Fly	Flying	70	95	15
TM27	Return	Normal	—	100	20	HM04	Strength	Normal	80	100	15
TM32	Double Team	Normal	—	—	15	HM06	Rock Smash	Fighting	20	100	15
TM35	Flamethrower	Fire	95	100	15						

EGG MOVES*

Name	Type	Power	ACC	PP
Curse	—	—	—	10
Dragonbreath	Dragon	60	100	20
Foresight	Normal	—	—	40
Pursuit	Dark	40	100	20
Steel Wing	Steel	70	90	25
Whirlwind	Normal	—	100	20

*Learned Via Breeding

MOVE TUTOR
FireRed/LeafGreen and *Emerald* Only

Double-Edge	Mimic	Rock Slide*
Substitute		

*Battle Frontier tutor move (Emerald)

143 Snorlax™

NORMAL

GENERAL INFO

SPECIES: Sleeping Pokémon
HEIGHT: 6'11"
WEIGHT: 1014 lbs.
ABILITY 1: Immunity
Prevents Snorlax from being poisoned.

ABILITY 2: Thick Fat
Fire-type and Ice-type attacks are half the damage on Snorlax.

STATS

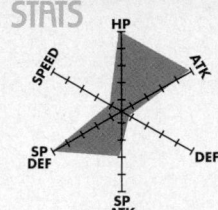

EVOLUTIONS

DOES NOT EVOLVE

LOCATION(S):

RUBY — Rarity: **None**
Trade from FireRed/LeafGreen

SAPPHIRE — Rarity: **None**
Trade from FireRed/LeafGreen

FIRERED — Rarity: **Only Two**
Route 12, Route 16

LEAFGREEN — Rarity: **Only Two**
Route 12, Route 16

COLOSSEUM — Rarity: **None**
Trade from FireRed/LeafGreen

EMERALD — Rarity: **None**
Trade from FireRed/LeafGreen

XD — Rarity: **Only One**
Citadark Island (Capture from Cipher Peon Ardos)

MOVES

Level	Attack	Type	Power	ACC	PP	Level	Attack	Type	Power	ACC	PP
—	Tackle	Normal	35	95	35	29	Snore	Normal	40	100	15
5	Amnesia	Psychic	—	—	20	33	Body Slam	Normal	85	100	15
9	Defense Curl	Normal	—	—	40	37	Sleep Talk	Normal	—	—	10
13	Belly Drum	Normal	—	—	10	41	Block	Normal	—	100	5
17	Headbutt	Normal	70	100	15	45	Covet	Normal	40	100	40
21	Yawn	Normal	—	100	10	49	Rollout	Rock	30	90	20
25	Rest	Psychic	—	—	10	53	Hyper Beam	Normal	150	90	5

TM/HM

TM/HM#	Name	Type	Power	ACC	PP	TM/HM#	Name	Type	Power	ACC	PP
TM01	Focus Punch	Fighting	150	100	20	TM29	Psychic	Psychic	90	100	10
TM03	Water Pulse	Water	60	95	20	TM30	Shadow Ball	Ghost	80	100	15
TM06	Toxic	Poison	—	85	10	TM31	Brick Break	Fighting	75	100	15
TM10	Hidden Power	Normal	—	100	15	TM32	Double Team	Normal	—	—	15
TM11	Sunny Day	Fire	—	—	5	TM34	Shock Wave	Electric	60	—	20
TM13	Ice Beam	Ice	95	100	10	TM35	Flamethrower	Fire	95	100	15
TM14	Blizzard	Ice	120	70	5	TM37	Sandstorm	Ground	—	—	10
TM15	Hyper Beam	Normal	150	90	5	TM38	Fire Blast	Fire	120	85	5
TM17	Protect	Normal	—	—	10	TM39	Rock Tomb	Rock	50	80	10
TM18	Rain Dance	Water	—	—	5	TM42	Facade	Normal	70	100	20
TM21	Frustration	Normal	—	100	20	TM43	Secret Power	Normal	70	100	20
TM22	Solarbeam	Grass	120	100	10	TM44	Rest	Psychic	—	—	10
TM24	Thunderbolt	Electric	95	100	15	TM45	Attract	Normal	—	100	15
TM25	Thunder	Electric	120	70	10	HM03	Surf	Water	95	100	15
TM26	Earthquake	Ground	100	100	10	HM04	Strength	Normal	80	100	20
TM27	Return	Normal	—	100	20						

EGG MOVES*

Name	Type	Power	ACC	PP
Charm	Normal	—	100	20
Curse	—	—	—	10
Double-Edge	Normal	120	100	15
Fissure	Ground	—	30	5
Lick	Ghost	20	100	30
Substitute	Normal	—	—	10

*Learned Via Breeding

MOVE TUTOR

FireRed/LeafGreen and *Emerald* Only

Body Slam*	Counter*	Double-Edge
Mega Kick*	Mega Punch*	Metronome
Mimic	Rock Slide*	Seismic Toss*
Substitute		

*Battle Frontier tutor move (*Emerald*)

---

144 Articuno™

ICE   FLYING

GENERAL INFO

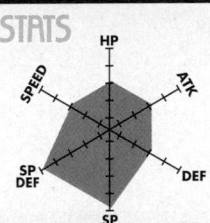

SPECIES: Freeze Pokémon
HEIGHT: 5'07"
WEIGHT: 122 lbs.
ABILITY: Pressure
Opponent uses 2 PPs for damage inflicted against Articuno.

STATS

EVOLUTIONS

DOES NOT EVOLVE

LOCATION(S):

RUBY — Rarity: **None**
Trade from FireRed/LeafGreen

SAPPHIRE — Rarity: **None**
Trade from FireRed/LeafGreen

FIRERED — Rarity: **Only One**
Seafoam Islands

LEAFGREEN — Rarity: **Only One**
Seafoam Islands

COLOSSEUM — Rarity: **None**
Trade from FireRed/LeafGreen

EMERALD — Rarity: **None**
Trade from FireRed/LeafGreen

XD — Rarity: **Only One**
Citadark Island (Capture from Master Greevil)

MOVES

Level	Attack	Type	Power	ACC	PP	Level	Attack	Type	Power	ACC	PP
—	Gust	Flying	40	100	35	37	Mind Reader	Normal	—	—	5
—	Powder Snow	Ice	40	100	25	49	Ice Beam	Ice	95	100	10
13	Mist	Ice	—	—	30	61	Reflect	Psychic	—	—	20
25	Agility	Psychic	—	—	30	73	Blizzard	Ice	120	70	5
						85	Sheer Cold	Ice	—	30	5

TM/HM

TM/HM#	Name	Type	Power	ACC	PP	TM/HM#	Name	Type	Power	ACC	PP
TM03	Water Pulse	Water	60	95	20	TM27	Return	Normal	—	100	20
TM05	Roar	Normal	—	100	20	TM32	Double Team	Normal	—	—	15
TM06	Toxic	Poison	—	85	10	TM33	Reflect	Psychic	—	—	20
TM07	Hail	Ice	—	—	10	TM37	Sandstorm	Ground	—	—	10
TM10	Hidden Power	Normal	—	100	15	TM40	Aerial Ace	Flying	60	—	20
TM11	Sunny Day	Fire	—	—	5	TM42	Facade	Normal	70	100	20
TM13	Ice Beam	Ice	95	100	10	TM43	Secret Power	Normal	70	100	20
TM14	Blizzard	Ice	120	70	5	TM44	Rest	Psychic	—	—	10
TM15	Hyper Beam	Normal	150	90	5	TM47	Steel Wing	Steel	70	90	25
TM17	Protect	Normal	—	—	10	HM02	Fly	Flying	70	95	15
TM18	Rain Dance	Water	—	—	5	HM06	Rock Smash	Fighting	20	100	15
TM21	Frustration	Normal	—	100	20						

MOVE TUTOR

FireRed/LeafGreen and *Emerald* Only

Double-Edge	Mimic	Substitute

145 Zapdos™

ELECTRIC | FLYING

GENERAL INFO
SPECIES: Electric Pokémon
HEIGHT: 5'03"
WEIGHT: 116 lbs.
ABILITY: Pressure
Opponent uses 2 PPs for damage inflicted against Zapdos.

STATS
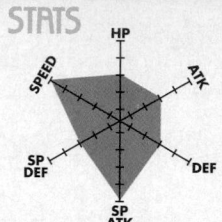

EVOLUTIONS

DOES NOT EVOLVE

LOCATION[S]:

RUBY — Rarity: **None**
Trade from *FireRed/LeafGreen*

SAPPHIRE — Rarity: **None**
Trade from *FireRed/LeafGreen*

FIRERED — Rarity: **Only One**
Power Plant

LEAFGREEN — Rarity: **Only One**
Power Plant

COLOSSEUM — Rarity: **None**
Trade from *FireRed/LeafGreen*

EMERALD — Rarity: **None**
Trade from *FireRed/LeafGreen*

XD — Rarity: **Only One**
Citadark Island (Capture from Master Greevil)

MOVES

Level	Attack	Type	Power	ACC	PP	Level	Attack	Type	Power	ACC	PP
—	Thundershock	Electric	40	100	30	37	Detect	Fight	—	—	5
—	Peck	Flying	35	100	35	49	Drill Peck	Flying	80	100	20
13	Thunder Wave	Electric	—	100	20	61	Charge	Electric	—	100	20
25	Agility	Psychic	—	—	30	73	Light Screen	Psychic	—	—	30
						85	Thunder	Electric	120	70	10

TM/HM#	Name	Type	Power	ACC	PP	TM/HM#	Name	Type	Power	ACC	PP
TM05	Roar	Normal	—	100	20	TM32	Double Team	Normal	—	—	15
TM06	Toxic	Poison	—	85	10	TM34	Shock Wave	Electric	60	—	20
TM10	Hidden Power	Normal	—	100	15	TM37	Sandstorm	Ground	—	—	10
TM11	Sunny Day	Fire	—	—	5	TM40	Aerial Ace	Flying	60	—	20
TM15	Hyper Beam	Normal	150	90	5	TM42	Facade	Normal	70	100	20
TM16	Light Screen	Psychic	—	—	30	TM43	Secret Power	Normal	70	100	20
TM17	Protect	Normal	—	—	10	TM44	Rest	Psychic	—	—	10
TM18	Rain Dance	Water	—	—	5	TM47	Steel Wing	Steel	70	90	25
TM21	Frustration	Normal	—	100	20	HM02	Fly	Flying	70	95	15
TM24	Thunderbolt	Electric	95	100	15	HM05	Flash	Normal	—	70	20
TM25	Thunder	Electric	120	70	10	HM06	Rock Smash	Fighting	20	100	15
TM27	Return	Normal	—	100	20						

MOVE TUTOR
FireRed/LeafGreen and *Emerald* Only

Double-Edge	Mimic	Substitute
Thunder Wave*		

*Battle Frontier tutor move (*Emerald*)

146 Moltres™

FIRE | FLYING

GENERAL INFO
SPECIES: Flame Pokémon
HEIGHT: 6'07"
WEIGHT: 132 lbs.
ABILITY: Pressure
Opponent uses 2 PPs for damage inflicted against Moltres.

STATS
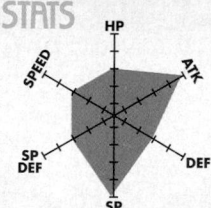

EVOLUTIONS

DOES NOT EVOLVE

LOCATION[S]:

RUBY — Rarity: **None**
Trade from *FireRed/LeafGreen*

SAPPHIRE — Rarity: **None**
Trade from *FireRed/LeafGreen*

FIRERED — Rarity: **Only One**
One Island

LEAFGREEN — Rarity: **Only One**
One Island

COLOSSEUM — Rarity: **None**
Trade from *FireRed/LeafGreen*

EMERALD — Rarity: **None**
Trade from *FireRed/LeafGreen*

XD — Rarity: **Only One**
Citadark Island (Capture from Master Greevil)

MOVES

Level	Attack	Type	Power	ACC	PP	Level	Attack	Type	Power	ACC	PP
—	Wing Attack	Flying	60	100	35	37	Endure	Normal	—	—	10
—	Ember	Fire	40	100	25	49	Flamethrower	Fire	95	100	15
13	Fire Spin	Fire	15	70	15	61	Safeguard	Normal	—	—	25
25	Agility	Psychic	—	—	30	73	Heat Wave	Fire	100	90	10
						85	Sky Attack	Flying	140	90	5

TM/HM#	Name	Type	Power	ACC	PP	TM/HM#	Name	Type	Power	ACC	PP
TM05	Roar	Normal	—	100	20	TM35	Flamethrower	Fire	95	100	15
TM06	Toxic	Poison	—	85	10	TM37	Sandstorm	Ground	—	—	10
TM10	Hidden Power	Normal	—	100	15	TM38	Fire Blast	Fire	120	85	5
TM11	Sunny Day	Fire	—	—	5	TM40	Aerial Ace	Flying	60	—	20
TM15	Hyper Beam	Normal	150	90	5	TM42	Facade	Normal	70	100	20
TM17	Protect	Normal	—	—	10	TM43	Secret Power	Normal	70	100	20
TM18	Rain Dance	Water	—	—	5	TM44	Rest	Psychic	—	—	10
TM20	Safeguard	Normal	—	—	25	TM47	Steel Wing	Steel	70	90	25
TM21	Frustration	Normal	—	100	20	TM50	Overheat	Fire	140	90	5
TM27	Return	Normal	—	100	20	HM02	Fly	Flying	70	95	15
TM32	Double Team	Normal	—	—	15	HM06	Rock Smash	Fighting	20	100	15

MOVE TUTOR
FireRed/LeafGreen and *Emerald* Only

Double-Edge	Mimic	Substitute

147 Dratini™

DRAGON

GENERAL INFO
SPECIES: Dragon Pokémon
HEIGHT: 5'11"
WEIGHT: 7 lbs.
ABILITY: Shed Skin

Status effects only last one turn on Dratini. Has a 30% chance of success.

STATS

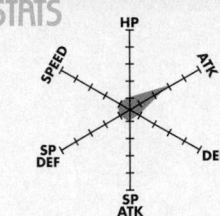

EVOLUTIONS

LV30 LV55

LOCATION(S):

RUBY Rarity: **None**
Trade from *FireRed/LeafGreen*

SAPPHIRE Rarity: **None**
Trade from *FireRed/LeafGreen*

FIRERED Rarity: **Rare**
Safari Zone

LEAFGREEN Rarity: **Rare**
Safari Zone

COLOSSEUM Rarity: **None**
Trade from *FireRed/LeafGreen*

EMERALD Rarity: **None**
Trade from *FireRed/LeafGreen*

XD Rarity: **None**
Trade from *FireRed/LeafGreen*

MOVES

Level	Attack	Type	Power	ACC	PP	Level	Attack	Type	Power	ACC	PP
—	Wrap	Normal	15	85	20	29	Slam	Normal	80	75	20
—	Leer	Normal	—	100	30	36	Agility	Psychic	—	—	30
8	Thunder Wave	Electric	—	100	20	43	Safeguard	Normal	—	—	25
15	Twister	Dragon	40	100	20	50	Outrage	Dragon	90	100	15
22	Dragon Rage	Dragon	—	100	10	57	Hyper Beam	Normal	150	90	5

TM/HM

TM/HM#	Name	Type	Power	ACC	PP	TM/HM#	Name	Type	Power	ACC	PP
TM03	Water Pulse	Water	60	95	20	TM24	Thunderbolt	Electric	95	100	15
TM06	Toxic	Poison	—	85	10	TM25	Thunder	Electric	120	70	10
TM07	Hail	Ice	—	—	10	TM27	Return	Normal	—	100	20
TM10	Hidden Power	Normal	—	100	15	TM32	Double Team	Normal	—	—	15
TM11	Sunny Day	Fire	—	—	5	TM34	Shock Wave	Electric	60	—	20
TM13	Ice Beam	Ice	95	100	10	TM35	Flamethrower	Fire	95	100	15
TM14	Blizzard	Ice	120	70	5	TM38	Fire Blast	Fire	120	85	5
TM15	Hyper Beam	Normal	150	90	5	TM42	Facade	Normal	70	100	20
TM17	Protect	Normal	—	—	10	TM43	Secret Power	Normal	70	100	20
TM18	Rain Dance	Water	—	—	5	TM44	Rest	Psychic	—	—	10
TM20	Safeguard	Normal	—	—	25	TM45	Attract	Normal	—	100	15
TM21	Frustration	Normal	—	100	20	HM03	Surf	Water	95	100	15
TM23	Iron Tail	Steel	75	75	15	HM07	Waterfall	Water	80	100	15

EGG MOVES*

Name	Type	Power	ACC	PP
Dragon Dance	Dragon	—	—	20
Dragonbreath	Dragon	60	100	20
Haze	Ice	—	—	30
Light Screen	Psychic	—	—	30
Mist	Ice	—	—	30
Supersonic	Normal	—	55	20

*Learned Via Breeding

MOVE TUTOR
FireRed/LeafGreen and *Emerald* Only

Body Slam*	Double-Edge	Mimic
Substitute	Thunder Wave*	

*Battle Frontier tutor move (*Emerald*)

---

148 Dragonair™

DRAGON

GENERAL INFO
SPECIES: Dragon Pokémon
HEIGHT: 13'01"
WEIGHT: 36 lbs.
ABILITY: Shed Skin

Status effects only last one turn on Dragonair. Has a 30% chance of success.

STATS

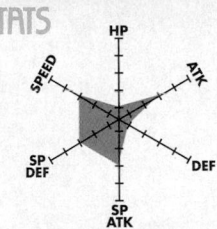

EVOLUTIONS

LV30 LV55

LOCATION(S):

RUBY Rarity: **None**
Trade from *FireRed/LeafGreen*

SAPPHIRE Rarity: **None**
Trade from *FireRed/LeafGreen*

FIRERED Rarity: **Rare**
Evolve Dratini, Safari Zone

LEAFGREEN Rarity: **Rare**
Evolve Dratini, Safari Zone

COLOSSEUM Rarity: **None**
Trade from *FireRed/LeafGreen*

EMERALD Rarity: **None**
Trade from *FireRed/LeafGreen*

XD Rarity: **None**
Trade from *FireRed/LeafGreen*

MOVES

Level	Attack	Type	Power	ACC	PP	Level	Attack	Type	Power	ACC	PP
—	Wrap	Normal	15	85	20	29	Slam	Normal	80	75	20
—	Leer	Normal	—	100	30	38	Agility	Psychic	—	—	30
—	Thunder Wave	Electric	—	100	20	47	Safeguard	Normal	—	—	25
—	Twister	Dragon	40	100	20	56	Outrage	Dragon	90	100	15
22	Dragon Rage	Dragon	—	100	10	65	Hyper Beam	Normal	150	90	5

TM/HM

TM/HM#	Name	Type	Power	ACC	PP	TM/HM#	Name	Type	Power	ACC	PP
TM03	Water Pulse	Water	60	95	20	TM24	Thunderbolt	Electric	95	100	15
TM06	Toxic	Poison	—	85	10	TM25	Thunder	Electric	120	70	10
TM07	Hail	Ice	—	—	10	TM27	Return	Normal	—	100	20
TM10	Hidden Power	Normal	—	100	15	TM32	Double Team	Normal	—	—	15
TM11	Sunny Day	Fire	—	—	5	TM34	Shock Wave	Electric	60	—	20
TM13	Ice Beam	Ice	95	100	10	TM35	Flamethrower	Fire	95	100	15
TM14	Blizzard	Ice	120	70	5	TM38	Fire Blast	Fire	120	85	5
TM15	Hyper Beam	Normal	150	90	5	TM42	Facade	Normal	70	100	20
TM17	Protect	Normal	—	—	10	TM43	Secret Power	Normal	70	100	20
TM18	Rain Dance	Water	—	—	5	TM44	Rest	Psychic	—	—	10
TM20	Safeguard	Normal	—	—	25	TM45	Attract	Normal	—	100	15
TM21	Frustration	Normal	—	100	20	HM03	Surf	Water	95	100	15
TM23	Iron Tail	Steel	75	75	15	HM07	Waterfall	Water	80	100	15

MOVE TUTOR
FireRed/LeafGreen and *Emerald* Only

Body Slam*	Double-Edge	Mimic
Substitute	Thunder Wave*	

*Battle Frontier tutor move (*Emerald*)

149 Dragonite™

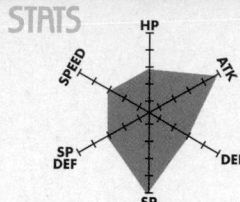

DRAGON | FLYING

GENERAL INFO
SPECIES: Dragon Pokémon
HEIGHT: 7'03"
WEIGHT: 463 lbs.
ABILITY: Inner Focus
Prevents Dragonite from flinching.

STATS

EVOLUTIONS

 LV30  LV55

LOCATION(S):

RUBY Rarity: **None**
Trade from *FireRed/LeafGreen*

SAPPHIRE Rarity: **None**
Trade from *FireRed/LeafGreen*

FIRERED Rarity: **None**
Evolve Dragonair

LEAFGREEN Rarity: **None**
Evolve Dragonair

COLOSSEUM Rarity: **None**
Trade from *FireRed/LeafGreen*

EMERALD Rarity: **None**
Trade from *FireRed/LeafGreen*

XD Rarity: **Only One**
Capture from Miror B.
after shutting down the
Cipher Key Lair

MOVES

Level	Attack	Type	Power	ACC	PP
—	Wrap	Normal	15	85	20
—	Leer	Normal	—	100	30
—	Thunder Wave	Electric	—	100	20
—	Twister	Dragon	40	100	20
22	Dragon Rage	Dragon	—	100	10

Level	Attack	Type	Power	ACC	PP
29	Slam	Normal	80	75	20
38	Agility	Psychic	—	—	30
47	Safeguard	Normal	—	—	25
55	Wing Attack	Flying	60	100	35
61	Outrage	Dragon	90	100	15
75	Hyper Beam	Normal	150	90	5

TM/HM

TM/HM#	Name	Type	Power	ACC	PP
TM01	Focus Punch	Fighting	150	100	20
TM02	Dragon Claw	Dragon	80	100	15
TM03	Water Pulse	Water	60	95	20
TM05	Roar	Normal	—	100	20
TM06	Toxic	Poison	—	85	10
TM07	Hail	Ice	—	—	10
TM10	Hidden Power	Normal	—	100	15
TM11	Sunny Day	Fire	—	—	5

TM/HM#	Name	Type	Power	ACC	PP
TM13	Ice Beam	Ice	95	100	10
TM14	Blizzard	Ice	120	70	5
TM15	Hyper Beam	Normal	150	90	5
TM17	Protect	Normal	—	—	10
TM18	Rain Dance	Water	—	—	5
TM20	Safeguard	Normal	—	—	25
TM21	Frustration	Normal	—	100	20
TM23	Iron Tail	Steel	75	75	15
TM24	Thunderbolt	Electric	95	100	15
TM25	Thunder	Electric	120	70	10
TM26	Earthquake	Ground	100	100	10
TM27	Return	Normal	—	100	20
TM31	Brick Break	Fighting	75	100	15
TM32	Double Team	Normal	—	—	15
TM34	Shock Wave	Electric	60	—	20
TM35	Flamethrower	Fire	95	100	15

TM/HM#	Name	Type	Power	ACC	PP
TM37	Sandstorm	Ground	—	—	10
TM38	Fire Blast	Fire	120	85	5
TM39	Rock Tomb	Rock	50	80	10
TM40	Aerial Ace	Flying	60	—	20
TM42	Facade	Normal	70	100	20
TM43	Secret Power	Normal	70	100	20
TM44	Rest	Psychic	—	—	10
TM45	Attract	Normal	—	100	15
TM47	Steel Wing	Steel	70	90	25
HM01	Cut	Normal	50	95	30
HM02	Fly	Flying	70	95	15
HM03	Surf	Water	95	100	15
HM04	Strength	Normal	80	100	15
HM06	Rock Smash	Fighting	20	100	15
HM07	Waterfall	Water	80	100	15
HM08	Dive	Water	60	100	10

EGG MOVES*

Name	Type	Power	ACC	PP
Dragon Dance	Dragon	—	—	20
Dragonbreath	Dragon	60	100	20
Haze	Ice	—	—	30
Light Screen	Psychic	—	—	30
Mist	Ice	—	—	30
Supersonic	Normal	—	55	20

*Learned Via Breeding

MOVE TUTOR
FireRed/LeafGreen and *Emerald* Only

Body Slam*	Double-Edge	Mimic
Substitute	Thunder Wave*	

*Battle Frontier tutor move (*Emerald*)

150 Mewtwo™

PSYCHIC

GENERAL INFO
SPECIES: Genetic Pokémon
HEIGHT: 6'07"
WEIGHT: 269 lbs.
ABILITY: Pressure
Opponent uses 2 PPs for damage inflicted against Mewtwo.

STATS

EVOLUTIONS

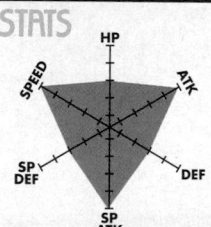 DOES NOT EVOLVE

LOCATION(S):

RUBY Rarity: **None**
Trade from *FireRed/LeafGreen*

SAPPHIRE Rarity: **None**
Trade from *FireRed/LeafGreen*

FIRERED Rarity: **Only One**
Cerulean Cave

LEAFGREEN Rarity: **Only One**
Cerulean Cave

COLOSSEUM Rarity: **None**
Trade from *FireRed/LeafGreen*

EMERALD Rarity: **None**
Trade from *FireRed/LeafGreen*

XD Rarity: **None**
Trade from *FireRed/LeafGreen*

MOVES

Level	Attack	Type	Power	ACC	PP
—	Confusion	Psychic	50	100	25
—	Disable	Normal	—	55	20
11	Barrier	Psychic	—	—	30
22	Mist	Ice	—	—	30
33	Swift	Normal	60	—	20

Level	Attack	Type	Power	ACC	PP
44	Recover	Normal	—	—	20
55	Safeguard	Normal	—	—	25
66	Psychic	Psychic	90	100	10
77	Psych Up	Normal	—	—	10
88	Future Sight	Psychic	80	90	15
99	Amnesia	Psychic	—	—	20

TM/HM

TM/HM#	Name	Type	Power	ACC	PP
TM01	Focus Punch	Fighting	150	100	20
TM03	Water Pulse	Water	60	95	20
TM04	Calm Mind	Psychic	—	—	20
TM06	Toxic	Poison	—	85	10
TM07	Hail	Ice	—	—	10
TM08	Bulk Up	Fighting	—	—	20
TM10	Hidden Power	Normal	—	100	15
TM11	Sunny Day	Fire	—	—	5
TM12	Taunt	Dark	—	100	20

TM/HM#	Name	Type	Power	ACC	PP
TM13	Ice Beam	Ice	95	100	10
TM14	Blizzard	Ice	120	70	5
TM15	Hyper Beam	Normal	150	90	5
TM16	Light Screen	Psychic	—	—	30
TM17	Protect	Normal	—	—	10
TM18	Rain Dance	Water	—	—	5
TM20	Safeguard	Normal	—	—	25
TM21	Frustration	Normal	—	100	20
TM22	Solarbeam	Grass	120	100	10
TM23	Iron Tail	Steel	75	75	15
TM24	Thunderbolt	Electric	95	100	15
TM25	Thunder	Electric	120	70	10
TM26	Earthquake	Ground	100	100	10
TM27	Return	Normal	—	100	20
TM29	Psychic	Psychic	90	100	10
TM30	Shadow Ball	Ghost	80	100	15
TM31	Brick Break	Fighting	75	100	15

TM/HM#	Name	Type	Power	ACC	PP
TM32	Double Team	Normal	—	—	15
TM33	Reflect	Normal	—	—	20
TM34	Shock Wave	Electric	60	—	20
TM35	Flamethrower	Fire	95	100	15
TM37	Sandstorm	Ground	—	—	10
TM38	Fire Blast	Fire	120	85	5
TM39	Rock Tomb	Rock	50	80	10
TM40	Aerial Ace	Flying	60	—	20
TM41	Torment	Dark	—	100	15
TM42	Facade	Normal	70	100	20
TM43	Secret Power	Normal	70	100	20
TM44	Rest	Psychic	—	—	10
TM48	Skill Swap	Psychic	—	100	10
TM49	Snatch	Dark	—	100	10
HM04	Strength	Normal	80	100	15
HM05	Flash	Normal	—	70	20
HM06	Rock Smash	Fighting	20	100	15

EGG MOVES*

Name	Type	Power	ACC	PP
None				

*Learned Via Breeding

MOVE TUTOR
FireRed/LeafGreen and *Emerald* Only

Body Slam*	Counter*	Double-Edge
Dream Eater*	Mega Kick*	Mega Punch*
Metronome	Mimic	Seismic Toss*
Substitute	Thunder Wave*	

*Battle Frontier tutor move (*Emerald*)

151 Mew™

note This character has not been released in the United States.

152 Chikorita™

GRASS

GENERAL INFO
SPECIES: Leaf Pokémon
HEIGHT: 2'11"
WEIGHT: 14 lbs.
ABILITY: Overgrow

When Chikorita's HPs are very low, its Grass-type attacks are multiplied by 1.5.

STATS
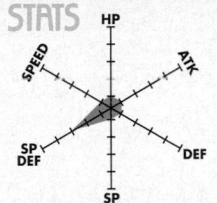

EVOLUTIONS

LV16 LV32

LOCATION(S):

RUBY	Rarity: **None**

Trade Bayleef or Meganium from *Colosseum* then breed

SAPPHIRE	Rarity: **None**

Trade Bayleef or Meganium from *Colosseum* then breed

FIRERED	Rarity: **None**

Trade Bayleef or Meganium from *Colosseum* then breed

LEAFGREEN	Rarity: **None**

Trade Bayleef or Meganium from *Colosseum* then breed

COLOSSEUM	Rarity: **Breed**

Breed in *Ruby/Sapphire/FireRed/LeafGreen* then trade back to *Colosseum*

EMERALD	Rarity: **Only One**

Trade Bayleef or Meganium from *Colosseum* then breed, Littleroot Town

XD	Rarity: **Only One**

Complete Mt. Battle in Story mode

MOVES

Level	Attack	Type	Power	ACC	PP
—	Tackle	Normal	35	95	35
—	Growl	Normal	—	100	40
8	Razor Leaf	Grass	55	95	25
12	Reflect	Psychic	—	—	20
15	Poisonpowder	Poison	—	75	35

Level	Attack	Type	Power	ACC	PP
22	Synthesis	Grass	—	—	5
29	Body Slam	Normal	85	100	15
36	Light Screen	Psychic	—	—	30
43	Safeguard	Normal	—	—	25
50	Solarbeam	Grass	120	100	10

TM/HM

TM/HM#	Name	Type	Power	ACC	PP
TM06	Toxic	Poison	—	85	10
TM09	Bullet Seed	Grass	10	100	30
TM10	Hidden Power	Normal	—	100	15
TM11	Sunny Day	Fire	—	—	5
TM16	Light Screen	Psychic	—	—	30
TM17	Protect	Normal	—	—	10
TM19	Giga Drain	Grass	60	100	5
TM20	Safeguard	Normal	—	—	25
TM21	Frustration	Normal	—	100	20
TM22	Solarbeam	Grass	120	100	10

TM/HM#	Name	Type	Power	ACC	PP
TM23	Iron Tail	Steel	75	75	15
TM27	Return	Normal	—	100	20
TM32	Double Team	Normal	—	—	15
TM33	Reflect	Normal	—	—	20
TM42	Facade	Normal	70	100	20
TM43	Secret Power	Normal	70	100	20
TM44	Rest	Psychic	—	—	10
TM45	Attract	Normal	—	100	15
HM01	Cut	Normal	50	95	30
HM05	Flash	Normal	—	70	20

EGG MOVES*

Name	Type	Power	ACC	PP
Ancientpower	Rock	60	100	5
Counter	Fighting	—	100	20
Flail	Normal	—	100	15
Grasswhistle	Grass	—	55	15
Ingrain	Grass	—	100	20
Leech Seed	Grass	—	90	10
Nature Power	Normal	—	95	20
Vine Whip	Grass	35	100	10

*Learned Via Breeding

MOVE TUTOR
FireRed/LeafGreen and *Emerald* Only

Body Slam*	Counter*	Double-Edge
Mimic	Substitute	Swords Dance*

*Battle Frontier tutor move (*Emerald*)

POKÉMON FACTS

Bulbasaur always has its lunch with it, thanks to the photosynthetic bulb on its back.

POKÉMON FACTS

As if the stench from a Grimer wasn't bad enough, it also leaves bits of itself behind as it slides about the ground, which gradually become new Grimer.

153 Bayleef™

GRASS

GENERAL INFO
SPECIES: Leaf Pokémon
HEIGHT: 3'11"
WEIGHT: 35 lbs.
ABILITY: Overgrow
When Bayleef's HPs are very low, its Grass-type attacks are multiplied by 1.5.

STATS
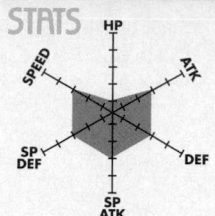

EVOLUTIONS
  LV16  LV32

LOCATION[S]:

RUBY   Rarity: **None**
Trade from *Colosseum*

SAPPHIRE   Rarity: **None**
Trade from *Colosseum*

FIRERED   Rarity: **None**
Trade from *Colosseum*

LEAFGREEN   Rarity: **None**
Trade from *Colosseum*

COLOSSEUM   Rarity: **Only One**
Obtained from Mystery Troop Verde in Phenac City

EMERALD   Rarity: **None**
Trade from *Colosseum*

XD   Rarity: **Evolve**
Evolve Chikorita

MOVES

Level	Attack	Type	Power	ACC	PP	Level	Attack	Type	Power	ACC	PP
—	Tackle	Normal	35	95	35	23	Synthesis	Grass	—	—	5
—	Growl	Normal	—	100	40	31	Body Slam	Normal	85	100	15
—	Razor Leaf	Grass	55	95	25	39	Light Screen	Psychic	—	—	30
—	Reflect	Psychic	—	—	20	47	Safeguard	Normal	—	—	25
15	Poisonpowder	Poison	—	75	35	55	Solarbeam	Grass	120	100	10

TM/HM

TM/HM#	Name	Type	Power	ACC	PP	TM/HM#	Name	Type	Power	ACC	PP
TM06	Toxic	Poison	—	85	10	TM27	Return	Normal	—	100	20
TM09	Bullet Seed	Grass	10	100	30	TM32	Double Team	Normal	—	—	15
TM10	Hidden Power	Normal	—	100	15	TM33	Reflect	Normal	—	—	20
TM11	Sunny Day	Fire	—	—	5	TM42	Facade	Normal	70	100	20
TM16	Light Screen	Psychic	—	—	30	TM43	Secret Power	Normal	70	100	20
TM17	Protect	Normal	—	—	10	TM44	Rest	Psychic	—	—	10
TM19	Giga Drain	Grass	60	100	5	TM45	Attract	Normal	—	100	15
TM20	Safeguard	Normal	—	—	25	HM01	Cut	Normal	50	95	30
TM21	Frustration	Normal	—	100	20	HM04	Strength	Normal	80	100	20
TM22	Solarbeam	Grass	120	100	10	HM05	Flash	Normal	—	70	20
TM23	Iron Tail	Steel	75	75	15	HM06	Rock Smash	Fighting	20	100	15

MOVE TUTOR
FireRed/LeafGreen and *Emerald* Only

Body Slam*	Counter*	Double-Edge
Mimic	Substitute	Swords Dance*

*Battle Frontier tutor move (*Emerald*)

154 Meganium™

GRASS

GENERAL INFO
SPECIES: Herb Pokémon
HEIGHT: 5'11"
WEIGHT: 222 lbs.
ABILITY: Overgrow
When Meganium's HPs are very low, its Grass-type attacks are multiplied by 1.5.

STATS
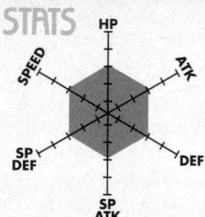

EVOLUTIONS
 LV16 LV32

LOCATION[S]:

RUBY   Rarity: **None**
Trade from *Colosseum*

SAPPHIRE   Rarity: **None**
Trade from *Colosseum*

FIRERED   Rarity: **None**
Trade from *Colosseum*

LEAFGREEN   Rarity: **None**
Trade from *Colosseum*

COLOSSEUM   Rarity: **Evolve**
Evolve Bayleef

EMERALD   Rarity: **Evolve**
Evolve Bayleef

XD   Rarity: **Evolve**
Evolve Bayleef

MOVES

Level	Attack	Type	Power	ACC	PP	Level	Attack	Type	Power	ACC	PP
—	Tackle	Normal	35	95	35	23	Synthesis	Grass	—	—	5
—	Growl	Normal	—	100	40	31	Body Slam	Normal	85	100	15
—	Razor Leaf	Grass	55	95	25	41	Light Screen	Psychic	—	—	30
—	Reflect	Psychic	—	—	20	51	Safeguard	Normal	—	—	25
15	Poisonpowder	Poison	—	75	35	61	Solarbeam	Grass	120	100	10

TM/HM

TM/HM#	Name	Type	Power	ACC	PP	TM/HM#	Name	Type	Power	ACC	PP
TM06	Toxic	Poison	—	85	10	TM26	Earthquake	Ground	100	100	10
TM09	Bullet Seed	Grass	10	100	30	TM27	Return	Normal	—	100	20
TM10	Hidden Power	Normal	—	100	15	TM32	Double Team	Normal	—	—	15
TM11	Sunny Day	Fire	—	—	5	TM33	Reflect	Normal	—	—	20
TM15	Hyper Beam	Normal	150	90	5	TM42	Facade	Normal	70	100	20
TM16	Light Screen	Psychic	—	—	30	TM43	Secret Power	Normal	70	100	20
TM17	Protect	Normal	—	—	10	TM44	Rest	Psychic	—	—	10
TM19	Giga Drain	Grass	60	100	5	TM45	Attract	Normal	—	100	15
TM20	Safeguard	Normal	—	—	25	HM01	Cut	Normal	50	95	30
TM21	Frustration	Normal	—	100	20	HM04	Strength	Normal	80	100	20
TM22	Solarbeam	Grass	120	100	10	HM05	Flash	Normal	—	70	20
TM23	Iron Tail	Steel	75	75	15	HM06	Rock Smash	Fighting	20	100	15

MOVE TUTOR
FireRed/LeafGreen and *Emerald* Only

Body Slam*	Counter*	Double-Edge
Mimic	Substitute	Swords Dance*

*Battle Frontier tutor move (*Emerald*)

155 Cyndaquil™

FIRE

GENERAL INFO

SPECIES: Fire Mouse Pokémon
HEIGHT: 1'08"
WEIGHT: 17 lbs.
ABILITY: Blaze

When Cyndaquil's HPs are very low, its Fire-type attacks are multiplied by 1.5.

STATS

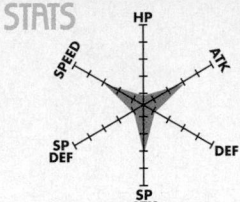

EVOLUTIONS

 LV14  LV36

LOCATION[S]:

RUBY   Rarity: **None**
Trade Quilava or Typhlosion from *Colosseum* then breed

SAPPHIRE   Rarity: **None**
Trade Quilava or Typhlosion from *Colosseum* then breed

FIRERED   Rarity: **None**
Trade Quilava or Typhlosion from *Colosseum* then breed

LEAFGREEN   Rarity: **None**
Trade Quilava or Typhlosion from *Colosseum* then breed

COLOSSEUM   Rarity: **Breed**
Breed in *Ruby/Sapphire/FireRed/LeafGreen* then trade back to *Colosseum*

EMERALD   Rarity: **Only One**
Trade Quilava or Typhlosion from *Colosseum* then breed, Littleroot Town

XD   Rarity: **Only One**
Reward from Battlus for climbing Mt. Battle without switching Pokémon

MOVES

Level	Attack	Type	Power	ACC	PP	Level	Attack	Type	Power	ACC	PP
—	Tackle	Normal	35	95	35	19	Quick Attack	Normal	40	100	30
—	Leer	Normal	—	100	30	27	Flame Wheel	Fire	60	100	25
6	Smokescreen	Normal	—	100	20	36	Swift	Normal	60	—	20
12	Ember	Fire	40	100	25	46	Flamethrower	Fire	95	100	15

TM/HM

TM/HM#	Name	Type	Power	ACC	PP	TM/HM#	Name	Type	Power	ACC	PP
TM06	Toxic	Poison	—	85	10	TM38	Fire Blast	Fire	120	85	5
TM10	Hidden Power	Normal	—	100	15	TM40	Aerial Ace	Flying	60	—	20
TM11	Sunny Day	Fire	—	—	5	TM42	Facade	Normal	70	100	20
TM17	Protect	Normal	—	—	10	TM43	Secret Power	Normal	70	100	20
TM21	Frustration	Normal	—	100	20	TM44	Rest	Psychic	—	—	10
TM27	Return	Normal	—	100	20	TM45	Attract	Normal	—	100	15
TM28	Dig	Ground	60	100	10	TM50	Overheat	Fire	140	90	5
TM32	Double Team	Normal	—	—	15	HM01	Cut	Normal	50	95	30
TM35	Flamethrower	Fire	95	100	15						

EGG MOVES*

Name	Type	Power	ACC	PP
Covet	Normal	40	100	40
Crush Claw	Normal	75	95	10
Foresight	Normal	—	100	40
Fury Swipes	Normal	18	80	15
Howl	Normal	—	—	40
Quick Attack	Normal	40	100	30
Reversal	Fighting	—	100	15
Thrash	Normal	90	100	20

*Learned Via Breeding

MOVE TUTOR

FireRed/LeafGreen and *Emerald* Only

Body Slam*	Double-Edge	Mimic
Substitute		

*Battle Frontier tutor move (*Emerald*)

---

156 Quilava™

FIRE

GENERAL INFO

SPECIES: Volcano Pokémon
HEIGHT: 2'11"
WEIGHT: 42 lbs.
ABILITY: Blaze

When Quilava's HPs are very low, its Fire-type attacks are multiplied by 1.5.

STATS

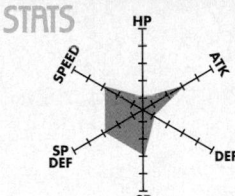

EVOLUTIONS

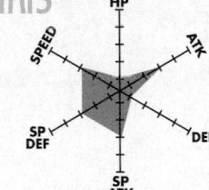 LV14  LV36

LOCATION[S]:

RUBY   Rarity: **None**
Trade from *Colosseum*

SAPPHIRE   Rarity: **None**
Trade from *Colosseum*

FIRERED   Rarity: **None**
Trade from *Colosseum*

LEAFGREEN   Rarity: **None**
Trade from *Colosseum*

COLOSSEUM   Rarity: **Only One**
Phenac City

EMERALD   Rarity: **None**
Trade from *Colosseum*

XD   Rarity: **Evolve**
Evolve Cyndaquil

MOVES

Level	Attack	Type	Power	ACC	PP	Level	Attack	Type	Power	ACC	PP
—	Tackle	Normal	35	95	35	21	Quick Attack	Normal	40	100	30
—	Leer	Normal	—	100	30	31	Flame Wheel	Fire	60	100	25
—	Smokescreen	Normal	—	100	20	42	Swift	Normal	60	—	20
12	Ember	Fire	40	100	25	54	Flamethrower	Fire	95	100	15

TM/HM

TM/HM#	Name	Type	Power	ACC	PP	TM/HM#	Name	Type	Power	ACC	PP
TM01	Focus Punch	Fighting	150	100	20	TM35	Flamethrower	Fire	95	100	15
TM05	Roar	Normal	—	100	20	TM38	Fire Blast	Fire	120	85	5
TM06	Toxic	Poison	—	85	10	TM40	Aerial Ace	Flying	60	—	20
TM10	Hidden Power	Normal	—	100	15	TM42	Facade	Normal	70	100	20
TM11	Sunny Day	Fire	—	—	5	TM43	Secret Power	Normal	70	100	20
TM17	Protect	Normal	—	—	10	TM44	Rest	Psychic	—	—	10
TM21	Frustration	Normal	—	100	20	TM45	Attract	Normal	—	100	15
TM27	Return	Normal	—	100	20	TM50	Overheat	Fire	140	90	5
TM28	Dig	Ground	60	100	10	HM01	Cut	Normal	50	95	30
TM31	Brick Break	Fighting	75	100	15	HM04	Strength	Normal	80	100	15
TM32	Double Team	Normal	—	—	15	HM06	Rock Smash	Fighting	20	100	15

MOVE TUTOR

FireRed/LeafGreen and *Emerald* Only

Body Slam*	Double-Edge	Mimic
Substitute		

*Battle Frontier tutor move (*Emerald*)

157 Typhlosion™

FIRE

GENERAL INFO
SPECIES: Volcano Pokémon
HEIGHT: 5'07"
WEIGHT: 175 lbs.
ABILITY: Blaze
When Typhlosion's HPs are very low, its Fire-type attacks are multiplied by 1.5.

STATS
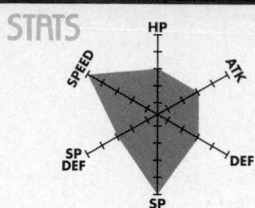

EVOLUTIONS

LV14   LV36

LOCATION[S]:

RUBY — Rarity: **None**
Trade from *Colosseum*

SAPPHIRE — Rarity: **None**
Trade from *Colosseum*

FIRERED — Rarity: **None**
Trade from *Colosseum*

LEAFGREEN — Rarity: **None**
Trade from *Colosseum*

COLOSSEUM — Rarity: **Evolve**
Evolve Quilava

EMERALD — Rarity: **Evolve**
Evolve Quilava

XD — Rarity: **Evolve**
Evolve Quilava

MOVES

Level	Attack	Type	Power	ACC	PP	Level	Attack	Type	Power	ACC	PP
—	Tackle	Normal	35	95	35	21	Quick Attack	Normal	40	100	30
—	Leer	Normal	—	100	30	31	Flame Wheel	Fire	60	100	25
—	Smokescreen	Normal	—	100	20	45	Swift	Normal	60	—	20
—	Ember	Fire	40	100	25	60	Flamethrower	Fire	95	100	15

TM/HM

TM/HM#	Name	Type	Power	ACC	PP	TM/HM#	Name	Type	Power	ACC	PP
TM01	Focus Punch	Fighting	150	100	20	TM32	Double Team	Normal	—	—	15
TM05	Roar	Normal	—	100	20	TM35	Flamethrower	Fire	95	100	15
TM06	Toxic	Poison	—	85	10	TM38	Fire Blast	Fire	120	85	5
TM10	Hidden Power	Normal	—	100	15	TM40	Aerial Ace	Flying	60	—	20
TM11	Sunny Day	Fire	—	—	5	TM42	Facade	Normal	70	100	20
TM15	Hyper Beam	Normal	150	90	5	TM43	Secret Power	Normal	70	100	20
TM17	Protect	Normal	—	—	10	TM44	Rest	Psychic	—	—	10
TM21	Frustration	Normal	—	100	20	TM45	Attract	Normal	—	100	15
TM26	Earthquake	Ground	100	100	10	TM50	Overheat	Fire	140	90	5
TM27	Return	Normal	—	100	20	HM01	Cut	Normal	50	95	30
TM28	Dig	Ground	60	100	10	HM04	Strength	Normal	80	100	15
TM31	Brick Break	Fighting	75	100	15	HM06	Rock Smash	Fighting	20	100	15

MOVE TUTOR
FireRed/LeafGreen and *Emerald* Only

Body Slam*	Counter*	Double-Edge
Mega Kick*	Mega Punch*	Mimic
Rock Slide*	Seismic Toss*	Substitute

*Battle Frontier tutor move (*Emerald*)

158 Totodile™

WATER

GENERAL INFO
SPECIES: Big Jaw Pokémon
HEIGHT: 2'00"
WEIGHT: 21 lbs.
ABILITY: Torrent
When Totodile's HPs are very low, its Water-type attacks are multiplied by 1.5.

STATS
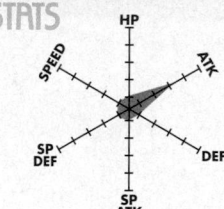

EVOLUTIONS

LV18   LV30

LOCATION[S]:

RUBY — Rarity: **None**
Trade Croconaw or Feraligatr from *Colosseum* then breed

SAPPHIRE — Rarity: **None**
Trade Croconaw or Feraligatr from *Colosseum* then breed

FIRERED — Rarity: **None**
Trade Croconaw or Feraligatr from *Colosseum* then breed

LEAFGREEN — Rarity: **None**
Trade Croconaw or Feraligatr from *Colosseum* then breed

COLOSSEUM — Rarity: **None**
Breed in *Ruby/Sapphire/FireRed/LeafGreen* then trade back to *Colosseum*

EMERALD — Rarity: **Only One**
Trade Croconaw or Feraligatr from *Colosseum* then breed, Littleroot Town

XD — Rarity: **Only One**
Reward from Battlus for climbing Mt. Battle without switching Pokémon

MOVES

Level	Attack	Type	Power	ACC	PP	Level	Attack	Type	Power	ACC	PP
—	Scratch	Normal	40	100	35	20	Bite	Dark	60	100	25
—	Leer	Normal	—	100	30	27	Scary Face	Normal	—	90	10
7	Rage	Normal	20	100	20	35	Slash	Normal	70	100	20
13	Water Gun	Water	40	100	25	43	Screech	Normal	—	85	40
						52	Hydro Pump	Water	120	80	5

TM/HM

TM/HM#	Name	Type	Power	ACC	PP	TM/HM#	Name	Type	Power	ACC	PP
TM01	Focus Punch	Fighting	150	100	20	TM28	Dig	Ground	60	100	10
TM03	Water Pulse	Water	60	95	20	TM31	Brick Break	Fighting	75	100	15
TM06	Toxic	Poison	—	85	10	TM32	Double Team	Normal	—	—	15
TM07	Hail	Ice	—	—	10	TM40	Aerial Ace	Flying	60	—	20
TM10	Hidden Power	Normal	—	100	15	TM42	Facade	Normal	70	100	20
TM13	Ice Beam	Ice	95	100	10	TM43	Secret Power	Normal	70	100	20
TM14	Blizzard	Ice	120	70	5	TM44	Rest	Psychic	—	—	10
TM17	Protect	Normal	—	—	10	TM45	Attract	Normal	—	100	15
TM18	Rain Dance	Water	—	—	5	HM01	Cut	Normal	50	95	30
TM21	Frustration	Normal	—	100	20	HM03	Surf	Water	95	100	15
TM23	Iron Tail	Steel	75	75	15	HM07	Waterfall	Water	80	100	15
TM27	Return	Normal	—	100	20	HM08	Dive	Water	60	100	10

EGG MOVES*

Name	Type	Power	ACC	PP
Ancientpower	Rock	60	100	5
Crunch	Dark	80	100	15
Dragon Claw	Dragon	80	100	15
Hydro Pump	Water	120	80	5
Mud Sport	Ground	—	100	15
Rock Slide	Rock	75	90	10
Thrash	Normal	90	100	20
Water Sport	Water	—	100	15

*Learned Via Breeding

MOVE TUTOR
FireRed/LeafGreen and *Emerald* Only

Body Slam*	Counter*	Double-Edge
Mega Kick*	Mega Punch*	Mimic
Rock Slide*	Seismic Toss*	Substitute
Swords Dance*		

*Battle Frontier tutor move (*Emerald*)

159 Croconaw™

WATER

GENERAL INFO
SPECIES: Big Jaw Pokémon
HEIGHT: 3'07"
WEIGHT: 55 lbs.
ABILITY: Torrent

When Croconaw's HPs are very low, its Water-type attacks are multiplied by 1.5.

STATS

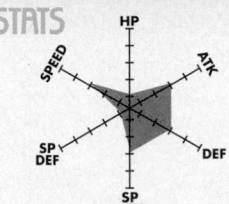

EVOLUTIONS

 LV18  LV30

LOCATION[S]:

RUBY	Rarity: **None**
Trade from *Colosseum*	
SAPPHIRE	Rarity: **None**
Trade from *Colosseum*	
FIRERED	Rarity: **None**
Trade from *Colosseum*	
LEAFGREEN	Rarity: **None**
Trade from *Colosseum*	
COLOSSEUM	Rarity: **Only One**
Phenac City	
EMERALD	Rarity: **None**
Trade from *Colosseum*	
XD	Rarity: **Evolve**
Evolve Totodile	

MOVES

Level	Attack	Type	Power	ACC	PP
—	Scratch	Normal	40	100	35
—	Leer	Normal	—	100	30
—	Rage	Normal	20	100	20
13	Water Gun	Water	40	100	25

Level	Attack	Type	Power	ACC	PP
21	Bite	Dark	60	100	25
28	Scary Face	Normal	—	90	10
37	Slash	Normal	70	100	20
45	Screech	Normal	—	85	40
55	Hydro Pump	Water	120	80	5

TM/HM

TM/HM#	Name	Type	Power	ACC	PP
TM01	Focus Punch	Fighting	150	100	20
TM03	Water Pulse	Water	60	95	20
TM05	Roar	Normal	—	100	20
TM06	Toxic	Poison	—	85	10
TM07	Hail	Ice	—	—	10
TM10	Hidden Power	Normal	—	100	15
TM13	Ice Beam	Ice	95	100	10
TM14	Blizzard	Ice	120	70	5
TM17	Protect	Normal	—	—	10
TM18	Rain Dance	Water	—	—	5
TM21	Frustration	Normal	—	100	20
TM23	Iron Tail	Steel	75	75	15
TM27	Return	Normal	—	100	20
TM28	Dig	Ground	60	100	10

TM/HM#	Name	Type	Power	ACC	PP
TM31	Brick Break	Fighting	75	100	15
TM32	Double Team	Normal	—	—	15
TM40	Aerial Ace	Flying	60	—	20
TM42	Facade	Normal	70	100	20
TM43	Secret Power	Normal	70	100	20
TM44	Rest	Psychic	—	—	10
TM45	Attract	Normal	—	100	15
HM01	Cut	Normal	50	95	30
HM03	Surf	Water	95	100	15
HM04	Strength	Normal	80	100	15
HM06	Rock Smash	Fighting	20	100	15
HM07	Waterfall	Water	80	100	15
HM08	Dive	Water	60	100	10

MOVE TUTOR
FireRed/LeafGreen and *Emerald* Only

Body Slam*	Counter*	Double-Edge
Mega Kick*	Mega Punch*	Mimic
Rock Slide*	Seismic Toss*	Substitute
Swords Dance*		

*Battle Frontier tutor move (*Emerald*)

160 Feraligatr™

WATER

GENERAL INFO
SPECIES: Big Jaw Pokémon
HEIGHT: 7'07"
WEIGHT: 196 lbs.
ABILITY: Torrent

When Feraligatr's HPs are very low, its Water-type attacks are multiplied by 1.5.

STATS

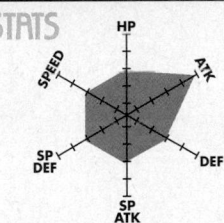

EVOLUTIONS

 LV18  LV30

LOCATION[S]:

RUBY	Rarity: **None**
Trade from *Colosseum*	
SAPPHIRE	Rarity: **None**
Trade from *Colosseum*	
FIRERED	Rarity: **None**
Trade from *Colosseum*	
LEAFGREEN	Rarity: **None**
Trade from *Colosseum*	
COLOSSEUM	Rarity: **Evolve**
Evolve Croconaw	
EMERALD	Rarity: **Evolve**
Evolve Croconaw	
XD	Rarity: **Evolve**
Evolve Croconaw	

MOVES

Level	Attack	Type	Power	ACC	PP
—	Scratch	Normal	40	100	35
—	Leer	Normal	—	100	30
—	Rage	Normal	20	100	20
—	Water Gun	Water	40	100	25

Level	Attack	Type	Power	ACC	PP
21	Bite	Dark	60	100	25
28	Scary Face	Normal	—	90	10
38	Slash	Normal	70	100	20
47	Screech	Normal	—	85	40
58	Hydro Pump	Water	120	80	5

TM/HM

TM/HM#	Name	Type	Power	ACC	PP
TM01	Focus Punch	Fighting	150	100	20
TM02	Dragon Claw	Dragon	80	100	15
TM03	Water Pulse	Water	60	95	20
TM05	Roar	Normal	—	100	20
TM06	Toxic	Poison	—	85	10
TM07	Hail	Ice	—	—	10
TM10	Hidden Power	Normal	—	100	15
TM13	Ice Beam	Ice	95	100	10
TM14	Blizzard	Ice	120	70	5
TM15	Hyper Beam	Normal	150	90	5
TM17	Protect	Normal	—	—	10
TM18	Rain Dance	Water	—	—	5
TM21	Frustration	Normal	—	100	20
TM23	Iron Tail	Steel	75	75	15
TM26	Earthquake	Ground	100	100	10

TM/HM#	Name	Type	Power	ACC	PP
TM27	Return	Normal	—	100	20
TM28	Dig	Ground	60	100	10
TM31	Brick Break	Fighting	75	100	15
TM32	Double Team	Normal	—	—	15
TM40	Aerial Ace	Flying	60	—	20
TM42	Facade	Normal	70	100	20
TM43	Secret Power	Normal	70	100	20
TM44	Rest	Psychic	—	—	10
TM45	Attract	Normal	—	100	15
HM01	Cut	Normal	50	95	30
HM03	Surf	Water	95	100	15
HM04	Strength	Normal	80	100	15
HM06	Rock Smash	Fight	20	100	15
HM07	Waterfall	Water	80	100	15
HM08	Dive	Water	60	100	10

MOVE TUTOR
FireRed/LeafGreen and *Emerald* Only

Body Slam*	Counter*	Double-Edge
Mega Kick*	Mega Punch*	Mimic
Rock Slide*	Seismic Toss*	Substitute
Swords Dance*		

*Battle Frontier tutor move (*Emerald*)

161 Sentret ™

NORMAL

GENERAL INFO
SPECIES: Scout Pokémon
HEIGHT: 2'07"
WEIGHT: 13 lbs.
ABILITY 1: Run Away
Allows Sentret to escape from wild Pokémon.
ABILITY 2: Keen Eye
Protects Sentret from having its Accuracy lowered.

STATS
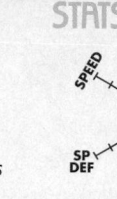

EVOLUTIONS

LV15

LOCATION(S):

RUBY — Rarity: **None**
Trade from *FireRed/LeafGreen*

SAPPHIRE — Rarity: **None**
Trade from *FireRed/LeafGreen*

FIRERED — Rarity: **Common**
Five Island, Six Island, Seven Island

LEAFGREEN — Rarity: **Common**
Five Island, Six Island, Seven Island

COLOSSEUM — Rarity: **Breed**
Trade from *FireRed/LeafGreen*

EMERALD — Rarity: **None**
Trade from *FireRed/LeafGreen*

XD — Rarity: **None**
Trade from *FireRed/LeafGreen*

MOVES

Level	Attack	Type	Power	ACC	PP	Level	Attack	Type	Power	ACC	PP
—	Scratch	Normal	40	100	35	17	Helping Hand	Normal	—	100	20
4	Defense Curl	Normal	—	—	40	24	Slam	Normal	80	75	20
7	Quick Attack	Normal	40	100	30	31	Follow Me	Normal	—	100	20
12	Fury Swipes	Normal	18	80	15	40	Rest	Psychic	—	—	10
						49	Amnesia	Psychic	—	—	20

TM/HM

TM/HM#	Name	Type	Power	ACC	PP	TM/HM#	Name	Type	Power	ACC	PP
TM01	Focus Punch	Fighting	150	100		TM28	Dig	Ground	60	100	10
TM03	Water Pulse	Water	60	95	20	TM30	Shadow Ball	Ghost	80	100	15
TM06	Toxic	Poison	—	85	10	TM31	Brick Break	Fighting	75	100	15
TM10	Hidden Power	Normal	—	100	15	TM32	Double Team	Normal	—	—	15
TM11	Sunny Day	Fire	—	—	5	TM34	Shock Wave	Electric	60	—	20
TM13	Ice Beam	Ice	95	100	10	TM35	Flamethrower	Fire	95	100	15
TM17	Protect	Normal	—	—	10	TM42	Facade	Normal	70	100	20
TM18	Rain Dance	Water	—	—	5	TM43	Secret Power	Normal	70	100	20
TM21	Frustration	Normal	—	100	20	TM44	Rest	Psychic	—	—	10
TM22	Solarbeam	Grass	120	100	10	TM45	Attract	Normal	—	100	15
TM23	Iron Tail	Steel	75	75	15	TM46	Thief	Dark	40	100	10
TM24	Thunderbolt	Electric	95	100	15	HM01	Cut	Normal	50	95	30
TM27	Return	Normal	—	100	20	HM03	Surf	Water	95	100	15

EGG MOVES*

Name	Type	Power	ACC	PP
Assist	Normal	—	100	20
Double-Edge	Normal	120	100	15
Focus Energy	Normal	—	—	30
Pursuit	Dark	40	100	20
Reversal	Fighting	—	100	15
Slash	Normal	70	100	20
Substitute	Normal	—	—	10
Trick	Psychic	—	100	10

*Learned Via Breeding

MOVE TUTOR
FireRed/LeafGreen and *Emerald* Only

Body Slam*	Double-Edge	Mimic
Substitute		

*Battle Frontier tutor move (*Emerald*)

162 Furret ™

NORMAL

GENERAL INFO
SPECIES: Long Body Pokémon
HEIGHT: 5'11"
WEIGHT: 72 lbs.
ABILITY 1: Run Away
Allows Furret to escape from wild Pokémon.
ABILITY 2: Keen Eye
Protects Furret from having its Accuracy lowered.

STATS
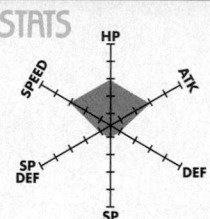

EVOLUTIONS

LV15

LOCATION(S):

RUBY — Rarity: **None**
Evolve Sentret

SAPPHIRE — Rarity: **None**
Evolve Sentret

FIRERED — Rarity: **Evolve**
Evolve Sentret

LEAFGREEN — Rarity: **Evolve**
Evolve Sentret

COLOSSEUM — Rarity: **Only One**
Pyrite Town

EMERALD — Rarity: **None**
Trade from *Colosseum*

XD — Rarity: **None**
Trade from *FireRed/LeafGreen*

MOVES

Level	Attack	Type	Power	ACC	PP	Level	Attack	Type	Power	ACC	PP
—	Scratch	Normal	40	100	35	19	Helping Hand	Normal	—	100	20
—	Defense Curl	Normal	—	—	40	28	Slam	Normal	80	75	20
—	Quick Attack	Normal	40	100	30	37	Follow Me	Normal	—	100	20
12	Fury Swipes	Normal	18	80	15	48	Rest	Psychic	—	—	10
						59	Amnesia	Psychic	—	—	20

TM/HM

TM/HM#	Name	Type	Power	ACC	PP	TM/HM#	Name	Type	Power	ACC	PP
TM01	Focus Punch	Fighting	150	100	20	TM28	Dig	Ground	60	100	10
TM03	Water Pulse	Water	60	95	20	TM30	Shadow Ball	Ghost	80	100	15
TM06	Toxic	Poison	—	85	10	TM31	Brick Break	Fighting	75	100	15
TM10	Hidden Power	Normal	—	100	15	TM32	Double Team	Normal	—	—	15
TM11	Sunny Day	Fire	—	—	5	TM34	Shock Wave	Electric	60	—	20
TM13	Ice Beam	Ice	95	100	10	TM35	Flamethrower	Fire	95	100	15
TM14	Blizzard	Ice	120	70	5	TM42	Facade	Normal	70	100	20
TM15	Hyper Beam	Normal	150	90	5	TM43	Secret Power	Normal	70	100	20
TM17	Protect	Normal	—	—	10	TM44	Rest	Psychic	—	—	10
TM18	Rain Dance	Water	—	—	5	TM45	Attract	Normal	—	100	15
TM21	Frustration	Normal	—	100	20	TM46	Thief	Dark	40	100	10
TM22	Solarbeam	Grass	120	100	10	HM01	Cut	Normal	50	95	30
TM23	Iron Tail	Steel	75	75	15	HM03	Surf	Water	95	100	15
TM24	Thunderbolt	Electric	95	100	15	HM04	Strength	Normal	80	100	15
TM25	Thunder	Electric	120	70	10	HM06	Rock Smash	Fighting	20	100	15
TM27	Return	Normal	—	100	20						

MOVE TUTOR
FireRed/LeafGreen and *Emerald* Only

Body Slam*	Double-Edge	Mimic
Substitute		

*Battle Frontier tutor move (*Emerald*)

163 Hoothoot™

NORMAL | FLYING

GENERAL INFO
SPECIES: Owl Pokémon
HEIGHT: 2'04"
WEIGHT: 47 lbs.
ABILITY 1: Insomnia
Prevents Hoothoot from being put to sleep.

ABILITY 2: Keen Eye
Protects Hoothoot from having its Accuracy lowered.

STATS

EVOLUTIONS

LV20

LOCATION(S):

RUBY — Rarity: **None**
Trade Noctowl from *Colosseum*, then breed

SAPPHIRE — Rarity: **None**
Trade Noctowl from *Colosseum*, then breed

FIRERED — Rarity: **None**
Trade Noctowl from *Colosseum*, then breed

LEAFGREEN — Rarity: **None**
Trade Noctowl from *Colosseum*, then breed

COLOSSEUM — Rarity: **Breed**
Breed Noctowl in *Ruby/Sapphire/FireRed/LeafGreen* then trade back

EMERALD — Rarity: **Rare**
Safari Zone

XD — Rarity: **None**
Trade Noctowl from *Colosseum*, then breed

MOVES

Level	Attack	Type	Power	ACC	PP	Level	Attack	Type	Power	ACC	PP
—	Tackle	Normal	35	95	35	16	Hypnosis	Psychic	—	60	20
—	Growl	Normal	—	100	40	22	Reflect	Psychic	—	—	20
6	Foresight	Normal	—	100	40	28	Take Down	Normal	90	85	20
11	Peck	Flying	35	100	35	34	Confusion	Psychic	50	100	25
						48	Dream Eater	Psychic	100	100	15

TM/HM

TM/HM#	Name	Type	Power	ACC	PP	TM/HM#	Name	Type	Power	ACC	PP
TM06	Toxic	Poison	—	85	10	TM33	Reflect	Normal	—	—	20
TM10	Hidden Power	Normal	—	100	15	TM40	Aerial Ace	Flying	60	—	20
TM11	Sunny Day	Fire	—	—	5	TM42	Facade	Normal	70	100	20
TM17	Protect	Normal	—	—	10	TM43	Secret Power	Normal	70	100	20
TM18	Rain Dance	Water	—	—	5	TM44	Rest	Psychic	—	—	10
TM21	Frustration	Normal	—	100	20	TM45	Attract	Normal	—	100	15
TM27	Return	Normal	—	100	20	TM46	Thief	Dark	40	100	10
TM29	Psychic	Psychic	90	100	10	TM47	Steel Wing	Steel	70	90	25
TM30	Shadow Ball	Ghost	80	100	15	HM02	Fly	Flying	70	95	15
TM32	Double Team	Normal	—	—	15	HM05	Flash	Normal	—	70	20

EGG MOVES*

Name	Type	Power	ACC	PP
Featherdance	Flying	—	100	15
Faint Attack	Dark	60	—	20
Mirror Move	Flying	—	—	20
Sky Attack	Flying	140	90	5
Supersonic	Normal	—	55	20
Whirlwind	Normal	—	100	20
Wing Attack	Flying	60	100	35

*Learned Via Breeding

MOVE TUTOR
FireRed/LeafGreen and *Emerald* Only

Double-Edge	Dream Eater*	Mimic
Substitute		

*Battle Frontier tutor move (*Emerald*)

---

164 Noctowl™

NORMAL | FLYING

GENERAL INFO
SPECIES: Owl Pokémon
HEIGHT: 5'03"
WEIGHT: 90 lbs.
ABILITY 1: Insomnia
Prevents Noctowl from being put to sleep.

ABILITY 2: Keen Eye
Protects Noctowl from having its Accuracy lowered.

STATS
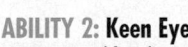

EVOLUTIONS
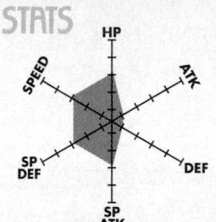  
LV20

LOCATION(S):

RUBY — Rarity: **None**
Trade from *Colosseum*

SAPPHIRE — Rarity: **None**
Trade from *Colosseum*

FIRERED — Rarity: **None**
Trade from *Colosseum*

LEAFGREEN — Rarity: **None**
Trade from *Colosseum*

COLOSSEUM — Rarity: **Only One**
Pyrite Town

EMERALD — Rarity: **Evolve**
Evolve Hoothoot

XD — Rarity: **None**
Trade from *Colosseum*

MOVES

Level	Attack	Type	Power	ACC	PP	Level	Attack	Type	Power	ACC	PP
—	Tackle	Normal	35	95	35	16	Hypnosis	Psychic	—	60	20
—	Growl	Normal	—	100	40	25	Reflect	Psychic	—	—	20
—	Foresight	Normal	—	100	40	33	Take Down	Normal	90	85	20
—	Peck	Flying	35	100	35	41	Confusion	Psychic	50	100	25
						57	Dream Eater	Psychic	100	100	15

TM/HM

TM/HM#	Name	Type	Power	ACC	PP	TM/HM#	Name	Type	Power	ACC	PP
TM06	Toxic	Poison	—	85	10	TM33	Reflect	Normal	—	—	20
TM10	Hidden Power	Normal	—	100	15	TM40	Aerial Ace	Flying	60	—	20
TM11	Sunny Day	Fire	—	—	5	TM42	Facade	Normal	70	100	20
TM15	Hyper Beam	Normal	150	90	5	TM43	Secret Power	Normal	70	100	20
TM17	Protect	Normal	—	—	10	TM44	Rest	Psychic	—	—	10
TM18	Rain Dance	Water	—	—	5	TM45	Attract	Normal	—	100	15
TM21	Frustration	Normal	—	100	20	TM46	Thief	Dark	40	100	10
TM27	Return	Normal	—	100	20	TM47	Steel Wing	Steel	70	90	25
TM29	Psychic	Psychic	90	100	10	HM02	Fly	Flying	70	95	15
TM30	Shadow Ball	Ghost	80	100	15	HM05	Flash	Normal	—	70	20
TM32	Double Team	Normal	—	—	15						

MOVE TUTOR
FireRed/LeafGreen and *Emerald* Only

Double-Edge	Dream Eater*	Mimic
Substitute		

*Battle Frontier tutor move (*Emerald*)

165 Ledyba

BUG · FLYING

GENERAL INFO
SPECIES: Five Star Pokémon
HEIGHT: 3'03"
WEIGHT: 24 lbs.
ABILITY 1: Early Bird
Allows Ledyba to wake up earlier when put to sleep.
ABILITY 2: Swarm
When Ledyba's HPs are low, its Bug-type moves are multiplied by 1.5.

STATS

EVOLUTIONS
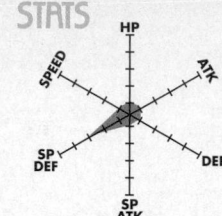 LV18

LOCATION[S]:

RUBY — Rarity: **None**
Trade from *FireRed/LeafGreen*

SAPPHIRE — Rarity: **None**
Trade from *FireRed/LeafGreen*

FIRERED — Rarity: **Rare**
Six Island

LEAFGREEN — Rarity: **Rare**
Six Island

COLOSSEUM — Rarity: **Breed**
Breed Ledian in *Ruby/Sapphire/FireRed/LeafGreen* then trade back

EMERALD — Rarity: **Rare**
Safari Zone

XD — Rarity: **Only One**
Gateon Port (Capture from Casual Guy Cyle)

MOVES

Level	Attack	Type	Power	ACC	PP		Level	Attack	Type	Power	ACC	PP
—	Tackle	Normal	35	95	35		22	Safeguard	Normal	—	—	25
8	Supersonic	Normal	—	55	20		29	Baton Pass	Normal	—	—	40
15	Comet Punch	Normal	18	85	15		36	Swift	Normal	60	—	20
22	Light Screen	Psychic	—	—	30		43	Agility	Psychic	—	—	30
22	Reflect	Psychic	—	—	20		50	Double-Edge	Normal	120	100	15

TM/HM

TM/HM#	Name	Type	Power	ACC	PP		TM/HM#	Name	Type	Power	ACC	PP
TM01	Focus Punch	Fighting	150	100	20		TM28	Dig	Ground	60	100	10
TM06	Toxic	Poison	—	85	10		TM31	Brick Break	Fighting	75	100	15
TM10	Hidden Power	Normal	—	100	15		TM32	Double Team	Normal	—	—	15
TM11	Sunny Day	Fire	—	—	5		TM33	Reflect	Normal	—	—	20
TM16	Light Screen	Psychic	—	—	30		TM40	Aerial Ace	Flying	60	—	20
TM17	Protect	Normal	—	—	10		TM42	Facade	Normal	70	100	20
TM19	Giga Drain	Grass	60	100	5		TM43	Secret Power	Normal	70	100	20
TM20	Safeguard	Normal	—	—	25		TM44	Rest	Psychic	—	—	10
TM21	Frustration	Normal	—	100	20		TM45	Attract	Normal	—	100	15
TM22	Solarbeam	Grass	120	100	10		TM46	Thief	Dark	40	100	10
TM27	Return	Normal	—	100	20		HM05	Flash	Normal	—	70	20

EGG MOVES*

Name	Type	Power	ACC	PP
Bide	Normal	—	100	10
Psybeam	Psychic	65	100	20
Silver Wind	Bug	60	100	5

*Learned Via Breeding

MOVE TUTOR
FireRed/LeafGreen and *Emerald* Only

Double-Edge	Mega Punch*	Mimic
Substitute	Swords Dance*	

*Battle Frontier tutor move (*Emerald*)

---

166 Ledian

BUG · FLYING

GENERAL INFO
SPECIES: Five Star Pokémon
HEIGHT: 4'07"
WEIGHT: 79 lbs.
ABILITY 1: Early Bird
Allows Ledian to wake up earlier when put to sleep.
ABILITY 2: Swarm
When Ledian's HPs are low, its Bug-type moves are multiplied by 1.5.

STATS

EVOLUTIONS
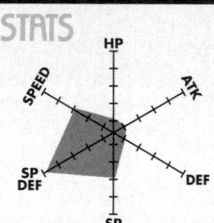 LV18

LOCATION[S]:

RUBY — Rarity: **Evolve**
Trade from *Colosseum*

SAPPHIRE — Rarity: **Evolve**
Trade from *Colosseum*

FIRERED — Rarity: **Evolve**
Trade from *Colosseum*

LEAFGREEN — Rarity: **Evolve**
Trade from *Colosseum*

COLOSSEUM — Rarity: **Only One**
The Under

EMERALD — Rarity: **Evolve**
Evolve Ledyba

XD — Rarity: **Evolve**
Evolve Ledyba

MOVES

Level	Attack	Type	Power	ACC	PP		Level	Attack	Type	Power	ACC	PP
—	Tackle	Normal	35	95	35		24	Safeguard	Normal	—	—	25
—	Supersonic	Normal	—	55	20		33	Baton Pass	Normal	—	—	40
15	Comet Punch	Normal	18	85	15		42	Swift	Normal	60	—	20
24	Light Screen	Psychic	—	—	30		51	Agility	Psychic	—	—	30
24	Reflect	Psychic	—	—	20		60	Double-Edge	Normal	120	100	15

TM/HM

TM/HM#	Name	Type	Power	ACC	PP		TM/HM#	Name	Type	Power	ACC	PP
TM01	Focus Punch	Fighting	150	100	20		TM28	Dig	Ground	60	100	10
TM06	Toxic	Poison	—	85	10		TM31	Brick Break	Fighting	75	100	15
TM10	Hidden Power	Normal	—	100	15		TM32	Double Team	Normal	—	—	15
TM11	Sunny Day	Fire	—	—	5		TM33	Reflect	Normal	—	—	20
TM15	Hyper Beam	Normal	150	90	5		TM40	Aerial Ace	Flying	60	—	20
TM16	Light Screen	Psychic	—	—	30		TM42	Facade	Normal	70	100	20
TM17	Protect	Normal	—	—	10		TM43	Secret Power	Normal	70	100	20
TM19	Giga Drain	Grass	60	100	5		TM44	Rest	Psychic	—	—	10
TM20	Safeguard	Normal	—	—	25		TM45	Attract	Normal	—	100	15
TM21	Frustration	Normal	—	100	20		TM46	Thief	Dark	40	100	10
TM22	Solarbeam	Grass	120	100	10		HM05	Flash	Normal	—	70	20
TM27	Return	Normal	—	100	20							

MOVE TUTOR
FireRed/LeafGreen and *Emerald* Only

Double-Edge	Mega Punch*	Mimic
Substitute	Swords Dance*	

*Battle Frontier tutor move (*Emerald*)

167 Spinarak™

BUG | POISON

GENERAL INFO
SPECIES: String Spit Pokémon
HEIGHT: 1'08"
WEIGHT: 19 lbs.
ABILITY: Insomnia
Prevents Spinarak from being put to sleep.
ABILITY 2: Swarm
When Spinarak's HPs are low, its Bug-type moves are multiplied by 1.5.

STATS
(HP, ATK, DEF, SP ATK, SP DEF, SPEED)

EVOLUTIONS

LV22

LOCATION(S):

RUBY Rarity: **None**
Trade from *FireRed/LeafGreen*

SAPPHIRE Rarity: **None**
Trade from *FireRed/LeafGreen*

FIRERED Rarity: **Rare**
Six Island

LEAFGREEN Rarity: **Rare**
Six Island

COLOSSEUM Rarity: **None**
Breed Ariados in *Ruby/Sapphire/FireRed/LeafGreen* then trade back

EMERALD Rarity: **Rare**
Safari Zone

XD Rarity: **Only One**
Cipher Lab (Capture from Cipher Peon Nexir)

MOVES

Level	Attack	Type	Power	ACC	PP	Level	Attack	Type	Power	ACC	PP
—	Poison Sting	Poison	15	100	35	23	Leech Life	Bug	20	100	15
—	String Shot	Bug	—	95	40	30	Fury Swipes	Normal	18	80	15
6	Scary Face	Normal	—	90	10	37	Spider Web	Bug	—	100	10
11	Constrict	Normal	10	100	35	45	Agility	Psychic	—	—	30
17	Night Shade	Ghost	—	100	15	53	Psychic	Psychic	90	100	10

TM/HM

TM/HM#	Name	Type	Power	ACC	PP	TM/HM#	Name	Type	Power	ACC	PP
TM06	Toxic	Poison	—	85	10	TM29	Psychic	Psychic	90	100	10
TM10	Hidden Power	Normal	—	100	15	TM32	Double Team	Normal	—	—	15
TM11	Sunny Day	Fire	—	—	5	TM36	Sludge Bomb	Poison	90	100	10
TM17	Protect	Normal	—	—	10	TM42	Facade	Normal	70	100	20
TM19	Giga Drain	Grass	60	100	5	TM43	Secret Power	Normal	70	100	20
TM21	Frustration	Normal	—	100	20	TM44	Rest	Psychic	—	—	10
TM22	Solarbeam	Grass	120	100	10	TM45	Attract	Normal	—	100	15
TM27	Return	Normal	—	100	20	TM46	Thief	Dark	40	100	10
TM28	Dig	Ground	60	100	10	HM05	Flash	Normal	—	70	20

EGG MOVES*

Name	Type	Power	ACC	PP
Baton Pass	Normal	—	—	40
Disable	Normal	—	55	20
Psybeam	Psychic	65	100	20
Pursuit	Dark	40	100	20
Signal Beam	Bug	75	100	15
Sonicboom	Normal	—	90	20

*Learned Via Breeding

MOVE TUTOR
FireRed/LeafGreen and *Emerald* Only

Body Slam*	Double-Edge	Mimic
Substitute		

*Battle Frontier tutor move (*Emerald*)

---

168 Ariados™

BUG | POISON

GENERAL INFO
SPECIES: Long Leg Pokémon
HEIGHT: 3'07"
WEIGHT: 74 lbs.
ABILITY: Insomnia
Prevents Ariados from being put to sleep.
ABILITY 2: Swarm
When Ariados's HPs are low, its Bug-type moves are multiplied by 1.5.

STATS
(HP, ATK, DEF, SP ATK, SP DEF, SPEED)

EVOLUTIONS
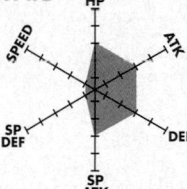 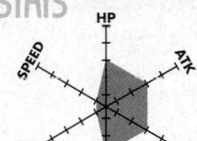 LV22

LOCATION(S):

RUBY Rarity: **Evolve**
Trade from *FireRed/LeafGreen/Colosseum*

SAPPHIRE Rarity: **Evolve**
Trade from *FireRed/LeafGreen/Colosseum*

FIRERED Rarity: **Evolve**
Evolve Spinarak

LEAFGREEN Rarity: **Evolve**
Evolve Spinarak

COLOSSEUM Rarity: **Only One**
Shadow Pokémon Lab

EMERALD Rarity: **Evolve**
Evolve Spinarak

XD Rarity: **Evolve**
Evolve Spinarak

MOVES

Level	Attack	Type	Power	ACC	PP	Level	Attack	Type	Power	ACC	PP
—	Poison Sting	Poison	15	100	35	25	Leech Life	Bug	20	100	15
—	String Shot	Bug	—	95	40	34	Fury Swipes	Normal	18	80	15
—	Scary Face	Normal	—	90	10	43	Spider Web	Bug	—	100	10
—	Constrict	Normal	10	100	35	53	Agility	Psychic	—	—	30
17	Night Shade	Ghost	—	100	15	63	Psychic	Psychic	90	100	10

TM/HM

TM/HM#	Name	Type	Power	ACC	PP	TM/HM#	Name	Type	Power	ACC	PP
TM06	Toxic	Poison	—	85	10	TM29	Psychic	Psychic	90	100	10
TM10	Hidden Power	Normal	—	100	15	TM32	Double Team	Normal	—	—	15
TM11	Sunny Day	Fire	—	—	5	TM36	Sludge Bomb	Poison	90	100	10
TM15	Hyper Beam	Normal	150	90	5	TM42	Facade	Normal	70	100	20
TM17	Protect	Normal	—	—	10	TM43	Secret Power	Normal	70	100	20
TM19	Giga Drain	Grass	60	100	5	TM44	Rest	Psychic	—	—	10
TM21	Frustration	Normal	—	100	20	TM45	Attract	Normal	—	100	15
TM22	Solarbeam	Grass	120	100	10	TM46	Thief	Dark	40	100	10
TM27	Return	Normal	—	100	20	HM05	Flash	Normal	—	70	20
TM28	Dig	Ground	60	100	10						

MOVE TUTOR
FireRed/LeafGreen and *Emerald* Only

Body Slam*	Double-Edge	Mimic
Substitute		

*Battle Frontier tutor move (*Emerald*)

169 Crobat™

POISON   FLYING

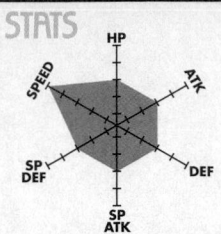

GENERAL INFO
SPECIES: Bat Pokémon
HEIGHT: 5'11"
WEIGHT: 165 lbs.
ABILITY: Inner Focus
Prevents Crobat from flinching.

STATS

EVOLUTIONS
LV22   FRIENDSHIP

LOCATION[S]:

RUBY   Rarity: **Evolve**
Evolve Golbat

SAPPHIRE   Rarity: **Evolve**
Evolve Golbat

FIRERED   Rarity: **Evolve**
Evolve Golbat

LEAFGREEN   Rarity: **Evolve**
Evolve Golbat

COLOSSEUM   Rarity: **None**
Trade from Ruby/Sapphire/FireRed/LeafGreen

EMERALD   Rarity: **Evolve**
Evolve Golbat

XD   Rarity: **Evolve**
Evolve Golbat

MOVES

Level	Attack	Type	Power	ACC	PP	Level	Attack	Type	Power	ACC	PP
—	Leech Life	Bug	20	100	15	28	Confuse Ray	Ghost	—	100	10
—	Screech	Normal	—	85	40	35	Air Cutter	Flying	55	95	25
—/6	Astonish	Ghost	30	100	15	42	Mean Look	Normal	—	100	5
—/11	Supersonic	Normal	—	55	20	49	Poison Fang	Poison	50	100	15
16	Bite	Dark	60	100	25	56	Haze	Ice	—	—	30
21	Wing Attack	Flying	60	100	35						

= *Emerald* Only

TM/HM

TM/HM#	Name	Type	Power	ACC	PP	TM/HM#	Name	Type	Power	ACC	PP
TM06	Toxic	Poison	—	85	10	TM36	Sludge Bomb	Poison	90	100	10
TM10	Hidden Power	Normal	—	100	15	TM40	Aerial Ace	Flying	60	—	20
TM11	Sunny Day	Fire	—	—	5	TM41	Torment	Dark	—	100	15
TM12	Taunt	Dark	—	100	20	TM42	Facade	Normal	70	100	20
TM15	Hyper Beam	Normal	150	90	5	TM43	Secret Power	Normal	70	100	20
TM17	Protect	Normal	—	—	10	TM44	Rest	Psychic	—	—	10
TM18	Rain Dance	Water	—	—	5	TM45	Attract	Normal	—	100	15
TM19	Giga Drain	Grass	60	100	5	TM46	Thief	Dark	40	100	10
TM21	Frustration	Normal	—	100	20	TM47	Steel Wing	Steel	70	90	25
TM27	Return	Normal	—	100	20	TM49	Snatch	Dark	—	100	10
TM30	Shadow Ball	Ghost	80	100	15	HM02	Fly	Flying	70	95	15
TM32	Double Team	Normal	—	—	15						

MOVE TUTOR
FireRed/LeafGreen and ***Emerald*** Only

Double-Edge	Mimic	Substitute

Emerald Only

Endure*	Sleep Talk	Snore*
Swagger	Swift*	

*Battle Frontier tutor move (*Emerald*)

---

170 Chinchou™

ELECTRIC   WATER

GENERAL INFO
SPECIES: Angler Pokémon
HEIGHT: 1'08"
WEIGHT: 26 lbs.
ABILITY 1: Volt Absorb
Chinchou's HPs are restored every time it gets struck by an Electric-type attack.

ABILITY 2: Illuminate
When Chinchou is in the first slot, the chances of running into a wild Pokémon increase.

STATS

EVOLUTIONS
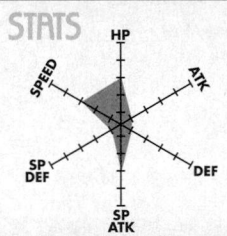 LV27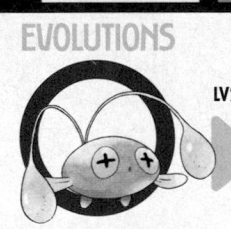

LOCATION[S]:

RUBY   Rarity: **Common**
Route 124, Route 126

SAPPHIRE   Rarity: **Common**
Route 124, Route 126

FIRERED   Rarity: **None**
Trade from Ruby/Sapphire

LEAFGREEN   Rarity: **None**
Trade from Ruby/Sapphire

COLOSSEUM   Rarity: **None**
Trade from Ruby/Sapphire

EMERALD   Rarity: **Common**
Route 124, Route 126

XD   Rarity: **None**
Trade from Ruby/Sapphire

MOVES

Level	Attack	Type	Power	ACC	PP	Level	Attack	Type	Power	ACC	PP
—	Bubble	Water	20	100	30	25	Spark	Electric	65	100	20
—	Thunder Wave	Electric	—	100	20	29	Confuse Ray	Ghost	—	100	10
5	Supersonic	Normal	—	55	20	37	Take Down	Normal	90	85	20
13	Flail	Normal	—	100	15	41	Hydro Pump	Water	120	80	5
17	Water Gun	Water	40	100	25	49	Charge	Electric	—	100	20

TM/HM

TM/HM#	Name	Type	Power	ACC	PP	TM/HM#	Name	Type	Power	ACC	PP
TM03	Water Pulse	Water	60	95	20	TM27	Return	Normal	—	100	20
TM06	Toxic	Poison	—	85	10	TM32	Double Team	Normal	—	—	15
TM07	Hail	Ice	—	—	10	TM34	Shock Wave	Electric	60	—	20
TM10	Hidden Power	Normal	—	100	15	TM42	Facade	Normal	70	100	20
TM13	Ice Beam	Ice	95	100	10	TM43	Secret Power	Normal	70	100	20
TM14	Blizzard	Ice	120	70	5	TM44	Rest	Psychic	—	—	10
TM17	Protect	Normal	—	—	10	TM45	Attract	Normal	—	100	15
TM18	Rain Dance	Water	—	—	5	HM03	Surf	Water	95	100	15
TM21	Frustration	Normal	—	100	20	HM05	Flash	Normal	—	70	20
TM24	Thunderbolt	Electric	95	100	15	HM07	Waterfall	Water	80	100	15
TM25	Thunder	Electric	120	70	10	HM08	Dive	Water	60	100	10

EGG MOVES*

Name	Type	Power	ACC	PP
Flail	Normal	—	100	15
Screech	Normal	—	85	40
Amnesia	Psychic	—	—	20

*Learned Via Breeding

MOVE TUTOR
FireRed/LeafGreen and ***Emerald*** Only

Double-Edge	Mimic	Substitute
Thunder Wave*		

Emerald Only

Endure*	Sleep Talk	Snore*
Swagger		

*Battle Frontier tutor move (*Emerald*)

171 Lanturn™

ELECTRIC | WATER

GENERAL INFO
SPECIES: Light Pokémon
HEIGHT: 3'11"
WEIGHT: 50 lbs.
ABILITY 1: Volt Absorb
Lanturn's HPs are restored every time it gets struck by an Electric-type attack.

ABILITY 2: Illuminate
When Lanturn is in the first slot, the chances of running into a wild Pokémon increase.

STATS

EVOLUTIONS
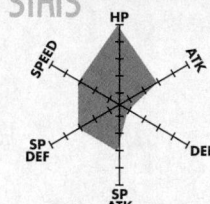
LV27

LOCATION(S):

RUBY	**Rarity: Evolve**
Evolve Chinchou	
SAPPHIRE	**Rarity: Evolve**
Evolve Chinchou	
FIRERED	**Rarity: None**
Trade from *Ruby/Sapphire*	
LEAFGREEN	**Rarity: None**
Trade from *Ruby/Sapphire*	
COLOSSEUM	**Rarity: None**
Trade from *Ruby/Sapphire*	
EMERALD	**Rarity: Evolve**
Evolve Chinchou	
XD	**Rarity: None**
Trade from *Ruby/Sapphire*	

MOVES

Level	Attack	Type	Power	ACC	PP	Level	Attack	Type	Power	ACC	PP
—	Bubble	Water	20	100	30	25	Spark	Electric	65	100	20
—	Thunder Wave	Electric	—	100	20	32	Confuse Ray	Ghost	—	100	10
—	Supersonic	Normal	—	55	20	43	Take Down	Normal	90	85	20
13	Flail	Normal	—	100	15	50	Hydro Pump	Water	120	80	5
17	Water Gun	Water	40	100	25	61	Charge	Electric	—	100	20

TM/HM

TM/HM#	Name	Type	Power	ACC	PP	TM/HM#	Name	Type	Power	ACC	PP
TM03	Water Pulse	Water	60	95	20	TM27	Return	Normal	—	100	20
TM06	Toxic	Poison	—	85	10	TM32	Double Team	Normal	—	—	15
TM07	Hail	Ice	—	—	10	TM34	Shock Wave	Electric	60	—	20
TM10	Hidden Power	Normal	—	100	15	TM42	Facade	Normal	70	100	20
TM13	Ice Beam	Ice	95	100	10	TM43	Secret Power	Normal	70	100	20
TM14	Blizzard	Ice	120	70		TM44	Rest	Psychic	—	—	10
TM15	Hyper Beam	Normal	150	90	5	TM45	Attract	Normal	—	100	15
TM17	Protect	Normal	—	—	10	HM03	Surf	Water	95	100	15
TM18	Rain Dance	Water	—	—	5	HM05	Flash	Normal	—	70	20
TM21	Frustration	Normal	—	100	20	HM07	Waterfall	Water	80	100	15
TM24	Thunderbolt	Electric	95	100	15	HM08	Dive	Water	60	100	10
TM25	Thunder	Electric	120	70	10						

MOVE TUTOR
FireRed/LeafGreen and *Emerald* Only

Double-Edge	Mimic	Substitute
Thunder Wave*		

Emerald Only

Endure*	Sleep Talk	Snore*
Swagger		

*Battle Frontier tutor move (*Emerald*)

---

172 Pichu™

ELECTRIC

GENERAL INFO
SPECIES: Tiny Mouse Pokémon
HEIGHT: 1'00"
WEIGHT: 4 lbs.
ABILITY: Static
An opponent has a 30% chance of being paralyzed if Pichu is hit directly.

STATS
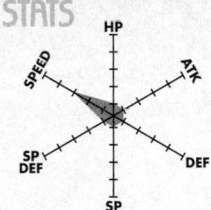

EVOLUTIONS

FRIENDSHIP | THUNDER STONE

LOCATION(S):

RUBY	**Rarity: Breed**
Breed Pikachu	
SAPPHIRE	**Rarity: Breed**
Breed Pikachu	
FIRERED	**Rarity: Breed**
Breed Pikachu	
LEAFGREEN	**Rarity: Breed**
Breed Pikachu	
COLOSSEUM	**Rarity: None**
Trade from *Ruby/Sapphire/FireRed/LeafGreen*	
EMERALD	**Rarity: Breed**
Breed Pikachu	
XD	**Rarity: None**
Trade from *Ruby/Sapphire/FireRed/LeafGreen*	

MOVES

Level	Attack	Type	Power	ACC	PP	Level	Attack	Type	Power	ACC	PP
—	Thundershock	Electric	40	100	30	6	Tail Whip	Normal	—	100	30
—	Charm	Normal	—	100	20	8	Thunder Wave	Electric	—	100	20
						11	Sweet Kiss	Normal	—	75	10

TM/HM

TM/HM#	Name	Type	Power	ACC	PP	TM/HM#	Name	Type	Power	ACC	PP
TM06	Toxic	Poison	—	85	10	TM27	Return	Normal	—	100	20
TM10	Hidden Power	Normal	—	100	15	TM32	Double Team	Normal	—	—	15
TM16	Light Screen	Psychic	—	—	30	TM34	Shock Wave	Electric	60	—	20
TM17	Protect	Normal	—	—	10	TM42	Facade	Normal	70	100	20
TM18	Rain Dance	Water	—	—	5	TM43	Secret Power	Normal	70	100	20
TM21	Frustration	Normal	—	100	20	TM44	Rest	Psychic	—	—	10
TM23	Iron Tail	Steel	75	75	15	TM45	Attract	Normal	—	100	15
TM24	Thunderbolt	Electric	95	100	15	HM05	Flash	Normal	—	70	20
TM25	Thunder	Electric	120	70	10						

EGG MOVES*

Name	Type	Power	ACC	PP
Reversal	Fighting	—	100	15
Bide	Normal	—	100	10
Encore	Normal	—	100	5
Doubleslap	Normal	15	85	10
Charge	Electric	—	100	20
Present	Normal	—	90	15
Wish	Normal	—	100	10

*Learned Via Breeding

MOVE TUTOR
FireRed/LeafGreen and *Emerald* Only

Body Slam*	Counter*	Double-Edge
Mega Kick*	Mega Punch*	Mimic
Seismic Toss*	Substitute	Thunder Wave*

Emerald Only

Defense Curl*	Endure*	Metronome
Mud-Slap*	Rollout	Sleep Talk
Snore*	Swagger	Swift*

*Battle Frontier tutor move (*Emerald*)

173 Cleffa™

GENERAL INFO

SPECIES: Star Shape Pokémon
HEIGHT: 1'0"
WEIGHT: 7 lbs.
ABILITY: Cute Charm

If an opponent physically strikes Cleffa, it has a 30% chance of becoming attracted to it.

STATS

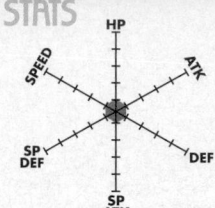

EVOLUTIONS

FRIENDSHIP   MOON STONE

LOCATION[S]:

RUBY — Rarity: **None**
Trade from *FireRed/LeafGreen*

SAPPHIRE — Rarity: **None**
Trade from *FireRed/LeafGreen*

FIRERED — Rarity: **Breed**
Breed Clefairy

LEAFGREEN — Rarity: **Breed**
Breed Clefairy

COLOSSEUM — Rarity: **None**
Trade from *FireRed/LeafGreen*

EMERALD — Rarity: **None**
Trade from *FireRed/LeafGreen*

XD — Rarity: **None**
Trade from *FireRed/LeafGreen*

MOVES

Level	Attack	Type	Power	ACC	PP		Level	Attack	Type	Power	ACC	PP
—	Pound	Normal	40	100	35		8	Sing	Normal	—	55	15
—	Charm	Normal	—	100	20		13	Sweet Kiss	Normal	—	75	10
4	Encore	Normal	—	100	5		17	Magical Leaf	Grass	60	—	20

TM/HM

TM/HM#	Name	Type	Power	ACC	PP		TM/HM#	Name	Type	Power	ACC	PP
TM03	Water Pulse	Water	60	95	20		TM29	Psychic	Psychic	90	100	10
TM06	Toxic	Poison	—	85	10		TM30	Shadow Ball	Ghost	80	100	15
TM10	Hidden Power	Normal	—	100	15		TM32	Double Team	Normal	—	—	15
TM11	Sunny Day	Fire	—	—	5		TM33	Reflect	Normal	—	—	20
TM16	Light Screen	Psychic	—	—	30		TM34	Shock Wave	Electric	60	—	20
TM17	Protect	Normal	—	—	10		TM35	Flamethrower	Fire	95	100	15
TM18	Rain Dance	Water	—	—	5		TM38	Fire Blast	Fire	120	85	5
TM20	Safeguard	Normal	—	—	25		TM42	Facade	Normal	70	100	20
TM21	Frustration	Normal	—	100	20		TM43	Secret Power	Normal	70	100	20
TM22	Solarbeam	Grass	120	100	10		TM44	Rest	Psychic	—	—	10
TM23	Iron Tail	Steel	75	75	15		TM45	Attract	Normal	—	100	15
TM27	Return	Normal	—	100	20		HM05	Flash	Normal	—	70	20
TM28	Dig	Ground	60	100	10							

EGG MOVES*

Name	Type	Power	ACC	PP
Amnesia	Psychic	—	—	20
Belly Drum	Normal	—	—	10
Metronome	Normal	—	—	10
Mimic	Normal	—	100	10
Present	Normal	—	90	15
Substitute	Normal	—	—	10
Wish	Normal	—	100	10
Bounce	Flying	85	85	5

*Learned Via Breeding

MOVE TUTOR

FireRed/LeafGreen and *Emerald* Only

Body Slam*	Counter*	Double-Edge
Dream Eater*	Mega Kick*	Mega Punch*
Metronome	Mimic	Seismic Toss*
Softboiled	Substitute	Thunder Wave*

*Battle Frontier tutor move (*Emerald*)

---

174 Igglybuff™

GENERAL INFO

SPECIES: Balloon Pokémon
HEIGHT: 1'00"
WEIGHT: 2 lbs.
ABILITY: Cute Charm

If an opponent physically strikes Igglybuff, it has a 30% chance of becoming attracted to it.

STATS

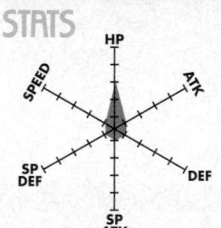

EVOLUTIONS

FRIENDSHIP   MOON STONE

LOCATION[S]:

RUBY — Rarity: **Breed**
Breed Jigglypuff

SAPPHIRE — Rarity: **Breed**
Breed Jigglypuff

FIRERED — Rarity: **Breed**
Breed Jigglypuff

LEAFGREEN — Rarity: **Breed**
Breed Jigglypuff

COLOSSEUM — Rarity: **None**
Trade from *Ruby/Sapphire/FireRed/LeafGreen*

EMERALD — Rarity: **Breed**
Breed Jigglypuff

XD — Rarity: **None**
Trade from *Ruby/Sapphire/FireRed/LeafGreen*

MOVES

Level	Attack	Type	Power	ACC	PP		Level	Attack	Type	Power	ACC	PP
—	Charm	Normal	—	100	20		4	Defense Curl	Normal	—	—	40
—	Sing	Normal	—	55	15		9	Pound	Normal	40	100	35
							14	Sweet Kiss	Normal	—	75	10

TM/HM

TM/HM#	Name	Type	Power	ACC	PP		TM/HM#	Name	Type	Power	ACC	PP
TM03	Water Pulse	Water	60	95	20		TM29	Psychic	Psychic	90	100	10
TM06	Toxic	Poison	—	85	10		TM30	Shadow Ball	Ghost	80	100	15
TM10	Hidden Power	Normal	—	100	15		TM32	Double Team	Normal	—	—	15
TM11	Sunny Day	Fire	—	—	5		TM33	Reflect	Normal	—	—	20
TM16	Light Screen	Psychic	—	—	30		TM34	Shock Wave	Electric	60	—	20
TM17	Protect	Normal	—	—	10		TM35	Flamethrower	Fire	95	100	15
TM18	Rain Dance	Water	—	—	5		TM38	Fire Blast	Fire	120	85	5
TM20	Safeguard	Normal	—	—	25		TM42	Facade	Normal	70	100	20
TM21	Frustration	Normal	—	100	20		TM43	Secret Power	Normal	70	100	20
TM22	Solarbeam	Grass	120	100	10		TM44	Rest	Psychic	—	—	10
TM27	Return	Normal	—	100	20		TM45	Attract	Normal	—	100	15
TM28	Dig	Ground	60	100	10		HM05	Flash	Normal	—	70	20

EGG MOVES*

Name	Type	Power	ACC	PP
Faint Attack	Dark	60	—	20
Fake Tears	Dark	—	100	20
Perish Song	Normal	—	—	5
Present	Normal	—	90	15
Wish	Normal	—	100	10

*Learned Via Breeding

MOVE TUTOR

FireRed/LeafGreen and *Emerald* Only

Body Slam*	Counter*	Double-Edge
Dream Eater*	Mega Kick*	Mega Punch*
Mimic	Seismic Toss*	Substitute
Thunder Wave*		

Emerald Only

Defense Curl*	Endure*	Icy Wind*
Mud-Slap*	Psych Up*	Rollout
Sleep Talk	Snore*	Swagger

*Battle Frontier tutor move (*Emerald*)

175 Togepi™

NORMAL

GENERAL INFO

SPECIES: Spike Ball Pokémon
HEIGHT: 1'00"
WEIGHT: 3 lbs.
ABILITY 1: Serene Grace
Togepi's Attacks that inflict extra status effects have twice the chance of occurring.

ABILITY 2: Hustle
Multiplies Togepi's attacks by 1.5, but lowers its Accuracy to 80%.

STATS

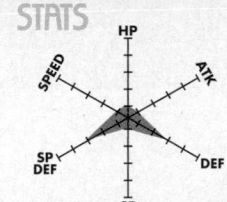

EVOLUTIONS

FRIENDSHIP

LOCATION(S):

RUBY Rarity: **None**
Trade from *FireRed/LeafGreen*

SAPPHIRE Rarity: **None**
Trade from *FireRed/LeafGreen*

FIRERED Rarity: **Only One**
Five Island (Old Man on Western Island)

LEAFGREEN Rarity: **Only One**
Five Island (Old Man on Western Island)

COLOSSEUM Rarity: **None**
Trade from *FireRed/LeafGreen*

EMERALD Rarity: **None**
Trade from *FireRed/LeafGreen*

XD Rarity: **Only One**
Outskirt Stand (Receive from Hordel)

MOVES

Level	Attack	Type	Power	ACC	PP
—	Growl	Normal	—	100	40
—	Charm	Normal	—	100	20
9	Sweet Kiss	Normal	—	75	10
13	Yawn	Normal	—	100	10
17	Encore	Normal	—	100	5

Level	Attack	Type	Power	ACC	PP
21	Ancientpower	Rock	60	100	5
25	Follow Me	Normal	—	100	20
29	Wish	Normal	—	100	10
33	Safeguard	Normal	—	—	25
37	Double-Edge	Normal	120	100	15
41	Baton Pass	Normal	—	—	40

TM/HM

TM/HM#	Name	Type	Power	ACC	PP
TM03	Water Pulse	Water	60	95	20
TM06	Toxic	Poison	—	85	10
TM10	Hidden Power	Normal	—	100	15
TM11	Sunny Day	Fire	—	—	5
TM16	Light Screen	Psychic	—	—	30
TM17	Protect	Normal	—	—	10
TM18	Rain Dance	Water	—	—	5
TM20	Safeguard	Normal	—	—	25
TM21	Frustration	Normal	—	100	20
TM22	Solarbeam	Grass	120	100	10
TM27	Return	Normal	—	100	20
TM29	Psychic	Psychic	90	100	10

TM/HM#	Name	Type	Power	ACC	PP
TM30	Shadow Ball	Ghost	80	100	15
TM32	Double Team	Normal	—	—	15
TM33	Reflect	Normal	—	—	20
TM34	Shock Wave	Electric	60	—	20
TM35	Flamethrower	Fire	95	100	15
TM38	Fire Blast	Fire	120	85	5
TM42	Facade	Normal	70	100	20
TM43	Secret Power	Normal	70	100	20
TM44	Rest	Psychic	—	—	10
TM45	Attract	Normal	—	100	15
HM05	Flash	Normal	—	70	20
HM06	Rock Smash	Fighting	20	100	15

EGG MOVES*

Name	Type	Power	ACC	PP
Foresight	Normal	—	100	40
Future Sight	Psychic	80	90	15
Mirror Move	Flying	—	—	20
Peck	Flying	35	100	35
Present	Normal	—	90	15
Psych Up	Normal	—	—	10
Substitute	Normal	—	—	10

*Learned Via Breeding

MOVE TUTOR

FireRed/LeafGreen and *Emerald* Only

Body Slam*	Counter*	Double-Edge
Dream Eater*	Mega Kick*	Mega Punch*
Metronome	Mimic	Seismic Toss*
Softboiled	Substitute	Thunder Wave*

*Battle Frontier tutor move (*Emerald*)

---

176 Togetic™

NORMAL FLYING

GENERAL INFO

SPECIES: Happiness Pokémon
HEIGHT: 2'00"
WEIGHT: 7 lbs.
ABILITY 1: Serene Grace
Togetic's attacks that inflict extra status effects have twice the chance of occurring.

ABILITY 2: Hustle
Multiplies Togetic's attacks by 1.5, but lowers its accuracy to 80%.

STATS

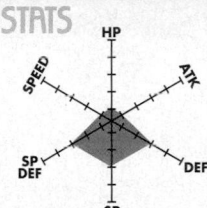

EVOLUTIONS

FRIENDSHIP

LOCATION(S):

RUBY Rarity: **None**
Trade from *FireRed/LeafGreen/Colosseum*

SAPPHIRE Rarity: **None**
Trade from *FireRed/LeafGreen/Colosseum*

FIRERED Rarity: **Evolve**
Evolve Togepi

LEAFGREEN Rarity: **Evolve**
Evolve Togepi

COLOSSEUM Rarity: **Only One**
Obtained from Fake Artist in Outskirt Stand

EMERALD Rarity: **None**
Trade from *FireRed/LeafGreen/Colosseum*

XD Rarity: **Evolve**
Evolve Togepi

MOVES

Level	Attack	Type	Power	ACC	PP
—	Magical Leaf	Grass	60	—	20
—	Growl	Normal	—	100	40
—	Charm	Normal	—	100	20
—	Metronome	Normal	—	—	10
—	Sweet Kiss	Normal	—	75	10
13	Yawn	Normal	—	100	10

Level	Attack	Type	Power	ACC	PP
17	Encore	Normal	—	100	5
21	Ancientpower	Rock	60	100	5
25	Follow Me	Normal	—	100	20
29	Wish	Normal	—	100	10
33	Safeguard	Normal	—	—	25
37	Double-Edge	Normal	120	100	15
41	Baton Pass	Normal	—	—	40

TM/HM

TM/HM#	Name	Type	Power	ACC	PP
TM01	Focus Punch	Fighting	150	100	20
TM03	Water Pulse	Water	60	95	20
TM06	Toxic	Poison	—	85	10
TM10	Hidden Power	Normal	—	100	15
TM11	Sunny Day	Fire	—	—	5
TM15	Hyper Beam	Normal	150	90	5
TM16	Light Screen	Psychic	—	—	30
TM17	Protect	Normal	—	—	10
TM18	Rain Dance	Water	—	—	5
TM20	Safeguard	Normal	—	—	25
TM21	Frustration	Normal	—	100	20
TM22	Solarbeam	Grass	120	100	10
TM27	Return	Normal	—	100	20
TM29	Psychic	Psychic	90	100	10
TM30	Shadow Ball	Ghost	80	100	15

TM/HM#	Name	Type	Power	ACC	PP
TM31	Brick Break	Fighting	75	100	15
TM32	Double Team	Normal	—	—	15
TM33	Reflect	Normal	—	—	20
TM34	Shock Wave	Electric	60	—	20
TM35	Flamethrower	Fire	95	100	15
TM38	Fire Blast	Fire	120	85	5
TM40	Aerial Ace	Flying	60	—	20
TM42	Facade	Normal	70	100	20
TM43	Secret Power	Normal	70	100	20
TM44	Rest	Psychic	—	—	10
TM45	Attract	Normal	—	100	15
TM47	Steel Wing	Steel	70	90	25
HM02	Fly	Flying	70	95	15
HM05	Flash	Normal	—	70	20
HM06	Rock Smash	Fighting	20	100	15

MOVE TUTOR

FireRed/LeafGreen and *Emerald* Only

Body Slam*	Counter*	Double-Edge
Dream Eater*	Mega Kick*	Mega Punch*
Metronome	Mimic	Seismic Toss*
Softboiled	Substitute	Thunder Wave*

*Battle Frontier tutor move (*Emerald*)

177 Natu™

PSYCHIC | FLYING

GENERAL INFO

SPECIES: Tiny Bird Pokémon
HEIGHT: 0'08"
WEIGHT: 4 lbs.
ABILITY 1: Synchronize
When Natu gets poisoned, burned, or paralyzed, the opponent also gets the same condition.

ABILITY 2: Early Bird
Allows Natu to wake up earlier when put to sleep.

STATS

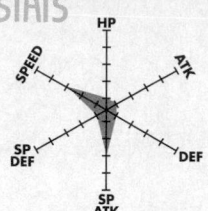

EVOLUTIONS

 LV25

LOCATION[S]:

RUBY	Rarity: **Common**
Safari Zone	
SAPPHIRE	Rarity: **Common**
Safari Zone	
FIRERED	Rarity: **Common**
Six Island	
LEAFGREEN	Rarity: **Common**
Six Island	
COLOSSEUM	Rarity: **None**
Trade from *Ruby/Sapphire/FireRed/LeafGreen*	
EMERALD	Rarity: **Common**
Safari Zone	
XD	Rarity: **Only One**
Phenac City (Capture from Cipher Peon Elosin)	

MOVES

Level	Attack	Type	Power	ACC	PP	Level	Attack	Type	Power	ACC	PP
—	Peck	Flying	35	100	35	30	Wish	Normal	—	100	10
—	Leer	Normal	—	100	30	30	Future Sight	Psychic	80	90	15
10	Night Shade	Ghost	—	100	15	40	Confuse Ray	Ghost	—	100	10
20	Teleport	Psychic	—	—	20	50	Psychic	Psychic	90	100	10

TM/HM

TM/HM#	Name	Type	Power	ACC	PP	TM/HM#	Name	Type	Power	ACC	PP
TM04	Calm Mind	Psychic	—	—	20	TM30	Shadow Ball	Ghost	80	100	15
TM06	Toxic	Poison	—	85	10	TM32	Double Team	Normal	—	—	15
TM10	Hidden Power	Normal	—	100	15	TM33	Reflect	Normal	—	—	20
TM11	Sunny Day	Fire	—	—	5	TM40	Aerial Ace	Flying	60	—	20
TM16	Light Screen	Psychic	—	—	30	TM42	Facade	Normal	70	100	20
TM17	Protect	Normal	—	—	10	TM43	Secret Power	Normal	70	100	20
TM18	Rain Dance	Water	—	—	5	TM44	Rest	Psychic	—	—	10
TM19	Giga Drain	Grass	60	100	5	TM45	Attract	Normal	—	100	15
TM21	Frustration	Normal	—	100	20	TM46	Thief	Dark	40	100	10
TM22	Solarbeam	Grass	120	100	10	TM47	Steel Wing	Steel	70	90	25
TM27	Return	Normal	—	100	20	TM48	Skill Swap	Psychic	—	100	10
TM29	Psychic	Psychic	90	100	10	HM05	Flash	Normal	—	70	20

EGG MOVES*

Name	Type	Power	ACC	PP
Haze	Ice	—	—	30
Drill Peck	Flying	80	100	20
Quick Attack	Normal	40	100	30
Steel Wing	Steel	70	90	25
Refresh	Normal	—	100	20
Featherdance	Flying	—	100	15
Psych Up	Normal	—	—	10
Faint Attack	Dark	60	—	20

*Learned Via Breeding

MOVE TUTOR

FireRed/LeafGreen and *Emerald* Only

Double-Edge	Dream Eater*	Mimic
Substitute	Thunder Wave*	

***Emerald* Only**

Endure*	Psych Up*	Sleep Talk
Snore*	Swagger	Swift*

*Battle Frontier tutor move (*Emerald*)

178 Xatu™

PSYCHIC | FLYING

GENERAL INFO

SPECIES: Mystic Pokémon
HEIGHT: 4'11"
WEIGHT: 33 lbs.
ABILITY 1: Synchronize
When Xatu gets poisoned, burned, or paralyzed, the opponent also gets the same condition.

ABILITY 2: Early Bird
Allows Xatu to wake up earlier when put to sleep.

STATS

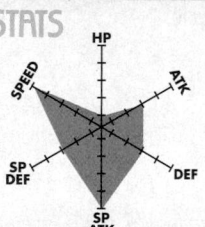

EVOLUTIONS

 LV25

LOCATION[S]:

RUBY	Rarity: **Rare**
Safari Zone	
SAPPHIRE	Rarity: **Rare**
Safari Zone	
FIRERED	Rarity: **Evolve**
Evolve Natu	
LEAFGREEN	Rarity: **Evolve**
Evolve Natu	
COLOSSEUM	Rarity: **None**
Trade from *Ruby/Sapphire/FireRed/LeafGreen*	
EMERALD	Rarity: **Rare**
Safari Zone	
XD	Rarity: **Evolve**
Evolve Natu	

MOVES

Level	Attack	Type	Power	ACC	PP	Level	Attack	Type	Power	ACC	PP
—	Peck	Flying	35	100	35	35	Wish	Normal	—	100	10
—	Leer	Normal	—	100	30	35	Future Sight	Psychic	80	90	15
10	Night Shade	Ghost	—	100	15	50	Confuse Ray	Ghost	—	100	10
20	Teleport	Psychic	—	—	20	65	Psychic	Psychic	90	100	10

TM/HM

TM/HM#	Name	Type	Power	ACC	PP	TM/HM#	Name	Type	Power	ACC	PP
TM04	Calm Mind	Psychic	—	—	20	TM30	Shadow Ball	Ghost	80	100	15
TM06	Toxic	Poison	—	85	10	TM32	Double Team	Normal	—	—	15
TM10	Hidden Power	Normal	—	100	15	TM33	Reflect	Normal	—	—	20
TM11	Sunny Day	Fire	—	—	5	TM40	Aerial Ace	Flying	60	—	20
TM15	Hyper Beam	Normal	150	90	5	TM42	Facade	Normal	70	100	20
TM16	Light Screen	Psychic	—	—	30	TM43	Secret Power	Normal	70	100	20
TM17	Protect	Normal	—	—	10	TM44	Rest	Psychic	—	—	10
TM18	Rain Dance	Water	—	—	5	TM45	Attract	Normal	—	100	15
TM19	Giga Drain	Grass	60	100	5	TM46	Thief	Dark	40	100	10
TM21	Frustration	Normal	—	100	20	TM47	Steel Wing	Steel	70	90	25
TM22	Solarbeam	Grass	120	100	10	TM48	Skill Swap	Psychic	—	100	10
TM27	Return	Normal	—	100	20	HM02	Fly	Flying	70	95	15
TM29	Psychic	Psychic	90	100	10	HM05	Flash	Normal	—	70	20

MOVE TUTOR

FireRed/LeafGreen and *Emerald* Only

Double-Edge	Dream Eater*	Mimic
Substitute	Thunder Wave*	

***Emerald* Only**

Endure*	Psych Up*	Sleep Talk
Snore*	Swagger	Swift*

*Battle Frontier tutor move (*Emerald*)

179 Mareep™

ELECTRIC

GENERAL INFO
SPECIES: Wool Pokémon
HEIGHT: 2'00"
WEIGHT: 17 lbs.
ABILITY: Static

An opponent has a 30% chance of being paralyzed if Mareep is hit directly.

STATS
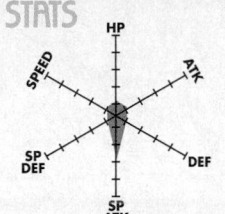

EVOLUTIONS
 LV15  LV30

LOCATION[S]:

RUBY **Rarity: None**
Trade Flaaffy or Ampharos from *Colosseum*, then breed

SAPPHIRE **Rarity: None**
Trade Flaaffy or Ampharos from *Colosseum*, then breed

FIRERED **Rarity: None**
Trade Flaaffy or Ampharos from *Colosseum*, then breed

LEAFGREEN **Rarity: None**
Trade Flaaffy or Ampharos from *Colosseum*, then breed

COLOSSEUM **Rarity: None**
Breed in *Ruby/Sapphire/FireRed/LeafGreen*, then trade back

EMERALD **Rarity: Common**
Safari Zone

XD **Rarity: Only One**
Cipher Lab (Capture from Cipher Peon Yellosix)

MOVES

Level	Attack	Type	Power	ACC	PP
—	Tackle	Normal	35	95	35
—	Growl	Normal	—	100	40
9	Thundershock	Electric	40	100	30

Level	Attack	Type	Power	ACC	PP
16	Thunder Wave	Electric	—	100	20
23	Cotton Spore	Grass	—	85	40
30	Light Screen	Psychic	—	—	30
37	Thunder	Electric	120	70	10

TM/HM

TM/HM#	Name	Type	Power	ACC	PP
TM06	Toxic	Poison	—	85	10
TM10	Hidden Power	Normal	—	100	15
TM16	Light Screen	Psychic	—	—	30
TM17	Protect	Normal	—	—	10
TM18	Rain Dance	Water	—	—	5
TM21	Frustration	Normal	—	100	20
TM23	Iron Tail	Steel	75	75	15
TM24	Thunderbolt	Electric	95	100	15
TM25	Thunder	Electric	120	70	10

TM/HM#	Name	Type	Power	ACC	PP
TM27	Return	Normal	—	100	20
TM32	Double Team	Normal	—	—	15
TM34	Shock Wave	Electric	60	—	20
TM42	Facade	Normal	70	100	20
TM43	Secret Power	Normal	70	100	20
TM44	Rest	Psychic	—	—	10
TM45	Attract	Normal	—	100	15
HM05	Flash	Normal	—	70	20

EGG MOVES*

Name	Type	Power	ACC	PP
Body Slam	Normal	85	100	15
Charge	Electric	—	100	20
Odor Sleuth	Normal	—	100	40
Reflect	Psychic	—	—	20
Safeguard	Normal	—	—	25
Screech	Normal	—	85	40
Take Down	Normal	90	85	20

*Learned Via Breeding

MOVE TUTOR
FireRed/LeafGreen and *Emerald* Only

Body Slam*	Double-Edge	Mimic
Substitute	Thunder Wave*	

*Battle Frontier tutor move (*Emerald*)

180 Flaaffy™

ELECTRIC

GENERAL INFO
SPECIES: Wool Pokémon
HEIGHT: 2'07"
WEIGHT: 29 lbs.
ABILITY: Static

An opponent has a 30% chance of being paralyzed if Flaaffy is hit directly.

STATS
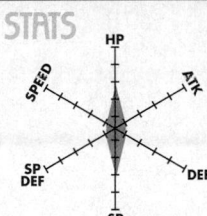

EVOLUTIONS
 LV15  LV30

LOCATION[S]:

RUBY **Rarity: None**
Trade from *Colosseum*

SAPPHIRE **Rarity: None**
Trade from *Colosseum*

FIRERED **Rarity: Evolve**
Evolve Mareep

LEAFGREEN **Rarity: Evolve**
Evolve Mareep

COLOSSEUM **Rarity: Only One**
Pyrite Town

EMERALD **Rarity: Evolve**
Evolve Mareep

XD **Rarity: Evolve**
Evolve Mareep

MOVES

Level	Attack	Type	Power	ACC	PP
—	Tackle	Normal	35	95	35
—	Growl	Normal	—	100	40
—	Thundershock	Electric	40	100	30

Level	Attack	Type	Power	ACC	PP
18	Thunder Wave	Electric	—	100	20
27	Cotton Spore	Grass	—	85	40
36	Light Screen	Psychic	—	—	30
45	Thunder	Electric	120	70	10

TM/HM

TM/HM#	Name	Type	Power	ACC	PP
TM01	Focus Punch	Fighting	150	100	20
TM06	Toxic	Poison	—	85	10
TM10	Hidden Power	Normal	—	100	15
TM16	Light Screen	Psychic	—	—	30
TM17	Protect	Normal	—	—	10
TM18	Rain Dance	Water	—	—	5
TM21	Frustration	Normal	—	100	20
TM23	Iron Tail	Steel	75	75	15
TM24	Thunderbolt	Electric	95	100	15
TM25	Thunder	Electric	120	70	10
TM27	Return	Normal	—	100	20

TM/HM#	Name	Type	Power	ACC	PP
TM31	Brick Break	Fighting	75	100	15
TM32	Double Team	Normal	—	—	15
TM34	Shock Wave	Electric	60	—	20
TM42	Facade	Normal	70	100	20
TM43	Secret Power	Normal	70	100	20
TM44	Rest	Psychic	—	—	10
TM45	Attract	Normal	—	100	15
HM04	Strength	Normal	80	100	15
HM05	Flash	Normal	—	70	20
HM06	Rock Smash	Fighting	20	100	15

MOVE TUTOR
FireRed/LeafGreen and *Emerald* Only

Body Slam*	Counter*	Double-Edge
Mega Kick*	Mega Punch*	Mimic
Seismic Toss*	Substitute	Thunder Wave*

*Battle Frontier tutor move (*Emerald*)

181 Ampharos™

ELECTRIC

GENERAL INFO

SPECIES: Light Pokémon
HEIGHT: 4'07"
WEIGHT: 136 lbs.
ABILITY: Static

An opponent has a 30% chance of being paralyzed if Ampharos is hit directly.

STATS

EVOLUTIONS

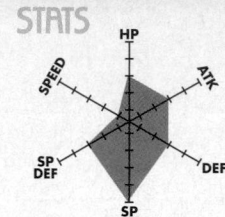 LV15  LV30

LOCATION[S]:

RUBY Rarity: **Evolve**
Trade from *Colosseum*

SAPPHIRE Rarity: **Evolve**
Trade from *Colosseum*

FIRERED Rarity: **Evolve**
Trade from *Colosseum*

LEAFGREEN Rarity: **Evolve**
Trade from *Colosseum*

COLOSSEUM Rarity: **Evolve**
Evolve Flaaffy

EMERALD Rarity: **Evolve**
Evolve Flaaffy

XD Rarity: **Evolve**
Evolve Flaaffy

MOVES

Level	Attack	Type	Power	ACC	PP
—	Tackle	Normal	35	95	35
—	Growl	Normal	—	100	40
—	Thundershock	Electric	40	100	30
—	Thunder Wave	Electric	—	100	20
27	Cotton Spore	Grass	—	85	40
30	Thunderpunch	Electric	75	100	15
42	Light Screen	Psychic	—	—	30
57	Thunder	Electric	120	70	10

TM/HM

TM/HM#	Name	Type	Power	ACC	PP
TM01	Focus Punch	Fighting	150	100	20
TM06	Toxic	Poison	—	85	10
TM10	Hidden Power	Normal	—	100	15
TM15	Hyper Beam	Normal	150	90	5
TM16	Light Screen	Psychic	—	—	30
TM17	Protect	Normal	—	—	10
TM18	Rain Dance	Water	—	—	5
TM21	Frustration	Normal	—	100	20
TM23	Iron Tail	Steel	75	75	15
TM24	Thunderbolt	Electric	95	100	15
TM25	Thunder	Electric	120	70	10
TM27	Return	Normal	—	100	20
TM31	Brick Break	Fighting	75	100	15
TM32	Double Team	Normal	—	—	15
TM34	Shock Wave	Electric	60	—	20
TM42	Facade	Normal	70	100	20
TM43	Secret Power	Normal	70	100	20
TM44	Rest	Psychic	—	—	10
TM45	Attract	Normal	—	100	15
HM04	Strength	Normal	80	100	20
HM05	Flash	Normal	—	70	20
HM06	Rock Smash	Fighting	20	100	15

MOVE TUTOR

FireRed/LeafGreen and *Emerald* Only

Body Slam*	Counter*	Double-Edge
Mega Kick*	Mega Punch*	Mimic
Seismic Toss*	Substitute	Thunder Wave*

*Battle Frontier tutor move (*Emerald*)

---

182 Bellossom™

GRASS

GENERAL INFO

SPECIES: Flower Pokémon
HEIGHT: 1'04"
WEIGHT: 13 lbs.
ABILITY: Chlorophyll

Bellossom's Speed is doubled when the sunlight is strong.

STATS

EVOLUTIONS

 LV21 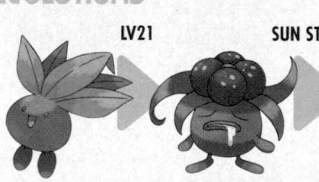 SUN STONE

LOCATION[S]:

RUBY Rarity: **Evolve**
Evolve Gloom

SAPPHIRE Rarity: **Evolve**
Evolve Gloom

FIRERED Rarity: **Evolve**
Evolve Gloom

LEAFGREEN Rarity: **None**
Trade from *Ruby/Sapphire/FireRed*

COLOSSEUM Rarity: **None**
Trade from *Ruby/Sapphire/FireRed*

EMERALD Rarity: **Evolve**
Evolve Gloom

XD Rarity: **None**
Trade from *Ruby/Sapphire/FireRed*

MOVES

Level	Attack	Type	Power	ACC	PP
—	Absorb	Grass	20	100	20
—	Sweet Scent	Normal	—	100	20
—	Stun Spore	Grass	—	75	30
—	Magical Leaf	Grass	60	—	20
44	Petal Dance	Grass	70	100	20
55	Solarbeam	Grass	120	100	10

TM/HM

TM/HM#	Name	Type	Power	ACC	PP
TM06	Toxic	Poison	—	85	10
TM09	Bullet Seed	Grass	10	100	30
TM10	Hidden Power	Normal	—	100	15
TM11	Sunny Day	Fire	—	—	5
TM15	Hyper Beam	Normal	150	90	5
TM17	Protect	Normal	—	—	10
TM19	Giga Drain	Grass	60	100	5
TM20	Safeguard	Normal	—	—	25
TM21	Frustration	Normal	—	100	20
TM22	Solarbeam	Grass	120	100	10
TM27	Return	Normal	—	100	20
TM32	Double Team	Normal	—	—	15
TM36	Sludge Bomb	Poison	90	100	10
TM42	Facade	Normal	70	100	20
TM43	Secret Power	Normal	70	100	20
TM44	Rest	Psychic	—	—	10
TM45	Attract	Normal	—	100	15
HM01	Cut	Normal	50	95	30
HM05	Flash	Normal	—	70	20

MOVE TUTOR

FireRed/LeafGreen and *Emerald* Only

Double-Edge	Mimic	Substitute
Swords Dance*		

Emerald Only

Endure*	Sleep Talk	Snore*
Swagger		

*Battle Frontier tutor move (*Emerald*)

183 Marill™

WATER

GENERAL INFO

SPECIES: Aqua Mouse Pokémon
HEIGHT: 1'04"
WEIGHT: 19 lbs.
ABILITY 1: Thick Fat

When Marill is attacked by Fire-type or Ice-type attacks, the damage is reduced by half.

ABILITY 2: Huge Power

Increases the Power of Marill's attack, but power is reduced when the ability is changed.

STATS

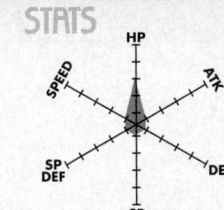

EVOLUTIONS

FRIENDSHIP   LV18

LOCATION(S):

RUBY	Rarity: **Common**
Routes 102, 111, 114, 117, 120	
SAPPHIRE	Rarity: **Common**
Routes 102, 111, 114, 117, 120	
FIRERED	Rarity: **None**
Trade from *Ruby/Sapphire/LeafGreen*	
LEAFGREEN	Rarity: **Common**
Six Island	
COLOSSEUM	Rarity: **None**
Trade from *Ruby/Sapphire/LeafGreen*	
EMERALD	Rarity: **Common**
Routes 102, 104, 111, 112, 114, 117, 120, Petalburg City, Safari Zone	
XD	Rarity: **None**
Trade from *Ruby/Sapphire/LeafGreen*	

MOVES

Level	Attack	Type	Power	ACC	PP	Level	Attack	Type	Power	ACC	PP
—	Tackle	Normal	35	95	35	15	Rollout	Rock	30	90	20
3	Defense Curl	Normal	—	—	40	21	Bubblebeam	Water	65	100	20
6	Tail Whip	Normal	—	100	30	28	Double-Edge	Normal	120	100	15
10	Water Gun	Water	40	100	25	36	Rain Dance	Water	—	—	5
						45	Hydro Pump	Water	120	80	5

TM/HM

TM/HM#	Name	Type	Power	ACC	PP	TM/HM#	Name	Type	Power	ACC	PP
TM01	Focus Punch	Fighting	150	100	20	TM28	Dig	Ground	60	100	10
TM03	Water Pulse	Water	60	95	20	TM31	Brick Break	Fighting	75	100	15
TM06	Toxic	Poison	—	85	10	TM32	Double Team	Normal	—	—	15
TM07	Hail	Ice	—	—	10	TM42	Facade	Normal	70	100	20
TM10	Hidden Power	Normal	—	100	15	TM43	Secret Power	Normal	70	100	20
TM13	Ice Beam	Ice	95	100	10	TM44	Rest	Psychic	—	—	10
TM14	Blizzard	Ice	120	70	5	TM45	Attract	Normal	—	100	15
TM17	Protect	Normal	—	—	10	HM03	Surf	Water	95	100	15
TM18	Rain Dance	Water	—	—	5	HM04	Strength	Normal	80	100	20
TM21	Frustration	Normal	—	100	20	HM06	Rock Smash	Fighting	20	100	15
TM23	Iron Tail	Steel	75	75	15	HM07	Waterfall	Water	80	100	15
TM27	Return	Normal	—	100	20	HM08	Dive	Water	60	100	10

EGG MOVES*

Name	Type	Power	ACC	PP
Light Screen	Psychic	—	—	30
Amnesia	Psychic	—	—	20
Future Sight	Psychic	80	90	15
Supersonic	Normal	—	55	20
Substitute	Normal	—	—	10
Present	Normal	—	90	15
Belly Drum	Normal	—	—	10
Perish Song	Normal	—	—	5

Learned Via Breeding

MOVE TUTOR

FireRed/LeafGreen and *Emerald* Only

Body Slam*	Double-Edge	Mega Kick*
Mega Punch*	Mimic	Seismic Toss*
Substitute		

Emerald Only

Defense Curl*	Dynamicpunch	Endure*
Ice Punch*	Icy Wind*	Mud-Slap*
Rollout	Sleep Talk	Snore*
Swagger	Swift*	

*Battle Frontier tutor move (*Emerald*)

---

184 Azumarill™

WATER

GENERAL INFO

SPECIES: Aqua Rabbit Pokémon
HEIGHT: 2'07"
WEIGHT: 63 lbs.
ABILITY 1: Thick Fat

When Azumarill is attacked by Fire-type or Ice-type attacks, the damage is reduced by half.

ABILITY 2: Huge Power

Increases the Power of Azumarill's attack, but power is reduced when the ability is changed.

STATS

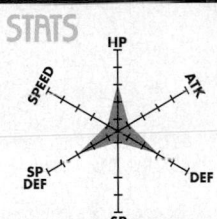

EVOLUTIONS

FRIENDSHIP   LV18

LOCATION(S):

RUBY	Rarity: **Evolve**
Evolve Marill	
SAPPHIRE	Rarity: **Evolve**
Evolve Marill	
FIRERED	Rarity: **None**
Trade from *Ruby/Sapphire/LeafGreen*	
LEAFGREEN	Rarity: **Evolve**
Evolve Marill	
COLOSSEUM	Rarity: **None**
Trade from *Ruby/Sapphire/LeafGreen*	
EMERALD	Rarity: **Evolve**
Evolve Marill	
XD	Rarity: **None**
Trade from *Ruby/Sapphire/LeafGreen*	

MOVES

Level	Attack	Type	Power	ACC	PP	Level	Attack	Type	Power	ACC	PP
—	Tackle	Normal	35	95	35	15	Rollout	Rock	30	90	20
—/3	Defense Curl	Normal	—	—	40	24	Bubblebeam	Water	65	100	20
—/6	Tail Whip	Normal	—	100	30	34	Double-Edge	Normal	120	100	15
—/10	Water Gun	Water	40	100	25	45	Rain Dance	Water	—	—	5
						57	Hydro Pump	Water	120	80	5

TM/HM

TM/HM#	Name	Type	Power	ACC	PP	TM/HM#	Name	Type	Power	ACC	PP
TM01	Focus Punch	Fighting	150	100	20	TM28	Dig	Ground	60	100	10
TM03	Water Pulse	Water	60	95	20	TM31	Brick Break	Fighting	75	100	15
TM06	Toxic	Poison	—	85	10	TM32	Double Team	Normal	—	—	15
TM07	Hail	Ice	—	—	10	TM42	Facade	Normal	70	100	20
TM10	Hidden Power	Normal	—	100	15	TM43	Secret Power	Normal	70	100	20
TM13	Ice Beam	Ice	95	100	10	TM44	Rest	Psychic	—	—	10
TM14	Blizzard	Ice	120	70	5	TM45	Attract	Normal	—	100	15
TM15	Hyper Beam	Normal	150	90	5	HM03	Surf	Water	95	100	15
TM17	Protect	Normal	—	—	10	HM04	Strength	Normal	80	100	20
TM18	Rain Dance	Water	—	—	5	HM06	Rock Smash	Fighting	20	100	15
TM21	Frustration	Normal	—	100	20	HM07	Waterfall	Water	80	100	15
TM23	Iron Tail	Steel	75	75	15	HM08	Dive	Water	60	100	10
TM27	Return	Normal	—	100	20	# = *Emerald Only*					

MOVE TUTOR

FireRed/LeafGreen and *Emerald* Only

Body Slam*	Double-Edge	Mega Kick*
Mega Punch*	Mimic	Seismic Toss*
Substitute		

Emerald Only

Defense Curl*	Dynamicpunch	Endure*
Ice Punch*	Icy Wind*	Mud-Slap*
Rollout	Sleep Talk	Snore*
Swagger	Swift*	

*Battle Frontier tutor move (*Emerald*)

185 Sudowoodo™

ROCK

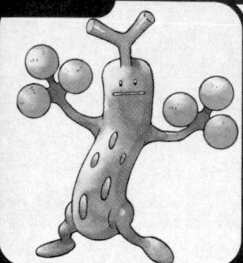

GENERAL INFO
SPECIES: Imitation Pokémon
HEIGHT: 3'11"
WEIGHT: 84 lbs.
ABILITY 1: Rock Head
Prevents Sudowoodo from receiving recoil damage.
ABILITY 2: Sturdy
Prevents Sudowoodo from receiving a one hit KO.

STATS
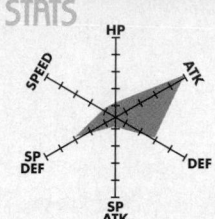

EVOLUTIONS

DOES NOT EVOLVE

LOCATION[S]:

RUBY Rarity: **None**
Trade from *Colosseum/Emerald*

SAPPHIRE Rarity: **None**
Trade from *Colosseum/Emerald*

FIRERED Rarity: **None**
Trade from *Colosseum/Emerald*

LEAFGREEN Rarity: **None**
Trade from *Colosseum/Emerald*

COLOSSEUM Rarity: **Only One**
Pyrite Cave

EMERALD Rarity: **Only One**
Battle Frontier

XD Rarity: **None**
Trade from *Colosseum/Emerald*

MOVES

Level	Attack	Type	Power	ACC	PP
—	Rock Throw	Rock	50	90	15
—	Mimic	Normal	—	100	10
9	Flail	Normal	—	100	15
17	Low Kick	Fighting	—	100	20
25	Rock Slide	Rock	75	90	10
33	Block	Normal	—	100	5
41	Faint Attack	Dark	60	—	20
49	Slam	Normal	80	75	20
57	Double-Edge	Normal	120	100	15

TM/HM

TM/HM#	Name	Type	Power	ACC	PP
TM01	Focus Punch	Fighting	150	100	20
TM04	Calm Mind	Psychic	—	—	20
TM06	Toxic	Poison	—	85	10
TM10	Hidden Power	Normal	—	100	15
TM11	Sunny Day	Fire	—	—	5
TM12	Taunt	Dark	—	100	20
TM17	Protect	Normal	—	—	10
TM21	Frustration	Normal	—	100	20
TM26	Earthquake	Ground	100	100	10
TM27	Return	Normal	—	100	20
TM28	Dig	Ground	60	100	10
TM31	Brick Break	Fighting	75	100	15
TM32	Double Team	Normal	—	—	15
TM37	Sandstorm	Ground	—	—	10
TM39	Rock Tomb	Rock	50	80	10
TM42	Facade	Normal	70	100	20
TM43	Secret Power	Normal	70	100	20
TM44	Rest	Psychic	—	—	10
TM45	Attract	Normal	—	100	15
TM46	Thief	Dark	40	100	10
HM04	Strength	Normal	80	100	15
HM06	Rock Smash	Fighting	20	100	15

EGG MOVES*

Name	Type	Power	ACC	PP
Selfdestruct	Normal	200	100	5

*Learned Via Breeding

MOVE TUTOR
FireRed/LeafGreen and *Emerald* Only

Body Slam*	Counter*	Double-Edge
Explosion	Mega Kick*	Mega Punch*
Mimic	Rock Slide*	Seismic Toss*
Substitute		

*Battle Frontier tutor move (*Emerald*)

---

186 Politoed™

WATER

GENERAL INFO
SPECIES: Frog Pokémon
HEIGHT: 3'07"
WEIGHT: 75 lbs.
ABILITY 1: Damp
No one can use Selfdestruct or Explosion while Politoed is in battle.
ABILITY 2: Water Absorb
Politoed gets 1/4 HPs back when hit by a Water-type attack.

STATS
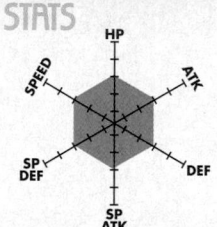

EVOLUTIONS

LV25 **TRADE WITH KING'S ROCK**

LOCATION[S]:

RUBY Rarity: **None**
Trade from *FireRed/LeafGreen*

SAPPHIRE Rarity: **None**
Trade from *FireRed/LeafGreen*

FIRERED Rarity: **Evolve**
Evolve Poliwhirl

LEAFGREEN Rarity: **Evolve**
Evolve Poliwhirl

COLOSSEUM Rarity: **None**
Trade from *FireRed/LeafGreen*

EMERALD Rarity: **None**
Trade from *FireRed/LeafGreen*

XD Rarity: **None**
Trade from *FireRed/LeafGreen*

MOVES

Level	Attack	Type	Power	ACC	PP
—	Water Gun	Water	40	100	25
—	Hypnosis	Psychic	—	60	20
—	Doubleslap	Normal	15	85	10
—	Perish Song	Normal	—	—	5
51	Swagger	Normal	—	90	15

TM/HM

TM/HM#	Name	Type	Power	ACC	PP
TM01	Focus Punch	Fighting	150	100	20
TM03	Water Pulse	Water	60	95	20
TM06	Toxic	Poison	—	85	10
TM07	Hail	Ice	—	—	10
TM10	Hidden Power	Normal	—	100	15
TM13	Ice Beam	Ice	95	100	10
TM14	Blizzard	Ice	120	70	5
TM15	Hyper Beam	Normal	150	90	5
TM17	Protect	Normal	—	—	10
TM18	Rain Dance	Water	—	—	5
TM21	Frustration	Normal	—	100	20
TM26	Earthquake	Ground	100	100	10
TM27	Return	Normal	—	100	20
TM28	Dig	Ground	60	100	10
TM29	Psychic	Psychic	90	100	10
TM31	Brick Break	Fighting	75	100	15
TM32	Double Team	Normal	—	—	15
TM42	Facade	Normal	70	100	20
TM43	Secret Power	Normal	70	100	20
TM44	Rest	Psychic	—	—	10
TM45	Attract	Normal	—	100	15
TM46	Thief	Dark	40	100	10
HM03	Surf	Water	95	100	15
HM04	Strength	Normal	80	100	15
HM06	Rock Smash	Fighting	20	100	15
HM07	Waterfall	Water	80	100	15
HM08	Dive	Water	60	100	10

MOVE TUTOR
FireRed/LeafGreen and *Emerald* Only

Body Slam*	Counter*	Double-Edge
Mega Kick*	Mega Punch*	Metronome
Mimic	Seismic Toss*	Substitute

*Battle Frontier tutor move (*Emerald*)

187 Hoppip™

GRASS | FLYING

GENERAL INFO
SPECIES: Cottonweed Pokémon
HEIGHT: 1'04"
WEIGHT: 1 lb.
ABILITY: Chlorophyll
When the sunlight is strong, Hoppip's Speed is doubled.

STATS
(HP, ATK, DEF, SP ATK, SP DEF, SPEED)

EVOLUTIONS
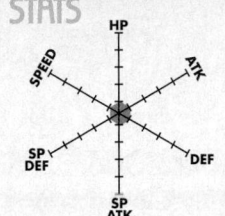  LV18  LV27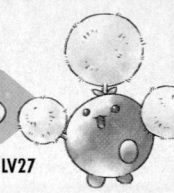

LOCATION(S):

RUBY — Rarity: **None**
Trade from FireRed/LeafGreen

SAPPHIRE — Rarity: **None**
Trade from FireRed/LeafGreen

FIRERED — Rarity: **Common**
Five Island

LEAFGREEN — Rarity: **Common**
Five Island

COLOSSEUM — Rarity: **None**
Breed Skiploom in Ruby/Sapphire/FireRed/LeafGreen, then trade back

EMERALD — Rarity: **None**
Trade from FireRed/LeafGreen

XD — Rarity: **Common**
Oasis Poké Spot

MOVES

Level	Attack	Type	Power	ACC	PP
—	Splash	Normal	—	—	40
5	Synthesis	Grass	—	—	5
5	Tail Whip	Normal	—	100	30
10	Tackle	Normal	35	95	35
13	Poisonpowder	Poison	—	75	35
15	Stun Spore	Grass	—	75	30
17	Sleep Powder	Grass	—	75	15
20	Leech Seed	Grass	—	90	10
25	Cotton Spore	Grass	—	85	40
30	Mega Drain	Grass	40	100	10

TM/HM

TM/HM#	Name	Type	Power	ACC	PP
TM06	Toxic	Poison	—	85	10
TM09	Bullet Seed	Grass	10	100	30
TM10	Hidden Power	Normal	—	100	15
TM11	Sunny Day	Fire	—	—	5
TM17	Protect	Normal	—	—	10
TM19	Giga Drain	Grass	60	100	5
TM21	Frustration	Normal	—	100	20
TM22	Solarbeam	Grass	120	100	10
TM27	Return	Normal	—	100	20
TM32	Double Team	Normal	—	—	15
TM40	Aerial Ace	Flying	60	—	20
TM42	Facade	Normal	70	100	20
TM43	Secret Power	Normal	70	100	20
TM44	Rest	Psychic	—	—	10
TM45	Attract	Normal	—	100	15
HM05	Flash	Normal	—	70	20

EGG MOVES*

Name	Type	Power	ACC	PP
Amnesia	Psychic	—	—	20
Confusion	Psychic	50	100	25
Double-Edge	Normal	120	100	15
Encore	Normal	—	100	5
Helping Hand	Normal	—	100	20
Psych Up	Normal	—	—	10
Reflect	Psychic	—	—	20

*Learned Via Breeding

MOVE TUTOR
FireRed/LeafGreen and Emerald Only

Double-Edge	Mimic	Substitute
Swords Dance*		

*Battle Frontier tutor move (Emerald)

---

188 Skiploom™

GRASS | FLYING

GENERAL INFO
SPECIES: Cottonweed Pokémon
HEIGHT: 2'00"
WEIGHT: 2 lbs.
ABILITY: Chlorophyll
When the Sunlight is Strong, Skiploom's Speed is doubled.

STATS
(HP, ATK, DEF, SP ATK, SP DEF, SPEED)

EVOLUTIONS
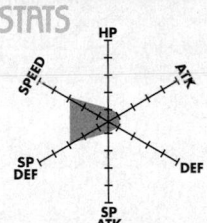  LV18  LV27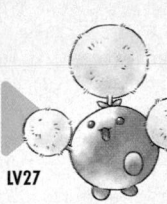

LOCATION(S):

RUBY — Rarity: **Evolve**
Trade from FireRed/LeafGreen/Colosseum

SAPPHIRE — Rarity: **Evolve**
Trade from FireRed/LeafGreen/Colosseum

FIRERED — Rarity: **Evolve**
Evolve Hoppip

LEAFGREEN — Rarity: **Evolve**
Evolve Hoppip

COLOSSEUM — Rarity: **Only One**
Pyrite Town

EMERALD — Rarity: **None**
Trade from FireRed/LeafGreen/Colosseum

XD — Rarity: **Evolve**
Evolve Hoppip

MOVES

Level	Attack	Type	Power	ACC	PP
—	Splash	Normal	—	—	40
—	Synthesis	Grass	—	—	5
—	Tail Whip	Normal	—	100	30
—	Tackle	Normal	35	95	35
13	Poisonpowder	Poison	—	75	35
15	Stun Spore	Grass	—	75	30
17	Sleep Powder	Grass	—	75	15
22	Leech Seed	Grass	—	90	10
29	Cotton Spore	Grass	—	85	40
36	Mega Drain	Grass	40	100	10

TM/HM

TM/HM#	Name	Type	Power	ACC	PP
TM06	Toxic	Poison	—	85	10
TM09	Bullet Seed	Grass	10	100	30
TM10	Hidden Power	Normal	—	100	15
TM11	Sunny Day	Fire	—	—	5
TM17	Protect	Normal	—	—	10
TM19	Giga Drain	Grass	60	100	5
TM21	Frustration	Normal	—	100	20
TM22	Solarbeam	Grass	120	100	10
TM27	Return	Normal	—	100	20
TM32	Double Team	Normal	—	—	15
TM40	Aerial Ace	Flying	60	—	20
TM42	Facade	Normal	70	100	20
TM43	Secret Power	Normal	70	100	20
TM44	Rest	Psychic	—	—	10
TM45	Attract	Normal	—	100	15
HM05	Flash	Normal	—	70	20

MOVE TUTOR
FireRed/LeafGreen and Emerald Only

Double-Edge	Mimic	Substitute
Swords Dance*		

*Battle Frontier tutor move (Emerald)

189 Jumpluff™

GRASS	FLYING

GENERAL INFO

SPECIES: Cottonweed Pokémon
HEIGHT: 2'07"
WEIGHT: 7 lbs.
ABILITY: Chlorophyll

When the sunlight is strong, Jumpluff's Speed is doubled.

STATS

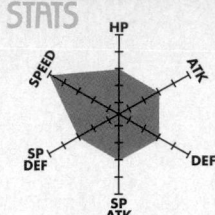

EVOLUTIONS

LV18   LV27

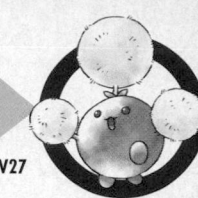

LOCATION[S]:

RUBY   Rarity: **Evolve**
Trade from *FireRed/LeafGreen/Colosseum*

SAPPHIRE   Rarity: **Evolve**
Trade from *FireRed/LeafGreen/Colosseum*

FIRERED   Rarity: **Evolve**
Evolve Skiploom

LEAFGREEN   Rarity: **Evolve**
Evolve Skiploom

COLOSSEUM   Rarity: **Evolve**
Evolve Skiploom

EMERALD   Rarity: **None**
Trade from *FireRed/LeafGreen/Colosseum*

XD   Rarity: **Evolve**
Evolve Skiploom

MOVES

Level	Attack	Type	Power	ACC	PP
—	Splash	Normal	—	—	40
—	Synthesis	Grass	—	—	5
—	Tail Whip	Normal	—	100	30
—	Tackle	Normal	35	95	35
13	Poisonpowder	Poison	—	75	35

Level	Attack	Type	Power	ACC	PP
15	Stun Spore	Grass	—	75	30
17	Sleep Powder	Grass	—	75	15
22	Leech Seed	Grass	—	90	10
33	Cotton Spore	Grass	—	85	40
44	Mega Drain	Grass	40	100	10

TM/HM

TM/HM#	Name	Type	Power	ACC	PP
TM06	Toxic	Poison	—	85	10
TM09	Bullet Seed	Grass	10	100	30
TM10	Hidden Power	Normal	—	100	15
TM11	Sunny Day	Fire	—	—	5
TM15	Hyper Beam	Normal	150	90	5
TM17	Protect	Normal	—	—	10
TM19	Giga Drain	Grass	60	100	5
TM21	Frustration	Normal	—	100	20
TM22	Solarbeam	Grass	120	100	10

TM/HM#	Name	Type	Power	ACC	PP
TM27	Return	Normal	—	100	20
TM32	Double Team	Normal	—	—	15
TM40	Aerial Ace	Flying	60	—	20
TM42	Facade	Normal	70	100	20
TM43	Secret Power	Normal	70	100	20
TM44	Rest	Psychic	—	—	10
TM45	Attract	Normal	—	100	15
HM05	Flash	Normal	—	70	20

EGG MOVES*

Name	Type	Power	ACC	PP
Amnesia	Psychic	—	—	20
Confusion	Psychic	50	100	25
Double-Edge	Normal	120	100	15
Encore	Normal	—	100	5
Helping Hand	Normal	—	100	20
Psych Up	Normal	—	—	10
Refresh	Normal	—	100	20

*Learned Via Breeding

MOVE TUTOR

FireRed/LeafGreen and *Emerald* Only

Double-Edge	Mimic	Substitute
Swords Dance*		

*Battle Frontier tutor move (*Emerald*)

190 Aipom™

	NORMAL

GENERAL INFO

SPECIES: Long Tail Pokémon
HEIGHT: 2'07"
WEIGHT: 25 lbs.
ABILITY 1: Run Away

Allows Aipom to escape from wild Pokémon.

ABILITY 2: Pickup

Attaches items when walking; allows Aipom to take opponent's item during battle.

STATS

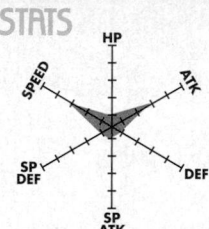

EVOLUTIONS

DOES NOT EVOLVE

LOCATION[S]:

RUBY   Rarity: **None**
Trade from *Colosseum*

SAPPHIRE   Rarity: **None**
Trade from *Colosseum*

FIRERED   Rarity: **None**
Trade from *Colosseum*

LEAFGREEN   Rarity: **None**
Trade from *Colosseum*

COLOSSEUM   Rarity: **Only One**
Shadow Pokémon Lab

EMERALD   Rarity: **Common**
Safari Zone

XD   Rarity: **None**
Trade from *Colosseum*

MOVES

Level	Attack	Type	Power	ACC	PP
—	Scratch	Normal	40	100	35
—	Tail Whip	Normal	—	100	30
6	Sand-Attack	Ground	—	100	15
13	Astonish	Ghost	30	100	15
18	Baton Pass	Normal	—	—	40

Level	Attack	Type	Power	ACC	PP
25	Tickle	Normal	—	100	20
31	Fury Swipes	Normal	18	80	15
38	Swift	Normal	60	—	20
43	Screech	Normal	—	85	40
50	Agility	Psychic	—	—	30

TM/HM

TM/HM#	Name	Type	Power	ACC	PP
TM01	Focus Punch	Fighting	150	100	20
TM03	Water Pulse	Water	60	95	20
TM06	Toxic	Poison	—	85	10
TM10	Hidden Power	Normal	—	100	15
TM11	Sunny Day	Fire	—	—	5
TM12	Taunt	Dark	—	100	20
TM17	Protect	Normal	—	—	10
TM18	Rain Dance	Water	—	—	5
TM21	Frustration	Normal	—	100	20
TM22	Solarbeam	Grass	120	100	10
TM23	Iron Tail	Steel	75	75	15
TM24	Thunderbolt	Electric	95	100	15
TM25	Thunder	Electric	120	70	10
TM27	Return	Normal	—	100	20
TM28	Dig	Ground	60	100	10

TM/HM#	Name	Type	Power	ACC	PP
TM30	Shadow Ball	Ghost	80	100	15
TM31	Brick Break	Fighting	75	100	15
TM32	Double Team	Normal	—	—	15
TM34	Shock Wave	Electric	60	—	20
TM40	Aerial Ace	Flying	60	—	20
TM42	Facade	Normal	70	100	20
TM43	Secret Power	Normal	70	100	20
TM44	Rest	Psychic	—	—	10
TM45	Attract	Normal	—	100	15
TM46	Thief	Dark	40	100	10
TM49	Snatch	Dark	—	100	10
HM01	Cut	Normal	50	95	30
HM04	Strength	Normal	80	100	15
HM06	Rock Smash	Fighting	20	100	15

EGG MOVES*

Name	Type	Power	ACC	PP
Agility	Psychic	—	—	30
Beat Up	Dark	10	100	10
Counter	Fighting	—	100	20
Doubleslap	Normal	15	85	10
Pursuit	Dark	40	100	20
Screech	Normal	—	85	40
Slam	Normal	80	75	20
Spite	Ghost	—	100	10

*Learned Via Breeding

MOVE TUTOR

FireRed/LeafGreen and *Emerald* Only

Body Slam*	Counter*	Double-Edge
Dream Eater*	Mega Kick*	Mega Punch*
Metronome	Mimic	Seismic Toss*
Substitute	Thunder Wave*	

*Battle Frontier tutor move (*Emerald*)

191 Sunkern™

GRASS

GENERAL INFO

SPECIES: Seed Pokémon
HEIGHT: 1'00"
WEIGHT: 4 lbs.
ABILITY: Chlorophyll

Sunkern's speed is doubled when the sunlight is strong.

STATS

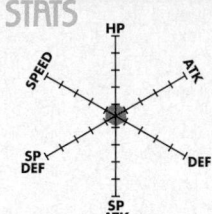

EVOLUTIONS

SUN STONE

LOCATION(S):

RUBY   Rarity: **None**
Trade Sunflora from *Colosseum*, then breed

SAPPHIRE   Rarity: **None**
Trade Sunflora from *Colosseum*, then breed

FIRERED   Rarity: **None**
Trade Sunflora from *Colosseum*, then breed

LEAFGREEN   Rarity: **None**
Trade Sunflora from *Colosseum*, then breed

COLOSSEUM   Rarity: **Breed**
Breed in *Ruby/Sapphire/FireRed/LeafGreen* then trade back

EMERALD   Rarity: **Common**
Safari Zone

XD   Rarity: **None**
Trade Sunflora from *Colosseum*, then breed

MOVES

Level	Attack	Type	Power	ACC	PP
—	Absorb	Grass	20	100	20
6	Growth	Normal	—	—	40
13	Mega Drain	Grass	40	100	10
18	Ingrain	Grass	—	100	20

Level	Attack	Type	Power	ACC	PP
25	Endeavor	Normal	—	100	5
30	Sunny Day	Fire	—	—	5
37	Synthesis	Grass	—	—	5
42	Giga Drain	Grass	60	100	5

TM/HM

TM/HM#	Name	Type	Power	ACC	PP
TM06	Toxic	Poison	—	85	10
TM09	Bullet Seed	Grass	10	100	30
TM10	Hidden Power	Normal	—	100	15
TM11	Sunny Day	Fire	—	—	5
TM16	Light Screen	Psychic	—	—	30
TM17	Protect	Normal	—	—	10
TM19	Giga Drain	Grass	60	100	5
TM20	Safeguard	Normal	—	—	25
TM21	Frustration	Normal	—	100	20
TM22	Solarbeam	Grass	120	100	10

TM/HM#	Name	Type	Power	ACC	PP
TM27	Return	Normal	—	100	20
TM32	Double Team	Normal	—	—	15
TM36	Sludge Bomb	Poison	90	100	10
TM42	Facade	Normal	70	100	20
TM43	Secret Power	Normal	70	100	20
TM44	Rest	Psychic	—	—	10
TM45	Attract	Normal	—	100	15
HM01	Cut	Normal	50	95	30
HM05	Flash	Normal	—	70	20

EGG MOVES*

Name	Type	Power	ACC	PP
Curse	—	—	—	10
Encore	Normal	—	100	5
Grasswhistle	Grass	—	55	15
Helping Hand	Normal	—	100	20
Leech Seed	Grass	—	90	10
Nature Power	Normal	—	95	20

*Learned Via Breeding

MOVE TUTOR

FireRed/LeafGreen and *Emerald* Only

Double-Edge	Mimic	Substitute
Swords Dance*		

*Battle Frontier tutor move (*Emerald*)

---

192 Sunflora™

GRASS

GENERAL INFO

SPECIES: Sun Pokémon
HEIGHT: 2'07"
WEIGHT: 19 lbs.
ABILITY: Chlorophyll

Sunflora's Speed is doubled when the sunlight is strong.

STATS

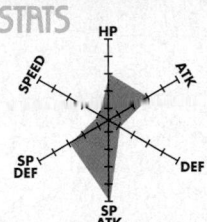

EVOLUTIONS

SUN STONE

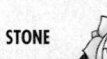

LOCATION(S):

RUBY   Rarity: **None**
Trade from *Colosseum*

SAPPHIRE   Rarity: **None**
Trade from *Colosseum*

FIRERED   Rarity: **None**
Trade from *Colosseum*

LEAFGREEN   Rarity: **None**
Trade from *Colosseum*

COLOSSEUM   Rarity: **Only One**
Obtained from Baila in Realgam Tower

EMERALD   Rarity: **Evolve**
Evolve Sunkern

XD   Rarity: **None**
Trade from *Colosseum*

MOVES

Level	Attack	Type	Power	ACC	PP
—	Absorb	Grass	20	100	20
—	Pound	Normal	40	100	35
6	Growth	Normal	—	—	40
13	Razor Leaf	Grass	55	95	25

Level	Attack	Type	Power	ACC	PP
18	Ingrain	Grass	—	100	20
25	Bullet Seed	Grass	10	100	30
30	Sunny Day	Fire	—	—	5
37	Petal Dance	Grass	70	100	20
42	Solarbeam	Grass	120	100	10

TM/HM

TM/HM#	Name	Type	Power	ACC	PP
TM06	Toxic	Poison	—	85	10
TM09	Bullet Seed	Grass	10	100	30
TM10	Hidden Power	Normal	—	100	15
TM11	Sunny Day	Fire	—	—	5
TM15	Hyper Beam	Normal	150	90	5
TM16	Light Screen	Psychic	—	—	30
TM17	Protect	Normal	—	—	10
TM19	Giga Drain	Grass	60	100	5
TM20	Safeguard	Normal	—	—	25
TM21	Frustration	Normal	—	100	20

TM/HM#	Name	Type	Power	ACC	PP
TM22	Solarbeam	Grass	120	100	10
TM27	Return	Normal	—	100	20
TM32	Double Team	Normal	—	—	15
TM36	Sludge Bomb	Poison	90	100	10
TM42	Facade	Normal	70	100	20
TM43	Secret Power	Normal	70	100	20
TM44	Rest	Psychic	—	—	10
TM45	Attract	Normal	—	100	15
HM01	Cut	Normal	50	95	30
HM05	Flash	Normal	—	70	20

MOVE TUTOR

FireRed/LeafGreen and *Emerald* Only

Double-Edge	Mimic	Substitute
Swords Dance*		

*Battle Frontier tutor move (*Emerald*)

193 Yanma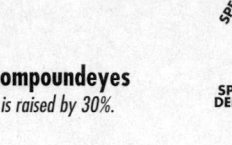

BUG | FLYING

GENERAL INFO

SPECIES: Clear Wing Pokémon
HEIGHT: 3'11"
WEIGHT: 84 lbs.
ABILITY 1: Speed Boost
Yanma's Speed raises one level after each turn.
ABILITY 2: Compoundeyes
Yanma's Accuracy is raised by 30%.

STATS

EVOLUTIONS

DOES NOT EVOLVE

LOCATION[S]:

RUBY Rarity: **None**
Trade from *FireRed/LeafGreen/Colosseum*

SAPPHIRE Rarity: **None**
Trade from *FireRed/LeafGreen/Colosseum*

FIRERED Rarity: **Rare**
Six Island

LEAFGREEN Rarity: **Rare**
Six Island

COLOSSEUM Rarity: **Only One**
Pyrite Town

EMERALD Rarity: **None**
Trade from *FireRed/LeafGreen/Colosseum*

XD Rarity: **None**
Trade from *FireRed/LeafGreen/Colosseum*

MOVES

Level	Attack	Type	Power	ACC	PP	Level	Attack	Type	Power	ACC	PP
—	Tackle	Normal	35	95	35	23	Hypnosis	Psychic	—	60	20
—	Foresight	Normal	—	100	40	28	Detect	Fight	—	—	5
6	Quick Attack	Normal	40	100	30	34	Uproar	Normal	50	100	10
12	Double Team	Normal	—	—	15	39	Wing Attack	Flying	60	100	35
17	Sonicboom	Normal	—	90	20	45	Supersonic	Normal	—	55	20
						50	Screech	Normal	—	85	40

TM/HM

TM/HM#	Name	Type	Power	ACC	PP	TM/HM#	Name	Type	Power	ACC	PP
TM06	Toxic	Poison	—	85	10	TM32	Double Team	Normal	—	—	15
TM10	Hidden Power	Normal	—	100	15	TM40	Aerial Ace	Flying	60	—	20
TM11	Sunny Day	Fire	—	—	5	TM42	Facade	Normal	70	100	20
TM17	Protect	Normal	—	—	10	TM43	Secret Power	Normal	70	100	20
TM19	Giga Drain	Grass	60	100	5	TM44	Rest	Psychic	—	—	10
TM21	Frustration	Normal	—	100	20	TM45	Attract	Normal	—	100	15
TM22	Solarbeam	Grass	120	100	10	TM46	Thief	Dark	40	100	10
TM27	Return	Normal	—	100	20	TM47	Steel Wing	Steel	70	90	25
TM29	Psychic	Psychic	90	100	10	HM05	Flash	Normal	—	70	20
TM30	Shadow Ball	Ghost	80	100	15						

EGG MOVES*

Name	Type	Power	ACC	PP
Leech Life	Bug	20	100	15
Reversal	Fighting	—	100	15
Signal Beam	Bug	75	100	15
Silver Wind	Bug	60	100	5
Whirlwind	Normal	—	100	20

*Learned Via Breeding

MOVE TUTOR

FireRed/LeafGreen and *Emerald* Only

Double-Edge | Dream Eater* | Mimic
Substitute

*Battle Frontier tutor move (*Emerald*)

---

194 Wooper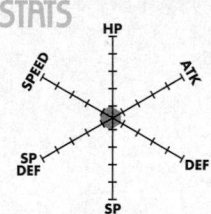

WATER | GROUND

GENERAL INFO

SPECIES: Water Fish Pokémon
HEIGHT: 1'04"
WEIGHT: 19 lbs.
ABILITY 1: Damp
No one can use Selfdestruct or Explosion while Wooper is in battle.
ABILITY 2: Water Absorb
Wooper gets 1/4 HPs back when hit by a Water-type attack.

STATS

EVOLUTIONS

 ▶
LV20

LOCATION[S]:

RUBY Rarity: **None**
Trade from *FireRed*

SAPPHIRE Rarity: **None**
Trade from *FireRed*

FIRERED Rarity: **Common**
Six Island

LEAFGREEN Rarity: **None**
Trade from *FireRed*

COLOSSEUM Rarity: **None**
Trade from *FireRed/LeafGreen*

EMERALD Rarity: **Common**
Safari Zone

XD Rarity: **Rare**
Cave Poké Spot

MOVES

Level	Attack	Type	Power	ACC	PP	Level	Attack	Type	Power	ACC	PP
—	Water Gun	Water	40	100	25	31	Yawn	Normal	—	100	10
—	Tail Whip	Normal	—	100	30	36	Earthquake	Ground	100	100	10
11	Slam	Normal	80	75	20	41	Rain Dance	Water	—	—	5
16	Mud Shot	Ground	55	95	15	51	Mist	Ice	—	—	30
21	Amnesia	Psychic	—	—	20	51	Haze	Ice	—	—	30

TM/HM

TM/HM#	Name	Type	Power	ACC	PP	TM/HM#	Name	Type	Power	ACC	PP
TM03	Water Pulse	Water	60	95	20	TM32	Double Team	Normal	—	—	15
TM06	Toxic	Poison	—	85	10	TM36	Sludge Bomb	Poison	90	100	10
TM07	Hail	Ice	—	—	10	TM37	Sandstorm	Ground	—	—	10
TM10	Hidden Power	Normal	—	100	15	TM42	Facade	Normal	70	100	20
TM13	Ice Beam	Ice	95	100	10	TM43	Secret Power	Normal	70	100	20
TM14	Blizzard	Ice	120	70	5	TM44	Rest	Psychic	—	—	10
TM17	Protect	Normal	—	—	10	TM45	Attract	Normal	—	100	15
TM18	Rain Dance	Water	—	—	5	HM03	Surf	Water	95	100	15
TM21	Frustration	Normal	—	100	20	HM05	Flash	Normal	—	70	20
TM23	Iron Tail	Steel	75	75	15	HM06	Rock Smash	Fighting	20	100	15
TM26	Earthquake	Ground	100	100	10	HM07	Waterfall	Water	80	100	15
TM27	Return	Normal	—	100	20	HM08	Dive	Water	60	100	10
TM28	Dig	Ground	60	100	10						

EGG MOVES*

Name	Type	Power	ACC	PP
Ancientpower	Rock	60	100	5
Body Slam	Normal	85	100	15
Curse	—	—	—	10
Mud Sport	Ground	—	100	15
Safeguard	Normal	—	—	25
Spit Up	Normal	100	100	10
Swallow	Normal	—	—	10
Stockpile	Normal	—	—	10

*Learned Via Breeding

MOVE TUTOR

FireRed/LeafGreen and *Emerald* Only

Body Slam* | Double-Edge | Mimic
Substitute

*Battle Frontier tutor move (*Emerald*)

195 Quagsire™

WATER | GROUND

GENERAL INFO

SPECIES: Water Fish Pokémon
HEIGHT: 4'07"
WEIGHT: 165 lbs.
ABILITY 1: Damp
No one can use Selfdestruct or Explosion while Quagsire is in battle.

ABILITY 2: Water Absorb
Quagsire gets 1/4 HPs back when hit by a Water attack.

STATS

EVOLUTIONS

LV20

LOCATION(S):

RUBY	Rarity: **Evolve**
Trade from *FireRed/Colosseum*	
SAPPHIRE	Rarity: **Evolve**
Trade from *FireRed/Colosseum*	
FIRERED	Rarity: **Evolve**
Evolve Wooper	
LEAFGREEN	Rarity: **None**
Trade from *FireRed/Colosseum*	
COLOSSEUM	Rarity: **Only One**
Pyrite Town	
EMERALD	Rarity: **Rare**
Safari Zone	
XD	Rarity: **Evolve**
Evolve Wooper	

MOVES

Level	Attack	Type	Power	ACC	PP	Level	Attack	Type	Power	ACC	PP
—	Water Gun	Water	40	100	25	35	Yawn	Normal	—	100	10
—	Tail Whip	Normal	—	100	30	42	Earthquake	Ground	100	100	10
11	Slam	Normal	80	75	20	49	Rain Dance	Water	—	—	5
16	Mud Shot	Ground	55	95	15	61	Mist	Ice	—	—	30
23	Amnesia	Psychic	—	—	20	61	Haze	Ice	—	—	30

TM/HM

TM/HM#	Name	Type	Power	ACC	PP	TM/HM#	Name	Type	Power	ACC	PP
TM01	Focus Punch	Fighting	150	100	20	TM31	Brick Break	Fighting	75	100	15
TM03	Water Pulse	Water	60	95	20	TM32	Double Team	Normal	—	—	15
TM06	Toxic	Poison	—	85	10	TM36	Sludge Bomb	Poison	90	100	10
TM07	Hail	Ice	—	—	10	TM37	Sandstorm	Ground	—	—	10
TM10	Hidden Power	Normal	—	100	15	TM39	Rock Tomb	Rock	50	80	10
TM13	Ice Beam	Ice	95	100	10	TM42	Facade	Normal	70	100	20
TM14	Blizzard	Ice	120	70	5	TM43	Secret Power	Normal	70	100	20
TM15	Hyper Beam	Normal	150	90	5	TM44	Rest	Psychic	—	—	10
TM17	Protect	Normal	—	—	10	TM45	Attract	Normal	—	100	15
TM18	Rain Dance	Water	—	—	5	HM03	Surf	Water	95	100	15
TM21	Frustration	Normal	—	100	20	HM04	Strength	Normal	80	100	20
TM23	Iron Tail	Steel	75	75	15	HM05	Flash	Normal	—	70	20
TM26	Earthquake	Ground	100	100	10	HM06	Rock Smash	Fighting	20	100	15
TM27	Return	Normal	—	100	20	HM07	Waterfall	Water	80	100	15
TM28	Dig	Ground	60	100	10	HM08	Dive	Water	60	100	10

MOVE TUTOR

FireRed/LeafGreen and Emerald Only

Body Slam*	Counter*	Double-Edge
Mega Kick*	Mega Punch*	Mimic
Seismic Toss*	Substitute	

*Battle Frontier tutor move (*Emerald*)

---

196 Espeon™

PSYCHIC

GENERAL INFO

SPECIES: Sun Pokémon
HEIGHT: 2'11"
WEIGHT: 58 lbs.
ABILITY: Synchronize
When Espeon is hit by Poison, Paralyze, or Burn, the opponent receives the same.

STATS

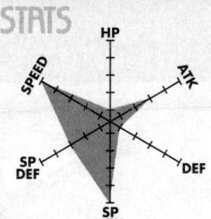

EVOLUTIONS

FRIENDSHIP (DAY)

LOCATION(S):

RUBY	Rarity: **Evolve**
Evolve Eevee	
SAPPHIRE	Rarity: **Evolve**
Evolve Eevee	
FIRERED	Rarity: **Evolve**
Trade from *Ruby/Sapphire/Colosseum*	
LEAFGREEN	Rarity: **Evolve**
Trade from *Ruby/Sapphire/Colosseum*	
COLOSSEUM	Rarity: **Only One**
Starter Pokémon in *Colosseum*	
EMERALD	Rarity: **None**
Trade from *Ruby/Sapphire/Colosseum*	
XD	Rarity: **Evolve**
Evolve Eevee	

MOVES

Level	Attack	Type	Power	ACC	PP	Level	Attack	Type	Power	ACC	PP
—	Tackle	Normal	35	95	35	23	Quick Attack	Normal	40	100	30
—	Tail Whip	Normal	—	100	30	30	Swift	Normal	60	—	20
—	Helping Hand	Normal	—	100	20	36	Psybeam	Psychic	65	100	20
8	Sand-Attack	Ground	—	100	15	42	Psych Up	Normal	—	—	10
16	Confusion	Psychic	50	100	25	47	Psychic	Psychic	90	100	10
						52	Morning Sun	Normal	—	—	5

TM/HM

TM/HM#	Name	Type	Power	ACC	PP	TM/HM#	Name	Type	Power	ACC	PP
TM04	Calm Mind	Psychic	—	—	20	TM29	Psychic	Psychic	90	100	10
TM06	Toxic	Poison	—	85	10	TM30	Shadow Ball	Ghost	80	100	15
TM10	Hidden Power	Normal	—	100	15	TM32	Double Team	Normal	—	—	15
TM11	Sunny Day	Fire	—	—	5	TM33	Reflect	Normal	—	—	20
TM15	Hyper Beam	Normal	150	90	5	TM42	Facade	Normal	70	100	20
TM16	Light Screen	Psychic	—	—	30	TM43	Secret Power	Normal	70	100	20
TM17	Protect	Normal	—	—	10	TM44	Rest	Psychic	—	—	10
TM18	Rain Dance	Water	—	—	5	TM45	Attract	Normal	—	100	15
TM21	Frustration	Normal	—	100	20	TM48	Skill Swap	Psychic	—	100	10
TM23	Iron Tail	Steel	75	75	15	HM01	Cut	Normal	50	95	30
TM27	Return	Normal	—	100	20	HM05	Flash	Normal	—	70	20
TM28	Dig	Ground	60	100	10						

MOVE TUTOR

FireRed/LeafGreen and Emerald Only

Body Slam*	Double-Edge	Dream Eater*
Mimic	Substitute	

*Battle Frontier tutor move (*Emerald*)

201 Unown™

PSYCHIC

GENERAL INFO
SPECIES: **Symbol Pokémon**
HEIGHT: **1'08"**
WEIGHT: **11 lbs.**
ABILITY: **Levitate**
Prevents Unown from being hit by Ground-type moves.

STATS

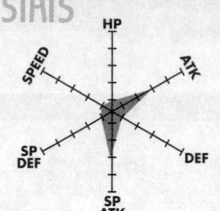

EVOLUTIONS

DOES NOT EVOLVE

LOCATION(S):

RUBY Rarity: **None**
Trade from *FireRed/LeafGreen*

SAPPHIRE Rarity: **None**
Trade from *FireRed/LeafGreen*

FIRERED Rarity: **Common**
Ruins of Seven Island

LEAFGREEN Rarity: **Common**
Ruins of Seven Island

COLOSSEUM Rarity: **None**
Trade from *FireRed/LeafGreen*

EMERALD Rarity: **None**
Trade from *FireRed/LeafGreen*

XD Rarity: **None**
Trade from *FireRed/LeafGreen*

MOVES

Level	Attack	Type	Power	ACC	PP
—	Hidden Power	Normal	—	100	15

TM/HM

TM/HM#	Name	Type	Power	ACC	PP
None					

EGG MOVES*

Name	Type	Power	ACC	PP
None				

*Learned Via Breeding

MOVE TUTOR
FireRed/LeafGreen and *Emerald* Only
None

202 Wobbuffet™

PSYCHIC

GENERAL INFO
SPECIES: **Patient Pokémon**
HEIGHT: **4'03"**
WEIGHT: **63 lbs.**
ABILITY: **Shadow Tag**
An opponent cannot escape while Wobbuffet is in battle.

STATS

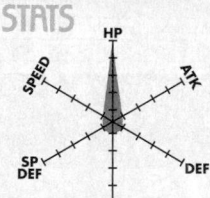

EVOLUTIONS

LV15

LOCATION(S):

RUBY Rarity: **Common**
Safari Zone

SAPPHIRE Rarity: **Common**
Safari Zone

FIRERED Rarity: **Common**
Six Island

LEAFGREEN Rarity: **Common**
Six Island

COLOSSEUM Rarity: **None**
Trade from *Ruby/Sapphire*

EMERALD Rarity: **Common**
Safari Zone

XD Rarity: **None**
Trade from *Ruby/Sapphire/Emerald*

MOVES

Level	Attack	Type	Power	ACC	PP
—	Counter	Fighting	—	100	20
—	Mirror Coat	Psychic	—	100	20
—	Safeguard	Normal	—	—	25
—	Destiny Bond	Ghost	—	—	5

TM/HM

TM/HM#	Name	Type	Power	ACC	PP
None					

EGG MOVES*

Name	Type	Power	ACC	PP
None				

*Learned Via Breeding

MOVE TUTOR
FireRed/LeafGreen and *Emerald* Only
None

203 Girafarig™

NORMAL PSYCHIC

GENERAL INFO
SPECIES: Long Neck Pokémon
HEIGHT: 4'11"
WEIGHT: 91 lbs.
ABILITY 1: Inner Focus
Prevents Girafarig from flinching.
ABILITY 2: Early Bird
Allows Girafarig to wake up sooner when put to sleep.

STATS

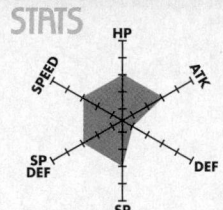

EVOLUTIONS

DOES NOT EVOLVE

LOCATION(S):

RUBY — Rarity: **Common**
Safari Zone

SAPPHIRE — Rarity: **Common**
Safari Zone

FIRERED — Rarity: **None**
Trade from *Ruby/Sapphire*

LEAFGREEN — Rarity: **None**
Trade from *Ruby/Sapphire*

COLOSSEUM — Rarity: **None**
Trade from *Ruby/Sapphire*

EMERALD — Rarity: **Common**
Safari Zone

XD — Rarity: **None**
Trade from *Ruby/Sapphire*

MOVES

Level	Attack	Type	Power	ACC	PP	Level	Attack	Type	Power	ACC	PP
—	Tackle	Normal	35	95	35	25	Odor Sleuth	Normal	—	100	40
—	Growl	Normal	—	100	40	31	Agility	Psychic	—	—	30
7	Astonish	Ghost	30	100	15	37	Baton Pass	Normal	—	—	40
13	Confusion	Psychic	50	100	25	43	Psybeam	Psychic	65	100	20
19	Stomp	Normal	65	100	20	49	Crunch	Dark	80	100	15

TM/HM

TM/HM#	Name	Type	Power	ACC	PP	TM/HM#	Name	Type	Power	ACC	PP
TM04	Calm Mind	Psychic	—	—	20	TM30	Shadow Ball	Ghost	80	100	15
TM06	Toxic	Poison	—	85	10	TM32	Double Team	Normal	—	—	15
TM10	Hidden Power	Normal	—	100	15	TM33	Reflect	Normal	—	—	20
TM11	Sunny Day	Fire	—	—	5	TM34	Shock Wave	Electric	60	—	20
TM16	Light Screen	Psychic	—	—	30	TM42	Facade	Normal	70	100	20
TM17	Protect	Normal	—	—	10	TM43	Secret Power	Normal	70	100	20
TM18	Rain Dance	Water	—	—	5	TM44	Rest	Psychic	—	—	10
TM21	Frustration	Normal	—	100	20	TM45	Attract	Normal	—	100	15
TM23	Iron Tail	Steel	75	75	15	TM46	Thief	Dark	40	100	10
TM24	Thunderbolt	Electric	95	100	15	TM48	Skill Swap	Psychic	—	100	10
TM25	Thunder	Electric	120	70	10	HM04	Strength	Normal	80	100	15
TM26	Earthquake	Ground	100	100	10	HM05	Flash	Normal	—	70	20
TM27	Return	Normal	—	100	20	HM06	Rock Smash	Fighting	20	100	15
TM29	Psychic	Psychic	90	100	10						

EGG MOVES*

Name	Type	Power	ACC	PP
Take Down	Normal	90	85	20
Amnesia	Psychic	—	—	20
Foresight	Normal	—	100	40
Future Sight	Psychic	80	90	15
Psych Up	Normal	—	—	10
Magic Coat	Psychic	—	100	15
Beat Up	Dark	10	100	10
Wish	Normal	—	100	10

*Learned Via Breeding

MOVE TUTOR

FireRed/LeafGreen and Emerald Only

Body Slam*	Double-Edge*	Dream Eater*
Mimic	Substitute	Thunder Wave*

Emerald Only

Endure*	Mud-Slap*	Psych Up*
Sleep Talk	Snore*	Swagger
Swift*		

*Battle Frontier tutor move (*Emerald*)

204 Pineco™

BUG

GENERAL INFO
SPECIES: Bagworm Pokémon
HEIGHT: 2'00"
WEIGHT: 16 lbs.
ABILITY: Sturdy
Prevents Pineco from being hit by a one hit KO.

STATS

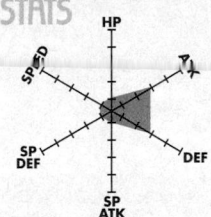

EVOLUTIONS

LV31

LOCATION(S):

RUBY — Rarity: **None**
Trade from *Colosseum*

SAPPHIRE — Rarity: **None**
Trade from *Colosseum*

FIRERED — Rarity: **None**
Trade from *Colosseum*

LEAFGREEN — Rarity: **None**
Trade from *Colosseum*

COLOSSEUM — Rarity: **Breed**
Must Breed Forretress

EMERALD — Rarity: **Common**
Safari Zone

XD — Rarity: **Only One**
Phenac City (Capture from Cipher Peon Gonrag)

MOVES

Level	Attack	Type	Power	ACC	PP	Level	Attack	Type	Power	ACC	PP
—	Tackle	Normal	35	95	35	22	Rapid Spin	Normal	20	100	40
—	Protect	Normal	—	—	10	29	Bide	Normal	—	100	10
8	Selfdestruct	Normal	200	100	5	36	Explosion	Normal	250	100	5
15	Take Down	Normal	90	85	20	43	Spikes	Ground	—	—	20
						50	Double-Edge	Normal	120	100	15

TM/HM

TM/HM#	Name	Type	Power	ACC	PP	TM/HM#	Name	Type	Power	ACC	PP
TM06	Toxic	Poison	—	85	10	TM28	Dig	Ground	60	100	10
TM10	Hidden Power	Normal	—	100	15	TM32	Double Team	Normal	—	—	15
TM11	Sunny Day	Fire	—	—	5	TM33	Reflect	Normal	—	—	20
TM16	Light Screen	Psychic	—	—	30	TM37	Sandstorm	Ground	—	—	10
TM17	Protect	Normal	—	—	10	TM42	Facade	Normal	70	100	20
TM19	Giga Drain	Grass	60	100	5	TM43	Secret Power	Normal	70	100	20
TM21	Frustration	Normal	—	100	20	TM44	Rest	Psychic	—	—	10
TM22	Solarbeam	Grass	120	100	10	TM45	Attract	Normal	—	100	15
TM26	Earthquake	Ground	100	100	10	HM04	Strength	Normal	80	100	15
TM27	Return	Normal	—	100	20	HM06	Rock Smash	Fighting	20	100	15

EGG MOVES*

Name	Type	Power	ACC	PP
Counter	Fighting	—	100	20
Flail	Normal	—	100	15
Pin Missile	Bug	14	85	20
Reflect	Psychic	—	—	20
Sand Tomb	Ground	15	70	15
Swift	Normal	60	—	20

*Learned Via Breeding

MOVE TUTOR

FireRed/LeafGreen and Emerald Only

Body Slam*	Counter*	Double-Edge*
Explosion	Mimic	Rock Slide*
Substitute		

*Battle Frontier tutor move (*Emerald*)

205 Forretress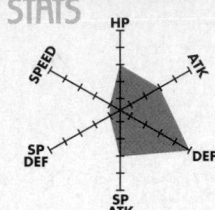

BUG	STEEL

GENERAL INFO
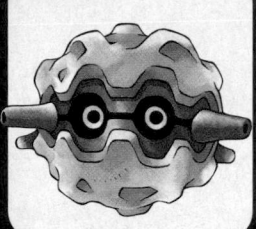

SPECIES: Bagworm Pokémon
HEIGHT: 3'11"
WEIGHT: 277 lbs.
ABILITY: Sturdy
Prevents Forretress from being hit by a one hit KO.

STATS

EVOLUTIONS
 ▶

LV31

LOCATION[S]:

RUBY — Rarity: **None**
Evolve Pineco, Obtain in *Colosseum*

SAPPHIRE — Rarity: **None**
Evolve Pineco, Obtain in *Colosseum*

FIRERED — Rarity: **None**
Trade from *Colosseum*

LEAFGREEN — Rarity: **None**
Trade from *Colosseum*

COLOSSEUM — Rarity: **Only One**
Shadow Pokémon Lab

EMERALD — Rarity: **Evolve**
Evolve Pineco, Obtain in *Colosseum*

XD — Rarity: **Evolve**
Evolve Pineco

MOVES

Level	Attack	Type	Power	ACC	PP	Level	Attack	Type	Power	ACC	PP
—	Tackle	Normal	35	95	35	29	Bide	Normal	—	100	10
—	Protect	Normal	—	—	10	31	Zap Cannon	Electric	100	50	5
—	Selfdestruct	Normal	200	100	5	39	Explosion	Normal	250	100	5
15	Take Down	Normal	90	85	20	49	Spikes	Ground	—	—	20
22	Rapid Spin	Normal	20	100	40	59	Double-Edge	Normal	120	100	15

TM/HM

TM/HM#	Name	Type	Power	ACC	PP	TM/HM#	Name	Type	Power	ACC	PP
TM06	Toxic	Poison	—	85	10	TM28	Dig	Ground	60	100	10
TM10	Hidden Power	Normal	—	100	15	TM32	Double Team	Normal	—	—	15
TM11	Sunny Day	Fire	—	—	5	TM33	Reflect	Normal	—	—	20
TM15	Hyper Beam	Normal	150	90	5	TM37	Sandstorm	Ground	—	—	10
TM16	Light Screen	Psychic	—	—	30	TM42	Facade	Normal	70	100	20
TM17	Protect	Normal	—	—	10	TM43	Secret Power	Normal	70	100	20
TM19	Giga Drain	Grass	60	100	5	TM44	Rest	Psychic	—	—	10
TM21	Frustration	Normal	—	100	20	TM45	Attract	Normal	—	100	15
TM22	Solarbeam	Grass	120	100	10	HM04	Strength	Normal	80	100	20
TM26	Earthquake	Ground	100	100	10	HM06	Rock Smash	Fighting	20	100	15
TM27	Return	Normal	—	100	20						

MOVE TUTOR
FireRed/LeafGreen and *Emerald* Only

Body Slam*	Counter*	Double-Edge
Explosion	Mimic	Rock Slide*
Substitute		

*Battle Frontier tutor move (*Emerald*)

---

206 Dunsparce

NORMAL

GENERAL INFO

SPECIES: Land Snake Pokémon
HEIGHT: 4'11"
WEIGHT: 31 lbs.
ABILITY 1: Run Away
Dunsparce can escape from wild Pokémon.

ABILITY 2: Serene Grace
When Dunsparce is in battle, attacks with extra effects have two times the chance of happening.

STATS
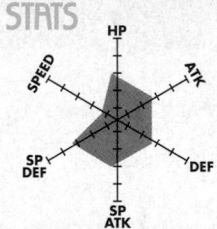

EVOLUTIONS

DOES NOT EVOLVE

LOCATION[S]:

RUBY — Rarity: **None**
Obtain in *Colosseum*

SAPPHIRE — Rarity: **None**
Obtain in *Colosseum*

FIRERED — Rarity: **Common**
Three Island

LEAFGREEN — Rarity: **Common**
Three Island

COLOSSEUM — Rarity: **Only One**
Pyrite Cave

EMERALD — Rarity: **None**
Trade from *FireRed/LeafGreen/Colosseum*

XD — Rarity: **None**
Trade from *FireRed/LeafGreen/Colosseum*

MOVES

Level	Attack	Type	Power	ACC	PP	Level	Attack	Type	Power	ACC	PP
—	Rage	Normal	20	100	20	24	Spite	Ghost	—	100	10
4	Defense Curl	Normal	—	—	40	31	Pursuit	Dark	40	100	20
11	Yawn	Normal	—	100	10	34	Screech	Normal	—	85	40
14	Glare	Normal	—	75	30	41	Take Down	Normal	90	85	20
21	Rollout	Rock	30	90	20	44	Flail	Normal	—	100	15
						51	Endeavor	Normal	—	100	5

TM/HM

TM/HM#	Name	Type	Power	ACC	PP	TM/HM#	Name	Type	Power	ACC	PP
TM03	Water Pulse	Water	60	95	20	TM28	Dig	Ground	60	100	10
TM04	Calm Mind	Psychic	—	—	20	TM30	Shadow Ball	Ghost	80	100	15
TM06	Toxic	Poison	—	85	10	TM31	Brick Break	Fighting	75	100	15
TM10	Hidden Power	Normal	—	100	15	TM32	Double Team	Normal	—	—	15
TM11	Sunny Day	Fire	—	—	5	TM34	Shock Wave	Electric	60	—	20
TM13	Ice Beam	Ice	95	100	10	TM35	Flamethrower	Fire	95	100	15
TM14	Blizzard	Ice	120	70	5	TM38	Fire Blast	Fire	120	85	5
TM17	Protect	Normal	—	—	10	TM39	Rock Tomb	Rock	50	80	10
TM18	Rain Dance	Water	—	—	5	TM42	Facade	Normal	70	100	20
TM21	Frustration	Normal	—	100	20	TM43	Secret Power	Normal	70	100	20
TM22	Solarbeam	Grass	120	100	10	TM44	Rest	Psychic	—	—	10
TM23	Iron Tail	Steel	75	75	15	TM45	Attract	Normal	—	100	15
TM24	Thunderbolt	Electric	95	100	15	TM46	Thief	Dark	40	100	10
TM25	Thunder	Electric	120	70	10	HM04	Strength	Normal	80	100	20
TM26	Earthquake	Ground	100	100	10	HM06	Rock Smash	Fighting	20	100	15
TM27	Return	Normal	—	100	20						

EGG MOVES*

Name	Type	Power	ACC	PP
Ancientpower	Rock	60	100	5
Astonish	Ghost	30	100	15
Bide	Normal	—	100	10
Bite	Dark	60	100	25
Curse	—	—	—	10
Headbutt	Normal	70	100	15
Rock Slide	Rock	75	90	10

*Learned Via Breeding

MOVE TUTOR
FireRed/LeafGreen and *Emerald* Only

Body Slam*	Counter*	Double-Edge
Dream Eater*	Mimic	Rock Slide*
Substitute	Thunder Wave*	

*Battle Frontier tutor move (*Emerald*)

207 Gligar™

GROUND | FLYING

GENERAL INFO
SPECIES: Flyscorpion Pokémon
HEIGHT: 3'07"
WEIGHT: 143 lbs.
ABILITY 1: Sand Veil
During a sandstorm, Gligar is able to evade more moves.

ABILITY 2: Hyper Cutter
Prevents Gligar from having its Attack lowered.

STATS
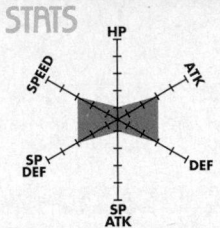

EVOLUTIONS

DOES NOT EVOLVE

LOCATION(S):

RUBY	**Rarity: None**	
Obtain in *Colosseum*		
SAPPHIRE	**Rarity: None**	
Obtain in *Colosseum*		
FIRERED	**Rarity: None**	
Trade from *Colosseum*		
LEAFGREEN	**Rarity: None**	
Trade from *Colosseum*		
COLOSSEUM	**Rarity: Only One**	
The Under		
EMERALD	**Rarity: Rare**	
Safari Zone		
XD	**Rarity: Rare**	
Rock Poké Spot		

MOVES

Level	Attack	Type	Power	ACC	PP	Level	Attack	Type	Power	ACC	PP
—	Poison Sting	Poison	15	100	35	28	Faint Attack	Dark	60	—	20
6	Sand Attack	Ground	—	100	15	36	Slash	Normal	70	100	20
13	Harden	Normal	—	—	30	44	Screech	Normal	—	85	40
20	Quick Attack	Normal	40	100	30	52	Guillotine	Normal	—	30	5

TM/HM

TM/HM#	Name	Type	Power	ACC	PP	TM/HM#	Name	Type	Power	ACC	PP
TM06	Toxic	Poison	—	85	10	TM37	Sandstorm	Ground	—	—	10
TM10	Hidden Power	Normal	—	100	15	TM39	Rock Tomb	Rock	50	80	10
TM11	Sunny Day	Fire	—	—	5	TM40	Aerial Ace	Flying	60	—	20
TM17	Protect	Normal	—	—	10	TM42	Facade	Normal	70	100	20
TM18	Rain Dance	Water	—	—	5	TM43	Secret Power	Normal	70	100	20
TM21	Frustration	Normal	—	100	20	TM44	Rest	Psychic	—	—	10
TM23	Iron Tail	Steel	75	75	15	TM45	Attract	Normal	—	100	15
TM26	Earthquake	Ground	100	100	10	TM46	Thief	Dark	40	100	10
TM27	Return	Normal	—	100	20	TM47	Steel Wing	Steel	70	90	25
TM28	Dig	Ground	60	100	10	HM01	Cut	Normal	50	95	30
TM32	Double Team	Normal	—	—	15	HM04	Strength	Normal	80	100	20
TM36	Sludge Bomb	Poison	90	100	10	HM06	Rock Smash	Fighting	20	100	15

EGG MOVES*

Name	Type	Power	ACC	PP
Counter	Fighting	—	100	20
Metal Claw	Steel	50	95	35
Sand Tomb	Ground	15	70	15
Wing Attack	Flying	60	100	35

*Learned Via Breeding

MOVE TUTOR
FireRed/LeafGreen and *Emerald* Only

Counter*	Double-Edge	Dream Eater*
Mimic	Rock Slide*	Substitute
Swords Dance*		

*Battle Frontier tutor move (*Emerald*)

---

208 Steelix™

STEEL | GROUND

GENERAL INFO
SPECIES: Iron Snake Pokémon
HEIGHT: 30'02"
WEIGHT: 882 lbs.
ABILITY 1: Sturdy
Prevents a one hit KO from hitting Steelix.

ABILITY 2: Rock Head
Prevents Steelix from receiving recoil damage.

STATS
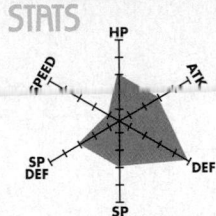

EVOLUTIONS

TRADE WITH METAL COAT

LOCATION(S):

RUBY	**Rarity: None**	
Evolve Onix or obtain from *Colosseum*		
SAPPHIRE	**Rarity: None**	
Evolve Onix or obtain from *Colosseum*		
FIRERED	**Rarity: None**	
Evolve Onix		
LEAFGREEN	**Rarity: None**	
Evolve Onix		
COLOSSEUM	**Rarity: None**	
Trade from *FireRed/LeafGreen*		
EMERALD	**Rarity: None**	
Trade from *FireRed/LeafGreen*		
XD	**Rarity: None**	
Trade from *FireRed/LeafGreen*		

MOVES

Level	Attack	Type	Power	ACC	PP	Level	Attack	Type	Power	ACC	PP
—	Tackle	Normal	35	95	35	30	Dragonbreath	Dragon	60	100	20
—	Screech	Normal	—	85	40	34	Sandstorm	Rock	—	—	10
8	Bind	Normal	15	75	20	41	Slam	Normal	80	75	20
12	Rock Throw	Rock	50	90	15	45	Iron Tail	Steel	100	75	15
19	Harden	Normal	—	—	30	52	Crunch	Dark	80	100	15
23	Rage	Normal	20	100	20	56	Double-Edge	Normal	120	100	15

TM/HM

TM/HM#	Name	Type	Power	ACC	PP	TM/HM#	Name	Type	Power	ACC	PP
TM05	Roar	Normal	—	100	20	TM32	Double Team	Normal	—	—	15
TM06	Toxic	Poison	—	85	10	TM37	Sandstorm	Ground	—	—	10
TM10	Hidden Power	Normal	—	100	15	TM39	Rock Tomb	Rock	50	80	10
TM11	Sunny Day	Fire	—	—	5	TM41	Torment	Dark	—	100	15
TM12	Taunt	Dark	—	100	20	TM42	Facade	Normal	70	100	20
TM15	Hyper Beam	Normal	150	90	5	TM43	Secret Power	Normal	70	100	20
TM17	Protect	Normal	—	—	10	TM44	Rest	Psychic	—	—	10
TM21	Frustration	Normal	—	100	20	TM45	Attract	Normal	—	100	15
TM23	Iron Tail	Steel	75	75	15	HM01	Cut	Normal	50	95	30
TM26	Earthquake	Ground	100	100	10	HM04	Strength	Normal	80	100	20
TM27	Return	Normal	—	100	20	HM06	Rock Smash	Fighting	20	100	15
TM28	Dig	Ground	60	100	10						

MOVE TUTOR
FireRed/LeafGreen and *Emerald* Only

Body Slam*	Double-Edge	Explosion
Mimic	Rock Slide*	Substitute

*Battle Frontier tutor move (*Emerald*)

209 Snubbull™

NORMAL

GENERAL INFO
SPECIES: Fairy Pokémon
HEIGHT: 2'00"
WEIGHT: 17 lbs.
ABILITY 1: Intimidate
When Snubbull is sent into battle, it lowers the opponent's Attack.
ABILITY 2: Run Away
Allows Snubbull to escape from wild Pokémon.

STATS
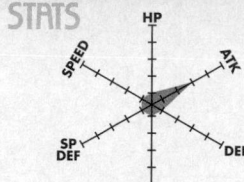

EVOLUTIONS
 LV23

LOCATION(S):

RUBY Rarity: **None**
Obtain in *Colosseum*

SAPPHIRE Rarity: **None**
Obtain in *Colosseum*

FIRERED Rarity: **None**
Trade Granbull from *Colosseum*, then Breed

LEAFGREEN Rarity: **None**
Trade Granbull from *Colosseum*, then Breed

COLOSSEUM Rarity: **Breed**
Breed Granbull

EMERALD Rarity: **Rare**
Safari Zone

XD Rarity: **None**
Obtain in *Colosseum*

MOVES

Level	Attack	Type	Power	ACC	PP	Level	Attack	Type	Power	ACC	PP
—	Tackle	Normal	35	95	35	19	Lick	Ghost	20	100	30
—	Scary Face	Normal	—	90	10	26	Roar	Normal	—	100	20
4	Tail Whip	Normal	—	100	30	34	Rage	Normal	20	100	20
8	Charm	Normal	—	100	20	43	Take Down	Normal	90	85	20
13	Bite	Dark	60	100	25	53	Crunch	Dark	80	100	15

TM/HM#	Name	Type	Power	ACC	PP	TM/HM#	Name	Type	Power	ACC	PP
TM11	Sunny Day	Fire	—	—	5	TM34	Shock Wave	Electric	60	—	20
TM12	Taunt	Dark	—	100	20	TM35	Flamethrower	Fire	95	100	15
TM17	Protect	Normal	—	—	10	TM36	Sludge Bomb	Poison	90	100	10
TM18	Rain Dance	Water	—	—	5	TM38	Fire Blast	Fire	120	85	5
TM21	Frustration	Normal	—	100	20	TM41	Torment	Dark	—	100	15
TM22	Solarbeam	Grass	120	100	10	TM42	Facade	Normal	70	100	20
TM24	Thunderbolt	Electric	95	100	15	TM43	Secret Power	Normal	70	100	20
TM25	Thunder	Electric	120	70	10	TM44	Rest	Psychic	—	—	10
TM26	Earthquake	Ground	100	100	10	TM45	Attract	Normal	—	100	15
TM27	Return	Normal	—	100	20	TM46	Thief	Dark	40	100	10
TM28	Dig	Ground	60	100	10	TM50	Overheat	Fire	140	90	5
TM30	Shadow Ball	Ghost	80	100	15	HM04	Strength	Normal	80	100	15
TM31	Brick Break	Fighting	75	100	15	HM06	Rock Smash	Fighting	20	100	15
TM32	Double Team	Normal	—	—	15						

TM/HM

TM/HM#	Name	Type	Power	ACC	PP
TM01	Focus Punch	Fighting	150	100	20
TM03	Water Pulse	Water	60	95	20
TM05	Roar	Normal	—	100	20
TM06	Toxic	Poison	—	85	10
TM08	Bulk Up	Fighting	—	—	20
TM10	Hidden Power	Normal	—	100	15

EGG MOVES*

Name	Type	Power	ACC	PP
Crunch	Dark	80	100	15
Faint Attack	Dark	60	—	20
Heal Bell	Normal	—	—	5
Metronome	Normal	—	—	10
Present	Normal	—	90	15
Reflect	Psychic	—	—	20
Smellingsalt	Normal	60	100	10
Snore	Normal	40	100	15

*Learned Via Breeding

MOVE TUTOR
FireRed/LeafGreen and *Emerald* Only

Body Slam*	Counter*	Double-Edge
Mega Kick*	Mega Punch*	Metronome
Mimic	Seismic Toss*	Substitute
Thunder Wave*		

*Battle Frontier tutor move (*Emerald*)

---

210 Granbull™

NORMAL

GENERAL INFO
SPECIES: Fairy Pokémon
HEIGHT: 4'07"
WEIGHT: 107 lbs.
ABILITY: Intimidate
When Granbull is sent into battle, it lowers the opponent's Attack.

STATS
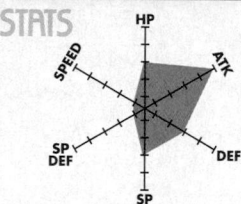

EVOLUTIONS
 LV23

LOCATION(S):

RUBY Rarity: **None**
Evolve Snubbull or Obtain in *Colosseum*

SAPPHIRE Rarity: **None**
Evolve Snubbull or Obtain in *Colosseum*

FIRERED Rarity: **None**
Trade from *Colosseum*

LEAFGREEN Rarity: **None**
Trade from *Colosseum*

COLOSSEUM Rarity: **Only One**
Shadow Pokémon Lab

EMERALD Rarity: **Rare**
Evolve Snubbull, Trade from *Colosseum*

XD Rarity: **None**
Trade from *Colosseum*

MOVES

Level	Attack	Type	Power	ACC	PP	Level	Attack	Type	Power	ACC	PP
—	Scary Face	Normal	—	90	10	19	Lick	Ghost	20	100	30
—	Tackle	Normal	35	95	35	28	Roar	Normal	—	100	20
4	Tail Whip	Normal	—	100	30	38	Rage	Normal	20	100	20
8	Charm	Normal	—	100	20	49	Take Down	Normal	90	85	20
13	Bite	Dark	60	100	25	61	Crunch	Dark	80	100	15

TM/HM#	Name	Type	Power	ACC	PP	TM/HM#	Name	Type	Power	ACC	PP
TM11	Sunny Day	Fire	—	—	5	TM32	Double Team	Normal	—	—	15
TM12	Taunt	Dark	—	100	20	TM34	Shock Wave	Electric	60	—	20
TM15	Hyper Beam	Normal	150	90	5	TM35	Flamethrower	Fire	95	100	15
TM17	Protect	Normal	—	—	10	TM36	Sludge Bomb	Poison	90	100	10
TM18	Rain Dance	Water	—	—	5	TM38	Fire Blast	Fire	120	85	5
TM21	Frustration	Normal	—	100	20	TM39	Rock Tomb	Rock	50	80	10
TM22	Solarbeam	Grass	120	100	10	TM41	Torment	Dark	—	100	15
TM23	Iron Tail	Steel	75	75	15	TM42	Facade	Normal	70	100	20
TM24	Thunderbolt	Electric	95	100	15	TM43	Secret Power	Normal	70	100	20
TM25	Thunder	Electric	120	70	10	TM44	Rest	Psychic	—	—	10
TM26	Earthquake	Ground	100	100	10	TM45	Attract	Normal	—	100	15
TM27	Return	Normal	—	100	20	TM46	Thief	Dark	40	100	10
TM28	Dig	Ground	60	100	10	TM50	Overheat	Fire	140	90	5
TM30	Shadow Ball	Ghost	80	100	15	HM04	Strength	Normal	80	100	15
TM31	Brick Break	Fighting	75	100	15	HM06	Rock Smash	Fighting	20	100	15

TM/HM

TM/HM#	Name	Type	Power	ACC	PP
TM01	Focus Punch	Fighting	150	100	20
TM03	Water Pulse	Water	60	95	20
TM05	Roar	Normal	—	100	20
TM06	Toxic	Poison	—	85	10
TM08	Bulk Up	Fighting	—	—	20
TM10	Hidden Power	Normal	—	100	15

MOVE TUTOR
FireRed/LeafGreen and *Emerald* Only

Body Slam*	Counter*	Double-Edge
Mega Kick*	Mega Punch*	Metronome
Mimic	Rock Slide*	Seismic Toss*
Substitute	Thunder Wave*	

*Battle Frontier tutor move (*Emerald*)

211 Qwilfish™

WATER | **POISON**

GENERAL INFO
SPECIES: Balloon Pokémon
HEIGHT: 1'08"
WEIGHT: 9 lbs.
ABILITY 1: Swift Swim
Increases Qwilfish's Speed when it's raining.
ABILITY 2: Poison Point
When Qwilfish is hit directly, the opponent has a 30% chance of being poisoned.

STATS
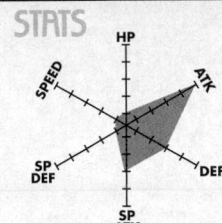

EVOLUTIONS

DOES NOT EVOLVE

LOCATION(S):

RUBY — Rarity: **None**
Obtain in *Colosseum*

SAPPHIRE — Rarity: **None**
Obtain in *Colosseum*

FIRERED — Rarity: **Common**
Five Island, Six Island, Seven Island

LEAFGREEN — Rarity: **None**
Trade from *FireRed/Colosseum*

COLOSSEUM — Rarity: **Only One**
Pyrite Town

EMERALD — Rarity: **None**
Trade from *FireRed/Colosseum*

XD — Rarity: **None**
Trade from *FireRed/Colosseum*

MOVES

Level	Attack	Type	Power	ACC	PP
—	Tackle	Normal	35	95	35
—	Poison Sting	Poison	15	100	35
—	Spikes	Ground	—	—	20
9	Harden	Normal	—	—	30
9	Minimize	Normal	—	—	20
13	Water Gun	Water	40	100	25
21	Pin Missile	Bug	14	85	20
25	Revenge	Fighting	60	100	10
33	Take Down	Normal	90	85	20
37	Hydro Pump	Water	120	80	5
45	Destiny Bond	Ghost	—	—	5

TM/HM

TM/HM#	Name	Type	Power	ACC	PP
TM03	Water Pulse	Water	60	95	20
TM06	Toxic	Poison	—	85	10
TM07	Hail	Ice	—	—	10
TM10	Hidden Power	Normal	—	100	15
TM13	Ice Beam	Ice	95	100	10
TM14	Blizzard	Ice	120	70	5
TM17	Protect	Normal	—	—	10
TM18	Rain Dance	Water	—	—	5
TM21	Frustration	Normal	—	100	20
TM27	Return	Normal	—	100	20
TM30	Shadow Ball	Ghost	80	100	15
TM32	Double Team	Normal	—	—	15
TM34	Shock Wave	Electric	60	—	20
TM36	Sludge Bomb	Poison	90	100	10
TM42	Facade	Normal	70	100	20
TM43	Secret Power	Normal	70	100	20
TM44	Rest	Psychic	—	—	10
TM45	Attract	Normal	—	100	15
HM03	Surf	Water	95	100	15
HM07	Waterfall	Water	80	100	15
HM08	Dive	Water	60	100	10

EGG MOVES*

Name	Type	Power	ACC	PP
Astonish	Ghost	30	100	15
Bubblebeam	Water	65	100	20
Flail	Normal	—	100	15
Haze	Ice	—	—	30
Supersonic	Normal	—	55	20

*Learned Via Breeding

MOVE TUTOR
FireRed/LeafGreen and *Emerald* Only

Body Slam*	Double-Edge	Mimic
Substitute	Swords Dance*	Thunder Wave*

*Battle Frontier tutor move (*Emerald*)

---

212 Scizor™

BUG | **STEEL**

GENERAL INFO
SPECIES: Scissors Pokémon
HEIGHT: 5'11"
WEIGHT: 260 lbs.
ABILITY: Swarm
When Scizor's HPs are low, its Bug-type moves are multiplied by 1.5.

STATS
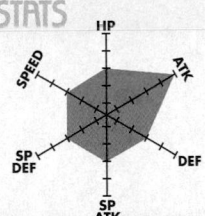

EVOLUTIONS

TRADE WITH METAL COAT

LOCATION(S):

RUBY — Rarity: **None**
Trade from *FireRed*

SAPPHIRE — Rarity: **None**
Trade from *FireRed*

FIRERED — Rarity: **None**
Evolve Scyther

LEAFGREEN — Rarity: **None**
Trade from *FireRed*

COLOSSEUM — Rarity: **None**
Trade from *FireRed*

EMERALD — Rarity: **None**
Trade from *FireRed*

XD — Rarity: **None**
Trade from *FireRed*

MOVES

Level	Attack	Type	Power	ACC	PP
—	Quick Attack	Normal	40	100	30
—	Leer	Normal	—	100	30
6	Focus Energy	Normal	—	—	30
11	Pursuit	Dark	40	100	20
16	False Swipe	Normal	40	100	40
21	Agility	Psychic	—	—	30
26	Metal Claw	Steel	50	95	35
31	Slash	Normal	70	100	20
36	Swords Dance	Normal	—	—	30
41	Iron Defense	Steel	—	—	15
46	Fury Cutter	Bug	10	95	20

TM/HM

TM/HM#	Name	Type	Power	ACC	PP
TM06	Toxic	Poison	—	85	10
TM10	Hidden Power	Normal	—	100	15
TM11	Sunny Day	Fire	—	—	5
TM15	Hyper Beam	Normal	150	90	5
TM17	Protect	Normal	—	—	10
TM18	Rain Dance	Water	—	—	5
TM21	Frustration	Normal	—	100	20
TM27	Return	Normal	—	100	20
TM32	Double Team	Normal	—	—	15
TM37	Sandstorm	Ground	—	—	10
TM40	Aerial Ace	Flying	60	—	20
TM42	Facade	Normal	70	100	20
TM43	Secret Power	Normal	70	100	20
TM44	Rest	Psychic	—	—	10
TM45	Attract	Normal	—	100	15
TM46	Thief	Dark	40	100	10
TM47	Steel Wing	Steel	70	90	25
HM01	Cut	Normal	50	95	30
HM04	Strength	Normal	80	100	15
HM06	Rock Smash	Fighting	20	100	15

MOVE TUTOR
FireRed/LeafGreen and *Emerald* Only

Counter*	Double-Edge	Mimic
Substitute	Swords Dance*	

*Battle Frontier tutor move (*Emerald*)

213 Shuckle™

BUG | ROCK

GENERAL INFO
SPECIES: Mold Pokémon
HEIGHT: 2'00"
WEIGHT: 45 lbs.
ABILITY: Sturdy
Prevents Shuckle from being hit by a one hit KO.

STATS
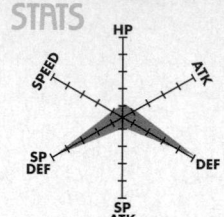

EVOLUTIONS
DOES NOT EVOLVE

LOCATION[S]:

RUBY — Rarity: **None**
Obtain in *Colosseum*

SAPPHIRE — Rarity: **None**
Obtain in *Colosseum*

FIRERED — Rarity: **None**
Trade from *Colosseum*

LEAFGREEN — Rarity: **None**
Trade from *Colosseum*

COLOSSEUM — Rarity: **Only One**
The Under

EMERALD — Rarity: **Common**
Safari Zone

XD — Rarity: **None**
Trade from *Colosseum*

MOVES

Level	Attack	Type	Power	ACC	PP	Level	Attack	Type	Power	ACC	PP
—	Constrict	Normal	10	100	35	14	Encore	Normal	—	100	5
—	Withdraw	Normal	—	—	40	23	Safeguard	Normal	—	—	25
9	Wrap	Normal	15	85	20	28	Bide	Normal	—	100	10
						37	Rest	Psychic	—	—	10

TM/HM

TM/HM#	Name	Type	Power	ACC	PP	TM/HM#	Name	Type	Power	ACC	PP
TM06	Toxic	Poison	—	85	10	TM36	Sludge Bomb	Poison	90	100	10
TM10	Hidden Power	Normal	—	100	15	TM37	Sandstorm	Ground	—	—	10
TM11	Sunny Day	Fire	—	—	5	TM39	Rock Tomb	Rock	50	80	10
TM17	Protect	Normal	—	—	10	TM42	Facade	Normal	70	100	20
TM20	Safeguard	Normal	—	—	25	TM43	Secret Power	Normal	70	100	20
TM21	Frustration	Normal	—	100	20	TM44	Rest	Psychic	—	—	10
TM26	Earthquake	Ground	100	100	10	TM45	Attract	Normal	—	100	15
TM27	Return	Normal	—	100	20	HM04	Strength	Normal	80	100	20
TM28	Dig	Ground	60	100	10	HM05	Flash	Normal	—	70	20
TM32	Double Team	Normal	—	—	15	HM06	Rock Smash	Fighting	20	100	15

EGG MOVES*

Name	Type	Power	ACC	PP
Sweet Scent	Normal	—	100	2

*Learned Via Breeding

MOVE TUTOR
FireRed/LeafGreen and *Emerald* Only

Body Slam*	Double-Edge	Mimic
Rock Slide*	Substitute	

*Battle Frontier tutor move (*Emerald*)

214 Heracross™

BUG | FIGHTING

GENERAL INFO
SPECIES: Single Horn Pokémon
HEIGHT: 4'11"
WEIGHT: 119 lbs.

ABILITY 1: Swarm
When Heracross's HPs are low, its Bug-type moves are multiplied by 1.5.

ABILITY 2: Guts
When Heracross has a status condition, its attack power is multiplied by 1.5.

STATS
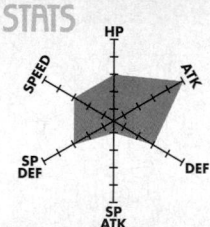

EVOLUTIONS

DOES NOT EVOLVE

LOCATION[S]:

RUBY — Rarity: **Rare**
Safari Zone

SAPPHIRE — Rarity: **Rare**
Safari Zone

FIRERED — Rarity: **Rare**
Six Island

LEAFGREEN — Rarity: **Rare**
Six Island

COLOSSEUM — Rarity: **Only one**
Realgam Tower

EMERALD — Rarity: **Rare**
Safari Zone

XD — Rarity: **None**
Trade from *Ruby/Sapphire/FireRed/LeafGreen/Colosseum*

MOVES

Level	Attack	Type	Power	ACC	PP	Level	Attack	Type	Power	ACC	PP
—	Tackle	Normal	35	95	35	23	Brick Break	Fighting	75	100	15
—	Leer	Normal	—	100	30	30	Counter	Fighting	—	100	20
6	Horn Attack	Normal	65	100	25	37	Take Down	Normal	90	85	20
11	Endure	Normal	—	—	10	45	Reversal	Fighting	—	100	15
17	Fury Attack	Normal	15	85	20	53	Megahorn	Bug	120	85	10

TM/HM

TM/HM#	Name	Type	Power	ACC	PP	TM/HM#	Name	Type	Power	ACC	PP
TM01	Focus Punch	Fighting	150	100	20	TM31	Brick Break	Fighting	75	100	15
TM06	Toxic	Poison	—	85	10	TM32	Double Team	Normal	—	—	15
TM08	Bulk Up	Fighting	—	—	20	TM39	Rock Tomb	Rock	50	80	10
TM10	Hidden Power	Normal	—	100	15	TM42	Facade	Normal	70	100	20
TM11	Sunny Day	Fire	—	—	5	TM43	Secret Power	Normal	70	100	20
TM15	Hyper Beam	Normal	150	90	5	TM44	Rest	Psychic	—	—	10
TM17	Protect	Normal	—	—	10	TM45	Attract	Normal	—	100	15
TM18	Rain Dance	Water	—	—	5	TM46	Thief	Dark	40	100	10
TM21	Frustration	Normal	—	100	20	HM01	Cut	Normal	50	95	30
TM26	Earthquake	Ground	100	100	10	HM04	Strength	Normal	80	100	20
TM27	Return	Normal	—	100	20	HM06	Rock Smash	Fighting	20	100	15
TM28	Dig	Ground	60	100	10						

EGG MOVES*

Name	Type	Power	ACC	PP
Harden	Normal	—	—	30
False Swipe	Normal	40	100	40
Bide	Normal	15	75	20
Flail	Normal	—	100	15

*Learned Via Breeding

MOVE TUTOR
FireRed/LeafGreen and *Emerald* Only

Body Slam*	Counter*	Double-Edge
Mimic	Rock Slide*	Seismic Toss*
Substitute	Swords Dance*	

Emerald Only

Endure*	Mud-Slap*	Sleep Talk
Snore*	Swagger*	Swift*

*Battle Frontier tutor move (*Emerald*)

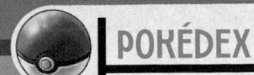

215 Sneasel™

DARK | ICE

GENERAL INFO
SPECIES: Sharp Claw Pokémon
HEIGHT: 2'11"
WEIGHT: 62 lbs.
ABILITY 1: Inner Focus
Prevents Sneasel from flinching.
ABILITY 2: Keen Eye
Prevents Sneasel from having its Accuracy lowered.

STATS
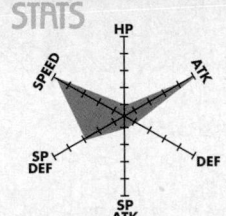

EVOLUTIONS

DOES NOT EVOLVE

LOCATION(S):

RUBY — Rarity: **None**
Obtain in *Colosseum*

SAPPHIRE — Rarity: **None**
Obtain in *Colosseum*

FIRERED — Rarity: **None**
Trade from *LeafGreen/Colosseum*

LEAFGREEN — Rarity: **Rare**
Four Island

COLOSSEUM — Rarity: **Only One**
The Under

EMERALD — Rarity: **None**
Trade from *LeafGreen/Colosseum*

XD — Rarity: **None**
Trade from *LeafGreen/Colosseum*

MOVES

Level	Attack	Type	Power	ACC	PP
—	Scratch	Normal	40	100	35
—	Leer	Normal	—	100	30
—	Taunt	Dark	—	100	20
8	Quick Attack	Normal	40	100	30
15	Screech	Normal	—	85	40
22	Faint Attack	Dark	60	—	20
29	Fury Swipes	Normal	18	80	15
36	Agility	Psychic	—	—	30
43	Icy Wind	Ice	55	95	15
50	Slash	Normal	70	100	20
57	Beat Up	Dark	10	100	10
64	Metal Claw	Steel	50	95	35

TM/HM

TM/HM#	Name	Type	Power	ACC	PP
TM01	Focus Punch	Fighting	150	100	20
TM04	Calm Mind	Psychic	—	—	20
TM06	Toxic	Poison	—	85	10
TM07	Hail	Ice	—	—	10
TM10	Hidden Power	Normal	—	100	15
TM11	Sunny Day	Fire	—	—	5
TM12	Taunt	Dark	—	100	20
TM13	Ice Beam	Ice	95	100	10
TM14	Blizzard	Ice	120	70	5
TM17	Protect	Normal	—	—	10
TM18	Rain Dance	Water	—	—	5
TM21	Frustration	Normal	—	100	20
TM23	Iron Tail	Steel	75	75	15
TM27	Return	Normal	—	100	20
TM28	Dig	Ground	60	100	10
TM30	Shadow Ball	Ghost	80	100	15
TM31	Brick Break	Fighting	75	100	15
TM32	Double Team	Normal	—	—	15
TM40	Aerial Ace	Flying	60	—	20
TM41	Torment	Dark	—	100	15
TM42	Facade	Normal	70	100	20
TM43	Secret Power	Normal	70	100	20
TM44	Rest	Psychic	—	—	10
TM45	Attract	Normal	—	100	15
TM46	Thief	Dark	40	100	10
TM49	Snatch	Dark	—	100	10
HM01	Cut	Normal	50	95	30
HM03	Surf	Water	95	100	15
HM04	Strength	Normal	80	100	20
HM06	Rock Smash	Fighting	20	100	15

EGG MOVES*

Name	Type	Power	ACC	PP
Bite	Dark	60	100	25
Counter	Fighting	—	100	20
Crush Claw	Normal	75	95	10
Fake Out	Normal	40	100	10
Foresight	Normal	—	100	40
Reflect	Psychic	—	—	20
Spite	Ghost	—	100	10

*Learned Via Breeding

MOVE TUTOR
FireRed/LeafGreen and *Emerald* Only

Counter*	Double-Edge	Dream Eater*
Mimic	Substitute	Swords Dance*

*Battle Frontier tutor move (*Emerald*)

---

216 Teddiursa™

NORMAL

GENERAL INFO
SPECIES: Little Bear Pokémon
HEIGHT: 2'00"
WEIGHT: 19 lbs.
ABILITY: Pickup
Allows Teddiursa to take items from an opponent.

STATS
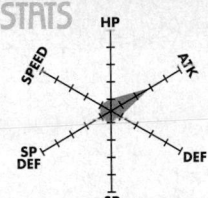

EVOLUTIONS
 LV30

LOCATION(S):

RUBY — Rarity: **None**
Obtain in *Colosseum*

SAPPHIRE — Rarity: **None**
Obtain in *Colosseum*

FIRERED — Rarity: **None**
Trade Ursaring from *Colosseum* then breed

LEAFGREEN — Rarity: **None**
Trade Ursaring from *Colosseum* then breed

COLOSSEUM — Rarity: **Breed**
Breed in *Ruby/Sapphire/FireRed/LeafGreen* then trade back

EMERALD — Rarity: **Common**
Safari Zone

XD — Rarity: **Only One**
Pokémon HQ (Capture from Cipher Peon Naps)

MOVES

Level	Attack	Type	Power	ACC	PP
—	Scratch	Normal	40	100	35
—	Leer	Normal	—	100	30
7	Lick	Ghost	20	100	30
13	Fury Swipes	Normal	18	80	15
19	Fake Tears	Dark	—	100	20
25	Faint Attack	Dark	60	—	20
31	Rest	Psychic	—	—	10
37	Slash	Normal	70	100	20
43	Snore	Normal	40	100	15
49	Thrash	Normal	90	100	20

TM/HM

TM/HM#	Name	Type	Power	ACC	PP
TM01	Focus Punch	Fighting	150	100	20
TM05	Roar	Normal	—	100	20
TM06	Toxic	Poison	—	85	10
TM08	Bulk Up	Fighting	—	—	20
TM10	Hidden Power	Normal	—	100	15
TM11	Sunny Day	Fire	—	—	5
TM12	Taunt	Dark	—	100	20
TM17	Protect	Normal	—	—	10
TM18	Rain Dance	Water	—	—	5
TM21	Frustration	Normal	—	100	20
TM26	Earthquake	Ground	100	100	10
TM27	Return	Normal	—	100	20
TM28	Dig	Ground	60	100	10
TM31	Brick Break	Fighting	75	100	15
TM32	Double Team	Normal	—	—	15
TM40	Aerial Ace	Flying	60	—	20
TM41	Torment	Dark	—	100	15
TM42	Facade	Normal	70	100	20
TM43	Secret Power	Normal	70	100	20
TM44	Rest	Psychic	—	—	10
TM45	Attract	Normal	—	100	15
TM46	Thief	Dark	40	100	10
HM01	Cut	Normal	50	95	30
HM04	Strength	Normal	80	100	20
HM06	Rock Smash	Fighting	20	100	15

EGG MOVES*

Name	Type	Power	ACC	PP
Counter	Fighting	—	100	20
Crunch	Dark	80	100	15
Fake Tears	Dark	—	100	20
Metal Claw	Steel	50	95	35
Seismic Toss	Fighting	—	100	20
Sleep Talk	Normal	—	—	10
Take Down	Normal	90	85	20
Yawn	Normal	—	100	10

*Learned Via Breeding

MOVE TUTOR
FireRed/LeafGreen and *Emerald* Only

Body Slam*	Counter*	Double-Edge
Mega Kick*	Mega Punch*	Metronome
Mimic	Seismic Toss*	Substitute
Swords Dance*		

*Battle Frontier tutor move (*Emerald*)

217 Ursaring

NORMAL

GENERAL INFO
SPECIES: Hibernator Pokémon
HEIGHT: 5'11"
WEIGHT: 277 lbs.
ABILITY: Guts
When Ursaring has a status condition, its attack power is multiplied by 1.5.

STATS
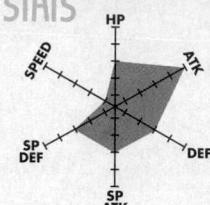

EVOLUTIONS
 LV30

LOCATION[S]:

RUBY   Rarity: **None**
Trade from *Colosseum/Emerald*

SAPPHIRE   Rarity: **None**
Trade from *Colosseum/Emerald*

FIRERED   Rarity: **None**
Trade from *Colosseum/Emerald*

LEAFGREEN   Rarity: **None**
Trade from *Colosseum/Emerald*

COLOSSEUM   Rarity: **Only One**
Snagem Hideout

EMERALD   Rarity: **Evolve**
Evolve Teddiursa

XD   Rarity: **Evolve**
Evolve Teddiursa

MOVES

Level	Attack	Type	Power	ACC	PP	Level	Attack	Type	Power	ACC	PP
—	Scratch	Normal	40	100	35	25	Faint Attack	Dark	60	—	20
—	Leer	Normal	—	100	30	31	Rest	Psychic	—	—	10
—	Lick	Ghost	20	100	30	37	Slash	Normal	70	100	20
—	Fury Swipes	Normal	18	80	15	43	Snore	Normal	40	100	15
19	Fake Tears	Dark	—	100	20	49	Thrash	Normal	90	100	20

TM/HM

TM/HM#	Name	Type	Power	ACC	PP	TM/HM#	Name	Type	Power	ACC	PP
TM01	Focus Punch	Fighting	150	100	20	TM31	Brick Break	Fighting	75	100	15
TM05	Roar	Normal	—	100	20	TM32	Double Team	Normal	—	—	15
TM06	Toxic	Poison	—	85	10	TM39	Rock Tomb	Rock	50	80	10
TM08	Bulk Up	Fighting	—	—	20	TM40	Aerial Ace	Flying	60	—	20
TM10	Hidden Power	Normal	—	100	15	TM41	Torment	Dark	—	100	15
TM11	Sunny Day	Fire	—	—	5	TM42	Facade	Normal	70	100	20
TM12	Taunt	Dark	—	100	20	TM43	Secret Power	Normal	70	100	20
TM15	Hyper Beam	Normal	150	90	5	TM44	Rest	Psychic	—	—	10
TM17	Protect	Normal	—	—	10	TM45	Attract	Normal	—	100	15
TM18	Rain Dance	Water	—	—	5	TM46	Thief	Dark	40	100	10
TM21	Frustration	Normal	—	100	20	HM01	Cut	Normal	50	95	30
TM26	Earthquake	Ground	100	100	10	HM04	Strength	Normal	80	100	20
TM27	Return	Normal	—	100	20	HM06	Rock Smash	Fighting	20	100	15
TM28	Dig	Ground	60	100	10						

MOVE TUTOR
FireRed/LeafGreen and *Emerald* Only

Body Slam*	Counter*	Double-Edge
Mega Kick*	Mega Punch*	Metronome
Mimic	Rock Slide*	Seismic Toss*
Substitute	Swords Dance*	

*Battle Frontier tutor move (*Emerald*)

218 Slugma

FIRE

GENERAL INFO
SPECIES: Lava Pokémon
HEIGHT: 2'04"
WEIGHT: 77 lbs.
ABILITY 1: Magma Armor   **ABILITY 2:** Flame Body
Slugma cannot be frozen.   *An opponent has a 30% chance of being burned if it attacks Slugma.*

STATS
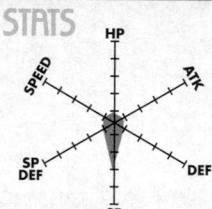

EVOLUTIONS
 LV38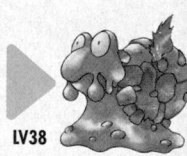

LOCATION[S]:

RUBY   Rarity: **Common**
Fiery Path

SAPPHIRE   Rarity: **Common**
Fiery Path

FIRERED   Rarity: **Common**
One Island

LEAFGREEN   Rarity: **Common**
One Island

COLOSSEUM   Rarity: **Only One**
Pyrite Town

EMERALD   Rarity: **Common**
Route 113, Fiery Path

XD   Rarity: **None**
Trade from *Ruby/Sapphire/FireRed/LeafGreen/Colosseum*

MOVES

Level	Attack	Type	Power	ACC	PP	Level	Attack	Type	Power	ACC	PP
—	Yawn	Normal	—	100	10	22	Harden	Normal	—	—	30
—	Smog	Poison	20	70	20	29	Amnesia	Psychic	—	—	20
8	Ember	Fire	40	100	25	36	Flamethrower	Fire	95	100	15
15	Rock Throw	Rock	50	90	15	43	Rock Slide	Rock	75	90	10
						50	Body Slam	Normal	85	100	15

TM/HM

TM/HM#	Name	Type	Power	ACC	PP	TM/HM#	Name	Type	Power	ACC	PP
TM06	Toxic	Poison	—	85	10	TM35	Flamethrower	Fire	95	100	15
TM10	Hidden Power	Normal	—	100	15	TM38	Fire Blast	Fire	120	85	5
TM11	Sunny Day	Fire	—	—	5	TM42	Facade	Normal	70	100	20
TM16	Light Screen	Psychic	—	—	30	TM43	Secret Power	Normal	70	100	20
TM17	Protect	Normal	—	—	10	TM44	Rest	Psychic	—	—	10
TM21	Frustration	Normal	—	100	20	TM45	Attract	Normal	—	100	15
TM27	Return	Normal	—	100	20	TM50	Overheat	Fire	140	90	5
TM32	Double Team	Normal	—	—	15	HM06	Rock Smash	Fighting	20	100	15
TM33	Reflect	Normal	—	—	20						

EGG MOVES*

Name	Type	Power	ACC	PP
Acid Armor	Poison	—	—	4

*Learned Via Breeding

MOVE TUTOR
FireRed/LeafGreen and *Emerald* Only

Body Slam*	Double-Edge	Mimic
Rock Slide *	Substitute	

Emerald Only

Defense Curl*	Endure*	Mud-Slap*
Rollout	Sleep Talk	Snore*
Swagger		

*Battle Frontier tutor move (*Emerald*)

219 Magcargo™

FIRE | ROCK

GENERAL INFO
SPECIES: Lava Pokémon
HEIGHT: 2'07"
WEIGHT: 121 lbs.
ABILITY 1: Magma Armor
Magcargo cannot be frozen.
ABILITY 2: Flame Body
An opponent has a 30% chance of being burned if it attacks Magcargo.

STATS
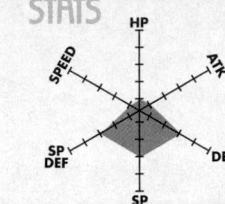

EVOLUTIONS

LV38

LOCATION(S):

RUBY   Rarity: **None**
Evolve Slugma

SAPPHIRE   Rarity: **None**
Evolve Slugma

FIRERED   Rarity: **None**
Evolve Slugma, One Island

LEAFGREEN   Rarity: **None**
Evolve Slugma, One Island

COLOSSEUM   Rarity: **None**
Evolve Slugma

EMERALD   Rarity: **Evolve**
Evolve Slugma

XD   Rarity: **Only One**
Citadark Island (Capture from Cipher Peon Kolest)

MOVES

Level	Attack	Type	Power	ACC	PP
—	Yawn	Normal	—	100	10
—	Smog	Poison	20	70	20
—	Ember	Fire	40	100	25
—	Rock Throw	Rock	50	90	15
22	Harden	Normal	—	—	30
29	Amnesia	Psychic	—	—	20
36	Flamethrower	Fire	95	100	15
48	Rock Slide	Rock	75	90	10
60	Body Slam	Normal	85	100	15

TM/HM

TM/HM#	Name	Type	Power	ACC	PP
TM06	Toxic	Poison	—	85	10
TM10	Hidden Power	Normal	—	100	15
TM11	Sunny Day	Fire	—	—	5
TM15	Hyper Beam	Normal	150	90	5
TM16	Light Screen	Psychic	—	—	30
TM17	Protect	Normal	—	—	10
TM21	Frustration	Normal	—	100	20
TM26	Earthquake	Ground	100	100	10
TM27	Return	Normal	—	100	20
TM32	Double Team	Normal	—	—	15
TM33	Reflect	Normal	—	—	20
TM35	Flamethrower	Fire	95	100	15
TM37	Sandstorm	Ground	—	—	10
TM38	Fire Blast	Fire	120	85	5
TM39	Rock Tomb	Rock	50	80	10
TM42	Facade	Normal	70	100	20
TM43	Secret Power	Normal	70	100	20
TM44	Rest	Psychic	—	—	10
TM45	Attract	Normal	—	100	15
TM50	Overheat	Fire	140	90	5
HM04	Strength	Normal	80	100	20
HM06	Rock Smash	Fighting	20	100	15

MOVE TUTOR
FireRed/LeafGreen and *Emerald* Only

Body Slam*	Double-Edge	Mimic
Rock Slide*	Substitute	

Emerald Only

Defense Curl*	Endure*	Mud-Slap*
Rollout	Sleep Talk	Snore*
Swagger		

*Battle Frontier tutor move (*Emerald*)

---

220 Swinub™

ICE | GROUND

GENERAL INFO
SPECIES: Pig Pokémon
HEIGHT: 1'04"
WEIGHT: 14 lbs.
ABILITY: Oblivious
Prevents Swinub from being attracted.

STATS
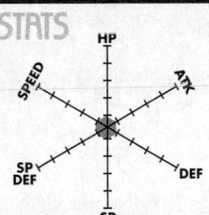

EVOLUTIONS

LV33

LOCATION(S):

RUBY   Rarity: **None**
Trade from *FireRed/LeafGreen*

SAPPHIRE   Rarity: **None**
Trade from *FireRed/LeafGreen*

FIRERED   Rarity: **None**
Four Island

LEAFGREEN   Rarity: **None**
Four Island

COLOSSEUM   Rarity: **None**
Trade from *FireRed/LeafGreen*

EMERALD   Rarity: **None**
Trade from *FireRed/LeafGreen*

XD   Rarity: **Only One**
Phenac City (Capture from Cipher Peon Greck)

MOVES

Level	Attack	Type	Power	ACC	PP
—	Tackle	Normal	35	95	35
—	Odor Sleuth	Normal	—	100	40
10	Powder Snow	Ice	40	100	25
19	Endure	Normal	—	—	10
28	Take Down	Normal	90	85	20
37	Mist	Ice	—	—	30
46	Blizzard	Ice	120	70	5
55	Amnesia	Psychic	—	—	20

TM/HM

TM/HM#	Name	Type	Power	ACC	PP
TM05	Roar	Normal	—	100	20
TM06	Toxic	Poison	—	85	10
TM07	Hail	Ice	—	—	10
TM10	Hidden Power	Normal	—	100	15
TM13	Ice Beam	Ice	95	100	10
TM14	Blizzard	Ice	120	70	5
TM16	Light Screen	Psychic	—	—	30
TM17	Protect	Normal	—	—	10
TM18	Rain Dance	Water	—	—	5
TM21	Frustration	Normal	—	100	20
TM26	Earthquake	Ground	100	100	10
TM27	Return	Normal	—	100	20
TM28	Dig	Ground	60	100	10
TM32	Double Team	Normal	—	—	15
TM33	Reflect	Normal	—	—	20
TM37	Sandstorm	Ground	—	—	10
TM39	Rock Tomb	Rock	50	80	10
TM42	Facade	Normal	70	100	20
TM43	Secret Power	Normal	70	100	20
TM44	Rest	Psychic	—	—	10
TM45	Attract	Normal	—	100	15
HM04	Strength	Normal	80	100	20
HM06	Rock Smash	Fighting	20	100	15

EGG MOVES*

Name	Type	Power	ACC	PP
Ancientpower	Rock	60	100	5
Bite	Dark	60	100	25
Body Slam	Normal	85	100	15
Double-Edge	Normal	120	100	15
Icicle Spear	Ice	15	100	30
Mud Shot	Ground	55	95	15
Rock Slide	Rock	75	90	10
Take Down	Normal	90	85	20

*Learned Via Breeding

MOVE TUTOR
FireRed/LeafGreen and *Emerald* Only

Body Slam*	Double-Edge	Mimic
Rock Slide*	Substitute	

*Battle Frontier tutor move (*Emerald*)

221 Piloswine™

| ICE | GROUND |

GENERAL INFO
SPECIES: Swine Pokémon
HEIGHT: 3'07"
WEIGHT: 123 lbs.
ABILITY: Oblivious
Prevents Piloswine from being attracted.

STATS
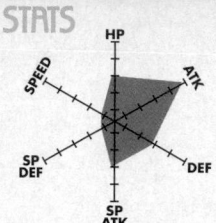

EVOLUTIONS

LV33

LOCATION(S):

RUBY   Rarity: **None**
Trade from *FireRed/LeafGreen/Colosseum*

SAPPHIRE   Rarity: **None**
Trade from *FireRed/LeafGreen/Colosseum*

FIRERED   Rarity: **None**
Evolve Swinub

LEAFGREEN   Rarity: **None**
Evolve Swinub

COLOSSEUM   Rarity: **Only One**
Snatched from Bodybuilder Lonia in The Under

EMERALD   Rarity: **None**
Trade from *FireRed/LeafGreen/Colosseum*

XD   Rarity: **Evolve**
Evolve Swinub

MOVES

Level	Attack	Type	Power	ACC	PP	Level	Attack	Type	Power	ACC	PP
—	Horn Attack	Normal	65	100	25	28	Take Down	Normal	90	85	20
—	Odor Sleuth	Normal	—	100	40	33	Fury Attack	Normal	15	85	20
—	Powder Snow	Ice	40	100	25	42	Mist	Ice	—	—	30
—	Endure	Normal	—	—	10	56	Blizzard	Ice	120	70	5
						70	Amnesia	Psychic	—	—	20

TM/HM

TM/HM#	Name	Type	Power	ACC	PP	TM/HM#	Name	Type	Power	ACC	PP
TM05	Roar	Normal	—	100	20	TM27	Return	Normal	—	100	20
TM06	Toxic	Poison	—	85	10	TM28	Dig	Ground	60	100	10
TM07	Hail	Ice	—	—	10	TM32	Double Team	Normal	—	—	15
TM10	Hidden Power	Normal	—	100	15	TM33	Reflect	Normal	—	—	20
TM13	Ice Beam	Ice	95	100	10	TM37	Sandstorm	Ground	—	—	10
TM14	Blizzard	Ice	120	70	5	TM39	Rock Tomb	Rock	50	80	10
TM15	Hyper Beam	Normal	150	90	5	TM42	Facade	Normal	70	100	20
TM16	Light Screen	Psychic	—	—	30	TM43	Secret Power	Normal	70	100	20
TM17	Protect	Normal	—	—	10	TM44	Rest	Psychic	—	—	10
TM18	Rain Dance	Water	—	—	5	TM45	Attract	Normal	—	100	15
TM21	Frustration	Normal	—	100	20	HM04	Strength	Normal	80	100	20
TM26	Earthquake	Ground	100	100	10	HM06	Rock Smash	Fighting	20	100	15

MOVE TUTOR
FireRed/LeafGreen and *Emerald* Only

Body Slam*	Double-Edge	Mimic
Rock Slide*	Substitute	

*Battle Frontier tutor move (*Emerald*)

---

222 Corsola™

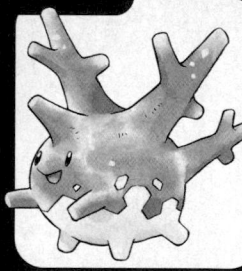

| WATER | ROCK |

GENERAL INFO
SPECIES: Coral Pokémon
HEIGHT: 2'00"
WEIGHT: 11 lbs.
ABILITY 1: Hustle
Multiplies Corsola's attack power by 1.5, but lowers its Accuracy to 80%.

ABILITY 2: Natural Cure
Any status condition Corsola may have is cured when Corsola is switched out.

STATS
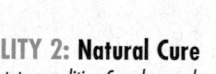

EVOLUTIONS
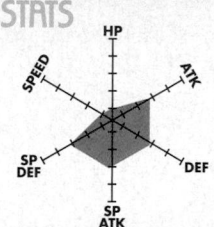
DOES NOT EVOLVE

LOCATION(S):

RUBY   Rarity: **Common**
Ever Grande City, Pacifidlog Town

SAPPHIRE   Rarity: **Common**
Ever Grande City, Pacifidlog Town

FIRERED   Rarity: **None**
Trade from *Ruby/Sapphire*

LEAFGREEN   Rarity: **None**
Trade from *Ruby/Sapphire*

COLOSSEUM   Rarity: **None**
Trade from *Ruby/Sapphire*

EMERALD   Rarity: **Common**
Route 128, Ever Grande City

XD   Rarity: **None**
Trade from *Ruby/Sapphire/Emerald*

MOVES

Level	Attack	Type	Power	ACC	PP	Level	Attack	Type	Power	ACC	PP
—	Tackle	Normal	35	95	35	23	Bubblebeam	Water	65	100	20
6	Harden	Normal	—	—	30	28	Spike Cannon	Normal	20	100	15
12	Bubble	Water	20	100	30	34	Rock Blast	Rock	25	80	10
17	Recover	Normal	—	—	20	39	Mirror Coat	Psychic	—	100	20
17	Refresh	Normal	—	100	20	45	Ancientpower	Rock	60	100	5

TM/HM

TM/HM#	Name	Type	Power	ACC	PP	TM/HM#	Name	Type	Power	ACC	PP
TM03	Water Pulse	Water	60	95	20	TM28	Dig	Ground	60	100	10
TM04	Calm Mind	Psychic	—	—	20	TM29	Psychic	Psychic	90	100	10
TM06	Toxic	Poison	—	85	10	TM30	Shadow Ball	Ghost	80	100	15
TM07	Hail	Ice	—	—	10	TM32	Double Team	Normal	—	—	15
TM10	Hidden Power	Normal	—	100	15	TM33	Reflect	Normal	—	—	20
TM11	Sunny Day	Fire	—	—	5	TM37	Sandstorm	Ground	—	—	10
TM13	Ice Beam	Ice	95	100	10	TM39	Rock Tomb	Rock	50	80	10
TM14	Blizzard	Ice	120	70	5	TM42	Facade	Normal	70	100	20
TM16	Light Screen	Psychic	—	—	30	TM43	Secret Power	Normal	70	100	20
TM17	Protect	Normal	—	—	10	TM44	Rest	Psychic	—	—	10
TM18	Rain Dance	Water	—	—	5	TM45	Attract	Normal	—	100	15
TM20	Safeguard	Normal	—	—	25	HM03	Surf	Water	95	100	15
TM21	Frustration	Normal	—	100	20	HM04	Strength	Normal	80	100	20
TM26	Earthquake	Ground	100	100	10	HM06	Rock Smash	Fighting	20	100	15
TM27	Return	Normal	—	100	20						

EGG MOVES*

Name	Type	Power	ACC	PP
Amnesia	Psychic	—	—	20
Rock Slide	Rock	75	90	10
Screech	Normal	—	85	40
Mist	Ice	—	—	30
Barrier	Psychic	—	—	30
Ingrain	Grass	—	100	20
Confuse Ray	Ghost	—	100	10
Icicle Spear	Ice	10	100	30

*Learned Via Breeding

MOVE TUTOR
FireRed/LeafGreen and *Emerald* Only

Body Slam*	Double-Edge	Explosion
Mimic	Rock Slide*	Substitute

Emerald Only

Defense Curl*	Endure*	Mud-Slap*
Rollout	Sleep Talk	Snore*
Swagger		

*Battle Frontier tutor move (*Emerald*)

223 Remoraid™

WATER

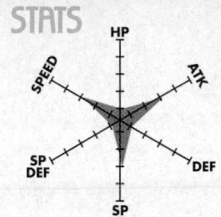

GENERAL INFO
SPECIES: Jet Pokémon
HEIGHT: 2'00"
WEIGHT: 26 lbs.
ABILITY: Hustle
Multiplies Remoraid's attacks by 1.5, but lowers its Accuracy to 80%.

STATS

EVOLUTIONS

LV25

LOCATION(S):

RUBY — Rarity: **None**
Obtain in *Colosseum*

SAPPHIRE — Rarity: **None**
Obtain in *Colosseum*

FIRERED — Rarity: **None**
Trade from *LeafGreen/Colosseum*

LEAFGREEN — Rarity: **Common**
Five Island

COLOSSEUM — Rarity: **Only One**
Pyrite Town

EMERALD — Rarity: **Common**
Safari Zone

XD — Rarity: **None**
Trade from *LeafGreen/Colosseum/Emerald*

MOVES

Level	Attack	Type	Power	ACC	PP	Level	Attack	Type	Power	ACC	PP
—	Water Gun	Water	40	100	25	22	Bubblebeam	Water	65	100	20
11	Lock-on	Normal	—	100	5	33	Focus Energy	Normal	—	—	30
22	Psybeam	Psychic	65	100	20	44	Ice Beam	Ice	95	100	10
22	Aurora Beam	Ice	65	100	20	55	Hyper Beam	Normal	150	90	5

TM/HM

TM/HM#	Name	Type	Power	ACC	PP	TM/HM#	Name	Type	Power	ACC	PP
TM03	Water Pulse	Water	60	95	20	TM32	Double Team	Normal	—	—	15
TM06	Toxic	Poison	—	85	10	TM35	Flamethrower	Fire	95	100	15
TM10	Hidden Power	Normal	—	100	15	TM38	Fire Blast	Fire	120	85	5
TM11	Sunny Day	Fire	—	—	5	TM42	Facade	Normal	70	100	20
TM13	Ice Beam	Ice	95	100	10	TM43	Secret Power	Normal	70	100	20
TM14	Blizzard	Ice	120	70	5	TM44	Rest	Psychic	—	—	10
TM15	Hyper Beam	Normal	150	90	5	TM45	Attract	Normal	—	100	15
TM17	Protect	Normal	—	—	10	TM46	Thief	Dark	40	100	10
TM18	Rain Dance	Water	—	—	5	HM03	Surf	Water	95	100	15
TM21	Frustration	Normal	—	100	20	HM07	Waterfall	Water	80	100	15
TM27	Return	Normal	—	100	20	HM08	Dive	Water	60	100	10
TM29	Psychic	Psychic	90	100	10						

EGG MOVES*

Name	Type	Power	ACC	PP
Aurora Beam	Ice	65	100	20
Haze	Ice	—	—	30
Octazooka	Water	65	85	10
Rock Blast	Rock	25	80	10
Screech	Normal	—	85	40
Supersonic	Normal	—	55	20
Thunder Wave	Electric	—	100	20

*Learned Via Breeding

MOVE TUTOR
FireRed/LeafGreen and *Emerald* Only

Double-Edge	Mimic	Substitute
Thunder Wave*		

*Battle Frontier tutor move (*Emerald*)

224 Octillery™

WATER

GENERAL INFO
SPECIES: Jet Pokémon
HEIGHT: 2'11"
WEIGHT: 63 lbs.
ABILITY: Suction Cups
Protects Octillery from being switched out by Whirlwind or Roar.

STATS
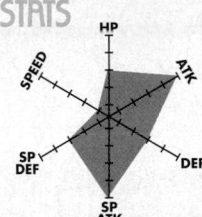

EVOLUTIONS

LV25

LOCATION(S):

RUBY — Rarity: **None**
Evolve Remoraid or Trade from *Colosseum*

SAPPHIRE — Rarity: **None**
Evolve Remoraid or Trade from *Colosseum*

FIRERED — Rarity: **None**
Trade from *LeafGreen/Colosseum*

LEAFGREEN — Rarity: **None**
Evolve Remoraid

COLOSSEUM — Rarity: **None**
Evolve Remoraid

EMERALD — Rarity: **Evolve**
Evolve Remoraid

XD — Rarity: **None**
Trade from *LeafGreen/Colosseum/Emerald*

MOVES

Level	Attack	Type	Power	ACC	PP	Level	Attack	Type	Power	ACC	PP
—	Water Gun	Water	40	100	25	22	Bubblebeam	Water	65	100	20
11	Constrict	Normal	10	100	35	25	Octazooka	Water	65	85	10
22	Psybeam	Psychic	65	100	20	38	Focus Energy	Normal	—	—	30
22	Aurora Beam	Ice	65	100	20	54	Ice Beam	Ice	95	100	10
						70	Hyper Beam	Normal	150	90	5

TM/HM

TM/HM#	Name	Type	Power	ACC	PP	TM/HM#	Name	Type	Power	ACC	PP
TM03	Water Pulse	Water	60	95	20	TM32	Double Team	Normal	—	—	15
TM06	Toxic	Poison	—	85	10	TM35	Flamethrower	Fire	95	100	15
TM10	Hidden Power	Normal	—	100	15	TM36	Sludge Bomb	Poison	90	100	10
TM11	Sunny Day	Fire	—	—	5	TM38	Fire Blast	Fire	120	85	5
TM13	Ice Beam	Ice	95	100	10	TM42	Facade	Normal	70	100	20
TM14	Blizzard	Ice	120	70	5	TM43	Secret Power	Normal	70	100	20
TM15	Hyper Beam	Normal	150	90	5	TM44	Rest	Psychic	—	—	10
TM17	Protect	Normal	—	—	10	TM45	Attract	Normal	—	100	15
TM18	Rain Dance	Water	—	—	5	TM46	Thief	Dark	40	100	10
TM21	Frustration	Normal	—	100	20	HM03	Surf	Water	95	100	15
TM27	Return	Normal	—	100	20	HM07	Waterfall	Water	80	100	15
TM29	Psychic	Psychic	90	100	10	HM08	Dive	Water	60	100	10

MOVE TUTOR
FireRed/LeafGreen and *Emerald* Only

Double-Edge	Mimic	Seismic Toss*
Substitute	Thunder Wave*	

*Battle Frontier tutor move (*Emerald*)

225 Delibird™

ICE **FLYING**

GENERAL INFO
SPECIES: Delivery Pokémon
HEIGHT: 2'11"
WEIGHT: 35 lbs.
ABILITY 1: Hustle
Multiplies Delibird's attacks by 1.5, but lowers its Accuracy to 80%.

ABILITY 2: Vital Spirit
Prevents Delibird from getting a Sleep condition.

STATS
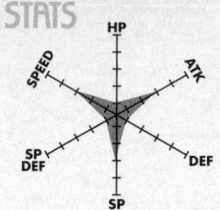

EVOLUTIONS

DOES NOT EVOLVE

LOCATION[S]:

RUBY — Rarity: **None**
Obtain in *Colosseum*

SAPPHIRE — Rarity: **None**
Obtain in *Colosseum*

FIRERED — Rarity: **Rare**
Four Island

LEAFGREEN — Rarity: **None**
Trade from *FireRed/Colosseum*

COLOSSEUM — Rarity: **Only One**
Realgam Tower

EMERALD — Rarity: **None**
Trade from *FireRed/Colosseum*

XD — Rarity: **None**
Trade from *FireRed/Colosseum*

MOVES

Level	Attack	Type	Power	ACC	PP
—	Present	Normal	—	90	15

TM/HM

TM/HM#	Name	Type	Power	ACC	PP	TM/HM#	Name	Type	Power	ACC	PP
TM01	Focus Punch	Fighting	150	100	20	TM27	Return	Normal	—	100	20
TM03	Water Pulse	Water	60	95	20	TM32	Double Team	Normal	—	—	15
TM06	Toxic	Poison	—	85	10	TM40	Aerial Ace	Flying	60	—	20
TM07	Hail	Ice	—	—	10	TM42	Facade	Normal	70	100	20
TM10	Hidden Power	Normal	—	100	15	TM43	Secret Power	Normal	70	100	20
TM13	Ice Beam	Ice	95	100	10	TM44	Rest	Psychic	—	—	10
TM14	Blizzard	Ice	120	70	5	TM45	Attract	Normal	—	100	15
TM17	Protect	Normal	—	—	10	TM46	Thief	Dark	40	100	10
TM18	Rain Dance	Water	—	—	5	HM02	Fly	Flying	70	95	15
TM21	Frustration	Normal	—	100	20						

EGG MOVES*

Name	Type	Power	ACC	PP
Aurora Beam	Ice	65	100	20
Future Sight	Psychic	80	90	15
Ice Ball	Ice	30	90	20
Quick Attack	Normal	40	100	30
Rapid Spin	Normal	20	100	40
Bounce	Flying	85	85	5

*Learned Via Breeding

MOVE TUTOR
FireRed/LeafGreen and *Emerald* Only

Body Slam*	Counter*	Double-Edge
Mega Kick*	Mega Punch*	Mimic
Seismic Toss*	Substitute	

*Battle Frontier tutor move (*Emerald*)

---

226 Mantine™

FLYING **WATER**

GENERAL INFO
SPECIES: Kite Pokémon
HEIGHT: 6'11"
WEIGHT: 485 lbs.
ABILITY 1: Water Absorb
When Mantine is hit with a Water attack, it gets 1/4 of its HPs back.

ABILITY 2: Swift Swim
Increases Mantine's Speed when it's raining.

STATS
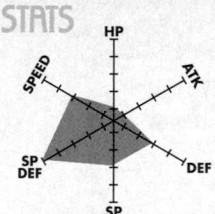

EVOLUTIONS

DOES NOT EVOLVE

LOCATION[S]:

RUBY — Rarity: **None**
Obtain in *Colosseum*

SAPPHIRE — Rarity: **None**
Obtain in *Colosseum*

FIRERED — Rarity: **Common**
Trade from *LeafGreen/Colosseum*

LEAFGREEN — Rarity: **Rare**
Seven Island

COLOSSEUM — Rarity: **Only One**
Pyrite Town

EMERALD — Rarity: **None**
Trade from *LeafGreen/Colosseum*

XD — Rarity: **None**
Trade from *LeafGreen/Colosseum*

MOVES

Level	Attack	Type	Power	ACC	PP	Level	Attack	Type	Power	ACC	PP
—	Tackle	Normal	35	95	35	22	Take Down	Normal	90	85	20
—	Bubble	Water	20	100	30	29	Agility	Psychic	—	—	30
8	Supersonic	Normal	—	55	20	36	Wing Attack	Flying	60	100	35
15	Bubblebeam	Water	65	100	20	43	Water Pulse	Water	60	100	20
						50	Confuse Ray	Ghost	—	100	10

TM/HM

TM/HM#	Name	Type	Power	ACC	PP	TM/HM#	Name	Type	Power	ACC	PP
TM03	Water Pulse	Water	60	95	20	TM27	Return	Normal	—	100	20
TM06	Toxic	Poison	—	85	10	TM32	Double Team	Normal	—	—	15
TM07	Hail	Ice	—	—	10	TM40	Aerial Ace	Flying	60	—	20
TM10	Hidden Power	Normal	—	100	15	TM42	Facade	Normal	70	100	20
TM11	Sunny Day	Fire	—	—	5	TM43	Secret Power	Normal	70	100	20
TM13	Ice Beam	Ice	95	100	10	TM44	Rest	Psychic	—	—	10
TM14	Blizzard	Ice	120	70	5	TM45	Attract	Normal	—	100	15
TM17	Protect	Normal	—	—	10	HM03	Surf	Water	95	100	15
TM18	Rain Dance	Water	—	—	5	HM07	Waterfall	Water	80	100	15
TM21	Frustration	Normal	—	100	20	HM08	Dive	Water	60	100	10
TM26	Earthquake	Ground	100	100	10						

EGG MOVES*

Name	Type	Power	ACC	PP
Haze	Ice	—	—	30
Hydro Pump	Water	120	80	5
Mud Sport	Ground	—	100	15
Rock Slide	Rock	75	90	10
Slam	Normal	80	75	20
Twister	Dragon	40	100	20

*Learned Via Breeding

MOVE TUTOR
FireRed/LeafGreen and *Emerald* Only

Body Slam*	Double-Edge	Mimic
Substitute		

*Battle Frontier tutor move (*Emerald*)

227 Skarmory™

STEEL | FLYING

GENERAL INFO
SPECIES: Armor Bird Pokémon
HEIGHT: 5'07"
WEIGHT: 111 lbs.
ABILITY 1: Keen Eye
Skarmory's Accuracy cannot be lowered.
ABILITY 2: Sturdy
One hit KO moves have no effect.

STATS

EVOLUTIONS

DOES NOT EVOLVE

LOCATION[S]:

RUBY — Rarity: **Rare**
Route 113

SAPPHIRE — Rarity: **Rare**
Route 113

FIRERED — Rarity: **Rare**
Seven Island

LEAFGREEN — Rarity: **Rare**
Seven Island

COLOSSEUM — Rarity: **Only One**
Realgam Tower

EMERALD — Rarity: **Rare**
Route 113

XD — Rarity: **None**
Trade from Ruby/Sapphire/FireRed/LeafGreen/Colosseum

MOVES

Level	Attack	Type	Power	ACC	PP	Level	Attack	Type	Power	ACC	PP
—	Leer	Normal	—	100	30	26	Fury Attack	Normal	15	85	20
—	Peck	Flying	35	100	35	29	Air Cutter	Flying	55	95	25
10	Sand-Attack	Ground	—	100	15	32	Steel Wing	Steel	70	90	25
13	Swift	Normal	60	—	20	42	Spikes	Ground	—	—	20
16	Agility	Psychic	—	—	30	45	Metal Sound	Steel	—	85	40

TM/HM

TM/HM#	Name	Type	Power	ACC	PP	TM/HM#	Name	Type	Power	ACC	PP
TM05	Roar	Normal	—	100	20	TM41	Torment	Dark	—	100	15
TM06	Toxic	Poison	—	85	10	TM42	Facade	Normal	70	100	20
TM10	Hidden Power	Normal	—	100	15	TM43	Secret Power	Normal	70	100	20
TM11	Sunny Day	Fire	—	—	5	TM44	Rest	Psychic	—	—	10
TM12	Taunt	Dark	—	100	20	TM45	Attract	Normal	—	100	15
TM17	Protect	Normal	—	—	10	TM46	Thief	Dark	40	100	10
TM21	Frustration	Normal	—	100	20	TM47	Steel Wing	Steel	70	90	25
TM27	Return	Normal	—	100	20	HM01	Cut	Normal	50	95	30
TM32	Double Team	Normal	—	—	15	HM02	Fly	Flying	70	95	15
TM37	Sandstorm	Rock	—	—	10	HM06	Rock Smash	Fighting	20	100	15
TM40	Aerial Ace	Flying	60	—	20						

EGG MOVES*

Name	Type	Power	ACC	PP
Drill Peck	Flying	80	100	20
Pursuit	Dark	40	100	20
Sky Attack	Flying	140	90	5
Whirlwind	Normal	—	100	20
Curse	—	—	—	10

*Learned Via Breeding

MOVE TUTOR

FireRed/LeafGreen and Emerald Only

Counter*	Double-Edge	Mimic
Rock Slide*	Substitute	

Emerald Only

Endure*	Mud-Slap*	Sleep Talk
Snore*	Swagger	Swift*

*Battle Frontier tutor move (Emerald)

---

228 Houndour™

DARK | FIRE

GENERAL INFO
SPECIES: Dark Pokémon
HEIGHT: 2'00"
WEIGHT: 24 lbs.
ABILITY 1: Flash Fire
Boosts the power of Houndour's Fire-type attacks and prevents it from being damaged by Fire-type attacks.
ABILITY 2: Early Bird
Allows Houndour to wake up sooner when put to sleep.

STATS

EVOLUTIONS

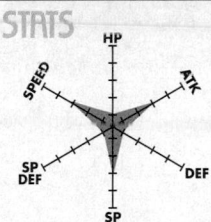LV24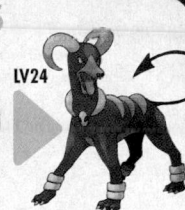

LOCATION[S]:

RUBY — Rarity: **None**
Obtain in Colosseum

SAPPHIRE — Rarity: **None**
Obtain in Colosseum

FIRERED — Rarity: **None**
Trade Houndoom from Colosseum and breed

LEAFGREEN — Rarity: **None**
Trade Houndoom from Colosseum and breed

COLOSSEUM — Rarity: **None**
Breed Houndoom

EMERALD — Rarity: **Rare**
Safari Zone

XD — Rarity: **Only One**
Cipher Lab (Capture from Cipher Peon Resix)

MOVES

Level	Attack	Type	Power	ACC	PP	Level	Attack	Type	Power	ACC	PP
—	Leer	Normal	—	100	30	25	Bite	Dark	60	100	25
—	Ember	Fire	40	100	25	31	Odor Sleuth	Normal	—	100	40
7	Howl	Normal	—	—	40	37	Faint Attack	Dark	60	—	20
13	Smog	Poison	20	70	20	43	Flamethrower	Fire	95	100	15
19	Roar	Normal	—	100	20	49	Crunch	Dark	80	100	15

TM/HM

TM/HM#	Name	Type	Power	ACC	PP	TM/HM#	Name	Type	Power	ACC	PP
TM05	Roar	Normal	—	100	20	TM35	Flamethrower	Fire	95	100	15
TM06	Toxic	Poison	—	85	10	TM36	Sludge Bomb	Poison	90	100	10
TM10	Hidden Power	Normal	—	100	15	TM38	Fire Blast	Fire	120	85	5
TM11	Sunny Day	Fire	—	—	5	TM41	Torment	Dark	—	100	15
TM12	Taunt	Dark	—	100	20	TM42	Facade	Normal	70	100	20
TM17	Protect	Normal	—	—	10	TM43	Secret Power	Normal	70	100	20
TM21	Frustration	Normal	—	100	20	TM44	Rest	Psychic	—	—	10
TM22	Solarbeam	Grass	120	100	10	TM45	Attract	Normal	—	100	15
TM23	Iron Tail	Steel	75	75	15	TM46	Thief	Dark	40	100	10
TM27	Return	Normal	—	100	20	TM49	Snatch	Dark	—	100	10
TM30	Shadow Ball	Ghost	80	100	15	TM50	Overheat	Fire	140	90	5
TM32	Double Team	Normal	—	—	15	HM06	Rock Smash	Fighting	20	100	15

EGG MOVES*

Name	Type	Power	ACC	PP
Beat Up	Dark	10	100	10
Counter	Fighting	—	100	20
Fire Spin	Fire	15	70	15
Pursuit	Dark	40	100	20
Rage	Normal	20	100	20
Reversal	Fighting	—	100	15
Spite	Ghost	—	100	10
Will-O-Wisp	Fire	—	75	15

*Learned Via Breeding

MOVE TUTOR

FireRed/LeafGreen and Emerald Only

Body Slam*	Counter*	Double-Edge
Dream Eater*	Mimic	Substitute

*Battle Frontier tutor move (Emerald)

229 Houndoom™

| | | DARK | FIRE |

GENERAL INFO
SPECIES: Dark Pokémon
HEIGHT: 4'07"
WEIGHT: 77 lbs.
ABILITY 1: Flash Fire
Boosts the power of Houndoom's Fire-type attacks and prevents it from being damaged by Fire-type attacks.

ABILITY 2: Early Bird
Allows Houndoom to wake up sooner when put to sleep.

STATS

EVOLUTIONS
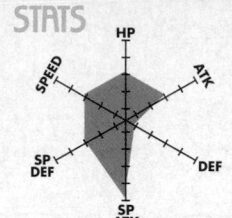
LV24

LOCATION[S]:

RUBY — Rarity: **None**
Trade from *Colosseum*

SAPPHIRE — Rarity: **None**
Trade from *Colosseum*

FIRERED — Rarity: **None**
Trade from *Colosseum*

LEAFGREEN — Rarity: **None**
Trade from *Colosseum*

COLOSSEUM — Rarity: **Only One**
Realgam Tower

EMERALD — Rarity: **Evolve**
Evolve Houndour

XD — Rarity: **Evolve**
Evolve Houndour

MOVES

Level	Attack	Type	Power	ACC	PP	Level	Attack	Type	Power	ACC	PP
—	Leer	Normal	—	100	30	27	Bite	Dark	60	100	25
—	Ember	Fire	40	100	25	35	Odor Sleuth	Normal	—	100	40
—	Howl	Normal	—	—	40	43	Faint Attack	Dark	60	—	20
13	Smog	Poison	20	70	20	51	Flamethrower	Fire	95	100	15
19	Roar	Normal	—	100	20	59	Crunch	Dark	80	100	15

TM/HM

TM/HM#	Name	Type	Power	ACC	PP	TM/HM#	Name	Type	Power	ACC	PP
TM05	Roar	Normal	—	100	20	TM35	Flamethrower	Fire	95	100	15
TM06	Toxic	Poison	—	85	10	TM36	Sludge Bomb	Poison	90	100	10
TM10	Hidden Power	Normal	—	100	15	TM38	Fire Blast	Fire	120	85	5
TM11	Sunny Day	Fire	—	—	5	TM41	Torment	Dark	—	100	15
TM12	Taunt	Dark	—	100	20	TM42	Facade	Normal	70	100	20
TM15	Hyper Beam	Normal	150	90	5	TM43	Secret Power	Normal	70	100	20
TM17	Protect	Normal	—	—	10	TM44	Rest	Psychic	—	—	10
TM21	Frustration	Normal	—	100	20	TM45	Attract	Normal	—	100	15
TM22	Solarbeam	Grass	120	100	10	TM46	Thief	Dark	40	100	10
TM23	Iron Tail	Steel	75	75	15	TM49	Snatch	Dark	—	100	10
TM27	Return	Normal	—	100	20	TM50	Overheat	Fire	140	90	5
TM30	Shadow Ball	Ghost	80	100	15	HM04	Strength	Normal	80	100	20
TM32	Double Team	Normal	—	—	15	HM06	Rock Smash	Fighting	20	100	15

MOVE TUTOR
FireRed/LeafGreen and *Emerald* Only

Body Slam*	Counter*	Double-Edge
Dream Eater*	Mimic	Substitute

*Battle Frontier tutor move (*Emerald*)

230 Kingdra™

| | | WATER | DRAGON |

GENERAL INFO
SPECIES: Dragon Pokémon
HEIGHT: 5'11"
WEIGHT: 335 lbs.
ABILITY: Swift Swim
Doubles the Kingdra's Speed when it's raining.

STATS

EVOLUTIONS
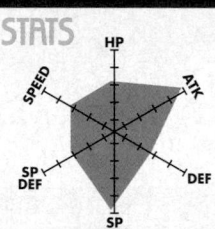
LV24
TRADE WITH DRAGON SCALE

LOCATION[S]:

RUBY — Rarity: **None**
Evolve Seadra

SAPPHIRE — Rarity: **None**
Evolve Seadra

FIRERED — Rarity: **None**
Evolve Seadra

LEAFGREEN — Rarity: **None**
Evolve Seadra

COLOSSEUM — Rarity: **None**
Trade from *Ruby/Sapphire/FireRed/LeafGreen*

EMERALD — Rarity: **Evolve**
Evolve Seadra

XD — Rarity: **None**
Trade from *Ruby/Sapphire/FireRed/LeafGreen*

MOVES

Level	Attack	Type	Power	ACC	PP	Level	Attack	Type	Power	ACC	PP
—	Bubble	Water	20	100	30	29	Twister	Dragon	40	100	20
—	Smokescreen	Normal	—	100	20	40	Agility	Psychic	—	—	30
—	Leer	Normal	—	100	30	51	Hydro Pump	Water	120	80	5
—/22	Water Gun	Water	40	100	25	62	Dragon Dance	Dragon	—	—	20

TM/HM

TM/HM#	Name	Type	Power	ACC	PP	TM/HM#	Name	Type	Power	ACC	PP
TM03	Water Pulse	Water	60	100	20	TM27	Return	Normal	—	100	20
TM06	Toxic	Poison	—	85	10	TM32	Double Team	Normal	—	—	15
TM07	Hail	Ice	—	—	10	TM42	Facade	Normal	70	100	20
TM10	Hidden Power	Normal	—	100	15	TM43	Secret Power	Normal	70	100	20
TM13	Ice Beam	Ice	95	100	10	TM44	Rest	Psychic	—	—	10
TM14	Blizzard	Ice	120	70	5	TM45	Attract	Normal	—	100	15
TM15	Hyper Beam	Normal	150	90	5	HM03	Surf	Water	95	100	15
TM17	Protect	Normal	—	—	10	HM07	Waterfall	Water	80	100	15
TM18	Rain Dance	Water	—	—	5	HM08	Dive	Water	60	100	10
TM21	Frustration	Normal	—	100	20						

= Emerald Only

MOVE TUTOR
FireRed/LeafGreen and *Emerald* Only

Body Slam*	Double-Edge	Mimic
Substitute		

Emerald Only

Endure*	Icy Wind*	Sleep Talk*
Snore*	Swagger	Swift*

*Battle Frontier tutor move (*Emerald*)

231 Phanpy™

GROUND

GENERAL INFO

SPECIES: Long Nose Pokémon
HEIGHT: 1'08"
WEIGHT: 74 lbs.
ABILITY: Pickup

Allows Phanpy to pick up items from the opponent in battle. Also picks up items on roads when in a party.

STATS

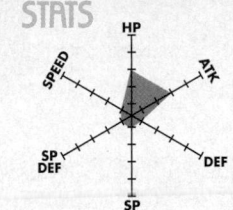

EVOLUTIONS

LV25

LOCATION[s]:

RUBY	Rarity: **Common**
Safari Zone	
SAPPHIRE	Rarity: **Common**
Safari Zone	
FIRERED	Rarity: **Common**
Seven Island	
LEAFGREEN	Rarity: **Common**
Seven Island	
COLOSSEUM	Rarity: **None**
Trade from *Ruby/Sapphire/FireRed/LeafGreen*	
EMERALD	Rarity: **Common**
Safari Zone	
XD	Rarity: **Rare**
Oasis Poké Spot	

MOVES

Level	Attack	Type	Power	ACC	PP
—	Odor Sleuth	Normal	—	100	40
—	Growl	Normal	—	100	40
—	Tackle	Normal	35	95	35
9	Defense Curl	Normal	—	—	40

Level	Attack	Type	Power	ACC	PP
17	Flail	Normal	—	100	15
25	Take Down	Normal	90	85	20
33	Rollout	Rock	30	90	20
41	Endure	Normal	—	—	10
49	Double-Edge	Normal	120	100	15

TM/HM

TM/HM#	Name	Type	Power	ACC	PP
TM05	Roar	Normal	—	100	20
TM06	Toxic	Poison	—	85	10
TM10	Hidden Power	Normal	—	100	15
TM11	Sunny Day	Fire	—	—	5
TM17	Protect	Normal	—	—	10
TM21	Frustration	Normal	—	100	20
TM23	Iron Tail	Steel	100	75	15
TM26	Earthquake	Ground	100	100	10
TM27	Return	Normal	—	100	20

TM/HM#	Name	Type	Power	ACC	PP
TM32	Double Team	Normal	—	—	15
TM37	Sandstorm	Rock	—	—	10
TM39	Rock Tomb	Rock	50	80	10
TM42	Facade	Normal	70	100	20
TM43	Secret Power	Normal	70	100	20
TM44	Rest	Psychic	—	—	10
TM45	Attract	Normal	—	100	15
HM04	Strength	Normal	80	100	15
HM06	Rock Smash	Fighting	20	100	15

EGG MOVES*

Name	Type	Power	ACC	PP
Focus Energy	Normal	—	—	30
Body Slam	Normal	85	100	15
Ancientpower	Rock	60	100	5
Snore	Normal	40	100	15
Counter	Fighting	—	100	20
Fissure	Ground	—	30	5

*Learned Via Breeding

MOVE TUTOR

FireRed/LeafGreen and Emerald Only

Body Slam*	Counter*	Double-Edge
Mimic	Substitute	

Emerald Only

Endure*	Mud-Slap*	Rollout
Sleep Talk	Snore*	Swagger

*Battle Frontier tutor move (*Emerald*)

---

232 Donphan™

GROUND

GENERAL INFO

SPECIES: Armor Pokémon
HEIGHT: 3'07"
WEIGHT: 265 lbs.
ABILITY: Sturdy

One hit KO Moves have no effect.

STATS

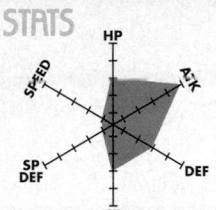

EVOLUTIONS

LV25

LOCATION[s]:

RUBY	Rarity: **Common**
Evolve Phanpy	
SAPPHIRE	Rarity: **Common**
Evolve Phanpy	
FIRERED	Rarity: **Common**
Evolve Phanpy	
LEAFGREEN	Rarity: **Common**
Evolve Phanpy	
COLOSSEUM	Rarity: **None**
Trade from *Ruby/Sapphire/FireRed/LeafGreen*	
EMERALD	Rarity: **Evolve**
Evolve Phanpy	
XD	Rarity: **Evolve**
Evolve Phanpy	

MOVES

Level	Attack	Type	Power	ACC	PP
—	Odor Sleuth	Normal	—	100	40
—	Horn Attack	Normal	65	100	25
—	Growl	Normal	—	100	40
9	Defense Curl	Normal	—	—	40

Level	Attack	Type	Power	ACC	PP
17	Flail	Normal	—	100	15
25	Fury Attack	Normal	15	85	20
33	Rollout	Rock	30	90	20
41	Rapid Spin	Normal	20	100	40
49	Earthquake	Ground	100	100	10

TM/HM

TM/HM#	Name	Type	Power	ACC	PP
TM05	Roar	Normal	—	100	20
TM06	Toxic	Poison	—	85	10
TM10	Hidden Power	Normal	—	100	15
TM11	Sunny Day	Fire	—	—	5
TM15	Hyper Beam	Normal	150	90	5
TM17	Protect	Normal	—	—	10
TM21	Frustration	Normal	—	100	20
TM23	Iron Tail	Steel	100	75	15
TM26	Earthquake	Ground	100	100	10
TM27	Return	Normal	—	100	20

TM/HM#	Name	Type	Power	ACC	PP
TM32	Double Team	Normal	—	—	15
TM37	Sandstorm	Rock	—	—	10
TM39	Rock Tomb	Rock	50	80	10
TM42	Facade	Normal	70	100	20
TM43	Secret Power	Normal	70	100	20
TM44	Rest	Psychic	—	—	10
TM45	Attract	Normal	—	100	15
HM04	Strength	Normal	80	100	15
HM06	Rock Smash	Fighting	20	100	15

MOVE TUTOR

FireRed/LeafGreen and Emerald Only

Body Slam*	Counter*	Double-Edge
Mimic	Rock Slide*	Substitute

Emerald Only

Defense Curl*	Endure*	Mud-Slap*
Rollout	Sleep Talk	Snore*
Swagger		

*Battle Frontier tutor move (*Emerald*)

233 Porygon2™

NORMAL

GENERAL INFO
SPECIES: Virtual Pokémon
HEIGHT: 2'00"
WEIGHT: 72 lbs.
ABILITY: Trace
Allows Porygon2 to copy the opponent's ability.

STATS
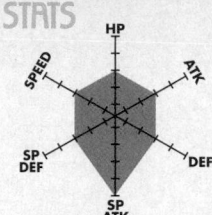

EVOLUTIONS

TRADE WITH UP-GRADE

LOCATION[S]:

RUBY   Rarity: **None**
Trade from *FireRed/LeafGreen*

SAPPHIRE   Rarity: **None**
Trade from *FireRed/LeafGreen*

FIRERED   Rarity: **None**
Evolve Porygon

LEAFGREEN   Rarity: **None**
Evolve Porygon

COLOSSEUM   Rarity: **None**
Evolve Porygon

EMERALD   Rarity: **None**
Trade from *FireRed/LeafGreen*

XD   Rarity: **None**
Trade from *FireRed/LeafGreen*

MOVES

Level	Attack	Type	Power	ACC	PP	Level	Attack	Type	Power	ACC	PP
—	Tackle	Normal	35	95	35	20	Recover	Normal	—	—	20
—	Conversion	Normal	—	—	30	24	Defense Curl	Normal	—	—	40
—	Conversion 2	Normal	—	—	30	32	Lock-on	Normal	—	100	5
9	Agility	Psychic	—	—	30	36	Tri Attack	Normal	80	100	10
12	Psybeam	Psychic	65	100	20	44	Recycle	Normal	—	100	10
						48	Zap Cannon	Electric	100	50	5

TM/HM

TM/HM#	Name	Type	Power	ACC	PP	TM/HM#	Name	Type	Power	ACC	PP
TM06	Toxic	Poison	—	85	10	TM25	Thunder	Electric	120	70	10
TM10	Hidden Power	Normal	—	100	15	TM27	Return	Normal	—	100	10
TM11	Sunny Day	Fire	—	—	5	TM29	Psychic	Psychic	90	100	10
TM13	Ice Beam	Ice	95	100	10	TM30	Shadow Ball	Ghost	80	100	15
TM14	Blizzard	Ice	120	70	5	TM32	Double Team	Normal	—	—	15
TM15	Hyper Beam	Normal	150	90	5	TM34	Shock Wave	Electric	60	—	20
TM17	Protect	Normal	—	—	10	TM40	Aerial Ace	Flying	60	—	20
TM18	Rain Dance	Water	—	—	5	TM42	Facade	Normal	70	100	20
TM21	Frustration	Normal	—	100	20	TM43	Secret Power	Normal	70	100	20
TM22	Solarbeam	Grass	120	100	10	TM44	Rest	Psychic	—	—	10
TM23	Iron Tail	Steel	75	75	15	TM46	Thief	Dark	40	100	10
TM24	Thunderbolt	Electric	95	100	15	HM05	Flash	Normal	—	70	20

MOVE TUTOR
FireRed/LeafGreen and *Emerald* Only

Double-Edge	Dream Eater*	Mimic
Substitute	Thunder Wave*	

*Battle Frontier tutor move (*Emerald*)

---

234 Stantler™

NORMAL

GENERAL INFO
SPECIES: Big Horn Pokémon
HEIGHT: 4'07"
WEIGHT: 157 lbs.
ABILITY: Intimidate
An opponent's Attack decreases when Stantler is summoned into battle.

STATS
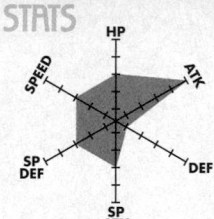
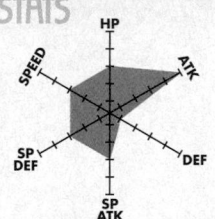

EVOLUTIONS

DOES NOT EVOLVE

LOCATION[S]:

RUBY   Rarity: **None**
Trade from *Colosseum*

SAPPHIRE   Rarity: **None**
Trade from *Colosseum*

FIRERED   Rarity: **None**
Trade from *Colosseum*

LEAFGREEN   Rarity: **None**
Trade from *Colosseum*

COLOSSEUM   Rarity: **Only One**
The Under

EMERALD   Rarity: **Rare**
Safari Zone

XD   Rarity: **None**
Trade from *Colosseum*

MOVES

Level	Attack	Type	Power	ACC	PP	Level	Attack	Type	Power	ACC	PP
—	Tackle	Normal	35	95	35	27	Sand-Attack	Ground	—	100	15
7	Leer	Normal	—	100	30	31	Role Play	Psychic	—	100	10
11	Astonish	Ghost	30	100	15	37	Take Down	Normal	90	85	20
17	Hypnosis	Psychic	—	60	20	41	Confuse Ray	Ghost	—	100	10
21	Stomp	Normal	65	100	20	47	Calm Mind	Psychic	—	—	20

TM/HM

TM/HM#	Name	Type	Power	ACC	PP	TM/HM#	Name	Type	Power	ACC	PP
TM04	Calm Mind	Psychic	—	—	20	TM27	Return	Normal	—	100	20
TM05	Roar	Normal	—	100	20	TM29	Psychic	Psychic	90	100	10
TM06	Toxic	Poison	—	85	10	TM30	Shadow Ball	Ghost	80	100	15
TM10	Hidden Power	Normal	—	100	15	TM32	Double Team	Normal	—	—	15
TM11	Sunny Day	Fire	—	—	5	TM33	Reflect	Normal	—	—	20
TM16	Light Screen	Psychic	—	—	30	TM34	Shock Wave	Electric	60	—	20
TM17	Protect	Normal	—	—	10	TM42	Facade	Normal	70	100	20
TM18	Rain Dance	Water	—	—	5	TM43	Secret Power	Normal	70	100	20
TM21	Frustration	Normal	—	100	20	TM44	Rest	Psychic	—	—	10
TM22	Solarbeam	Grass	120	100	10	TM45	Attract	Normal	—	100	15
TM23	Iron Tail	Steel	75	75	15	TM46	Thief	Dark	40	100	10
TM24	Thunderbolt	Electric	95	100	15	TM48	Skill Swap	Psychic	—	100	10
TM25	Thunder	Electric	120	70	10	HM05	Flash	Normal	—	70	20
TM26	Earthquake	Ground	100	100	10						

EGG MOVES*

Name	Type	Power	ACC	PP
Bite	Dark	60	100	25
Disable	Normal	—	55	20
Extrasensory	Psychic	80	100	30
Psych Up	Normal	—	—	10
Spite	Ghost	—	100	10
Swagger	Normal	—	90	15

*Learned Via Breeding

MOVE TUTOR
FireRed/LeafGreen and *Emerald* Only

Body Slam*	Double-Edge	Dream Eater*
Mimic	Substitute	Thunder Wave*

*Battle Frontier tutor move (*Emerald*)

235 Smeargle™

NORMAL

GENERAL INFO
SPECIES: Painter Pokémon
HEIGHT: 3'11"
WEIGHT: 128 lbs.
ABILITY: Own Tempo
Smeargle can't be confused.

STATS
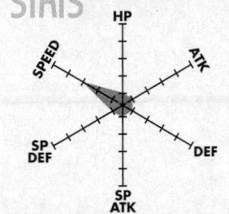

EVOLUTIONS

DOES NOT EVOLVE

LOCATION[S]:
RUBY **Rarity: None**
Trade from *Colosseum/Emerald*

SAPPHIRE **Rarity: None**
Trade from *Colosseum/Emerald*

FIRERED **Rarity: None**
Trade from *Colosseum/Emerald*

LEAFGREEN **Rarity: None**
Trade from *Colosseum/Emerald*

COLOSSEUM **Rarity: None**
Snagem Hideout

EMERALD **Rarity: Common**
Battle Frontier

XD **Rarity: None**
Trade from *Colosseum/Emerald*

MOVES
Level	Attack	Type	Power	ACC	PP	Level	Attack	Type	Power	ACC	PP
—	Sketch	Normal	—	—	1	51	Sketch	Normal	—	—	1
11	Sketch	Normal	—	—	1	61	Sketch	Normal	—	—	1
21	Sketch	Normal	—	—	1	71	Sketch	Normal	—	—	1
31	Sketch	Normal	—	—	1	81	Sketch	Normal	—	—	1
41	Sketch	Normal	—	—	1	91	Skotch	Normal	—	—	1

TM/HM
TM/HM#	Name	Type	Power	ACC	PP
None					

EGG MOVES*
Name	Type	Power	ACC	PP
None				

*Learned Via Breeding

MOVE TUTOR
FireRed/LeafGreen and *Emerald* Only
None

236 Tyrogue™

FIGHTING

GENERAL INFO
SPECIES: Scuffle Pokémon
HEIGHT: 2'04"
WEIGHT: 46 lbs.
ABILITY: Guts
When Tyrogue has a status condition, its attack power is multiplied by 1.5.

STATS
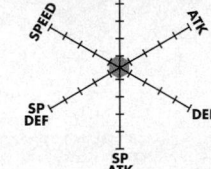

EVOLUTIONS
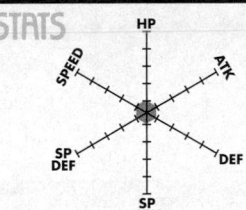
(ATTACK>DEFENSE) LV20
(ATTACK<DEFENSE) LV20
(ATTACK=DEFENSE) LV20

LOCATION[S]:
RUBY **Rarity: None**
Trade and then breed Hitmonchan or Hitmonlee

SAPPHIRE **Rarity: None**
Trade and then breed Hitmonchan or Hitmonlee

FIRERED **Rarity: None**
Breed Hitmonchan or Hitmonlee

LEAFGREEN **Rarity: None**
Breed Hitmonchan or Hitmonlee

COLOSSEUM **Rarity: None**
Trade from *Ruby/Sapphire/FireRed/LeafGreen*

EMERALD **Rarity: None**
Trade and then breed Hitmonchan or Hitmonlee

XD **Rarity: None**
Trade from *Ruby/Sapphire/FireRed/LeafGreen*

MOVES
Level	Attack	Type	Power	ACC	PP
—	Tackle	Normal	35	95	35

TM/HM
TM/HM#	Name	Type	Power	ACC	PP	TM/HM#	Name	Type	Power	ACC	PP
TM06	Toxic	Poison	—	85	10	TM31	Brick Break	Fighting	75	100	15
TM08	Bulk Up	Fighting	—	—	20	TM32	Double Team	Normal	—	—	15
TM10	Hidden Power	—	—	100	15	TM42	Facade	Normal	70	100	20
TM11	Sunny Day	Fire	—	—	5	TM43	Secret Power	Normal	70	100	20
TM17	Protect	Normal	—	—	10	TM44	Rest	Psychic	—	—	10
TM18	Rain Dance	Water	—	—	5	TM45	Attract	Normal	—	100	15
TM21	Frustration	Normal	—	100	20	TM46	Thief	Dark	40	100	10
TM26	Earthquake	Ground	100	100	10	HM04	Strength	Normal	80	100	15
TM27	Return	Normal	—	100	20	HM06	Rock Smash	Fighting	20	100	15

EGG MOVES*
Name	Type	Power	ACC	PP
Hi Jump Kick	Fighting	85	90	20
Mach Punch	Fighting	40	100	30
Mind Reader	Normal	—	100	5
Rapid Spin	Normal	20	100	40

*Learned Via Breeding

MOVE TUTOR
FireRed/LeafGreen and *Emerald* Only
Body Slam*	Counter*	Double-Edge
Mega Kick*	Mimic	Rock Slide*
Seismic Toss*	Substitute	

*Battle Frontier tutor move (*Emerald*)

237 Hitmontop ™

FIGHTING

GENERAL INFO

SPECIES: Handstand Pokémon
HEIGHT: 4'07"
WEIGHT: 105 lbs.
ABILITY: Intimidate

When Hitmontop is sent into battle, it lowers the opponent's Attack.

STATS

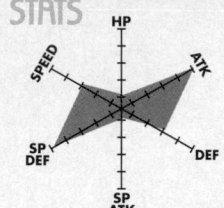

EVOLUTIONS

(ATTACK=DEFENSE)
LV20

LOCATION(S):

RUBY   **Rarity: None**
Trade from *Colosseum*

SAPPHIRE   **Rarity: None**
Trade from *Colosseum*

FIRERED   **Rarity: None**
Trade from *Colosseum*

LEAFGREEN   **Rarity: None**
Trade from *Colosseum*

COLOSSEUM   **Rarity: Only One**
Agate Village

EMERALD   **Rarity: None**
Trade from *Colosseum*

XD   **Rarity: None**
Trade from *Colosseum*

MOVES

Level	Attack	Type	Power	ACC	PP	Level	Attack	Type	Power	ACC	PP
—	Rolling Kick	Fight	60	85	15	20	Triple Kick	Fight	10	100	10
—	Revenge	Fighting	60	100	10	25	Rapid Spin	Normal	20	100	40
7	Focus Energy	Normal	—	—	30	31	Counter	Fighting	—	100	20
13	Pursuit	Dark	40	100	20	37	Agility	Psychic	—	—	30
19	Quick Attack	Normal	40	100	30	43	Detect	Fight	—	—	5
						49	Endeavor	Normal	—	100	5

TM/HM

TM/HM#	Name	Type	Power	ACC	PP	TM/HM#	Name	Type	Power	ACC	PP
TM06	Toxic	Poison	—	85	10	TM31	Brick Break	Fighting	75	100	15
TM08	Bulk Up	Fighting	—	—	20	TM32	Double Team	Normal	—	—	15
TM10	Hidden Power	Normal	—	100	15	TM37	Sandstorm	Ground	—	—	10
TM11	Sunny Day	Fire	—	—	5	TM42	Facade	Normal	70	100	20
TM17	Protect	Normal	—	—	10	TM43	Secret Power	Normal	70	100	20
TM18	Rain Dance	Water	—	—	5	TM44	Rest	Psychic	—	—	10
TM21	Frustration	Normal	—	100	20	TM45	Attract	Normal	—	100	15
TM26	Earthquake	Ground	100	100	10	TM46	Thief	Dark	40	100	10
TM27	Return	Normal	—	100	20	HM04	Strength	Normal	80	100	15
TM28	Dig	Ground	60	100	10	HM06	Rock Smash	Fighting	20	100	15

MOVE TUTOR

FireRed/LeafGreen and *Emerald* Only

Body Slam*	Counter*	Double-Edge
Mega Kick*	Mimic	Rock Slide*
Seismic Toss*	Substitute	

*Battle Frontier tutor move (*Emerald*)

238 Smoochum ™

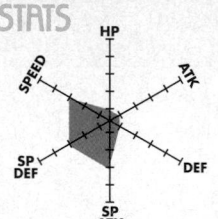

ICE   PSYCHIC

GENERAL INFO

SPECIES: Kiss Pokémon
HEIGHT: 1'04"
WEIGHT: 14 lbs.
ABILITY: Oblivious

Prevents Smoochum from being attracted.

STATS

EVOLUTIONS

LV30

LOCATION(S):

RUBY   **Rarity: None**
Trade from *FireRed/LeafGreen*

SAPPHIRE   **Rarity: None**
Trade from *FireRed/LeafGreen*

FIRERED   **Rarity: None**
Breed Jynx

LEAFGREEN   **Rarity: None**
Breed Jynx

COLOSSEUM   **Rarity: None**
Trade from *FireRed/LeafGreen*

EMERALD   **Rarity: None**
Trade from *FireRed/LeafGreen*

XD   **Rarity: None**
Trade from *FireRed/LeafGreen*

MOVES

Level	Attack	Type	Power	ACC	PP	Level	Attack	Type	Power	ACC	PP
—	Pound	Normal	40	100	35	25	Sing	Normal	—	55	15
—	Lick	Ghost	20	100	30	33	Mean Look	Normal	—	100	5
9	Sweet Kiss	Normal	—	75	10	37	Fake Tears	Dark	—	100	20
13	Powder Snow	Ice	40	100	25	45	Psychic	Psychic	90	100	10
21	Confusion	Psychic	50	100	25	49	Perish Song	Normal	—	—	5
						57	Blizzard	Ice	120	70	5

TM/HM

TM/HM#	Name	Type	Power	ACC	PP	TM/HM#	Name	Type	Power	ACC	PP
TM03	Water Pulse	Water	60	95	20	TM29	Psychic	Psychic	90	100	10
TM04	Calm Mind	Psychic	—	—	20	TM30	Shadow Ball	Ghost	80	100	10
TM06	Toxic	Poison	—	85	10	TM32	Double Team	Normal	—	—	15
TM07	Hail	Ice	—	—	10	TM33	Reflect	Normal	—	—	20
TM10	Hidden Power	Normal	—	100	15	TM42	Facade	Normal	70	100	20
TM13	Ice Beam	Ice	95	100	10	TM43	Secret Power	Normal	70	100	20
TM14	Blizzard	Ice	120	70	5	TM44	Rest	Psychic	—	—	10
TM16	Light Screen	Psychic	—	—	30	TM45	Attract	Normal	—	100	15
TM17	Protect	Normal	—	—	10	TM46	Thief	Dark	40	100	10
TM18	Rain Dance	Water	—	—	5	TM48	Skill Swap	Psychic	—	100	10
TM21	Frustration	Normal	—	100	20	HM05	Flash	Normal	—	70	20
TM27	Return	Normal	—	100	20						

EGG MOVES*

Name	Type	Power	ACC	PP
Fake Out	Normal	40	100	10
Ice Punch	Ice	75	100	15
Meditate	Psychic	—	—	40
Psych Up	Normal	—	—	10
Wish	Normal	—	100	10

*Learned Via Breeding

MOVE TUTOR

FireRed/LeafGreen and *Emerald* Only

Body Slam*	Counter*	Double-Edge
Dream Eater*	Mega Kick*	Mega Punch*
Metronome	Mimic	Seismic Toss*
Substitute		

*Battle Frontier tutor move (*Emerald*)

239 Elekid™

GENERAL INFO
SPECIES: Electric Pokémon
HEIGHT: 2'00"
WEIGHT: 52 lbs.
ABILITY: Static

An opponent has a 30% chance of being paralyzed when it directly strikes Elekid.

STATS
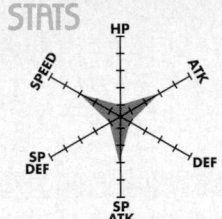

EVOLUTIONS

LV30

LOCATION[S]:

RUBY — Rarity: **None**
Trade from *FireRed/LeafGreen*

SAPPHIRE — Rarity: **None**
Trade from *FireRed/LeafGreen*

FIRERED — Rarity: **None**
Breed Electabuzz

LEAFGREEN — Rarity: **None**
Trade from *FireRed/LeafGreen*

COLOSSEUM — Rarity: **None**
Trade from *FireRed/LeafGreen*

EMERALD — Rarity: **None**
Trade from *FireRed/LeafGreen*

XD — Rarity: **Only One**
Give Hordel the Purified Togepi in trade for Elekid

MOVES

Level	Attack	Type	Power	ACC	PP	Level	Attack	Type	Power	ACC	PP
—	Quick Attack	Normal	40	100	30	25	Swift	Normal	60	—	20
—	Leer	Normal	—	100	30	33	Screech	Normal	—	85	40
9	Thunderpunch	Electric	75	100	15	41	Thunderbolt	Electric	95	100	15
17	Light Screen	Psychic	—	—	30	49	Thunder	Electric	120	70	10

TM/HM

TM/HM#	Name	Type	Power	ACC	PP	TM/HM#	Name	Type	Power	ACC	PP
TM01	Focus Punch	Fighting	150	100	20	TM31	Brick Break	Fighting	75	100	15
TM06	Toxic	Poison	—	85	10	TM32	Double Team	Normal	—	—	15
TM10	Hidden Power	Normal	—	100	15	TM34	Shock Wave	Electric	60	—	20
TM16	Light Screen	Psychic	—	—	30	TM42	Facade	Normal	70	100	20
TM17	Protect	Normal	—	—	10	TM43	Secret Power	Normal	70	100	20
TM18	Rain Dance	Water	—	—	5	TM44	Rest	Psychic	—	—	10
TM21	Frustration	Normal	—	100	20	TM45	Attract	Normal	—	100	15
TM24	Thunderbolt	Electric	95	100	15	TM46	Thief	Dark	40	100	15
TM25	Thunder	Electric	120	70	10	HM05	Flash	Normal	—	70	20
TM27	Return	Normal	—	100	20	HM06	Rock Smash	Fighting	20	100	15
TM29	Psychic	Psychic	90	100	10						

EGG MOVES*

Name	Type	Power	ACC	PP
Barrier	Psychic	—	—	30
Cross Chop	Fighting	100	80	5
Fire Punch	Fire	75	100	15
Ice Punch	Ice	75	100	15
Karate Chop	Fighting	50	100	25
Medtiate	Psychic	—	—	40
Rolling Kick	Fight	60	85	15

*Learned Via Breeding

MOVE TUTOR
FireRed/LeafGreen and Emerald Only

Body Slam*	Counter*	Double-Edge
Mega Kick*	Mega Punch*	Mimic
Seismic Toss*	Substitute	Thunder Wave*

*Battle Frontier tutor move (*Emerald*)

---

240 Magby™

GENERAL INFO
SPECIES: Live Coal Pokémon
HEIGHT: 2'04"
WEIGHT: 47 lbs.
ABILITY: Flame Body

If Magby is struck directly, the opponent has a 30% chance of being burned.

STATS
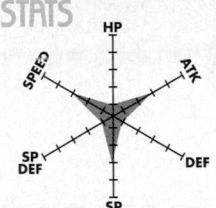

EVOLUTIONS

LV30

LOCATION[S]:

RUBY — Rarity: **None**
Trade from *LeafGreen*

SAPPHIRE — Rarity: **None**
Trade from *LeafGreen*

FIRERED — Rarity: **None**
Trade from *LeafGreen*

LEAFGREEN — Rarity: **None**
Breed Magmar

COLOSSEUM — Rarity: **None**
Trade from *LeafGreen*

EMERALD — Rarity: **None**
Trade from *LeafGreen*

XD — Rarity: **None**
Trade from *LeafGreen*

MOVES

Level	Attack	Type	Power	ACC	PP	Level	Attack	Type	Power	ACC	PP
—	Ember	Fire	40	100	25	25	Smokescreen	Normal	—	100	20
7	Leer	Normal	—	100	30	31	Sunny Day	Fire	—	—	5
13	Smog	Poison	20	70	20	37	Flamethrower	Fire	95	100	15
19	Fire Punch	Fire	75	100	15	43	Confuse Ray	Ghost	—	100	10
						49	Fire Blast	Fire	120	85	5

TM/HM

TM/HM#	Name	Type	Power	ACC	PP	TM/HM#	Name	Type	Power	ACC	PP
TM01	Focus Punch	Fighting	150	100	20	TM32	Double Team	Normal	—	—	15
TM06	Toxic	Poison	—	85	10	TM35	Flamethrower	Fire	95	100	15
TM10	Hidden Power	Normal	—	100	15	TM38	Fire Blast	Fire	120	85	5
TM11	Sunny Day	Fire	—	—	5	TM42	Facade	Normal	70	100	20
TM17	Protect	Normal	—	—	10	TM43	Secret Power	Normal	70	100	20
TM21	Frustration	Normal	—	100	20	TM44	Rest	Psychic	—	—	10
TM23	Iron Tail	Steel	75	75	15	TM45	Attract	Normal	—	100	15
TM27	Return	Normal	—	100	20	TM46	Thief	Dark	40	100	15
TM29	Psychic	Psychic	90	100	10	HM06	Rock Smash	Fighting	20	100	15
TM31	Brick Break	Fighting	75	100	15						

EGG MOVES*

Name	Type	Power	ACC	PP
Barrier	Psychic	—	—	30
Cross Chop	Fighting	100	80	5
Karate Chop	Fighting	50	100	25
Mega Punch	Normal	80	85	20
Screech	Normal	—	85	40
Thunderpunch	Electric	75	100	15

*Learned Via Breeding

MOVE TUTOR
FireRed/LeafGreen and Emerald Only

Body Slam*	Counter*	Double-Edge
Mega Kick*	Mega Punch*	Mimic
Seismic Toss*	Substitute	

*Battle Frontier tutor move (*Emerald*)

241 Miltank™

NORMAL

GENERAL INFO
SPECIES: Milk Cow Pokémon
HEIGHT: 3'11"
WEIGHT: 166 lbs.
ABILITY: Thick Fat

Miltank takes half damage on all Fire-type and Ice-type attacks.

STATS
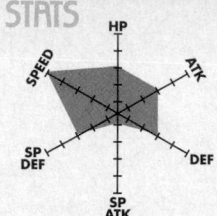

EVOLUTIONS

DOES NOT EVOLVE

LOCATION[S]:

RUBY — Rarity: **None**
Obtain in *Colosseum/Emerald*

SAPPHIRE — Rarity: **None**
Obtain in *Colosseum/Emerald*

FIRERED — Rarity: **None**
Obtain in *Colosseum/Emerald*

LEAFGREEN — Rarity: **None**
Obtain in *Colosseum/Emerald*

COLOSSEUM — Rarity: **Only One**
Realgam Tower

EMERALD — Rarity: **Rare**
Safari Zone

XD — Rarity: **None**
Obtain in *Colosseum/Emerald*

MOVES

Level	Attack	Type	Power	ACC	PP	Level	Attack	Type	Power	ACC	PP
—	Tackle	Normal	35	95	35	19	Milk Drink	Normal	—	—	10
4	Growl	Normal	—	100	40	26	Bide	Normal	—	100	10
8	Defense Curl	Normal	—	—	40	34	Rollout	Rock	30	90	20
13	Stomp	Normal	65	100	20	43	Body Slam	Normal	85	100	15
						53	Heal Bell	Normal	—	—	5

TM/HM

TM/HM#	Name	Type	Power	ACC	PP	TM/HM#	Name	Type	Power	ACC	PP
TM01	Focus Punch	Fighting	150	100	20	TM26	Earthquake	Ground	100	100	10
TM03	Water Pulse	Water	60	95	20	TM27	Return	Normal	—	100	20
TM06	Toxic	Poison	—	85	10	TM30	Shadow Ball	Ghost	80	100	15
TM10	Hidden Power	Normal	—	100	15	TM31	Brick Break	Fighting	75	100	15
TM11	Sunny Day	Fire	—	—	5	TM32	Double Team	Normal	—	—	15
TM13	Ice Beam	Ice	95	100	10	TM34	Shock Wave	Electric	60	—	20
TM14	Blizzard	Ice	120	70	5	TM37	Sandstorm	Ground	—	—	10
TM15	Hyper Beam	Normal	150	90	5	TM39	Rock Tomb	Rock	50	80	10
TM17	Protect	Normal	—	—	10	TM42	Facade	Normal	70	100	15
TM18	Rain Dance	Water	—	—	5	TM43	Secret Power	Normal	70	100	20
TM21	Frustration	Normal	—	100	20	TM44	Rest	Psychic	—	—	10
TM22	Solarbeam	Grass	120	100	10	TM45	Attract	Normal	—	100	15
TM23	Iron Tail	Steel	75	75	15	HM03	Surf	Water	95	100	15
TM24	Thunderbolt	Electric	95	100	15	HM04	Strength	Normal	80	100	15
TM25	Thunder	Electric	120	70	10	HM06	Rock Smash	Fighting	20	100	15

EGG MOVES*

Name	Type	Power	ACC	PP
Curse	—	—	—	10
Endure	Normal	—	—	10
Helping Hand	Normal	—	100	20
Present	Normal	—	90	15
Psych Up	Normal	—	—	10
Reversal	Fighting	—	100	15
Seismic Toss	Fighting	—	100	20
Sleep Talk	Normal	—	—	10

*Learned Via Breeding

MOVE TUTOR
FireRed/LeafGreen and *Emerald* Only

Body Slam*	Counter*	Double-Edge
Mega Kick*	Mega Punch*	Metronome
Mimic	Rock Slide*	Seismic Toss*
Substitute	Thunder Wave*	

*Battle Frontier tutor move (*Emerald*)

---

242 Blissey™

NORMAL

GENERAL INFO
SPECIES: Happiness Pokémon
HEIGHT: 4'11"
WEIGHT: 103 lbs.
ABILITY 1: Natural Cure **ABILITY 2:** Serene Grace

Any status condition is cured when Blissey is switched out.

When Blissey is in battle, the chances of extra effects occurring are doubled.

STATS

EVOLUTIONS
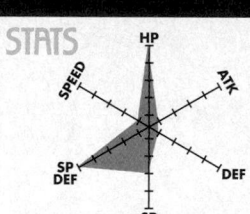

FRIENDSHIP

LOCATION[S]:

RUBY — Rarity: **None**
Trade from *FireRed/LeafGreen*

SAPPHIRE — Rarity: **None**
Trade from *FireRed/LeafGreen*

FIRERED — Rarity: **Evolve**
Evolve Chansey

LEAFGREEN — Rarity: **Evolve**
Evolve Chansey

COLOSSEUM — Rarity: **None**
Trade from *FireRed/LeafGreen*

EMERALD — Rarity: **None**
Trade from *FireRed/LeafGreen*

XD — Rarity: **Evolve**
Evolve Chansey

MOVES

Level	Attack	Type	Power	ACC	PP	Level	Attack	Type	Power	ACC	PP
—	Pound	Normal	40	100	35	18	Minimize	Normal	—	—	20
—	Growl	Normal	—	100	40	23	Sing	Normal	—	55	15
4	Tail Whip	Normal	—	100	30	28	Egg Bomb	Normal	100	75	10
7	Refresh	Normal	—	100	20	33	Defense Curl	Normal	—	—	40
10	Softboiled	Normal	—	100	10	40	Light Screen	Psychic	—	—	30
13	Doubleslap	Normal	15	85	10	47	Double-Edge	Normal	120	100	15

TM/HM

TM/HM#	Name	Type	Power	ACC	PP	TM/HM#	Name	Type	Power	ACC	PP
TM14	Blizzard	Ice	120	70	5	TM32	Double Team	Normal	—	—	15
TM15	Hyper Beam	Normal	150	90	5	TM34	Shock Wave	Electric	60	—	20
TM16	Light Screen	Psychic	—	—	30	TM35	Flamethrower	Fire	95	100	15
TM17	Protect	Normal	—	—	10	TM37	Sandstorm	Ground	—	—	10
TM18	Rain Dance	Water	—	—	5	TM38	Fire Blast	Fire	120	85	5
TM20	Safeguard	Normal	—	—	25	TM39	Rock Tomb	Rock	50	80	10
TM21	Frustration	Normal	—	100	20	TM42	Facade	Normal	70	100	20
TM22	Solarbeam	Grass	120	100	10	TM43	Secret Power	Normal	70	100	20
TM23	Iron Tail	Steel	75	75	15	TM44	Rest	Psychic	—	—	10
TM24	Thunderbolt	Electric	95	100	15	TM45	Attract	Normal	—	100	15
TM25	Thunder	Electric	120	70	10	TM48	Skill Swap	Psychic	—	100	10
TM26	Earthquake	Ground	100	100	10	TM49	Snatch	Dark	—	100	10
TM27	Return	Normal	—	100	20	HM04	Strength	Normal	80	100	15
TM29	Psychic	Psychic	90	100	10	HM05	Flash	—	—	70	20
TM30	Shadow Ball	Ghost	80	100	15	HM06	Rock Smash	Fighting	20	100	15
TM31	Brick Break	Fighting	75	100	15						

TM/HM#	Name	Type	Power	ACC	PP
TM01	Focus Punch	Fighting	150	100	20
TM03	Water Pulse	Water	60	95	20
TM04	Calm Mind	Psychic	—	—	20
TM06	Toxic	Poison	—	85	10
TM07	Hail	Ice	—	—	10
TM10	Hidden Power	Normal	—	100	15
TM11	Sunny Day	Fire	—	—	5
TM13	Ice Beam	Ice	95	100	10

MOVE TUTOR
FireRed/LeafGreen and *Emerald* Only

Body Slam*	Counter*	Double-Edge
Dream Eater*	Mega Kick*	Mega Punch*
Metronome	Mimic	Seismic Toss*
Softboiled	Substitute	Thunder Wave*

*Battle Frontier tutor move (*Emerald*)

243 Raikou™

ELECTRIC

GENERAL INFO
SPECIES: Thunder Pokémon
HEIGHT: 6'03"
WEIGHT: 392 lbs.
ABILITY: Pressure
Opponent uses 2 PPs for damage inflicted against Raikou.

STATS
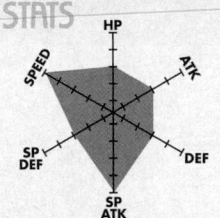

EVOLUTIONS

DOES NOT EVOLVE

LOCATION(S):

RUBY Rarity: **None**
Trade from *FireRed/LeafGreen/Colosseum*

SAPPHIRE Rarity: **None**
Trade from *FireRed/LeafGreen/Colosseum*

FIRERED Rarity: **Only One**
Wild in Kanto (after beating Elite Four) if starter Pokémon is Squirtle

LEAFGREEN Rarity: **Only One**
Wild in Kanto (after beating Elite Four) if starter Pokémon is Squirtle

COLOSSEUM Rarity: **Only One**
Shadow Pokémon Lab

EMERALD Rarity: **None**
Trade from *FireRed/LeafGreen/Colosseum*

XD Rarity: **None**
Trade from *FireRed/LeafGreen/Colosseum*

MOVES

Level	Attack	Type	Power	ACC	PP	Level	Attack	Type	Power	ACC	PP
—	Bite	Dark	60	100	25	41	Spark	Electric	65	100	20
—	Leer	Normal	—	100	30	51	Reflect	Psychic	—	—	20
11	Thundershock	Electric	40	100	30	61	Crunch	Dark	80	100	15
21	Roar	Normal	—	100	20	71	Thunder	Electric	120	70	10
31	Quick Attack	Normal	40	100	30	81	Calm Mind	Psychic	—	—	20

TM/HM

TM/HM#	Name	Type	Power	ACC	PP	TM/HM#	Name	Type	Power	ACC	PP
TM04	Calm Mind	Psychic	—	—	20	TM28	Dig	Ground	60	100	10
TM05	Roar	Normal	—	100	20	TM32	Double Team	Normal	—	—	15
TM06	Toxic	Poison	—	85	10	TM33	Reflect	Normal	—	—	20
TM10	Hidden Power	Normal	—	100	15	TM34	Shock Wave	Electric	60	—	20
TM11	Sunny Day	Fire	—	—	5	TM37	Sandstorm	Ground	—	—	10
TM15	Hyper Beam	Normal	150	90	5	TM42	Facade	Normal	70	100	20
TM17	Protect	Normal	—	—	10	TM43	Secret Power	Normal	70	100	20
TM18	Rain Dance	Water	—	—	5	TM44	Rest	Psychic	—	—	10
TM21	Frustration	Normal	—	100	20	HM01	Cut	Normal	50	95	30
TM23	Iron Tail	Steel	75	75	15	HM04	Strength	Normal	80	100	15
TM24	Thunderbolt	Electric	95	100	15	HM05	Flash	Normal	—	70	20
TM25	Thunder	Electric	120	70	10	HM06	Rock Smash	Fighting	20	100	15
TM27	Return	Normal	—	100	20						

MOVE TUTOR
FireRed/LeafGreen and Emerald Only

Body Slam* | Double-Edge | Mimic
Substitute | Thunder Wave*
*Battle Frontier tutor move (*Emerald*)

244 Entei™

FIRE

GENERAL INFO
SPECIES: Volcano Pokémon
HEIGHT: 6'11"
WEIGHT: 437 lbs.
ABILITY: Pressure
Opponent uses 2 PPs for damage inflicted against Entei.

STATS
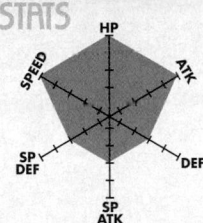

EVOLUTIONS

DOES NOT EVOLVE

LOCATION(S):

RUBY Rarity: **None**
Trade from *FireRed/LeafGreen/Colosseum*

SAPPHIRE Rarity: **None**
Trade from *FireRed/LeafGreen/Colosseum*

FIRERED Rarity: **Only One**
Wild in Kanto (after beating Elite Four) if starter Pokémon is Bulbasaur

LEAFGREEN Rarity: **Only One**
Wild in Kanto (after beating Elite Four) if starter Pokémon is Bulbasaur

COLOSSEUM Rarity: **Only One**
Mt. Battle

EMERALD Rarity: **None**
Trade from *FireRed/LeafGreen/Colosseum*

XD Rarity: **None**
Trade from *FireRed/LeafGreen/Colosseum*

MOVES

Level	Attack	Type	Power	ACC	PP	Level	Attack	Type	Power	ACC	PP
—	Bite	Dark	60	100	25	41	Stomp	Normal	65	100	20
—	Leer	Normal	—	100	30	51	Flamethrower	Fire	95	100	15
11	Ember	Fire	40	100	25	61	Swagger	Normal	—	90	15
21	Roar	Normal	—	100	20	71	Fire Blast	Fire	120	85	5
31	Fire Spin	Fire	15	70	15	81	Calm Mind	Psychic	—	—	20

TM/HM

TM/HM#	Name	Type	Power	ACC	PP	TM/HM#	Name	Type	Power	ACC	PP
TM04	Calm Mind	Psychic	—	—	20	TM32	Double Team	Normal	—	—	15
TM05	Roar	Normal	—	100	20	TM33	Reflect	Normal	—	—	20
TM06	Toxic	Poison	—	85	10	TM35	Flamethrower	Fire	95	100	15
TM10	Hidden Power	Normal	—	100	15	TM37	Sandstorm	Ground	—	—	10
TM11	Sunny Day	Fire	—	—	5	TM38	Fire Blast	Fire	120	85	5
TM15	Hyper Beam	Normal	150	90	5	TM42	Facade	Normal	70	100	20
TM17	Protect	Normal	—	—	10	TM43	Secret Power	Normal	70	100	20
TM18	Rain Dance	Water	—	—	5	TM44	Rest	Psychic	—	—	10
TM21	Frustration	Normal	—	100	20	HM01	Cut	Normal	50	95	30
TM22	Solar Beam	Grass	120	100	10	HM04	Strength	Normal	80	100	15
TM23	Iron Tail	Steel	75	75	15	HM05	Flash	Normal	—	70	20
TM27	Return	Normal	—	100	20	HM06	Rock Smash	Fighting	20	100	15
TM28	Dig	Ground	60	100	10						

MOVE TUTOR
FireRed/LeafGreen and Emerald Only

Body Slam* | Double-Edge | Mimic
Substitute
*Battle Frontier tutor move (*Emerald*)

245 Suicune™

WATER

GENERAL INFO
SPECIES: Aurora Pokémon
HEIGHT: 6'07"
WEIGHT: 412 lbs.
ABILITY: Pressure
Opponent uses 2 PPs for damage inflicted against Suicune.

STATS
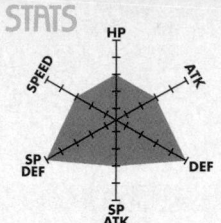

EVOLUTIONS

DOES NOT EVOLVE

LOCATION[S]:

RUBY — **Rarity: None**
Trade from *FireRed/LeafGreen/Colosseum*

SAPPHIRE — **Rarity: None**
Trade from *FireRed/LeafGreen/Colosseum*

FIRERED — **Rarity: Only One**
Wild in Kanto (after beating Elite Four) if starter Pokémon is Charmander

LEAFGREEN — **Rarity: Only One**
Wild in Kanto (after beating Elite Four) if starter Pokémon is Charmander

COLOSSEUM — **Rarity: Only One**
The Under

EMERALD — **Rarity: None**
Trade from *FireRed/LeafGreen/Colosseum*

XD — **Rarity: None**
Trade from *FireRed/LeafGreen/Colosseum*

MOVES

Level	Attack	Type	Power	ACC	PP	Level	Attack	Type	Power	ACC	PP
—	Bite	Dark	60	100	25	41	Aurora Beam	Ice	65	100	20
—	Leer	Normal	—	100	30	51	Mist	Ice	—	—	30
11	Bubblebeam	Water	65	100	20	61	Mirror Coat	Psychic	—	100	20
21	Rain Dance	Water	—	—	5	71	Hydro Pump	Water	120	80	5
31	Gust	Flying	40	100	35	81	Calm Mind	Psychic	—	—	20

TM/HM

TM/HM#	Name	Type	Power	ACC	PP	TM/HM#	Name	Type	Power	ACC	PP
TM03	Water Pulse	Water	60	95	20	TM27	Return	Normal	—	100	20
TM04	Calm Mind	Psychic	—	—	20	TM28	Dig	Ground	60	100	10
TM05	Roar	Normal	—	100	20	TM32	Double Team	Normal	—	—	15
TM06	Toxic	Poison	—	85	10	TM33	Reflect	Normal	—	—	20
TM07	Hail	Ice	—	—	10	TM37	Sandstorm	Ground	—	—	10
TM10	Hidden Power	Normal	—	100	15	TM42	Facade	Normal	70	100	20
TM11	Sunny Day	Fire	—	—	5	TM43	Secret Power	Normal	70	100	20
TM13	Ice Beam	Ice	95	100	10	TM44	Rest	Psychic	—	—	10
TM14	Blizzard	Ice	120	70	5	HM01	Cut	Normal	50	95	30
TM15	Hyper Beam	Normal	150	90	5	HM03	Surf	Water	95	100	15
TM17	Protect	Normal	—	—	10	HM06	Rock Smash	Fighting	20	100	15
TM18	Rain Dance	Water	—	—	5	HM07	Waterfall	Water	80	100	15
TM21	Frustration	Normal	—	100	20	HM08	Dive	Water	60	100	10
TM23	Iron Tail	Steel	75	75	15						

MOVE TUTOR
FireRed/LeafGreen and *Emerald* Only

Body Slam* — Double-Edge — Mimic
Substitute

*Battle Frontier tutor move (*Emerald*)

---

246 Larvitar™

ROCK **GROUND**

GENERAL INFO
SPECIES: Rock Skin Pokémon
HEIGHT: 2'00"
WEIGHT: 159 lbs.
ABILITY: Guts
When Larvitar has a status condition, its attack power is multiplied by 1.5.

STATS
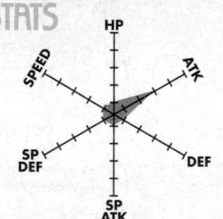

EVOLUTIONS
 LV30  LV55

LOCATION[S]:

RUBY — **Rarity: None**
Trade from *FireRed/LeafGreen*

SAPPHIRE — **Rarity: None**
Trade from *FireRed/LeafGreen*

FIRERED — **Rarity: Rare**
Seven Island

LEAFGREEN — **Rarity: Rare**
Seven Island

COLOSSEUM — **Rarity: None**
Trade from *FireRed/LeafGreen*

EMERALD — **Rarity: None**
Trade from *FireRed/LeafGreen*

XD — **Rarity: Only One**
Trade from Duking

MOVES

Level	Attack	Type	Power	ACC	PP	Level	Attack	Type	Power	ACC	PP
—	Bite	Dark	60	100	25	29	Thrash	Normal	90	100	20
—	Leer	Normal	—	100	30	36	Scary Face	Normal	—	90	10
—	Sandstorm	Rock	—	—	10	43	Crunch	Dark	80	100	15
5	Screech	Normal	—	85	40	50	Earthquake	Ground	100	100	10
22	Rock Slide	Rock	75	90	10	57	Hyper Beam	Normal	150	90	5

TM/HM

TM/HM#	Name	Type	Power	ACC	PP	TM/HM#	Name	Type	Power	ACC	PP
TM06	Toxic	Poison	—	85	10	TM28	Dig	Ground	60	100	10
TM10	Hidden Power	Normal	—	100	15	TM31	Brick Break	Fighting	75	100	15
TM11	Sunny Day	Fire	—	—	5	TM32	Double Team	Normal	—	—	15
TM12	Taunt	Dark	—	100	20	TM37	Sandstorm	Ground	—	—	10
TM15	Hyper Beam	Normal	150	90	5	TM41	Torment	Dark	—	100	15
TM17	Protect	Normal	—	—	10	TM42	Facade	Normal	70	100	20
TM18	Rain Dance	Water	—	—	5	TM43	Secret Power	Normal	70	100	20
TM21	Frustration	Normal	—	100	20	TM44	Rest	Psychic	—	—	10
TM26	Earthquake	Ground	100	100	10	TM45	Attract	Normal	—	100	15
TM27	Return	Normal	—	100	20	HM06	Rock Smash	Fighting	20	100	15

EGG MOVES*

Name	Type	Power	ACC	PP
Ancientpower	Rock	60	100	5
Curse	—	—	—	10
Dragon Dance	Dragon	—	—	20
Focus Energy	Normal	—	—	30
Outrage	Dragon	90	100	15
Pursuit	Dark	40	100	20
Stomp	Normal	65	100	20

*Learned Via Breeding

MOVE TUTOR
FireRed/LeafGreen and *Emerald* Only

Body Slam* — Double-Edge — Mimic
Rock Slide* — Substitute

*Battle Frontier tutor move (*Emerald*)

247 Pupitar™

ROCK GROUND

GENERAL INFO
SPECIES: Hard Shell Pokémon
HEIGHT: 3'11"
WEIGHT: 335 lbs.
ABILITY: Shed Skin

Enables Pupitar to have a status effect for only one turn. Shed Skin has 30% of success.

STATS

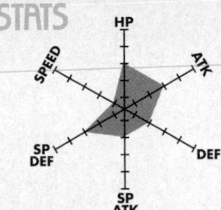

EVOLUTIONS

 LV30  LV55

LOCATION(S):

RUBY — Rarity: **None**
Evolve Larvitar or Trade from *FireRed/LeafGreen*

SAPPHIRE — Rarity: **None**
Evolve Larvitar or Trade from *FireRed/LeafGreen*

FIRERED — Rarity: **Rare**
Evolve Larvitar

LEAFGREEN — Rarity: **Rare**
Evolve Larvitar

COLOSSEUM — Rarity: **None**
Evolve Larvitar

EMERALD — Rarity: **None**
Trade from *FireRed/LeafGreen*

XD — Rarity: **Evolve**
Evolve Larvitar

MOVES

Level	Attack	Type	Power	ACC	PP	Level	Attack	Type	Power	ACC	PP
—	Bite	Dark	60	100	25	29	Thrash	Normal	90	100	20
—	Leer	Normal	—	100	30	38	Scary Face	Normal	—	90	10
—	Sandstorm	Rock	—	—	10	47	Crunch	Dark	80	100	15
—	Screech	Normal	—	85	40	56	Earthquake	Ground	100	100	10
22	Rock Slide	Rock	75	90	10	56	Hyper Beam	Normal	150	90	5

TM/HM

TM/HM#	Name	Type	Power	ACC	PP	TM/HM#	Name	Type	Power	ACC	PP
TM06	Toxic	Poison	—	85	10	TM28	Dig	Ground	60	100	10
TM10	Hidden Power	Normal	—	100	15	TM31	Brick Break	Fighting	75	100	15
TM11	Sunny Day	Fire	—	—	5	TM32	Double Team	Normal	—	—	15
TM12	Taunt	Dark	—	100	20	TM37	Sandstorm	Ground	—	—	10
TM15	Hyper Beam	Normal	150	90	5	TM41	Torment	Dark	—	100	15
TM17	Protect	Normal	—	—	10	TM42	Facade	Normal	70	100	20
TM18	Rain Dance	Water	—	—	5	TM43	Secret Power	Normal	70	100	20
TM21	Frustration	Normal	—	100	20	TM44	Rest	Psychic	—	—	10
TM26	Earthquake	Ground	100	100	10	TM45	Attract	Normal	—	100	15
TM27	Return	Normal	—	100	20	HM06	Rock Smash	Fighting	20	100	15

MOVE TUTOR
FireRed/LeafGreen and *Emerald* Only

Body Slam*	Double-Edge	Mimic
Rock Slide*	Substitute	

*Battle Frontier tutor move (*Emerald*)

---

248 Tyranitar™

ROCK DARK

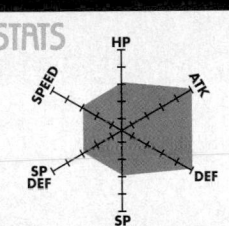

GENERAL INFO
SPECIES: Armor Pokémon
HEIGHT: 6'07"
WEIGHT: 445 lbs.
ABILITY: Sand Stream

A sandstorm begins when Tyranitar enters battle.

STATS

EVOLUTIONS

 LV30 LV55

LOCATION(S):

RUBY — Rarity: **None**
Trade from *Colosseum*

SAPPHIRE — Rarity: **None**
Trade from *Colosseum*

FIRERED — Rarity: **None**
Trade from *Colosseum*

LEAFGREEN — Rarity: **None**
Trade from *Colosseum*

COLOSSEUM — Rarity: **Only One**
Realgam Tower

EMERALD — Rarity: **None**
Trade from *FireRed/LeafGreen*

XD — Rarity: **Evolve**
Evolve Pupitar

MOVES

Level	Attack	Type	Power	ACC	PP	Level	Attack	Type	Power	ACC	PP
—	Bite	Dark	60	100	25	29	Thrash	Normal	90	100	20
—	Leer	Normal	—	100	30	38	Scary Face	Normal	—	90	10
—	Sandstorm	Rock	—	—	10	47	Crunch	Dark	80	100	15
—	Screech	Normal	—	85	40	61	Earthquake	Ground	100	100	10
22	Rock Slide	Rock	75	90	10	75	Hyper Beam	Normal	150	90	5

TM/HM

TM/HM#	Name	Type	Power	ACC	PP	TM/HM#	Name	Type	Power	ACC	PP
TM01	Focus Punch	Fighting	150	100	20	TM28	Dig	Ground	60	100	10
TM02	Dragon Claw	Dragon	80	100	15	TM31	Brick Break	Fighting	75	100	15
TM03	Water Pulse	Water	60	95	20	TM32	Double Team	Normal	—	—	15
TM05	Roar	Normal	—	100	20	TM34	Shock Wave	Electric	60	—	20
TM06	Toxic	Poison	—	85	10	TM35	Flamethrower	Fire	95	100	15
TM10	Hidden Power	Normal	—	100	15	TM37	Sandstorm	Ground	—	—	10
TM11	Sunny Day	Fire	—	—	5	TM38	Fire Blast	Fire	120	85	5
TM12	Taunt	Dark	—	100	20	TM39	Rock Tomb	Rock	50	80	10
TM13	Ice Beam	Ice	95	100	10	TM40	Aerial Ace	Flying	60	—	20
TM14	Blizzard	Ice	120	70	5	TM41	Torment	Dark	—	100	15
TM15	Hyper Beam	Normal	150	90	5	TM42	Facade	Normal	70	100	20
TM17	Protect	Normal	—	—	10	TM43	Secret Power	Normal	70	100	20
TM18	Rain Dance	Water	—	—	5	TM44	Rest	Psychic	—	—	10
TM21	Frustration	Normal	—	100	20	TM45	Attract	Normal	—	100	15
TM23	Iron Tail	Steel	75	75	15	HM01	Cut	Normal	50	95	30
TM24	Thunderbolt	Electric	95	100	15	HM03	Surf	Water	95	100	15
TM25	Thunder	Electric	120	70	10	HM04	Strength	Normal	80	100	15
TM26	Earthquake	Ground	100	100	10	HM06	Rock Smash	Fighting	20	100	15
TM27	Return	Normal	—	100	20						

MOVE TUTOR
FireRed/LeafGreen and *Emerald* Only

Body Slam*	Counter*	Double-Edge
Mega Kick*	Mega Punch*	Mimic
Rock Slide*	Seismic Toss*	Substitute
Thunder Wave*		

*Battle Frontier tutor move (*Emerald*)

249 Lugia™

PSYCHIC **FLYING**

GENERAL INFO
SPECIES: Diving Pokémon
HEIGHT: 17'01"
WEIGHT: 476 lbs.
ABILITY: Pressure
Opponent uses 2 PPs for damage inflicted against Lugia.

STATS
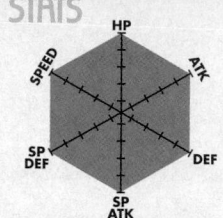

EVOLUTIONS

DOES NOT EVOLVE

LOCATION[S]:

RUBY   Rarity: **None**
Trade from *XD*

SAPPHIRE   Rarity: **None**
Trade from *XD*

FIRERED   Rarity: **None**
Trade from *XD*

LEAFGREEN   Rarity: **None**
Trade from *XD*

COLOSSEUM   Rarity: **None**
Trade from *XD*

EMERALD   Rarity: **None**
Trade from *XD*

XD   Rarity: **Only One**
Citadark Island (Capture from Master Greevil)

MOVES

Level	Attack	Type	Power	ACC	PP
—	Whirlwind	Normal	—	100	20
11	Safeguard	Normal	—	—	25
22	Gust	Flying	40	100	35
33	Recover	Normal	—	—	20
55	Rain Dance	Water	—	—	5
66	Swift	Normal	60	—	20
44	Hydro Pump	Water	120	80	5
77	Aeroblast	Flying	100	95	5
88	Ancientpower	Rock	60	100	5
99	Future Sight	Psychic	80	90	15

TM/HM

TM/HM#	Name	Type	Power	ACC	PP
TM03	Water Pulse	Water	60	100	20
TM04	Calm Mind	Psychic	—	—	20
TM05	Roar	Normal	—	100	20
TM06	Toxic	Poison	—	85	10
TM07	Hail	Ice	—	—	10
TM10	Hidden Power	Normal	—	100	15
TM11	Sunny Day	Fire	—	—	5
TM13	Ice Beam	Ice	95	100	10
TM14	Blizzard	Ice	120	70	5
TM15	Hyper Beam	Normal	150	90	5
TM16	Light Screen	Psychic	—	—	30
TM17	Protect	Normal	—	—	10
TM18	Rain Dance	Water	—	—	5
TM19	Giga Drain	Ground	600	100	5
TM20	Safeguard	Normal	—	—	25
TM21	Frustration	Normal	—	100	20
TM23	Iron Tail	Steel	100	75	15
TM24	Thunderbolt	Electric	95	100	15
TM25	Thunder	Electric	120	70	10
TM26	Earthquake	Ground	100	100	10
TM27	Return	Normal	—	100	20
TM29	Psychic	Psychic	90	100	10
TM30	Shadow Punch	Ghost	60	—	20
TM32	Double Team	Normal	—	—	—
TM33	Reflect	Psychic	—	—	20
TM34	Shockwave	Electric	60	—	20
TM37	Sandstorm	Ground	—	—	10
TM40	Aerial Ace	Flying	60	—	20
TM42	Facade	Normal	70	100	20
TM43	Secret Power	Normal	70	100	20
TM44	Rest	Psychic	—	—	10
TM47	Steel Wing	Steel	70	90	25
TM48	Skill Swap	Psychic	—	100	10

---

250 Ho-Oh™

FIRE **FLYING**

GENERAL INFO
SPECIES: Rainbow Pokémon
HEIGHT: 12'06"
WEIGHT: 439 lbs.
ABILITY: Pressure
Opponent uses 2 PPs for damage inflicted on Ho-Oh.

STATS
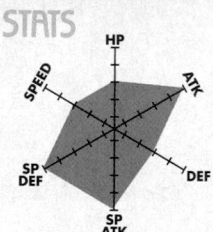

EVOLUTIONS
DOES NOT EVOLVE

LOCATION[S]:

RUBY   Rarity: **None**
Trade from *Colosseum*

SAPPHIRE   Rarity: **None**
Trade from *Colosseum*

FIRERED   Rarity: **None**
Trade from *Colosseum*

LEAFGREEN   Rarity: **None**
Trade from *Colosseum*

COLOSSEUM   Rarity: **Only One**
10 Man Mt. Battle Challenge

EMERALD   Rarity: **None**
Trade from *Colosseum*

XD   Rarity: **None**
Trade from *Colosseum*

MOVES

Level	Attack	Type	Power	ACC	PP
—	Whirlwind	Normal	—	100	20
11	Safeguard	Normal	—	—	25
22	Gust	Flying	40	100	35
33	Recover	Normal	—	—	20
44	Fire Blast	Fire	120	85	5
55	Sunny Day	Fire	—	—	5
66	Swift	Normal	60	—	20
77	Sacred Fire	Fire	100	100	5
88	Ancientpower	Rock	60	100	5
99	Future Sight	Psychic	80	90	15

TM/HM

TM/HM#	Name	Type	Power	ACC	PP
TM17	Protect	Normal	—	—	10
TM18	Rain Dance	Water	—	—	5
TM19	Giga Drain	Grass	60	100	5
TM20	Safeguard	Normal	—	—	25
TM21	Frustration	Normal	—	100	20
TM22	Solarbeam	Grass	120	100	10
TM24	Thunderbolt	Electric	95	100	15
TM25	Thunder	Electric	120	70	10
TM26	Earthquake	Ground	100	100	10
TM27	Return	Normal	—	100	20
TM29	Psychic	Psychic	90	100	10
TM30	Shadow Ball	Ghost	80	100	15
TM32	Double Team	Normal	—	—	15
TM33	Reflect	Normal	—	—	20
TM34	Shock Wave	Electric	60	—	20
TM35	Flamethrower	Fire	95	100	15
TM37	Sandstorm	Ground	—	—	10
TM38	Fire Blast	Fire	120	85	5
TM40	Aerial Ace	Flying	60	—	20
TM42	Facade	Normal	70	100	20
TM43	Secret Power	Normal	70	100	20
TM44	Rest	Psychic	—	—	10
TM47	Steel Wing	Steel	70	90	25
TM50	Overheat	Fire	140	90	5
HM02	Fly	Flying	70	95	15
HM04	Strength	Normal	80	100	20
HM05	Flash	Normal	—	70	20
HM06	Rock Smash	Fighting	20	100	15

TM/HM

TM/HM#	Name	Type	Power	ACC	PP
TM04	Calm Mind	Psychic	—	—	20
TM05	Roar	Normal	—	100	20
TM06	Toxic	Poison	—	85	10
TM10	Hidden Power	Normal	—	100	15
TM11	Sunny Day	Fire	—	—	5
TM15	Hyper Beam	Normal	150	90	5
TM16	Light Screen	Psychic	—	—	30

MOVE TUTOR
FireRed/LeafGreen and *Emerald* Only

Body Slam*	Double-Edge	Dream Eater*
Mimic	Substitute	Thunder Wave*

*Battle Frontier tutor move (*Emerald*)

251 Celebi™

GRASS | PSYCHIC

GENERAL INFO
SPECIES: Time Travel Pokémon
HEIGHT: 2'00"
WEIGHT: 11 lbs.
ABILITY: Natural Cure
If Celebi is switched out, the Status condition is gone.

STATS
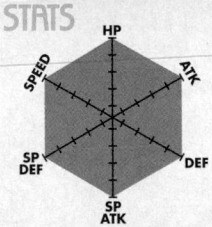

EVOLUTIONS

DOES NOT EVOLVE

LOCATION[S]:
RUBY Rarity: **None**
Only available via distribution at live events

SAPPHIRE Rarity: **None**
Only available via distribution at live events

FIRERED Rarity: **None**
Only available via distribution at live events

LEAFGREEN Rarity: **None**
Only available via distribution at live events

COLOSSEUM Rarity: **None**
Only available via distribution at live events

EMERALD Rarity: **None**
Only available via distribution at live events

XD Rarity: **None**
Only available via distribution at live events

MOVES
Level	Attack	Type	Power	ACC	PP
—	Leech Seeds	Grass		90	10
—	Confusion	Psychic	50	100	25
—	Recover	Normal	—	—	20
—	Heal Bell	Normal	—	—	5
10	Safeguard	Normal	—	—	25
20	Ancient Power	Rock	60	100	5
30	Future Sight	Psychic	80	90	15
40	Baton Pass	Normal	—	—	40
50	Perish Song	Normal	—	—	5

TM/HM
TM/HM#	Name	Type	Power	ACC	PP
TM03	Water Pulse	Water	60	100	20
TM04	Calm Mind	Psychic	—	—	20
TM06	Toxic	Poison	—	85	10
TM10	Hidden Power	Normal	—	100	15
TM11	Sunny Day	Fire	—	—	5
TM15	Hyper Beam	Normal	150	90	5
TM16	Light Screen	Psychic	—	—	30
TM17	Protect	Normal	—	—	10
TM18	Rain Dance	Water	—	—	5
TM19	Giga Drain	Grass	60	100	5
TM20	Safeguard	Normal	—	—	25
TM21	Frustration	Normal	—	100	20
TM22	Solarbeam	Grass	120	100	10
TM27	Return	Normal	—	100	20
TM29	Psychic	Psychic	90	100	10
TM30	Shadow Ball	Ghost	80	100	15
TM32	Double Team	Normal	—	—	15
TM33	Reflect	Psychic	—	—	20
TM34	Shock Wave	Electric	60	—	20
TM37	Sandstorm	Rock	—	—	10
TM40	Aerial Ace	Flying	60	—	20
TM42	Facade	Normal	70	100	20
TM43	Secret Power	Normal	70	100	20
TM44	Rest	Psychic	—	—	10
TM48	Skill Swap	Psychic	—	100	10
HM01	Cut	Normal	50	95	30
HM05	Flash	Normal	—	70	20

MOVE TUTOR
FireRed/LeafGreen and Emerald Only
Double-Edge	Dream Eater*	Metronome
Mimic	Substitute	Swords Dance*

*Battle Frontier tutor move (Emerald)

252 Treecko™

GRASS

GENERAL INFO
SPECIES: Wood Gecko Pokémon
HEIGHT: 1'08"
WEIGHT: 11 lbs.
ABILITY: Overgrow
Treecko's Grass-type attack power is multiplied by 1.5 when its HPs get low.

STATS
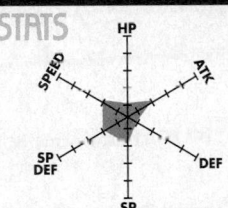

EVOLUTIONS
 LV16  LV36

LOCATION[S]:
RUBY Rarity: **Only One**
Starter Pokémon obtained from Prof. Birch on Route 101

SAPPHIRE Rarity: **Only One**
Starter Pokémon obtained from Prof. Birch on Route 101

FIRERED Rarity: **None**
Trade from Ruby/Sapphire

LEAFGREEN Rarity: **None**
Trade from Ruby/Sapphire

COLOSSEUM Rarity: **None**
Trade from Ruby/Sapphire

EMERALD Rarity: **Only One**
Starter Pokémon obtained from Prof. Birch on Route 101

XD Rarity: **None**
Trade from Ruby/Sapphire

MOVES
Level	Attack	Type	Power	ACC	PP
—/5	Pound	Normal	40	100	35
—/5	Leer	Normal	—	100	30
6	Absorb	Grass	20	100	20
11	Quick Attack	Normal	40	100	30
16	Pursuit	Dark	40	100	20
21	Screech	Normal	—	85	40
26	Mega Drain	Grass	40	100	10
31	Agility	Psychic	—	—	30
36	Slam	Normal	80	75	20
41	Detect	Fight	—	—	5
46	Giga Drain	Grass	60	100	5

= Emerald Only

TM/HM
TM/HM#	Name	Type	Power	ACC	PP
TM01	Focus Punch	Fighting	150	100	20
TM06	Toxic	Poison	—	85	10
TM09	Bullet Seed	Grass	10	100	30
TM10	Hidden Power	Normal	—	100	15
TM11	Sunny Day	Fire	—	—	5
TM17	Protect	Normal	—	—	10
TM19	Giga Drain	Grass	60	100	5
TM20	Safeguard	Normal	—	—	25
TM21	Frustration	Normal	—	100	20
TM22	Solarbeam	Grass	120	100	10
TM23	Iron Tail	Steel	75	75	15
TM27	Return	Normal	—	100	20
TM28	Dig	Ground	60	100	10
TM31	Brick Break	Fighting	75	100	15
TM32	Double Team	Normal	—	—	15
TM39	Rock Tomb	Rock	50	80	10
TM40	Aerial Ace	Flying	60	—	20
TM42	Facade	Normal	70	100	20
TM43	Secret Power	Normal	70	100	20
TM44	Rest	Psychic	—	—	10
TM45	Attract	Normal	—	100	15
HM01	Cut	Normal	50	95	30
HM04	Strength	Normal	80	100	15
HM05	Flash	Normal	—	70	20
HM06	Rock Smash	Fighting	20	100	15

EGG MOVES*
Name	Type	Power	ACC	PP
Mud Sport	Ground	—	100	15
Endeavor	Normal	—	100	5
Crunch	Dark	80	100	15
Leech Seed	Grass	—	90	10
Crush Claw	Normal	75	95	10
Dragonbreath	Dragon	60	100	20

*Learned Via Breeding

MOVE TUTOR
FireRed/LeafGreen and Emerald Only
Body Slam*	Counter*	Double-Edge
Mega Kick*	Mega Punch*	Mimic
Seismic Toss*	Substitute	Swords Dance*

Emerald Only
Dynamicpunch*	Endure*	Fury Cutter
Mud-Slap*	Sleep Talk	Snore
Swagger	Swift*	Thunderpunch*

*Battle Frontier tutor move (Emerald)

253 Grovyle™

GENERAL INFO
SPECIES: Wood Gecko Pokémon
HEIGHT: 2'11"
WEIGHT: 48 lbs.
ABILITY: Overgrow

Grovyle's Grass-type attack power is multiplied by 1.5 when its HPs get low.

STATS

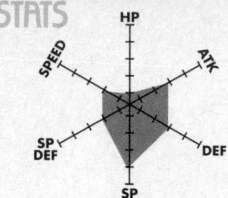

EVOLUTIONS

LV16   LV36

LOCATION[S]:

RUBY — Rarity: **Evolve**
Evolve Treecko

SAPPHIRE — Rarity: **Evolve**
Evolve Treecko

FIRERED — Rarity: **None**
Trade from *Ruby/Sapphire*

LEAFGREEN — Rarity: **None**
Trade from *Ruby/Sapphire*

COLOSSEUM — Rarity: **None**
Trade from *Ruby/Sapphire*

EMERALD — Rarity: **Evolve**
Evolve Treecko

XD — Rarity: **None**
Trade from *Ruby/Sapphire*

MOVES

Level	Attack	Type	Power	ACC	PP	Level	Attack	Type	Power	ACC	PP
—	Pound	Normal	40	100	35	23	Screech	Normal	—	85	40
—	Leer	Normal	—	100	30	29	Leaf Blade	Grass	70	100	15
—/6	Absorb	Grass	20	100	20	35	Agility	Psychic	—	—	30
—/11	Quick Attack	Normal	40	100	30	41	Slam	Normal	80	75	20
16	Fury Cutter	Bug	10	95	20	47	Detect	Fight	—	—	5
17	Pursuit	Dark	40	100	20	53	False Swipe	Normal	40	100	40

 # = Emerald Only

TM/HM

TM/HM#	Name	Type	Power	ACC	PP	TM/HM#	Name	Type	Power	ACC	PP
TM01	Focus Punch	Fighting	150	100	20	TM31	Brick Break	Fighting	75	100	15
TM06	Toxic	Poison	—	85	10	TM32	Double Team	Normal	—	—	15
TM09	Bullet Seed	Grass	10	100	30	TM39	Rock Tomb	Rock	50	80	10
TM10	Hidden Power	Normal	—	100	15	TM40	Aerial Ace	Flying	60	—	20
TM11	Sunny Day	Fire	—	—	5	TM42	Facade	Normal	70	100	20
TM17	Protect	Normal	—	—	10	TM43	Secret Power	Normal	70	100	20
TM19	Giga Drain	Grass	60	100	5	TM44	Rest	Psychic	—	—	10
TM20	Safeguard	Normal	—	—	25	TM45	Attract	Normal	—	100	15
TM21	Frustration	Normal	—	100	20	HM01	Cut	Normal	50	95	30
TM22	Solarbeam	Grass	120	100	10	HM04	Strength	Normal	80	100	20
TM23	Iron Tail	Steel	75	75	15	HM05	Flash	Normal	—	70	20
TM27	Return	Normal	—	100	20	HM06	Rock Smash	Fighting	20	100	15
TM28	Dig	Ground	60	100	10						

MOVE TUTOR
FireRed/LeafGreen and Emerald Only

Body Slam*	Counter*	Double-Edge
Mega Kick*	Mega Punch*	Mimic
Seismic Toss*	Substitute	Swords Dance

Emerald Only

Dynamicpunch	Endure*	Fury Cutter
Mud-Slap*	Sleep Talk	Snore*
Swagger	Swift*	Thunderpunch*

*Battle Frontier tutor move (Emerald)

---

254 Sceptile™

GENERAL INFO
SPECIES: Forest Pokémon
HEIGHT: 5'07"
WEIGHT: 115 lbs.
ABILITY: Overgrow

Sceptile's Grass-type attack power is multiplied by 1.5 when its HPs get low.

STATS

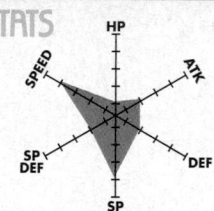

EVOLUTIONS

LV16   LV36

LOCATION[S]:

RUBY — Rarity: **Evolve**
Evolve Grovyle

SAPPHIRE — Rarity: **Evolve**
Evolve Grovyle

FIRERED — Rarity: **None**
Trade from *Ruby/Sapphire*

LEAFGREEN — Rarity: **None**
Trade from *Ruby/Sapphire*

COLOSSEUM — Rarity: **None**
Trade from *Ruby/Sapphire*

EMERALD — Rarity: **Evolve**
Evolve Grovyle

XD — Rarity: **None**
Trade from *Ruby/Sapphire*

MOVES

Level	Attack	Type	Power	ACC	PP	Level	Attack	Type	Power	ACC	PP
—	Pound	Normal	40	100	35	23	Screech	Normal	—	85	40
—	Leer	Normal	—	100	30	29	Leaf Blade	Grass	70	100	15
—/6	Absorb	Grass	20	100	20	35	Agility	Psychic	—	—	30
—/11	Quick Attack	Normal	40	100	30	43	Slam	Normal	80	75	20
16	Fury Cutter	Bug	10	95	20	51	Detect	Fight	—	—	5
17	Pursuit	Dark	40	100	20	59	False Swipe	Normal	40	100	40

 # = Emerald Only

TM/HM

TM/HM#	Name	Type	Power	ACC	PP	TM/HM#	Name	Type	Power	ACC	PP
TM01	Focus Punch	Fighting	150	100	20	TM27	Return	Normal	—	100	20
TM02	Dragon Claw	Dragon	80	100	15	TM28	Dig	Ground	60	100	10
TM05	Roar	Normal	—	100	20	TM31	Brick Break	Fighting	75	100	15
TM06	Toxic	Poison	—	85	10	TM32	Double Team	Normal	—	—	15
TM09	Bullet Seed	Grass	10	100	30	TM39	Rock Tomb	Rock	50	80	10
TM10	Hidden Power	Normal	—	100	15	TM40	Aerial Ace	Flying	60	—	20
TM11	Sunny Day	Fire	—	—	5	TM42	Facade	Normal	70	100	20
TM15	Hyper Beam	Normal	150	90	5	TM43	Secret Power	Normal	70	100	20
TM17	Protect	Normal	—	—	10	TM44	Rest	Psychic	—	—	10
TM19	Giga Drain	Grass	60	100	5	TM45	Attract	Normal	—	100	15
TM20	Safeguard	Normal	—	—	25	HM01	Cut	Normal	50	95	30
TM21	Frustration	Normal	—	100	20	HM04	Strength	Normal	80	100	20
TM22	Solarbeam	Grass	120	100	10	HM05	Flash	Normal	—	70	20
TM23	Iron Tail	Steel	75	75	15	HM06	Rock Smash	Fighting	20	100	15
TM26	Earthquake	Ground	100	100	10						

MOVE TUTOR
FireRed/LeafGreen and Emerald Only

Body Slam*	Counter*	Double-Edge
Mega Kick*	Mega Punch*	Mimic
Seismic Toss*	Substitute	Swords Dance

Emerald Only

Dynamicpunch	Endure*	Fury Cutter
Mud-Slap*	Sleep Talk	Snore*
Swagger	Swift*	Thunderpunch*

*Battle Frontier tutor move (Emerald)

255 Torchic™

FIRE

GENERAL INFO
SPECIES: Chick Pokémon
HEIGHT: 1'04"
WEIGHT: 6 lbs.
ABILITY: Blaze

Torchic's Fire-type attack power is multiplied by 1.5 when its HPs get low.

STATS

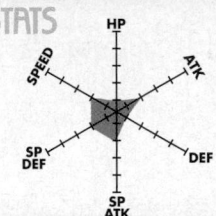

EVOLUTIONS

LV16 LV36

LOCATION[S]:

RUBY **Rarity: Only One**
Starter Pokémon obtained from Prof. Birch on Route 101

SAPPHIRE **Rarity: Only One**
Starter Pokémon obtained from Prof. Birch on Route 101

FIRERED **Rarity: None**
Trade from *Ruby/Sapphire*

LEAFGREEN **Rarity: None**
Trade from *Ruby/Sapphire*

COLOSSEUM **Rarity: None**
Trade from *Ruby/Sapphire*

EMERALD **Rarity: Only One**
Starter Pokémon obtained from Prof. Birch on Route 101

XD **Rarity: None**
Trade from *Ruby/Sapphire/Emerald*

MOVES

Level	Attack	Type	Power	ACC	PP	Level	Attack	Type	Power	ACC	PP
—	Scratch	Normal	40	100	35	19	Sand-Attack	Ground	—	100	15
—	Growl	Normal	—	100	40	25	Fire Spin	Fire	15	70	15
7	Focus Energy	Normal	—	—	30	28	Quick Attack	Normal	40	100	30
10	Ember	Fire	40	100	25	34	Slash	Normal	70	100	20
16	Peck	Flying	35	100	35	37	Mirror Move	Flying	—	—	20
						43	Flamethrower	Fire	95	100	15

TM/HM

TM/HM#	Name	Type	Power	ACC	PP	TM/HM#	Name	Type	Power	ACC	PP
TM06	Toxic	Poison	—	85	10	TM39	Rock Tomb	Rock	50	80	10
TM10	Hidden Power	Normal	—	100	15	TM40	Aerial Ace	Flying	60	—	20
TM11	Sunny Day	Fire	—	—	5	TM42	Facade	Normal	70	100	20
TM17	Protect	Normal	—	—	10	TM43	Secret Power	Normal	70	100	20
TM21	Frustration	Normal	—	100	20	TM44	Rest	Psychic	—	—	10
TM27	Return	Normal	—	100	20	TM45	Attract	Normal	—	100	15
TM28	Dig	Ground	60	100	10	TM50	Overheat	Fire	140	90	5
TM32	Double Team	Normal	—	—	15	HM01	Cut	Normal	50	95	30
TM35	Flamethrower	Fire	95	100	15	HM04	Strength	Normal	80	100	20
TM38	Fire Blast	Fire	120	85	5	HM06	Rock Smash	Fighting	20	100	15

EGG MOVES*

Name	Type	Power	ACC	PP
Counter	Fighting	—	100	20
Reversal	Fighting	—	100	15
Endure	Normal	—	—	10
Swagger	Normal	—	90	15
Smellingsalt	Normal	60	100	10
Rock Slide	Rock	75	90	10

*Learned Via Breeding

MOVE TUTOR

FireRed/LeafGreen and *Emerald* Only

Body Slam*	Counter*	Double-Edge
Mega Kick*	Mega Punch*	Mimic
Rock Slide*	Seismic Toss*	Substitute
Swords Dance*		

Emerald Only

Endure*	Mud-Slap*	Sleep Talk
Snore*	Swagger	Swift*

*Battle Frontier tutor move (*Emerald*)

---

256 Combusken™

FIRE   FIGHTING

GENERAL INFO
SPECIES: Young Fowl Pokémon
HEIGHT: 2'11"
WEIGHT: 43 lbs.
ABILITY: Blaze

Combusken's Fire-type attack power is multiplied by 1.5 when its HPs get low.

STATS

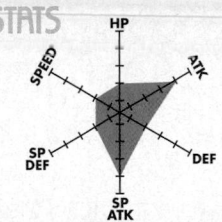

EVOLUTIONS

  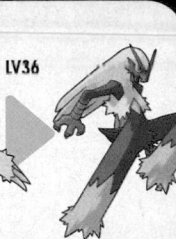

LV16 LV36

LOCATION[S]:

RUBY **Rarity: Evolve**
Evolve Torchic

SAPPHIRE **Rarity: Evolve**
Evolve Torchic

FIRERED **Rarity: None**
Trade from *Ruby/Sapphire*

LEAFGREEN **Rarity: None**
Trade from *Ruby/Sapphire*

COLOSSEUM **Rarity: None**
Trade from *Ruby/Sapphire*

EMERALD **Rarity: Evolve**
Evolve Torchic

XD **Rarity: None**
Trade from *Ruby/Sapphire/Emerald*

MOVES

Level	Attack	Type	Power	ACC	PP	Level	Attack	Type	Power	ACC	PP
—	Scratch	Normal	40	100	35	21	Sand-Attack	Ground	—	100	15
—	Growl	Normal	—	100	40	28	Bulk Up	Fighting	—	—	20
—/7	Focus Energy	Normal	—	—	30	32	Quick Attack	Normal	40	100	30
—/13	Ember	Fire	40	100	25	39	Slash	Normal	70	100	20
16	Double Kick	Fighting	30	100	30	43	Mirror Move	Flying	—	—	20
17	Peck	Flying	35	100	35	50	Sky Uppercut	Fighting	85	90	15

= *Emerald* Only

TM/HM

TM/HM#	Name	Type	Power	ACC	PP	TM/HM#	Name	Type	Power	ACC	PP
TM01	Focus Punch	Fighting	150	100	20	TM38	Fire Blast	Fire	120	85	5
TM06	Toxic	Poison	—	85	10	TM39	Rock Tomb	Rock	50	80	10
TM08	Bulk Up	Fighting	—	—	20	TM40	Aerial Ace	Flying	60	—	20
TM10	Hidden Power	Normal	—	100	15	TM42	Facade	Normal	70	100	20
TM11	Sunny Day	Fire	—	—	5	TM43	Secret Power	Normal	70	100	20
TM17	Protect	Normal	—	—	10	TM44	Rest	Psychic	—	—	10
TM21	Frustration	Normal	—	100	20	TM45	Attract	Normal	—	100	15
TM27	Return	Normal	—	100	20	TM50	Overheat	Fire	140	90	5
TM28	Dig	Ground	60	100	10	HM01	Cut	Normal	50	95	30
TM31	Brick Break	Fighting	75	100	15	HM04	Strength	Normal	80	100	20
TM32	Double Team	Normal	—	—	15	HM06	Rock Smash	Fighting	20	100	15
TM35	Flamethrower	Fire	95	100	15						

MOVE TUTOR

FireRed/LeafGreen and *Emerald* Only

Body Slam*	Counter*	Double-Edge
Mega Kick*	Mega Punch*	Mimic
Rock Slide*	Seismic Toss*	Substitute
Swords Dance*		

Emerald Only

Dynamicpunch*	Endure*	Fire Punch*
Fury Cutter	Sleep Talk	Snore*
Swagger	Swift*	Thunderpunch*

*Battle Frontier tutor move (*Emerald*)

257 Blaziken™

FIRE | FIGHTING

GENERAL INFO
SPECIES: Blaze Pokémon
HEIGHT: 6'03"
WEIGHT: 116 lbs.
ABILITY: Blaze

Blaziken's Fire-type attack power is multiplied when its HPs get low.

STATS
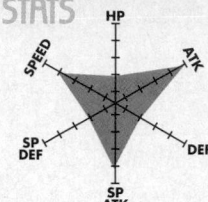

EVOLUTIONS
 LV16 LV36

LOCATION(S):

RUBY Rarity: **Evolve**
Evolve Combusken

SAPPHIRE Rarity: **Evolve**
Evolve Combusken

FIRERED Rarity: **None**
Trade from *Ruby/Sapphire*

LEAFGREEN Rarity: **None**
Trade from *Ruby/Sapphire*

COLOSSEUM Rarity: **None**
Trade from *Ruby/Sapphire*

EMERALD Rarity: **Evolve**
Evolve Combusken

XD Rarity: **None**
Trade from *Ruby/Sapphire/Emerald*

MOVES

Level	Attack	Type	Power	ACC	PP	Level	Attack	Type	Power	ACC	PP
—	Fire Punch	Fire	75	100	15	21	Sand-Attack	Ground	—	100	15
—	Scratch	Normal	40	100	35	28	Bulk Up	Fight	—	—	10
—	Growl	Normal	—	100	40	32	Quick Attack	Normal	40	100	30
—/7	Focus Energy	Normal	—	—	30	36	Blaze Kick	Fire	85	90	10
—/13	Ember	Fire	40	100	25	42	Slash	Normal	70	100	20
16	Double Kick	Fighting	30	100	30	49	Mirror Move	Flying	—	—	20
17	Peck	Flying	35	100	35	59	Sky Uppercut	Fighting	85	90	15

= Emerald Only

TM/HM

TM/HM#	Name	Type	Power	ACC	PP	TM/HM#	Name	Type	Power	ACC	PP
TM01	Focus Punch	Fighting	150	100	20	TM32	Double Team	Normal	—	—	15
TM05	Roar	Normal	—	100	20	TM35	Flamethrower	Fire	95	100	15
TM06	Toxic	Poison	—	85	10	TM38	Fire Blast	Fire	120	85	5
TM08	Bulk Up	Fighting	—	—	20	TM39	Rock Tomb	Rock	50	80	10
TM10	Hidden Power	Normal	—	100	15	TM40	Aerial Ace	Flying	60	—	20
TM11	Sunny Day	Fire	—	—	5	TM42	Facade	Normal	70	100	20
TM15	Hyper Beam	Normal	150	90	5	TM43	Secret Power	Normal	70	100	20
TM17	Protect	Normal	—	—	10	TM44	Rest	Psychic	—	—	10
TM21	Frustration	Normal	—	100	20	TM45	Attract	Normal	—	100	15
TM26	Earthquake	Ground	100	100	10	TM50	Overheat	Fire	140	90	5
TM27	Return	Normal	—	100	20	HM01	Cut	Normal	50	95	30
TM28	Dig	Ground	60	100	10	HM04	Strength	Normal	80	100	20
TM31	Brick Break	Fighting	75	100	15	HM06	Rock Smash	Fighting	20	100	15

MOVE TUTOR
FireRed/LeafGreen and *Emerald* Only

Body Slam*	Counter*	Double-Edge
Mega Kick*	Mega Punch*	Mimic
Rock Slide*	Seismic Toss*	Substitute
Swords Dance*		

Emerald Only

Dynamicpunch	Endure*	Fire Punch*
Fury Cutter*	Mud-Slap*	Sleep Talk
Snore*	Swagger	Swift*
Thunderpunch*		

*Battle Frontier tutor move (*Emerald*)

---

258 Mudkip™

WATER

GENERAL INFO
SPECIES: Mud Fish Pokémon
HEIGHT: 1'04"
WEIGHT: 17 lbs.
ABILITY: Torrent

When Mudkip's HPs fall below 1/3, its Water-type attack power increases 1.5 times.

STATS
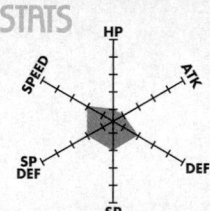

EVOLUTIONS
 LV16 LV36

LOCATION(S):

RUBY Rarity: **Only One**
Starter Pokémon obtained from Prof. Birch on Route 101

SAPPHIRE Rarity: **Only One**
Starter Pokémon obtained from Prof. Birch on Route 101

FIRERED Rarity: **None**
Trade from *Ruby/Sapphire*

LEAFGREEN Rarity: **None**
Trade from *Ruby/Sapphire*

COLOSSEUM Rarity: **None**
Trade from *Ruby/Sapphire*

EMERALD Rarity: **Only One**
Starter Pokémon obtained from Prof. Birch on Route 101

XD Rarity: **None**
Trade from *Ruby/Sapphire/Emerald*

MOVES

Level	Attack	Type	Power	ACC	PP	Level	Attack	Type	Power	ACC	PP
—	Tackle	Normal	35	95	35	24	Mud Sport	Ground	—	100	15
—	Growl	Normal	—	100	40	28	Take Down	Normal	90	85	20
6	Mud-Slap	Ground	20	100	10	33	Whirlpool	Water	15	70	15
10	Water Gun	Water	40	100	25	37	Protect	Normal	—	—	10
15	Bide	Normal	—	—	10	42	Hydro Pump	Water	120	80	5
19	Foresight	Normal	—	100	40	46	Endeavor	Normal	—	100	5

TM/HM

TM/HM#	Name	Type	Power	ACC	PP	TM/HM#	Name	Type	Power	ACC	PP
TM03	Water Pulse	Water	60	100	20	TM32	Double Team	Normal	—	—	15
TM06	Toxic	Poison	—	85	10	TM39	Rock Tomb	Rock	50	80	10
TM07	Hail	Ice	—	—	10	TM42	Facade	Normal	70	100	20
TM10	Hidden Power	Normal	—	100	15	TM43	Secret Power	Normal	70	100	20
TM13	Ice Beam	Ice	95	100	10	TM44	Rest	Psychic	—	—	10
TM14	Blizzard	Ice	120	70	5	TM45	Attract	Normal	—	100	15
TM17	Protect	Normal	—	—	10	HM03	Surf	Water	95	100	15
TM18	Rain Dance	Water	—	—	5	HM04	Strength	Normal	80	100	15
TM21	Frustration	Normal	—	100	20	HM06	Rock Smash	Fighting	20	100	15
TM23	Iron Tail	Steel	100	75	15	HM07	Waterfall	Water	80	100	15
TM27	Return	Normal	—	100	20	HM08	Dive	Water	60	100	10
TM28	Dig	Ground	60	100	10						

EGG MOVES*

Name	Type	Power	ACC	PP
Refresh	Normal	—	100	20
Uproar	Normal	50	100	10
Curse	—	—	—	10
Stomp	Normal	65	100	20
Ice Ball	Ice	30	90	20
Mirror Coat	Psychic	—	100	20

*Learned Via Breeding

MOVE TUTOR
FireRed/LeafGreen and *Emerald* Only

Body Slam*	Double-Edge	Mimic
Substitute		

Emerald Only

Defense Curl*	Endure*	Icy Wind*
Mud-Slap*	Rollout	Sleep Talk
Snore*	Swagger	

*Battle Frontier tutor move (*Emerald*)

259 Marshtomp™

WATER | GROUND

GENERAL INFO

SPECIES: Mud Fish Pokémon
HEIGHT: 2'04"
WEIGHT: 63 lbs.
ABILITY: Torrent
When Marshtomp's HPs fall below 1/3, its Water-type attack power increases 1.5 times.

STATS

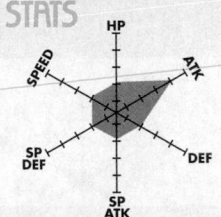

EVOLUTIONS

 LV16  LV36

LOCATION[S]:

RUBY — **Rarity: Evolve**
Evolve Mudkip

SAPPHIRE — **Rarity: Evolve**
Evolve Mudkip

FIRERED — **Rarity: None**
Trade from *Ruby/Sapphire*

LEAFGREEN — **Rarity: None**
Trade from *Ruby/Sapphire*

COLOSSEUM — **Rarity: None**
Trade from *Ruby/Sapphire*

EMERALD — **Rarity: Evolve**
Evolve Mudkip

XD — **Rarity: None**
Trade from *Ruby/Sapphire/Emerald*

MOVES

Level	Attack	Type	Power	ACC	PP	Level	Attack	Type	Power	ACC	PP
—	Tackle	Normal	35	95	35	20	Foresight	Normal	—	100	40
—	Growl	Normal	—	100	40	25	Mud Sport	Ground	—	100	15
—	Mud-Slap	Ground	20	100	10	31	Take Down	Normal	90	85	20
—	Water Gun	Water	40	100	25	37	Muddy Water	Water	95	85	10
15	Bide	Normal	—	100	10	42	Protect	Normal	—	—	10
16	Mud Shot	Ground	55	95	15	46	Earthquake	Ground	100	100	10
						53	Endeavor	Normal	—	100	5

TM/HM

TM/HM#	Name	Type	Power	ACC	PP	TM/HM#	Name	Type	Power	ACC	PP
TM03	Water Pulse	Water	60	100	20	TM28	Dig	Ground	60	100	10
TM06	Toxic	Poison	—	85	10	TM32	Double Team	Normal	—	—	15
TM07	Hail	Ice	—	—	10	TM39	Rock Tomb	Rock	50	80	10
TM10	Hidden Power	Normal	—	100	15	TM42	Facade	Normal	70	100	20
TM13	Ice Beam	Ice	95	100	10	TM43	Secret Power	Normal	70	100	20
TM14	Blizzard	Ice	120	70	5	TM44	Rest	Psychic	—	—	10
TM17	Protect	Normal	—	—	10	TM45	Attract	Normal	—	100	15
TM18	Rain Dance	Water	—	—	5	HM03	Surf	Water	95	100	15
TM21	Frustration	Normal	—	100	20	HM04	Strength	Normal	80	100	15
TM23	Iron Tail	Steel	100	75	15	HM06	Rock Smash	Fighting	20	100	15
TM26	Earthquake	Ground	100	100	10	HM07	Waterfall	Water	80	100	15
TM27	Return	Normal	—	100	20	HM08	Dive	Water	60	100	10

MOVE TUTOR

FireRed/LeafGreen and *Emerald* **Only**

Body Slam*	Counter*	Double-Edge
Mega Kick*	Mega Punch*	Mimic
Rock Slide*	Seismic Toss*	Substitute

Emerald **Only**

Defense Curl*	Dynamicpunch	Endure*
Ice Punch*	Icy Wind*	Mud-Slap*
Rollout	Sleep Talk	Snore*
Swagger		

*Battle Frontier tutor move (*Emerald*)

---

260 Swampert™

WATER | GROUND

GENERAL INFO

SPECIES: Mud Fish Pokémon
HEIGHT: 4'11"
WEIGHT: 181 lbs.
ABILITY: Torrent
When Swampert's HPs fall below 1/3, its Water-type attack power increases 1.5 times.

STATS

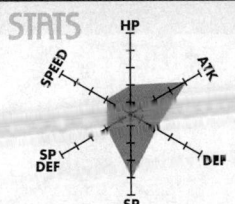

EVOLUTIONS

 LV16  LV36

LOCATION[S]:

RUBY — **Rarity: Evolve**
Evolve Marshtomp

SAPPHIRE — **Rarity: Evolve**
Evolve Marshtomp

FIRERED — **Rarity: None**
Trade from *Ruby/Sapphire*

LEAFGREEN — **Rarity: None**
Trade from *Ruby/Sapphire*

COLOSSEUM — **Rarity: None**
Trade from *Ruby/Sapphire*

EMERALD — **Rarity: Evolve**
Evolve Marshtomp

XD — **Rarity: None**
Trade from *Ruby/Sapphire/Emerald*

MOVES

Level	Attack	Type	Power	ACC	PP	Level	Attack	Type	Power	ACC	PP
—	Tackle	Normal	35	95	35	20	Foresight	Normal	—	100	40
—	Growl	Normal	—	100	40	25	Mud Sport	Ground	—	100	15
—	Mud-Slap	Ground	20	100	10	31	Take Down	Normal	90	85	20
—	Water Gun	Water	40	100	25	39	Muddy Water	Water	95	85	10
15	Bide	Normal	—	100	10	46	Protect	Normal	—	—	10
16	Mud Shot	Ground	55	95	15	52	Earthquake	Ground	100	100	10
						61	Endeavor	Normal	—	100	5

TM/HM

TM/HM#	Name	Type	Power	ACC	PP	TM/HM#	Name	Type	Power	ACC	PP
TM01	Focus Punch	Fighting	150	100	20	TM27	Return	Normal	—	100	20
TM03	Water Pulse	Water	60	100	20	TM28	Dig	Ground	60	100	10
TM05	Roar	Normal	—	100	20	TM31	Brick Break	Fighting	75	100	15
TM06	Toxic	Poison	—	85	10	TM32	Double Team	Normal	—	—	15
TM07	Hail	Ice	—	—	10	TM39	Rock Tomb	Rock	50	80	10
TM10	Hidden Power	Normal	—	100	15	TM42	Facade	Normal	70	100	20
TM13	Ice Beam	Ice	95	100	10	TM43	Secret Power	Normal	70	100	20
TM14	Blizzard	Ice	120	70	5	TM44	Rest	Psychic	—	—	10
TM15	Hyper Beam	Normal	150	90	5	TM45	Attract	Normal	—	100	15
TM17	Protect	Normal	—	—	10	HM03	Surf	Water	95	100	15
TM18	Rain Dance	Water	—	—	5	HM04	Strength	Normal	80	100	15
TM21	Frustration	Normal	—	100	20	HM06	Rock Smash	Fighting	20	100	15
TM23	Iron Tail	Steel	100	75	15	HM07	Waterfall	Water	80	100	15
TM26	Earthquake	Ground	100	100	10	HM08	Dive	Water	60	100	10

MOVE TUTOR

FireRed/LeafGreen and *Emerald* **Only**

Body Slam*	Counter*	Double-Edge
Mega Kick*	Mega Punch*	Mimic
Rock Slide*	Seismic Toss*	Substitute

Emerald **Only**

Defense Curl*	Dynamicpunch	Endure*
Icy Wind*	Mud-Slap*	Rollout
Sleep Talk	Snore*	Swagger

*Battle Frontier tutor move (*Emerald*)

265 Wurmple™

BUG

GENERAL INFO
SPECIES: Worm Pokémon
HEIGHT: 1'00"
WEIGHT: 8 lbs.
ABILITY: Shield Dust
Protects Wurmple from any additional effects of moves.

STATS
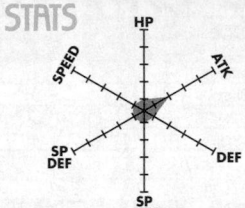

EVOLUTIONS
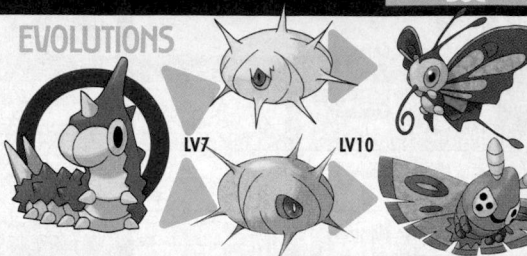
LV7   LV10

LOCATION[S]:

RUBY Rarity: **Common**
Route 101, Route 102, Route 104, Petalburg Woods

SAPPHIRE Rarity: **Common**
Route 101, Route 102, Route 104, Petalburg Woods

FIRERED Rarity: **None**
Trade from *Ruby/Sapphire*

LEAFGREEN Rarity: **None**
Trade from *Ruby/Sapphire*

COLOSSEUM Rarity: **None**
Trade from *Ruby/Sapphire*

EMERALD Rarity: **Common**
Route 101, Route 102, Route 104, Petalburg Woods

XD Rarity: **None**
Trade from *Ruby/Sapphire/Emerald*

MOVES
Level	Attack	Type	Power	ACC	PP
—	Tackle	Normal	35	95	35
—	String Shot	Bug	—	95	40
5	Poison Sting	Poison	15	100	35

TM/HM
TM/HM#	Name	Type	Power	ACC	PP
None					

EGG MOVES*
Name	Type	Power	ACC	PP
None				

*Learned Via Breeding

MOVE TUTOR
FireRed/LeafGreen and *Emerald* Only
None

266 Silcoon™

BUG

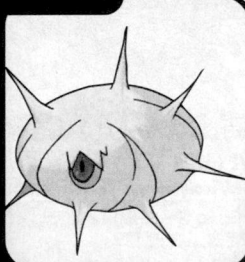

GENERAL INFO
SPECIES: Cocoon Pokémon
HEIGHT: 2'00"
WEIGHT: 22 lbs.
ABILITY: Shed Skin
Every turn, Silcoon has a 1/3 chance of recovering from a status condition.

STATS
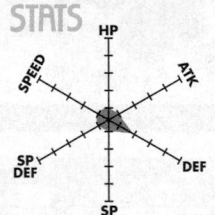

EVOLUTIONS

LV7   LV10

LOCATION[S]:

RUBY Rarity: **Rare**
Evolve Wurmple, Petalburg Woods

SAPPHIRE Rarity: **Rare**
Evolve Wurmple, Petalburg Woods

FIRERED Rarity: **None**
Trade from *Ruby/Sapphire*

LEAFGREEN Rarity: **None**
Trade from *Ruby/Sapphire*

COLOSSEUM Rarity: **None**
Trade from *Ruby/Sapphire*

EMERALD Rarity: **Rare**
Evolve Wurmple, Petalburg Woods

XD Rarity: **None**
Trade from *Ruby/Sapphire/Emerald*

MOVES
Level	Attack	Type	Power	ACC	PP
—/1	Harden	Normal	—	—	30

= Emerald Only

TM/HM
TM/HM#	Name	Type	Power	ACC	PP
None					

MOVE TUTOR
FireRed/LeafGreen and *Emerald* Only
None

267 Beautifly™

BUG | FLYING

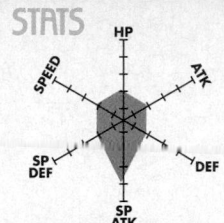

GENERAL INFO
SPECIES: Butterfly Pokémon
HEIGHT: 3'03"
WEIGHT: 63 lbs.
ABILITY: Swarm
When Beautifly's HPs fall below 1/3, the power of its Bug-type moves increases 1.5 times.

STATS

EVOLUTIONS

LV7 | LV10

* Evolution Depends on Gender and Personality

LOCATION[S]:

RUBY Rarity: **Evolve**
Evolve Silcoon

SAPPHIRE Rarity: **Evolve**
Evolve Silcoon

FIRERED Rarity: **None**
Trade from Ruby/Sapphire

LEAFGREEN Rarity: **None**
Trade from Ruby/Sapphire

COLOSSEUM Rarity: **None**
Trade from Ruby/Sapphire

EMERALD Rarity: **Evolve**
Evolve Silcoon

XD Rarity: **None**
Trade from Ruby/
Sapphire/Emerald

MOVES

Level	Attack	Type	Power	ACC	PP
—/10	Absorb	Grass	20	100	20
13	Gust	Flying	40	100	35
17	Stun Spore	Grass	—	75	30
20	Morning Sun	Normal	—	—	5
24	Mega Drain	Grass	40	100	10

Level	Attack	Type	Power	ACC	PP
27	Whirlwind	Normal	—	100	20
31	Attract	Normal	—	100	15
34	Silver Wind	Bug	60	100	5
38	Giga Drain	Grass	60	100	5

\# = Emerald Only

TM/HM

TM/HM#	Name	Type	Power	ACC	PP
TM06	Toxic	Poison	—	85	10
TM10	Hidden Power	Normal	—	100	15
TM11	Sunny Day	Fire	—	—	5
TM15	Hyper Beam	Normal	150	90	5
TM17	Protect	Normal	—	—	10
TM19	Giga Drain	Grass	60	100	5
TM20	Safeguard	Normal	—	—	25
TM21	Frustration	Normal	—	100	20
TM22	Solarbeam	Grass	120	100	10
TM27	Return	Normal	—	100	20

TM/HM#	Name	Type	Power	ACC	PP
TM29	Psychic	Psychic	90	100	10
TM30	Shadow Ball	Ghost	60	—	20
TM32	Double Team	Normal	—	—	15
TM40	Aerial Ace	Flying	60	—	20
TM42	Facade	Normal	70	100	20
TM43	Secret Power	Normal	70	100	20
TM44	Rest	Psychic	—	—	10
TM45	Attract	Normal	—	100	15
TM46	Thief	Dark	40	100	10
HM05	Flash	Normal	—	70	20

MOVE TUTOR
Emerald Only

Endure*	Sleep Talk	Snore*
Swagger	Swift*	

*Battle Frontier tutor move (Emerald)

---

268 Cascoon™

BUG

GENERAL INFO
SPECIES: Cocoon Pokémon
HEIGHT: 2'04"
WEIGHT: 25 lbs.
ABILITY: Shed Skin
Every turn, Cascoon has a 1/3 chance of recovering from a status condition.

STATS

EVOLUTIONS

LV7 | LV10

LOCATION[S]:

RUBY Rarity: **Rare**
Evolve Wurmple,
Petalburg Woods

SAPPHIRE Rarity: **Rare**
Evolve Wurmple,
Petalburg Woods

FIRERED Rarity: **None**
Trade from Ruby/Sapphire

LEAFGREEN Rarity: **None**
Trade from Ruby/Sapphire

COLOSSEUM Rarity: **None**
Trade from Ruby/Sapphire

EMERALD Rarity: **Rare**
Evolve Wurmple,
Petalburg Woods

XD Rarity: **None**
Trade from Ruby/
Sapphire/Emerald

MOVES

Level	Attack	Type	Power	ACC	PP
—/7	Harden	Normal	—	—	30

TM/HM

TM/HM#	Name	Type	Power	ACC	PP
None					

\# = Emerald Only

MOVE TUTOR
FireRed/LeafGreen and Emerald Only

None

269 Dustox™

| BUG | POISON |

GENERAL INFO
SPECIES: Poison Moth Pokémon
HEIGHT: 3'11"
WEIGHT: 70 lbs.
ABILITY: Shield Dust
Protects Dustox from any additional effects of moves.

STATS
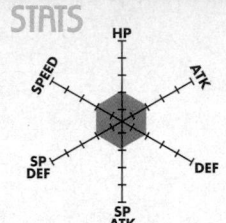

EVOLUTIONS
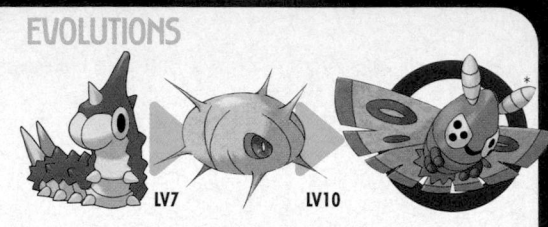

LV7   LV10

LOCATION[S]:

RUBY   Rarity: **Evolve**
Evolve Cascoon

SAPPHIRE   Rarity: **Evolve**
Evolve Cascoon

FIRERED   Rarity: **None**
Trade from *Ruby/Sapphire*

LEAFGREEN Rarity: **None**
Trade from *Ruby/Sapphire*

COLOSSEUM Rarity: **None**
Trade from *Ruby/Sapphire*

EMERALD   Rarity: **Evolve**
Evolve Cascoon

XD   Rarity: **None**
Trade from *Ruby/Sapphire/Emerald*

MOVES

Level	Attack	Type	Power	ACC	PP
—/10	Confusion	Psychic	50	100	25
13	Gust	Flying	40	100	35
17	Protect	Normal	—	—	10
20	Moonlight	Normal	—	—	5
24	Psybeam	Psychic	65	100	20
27	Whirlwind	Normal	—	100	20
31	Light Screen	Psychic	—	—	30
34	Silver Wind	Bug	60	100	5
38	Toxic	Poison	—	85	10

= *Emerald* Only

TM/HM

TM/HM#	Name	Type	Power	ACC	PP
TM06	Toxic	Poison	—	85	10
TM10	Hidden Power	Normal	—	100	15
TM11	Sunny Day	Fire	—	—	5
TM15	Hyper Beam	Normal	150	90	5
TM16	Light Screen	Psychic	—	—	30
TM17	Protect	Normal	—	—	10
TM19	Giga Drain	Grass	60	100	5
TM21	Frustration	Normal	—	100	20
TM22	Solarbeam	Grass	120	100	10
TM27	Return	Normal	—	100	20
TM29	Psychic	Psychic	90	100	10
TM30	Shadow Ball	Ghost	60	—	20
TM32	Double Team	Normal	—	—	15
TM36	Sludge Bomb	Poison	90	100	10
TM40	Aerial Ace	Flying	60	—	20
TM42	Facade	Normal	70	100	20
TM43	Secret Power	Normal	70	100	20
TM44	Rest	Psychic	—	—	10
TM45	Attract	Normal	—	100	15
TM46	Thief	Dark	40	100	10
HM05	Flash	Normal	—	70	20

MOVE TUTOR
Emerald Only

Endure*	Sleep Talk	Snore*
Swagger	Swift*	

*Battle Frontier tutor move (*Emerald*)

270 Lotad™

| WATER | GRASS |

GENERAL INFO
SPECIES: Water Weed Pokémon
HEIGHT: 1'08"
WEIGHT: 6 lbs.
ABILITY 1: Swift Swim   **ABILITY 2:** Rain Dish
Doubles Lotad's Speed when it is raining.   *Restores a few HPs every turn that it is raining.*

STATS
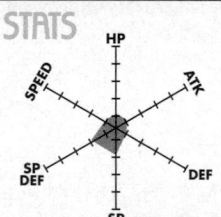

EVOLUTIONS

LV14   WATER STONE

LOCATION[S]:

RUBY   Rarity: **None**
Trade from *Sapphire*

SAPPHIRE   Rarity: **Common**
Route 102, Route 114

FIRERED   Rarity: **None**
Trade from *Sapphire*

LEAFGREEN Rarity: **None**
Trade from *Sapphire*

COLOSSEUM Rarity: **None**
Trade from *Sapphire*

EMERALD   Rarity: **Common**
Route 102, Route 114

XD   Rarity: **None**
Trade from *Sapphire/Emerald*

MOVES

Level	Attack	Type	Power	ACC	PP
—	Astonish	Ghost	30	100	15
3	Growl	Normal	—	100	40
7	Absorb	Grass	20	100	20
13	Nature Power	Normal	—	95	20
21	Mist	Ice	—	—	30
31	Rain Dance	Water	—	—	5
43	Mega Drain	Grass	40	100	10

TM/HM

TM/HM#	Name	Type	Power	ACC	PP
TM03	Water Pulse	Water	60	100	20
TM06	Toxic	Poison	—	85	10
TM07	Hail	Ice	—	—	10
TM09	Bullet Seed	Grass	10	100	30
TM10	Hidden Power	Normal	—	100	15
TM11	Sunny Day	Fire	—	—	5
TM13	Ice Beam	Ice	95	100	10
TM14	Blizzard	Ice	120	70	5
TM17	Protect	Normal	—	—	10
TM18	Rain Dance	Water	—	—	5
TM19	Giga Drain	Grass	60	100	5
TM21	Frustration	Normal	—	100	20
TM22	Solarbeam	Grass	120	100	10
TM27	Return	Normal	—	100	20
TM32	Double Team	Normal	—	—	15
TM42	Facade	Normal	70	100	20
TM43	Secret Power	Normal	70	100	20
TM44	Rest	Psychic	—	—	10
TM45	Attract	Normal	—	100	15
TM46	Thief	Dark	40	100	10
HM03	Surf	Water	95	100	15
HM05	Flash	Normal	—	70	20

EGG MOVES*

Name	Type	Power	ACC	PP
Synthesis	Grass	—	—	5
Razor Leaf	Grass	55	95	25
Sweet Scent	Normal	—	100	20
Leech Seed	Grass	—	90	10
Flail	Normal	—	100	15
Water Gun	Water	40	100	25

*Learned Via Breeding

MOVE TUTOR
FireRed/LeafGreen and *Emerald* Only

Body Slam*	Double-Edge	Mimic
Substitute	Swords Dance*	

Emerald Only

Endure*	Icy Wind*	Sleep Talk
Snore*	Swagger	

*Battle Frontier tutor move (*Emerald*)

271 Lombre™

WATER | **GRASS**

GENERAL INFO
SPECIES: Jolly Pokémon
HEIGHT: 3'11"
WEIGHT: 72 lbs.
ABILITY 1: Swift Swim
Doubles Lombre's Speed when it is raining.
ABILITY 2: Rain Dish
Restores a few HPs every turn that it is raining.

STATS

EVOLUTIONS

LV14 | WATER STONE

LOCATION[S]:

RUBY — **Rarity:** None
Trade from *Sapphire*

SAPPHIRE — **Rarity:** Rare
Route 114

FIRERED — **Rarity:** None
Trade from *Sapphire*

LEAFGREEN — **Rarity:** None
Trade from *Sapphire*

COLOSSEUM — **Rarity:** None
Trade from *Sapphire*

EMERALD — **Rarity:** Rare
Evolve Lotad, Route 114

XD — **Rarity:** None
Trade from *Sapphire/Emerald*

MOVES

Level	Attack	Type	Power	ACC	PP	Level	Attack	Type	Power	ACC	PP
—	Astonish	Ghost	30	100	15	25	Fury Swipes	Normal	18	80	15
3	Growl	Normal	—	100	40	31	Water Sport	Water	—	100	15
7	Absorb	Grass	20	100	20	37	Thief	Dark	40	100	10
13	Nature Power	Normal	—	95	20	43	Uproar	Normal	50	100	10
19	Fake Out	Normal	40	100	10	49	Hydro Pump	Water	120	80	5

TM/HM

TM/HM#	Name	Type	Power	ACC	PP	TM/HM#	Name	Type	Power	ACC	PP
TM03	Water Pulse	Water	60	100	20	TM31	Brick Break	Fighting	75	100	15
TM06	Toxic	Poison	—	85	10	TM32	Double Team	Normal	—	—	15
TM07	Hail	Ice	—	—	10	TM42	Facade	Normal	70	100	20
TM09	Bullet Seed	Grass	10	100	30	TM43	Secret Power	Normal	70	100	20
TM10	Hidden Power	Normal	—	100	15	TM44	Rest	Psychic	—	—	10
TM11	Sunny Day	Fire	—	—	5	TM45	Attract	Normal	—	100	15
TM13	Ice Beam	Ice	95	100	10	TM46	Thief	Dark	40	100	10
TM14	Blizzard	Ice	120	70	5	HM03	Surf	Water	95	100	15
TM17	Protect	Normal	—	—	10	HM04	Strength	Normal	80	100	15
TM18	Rain Dance	Water	—	—	5	HM05	Flash	Normal	—	70	20
TM19	Giga Drain	Grass	60	100	5	HM06	Rock Smash	Fighting	20	100	15
TM21	Frustration	Normal	—	100	20	HM07	Waterfall	Water	80	100	15
TM22	Solarbeam	Grass	120	100	10	HM08	Dive	Water	60	100	10
TM27	Return	Normal	—	100	20						

MOVE TUTOR
FireRed/LeafGreen and *Emerald* Only

Body Slam*	Double-Edge*	Mimic
Substitute	Swords Dance*	

Emerald Only

Dynamicpunch	Endure*	Fire Punch*
Ice Punch*	Icy Wind*	Mud-Slap*
Sleep Talk	Snore*	Swagger
Thunderpunch*		

*Battle Frontier tutor move (*Emerald*)

---

272 Ludicolo™

WATER | **GRASS**

GENERAL INFO
SPECIES: Carefree Pokémon
HEIGHT: 4'11"
WEIGHT: 121 lbs.
ABILITY 1: Swift Swim
Doubles Ludicolo's Speed when it is raining.
ABILITY 2: Rain Dish
Restores a few HPs every turn that it is raining.

STATS

EVOLUTIONS

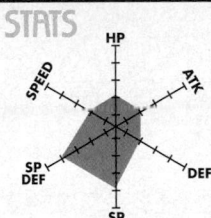

LV14 | WATER STONE

LOCATION[S]:

RUBY — **Rarity:** None
Trade from *Sapphire*

SAPPHIRE — **Rarity:** Evolve
Evolve Lombre

FIRERED — **Rarity:** None
Trade from *Sapphire*

LEAFGREEN — **Rarity:** None
Trade from *Sapphire*

COLOSSEUM — **Rarity:** None
Trade from *Sapphire*

EMERALD — **Rarity:** Evolve
Evolve Lombre

XD — **Rarity:** None
Trade from *Sapphire/Emerald*

MOVES

Level	Attack	Type	Power	ACC	PP	Level	Attack	Type	Power	ACC	PP
—	Astonish	Ghost	30	100	15	—	Absorb	Grass	20	100	20
—	Growl	Normal	—	100	40	—	Nature Power	Normal	—	95	20

TM/HM

TM/HM#	Name	Type	Power	ACC	PP	TM/HM#	Name	Type	Power	ACC	PP
TM01	Focus Punch	Fighting	150	100	20	TM27	Return	Normal	—	100	20
TM03	Water Pulse	Water	60	100	20	TM31	Brick Break	Fighting	75	100	15
TM06	Toxic	Poison	—	85	10	TM32	Double Team	Normal	—	—	15
TM07	Hail	Ice	—	—	10	TM42	Facade	Normal	70	100	20
TM09	Bullet Seed	Grass	10	100	30	TM43	Secret Power	Normal	70	100	20
TM10	Hidden Power	Normal	—	100	15	TM44	Rest	Psychic	—	—	10
TM11	Sunny Day	Fire	—	—	5	TM45	Attract	Normal	—	100	15
TM13	Ice Beam	Ice	95	100	10	TM46	Thief	Dark	40	100	10
TM14	Blizzard	Ice	120	70	5	HM03	Surf	Water	95	100	15
TM15	Hyper Beam	Normal	150	90	5	HM04	Strength	Normal	80	100	15
TM17	Protect	Normal	—	—	10	HM05	Flash	Normal	—	70	20
TM18	Rain Dance	Water	—	—	5	HM06	Rock Smash	Fighting	20	100	15
TM19	Giga Drain	Grass	60	100	5	HM07	Waterfall	Water	80	100	15
TM21	Frustration	Normal	—	100	20	HM08	Dive	Water	60	100	10
TM22	Solarbeam	Grass	120	100	10						

MOVE TUTOR
FireRed/LeafGreen and *Emerald* Only

Body Slam*	Counter*	Double-Edge*
Mega Kick*	Mega Punch*	Metronome
Mimic	Seismic Toss*	Substitute
Swords Dance*		

Emerald Only

Dynamicpunch	Endure*	Fire Punch*
Ice Punch*	Icy Wind*	Metronome
Mud-Slap*	Sleep Talk	Snore*
Swagger	Thunderpunch*	

*Battle Frontier tutor move (*Emerald*)

273 Seedot™

GRASS

GENERAL INFO
SPECIES: Acorn Pokémon
HEIGHT: 1'08"
WEIGHT: 9 lbs.
ABILITY 1: Chlorophyll
Doubles Seedot's Speed when the sunlight is strong.
ABILITY 2: Early Bird
Seedot recovers from Sleep earlier.

STATS

EVOLUTIONS

LV14   LEAF STONE

LOCATION[S]:

RUBY   Rarity: **Common**
Route 102, Route 114

SAPPHIRE   Rarity: **None**
Trade from *Ruby*

FIRERED   Rarity: **None**
Trade from *Ruby*

LEAFGREEN   Rarity: **None**
Trade from *Ruby*

COLOSSEUM   Rarity: **None**
Trade from *Ruby*

EMERALD   Rarity: **Rare**
Routes 102, 117, 120, Rustboro City

XD   Rarity: **Only One**
Cipher Lab (Capture from Cipher Peon Greesix)

MOVES

Level	Attack	Type	Power	ACC	PP	Level	Attack	Type	Power	ACC	PP
—	Bide	Normal	—	100	10	13	Nature Power	Normal	—	95	20
—	Pound*	Normal	40	100	35	21	Synthesis	Grass	—	—	5
3	Harden	Normal	—	—	30	31	Sunny Day	Fire	—	—	5
7	Growth	Normal	—	—	40	43	Explosion	Normal	250	100	5

= Emerald Only

TM/HM

TM/HM#	Name	Type	Power	ACC	PP	TM/HM#	Name	Type	Power	ACC	PP
TM06	Toxic	Poison	—	85	10	TM28	Dig	Ground	60	100	10
TM09	Bullet Seed	Grass	10	100	30	TM30	Shadow Ball	Ghost	60	—	20
TM10	Hidden Power	Normal	—	100	15	TM32	Double Team	Normal	—	—	15
TM11	Sunny Day	Fire	—	—	5	TM42	Facade	Normal	70	100	20
TM17	Protect	Normal	—	—	10	TM43	Secret Power	Normal	70	100	20
TM19	Giga Drain	Grass	60	100	5	TM44	Rest	Psychic	—	—	10
TM21	Frustration	Normal	—	100	20	TM45	Attract	Normal	—	100	15
TM22	Solarbeam	Grass	120	100	10	HM05	Flash	Normal	—	70	20
TM27	Return	Normal	—	100	20	HM06	Rock Smash	Fighting	20	100	15

EGG MOVES*

Name	Type	Power	ACC	PP
Leech Seed	Grass	—	90	10
Amnesia	Psychic	—	—	20
Quick Attack	Normal	40	100	30
Razor Wind	Normal	80	100	10
Take Down	Normal	90	85	20
False Swipe	Normal	40	100	40

Learned Via Breeding

MOVE TUTOR
FireRed/LeafGreen and Emerald Only

Body Slam*	Double-Edge	Explosion
Mimic	Substitute	Swords Dance*

Emerald Only

Defense Curl*	Endure*	Rollout
Sleep Talk	Snore*	Swagger

Battle Frontier tutor move (Emerald)

274 Nuzleaf™

GRASS   DARK

GENERAL INFO
SPECIES: Wily Pokémon
HEIGHT: 3'03"
WEIGHT: 62 lbs.
ABILITY 1: Chlorophyll
Doubles Nuzleaf's Speed when the sunlight is strong.
ABILITY 2: Early Bird
Nuzleaf recovers from Sleep earlier.

STATS
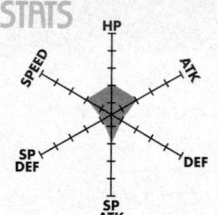

EVOLUTIONS

LV14   LEAF STONE

LOCATION[S]:

RUBY   Rarity: **Rare**
Route 114

SAPPHIRE   Rarity: **None**
Trade from *Ruby*

FIRERED   Rarity: **None**
Trade from *Ruby*

LEAFGREEN   Rarity: **None**
Trade from *Ruby*

COLOSSEUM   Rarity: **None**
Trade from *Ruby*

EMERALD   Rarity: **Rare**
Evolve Seedot, Route 114

XD   Rarity: **Evolve**
Evolve Seedot

MOVES

Level	Attack	Type	Power	ACC	PP	Level	Attack	Type	Power	ACC	PP
—	Bide*	Normal	—	100	10	25	Torment	Dark	—	100	15
—	Pound	Normal	40	100	35	31	Faint Attack	Dark	60	—	20
—/3	Harden	Normal	—	—	30	37	Razor Wind	Normal	80	100	10
—/7	Growth	Normal	—	—	40	43	Swagger	Normal	—	90	15
—/13	Nature Power	Normal	—	95	20	49	Extrasensory	Psychic	80	100	30
19	Fake Out	Normal	40	100	10						

 # = Emerald Only   ** Not Available in *Emerald*

TM/HM

TM/HM#	Name	Type	Power	ACC	PP	TM/HM#	Name	Type	Power	ACC	PP
TM06	Toxic	Poison	—	85	10	TM32	Double Team	Normal	—	—	15
TM09	Bullet Seed	Grass	10	100	30	TM39	Rock Tomb	Rock	50	80	10
TM10	Hidden Power	Normal	—	100	15	TM41	Torment	Dark	—	100	15
TM11	Sunny Day	Fire	—	—	5	TM42	Facade	Normal	70	100	20
TM15	Hyper Beam	Normal	150	90	5	TM43	Secret Power	Normal	70	100	20
TM17	Protect	Normal	—	—	10	TM44	Rest	Psychic	—	—	10
TM19	Giga Drain	Grass	60	100	5	TM45	Attract	Normal	—	100	15
TM21	Frustration	Normal	—	100	20	TM46	Thief	Dark	40	100	10
TM22	Solarbeam	Grass	120	100	10	HM01	Cut	Normal	50	95	30
TM27	Return	Normal	—	100	20	HM04	Strength	Normal	80	100	15
TM28	Dig	Ground	60	100	10	HM05	Flash	Normal	—	70	20
TM30	Shadow Punch	Ghost	60	—	20	HM06	Rock Smash	Fighting	20	100	15
TM31	Brick Break	Fighting	75	100	15						

MOVE TUTOR
FireRed/LeafGreen and Emerald Only

Body Slam*	Double-Edge	Explosion
Mega Kick*	Mimic	Substitute
Swords Dance*		

Emerald Only

Defense Curl*	Endure*	Fury Cutter
Mud-Slap*	Psych Up*	Rollout
Sleep Talk	Snore*	Swagger
Swift*		

Battle Frontier tutor move (Emerald)

275 Shiftry™

GRASS   DARK

GENERAL INFO
SPECIES: Wicked Pokémon
HEIGHT: 4'03"
WEIGHT: 131 lbs.
ABILITY 1: Chlorophyll
Doubles Shiftry's Speed when the sunlight is strong.
ABILITY 2: Early Bird
Shiftry recovers from Sleep earlier.

STATS
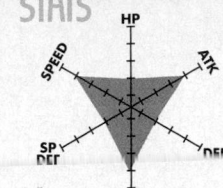

EVOLUTIONS

LV14   LEAF STONE

LOCATION(S):

RUBY   Rarity: **Evolve**
Evolve Nuzleaf

SAPPHIRE Rarity: **None**
Trade from *Ruby*

FIRERED   Rarity: **None**
Trade from *Ruby*

LEAFGREEN Rarity: **None**
Trade from *Ruby*

COLOSSEUM Rarity: **None**
Trade from *Ruby*

EMERALD   Rarity: **Evolve**
Evolve Nuzleaf

XD   Rarity: **Evolve**
Evolve Nuzleaf

MOVES

Level	Attack	Type	Power	ACC	PP	Level	Attack	Type	Power	ACC	PP
—	Pound	Normal	40	100	35	—	Growth	Normal	—	—	40
—	Harden	Normal	—	—	30	—	Nature Power	Normal	—	95	20

TM/HM

TM/HM#	Name	Type	Power	ACC	PP	TM/HM#	Name	Type	Power	ACC	PP
TM06	Toxic	Poison	—	85	10	TM32	Double Team	Normal	—	—	15
TM09	Bullet Seed	Grass	10	100	30	TM39	Rock Tomb	Rock	50	80	10
TM10	Hidden Power	Normal	—	100	15	TM40	Aerial Ace	Flying	60	—	20
TM11	Sunny Day	Fire	—	—	5	TM41	Torment	Dark	—	100	15
TM15	Hyper Beam	Normal	150	90	5	TM42	Facade	Normal	70	100	20
TM17	Protect	Normal	—	—	10	TM43	Secret Power	Normal	70	100	20
TM19	Giga Drain	Grass	60	100	5	TM44	Rest	Psychic	—	—	10
TM21	Frustration	Normal	—	100	20	TM45	Attract	Normal	—	100	15
TM22	Solarbeam	Grass	120	100	10	TM46	Thief	Dark	40	100	10
TM27	Return	Normal	—	100	20	HM01	Cut	Normal	50	95	30
TM20	Dig	Ground	60	100	10	HM04	Strength	Normal	80	100	15
TM30	Shadow Ball	Ghost	60	—	20	HM05	Flash	Normal	—	70	20
TM31	Brick Break	Fighting	75	100	15	HM06	Rock Smash	Fighting	20	100	15

MOVE TUTOR
FireRed/LeafGreen and *Emerald* Only

Body Slam*	Double-Edge*	Explosion
Mega Kick*	Mimic	Substitute
Swords Dance*		

Emerald Only

Defense Curl*	Endure*	Fury Cutter
Mud-Slap*	Psych Up*	Rollout
Sleep Talk	Snore*	Swagger
Swift*		

*Battle Frontier tutor move (*Emerald*)

---

276 Taillow™

NORMAL   FLYING

GENERAL INFO
SPECIES: Tinyswallow Pokémon
HEIGHT: 1'00"
WEIGHT: 5 lbs.
ABILITY: Guts
Taillow's attack power increases 1.5 times when inflicted with a status condition.

STATS
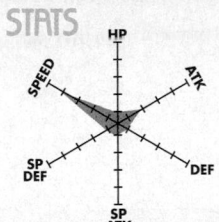

EVOLUTIONS

LV22

LOCATION(S):

RUBY   Rarity: **Common**
Route 104, Route 115, Route 116, Petalburg Woods

SAPPHIRE Rarity: **Common**
Route 104, Route 115, Route 116, Petalburg Woods

FIRERED   Rarity: **None**
Trade from *Ruby/Sapphire/Emerald*

LEAFGREEN Rarity: **None**
Trade from *Ruby/Sapphire/Emerald*

COLOSSEUM Rarity: **None**
Trade from *Ruby/Sapphire/Emerald*

EMERALD   Rarity: **Common**
Route 104, Route 115, Route 116, Petalburg Woods

XD   Rarity: **None**
Trade from *Ruby/Sapphire/Emerald*

MOVES

Level	Attack	Type	Power	ACC	PP	Level	Attack	Type	Power	ACC	PP
—	Peck	Flying	35	100	35	13	Wing Attack	Flying	60	100	35
—	Growl	Normal	—	100	40	19	Double Team	Normal	—	—	15
4	Focus Energy	Normal	—	—	30	26	Endeavor	Normal	—	100	5
8	Quick Attack	Normal	40	100	30	34	Aerial Ace	Flying	60	—	20
						43	Agility	Psychic	—	—	30

TM/HM

TM/HM#	Name	Type	Power	ACC	PP	TM/HM#	Name	Type	Power	ACC	PP
TM06	Toxic	Poison	—	85	10	TM40	Aerial Ace	Flying	60	—	20
TM10	Hidden Power	Normal	—	100	15	TM42	Facade	Normal	70	100	20
TM11	Sunny Day	Fire	—	—	5	TM43	Secret Power	Normal	70	100	20
TM17	Protect	Normal	—	—	10	TM44	Rest	Psychic	—	—	10
TM18	Rain Dance	Water	—	—	5	TM45	Attract	Normal	—	100	15
TM21	Frustration	Normal	—	100	20	TM46	Thief	Dark	40	100	10
TM27	Return	Normal	—	100	20	TM47	Steel Wing	Steel	70	90	25
TM32	Double Team	Normal	—	—	15	HM02	Fly	Flying	70	95	15

EGG MOVES*

Name	Type	Power	ACC	PP
Pursuit	Dark	40	100	20
Supersonic	Normal	—	55	20
Refresh	Normal	—	100	20
Mirror Move	Flying	—	—	20
Rage	Normal	20	100	20
Sky Attack	Flying	140	90	5

*Learned Via Breeding

MOVE TUTOR
FireRed/LeafGreen and *Emerald* Only

Counter*	Double-Edge*	Mimic
Substitute		

Emerald Only

Endure*	Mud-Slap*	Sleep Talk
Snore*	Swagger	Swift*

*Battle Frontier tutor move (*Emerald*)

277 Swellow™

NORMAL   FLYING

GENERAL INFO
SPECIES: Swallow Pokémon
HEIGHT: 2'04"
WEIGHT: 44 lbs.
ABILITY: Guts

Swellow's attack power increases 1.5 times when inflicted with a status condition.

STATS
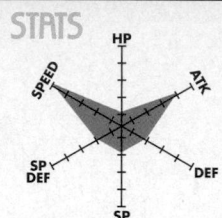

EVOLUTIONS

LV22

LOCATION[S]:

RUBY   Rarity: **Rare**
Evolve Taillow, Route 115

SAPPHIRE   Rarity: **Rare**
Evolve Taillow, Route 115

FIRERED   Rarity: **None**
Trade from *Ruby/Sapphire/Emerald*

LEAFGREEN   Rarity: **None**
Trade from *Ruby/Sapphire/Emerald*

COLOSSEUM   Rarity: **None**
Trade from *Ruby/Sapphire/Emerald*

EMERALD   Rarity: **Rare**
Evolve Taillow, Route 115

XD   Rarity: **Only One**
Citadark Island (Capture from Cipher Admin Ardos)

MOVES

Level	Attack	Type	Power	ACC	PP
—	Peck	Flying	35	100	35
—	Growl	Normal	—	100	40
—/4	Focus Energy	Normal	—	—	30
—/8	Quick Attack	Normal	40	100	30
13	Wing Attack	Flying	60	100	35

Level	Attack	Type	Power	ACC	PP
19	Double Team	Normal	—	—	15
28	Endeavor	Normal	—	100	5
38	Aerial Ace	Flying	60	—	20
49	Agility	Psychic	—	—	30

= *Emerald* Only

TM/HM

TM/HM#	Name	Type	Power	ACC	PP
TM06	Toxic	Poison	—	85	10
TM10	Hidden Power	Normal	—	100	15
TM11	Sunny Day	Fire	—	—	5
TM15	Hyper Beam	Normal	150	90	5
TM17	Protect	Normal	—	—	10
TM18	Rain Dance	Water	—	—	5
TM21	Frustration	Normal	—	100	20
TM27	Return	Normal	—	100	20
TM32	Double Team	Normal	—	—	15

TM/HM#	Name	Type	Power	ACC	PP
TM40	Aerial Ace	Flying	60	—	20
TM42	Facade	Normal	70	100	20
TM43	Secret Power	Normal	70	100	20
TM44	Rest	Psychic	—	—	10
TM45	Attract	Normal	—	100	15
TM46	Thief	Dark	40	100	10
TM47	Steel Wing	Steel	70	90	25
HM02	Fly	Flying	70	95	15

MOVE TUTOR
FireRed/LeafGreen and *Emerald* Only

Counter*	Double-Edge	Mimic
Substitute		

Emerald Only

Endure*	Mud-Slap*	Sleep Talk
Snore*	Swagger	Swift*

*Battle Frontier tutor move (*Emerald*)

278 Wingull™

WATER   FLYING

GENERAL INFO
SPECIES: Seagull Pokémon
HEIGHT: 2'00"
WEIGHT: 21 lbs.
ABILITY: Keen Eye

Wingull's Accuracy cannot be lowered.

STATS
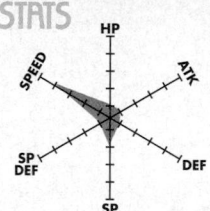

EVOLUTIONS

LV25

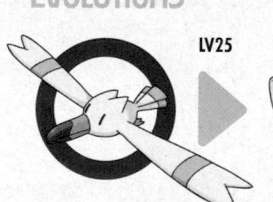

LOCATION[S]:

RUBY   Rarity: **Common**
Route 103, Route 104, Route 115, All Water Routes

SAPPHIRE   Rarity: **Common**
Route 103, Route 104, Route 115, All Water Routes

FIRERED   Rarity: **None**
Trade from *Ruby/Sapphire/Emerald*

LEAFGREEN   Rarity: **None**
Trade from *Ruby/Sapphire/Emerald*

COLOSSEUM   Rarity: **None**
Trade from *Ruby/Sapphire/Emerald*

EMERALD   Rarity: **Common**
Routes 103–110, 115, 118, 119, 121–134, Dewford Town, Ever Grande City, Lilycove City, Mossdeep City, Mt. Pyre, Pacifidlog Town, Slateport City

XD   Rarity: **None**
Trade from *Ruby/Sapphire/Emerald*

MOVES

Level	Attack	Type	Power	ACC	PP
—	Growl	Normal	—	100	40
—	Water Gun	Water	40	100	25
7	Supersonic	Normal	—	55	20
13	Wing Attack	Flying	60	100	35

Level	Attack	Type	Power	ACC	PP
21	Mist	Ice	—	—	30
31	Quick Attack	Normal	40	100	30
43	Pursuit	Dark	40	100	20
55	Agility	Psychic	—	—	30

TM/HM

TM/HM#	Name	Type	Power	ACC	PP
TM03	Water Pulse	Water	60	100	20
TM06	Toxic	Poison	—	85	10
TM07	Hail	Ice	—	—	10
TM10	Hidden Power	Normal	—	100	15
TM13	Ice Beam	Ice	95	100	10
TM14	Blizzard	Ice	120	70	5
TM17	Protect	Normal	—	—	10
TM18	Rain Dance	Water	—	—	5
TM21	Frustration	Normal	—	100	20
TM27	Return	Normal	—	100	20

TM/HM#	Name	Type	Power	ACC	PP
TM32	Double Team	Normal	—	—	15
TM34	Shock Wave	Electric	60	—	20
TM40	Aerial Ace	Flying	60	—	20
TM42	Facade	Normal	70	100	20
TM43	Secret Power	Normal	70	100	20
TM44	Rest	Psychic	—	—	10
TM45	Attract	Normal	—	100	15
TM46	Thief	Dark	40	100	10
TM47	Steel Wing	Steel	70	90	25
HM02	Fly	Flying	70	95	15

EGG MOVES*

Name	Type	Power	ACC	PP
Twister	Dragon	40	100	20
Water Sport	Water	—	100	15
Mist	Ice	—	—	30
Agility	Psychic	—	—	30
Whirlwind	Normal	—	100	20

*Learned Via Breeding

MOVE TUTOR
FireRed/LeafGreen and *Emerald* Only

Double-Edge	Mimic	Substitute

Emerald Only

Endure*	Icy Wind*	Mud-Slap*
Sleep Talk	Snore*	Swagger
Swift*		

*Battle Frontier tutor move (*Emerald*)

279 Pelipper™

WATER | FLYING

GENERAL INFO
SPECIES: Water Bird Pokémon
HEIGHT: 3'11"
WEIGHT: 62 lbs.
ABILITY: Keen Eye

Pelipper's Accuracy cannot be lowered.

STATS

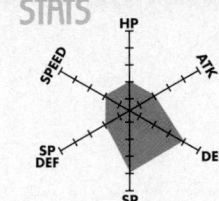

EVOLUTIONS

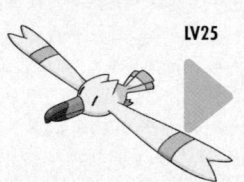 LV25

LOCATION(S):

RUBY Rarity: **Rare**
Evolve Wingull, Route 103, Route 104, Route 115, All Water Routes

SAPPHIRE Rarity: **Rare**
Evolve Wingull, Route 103, Route 104, Route 115, All Water Routes

FIRERED Rarity: **None**
Trade from *Ruby/Sapphire/Emerald*

LEAFGREEN Rarity: **None**
Trade from *Ruby/Sapphire/Emerald*

COLOSSEUM Rarity: **None**
Trade from *Ruby/Sapphire/Emerald*

EMERALD Rarity: **Common**
Evolve Wingull, Routes 103–110, 115, 118, 119, 121–134, Dewford Town, Ever Grande City, Lilycove City, Mossdeep City, Mt. Pyre, Pacifidlog Town, Slateport City

XD Rarity: **None**
Trade from *Ruby/Sapphire/Emerald*

MOVES

Level	Attack	Type	Power	ACC	PP	Level	Attack	Type	Power	ACC	PP
—	Growl	Normal	—	100	40	21	Mist	Ice	—	—	30
—/3	Water Gun	Water	40	100	25	25	Protect	Normal	—	—	10
—	Water Spout	Water	150	100	5	33	Stockpile	Normal	—	—	10
—	Water Sport*	Water	150	100	5	33	Swallow	Normal	—	—	10
—/7	Supersonic	Normal	—	55	20	47	Spit Up	Normal	100	100	10
—/13	Wing Attack	Flying	60	100	35	61	Hydro Pump	Water	120	80	5

= *Emerald* Only   * = *Emerald* Only

TM/HM

TM/HM#	Name	Type	Power	ACC	PP	TM/HM#	Name	Type	Power	ACC	PP
TM03	Water Pulse	Water	60	100	20	TM32	Double Team	Normal	—	—	15
TM06	Toxic	Poison	—	85	10	TM34	Shock Wave	Electric	60	—	20
TM07	Hail	Ice	—	—	10	TM40	Aerial Ace	Flying	60	—	20
TM10	Hidden Power	Normal	—	100	15	TM42	Facade	Normal	70	100	20
TM13	Ice Beam	Ice	95	100	10	TM43	Secret Power	Normal	70	100	20
TM14	Blizzard	Ice	120	70	5	TM44	Rest	Psychic	—	—	10
TM15	Hyper Beam	Normal	150	90	5	TM45	Attract	Normal	—	100	15
TM17	Protect	Normal	—	—	10	TM46	Thief	Dark	40	100	10
TM18	Rain Dance	Water	—	—	5	TM47	Steel Wing	Steel	70	90	25
TM21	Frustration	Normal	—	100	20	HM02	Fly	Flying	70	95	15
TM27	Return	Normal	—	100	20	HM03	Surf	Water	95	100	15

MOVE TUTOR
FireRed/LeafGreen and *Emerald* Only

Double-Edge	Mimic	Substitute

Emerald Only

Endure*	Icy Wind*	Mud-Slap*
Sleep Talk*	Snore*	Swagger
Swift*		

*Battle Frontier tutor move (*Emerald*)

280 Ralts™

PSYCHIC

GENERAL INFO
SPECIES: Feeling Pokémon
HEIGHT: 1'04"
WEIGHT: 15 lbs.
ABILITY 1: Synchronize

Shares Ralts's Poison, Paralyze, or Burn condition with the opponent Pokémon.

ABILITY 2: Trace

Ralts's ability becomes the same as the opponent's.

STATS

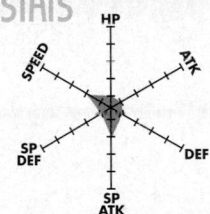

EVOLUTIONS

 LV20  LV30

LOCATION(S):

RUBY Rarity: **Rare**
Route 102

SAPPHIRE Rarity: **Rare**
Route 102

FIRERED Rarity: **None**
Trade from *Ruby/Sapphire/Emerald*

LEAFGREEN Rarity: **None**
Trade from *Ruby/Sapphire/Emerald*

COLOSSEUM Rarity: **None**
Trade from *Ruby/Sapphire/Emerald*

EMERALD Rarity: **Rare**
Route 102

XD Rarity: **Only One**
Pyrite Town (Capture from Cipher Peon Feldas)

MOVES

Level	Attack	Type	Power	ACC	PP	Level	Attack	Type	Power	ACC	PP
—	Growl	Normal	—	100	40	26	Psychic	Psychic	90	100	10
6	Confusion	Psychic	50	100	25	31	Imprison	Psychic	—	100	15
11	Double Team	Normal	—	—	15	36	Future Sight	Psychic	80	90	15
16	Teleport	Psychic	—	—	20	41	Hypnosis	Psychic	—	60	20
21	Calm Mind	Psychic	—	—	20	46	Dream Eater	Psychic	100	100	15

TM/HM

TM/HM#	Name	Type	Power	ACC	PP	TM/HM#	Name	Type	Power	ACC	PP
TM04	Calm Mind	Psychic	—	—	20	TM30	Shadow Ball	Ghost	60	—	20
TM06	Toxic	Poison	—	85	10	TM32	Double Team	Normal	—	—	15
TM10	Hidden Power	Normal	—	100	15	TM33	Reflect	Psychic	—	—	20
TM11	Sunny Day	Fire	—	—	5	TM34	Shock Wave	Electric	60	—	20
TM12	Taunt	Dark	—	100	20	TM41	Torment	Dark	—	100	15
TM16	Light Screen	Psychic	—	—	30	TM42	Facade	Normal	70	100	20
TM17	Protect	Normal	—	—	10	TM43	Secret Power	Normal	70	100	20
TM18	Rain Dance	Water	—	—	5	TM44	Rest	Psychic	—	—	10
TM20	Safeguard	Normal	—	—	25	TM45	Attract	Normal	—	100	15
TM21	Frustration	Normal	—	100	20	TM46	Thief	Dark	40	100	10
TM24	Thunderbolt	Electric	95	100	15	TM48	Skill Swap	Psychic	—	—	10
TM27	Return	Normal	—	100	20	TM49	Snatch	Dark	—	100	10
TM29	Psychic	Psychic	90	100	10	HM05	Flash	Normal	—	70	20

EGG MOVES*

Name	Type	Power	ACC	PP
Disable	Normal	—	55	20
Will-O-Wisp	Fire	—	75	15
Mean Look	Normal	—	100	5
Memento	Dark	—	100	10
Destiny Bond	Ghost	—	—	5

*Learned Via Breeding

MOVE TUTOR
FireRed/LeafGreen and *Emerald* Only

Body Slam*	Double-Edge	Dream Eater*
Mimic	Substitute	Swords Dance*

Emerald Only

Defense Curl*	Endure*	Fire Punch*
Ice Punch*	Icy Wind*	Mud-Slap*
Psych Up*	Sleep Talk*	Snore*
Swagger	Thunderpunch*	

*Battle Frontier tutor move (*Emerald*)

281 Kirlia™

PSYCHIC

GENERAL INFO
SPECIES: Emotion Pokémon
HEIGHT: 2'07"
WEIGHT: 45 lbs.
ABILITY 1: Synchronize
Shares Kirlia's Poison, Paralyze, or Burn condition with the opponent Pokémon.

ABILITY 2: Trace
Kirlia's ability becomes the same as the opponent's.

STATS
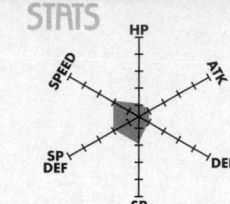

EVOLUTIONS

LV20
LV30

LOCATION(S):

RUBY — Rarity: **Evolve**
Evolve Ralts

SAPPHIRE — Rarity: **Evolve**
Evolve Ralts

FIRERED — Rarity: **None**
Trade from Ruby/Sapphire/Emerald

LEAFGREEN — Rarity: **None**
Trade from Ruby/Sapphire/Emerald

COLOSSEUM — Rarity: **None**
Trade from Ruby/Sapphire/Emerald

EMERALD — Rarity: **Evolve**
Evolve Ralts

XD — Rarity: **Evolve**
Evolve Ralts

MOVES

Level	Attack	Type	Power	ACC	PP	Level	Attack	Type	Power	ACC	PP
—	Growl	Normal	—	100	40	26	Psychic	Psychic	90	100	10
—/6	Confusion	Psychic	50	100	25	33	Imprison	Psychic	—	100	15
—/11	Double Team	Normal	—	—	15	40	Future Sight	Psychic	80	90	15
—/16	Teleport	Psychic	—	—	20	47	Hypnosis	Psychic	—	60	20
—	Magical Leaf	Grass	60	—	20	54	Dream Eater	Psychic	100	100	15
21	Calm Mind	Psychic	—	—	20						

= Emerald Only

TM/HM

TM/HM#	Name	Type	Power	ACC	PP	TM/HM#	Name	Type	Power	ACC	PP
TM04	Calm Mind	Psychic	—	—	20	TM30	Shadow Ball	Ghost	60	—	20
TM06	Toxic	Poison	—	85	10	TM32	Double Team	Normal	—	—	15
TM10	Hidden Power	Normal	—	100	15	TM33	Reflect	Psychic	—	—	20
TM11	Sunny Day	Fire	—	—	5	TM34	Shock Wave	Electric	60	—	20
TM12	Taunt	Dark	—	100	20	TM41	Torment	Dark	—	100	15
TM16	Light Screen	Psychic	—	—	30	TM42	Facade	Normal	70	100	20
TM17	Protect	Normal	—	—	10	TM43	Secret Power	Normal	70	100	20
TM18	Rain Dance	Water	—	—	5	TM44	Rest	Psychic	—	—	10
TM20	Safeguard	Normal	—	—	25	TM45	Attract	Normal	—	100	15
TM21	Frustration	Normal	—	100	20	TM46	Thief	Dark	40	100	10
TM24	Thunderbolt	Electric	95	100	15	TM48	Skill Swap	Psychic	—	100	10
TM27	Return	Normal	—	100	20	TM49	Snatch	Dark	—	100	10
TM29	Psychic	Psychic	90	100	10	HM05	Flash	Normal	—	70	20

MOVE TUTOR
FireRed/LeafGreen and Emerald Only

Body Slam* | Double-Edge* | Dream Eater*
Mimic | Substitute | Thunder Wave*

Emerald Only

Defense Curl* | Endure* | Fire Punch*
Ice Punch* | Icy Wind* | Mud-Slap*
Psych Up* | Sleep Talk | Snore*
Swagger | Thunderpunch* |

*Battle Frontier tutor move (Emerald)

---

282 Gardevoir™

PSYCHIC

GENERAL INFO
SPECIES: Embrace Pokémon
HEIGHT: 5'03"
WEIGHT: 107 lbs.
ABILITY 1: Synchronize
Shares Gardevoir's Poison, Paralyze, or Burn condition with the opponent Pokémon.

ABILITY 2: Trace
Gardevoir's ability becomes the same as the opponent's.

STATS

EVOLUTIONS
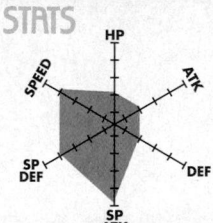
LV20
LV30

LOCATION(S):

RUBY — Rarity: **Evolve**
Evolve Kirlia

SAPPHIRE — Rarity: **Evolve**
Evolve Kirlia

FIRERED — Rarity: **None**
Trade from Ruby/Sapphire/Emerald

LEAFGREEN — Rarity: **None**
Trade from Ruby/Sapphire/Emerald

COLOSSEUM — Rarity: **None**
Trade from Ruby/Sapphire/Emerald

EMERALD — Rarity: **Evolve**
Evolve Kirlia

XD — Rarity: **Evolve**
Evolve Kirlia

MOVES

Level	Attack	Type	Power	ACC	PP	Level	Attack	Type	Power	ACC	PP
—	Growl	Normal	—	100	40	26	Psychic	Psychic	90	100	10
—/6	Confusion	Psychic	50	100	25	33	Imprison	Psychic	—	100	15
—/11	Double Team	Normal	—	—	15	42	Future Sight	Psychic	80	90	15
—/13	Teleport	Psychic	—	—	20	51	Hypnosis	Psychic	—	60	20
21	Calm Mind	Psychic	—	—	20	60	Dream Eater	Psychic	100	100	15

= Emerald Only

TM/HM

TM/HM#	Name	Type	Power	ACC	PP	TM/HM#	Name	Type	Power	ACC	PP
TM04	Calm Mind	Psychic	—	—	20	TM30	Shadow Ball	Ghost	60	—	20
TM06	Toxic	Poison	—	85	10	TM32	Double Team	Normal	—	—	15
TM10	Hidden Power	Normal	—	100	15	TM33	Reflect	Psychic	—	—	20
TM11	Sunny Day	Fire	—	—	5	TM34	Shock Wave	Electric	60	—	20
TM12	Taunt	Dark	—	100	20	TM41	Torment	Dark	—	100	15
TM15	Hyper Beam	Normal	150	90	5	TM42	Facade	Normal	70	100	20
TM16	Light Screen	Psychic	—	—	30	TM43	Secret Power	Normal	70	100	20
TM17	Protect	Normal	—	—	10	TM44	Rest	Psychic	—	—	10
TM18	Rain Dance	Water	—	—	5	TM45	Attract	Normal	—	100	15
TM20	Safeguard	Normal	—	—	25	TM46	Thief	Dark	40	100	10
TM21	Frustration	Normal	—	100	20	TM48	Skill Swap	Psychic	—	100	10
TM24	Thunderbolt	Electric	95	100	15	TM49	Snatch	Dark	—	100	10
TM27	Return	Normal	—	100	20	HM05	Flash	Normal	—	70	20
TM29	Psychic	Psychic	90	100	10						

MOVE TUTOR
FireRed/LeafGreen and Emerald Only

Body Slam* | Double-Edge* | Dream Eater*
Mimic | Substitute | Thunder Wave*

Emerald Only

Defense Curl* | Endure* | Fire Punch*
Ice Punch* | Icy Wind* | Mud-Slap*
Psych Up* | Sleep Talk | Snore*
Swagger | Thunderpunch* |

*Battle Frontier tutor move (Emerald)

283 Surskit™

BUG | WATER

GENERAL INFO
SPECIES: Pond Skater Pokémon
HEIGHT: 1'08"
WEIGHT: 4 lbs.
ABILITY: Swift Swim
Doubles Surskit's Speed when it is raining.

STATS
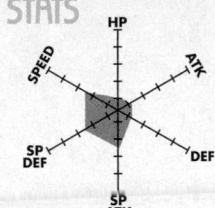

EVOLUTIONS
 LV22

LOCATION(S):

RUBY — Rarity: **Rare**
Routes 102, 111, 114, 117, 120

SAPPHIRE — Rarity: **Rare**
Routes 102, 111, 114, 117, 120

FIRERED — Rarity: **None**
Trade from *Ruby/Sapphire*

LEAFGREEN — Rarity: **None**
Trade from *Ruby/Sapphire*

COLOSSEUM — Rarity: **None**
Trade from *Ruby/Sapphire*

EMERALD — Rarity: **None**
Trade from *Ruby/Sapphire*

XD — Rarity: **Rare**
Oasis Poké Spot

MOVES

Level	Attack	Type	Power	ACC	PP	Level	Attack	Type	Power	ACC	PP
—	Bubble	Water	20	100	30	25	Bubblebeam	Water	65	100	20
7	Quick Attack	Normal	40	100	30	31	Agility	Psychic	—	—	30
13	Sweet Scent	Normal	—	100	20	37	Mist	Ice	—	—	30
19	Water Sport	Water	—	100	15	37	Haze	Ice	—	—	30

TM/HM

TM/HM#	Name	Type	Power	ACC	PP	TM/HM#	Name	Type	Power	ACC	PP
TM03	Water Pulse	Water	60	100	20	TM22	Solarbeam	Grass	120	100	10
TM06	Toxic	Poison	—	85	10	TM27	Return	Normal	—	100	20
TM10	Hidden Power	Normal	—	100	15	TM30	Shadow Ball	Ghost	60	—	20
TM11	Sunny Day	Fire	—	—	5	TM32	Double Team	Normal	—	—	15
TM13	Ice Beam	Ice	95	100	10	TM42	Facade	Normal	70	100	20
TM14	Blizzard	Ice	120	70	5	TM43	Secret Power	Normal	70	100	20
TM17	Protect	Normal	—	—	10	TM44	Rest	Psychic	—	—	10
TM18	Rain Dance	Water	—	—	5	TM45	Attract	Normal	—	100	15
TM19	Giga Drain	Grass	60	100	5	TM46	Thief	Dark	40	100	10
TM21	Frustration	Normal	—	100	20	HM05	Flash	Normal	—	70	20

EGG MOVES*

Name	Type	Power	ACC	PP
Foresight	Normal	—	100	40
Mud Shot	Ground	55	95	15
Psybeam	Psychic	65	100	20
Hydro Pump	Water	120	80	5
Mind Reader	Normal	—	100	5

*Learned Via Breeding

MOVE TUTOR
FireRed/LeafGreen and *Emerald* Only

Double-Edge	Mimic	Substitute

Emerald Only

Endure*	Icy Wind*	Psych Up*
Sleep Talk	Snore*	Swagger
Swift*		

*Battle Frontier tutor move (*Emerald*)

284 Masquerain™

BUG | FLYING

GENERAL INFO
SPECIES: Eyeball Pokémon
HEIGHT: 2'07"
WEIGHT: 8 lbs.
ABILITY: Intimidate
Lowers the opponent's Attack by one point at the start of a battle.

STATS
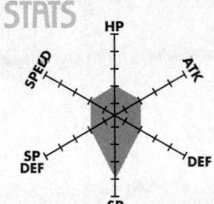

EVOLUTIONS
 LV22

LOCATION(S):

RUBY — Rarity: **Evolve**
Evolve Surskit

SAPPHIRE — Rarity: **Evolve**
Evolve Surskit

FIRERED — Rarity: **None**
Trade from *Ruby/Sapphire*

LEAFGREEN — Rarity: **None**
Trade from *Ruby/Sapphire*

COLOSSEUM — Rarity: **None**
Trade from *Ruby/Sapphire*

EMERALD — Rarity: **None**
Trade from *Ruby/Sapphire*

XD — Rarity: **Evolve**
Evolve Surskit

MOVES

Level	Attack	Type	Power	ACC	PP	Level	Attack	Type	Power	ACC	PP
—	Bubble	Water	20	100	30	33	Scary Face	Normal	—	90	10
—/7	Quick Attack	Normal	40	100	30	40	Stun Spore	Grass	—	75	30
—/13	Sweet Scent	Normal	—	100	20	47	Silver Wind	Bug	60	100	5
—/19	Water Sport	Water	—	100	15	53	Whirlwind	Normal	—	100	20
26	Gust	Flying	40	100	35			# = *Emerald* Only			

TM/HM

TM/HM#	Name	Type	Power	ACC	PP	TM/HM#	Name	Type	Power	ACC	PP
TM03	Water Pulse	Water	60	100	20	TM22	Solarbeam	Grass	120	100	10
TM06	Toxic	Poison	—	85	10	TM27	Return	Normal	—	100	20
TM10	Hidden Power	Normal	—	100	15	TM30	Shadow Ball	Ghost	60	—	20
TM11	Sunny Day	Fire	—	—	5	TM32	Double Team	Normal	—	—	15
TM13	Ice Beam	Ice	95	100	10	TM40	Aerial Ace	Flying	60	—	20
TM14	Blizzard	Ice	120	70	5	TM42	Facade	Normal	70	100	20
TM15	Hyper Beam	Normal	150	90	5	TM43	Secret Power	Normal	70	100	20
TM17	Protect	Normal	—	—	10	TM44	Rest	Psychic	—	—	10
TM18	Rain Dance	Water	—	—	5	TM45	Attract	Normal	—	100	15
TM19	Giga Drain	Grass	60	100	5	TM46	Thief	Dark	40	100	10
TM21	Frustration	Normal	—	100	20	HM05	Flash	Normal	—	70	20

MOVE TUTOR
FireRed/LeafGreen and *Emerald* Only

Double-Edge	Mimic	Substitute

Emerald Only

Endure*	Icy Wind*	Psych Up*
Sleep Talk	Snore*	Swagger
Swift*		

*Battle Frontier tutor move (*Emerald*)

285 Shroomish™

GRASS

GENERAL INFO
SPECIES: Mushroom Pokémon
HEIGHT: 1'04"
WEIGHT: 10 lbs.
ABILITY: Effect Spore

If physically attacked, Shroomish has a 10% chance of inflicting Paralysis, Poison, or Sleep on its opponent.

STATS
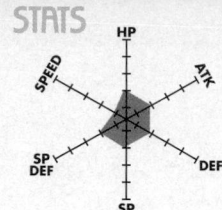

EVOLUTIONS
 LV23

LOCATION(S):

RUBY   **Rarity: Rare**
Petalburg Woods

SAPPHIRE   **Rarity: Rare**
Petalburg Woods

FIRERED   **Rarity: None**
Trade from *Ruby/Sapphire*

LEAFGREEN   **Rarity: None**
Trade from *Ruby/Sapphire*

COLOSSEUM   **Rarity: None**
Trade from *Ruby/Sapphire*

EMERALD   **Rarity: Common**
Petalburg Woods

XD   **Rarity: Only One**
Cipher Lab (Capture from Cipher R&D Klots)

MOVES

Level	Attack	Type	Power	ACC	PP	Level	Attack	Type	Power	ACC	PP
—	Absorb	Grass	20	100	20	22	Headbutt	Normal	70	100	15
4	Tackle	Normal	35	95	35	28	Poisonpowder	Poison	—	75	35
7	Stun Spore	Grass	—	75	30	36	Growth	Normal	—	—	40
10	Leech Seed	Grass	—	90	10	45	Giga Drain	Grass	60	100	5
16	Mega Drain	Grass	40	100	10	54	Spore	Grass	—	100	15

TM/HM

TM/HM#	Name	Type	Power	ACC	PP	TM/HM#	Name	Type	Power	ACC	PP
TM06	Toxic	Poison	—	85	10	TM27	Return	Normal	—	100	20
TM09	Bullet Seed	Grass	10	100	30	TM32	Double Team	Normal	—	—	15
TM10	Hidden Power	Normal	—	100	15	TM36	Sludge Bomb	Poison	90	100	10
TM11	Sunny Day	Fire	—	—	5	TM42	Facade	Normal	70	100	20
TM17	Protect	Normal	—	—	10	TM43	Secret Power	Normal	70	100	20
TM19	Giga Drain	Grass	60	100	5	TM44	Rest	Psychic	—	—	10
TM20	Safeguard	Normal	—	—	25	TM45	Attract	Normal	—	100	15
TM21	Frustration	Normal	—	100	20	TM49	Snatch	Dark	—	100	10
TM22	Solarbeam	Grass	120	100	10	HM05	Flash	Normal	—	70	20

EGG MOVES*

Name	Type	Power	ACC	PP
Fake Tears	Dark	—	100	20
Swagger	Normal	—	90	15
Charm	Normal	—	100	20
False Swipe	Normal	40	100	40
Helping Hand	Normal	—	100	20

Learned Via Breeding

MOVE TUTOR
FireRed/LeafGreen and *Emerald* Only

Body Slam*	Double-Edge	Mimic
Substitute	Swords Dance*	

Emerald Only

Endure*	Sleep Talk	Snore*
Swagger		

*Battle Frontier tutor move (*Emerald*)

---

286 Breloom™

GRASS   **FIGHTING**

GENERAL INFO
SPECIES: Mushroom Pokémon
HEIGHT: 3'11"
WEIGHT: 86 lbs.
ABILITY: Effect Spore

If physically attacked, Breloom has a 10% chance of inflicting Paralysis, Poison, or Sleep on its opponent.

STATS
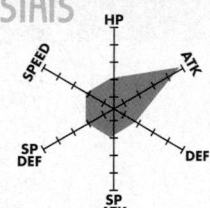

EVOLUTIONS
 LV23

LOCATION(S):

RUBY   **Rarity: Evolve**
Evolve Shroomish

SAPPHIRE   **Rarity: Evolve**
Evolve Shroomish

FIRERED   **Rarity: None**
Trade from *Ruby/Sapphire*

LEAFGREEN   **Rarity: None**
Trade from *Ruby/Sapphire*

COLOSSEUM   **Rarity: None**
Trade from *Ruby/Sapphire*

EMERALD   **Rarity: Evolve**
Evolve Shroomish

XD   **Rarity: Evolve**
Evolve Shroomish

MOVES

Level	Attack	Type	Power	ACC	PP	Level	Attack	Type	Power	ACC	PP
—	Absorb	Grass	20	100	20	23	Mach Punch	Fighting	40	100	30
—/4	Tackle	Normal	35	95	35	28	Counter	Fighting	—	100	20
—/7	Stun Spore	Grass	—	75	30	36	Sky Uppercut	Fighting	85	90	15
—/10	Leech Seed	Grass	—	90	10	45	Mind Reader	Normal	—	100	5
16	Mega Drain	Grass	40	100	10	54	Dynamicpunch	Fighting	100	50	5
22	Headbutt	Normal	70	100	15						

 # = Emerald Only

TM/HM

TM/HM#	Name	Type	Power	ACC	PP	TM/HM#	Name	Type	Power	ACC	PP
TM01	Focus Punch	Fighting	150	100	20	TM27	Return	Normal	—	100	20
TM06	Toxic	Poison	—	85	10	TM31	Brick Break	Fighting	75	100	15
TM08	Bulk Up	Fighting	—	—	20	TM32	Double Team	Normal	—	—	15
TM09	Bullet Seed	Grass	10	100	30	TM36	Sludge Bomb	Poison	90	100	10
TM10	Hidden Power	Normal	—	100	15	TM42	Facade	Normal	70	100	20
TM11	Sunny Day	Fire	—	—	5	TM43	Secret Power	Normal	70	100	20
TM15	Hyper Beam	Normal	150	90	5	TM44	Rest	Psychic	—	—	10
TM17	Protect	Normal	—	—	10	TM45	Attract	Normal	—	100	15
TM19	Giga Drain	Grass	60	100	5	TM49	Snatch	Dark	—	100	10
TM20	Safeguard	Normal	—	—	25	HM01	Cut	Normal	50	95	30
TM21	Frustration	Normal	—	100	20	HM04	Strength	Normal	80	100	15
TM22	Solarbeam	Grass	120	100	10	HM05	Flash	Normal	—	70	20
TM23	Iron Tail	Steel	100	75	15	HM06	Rock Smash	Fighting	20	100	15

MOVE TUTOR
FireRed/LeafGreen and *Emerald* Only

Body Slam*	Counter*	Double-Edge
Mega Kick*	Mega Punch*	Mimic
Seismic Toss*	Substitute	Swords Dance*

Emerald Only

Dynamicpunch	Endure*	Fury Cutter
Mud-Slap*	Sleep Talk	Snore*
Swagger		

*Battle Frontier tutor move (*Emerald*)

287 Slakoth™

NORMAL

GENERAL INFO

SPECIES: Slacker Pokémon
HEIGHT: 2'07"
WEIGHT: 53 lbs.
ABILITY: Truant
Can only attack every other turn.

STATS

(radar chart: HP, ATK, DEF, SP ATK, SP DEF, SPEED)

EVOLUTIONS

LV18 LV36

LOCATION[S]:

RUBY	Rarity: **Rare**
Petalburg Woods	
SAPPHIRE	Rarity: **Rare**
Petalburg Woods	
FIRERED	Rarity: **None**
Trade from *Ruby/Sapphire/Emerald*	
LEAFGREEN	Rarity: **None**
Trade from *Ruby/Sapphire/Emerald*	
COLOSSEUM	Rarity: **None**
Trade from *Ruby/Sapphire/Emerald*	
EMERALD	Rarity: **Rare**
Petalburg Woods	
XD	Rarity: **None**
Trade from *Ruby/Sapphire/Emerald*	

MOVES

Level	Attack	Type	Power	ACC	PP	Level	Attack	Type	Power	ACC	PP
—	Scratch	Normal	40	100	35	19	Faint Attack	Dark	60	—	20
—	Yawn	Normal	—	100	10	25	Amnesia	Psychic	—	—	20
7	Encore	Normal	—	100	5	31	Covet	Normal	40	100	40
13	Slack Off	Normal	—	100	10	37	Counter	Fighting	—	100	20
						43	Flail	Normal	—	100	15

TM/HM

TM/HM#	Name	Type	Power	ACC	PP	TM/HM#	Name	Type	Power	ACC	PP
TM01	Focus Punch	Fighting	150	100	20	TM30	Shadow Ball	Ghost	60	—	20
TM03	Water Pulse	Water	60	100	20	TM31	Brick Break	Fighting	75	100	15
TM06	Toxic	Poison	—	85	10	TM32	Double Team	Normal	—	—	15
TM08	Bulk Up	Fighting	—	—	20	TM34	Shock Wave	Electric	60	—	20
TM10	Hidden Power	Normal	—	100	15	TM35	Flamethrower	Fire	95	100	15
TM11	Sunny Day	Fire	—	—	5	TM38	Fire Blast	Fire	120	85	5
TM13	Ice Beam	Ice	95	100	10	TM40	Aerial Ace	Flying	60	—	20
TM14	Blizzard	Ice	120	70	5	TM42	Facade	Normal	70	100	20
TM17	Protect	Normal	—	—	10	TM43	Secret Power	Normal	70	100	20
TM18	Rain Dance	Water	—	—	5	TM44	Rest	Psychic	—	—	10
TM21	Frustration	Normal	—	100	20	TM45	Attract	Normal	—	100	15
TM22	Solarbeam	Grass	120	100	10	HM01	Cut	Normal	50	95	30
TM24	Thunderbolt	Electric	95	100	15	HM04	Strength	Normal	80	100	15
TM25	Thunder	Electric	120	70	10	HM06	Rock Smash	Fighting	20	100	15
TM27	Return	Normal	—	100	20						

EGG MOVES*

Name	Type	Power	ACC	PP
Pursuit	Dark	40	100	20
Slash	Normal	70	100	20
Body Slam	Normal	85	100	15
Snore	Normal	40	100	15
Crush Claw	Normal	75	95	10
Curse	—	—	—	10
Sleep Talk	Normal	—	—	10

*Learned Via Breeding

MOVE TUTOR

FireRed/LeafGreen and Emerald Only

Body Slam*	Counter*	Double-Edge
Mega Kick*	Mega Punch*	Mimic
Rock Slide*	Seismic Toss*	Substitute

Emerald Only

Dynamicpunch	Endure*	Fire Punch*
Fury Cutter	Ice Punch*	Icy Wind*
Mud-Slap*	Sleep Talk	Snore*
Swagger	Thunderpunch*	

*Battle Frontier tutor move (*Emerald*)

---

288 Vigoroth™

NORMAL

GENERAL INFO

SPECIES: Wild Monkey Pokémon
HEIGHT: 4'07"
WEIGHT: 103 lbs.
ABILITY: Vital Spirit
Vigoroth cannot be put to Sleep.

STATS

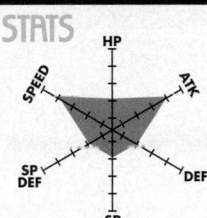

(radar chart: HP, ATK, DEF, SP ATK, SP DEF, SPEED)

EVOLUTIONS

 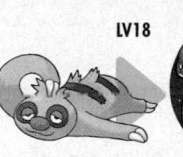  

LV18 LV36

LOCATION[S]:

RUBY	Rarity: **Evolve**
Evolve Slakoth	
SAPPHIRE	Rarity: **Evolve**
Evolve Slakoth	
FIRERED	Rarity: **None**
Trade from *Ruby/Sapphire/Emerald*	
LEAFGREEN	Rarity: **None**
Trade from *Ruby/Sapphire/Emerald*	
COLOSSEUM	Rarity: **None**
Trade from *Ruby/Sapphire/Emerald*	
EMERALD	Rarity: **Evolve**
Evolve Slakoth	
XD	Rarity: **None**
Trade from *Ruby/Sapphire/Emerald*	

MOVES

Level	Attack	Type	Power	ACC	PP	Level	Attack	Type	Power	ACC	PP
—	Scratch	Normal	40	100	35	25	Endure	Normal	—	—	10
—	Focus Energy	Normal	—	—	30	31	Slash	Normal	70	100	20
—/3	Uproar	Normal	50	100	10	37	Counter	Fighting	—	100	20
—/7	Encore	Normal	—	100	5	43	Focus Punch	Fighting	150	100	20
19	Fury Swipes	Normal	18	80	15	49	Reversal	Fighting	—	100	15

= *Emerald* Only

TM/HM

TM/HM#	Name	Type	Power	ACC	PP	TM/HM#	Name	Type	Power	ACC	PP
TM01	Focus Punch	Fighting	150	100	20	TM26	Earthquake	Ground	100	100	10
TM03	Water Pulse	Water	60	100	20	TM27	Return	Normal	—	100	20
TM05	Roar	Normal	—	100	20	TM30	Shadow Punch	Ghost	60	—	20
TM06	Toxic	Poison	—	85	10	TM31	Brick Break	Fighting	75	100	15
TM08	Bulk Up	Fighting	—	—	20	TM32	Double Team	Normal	—	—	15
TM10	Hidden Power	Normal	—	100	15	TM34	Shock Wave	Electric	60	—	20
TM11	Sunny Day	Fire	—	—	5	TM35	Flamethrower	Fire	95	100	15
TM12	Taunt	Dark	—	100	20	TM38	Fire Blast	Fire	120	85	5
TM13	Ice Beam	Ice	95	100	10	TM40	Aerial Ace	Flying	60	—	20
TM14	Blizzard	Ice	120	70	5	TM42	Facade	Normal	70	100	20
TM17	Protect	Normal	—	—	10	TM43	Secret Power	Normal	70	100	20
TM18	Rain Dance	Water	—	—	5	TM44	Rest	Psychic	—	—	10
TM21	Frustration	Normal	—	100	20	TM45	Attract	Normal	—	100	15
TM22	Solarbeam	Grass	120	100	10	HM01	Cut	Normal	50	95	30
TM24	Thunderbolt	Electric	95	100	15	HM04	Strength	Normal	80	100	15
TM25	Thunder	Electric	120	70	10	HM06	Rock Smash	Fighting	20	100	15

MOVE TUTOR

FireRed/LeafGreen and Emerald Only

Body Slam*	Counter*	Double-Edge
Mega Kick*	Mega Punch*	Mimic
Rock Slide*	Seismic Toss*	Substitute

Emerald Only

Dynamicpunch	Endure*	Fire Punch*
Fury Cutter	Ice Punch*	Icy Wind*
Mud-Slap*	Sleep Talk	Snore*
Swagger	Thunderpunch*	

*Battle Frontier tutor move (*Emerald*)

289 Slaking™

NORMAL

GENERAL INFO
SPECIES: Lazy Pokémon
HEIGHT: 6'07"
WEIGHT: 288 lbs.
ABILITY: Truant
Slaking can only attack every other turn.

STATS
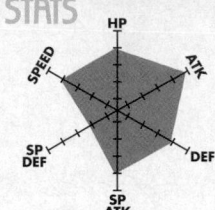

EVOLUTIONS
 LV18  LV36

LOCATION(S):

RUBY — Rarity: **Evolve**
Evolve Vigoroth

SAPPHIRE — Rarity: **Evolve**
Evolve Vigoroth

FIRERED — Rarity: **None**
Trade from *Ruby/Sapphire/Emerald*

LEAFGREEN — Rarity: **None**
Trade from *Ruby/Sapphire/Emerald*

COLOSSEUM — Rarity: **None**
Trade from *Ruby/Sapphire/Emerald*

EMERALD — Rarity: **Evolve**
Evolve Vigoroth

XD — Rarity: **None**
Trade from *Ruby/Sapphire/Emerald*

MOVES

Level	Attack	Type	Power	ACC	PP
—	Scratch	Normal	40	100	35
—	Yawn	Normal	—	100	10
—/1	Encore	Normal	—	100	5
—/13	Slack Off	Normal	—	100	10
19	Faint Attack	Dark	60	—	20
25	Amnesia	Psychic	—	—	20
31	Covet	Normal	40	100	40
36	Swagger	Normal	—	90	15
37	Counter	Fighting	—	100	20
43	Flail	Normal	—	100	15

= *Emerald* Only

TM/HM

TM/HM#	Name	Type	Power	ACC	PP
TM01	Focus Punch	Fighting	150	100	20
TM03	Water Pulse	Water	60	100	20
TM05	Roar	Normal	—	100	20
TM06	Toxic	Poison	—	85	10
TM08	Bulk Up	Fighting	—	—	20
TM10	Hidden Power	Normal	—	100	15
TM11	Sunny Day	Fire	—	—	5
TM12	Taunt	Dark	—	100	20
TM13	Ice Beam	Ice	95	100	10
TM14	Blizzard	Ice	120	70	5
TM15	Hyper Beam	Normal	150	90	5
TM17	Protect	Normal	—	—	10
TM18	Rain Dance	Water	—	—	5
TM21	Frustration	Normal	—	100	20
TM22	Solarbeam	Grass	120	100	10
TM24	Thunderbolt	Electric	95	100	15
TM25	Thunder	Electric	120	70	10
TM26	Earthquake	Ground	100	100	10
TM27	Return	Normal	—	100	20
TM30	Shadow Ball	Ghost	60	—	20
TM31	Brick Break	Fighting	75	100	15
TM32	Double Team	Normal	—	—	15
TM34	Shock Wave	Electric	60	—	20
TM35	Flamethrower	Fire	95	100	15
TM38	Fire Blast	Fire	120	85	5
TM40	Aerial Ace	Flying	60	—	20
TM42	Facade	Normal	70	100	20
TM43	Secret Power	Normal	70	100	20
TM44	Rest	Psychic	—	—	10
TM45	Attract	Normal	—	100	15
HM01	Cut	Normal	50	95	30
HM04	Strength	Normal	80	100	15
HM06	Rock Smash	Fighting	20	100	15

MOVE TUTOR
FireRed/LeafGreen and ***Emerald*** **Only**

Body Slam*	Counter*	Double-Edge
Mega Kick*	Mega Punch*	Mimic
Rock Slide*	Substitute	Swords Dance*

Emerald **Only**

Dynamicpunch	Endure*	Fire Punch*
Fury Cutter	Ice Punch*	Icy Wind*
Mud-Slap*	Sleep Talk	Snore*
Swagger	Thunderpunch*	

*Battle Frontier tutor move (*Emerald*)

---

290 Nincada™

BUG GROUND

GENERAL INFO
SPECIES: Trainee Pokémon
HEIGHT: 1'08"
WEIGHT: 12 lbs.
ABILITY: Compoundeyes
Raises Nincada's Accuracy 30% in battle.

STATS
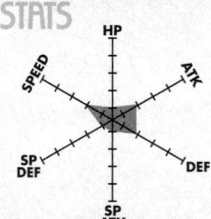

EVOLUTIONS
 LV20
LV20
(WHEN SPARE SLOT IN TEAM WITH
AN EMPTY POKÉ BALL AVAILABLE)

LOCATION(S):

RUBY — Rarity: **Rare**
Route 116

SAPPHIRE — Rarity: **Rare**
Route 116

FIRERED — Rarity: **None**
Trade from *Ruby/Sapphire/Emerald*

LEAFGREEN — Rarity: **None**
Trade from *Ruby/Sapphire/Emerald*

COLOSSEUM — Rarity: **None**
Trade from *Ruby/Sapphire/Emerald*

EMERALD — Rarity: **Rare**
Route 116

XD — Rarity: **None**
Trade from *Ruby/Sapphire/Emerald*

MOVES

Level	Attack	Type	Power	ACC	PP
—	Scratch	Normal	40	100	35
—	Harden	Normal	—	—	30
5	Leech Life	Bug	20	100	15
9	Sand-Attack	Ground	—	100	15
14	Fury Swipes	Normal	18	80	15
19	Mind Reader	Normal	—	100	5
25	False Swipe	Normal	40	100	40
31	Mud-Slap	Ground	20	100	10
38	Metal-Claw	Steel	50	95	35
45	Dig	Ground	60	100	10

TM/HM

TM/HM#	Name	Type	Power	ACC	PP
TM06	Toxic	Poison	—	85	10
TM10	Hidden Power	Normal	—	100	15
TM11	Sunny Day	Fire	—	—	5
TM17	Protect	Normal	—	—	10
TM19	Giga Drain	Grass	60	100	5
TM21	Frustration	Normal	—	100	20
TM22	Solarbeam	Grass	120	100	10
TM27	Return	Normal	—	100	20
TM28	Dig	Ground	60	100	10
TM30	Shadow Ball	Ghost	60	—	20
TM32	Double Team	Normal	—	—	15
TM37	Sandstorm	Rock	—	—	10
TM40	Aerial Ace	Flying	60	—	20
TM42	Facade	Normal	70	100	20
TM43	Secret Power	Normal	70	100	20
TM44	Rest	Psychic	—	—	10
HM01	Cut	Normal	50	95	30
HM05	Flash	Normal	—	70	20

EGG MOVES*

Name	Type	Power	ACC	PP
Endure	Normal	—	—	10
Faint Attack	Dark	60	—	20
Silver Wind	Bug	60	100	5
Whirlwind	Normal	—	100	20

*Learned Via Breeding

MOVE TUTOR
FireRed/LeafGreen and ***Emerald*** **Only**

Double-Edge	Mimic	Substitute

Emerald **Only**

Endure*	Fury Cutter	Mud-Slap*
Sleep Talk	Snore*	Swagger

*Battle Frontier tutor move (*Emerald*)

291 Ninjask™

BUG | FLYING

GENERAL INFO
SPECIES: Ninja Pokémon
HEIGHT: 2'07"
WEIGHT: 26 lbs.
ABILITY: Speed Boost
Increases Ninjask's Speed by one point each turn.

STATS

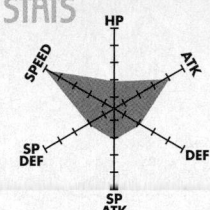

EVOLUTIONS

LV20

LOCATION[S]:

RUBY Rarity: **Evolve**
Evolve Nincada

SAPPHIRE Rarity: **Evolve**
Evolve Nincada

FIRERED Rarity: **None**
Trade from *Ruby/Sapphire/Emerald*

LEAFGREEN Rarity: **None**
Trade from *Ruby/Sapphire/Emerald*

COLOSSEUM Rarity: **None**
Trade from *Ruby/Sapphire/Emerald*

EMERALD Rarity: **Evolve**
Evolve Nincada

XD Rarity: **None**
Trade from *Ruby/Sapphire/Emerald*

MOVES

Level	Attack	Type	Power	ACC	PP	Level	Attack	Type	Power	ACC	PP
—	Scratch	Normal	40	100	35	20	Fury Cutter	Bug	10	95	20
—	Harden	Normal	—	—	30	20	Screech	Normal	—	85	40
—/5	Leech Life	Bug	20	100	15	25	Swords Dance	Normal	—	—	30
—/9	Sand-Attack	Ground	—	100	15	31	Slash	Normal	70	100	20
14	Fury Swipes	Normal	18	80	15	38	Agility	Psychic	—	—	30
19	Mind Reader	Normal	—	100	5	45	Baton Pass	Normal	—	—	40
20	Double Team	Normal	—	—	15						
							# = Emerald Only				

TM/HM

TM/HM#	Name	Type	Power	ACC	PP	TM/HM#	Name	Type	Power	ACC	PP
TM06	Toxic	Poison	—	85	10	TM32	Double Team	Normal	—	—	15
TM10	Hidden Power	Normal	—	100	15	TM37	Sandstorm	Rock	—	—	10
TM11	Sunny Day	Fire	—	—	5	TM40	Aerial Ace	Flying	60	—	20
TM15	Hyper Beam	Normal	150	90	5	TM42	Facade	Normal	70	100	20
TM17	Protect	Normal	—	—	10	TM43	Secret Power	Normal	70	100	20
TM19	Giga Drain	Grass	60	100	5	TM44	Rest	Psychic	—	—	10
TM21	Frustration	Normal	—	100	20	TM45	Attract	Normal	—	100	15
TM22	Solarbeam	Grass	120	100	10	TM46	Thief	Dark	40	100	10
TM27	Return	Normal	—	100	20	HM01	Cut	Normal	50	95	30
TM28	Dig	Ground	60	100	10	HM05	Flash	Normal	—	70	20
TM30	Shadow Ball	Ghost	60	—	20						

MOVE TUTOR
FireRed/LeafGreen and *Emerald* Only

Double-Edge	Mimic	Substitute
Swords Dance*		

Emerald Only

Endure*	Fury Cutter*	Mud-Slap*
Sleep Talk	Snore*	Swagger
Swift*		

*Battle Frontier tutor move (*Emerald*)

---

292 Shedinja™

BUG | GHOST

GENERAL INFO
SPECIES: Shed Pokémon
HEIGHT: 2'07"
WEIGHT: 3 lbs.
ABILITY: Wonder Guard
Shedinja is only harmed by moves that cause "Super Effective" damage.

STATS

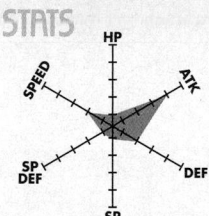

EVOLUTIONS

LV20
**(WHEN SPARE SLOT IN TEAM WITH
AN EMPTY POKÉ BALL AVAILABLE)**

LOCATION[S]:

RUBY Rarity: **Evolve**
Evolve Nincada

SAPPHIRE Rarity: **Evolve**
Evolve Nincada

FIRERED Rarity: **None**
Trade from *Ruby/Sapphire/Emerald*

LEAFGREEN Rarity: **None**
Trade from *Ruby/Sapphire/Emerald*

COLOSSEUM Rarity: **None**
Trade from *Ruby/Sapphire/Emerald*

EMERALD Rarity: **Evolve**
Evolve Nincada

XD Rarity: **None**
Trade from *Ruby/Sapphire/Emerald*

MOVES

Level	Attack	Type	Power	ACC	PP	Level	Attack	Type	Power	ACC	PP
—	Scratch	Normal	40	100	35	19	Mind Reader	Normal	—	100	5
—	Harden	Normal	—	—	30	25	Spite	Ghost	—	100	10
5	Leech Life	Bug	20	100	15	31	Confuse Ray	Ghost	—	100	10
9	Sand Attack	Ground	—	100	15	38	Shadow Ball	Ghost	80	100	15
14	Fury Swipes	Normal	18	80	15	45	Grudge	Ghost	—	100	5

TM/HM

TM/HM#	Name	Type	Power	ACC	PP	TM/HM#	Name	Type	Power	ACC	PP
TM06	Toxic	Poison	—	85	10	TM30	Shadow Ball	Ghost	60	—	20
TM10	Hidden Power	Normal	—	100	15	TM32	Double Team	Normal	—	—	15
TM11	Sunny Day	Fire	—	—	5	TM37	Sandstorm	Rock	—	—	10
TM15	Hyper Beam	Normal	150	90	5	TM40	Aerial Ace	Flying	60	—	20
TM17	Protect	Normal	—	—	10	TM42	Facade	Normal	70	100	20
TM19	Giga Drain	Grass	60	100	5	TM43	Secret Power	Normal	70	100	20
TM21	Frustration	Normal	—	100	20	TM44	Rest	Psychic	—	—	10
TM22	Solarbeam	Grass	120	100	10	TM46	Thief	Dark	40	100	10
TM27	Return	Normal	—	100	20	HM01	Cut	Normal	50	95	30
TM28	Dig	Ground	60	100	10	HM05	Flash	Normal	—	70	20

MOVE TUTOR
FireRed/LeafGreen and *Emerald* Only

Double-Edge	Dream Eater*	Mimic
Substitute		

Emerald Only

Endure*	Fury Cutter*	Mud-Slap*
Sleep Talk	Snore*	Swagger
Swift*		

*Battle Frontier tutor move (*Emerald*)

293 Whismur™

NORMAL

GENERAL INFO

SPECIES: Whisper Pokémon
HEIGHT: 2'00"
WEIGHT: 36 lbs.
ABILITY: Soundproof

Prevents Whismur from being hit by Grasswhistle, Growl, Heal Bell, Hyper Voice, Metal Sound, Perish Song, Roar, Screech, Sing, Snore, Supersonic, and Uproar.

STATS

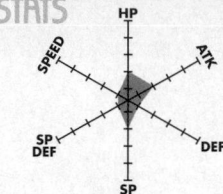

EVOLUTIONS

LV20   LV40

LOCATION(S):

RUBY	Rarity: **Common**

Route 116, Victory Road

SAPPHIRE	Rarity: **Common**

Route 116, Victory Road

FIRERED	Rarity: **None**

Trade from *Ruby/Sapphire/Emerald*

LEAFGREEN	Rarity: **None**

Trade from *Ruby/Sapphire/Emerald*

COLOSSEUM	Rarity: **None**

Trade from *Ruby/Sapphire/Emerald*

EMERALD	Rarity: **Common**

Route 116, Desert Pass, Rusturf Tunnel, Victory Road

XD	Rarity: **None**

Trade from *Ruby/Sapphire/Emerald*

MOVES

Level	Attack	Type	Power	ACC	PP	Level	Attack	Type	Power	ACC	PP
—	Pound	Normal	40	100	35	25	Stomp	Normal	65	100	20
5	Uproar	Normal	50	100	10	31	Screech	Normal	—	85	40
11	Astonish	Ghost	30	100	15	35	Roar	Normal	—	100	20
15	Howl	Normal	—	—	40	41	Rest	Psychic	—	—	10
21	Supersonic	Normal	—	55	20	41	Sleep Talk	Normal	—	—	10
						45	Hyper Voice	Normal	90	100	10

TM/HM

TM/HM#	Name	Type	Power	ACC	PP	TM/HM#	Name	Type	Power	ACC	PP
TM03	Water Pulse	Water	60	100	20	TM27	Return	Normal	—	100	20
TM05	Roar	Normal	—	100	20	TM30	Shadow Ball	Ghost	60	—	20
TM06	Toxic	Poison	—	85	10	TM32	Double Team	Normal	—	—	15
TM10	Hidden Power	Normal	—	100	15	TM34	Shock Wave	Electric	60	—	20
TM11	Sunny Day	Fire	—	—	5	TM35	Flamethrower	Fire	95	100	15
TM13	Ice Beam	Ice	95	100	10	TM38	Fire Blast	Fire	120	85	5
TM14	Blizzard	Ice	120	70	5	TM42	Facade	Normal	70	100	20
TM17	Protect	Normal	—	—	10	TM43	Secret Power	Normal	70	100	20
TM18	Rain Dance	Water	—	—	5	TM44	Rest	Psychic	—	—	10
TM21	Frustration	Normal	—	100	20	TM45	Attract	Normal	—	100	15
TM22	Solarbeam	Grass	120	100	10						

EGG MOVES*

Name	Type	Power	ACC	PP
Take Down	Normal	90	85	20
Snore	Normal	40	100	15
Swagger	Normal	—	90	15
Extrasensory	Psychic	80	100	30
Smellingsalt	Normal	60	100	10

*Learned Via Breeding

MOVE TUTOR

***FireRed/LeafGreen* and *Emerald* Only**

Body Slam*	Counter*	Double-Edge
Mega Kick*	Mega Punch*	Mimic
Seismic Toss*	Substitute	

***Emerald* Only**

Dynamicpunch*	Endure*	Fire Punch*
Fury Cutter*	Ice Punch*	Icy Wind*
Mud-Slap*	Sleep Talk	Snore*
Swagger	Thunderpunch*	

*Battle Frontier tutor move (*Emerald*)

294 Loudred™

NORMAL

GENERAL INFO

SPECIES: Big Voice Pokémon
HEIGHT: 3'03"
WEIGHT: 89 lbs.
ABILITY: Soundproof

Prevents Loudred from being hit by Grasswhistle, Growl, Heal Bell, Hyper Voice, Metal Sound, Perish Song, Roar, Screech, Sing, Snore, Supersonic, and Uproar.

STATS

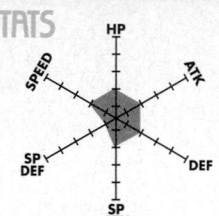

EVOLUTIONS

LV20   LV40

LOCATION(S):

RUBY	Rarity: **Rare**

Victory Road

SAPPHIRE	Rarity: **Rare**

Victory Road

FIRERED	Rarity: **None**

Trade from *Ruby/Sapphire/Emerald*

LEAFGREEN	Rarity: **None**

Trade from *Ruby/Sapphire/Emerald*

COLOSSEUM	Rarity: **None**

Trade from *Ruby/Sapphire/Emerald*

EMERALD	Rarity: **Rare**

Desert Pass, Victory Road

XD	Rarity: **None**

Trade from *Ruby/Sapphire/Emerald*

MOVES

Level	Attack	Type	Power	ACC	PP	Level	Attack	Type	Power	ACC	PP
—	Pound	Normal	40	100	35	29	Stomp	Normal	65	100	20
—/5	Uproar	Normal	50	100	10	37	Screech	Normal	—	85	40
—/11	Astonish	Ghost	30	100	15	43	Roar	Normal	—	100	20
—/15	Howl	Normal	—	—	40	51	Rest	Psychic	—	—	10
23	Supersonic	Normal	—	55	20	51	Sleep Talk	Normal	—	—	10
29	Stomp	Normal	65	100	20	57	Hyper Voice	Normal	90	100	10

= *Emerald* Only

TM/HM

TM/HM#	Name	Type	Power	ACC	PP	TM/HM#	Name	Type	Power	ACC	PP
TM03	Water Pulse	Water	60	100	20	TM30	Shadow Ball	Ghost	60	—	20
TM05	Roar	Normal	—	100	20	TM31	Brick Break	Fighting	75	100	15
TM06	Toxic	Poison	—	85	10	TM32	Double Team	Normal	—	—	15
TM10	Hidden Power	Normal	—	100	15	TM34	Shock Wave	Electric	60	—	20
TM11	Sunny Day	Fire	—	—	5	TM35	Flamethrower	Fire	95	100	15
TM12	Taunt	Dark	—	100	20	TM38	Fire Blast	Fire	120	85	5
TM13	Ice Beam	Ice	95	100	10	TM41	Torment	Dark	—	100	15
TM14	Blizzard	Ice	120	70	5	TM42	Facade	Normal	70	100	20
TM17	Protect	Normal	—	—	10	TM43	Secret Power	Normal	70	100	20
TM18	Rain Dance	Water	—	—	5	TM44	Rest	Psychic	—	—	10
TM21	Frustration	Normal	—	100	20	TM45	Attract	Normal	—	100	15
TM22	Solarbeam	Grass	120	100	10	TM50	Overheat	Fire	140	90	5
TM26	Earthquake	Ground	100	100	10	HM04	Strength	Normal	80	100	15
TM27	Return	Normal	—	100	20	HM06	Rock Smash	Fighting	20	100	15

MOVE TUTOR

***FireRed/LeafGreen* and *Emerald* Only**

Body Slam*	Counter*	Double-Edge
Mega Kick*	Mega Punch*	Mimic
Seismic Toss*	Substitute	

***Emerald* Only**

Dynamicpunch*	Endure*	Fire Punch*
Ice Punch*	Icy Wind*	Mud-Slap*
Psych Up*	Rollout	Sleep Talk
Snore*	Swagger	Thunderpunch*

*Battle Frontier tutor move (*Emerald*)

295 Exploud™

GENERAL INFO
SPECIES: Loud Noise Pokémon
HEIGHT: 4'11"
WEIGHT: 185 lbs.
ABILITY: Soundproof
Prevents Exploud from being hit by Grasswhistle, Growl, Heal Bell, Hyper Voice, Metal Sound, Perish Song, Roar, Screech, Sing, Snore, Supersonic, and Uproar.

STATS
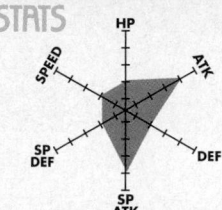

EVOLUTIONS

LV20   LV40

LOCATION[S]:

RUBY — Rarity: **Evolve**
Evolve Loudred

SAPPHIRE — Rarity: **Evolve**
Evolve Loudred

FIRERED — Rarity: **None**
Trade from *Ruby/Sapphire/Emerald*

LEAFGREEN — Rarity: **None**
Trade from *Ruby/Sapphire/Emerald*

COLOSSEUM — Rarity: **None**
Trade from *Ruby/Sapphire/Emerald*

EMERALD — Rarity: **Evolve**
Evolve Loudred

XD — Rarity: **None**
Trade from *Ruby/Sapphire/Emerald*

MOVES

Level	Attack	Type	Power	ACC	PP	Level	Attack	Type	Power	ACC	PP
—	Pound	Normal	40	100	35	37	Screech	Normal	—	85	40
—/5	Uproar	Normal	50	100	10	40	Hyper Beam	Normal	150	90	5
—/11	Astonish	Ghost	30	100	15	45	Roar	Normal	—	100	20
—/15	Howl	Normal	—	—	40	55	Rest	Psychic	—	—	10
23	Supersonic	Normal	—	55	20	55	Sleep Talk	Normal	—	—	10
29	Stomp	Normal	65	100	20	63	Hyper Voice	Normal	90	100	10

 # = Emerald Only

TM/HM

TM/HM#	Name	Type	Power	ACC	PP	TM/HM#	Name	Type	Power	ACC	PP
TM03	Water Pulse	Water	60	100	20	TM30	Shadow Ball	Ghost	60	—	20
TM05	Roar	Normal	—	100	20	TM31	Brick Break	Fighting	75	100	15
TM06	Toxic	Poison	—	85	10	TM32	Double Team	Normal	—	—	15
TM10	Hidden Power	Normal	—	100	15	TM34	Shock Wave	Electric	60	—	20
TM11	Sunny Day	Fire	—	—	5	TM35	Flamethrower	Fire	95	100	15
TM12	Taunt	Dark	—	100	20	TM38	Fire Blast	Fire	120	85	5
TM13	Ice Beam	Ice	95	100	10	TM41	Torment	Dark	—	100	15
TM14	Blizzard	Ice	120	70	5	TM42	Facade	Normal	70	100	20
TM15	Hyper Beam	Normal	150	90	5	TM43	Secret Power	Normal	70	100	20
TM17	Protect	Normal	—	—	10	TM44	Rest	Psychic	—	—	10
TM18	Rain Dance	Water	—	—	5	TM45	Attract	Normal	—	100	15
TM21	Frustration	Normal	—	100	20	TM50	Overheat	Fire	140	90	5
TM22	Solarbeam	Grass	120	100	10	HM04	Strength	Normal	80	100	15
TM26	Earthquake	Ground	100	100	10	HM06	Rock Smash	Fighting	20	100	15
TM27	Return	Normal	—	100	20						

MOVE TUTOR

FireRed/LeafGreen and Emerald Only

Body Slam*	Counter*	Double-Edge
Mega Kick*	Mega Punch*	Mimic
Seismic Toss*	Substitute	

Emerald Only

Dynamicpunch	Endure*	Fire Punch*
Ice Punch*	Icy Wind*	Mud-Slap*
Psych Up*	Rollout	Sleep Talk
Snore*	Swagger	Thunderpunch*

*Battle Frontier tutor move (Emerald)

---

296 Makuhita™

GENERAL INFO
SPECIES: Guts Pokémon
HEIGHT: 3'03"
WEIGHT: 191 lbs.
ABILITY 1: Thick Fat
Fire- and Ice-type moves inflict only 50% damage.

ABILITY 2: Guts
Makuhita's attack power increases 1.5 times when inflicted with a status condition.

STATS
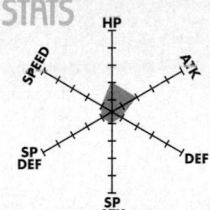

EVOLUTIONS

LV24

LOCATION[S]:

RUBY — Rarity: **Common**
Granite Cave, Victory Road

SAPPHIRE — Rarity: **Common**
Granite Cave, Victory Road

FIRERED — Rarity: **None**
Trade from *Ruby/Sapphire/Emerald/Colosseum*

LEAFGREEN — Rarity: **None**
Trade from *Ruby/Sapphire/Emerald/Colosseum*

COLOSSEUM — Rarity: **Only One**
Phenac City

EMERALD — Rarity: **Common**
Granite Cave, Victory Road

XD — Rarity: **Only One**
Pyrite Town (Capture from Cipher Peon Torkin)

MOVES

Level	Attack	Type	Power	ACC	PP	Level	Attack	Type	Power	ACC	PP
—	Tackle	Normal	35	95	35	22	Whirlwind	Normal	—	100	20
—	Focus Energy	Normal	—	—	30	28	Knock Off	Dark	20	100	20
4	Sand Attack	Ground	—	100	15	31	Smellingsalt	Normal	60	100	10
10	Arm Thrust	Fighting	15	100	20	37	Belly Drum	Normal	—	—	10
13	Vital Throw	Fighting	70	100	10	40	Endure	Normal	—	—	10
19	Fake Out	Normal	40	100	10	46	Seismic Toss	Fighting	—	100	20
						49	Reversal	Fighting	—	100	15

TM/HM

TM/HM#	Name	Type	Power	ACC	PP	TM/HM#	Name	Type	Power	ACC	PP
TM01	Focus Punch	Fighting	150	100	20	TM31	Brick Break	Fighting	75	100	15
TM06	Toxic	Poison	—	85	10	TM32	Double Team	Normal	—	—	15
TM08	Bulk Up	Fighting	—	—	20	TM39	Rock Tomb	Rock	50	80	10
TM10	Hidden Power	Normal	—	100	15	TM42	Facade	Normal	70	100	20
TM11	Sunny Day	Fire	—	—	5	TM43	Secret Power	Normal	70	100	20
TM17	Protect	Normal	—	—	10	TM44	Rest	Psychic	—	—	10
TM18	Rain Dance	Water	—	—	5	TM45	Attract	Normal	—	100	15
TM21	Frustration	Normal	—	100	20	HM03	Surf	Water	95	100	15
TM26	Earthquake	Ground	100	100	10	HM04	Strength	Normal	80	100	15
TM27	Return	Normal	—	100	20	HM06	Rock Smash	Fighting	20	100	15
TM28	Dig	Ground	60	100	10						

EGG MOVES*

Name	Type	Power	ACC	PP
Faint Attack	Dark	60	—	20
Detect	Fighting	—	—	5
Foresight	Normal	—	100	40
Helping Hand	Normal	—	100	20
Cross Chop	Fighting	100	80	5
Revenge	Fighting	60	100	10
Dynamicpunch	Fighting	100	50	5
Counter	Fighting	—	100	20

*Learned Via Breeding

MOVE TUTOR

FireRed/LeafGreen and Emerald Only

Body Slam*	Counter*	Double-Edge
Mega Kick*	Mega Punch*	Mimic
Rock Slide*	Seismic Toss*	Substitute

Emerald Only

Dynamicpunch	Endure*	Fire Punch*
Ice Punch*	Metronome	Mud-Slap*
Sleep Talk	Snore*	Swagger
Thunderpunch*		

*Battle Frontier tutor move (Emerald)

297 Hariyama ™

FIGHTING

GENERAL INFO

SPECIES: Arm Thrust Pokémon
HEIGHT: 7'07"
WEIGHT: 560 lbs.
ABILITY 1: Thick Fat
Fire- and Ice-type moves inflict only 50% damage.

ABILITY 2: Guts
Hariyama's attack power increases 1.5 times when inflicted with a Status condition.

STATS

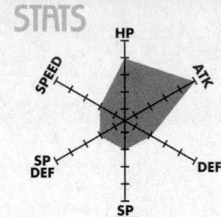

EVOLUTIONS

 LV24

LOCATION(S):

RUBY Rarity: **Rare**
Evolve Makuhita, Victory Road

SAPPHIRE Rarity: **Rare**
Evolve Makuhita, Victory Road

FIRERED Rarity: **None**
Trade from Ruby/Sapphire/Emerald/Colosseum

LEAFGREEN Rarity: **None**
Trade from Ruby/Sapphire/Emerald/Colosseum

COLOSSEUM Rarity: **Evolve**
Evolve Makuhita

EMERALD Rarity: **Common**
Evolve Makuhita, Victory Road

XD Rarity: **Evolve**
Evolve Makuhita

MOVES

Level	Attack	Type	Power	ACC	PP	Level	Attack	Type	Power	ACC	PP
—	Tackle	Normal	35	95	35	29	Knock Off	Dark	20	100	20
—	Focus Energy	Normal	—	—	30	33	Smellingsalt	Normal	60	100	10
—/4	Sand-Attack	Ground	—	100	15	40	Belly Drum	Normal	—	—	10
—/10	Arm Thrust	Fighting	15	100	20	44	Endure	Normal	—	—	10
13	Vital Throw	Fighting	70	—	10	51	Seismic Toss	Fighting	—	100	10
19	Fake Out	Normal	40	100	10	55	Reversal	Fighting	—	100	15
22	Whirlwind	Normal	—	100	20						

= Emerald Only

TM/HM

TM/HM#	Name	Type	Power	ACC	PP	TM/HM#	Name	Type	Power	ACC	PP
TM01	Focus Punch	Fighting	150	100	20	TM28	Dig	Ground	60	100	10
TM06	Toxic	Poison	—	85	10	TM31	Brick Break	Fighting	75	100	15
TM08	Bulk Up	Fighting	—	—	20	TM32	Double Team	Normal	—	—	15
TM10	Hidden Power	Normal	—	100	15	TM39	Rock Tomb	Rock	50	80	10
TM11	Sunny Day	Fire	—	—	5	TM42	Facade	Normal	70	100	20
TM15	Hyper Beam	Normal	150	90	5	TM43	Secret Power	Normal	70	100	20
TM17	Protect	Normal	—	—	10	TM44	Rest	Psychic	—	—	10
TM18	Rain Dance	Water	—	—	5	TM45	Attract	Normal	—	100	15
TM21	Frustration	Normal	—	100	20	HM03	Surf	Water	95	100	15
TM26	Earthquake	Ground	100	100	10	HM04	Strength	Normal	80	100	15
TM27	Return	Normal	—	100	20	HM06	Rock Smash	Fighting	20	100	15

MOVE TUTOR

FireRed/LeafGreen and Emerald Only

Body Slam*	Counter*	Double-Edge
Mega Kick*	Mega Punch*	Mimic
Rock Slide*	Seismic Toss*	Substitute

Emerald Only

Dynamicpunch*	Endure*	Fire Punch*
Ice Punch*	Metronome	Mud-Slap*
Sleep Talk	Snore*	Swagger
Thunderpunch*		

*Battle Frontier tutor move (Emerald)

298 Azurill ™

NORMAL

GENERAL INFO

SPECIES: Polka Dot Pokémon
HEIGHT: 0'08"
WEIGHT: 4 lbs.
ABILITY 1: Thick Fat
Fire- and Ice-type moves inflict only 50% damage.

ABILITY 2: Huge Power
Azurill's attack power is increased in battle.

STATS

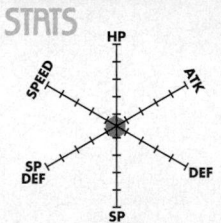

EVOLUTIONS

FRIENDSHIP LV18

LOCATION(S):

RUBY Rarity: **Breed**
Breed a female Marill or Azumarill with Sea Incense attached

SAPPHIRE Rarity: **Breed**
Breed a female Marill or Azumarill with Sea Incense attached

FIRERED Rarity: **Trade**
Trade from Ruby/Sapphire/LeafGreen/Emerald

LEAFGREEN Rarity: **Breed**
Breed a female Marill or Azumarill with Sea Incense attached

COLOSSEUM Rarity: **None**
Trade from Ruby/Sapphire/LeafGreen/Emerald

EMERALD Rarity: **Breed**
Breed a female Marill or Azumarill with Sea Incense attached

XD Rarity: **None**
Trade from Ruby/Sapphire/LeafGreen/Emerald

MOVES

Level	Attack	Type	Power	ACC	PP	Level	Attack	Type	Power	ACC	PP
—	Splash	Normal	—	—	40	10	Bubble	Water	20	100	30
3	Charm	Normal	—	100	20	15	Slam	Normal	80	75	20
6	Tail Whip	Normal	—	100	30	21	Water Gun	Water	40	100	25

TM/HM

TM/HM#	Name	Type	Power	ACC	PP	TM/HM#	Name	Type	Power	ACC	PP
TM03	Water Pulse	Water	60	100	20	TM23	Iron Tail	Steel	100	75	15
TM06	Toxic	Poison	—	85	10	TM27	Return	Normal	—	100	20
TM07	Hail	Ice	—	—	10	TM32	Double Team	Normal	—	—	15
TM10	Hidden Power	Normal	—	100	15	TM42	Facade	Normal	70	100	20
TM13	Ice Beam	Ice	95	100	10	TM43	Secret Power	Normal	70	100	20
TM14	Blizzard	Ice	120	70	5	TM44	Rest	Psychic	—	—	10
TM17	Protect	Normal	—	—	10	TM45	Attract	Normal	—	100	15
TM18	Rain Dance	Water	—	—	5	HM03	Surf	Water	95	100	15
TM21	Frustration	Normal	—	100	20	HM07	Waterfall	Water	80	100	15

EGG MOVES*

Name	Type	Power	ACC	PP
Encore	Normal	—	100	5
Sing	Normal	—	55	15
Refresh	Normal	—	100	20
Tickle	Normal	—	100	20
Slam	Normal	80	75	30

*Learned Via Breeding

MOVE TUTOR

FireRed/LeafGreen and Emerald Only

Body Slam*	Double-Edge	Mimic
Substitute		

Emerald Only

Defense Curl*	Endure*	Icy Wind*
Mud-Slap*	Rollout	Sleep Talk
Snore*	Swagger	Swift*

*Battle Frontier tutor move (Emerald)

299 Nosepass™

ROCK

GENERAL INFO
SPECIES: Compass Pokémon
HEIGHT: 3'03"
WEIGHT: 214 lbs.
ABILITY 1: Sturdy
One hit KO moves have no effect.
ABILITY 2: Magnet Pull
Prevents Steel-type Pokémon from fleeing in battle.

STATS

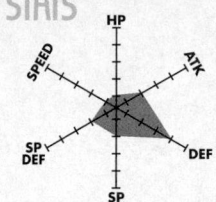

EVOLUTIONS

DOES NOT EVOLVE

LOCATION(S):

RUBY	**Rarity:**	**Rare**
Granite Cave		
SAPPHIRE	**Rarity:**	**Rare**
Granite Cave		
FIRERED	**Rarity:**	**None**
Trade from *Ruby/Sapphire/Emerald*		
LEAFGREEN	**Rarity:**	**None**
Trade from *Ruby/Sapphire/Emerald*		
COLOSSEUM	**Rarity:**	**None**
Trade from *Ruby/Sapphire/Emerald*		
EMERALD	**Rarity:**	**Rare**
Granite Cave		
XD	**Rarity:**	**Only One**
Capture from Wanderer Miror B. at the Outskirt Stand		

MOVES

Level	Attack	Type	Power	ACC	PP	Level	Attack	Type	Power	ACC	PP
—	Tackle	Normal	35	95	35	28	Rock Slide	Rock	75	90	10
7	Harden	Normal	—	—	30	31	Sandstorm	Rock	—	—	10
13	Rock Throw	Rock	50	90	15	37	Rest	Psychic	—	—	10
16	Block	Normal	—	100	5	43	Zap Cannon	Electric	100	50	5
22	Thunder Wave	Electric	—	100	20	46	Lock-on	Normal	—	100	5

TM/HM

TM/HM#	Name	Type	Power	ACC	PP	TM/HM#	Name	Type	Power	ACC	PP
TM06	Toxic	Poison	—	85	10	TM34	Shock Wave	Electric	60	—	20
TM10	Hidden Power	Normal	—	100	15	TM37	Sandstorm	Rock	—	—	10
TM11	Sunny Day	Fire	—	—	5	TM39	Rock Tomb	Rock	50	80	10
TM12	Taunt	Dark	—	100	20	TM41	Torment	Dark	—	100	15
TM17	Protect	Normal	—	—	10	TM42	Facade	Normal	70	100	20
TM21	Frustration	Normal	—	100	20	TM43	Secret Power	Normal	70	100	20
TM24	Thunderbolt	Electric	95	100	15	TM44	Rest	Psychic	—	—	10
TM25	Thunder	Electric	120	70	10	TM45	Attract	Normal	—	100	15
TM26	Earthquake	Ground	100	100	10	HM04	Strength	Normal	80	100	15
TM27	Return	Normal	—	100	20	HM06	Rock Smash	Fighting	20	100	15
TM32	Double Team	Normal	—	—	15						

EGG MOVES*

Name	Type	Power	ACC	PP
Magnitude	Ground	—	100	30
Rollout	Rock	30	90	20
Explosion	Normal	250	100	5

*Learned Via Breeding

MOVE TUTOR

FireRed/LeafGreen and **Emerald** Only

Body Slam*	Double-Edge	Explosion
Mimic	Rock Slide*	Substitute
Thunder Wave*		

Emerald Only

Defense Curl*	Dynamicpunch	Endure*
Fire Punch*	Ice Punch*	Mud-Slap*
Rollout	Sleep Talk	Snore*
Thunderpunch*		

*Battle Frontier tutor move (*Emerald*)

---

300 Skitty™

NORMAL

GENERAL INFO
SPECIES: Kitten Pokémon
HEIGHT: 2'00"
WEIGHT: 24 lbs.
ABILITY: Cute Charm
If an opponent physically strikes Skitty, it has a 30% chance of becoming attracted to it.

STATS

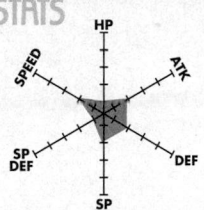

EVOLUTIONS

MOON STONE

LOCATION(S):

RUBY	**Rarity:**	**Rare**
Route 116		
SAPPHIRE	**Rarity:**	**Rare**
Route 116		
FIRERED	**Rarity:**	**None**
Trade from *Ruby/Sapphire/Emerald*		
LEAFGREEN	**Rarity:**	**None**
Trade from *Ruby/Sapphire/Emerald*		
COLOSSEUM	**Rarity:**	**None**
Trade from *Ruby/Sapphire/Emerald*		
EMERALD	**Rarity:**	**Rare**
Route 116		
XD	**Rarity:**	**None**
Trade from *Ruby/Sapphire/Emerald*		

MOVES

Level	Attack	Type	Power	ACC	PP	Level	Attack	Type	Power	ACC	PP
—	Growl	Normal	—	100	40	19	Assist	Normal	—	100	20
—	Tackle	Normal	35	95	35	25	Charm	Normal	—	100	20
3	Tail Whip	Normal	—	100	30	27	Faint Attack	Dark	60	—	20
7	Attract	Normal	—	100	15	31	Covet	Normal	40	100	40
13	Sing	Normal	—	55	15	37	Heal Bell	Normal	—	—	5
15	Doubleslap	Normal	15	85	10	39	Double-Edge	Normal	120	100	15

TM/HM

TM/HM#	Name	Type	Power	ACC	PP	TM/HM#	Name	Type	Power	ACC	PP
TM03	Water Pulse	Water	60	100	20	TM24	Thunderbolt	Electric	95	100	15
TM04	Calm Mind	Psychic	—	—	20	TM25	Thunder	Electric	120	70	10
TM06	Toxic	Poison	—	85	10	TM27	Return	Normal	—	100	20
TM10	Hidden Power	Normal	—	100	15	TM28	Dig	Ground	60	100	10
TM11	Sunny Day	Fire	—	—	5	TM30	Shadow Ball	Ghost	60	—	20
TM13	Ice Beam	Ice	95	100	10	TM32	Double Team	Normal	—	—	15
TM14	Blizzard	Ice	120	70	5	TM34	Shock Wave	Electric	60	—	20
TM17	Protect	Normal	—	—	10	TM42	Facade	Normal	70	100	20
TM18	Rain Dance	Water	—	—	5	TM43	Secret Power	Normal	70	100	20
TM20	Safeguard	Normal	—	—	25	TM44	Rest	Psychic	—	—	10
TM21	Frustration	Normal	—	100	20	TM45	Attract	Normal	—	100	15
TM22	Solarbeam	Grass	120	100	10	HM05	Flash	Normal	—	70	20
TM23	Iron Tail	Steel	100	75	15						

EGG MOVES*

Name	Type	Power	ACC	PP
Helping Hand	Normal	—	100	20
Psych Up	Normal	—	—	10
Uproar	Normal	50	100	10
Fake Tears	Dark	—	100	20
Baton Pass	Normal	—	—	40
Substitute	Normal	—	—	10
Tickle	Normal	—	100	20
Wish	Normal	—	100	10

*Learned Via Breeding

MOVE TUTOR

FireRed/LeafGreen and **Emerald** Only

Body Slam*	Double-Edge	Dream Eater*
Mimic	Substitute	Thunder Wave*

Emerald Only

Defense Curl*	Endure*	Icy Wind*
Mud-Slap*	Psych Up*	Rollout
Sleep Talk	Snore*	Swagger
Swift*		

*Battle Frontier tutor move (*Emerald*)

301 Delcatty

GENERAL INFO
SPECIES: Prim Pokémon
HEIGHT: 3'07"
WEIGHT: 72 lbs.
ABILITY: Cute Charm
If an opponent physically strikes Delcatty, it has a 30% chance of becoming attracted to it.

STATS
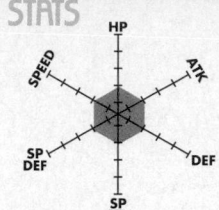

EVOLUTIONS

MOON STONE

LOCATION[S]:

RUBY — Rarity: **Evolve**
Evolve Skitty

SAPPHIRE — Rarity: **Evolve**
Evolve Skitty

FIRERED — Rarity: **None**
Trade from *Ruby/Sapphire/Emerald*

LEAFGREEN — Rarity: **None**
Trade from *Ruby/Sapphire/Emerald*

COLOSSEUM — Rarity: **None**
Trade from *Ruby/Sapphire/Emerald*

EMERALD — Rarity: **Evolve**
Evolve Skitty

XD — Rarity: **Only One**
Cipher Lab (Capture from Cipher Admin Lovrina)

MOVES

Level	Attack	Type	Power	ACC	PP	Level	Attack	Type	Power	ACC	PP
—	Growl	Normal	—	100	40	—	Sing	Normal	—	55	15
—	Attract	Normal	—	100	15	—	Doubleslap	Normal	15	85	10

TM/HM

TM/HM#	Name	Type	Power	ACC	PP	TM/HM#	Name	Type	Power	ACC	PP
TM03	Water Pulse	Water	60	100	20	TM24	Thunderbolt	Electric	95	100	15
TM04	Calm Mind	Psychic	—	—	20	TM25	Thunder	Electric	120	70	10
TM06	Toxic	Poison	—	85	10	TM27	Return	Normal	—	100	20
TM10	Hidden Power	Normal	—	100	15	TM28	Dig	Ground	60	100	10
TM11	Sunny Day	Fire	—	—	5	TM30	Shadow Ball	Ghost	60	—	20
TM13	Ice Beam	Ice	95	100	10	TM32	Double Team	Normal	—	—	15
TM14	Blizzard	Ice	120	70	5	TM34	Shock Wave	Electric	60	—	20
TM15	Hyper Beam	Normal	150	90	5	TM42	Facade	Normal	70	100	20
TM17	Protect	Normal	—	—	10	TM43	Secret Power	Normal	70	100	20
TM18	Rain Dance	Water	—	—	5	TM44	Rest	Psychic	—	—	10
TM20	Safeguard	Normal	—	—	25	TM45	Attract	Normal	—	100	15
TM21	Frustration	Normal	—	100	20	HM04	Strength	Normal	80	100	15
TM22	Solarbeam	Grass	120	100	10	HM05	Flash	Normal	—	70	20
TM23	Iron Tail	Steel	100	75	15	HM06	Rock Smash	Fighting	20	100	15

MOVE TUTOR
FireRed/LeafGreen and *Emerald* Only

Body Slam*	Double-Edge*	Dream Eater*
Mimic	Substitute	Thunder Wave*

Emerald Only

Defense Curl*	Endure*	Icy Wind*
Mud-Slap*	Psych Up*	Rollout
Sleep Talk	Snore*	Swagger
Swift*		

*Battle Frontier tutor move (*Emerald*)

---

302 Sableye

GENERAL INFO
SPECIES: Darkness Pokémon
HEIGHT: 1'08"
WEIGHT: 24 lbs.
ABILITY 1: Keen Eye
Sableye's Accuracy cannot be lowered.

STATS
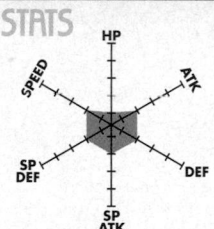

EVOLUTIONS

DOES NOT EVOLVE

LOCATION[S]:

RUBY — Rarity: **None**
Trade from *Sapphire/Emerald*

SAPPHIRE — Rarity: **Rare**
Cave of Origin, Granite Cave, Victory Road

FIRERED — Rarity: **None**
Trade from *Sapphire/Emerald*

LEAFGREEN — Rarity: **None**
Trade from *Sapphire/Emerald*

COLOSSEUM — Rarity: **None**
Trade from *Sapphire/Emerald*

EMERALD — Rarity: **Common**
Cave of Origin, Granite Cave, Sky Pillar, Victory Road

XD — Rarity: **Only One**
Citadark Island (Capture from Navigator Abson)

MOVES

Level	Attack	Type	Power	ACC	PP	Level	Attack	Type	Power	ACC	PP
—	Leer	Normal	—	100	30	21	Fake Out	Normal	40	100	10
—	Scratch	Normal	40	100	35	25	Detect	Fighting	—	—	5
5	Foresight	Normal	—	100	40	29	Faint Attack	Dark	60	—	20
9	Night Shade	Ghost	—	100	15	33	Knock Off	Dark	20	100	20
13	Astonish	Ghost	30	100	15	37	Confuse Ray	Ghost	—	100	10
17	Fury Swipes	Normal	18	80	15	41	Shadow Ball	Ghost	80	100	15
						45	Mean Look	Normal	—	100	5

TM/HM

TM/HM#	Name	Type	Power	ACC	PP	TM/HM#	Name	Type	Power	ACC	PP
TM01	Focus Punch	Fighting	150	100	20	TM32	Double Team	Normal	—	—	15
TM03	Water Pulse	Water	60	100	20	TM34	Shock Wave	Electric	60	—	20
TM04	Calm Mind	Psychic	—	—	20	TM39	Rock Tomb	Rock	50	80	10
TM06	Toxic	Poison	—	85	10	TM40	Aerial Ace	Flying	60	—	20
TM10	Hidden Power	Normal	—	100	15	TM41	Torment	Dark	—	100	15
TM11	Sunny Day	Fire	—	—	5	TM42	Facade	Normal	70	100	20
TM12	Taunt	Dark	—	100	20	TM43	Secret Power	Normal	70	100	20
TM17	Protect	Normal	—	—	10	TM44	Rest	Psychic	—	—	10
TM18	Rain Dance	Water	—	—	5	TM45	Attract	Normal	—	100	15
TM21	Frustration	Normal	—	100	20	TM46	Thief	Dark	40	100	10
TM27	Return	Normal	—	100	20	TM49	Snatch	Dark	—	100	10
TM28	Dig	Ground	60	100	10	HM01	Cut	Normal	50	95	30
TM29	Psychic	Psychic	90	100	10	HM05	Flash	Normal	—	70	20
TM30	Shadow Ball	Ghost	60	—	20	HM06	Rock Smash	Fighting	20	100	15
TM31	Brick Break	Fighting	75	100	15						

EGG MOVES*

Name	Type	Power	ACC	PP
Psych Up	Normal	—	—	10
Recover	Normal	—	—	20
Moonlight	Normal	—	—	5

*Learned Via Breeding

MOVE TUTOR
FireRed/LeafGreen and *Emerald* Only

Body Slam*	Counter*	Double-Edge*
Dream Eater*	Mega Kick*	Mega Punch*
Mimic	Seismic Toss*	Substitute

Emerald Only

Dynamicpunch*	Endure*	Fire Punch*
Ice Punch*	Metronome	Mud-Slap*
Psych Up*	Sleep Talk	Snore*
Swagger	Thunderpunch*	

*Battle Frontier tutor move (*Emerald*)

303 Mawile™

STEEL

GENERAL INFO
SPECIES: Deceiver Pokémon
HEIGHT: 2'00"
WEIGHT: 25 lbs.
ABILITY 1: Hyper Cutter
Mawile's attack power cannot be lowered.
ABILITY 2: Intimidate
Lowers the opponent's attack by one at a battle's start.

STATS
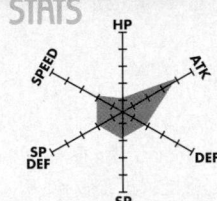

EVOLUTIONS
DOES NOT EVOLVE

LOCATION[S]:

RUBY — Rarity: **Rare**
Cave of Origin, Granite Cave, Victory Road

SAPPHIRE — Rarity: **None**
Trade from *Ruby/Emerald*

FIRERED — Rarity: **None**
Trade from *Ruby/Emerald*

LEAFGREEN — Rarity: **None**
Trade from *Ruby/Emerald*

COLOSSEUM — Rarity: **None**
Trade from *Ruby/Emerald*

EMERALD — Rarity: **Rare**
Victory Road

XD — Rarity: **Only One**
Pyrite Town (Capture from Cipher Peon Exol)

MOVES

Level	Attack	Type	Power	ACC	PP	Level	Attack	Type	Power	ACC	PP
—	Astonish	Ghost	30	100	15	31	Baton Pass	Normal	—	—	40
6	Fake Tears	Dark	—	100	20	36	Crunch	Dark	80	100	15
11	Bite	Dark	60	100	25	41	Iron Defense	Steel	—	—	15
16	Sweet Scent	Normal	—	100	20	46	Stockpile	Normal	—	—	10
21	Vicegrip	Normal	55	100	30	46	Swallow	Normal	—	—	10
26	Faint Attack	Dark	60	—	20	46	Spit Up	Normal	100	100	10

TM/HM

TM/HM#	Name	Type	Power	ACC	PP	TM/HM#	Name	Type	Power	ACC	PP
TM01	Focus Punch	Fighting	150	100	20	TM32	Double Team	Normal	—	—	15
TM06	Toxic	Poison	—	85	10	TM35	Flamethrower	Fire	95	100	15
TM10	Hidden Power	Normal	—	100	15	TM36	Sludge Bomb	Poison	90	100	10
TM11	Sunny Day	Fire	—	—	5	TM37	Sandstorm	Rock	—	—	10
TM12	Taunt	Dark	—	100	20	TM38	Fire Blast	Fire	120	85	5
TM13	Ice Beam	Ice	95	100	10	TM39	Rock Tomb	Rock	50	80	10
TM15	Hyper Beam	Normal	150	90	5	TM41	Torment	Dark	—	100	15
TM17	Protect	Normal	—	—	10	TM42	Facade	Normal	70	100	20
TM18	Rain Dance	Water	—	—	5	TM43	Secret Power	Normal	70	100	20
TM21	Frustration	Normal	—	100	20	TM44	Rest	Psychic	—	—	10
TM22	Solarbeam	Grass	120	100	10	TM45	Attract	Normal	—	100	15
TM27	Return	Normal	—	100	20	HM04	Strength	Normal	80	100	15
TM31	Brick Break	Fighting	75	100	15	HM06	Rock Smash	Fighting	20	100	15

EGG MOVES*

Name	Type	Power	ACC	PP
Swords Dance	Normal	—	—	30
False Swipe	Normal	40	100	40
Poison Fang	Poison	50	100	15
Psych Up	Normal	—	—	10
Ancientpower	Rock	60	100	5
Tickle	Normal	—	100	20

*Learned Via Breeding

MOVE TUTOR
FireRed/LeafGreen and *Emerald* Only

Body Slam*	Counter*	Double-Edge*
Mega Kick*	Mega Punch*	Mimic
Rock Slide*	Seismic Toss*	Substitute
Swords Dance*		

Emerald Only

Dynamicpunch*	Endure*	Ice Punch*
Icy Wind*	Mud-Slap*	Psych Up*
Sleep Talk	Snore*	Swagger*
Thunderpunch*		

*Battle Frontier tutor move (*Emerald*)

---

304 Aron™

STEEL   ROCK

GENERAL INFO
SPECIES: Iron Armor Pokémon
HEIGHT: 1'04"
WEIGHT: 132 lbs.
ABILITY 1: Sturdy
One hit KO moves have no effect.
ABILITY 2: Rock Head
Aron does not receive recoil damage from moves such as Double-Edge.

STATS
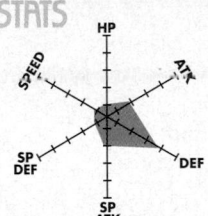

EVOLUTIONS

LV32   LV42

LOCATION[S]:

RUBY — Rarity: **Common**
Granite Cave, Victory Road

SAPPHIRE — Rarity: **Common**
Granite Cave, Victory Road

FIRERED — Rarity: **None**
Trade from *Ruby/Sapphire/Emerald*

LEAFGREEN — Rarity: **None**
Trade from *Ruby/Sapphire/Emerald*

COLOSSEUM — Rarity: **None**
Trade from *Ruby/Sapphire/Emerald*

EMERALD — Rarity: **Common**
Granite Cave, Victory Road

XD — Rarity: **Rare**
Cave Poké Spot

MOVES

Level	Attack	Type	Power	ACC	PP	Level	Attack	Type	Power	ACC	PP
—	Tackle	Normal	35	95	35	21	Roar	Normal	—	100	20
4	Harden	Normal	—	—	30	25	Take Down	Normal	90	85	20
7	Mud-Slap	Ground	20	100	10	29	Iron Tail	Steel	100	75	15
10	Headbutt	Normal	70	100	15	34	Protect	Normal	—	—	10
13	Metal Claw	Steel	50	95	35	39	Metal Sound	Steel	—	85	40
17	Iron Defense	Steel	—	—	15	44	Double-Edge	Normal	120	100	15

TM/HM

TM/HM#	Name	Type	Power	ACC	PP	TM/HM#	Name	Type	Power	ACC	PP
TM03	Water Pulse	Water	60	100	20	TM32	Double Team	Normal	—	—	15
TM05	Roar	Normal	—	100	20	TM34	Shock Wave	Electric	60	—	20
TM06	Toxic	Poison	—	85	10	TM37	Sandstorm	Rock	—	—	10
TM10	Hidden Power	Normal	—	100	15	TM39	Rock Tomb	Rock	50	80	10
TM11	Sunny Day	Fire	—	—	5	TM40	Aerial Ace	Flying	60	—	20
TM17	Protect	Normal	—	—	10	TM42	Facade	Normal	70	100	20
TM18	Rain Dance	Water	—	—	5	TM43	Secret Power	Normal	70	100	20
TM21	Frustration	Normal	—	100	20	TM44	Rest	Psychic	—	—	10
TM23	Iron Tail	Steel	100	75	15	TM45	Attract	Normal	—	100	15
TM26	Earthquake	Ground	100	100	10	HM01	Cut	Normal	50	95	30
TM27	Return	Normal	—	100	20	HM04	Strength	Normal	80	100	15
TM28	Dig	Ground	60	100	10	HM06	Rock Smash	Fighting	20	100	15

EGG MOVES*

Name	Type	Power	ACC	PP
Endeavor	Normal	—	100	5
Body Slam	Normal	85	100	15
Stomp	Normal	65	100	20
Smellingsalt	Normal	60	100	10

*Learned Via Breeding

MOVE TUTOR
FireRed/LeafGreen and *Emerald* Only

Body Slam*	Double-Edge*	Mimic
Rock Slide*	Substitute	

Emerald Only

Defense Curl*	Endure*	Fury Cutter*
Mud-Slap*	Rollout	Sleep Talk
Snore*	Swagger*	

*Battle Frontier tutor move (*Emerald*)

305 Lairon™

STEEL | ROCK

GENERAL INFO
SPECIES: Iron Armor Pokémon
HEIGHT: 2'11"
WEIGHT: 265 lbs.
ABILITY 1: Sturdy
One hit KO moves have no effect.
ABILITY 2: Rock Head
Lairon does not receive recoil damage from moves such as Double-Edge.

STATS
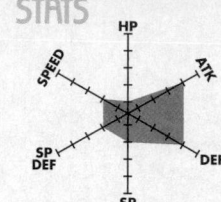

EVOLUTIONS

LV32 | LV42

LOCATION(S):

RUBY	Rarity: **Rare**
Victory Road	
SAPPHIRE	Rarity: **Rare**
Victory Road	
FIRERED	Rarity: **None**
Trade from Ruby/Sapphire/Emerald	
LEAFGREEN	Rarity: **None**
Trade from Ruby/Sapphire/Emerald	
COLOSSEUM	Rarity: **None**
Trade from Ruby/Sapphire/Emerald	
EMERALD	Rarity: **Rare**
Victory Road	
XD	Rarity: **Evolve**
Evolve Aron	

MOVES

Level	Attack	Type	Power	ACC	PP
—	Tackle	Normal	35	95	35
—/4	Harden	Normal	—	—	30
—/7	Mud-Slap	Ground	20	100	10
—/10	Headbutt	Normal	70	100	15
13	Metal Claw	Steel	50	95	35
17	Iron Defense	Steel	—	—	15
21	Roar	Normal	—	100	20
25	Take Down	Normal	90	85	20
29	Iron Tail	Steel	100	75	15
37	Protect	Normal	—	—	10
45	Metal Sound	Steel	—	85	40
53	Double-Edge	Normal	120	100	15

\# = Emerald Only

TM/HM

TM/HM#	Name	Type	Power	ACC	PP
TM03	Water Pulse	Water	60	100	20
TM05	Roar	Normal	—	100	20
TM06	Toxic	Poison	—	85	10
TM10	Hidden Power	Normal	—	100	15
TM11	Sunny Day	Fire	—	—	5
TM17	Protect	Normal	—	—	10
TM18	Rain Dance	Water	—	—	5
TM21	Frustration	Normal	—	100	20
TM23	Iron Tail	Steel	100	75	15
TM26	Earthquake	Ground	100	100	10
TM27	Return	Normal	—	100	20
TM28	Dig	Ground	60	100	10
TM32	Double Team	Normal	—	—	15
TM34	Shock Wave	Electric	60	—	20
TM37	Sandstorm	Rock	—	—	10
TM39	Rock Tomb	Rock	50	80	10
TM40	Aerial Ace	Flying	60	—	20
TM42	Facade	Normal	70	100	20
TM43	Secret Power	Normal	70	100	20
TM44	Rest	Psychic	—	—	10
TM45	Attract	Normal	—	100	15
HM01	Cut	Normal	50	95	30
HM04	Strength	Normal	80	100	15
HM06	Rock Smash	Fighting	20	100	15

MOVE TUTOR
FireRed/LeafGreen and Emerald Only

Body Slam*	Double-Edge	Mimic
Rock Slide*	Substitute	

Emerald Only

Defense Curl*	Endure*	Fury Cutter
Mud-Slap*	Rollout	Sleep Talk
Snore*	Swagger	

*Battle Frontier tutor move (*Emerald*)

---

306 Aggron™

STEEL | ROCK

GENERAL INFO
SPECIES: Iron Armor Pokémon
HEIGHT: 6'11"
WEIGHT: 794 lbs.
ABILITY 1: Sturdy
One hit KO moves have no effect.
ABILITY 2: Rock Head
Aggron does not receive recoil damage from moves such as Double-Edge.

STATS
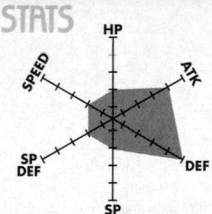

EVOLUTIONS
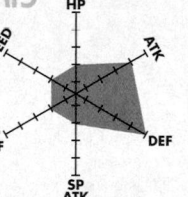   
LV32 | LV42

LOCATION(S):

RUBY	
Rarity: **Evolve**	
Evolve Lairon	
SAPPHIRE	
Rarity: **Evolve**	
Evolve Lairon	
FIRERED	
Rarity: **None**	
Trade from Ruby/Sapphire/Emerald	
LEAFGREEN	
Rarity: **None**	
Trade from Ruby/Sapphire/Emerald	
COLOSSEUM	
Rarity: **None**	
Trade from Ruby/Sapphire/Emerald	
EMERALD	
Rarity: **Evolve**	
Evolve Lairon	
XD	
Rarity: **Evolve**	
Evolve Lairon	

MOVES

Level	Attack	Type	Power	ACC	PP
—	Tackle	Normal	35	95	35
—/4	Harden	Normal	—	—	30
—/7	Mud-Slap	Ground	20	100	10
—/10	Headbutt	Normal	70	100	15
13	Metal Claw	Steel	50	95	35
17	Iron Defense	Steel	—	—	15
21	Roar	Normal	—	100	20
25	Take Down	Normal	90	85	20
29	Iron Tail	Steel	100	75	15
37	Protect	Normal	—	—	10
50	Metal Sound	Steel	—	85	40
63	Double-Edge	Normal	120	100	15

\# = Emerald Only

TM/HM

TM/HM#	Name	Type	Power	ACC	PP
TM12	Taunt	Dark	—	100	20
TM13	Ice Beam	Ice	95	100	10
TM14	Blizzard	Ice	120	70	5
TM15	Hyper Beam	Normal	150	90	5
TM17	Protect	Normal	—	—	10
TM18	Rain Dance	Water	—	—	5
TM21	Frustration	Normal	—	100	20
TM22	Solarbeam	Grass	120	100	10
TM23	Iron Tail	Steel	100	75	15
TM24	Thunderbolt	Electric	95	100	15
TM25	Thunder	Electric	120	70	10
TM26	Earthquake	Ground	100	100	10
TM27	Return	Normal	—	100	20
TM28	Dig	Ground	60	100	10
TM31	Brick Break	Fighting	75	100	15
TM32	Double Team	Normal	—	—	15
TM34	Shock Wave	Electric	60	—	20
TM35	Flamethrower	Fire	95	100	15
TM37	Sandstorm	Rock	—	—	10
TM38	Fire Blast	Fire	120	85	5
TM39	Rock Tomb	Rock	50	80	10
TM40	Aerial Ace	Flying	60	—	20
TM42	Facade	Normal	70	100	20
TM43	Secret Power	Normal	70	100	20
TM44	Rest	Psychic	—	—	10
TM45	Attract	Normal	—	100	15
HM01	Cut	Normal	50	95	30
HM03	Surf	Water	95	100	15
HM04	Strength	Normal	80	100	15
HM06	Rock Smash	Fighting	20	100	15

TM/HM#	Name	Type	Power	ACC	PP
TM01	Focus Punch	Fighting	150	100	20
TM02	Dragon Claw	Dragon	80	100	15
TM03	Water Pulse	Water	60	100	20
TM05	Roar	Normal	—	100	20
TM06	Toxic	Poison	—	85	10
TM10	Hidden Power	Normal	—	100	15
TM11	Sunny Day	Fire	—	—	5

MOVE TUTOR
FireRed/LeafGreen and Emerald Only

Body Slam*	Counter*	Double-Edge
Mega Kick*	Mega Punch*	Mimic
Rock Slide*	Seismic Toss*	Substitute
Thunder Wave*		

Emerald Only

Dynamicpunch*	Endure*	Fire Punch*
Fury Cutter	Ice Punch*	Icy Wind*
Mud-Slap*	Rollout	Sleep Talk
Snore*	Swagger	Thunderpunch*

*Battle Frontier tutor move (*Emerald*)

307 Meditite™

FIGHTING | PSYCHIC

GENERAL INFO
SPECIES: Meditate Pokémon
HEIGHT: 2'00"
WEIGHT: 25 lbs.
ABILITY: Pure Power
Raises attack power, but effect is lessened by half when ability is changed.

STATS
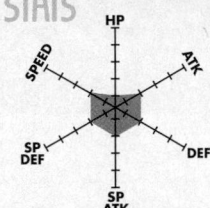

EVOLUTIONS

LV37

LOCATION[S]:

RUBY **Rarity: Rare**
Mt. Pyre, Victory Road

SAPPHIRE **Rarity: Rare**
Mt. Pyre, Victory Road

FIRERED **Rarity: None**
Trade from *Ruby/Sapphire/Colosseum*

LEAFGREEN **Rarity: None**
Trade from *Ruby/Sapphire/Colosseum*

COLOSSEUM **Rarity: Only One**
Pyrite Cave

EMERALD **Rarity: None**
Trade from *Ruby/Sapphire/Colosseum*

XD **Rarity: Only One**
Trade with Duking

MOVES

Level	Attack	Type	Power	ACC	PP
—	Bide	Normal	—	100	10
4	Meditate	Psychic	—	—	40
9	Confusion	Psychic	50	100	25
12	Detect	Fighting	—	—	5
17/18	Hidden Power	Normal	—	100	15
20	Swagger*	Normal	—	90	15

Level	Attack	Type	Power	ACC	PP
25	Mind Reader	Normal	—	100	5
28	Calm Mind	Psychic	—	—	20
33	Hi Jump Kick	Fighting	85	90	20
36	Psych Up	Normal	—	—	10
41	Reversal	Fighting	—	100	15
49/44	Recover	Normal	—	—	20

= *Emerald* Only   * Not Available in *Emerald*

TM/HM

TM/HM#	Name	Type	Power	ACC	PP
TM01	Focus Punch	Fighting	150	100	20
TM04	Calm Mind	Psychic	—	—	20
TM06	Toxic	Poison	—	85	10
TM08	Bulk Up	Fighting	—	—	20
TM10	Hidden Power	Normal	—	100	15
TM11	Sunny Day	Fire	—	—	5
TM16	Light Screen	Psychic	—	—	30
TM17	Protect	Normal	—	—	10
TM18	Rain Dance	Water	—	—	5
TM21	Frustration	Normal	—	100	20
TM27	Return	Normal	—	100	20
TM29	Psychic	Psychic	90	100	10

TM/HM#	Name	Type	Power	ACC	PP
TM30	Shadow Ball	Ghost	60	—	20
TM31	Brick Break	Fighting	75	100	15
TM32	Double Team	Normal	—	—	15
TM33	Reflect	Psychic	—	—	20
TM39	Rock Tomb	Rock	50	80	10
TM42	Facade	Normal	70	100	20
TM43	Secret Power	Normal	70	100	20
TM44	Rest	Psychic	—	—	10
TM45	Attract	Normal	—	100	15
HM04	Strength	Normal	80	100	15
HM05	Flash	Normal	—	70	20
HM06	Rock Smash	Fighting	20	100	15

EGG MOVES*

Name	Type	Power	ACC	PP
Fire Punch	Fire	75	100	15
Thunderpunch	Electric	75	100	15
Ice Punch	Ice	75	100	15
Foresight	Normal	—	100	40
Fake Out	Normal	40	100	10
Baton Pass	Normal	—	—	40
Dynamicpunch	Fighting	100	50	5

*Learned Via Breeding

MOVE TUTOR
FireRed/LeafGreen and *Emerald* Only

Body Slam*	Counter*	Double-Edge
Dream Eater*	Mega Kick*	Mega Punch*
Mimic	Seismic Toss*	Substitute

Emerald Only

Dynamicpunch	Endure*	Fire Punch*
Ice Punch*	Metronome	Mud-Slap*
Psych Up*	Sleep Talk	Snore*
Swagger	Swift*	Thunderpunch*

*Battle Frontier tutor move (*Emerald*)

---

308 Medicham™

FIGHTING | PSYCHIC

GENERAL INFO
SPECIES: Meditate Pokémon
HEIGHT: 4'03"
WEIGHT: 69 lbs.
ABILITY: Pure Power
Raises attack power, but effect is lessened by half when ability is changed.

STATS

EVOLUTIONS

LV37

LOCATION[S]:

RUBY **Rarity: Rare**
Evolve Meditite, Victory Road

SAPPHIRE **Rarity: Rare**
Evolve Meditite, Victory Road

FIRERED **Rarity: None**
Trade from *Ruby/Sapphire/Colosseum*

LEAFGREEN **Rarity: None**
Trade from *Ruby/Sapphire/Colosseum*

COLOSSEUM **Rarity: Evolve**
Evolve Meditite

EMERALD **Rarity: None**
Trade from *Ruby/Sapphire/Colosseum*

XD **Rarity: Only One**
Trade with Duking

MOVES

Level	Attack	Type	Power	ACC	PP
—	Fire Punch	Fire	75	100	15
—	Thunderpunch	Electric	75	100	15
—	Ice Punch	Ice	75	100	15
—	Bide	Normal	—	100	10
4	Meditate*	Psychic	—	—	40
9	Confusion*	Psychic	50	100	25
12	Detect*	Fighting	—	—	5
17	Hidden Power	Normal	—	100	15

Level	Attack	Type	Power	ACC	PP
20	Swagger	Normal	—	20	15
25	Mind Reader	Normal	—	100	5
28	Calm Mind	Psychic	—	—	20
33	Hi Jump Kick	Fighting	85	90	20
36	Psych Up	Normal	—	—	10
47/44	Reversal	Fighting	—	100	15
56	Recover	Normal	—	—	20

= *Emerald* Only   * = *Emerald* Only

TM/HM

TM/HM#	Name	Type	Power	ACC	PP
TM01	Focus Punch	Fighting	150	100	20
TM04	Calm Mind	Psychic	—	—	20
TM06	Toxic	Poison	—	85	10
TM08	Bulk Up	Fighting	—	—	20
TM10	Hidden Power	Normal	—	100	15
TM11	Sunny Day	Fire	—	—	5
TM15	Hyper Beam	Normal	150	90	5
TM16	Light Screen	Psychic	—	—	30
TM17	Protect	Normal	—	—	10
TM18	Rain Dance	Water	—	—	5
TM21	Frustration	Normal	—	100	20
TM27	Return	Normal	—	100	20
TM29	Psychic	Psychic	90	100	10

TM/HM#	Name	Type	Power	ACC	PP
TM30	Shadow Ball	Ghost	60	—	20
TM31	Brick Break	Fighting	75	100	15
TM32	Double Team	Normal	—	—	15
TM33	Reflect	Psychic	—	—	20
TM39	Rock Tomb	Rock	50	80	10
TM42	Facade	Normal	70	100	20
TM43	Secret Power	Normal	70	100	20
TM44	Rest	Psychic	—	—	10
TM45	Attract	Normal	—	100	15
HM04	Strength	Normal	80	100	15
HM05	Flash	Normal	—	70	20
HM06	Rock Smash	Fighting	20	100	15

EGG MOVES*

Name	Type	Power	ACC	PP
Fire Punch	Fire	75	100	15
Thunderpunch	Electric	75	100	15
Ice Punch	Ice	75	100	15
Foresight	Normal	—	100	40
Fake Out	Normal	40	100	10
Baton Pass	Normal	—	—	40
Dynamicpunch	Fighting	100	50	5

*Learned Via Breeding

MOVE TUTOR
FireRed/LeafGreen and *Emerald* Only

Body Slam*	Counter*	Double-Edge
Dream Eater*	Mega Kick*	Mega Punch*
Mimic	Rock Slide*	Seismic Toss*
Substitute	Thunder Wave*	

Emerald Only

Dynamicpunch	Endure*	Fire Punch*
Ice Punch*	Metronome	Mud-Slap*
Psych Up*	Sleep Talk	Snore*
Swagger	Swift*	Thunderpunch*

*Battle Frontier tutor move (*Emerald*)

309 Electrike™

ELECTRIC

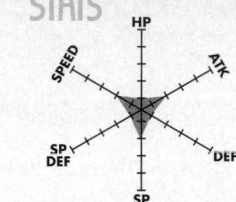

GENERAL INFO
SPECIES: Lightning Pokémon
HEIGHT: 2'00"
WEIGHT: 34 lbs.
ABILITY 1: Static
An opponent has a 30% chance of being paralyzed if it strikes Electrike.

ABILITY 2: Lightningrod
Draws Electric-type moves to itself.

STATS

EVOLUTIONS

LV26

LOCATION(S):

RUBY	**Rarity: Common**	
Route 110, Route 118		
SAPPHIRE	**Rarity: Common**	
Route 110, Route 118		
FIRERED	**Rarity: None**	
Trade from *Ruby/Sapphire/Emerald*		
LEAFGREEN	**Rarity: None**	
Trade from *Ruby/Sapphire/Emerald*		
COLOSSEUM	**Rarity: None**	
Trade from *Ruby/Sapphire/Emerald*		
EMERALD	**Rarity: Common**	
Route 110, Route 118		
XD	**Rarity: None**	
Trade from *Ruby/Sapphire/Emerald*		

MOVES

Level	Attack	Type	Power	ACC	PP	Level	Attack	Type	Power	ACC	PP
—	Tackle	Normal	35	95	35	20	Spark	Electric	65	100	20
4	Thunder Wave	Electric	—	100	20	25	Odor Sleuth	Normal	—	100	40
9	Leer	Normal	—	100	30	28	Roar	Normal	—	100	20
12	Howl	Normal	—	—	40	33	Bite	Dark	60	100	25
17	Quick Attack	Normal	40	100	30	36	Thunder	Electric	120	70	10
						41	Charge	Electric	—	100	20

TM/HM

TM/HM#	Name	Type	Power	ACC	PP	TM/HM#	Name	Type	Power	ACC	PP
TM05	Roar	Normal	—	100	20	TM27	Return	Normal	—	100	20
TM06	Toxic	Poison	—	85	10	TM32	Double Team	Normal	—	—	15
TM10	Hidden Power	Normal	—	100	15	TM34	Shock Wave	Electric	60	—	20
TM17	Protect	Normal	—	—	10	TM42	Facade	Normal	70	100	20
TM18	Rain Dance	Water	—	—	5	TM43	Secret Power	Normal	70	100	20
TM21	Frustration	Normal	—	100	20	TM44	Rest	Psychic	—	—	10
TM23	Iron Tail	Steel	100	75	15	TM45	Attract	Normal	—	100	15
TM24	Thunderbolt	Electric	95	100	15	TM46	Thief	Dark	40	100	10
TM25	Thunder	Electric	120	70	10	HM04	Strength	Normal	80	100	15
						HM05	Flash	Normal	—	70	20

EGG MOVES*

Name	Type	Power	ACC	PP
Crunch	Dark	80	100	15
Uproar	Normal	50	100	10
Headbutt	Normal	70	100	15
Curse	—	—	—	10
Swift	Normal	60	—	20

*Learned Via Breeding

MOVE TUTOR
FireRed/LeafGreen and *Emerald* Only

Body Slam*	Double-Edge	Mimic
Substitute	Thunder Wave*	

Emerald Only

Endure	Mud-Slap*	Sleep Talk
Snore	Swagger	Swift*

*Battle Frontier tutor move (*Emerald*)

---

310 Manectric™

ELECTRIC

GENERAL INFO
SPECIES: Discharge Pokémon
HEIGHT: 4'11"
WEIGHT: 89 lbs.
ABILITY 1: Static
An opponent has a 30% chance of being paralyzed if it strikes Manectric.

ABILITY 2: Lightningrod
Draws Electric-type moves to itself.

STATS

EVOLUTIONS

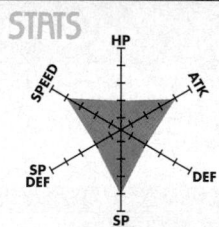

LV26

LOCATION(S):

RUBY	**Rarity: Rare**	
Route 118		
SAPPHIRE	**Rarity: Rare**	
Route 118		
FIRERED	**Rarity: None**	
Trade from *Ruby/Sapphire/Emerald*		
LEAFGREEN	**Rarity: None**	
Trade from *Ruby/Sapphire/Emerald*		
COLOSSEUM	**Rarity: None**	
Trade from *Ruby/Sapphire/Emerald*		
EMERALD	**Rarity: Rare**	
Evolve Electrike, Route 118		
XD	**Rarity: Only One**	
Citadark Island (Capture from Cipher Admin Eldes)		

MOVES

Level	Attack	Type	Power	ACC	PP	Level	Attack	Type	Power	ACC	PP
—	Tackle	Normal	35	95	35	25	Odor Sleuth	Normal	—	100	40
—/4	Thunder Wave	Electric	—	100	20	31	Roar	Normal	—	100	20
—/9	Leer	Normal	—	100	30	39	Bite	Dark	60	100	25
—/12	Howl	Normal	—	—	40	45	Thunder	Electric	120	70	10
17	Quick Attack	Normal	40	100	30	53	Charge	Electric	—	100	20
20	Spark	Electric	65	100	20	# = *Emerald* Only					

TM/HM

TM/HM#	Name	Type	Power	ACC	PP	TM/HM#	Name	Type	Power	ACC	PP
TM05	Roar	Normal	—	100	20	TM27	Return	Normal	—	100	20
TM06	Toxic	Poison	—	85	10	TM32	Double Team	Normal	—	—	15
TM10	Hidden Power	Normal	—	100	15	TM34	Shock Wave	Electric	60	—	20
TM15	Hyper Beam	Normal	150	90	5	TM42	Facade	Normal	70	100	20
TM17	Protect	Normal	—	—	10	TM43	Secret Power	Normal	70	100	20
TM18	Rain Dance	Water	—	—	5	TM44	Rest	Psychic	—	—	10
TM21	Frustration	Normal	—	100	20	TM45	Attract	Normal	—	100	15
TM23	Iron Tail	Steel	100	75	15	TM46	Thief	Dark	40	100	10
TM24	Thunderbolt	Electric	95	100	15	HM04	Strength	Normal	80	100	15
TM25	Thunder	Electric	120	70	10	HM05	Flash	Normal	—	70	20

MOVE TUTOR
FireRed/LeafGreen and *Emerald* Only

Body Slam*	Double-Edge	Mimic
Substitute	Thunder Wave*	

Emerald Only

Endure*	Mud-Slap*	Sleep Talk
Snore*	Swagger	Swift*

*Battle Frontier tutor move (*Emerald*)

311 Plusle™

ELECTRIC

GENERAL INFO

SPECIES: Cheering Pokémon
HEIGHT: 1'04"
WEIGHT: 9 lbs.
ABILITY: Plus
Increases Special Attack 1.5 times when faced with a Pokémon with the Minus Ability.

STATS

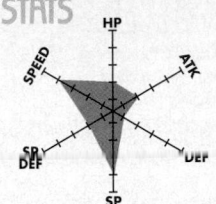

EVOLUTIONS

DOES NOT EVOLVE

LOCATION(S):

RUBY	**Rarity:** Rare	
Route 110		
SAPPHIRE	**Rarity:** Common	
Route 110		
FIRERED	**Rarity:** None	
Trade from *Ruby/Sapphire/Colosseum/Emerald*		
LEAFGREEN	**Rarity:** None	
Trade from *Ruby/Sapphire/Colosseum/Emerald*		
COLOSSEUM	**Rarity:** Only One	
Pyrite Town		
EMERALD	**Rarity:** Rare	
Route 110, Fortree City		
XD	**Rarity:** None	
Trade from *Ruby/Sapphire/Colosseum/Emerald*		

MOVES

Level	Attack	Type	Power	ACC	PP
—	Growl	Normal	—	100	40
4	Thunder Wave	Electric	—	100	20
10	Quick Attack	Normal	40	100	30
13	Helping Hand	Normal	—	100	20
19	Spark	Electric	65	100	20
22	Encore	Normal	—	100	5
28	Fake Tears	Dark	—	100	20
31	Charge	Electric	—	100	20
37	Thunder	Electric	120	70	10
40	Baton Pass	Normal	—	—	40
47	Agility	Psychic	—	—	30

TM/HM

TM/HM#	Name	Type	Power	ACC	PP
TM06	Toxic	Poison	—	85	10
TM10	Hidden Power	Normal	—	100	15
TM16	Light Screen	Psychic	—	—	30
TM17	Protect	Normal	—	—	10
TM18	Rain Dance	Water	—	—	5
TM21	Frustration	Normal	—	100	20
TM23	Iron Tail	Steel	100	75	15
TM24	Thunderbolt	Electric	95	100	15
TM25	Thunder	Electric	120	70	10
TM27	Return	Normal	—	100	20
TM32	Double Team	Normal	—	—	15
TM34	Shock Wave	Electric	60	—	20
TM42	Facade	Normal	70	100	20
TM43	Secret Power	Normal	70	100	20
TM44	Rest	Psychic	—	—	10
TM45	Attract	Normal	—	100	15
HM05	Flash	Normal	—	70	20

EGG MOVES*

Name	Type	Power	ACC	PP
Substitute	Normal	—	—	10
Wish	Normal	—	100	10

*Learned Via Breeding

MOVE TUTOR

FireRed/LeafGreen and *Emerald* Only

Body Slam*	Counter*	Double-Edge
Mega Kick*	Mega Punch*	Mimic
Seismic Toss*	Substitute	Thunder Wave*

Emerald Only

Defense Curl*	Dynamicpunch*	Endure*
Metronome	Mud-Slap*	Rollout
Sleep Talk	Snore*	Swagger
Swift*	Thunderpunch*	

*Battle Frontier tutor move (*Emerald*)

---

312 Minun™

ELECTRIC

GENERAL INFO

SPECIES: Cheering Pokémon
HEIGHT: 1'04"
WEIGHT: 9 lbs.
ABILITY: Minus
Increases Special Attack 1.5 times when faced with a Pokémon with the Plus Ability.

STATS

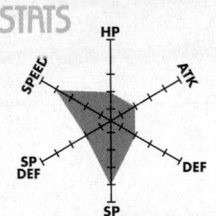

EVOLUTIONS

DOES NOT EVOLVE

LOCATION(S):

RUBY	**Rarity:** Common	
Route 110		
SAPPHIRE	**Rarity:** Rare	
Route 110		
FIRERED	**Rarity:** None	
Trade from *Ruby/Sapphire/Emerald*		
LEAFGREEN	**Rarity:** None	
Trade from *Ruby/Sapphire/Emerald*		
COLOSSEUM	**Rarity:** None	
Trade from *Ruby/Sapphire/Emerald*		
EMERALD	**Rarity:** Rare	
Route 110		
XD	**Rarity:** None	
Trade from *Ruby/Sapphire/Emerald*		

MOVES

Level	Attack	Type	Power	ACC	PP
—	Growl	Normal	—	100	40
4	Thunder Wave	Electric	—	100	20
10	Quick Attack	Normal	40	100	30
13	Helping Hand	Normal	—	100	20
19	Spark	Electric	65	100	20
22	Encore	Normal	—	100	5
28	Charm	Normal	—	100	20
31	Charge	Electric	—	100	20
37	Thunder	Electric	120	70	10
40	Baton Pass	Normal	—	—	40
47	Agility	Psychic	—	—	30

TM/HM

TM/HM#	Name	Type	Power	ACC	PP
TM06	Toxic	Poison	—	85	10
TM10	Hidden Power	Normal	—	100	15
TM16	Light Screen	Psychic	—	—	30
TM17	Protect	Normal	—	—	10
TM18	Rain Dance	Water	—	—	5
TM21	Frustration	Normal	—	100	20
TM23	Iron Tail	Steel	100	75	15
TM24	Thunderbolt	Electric	95	100	15
TM25	Thunder	Electric	120	70	10
TM27	Return	Normal	—	100	20
TM32	Double Team	Normal	—	—	15
TM34	Shock Wave	Electric	60	—	20
TM42	Facade	Normal	70	100	20
TM43	Secret Power	Normal	70	100	20
TM44	Rest	Psychic	—	—	10
TM45	Attract	Normal	—	100	15
HM05	Flash	Normal	—	70	20

EGG MOVES*

Name	Type	Power	ACC	PP
Substitute	Normal	—	—	10
Wish	Normal	—	100	10

*Learned Via Breeding

MOVE TUTOR

FireRed/LeafGreen and *Emerald* Only

Body Slam*	Counter*	Double-Edge
Mega Kick*	Mega Punch*	Mimic
Seismic Toss*	Substitute	Thunder Wave*

Emerald Only

Defense Curl*	Dynamicpunch*	Endure*
Metronome	Mud-Slap*	Rollout
Sleep Talk	Snore*	Swagger
Swift*	Thunderpunch*	

*Battle Frontier tutor move (*Emerald*)

313 Volbeat™

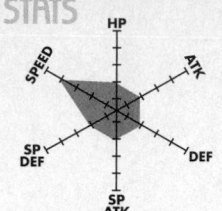

BUG

GENERAL INFO
SPECIES: Firefly Pokémon
HEIGHT: 2'04"
WEIGHT: 39 lbs.
ABILITY 1: Illuminate
Increases the chance of encountering wild Pokémon.

ABILITY 2: Swarm
When Volbeat's HPs fall below 1/3, the power of Bug-type moves increases 1.5 times.

STATS

EVOLUTIONS

DOES NOT EVOLVE

LOCATION[S]:

RUBY — Rarity: **Rare**
Route 117

SAPPHIRE — Rarity: **Rare**
Route 117

FIRERED — Rarity: **None**
Trade from *Ruby/Sapphire/Emerald*

LEAFGREEN — Rarity: **None**
Trade from *Ruby/Sapphire/Emerald*

COLOSSEUM — Rarity: **None**
Trade from *Ruby/Sapphire/Emerald*

EMERALD — Rarity: **Rare**
Route 117

XD — Rarity: **None**
Trade from *Ruby/Sapphire/Emerald*

MOVES

Level	Attack	Type	Power	ACC	PP
—	Tackle	Normal	35	95	35
5	Confuse Ray	Ghost	—	100	10
9	Double Team	Normal	—	—	15
13	Moonlight	Normal	—	—	5
17	Quick Attack	Normal	40	100	30
21	Tail Glow	Bug	—	100	20
25	Signal Beam	Bug	75	100	15
29	Protect	Normal	—	—	10
33	Helping Hand	Normal	—	100	20
37	Double-Edge	Normal	120	100	15

TM/HM

TM/HM#	Name	Type	Power	ACC	PP
TM01	Focus Punch	Fighting	150	100	20
TM03	Water Pulse	Water	60	100	20
TM06	Toxic	Poison	—	85	10
TM10	Hidden Power	Normal	—	100	15
TM11	Sunny Day	Fire	—	—	5
TM16	Light Screen	Psychic	—	—	30
TM17	Protect	Normal	—	—	10
TM18	Rain Dance	Water	—	—	5
TM19	Giga Drain	Grass	60	100	5
TM21	Frustration	Normal	—	100	20
TM22	Solarbeam	Grass	120	100	10
TM24	Thunderbolt	Electric	95	100	15
TM25	Thunder	Electric	120	70	10
TM27	Return	Normal	—	100	20
TM30	Shadow Ball	Ghost	60	—	20
TM31	Brick Break	Fighting	75	100	15
TM32	Double Team	Normal	—	—	15
TM34	Shock Wave	Electric	60	—	20
TM40	Aerial Ace	Flying	60	—	20
TM42	Facade	Normal	70	100	20
TM43	Secret Power	Normal	70	100	20
TM44	Rest	Psychic	—	—	10
TM45	Attract	Normal	—	100	15
TM46	Thief	Dark	40	100	10
HM05	Flash	Normal	—	70	20

EGG MOVES*

Name	Type	Power	ACC	PP
Baton Pass	Normal	—	—	40
Silver Wind	Bug	60	100	5
Trick	Psychic	—	100	10

*Learned Via Breeding

MOVE TUTOR
FireRed/LeafGreen and *Emerald* Only

Body Slam*	Counter*	Double-Edge
Mega Kick*	Mega Punch*	Mimic
Seismic Toss*	Substitute	Thunder Wave*

***Emerald* Only**

Dynamicpunch	Endure*	Ice Punch*
Metronome	Mud-Slap*	Psych Up*
Sleep Talk	Snore*	Swagger
Swift*	Thunderpunch*	

*Battle Frontier tutor move (*Emerald*)

314 Illumise™

BUG

GENERAL INFO
SPECIES: Firefly Pokémon
HEIGHT: 2'00"
WEIGHT: 39 lbs.
ABILITY: Oblivious
Illumise is not affected by the Attract condition.

STATS

EVOLUTIONS

DOES NOT EVOLVE

LOCATION[S]:

RUBY — Rarity: **Rare**
Route 117

SAPPHIRE — Rarity: **Rare**
Route 117

FIRERED — Rarity: **None**
Trade from *Ruby/Sapphire/Emerald*

LEAFGREEN — Rarity: **None**
Trade from *Ruby/Sapphire/Emerald*

COLOSSEUM — Rarity: **None**
Trade from *Ruby/Sapphire/Emerald*

EMERALD — Rarity: **Rare**
Route 117

XD — Rarity: **None**
Trade from *Ruby/Sapphire/Emerald*

MOVES

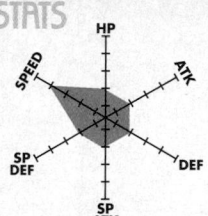
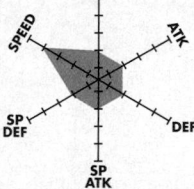

Level	Attack	Type	Power	ACC	PP
—	Tackle	Normal	35	95	35
5	Sweet Scent	Normal	—	100	20
9	Charm	Normal	—	100	20
13	Moonlight	Normal	—	—	5
17	Quick Attack	Normal	40	100	30
21	Wish	Normal	—	100	10
25	Encore	Normal	—	100	5
29	Flatter	Dark	—	100	15
33	Helping Hand	Normal	—	100	20
37	Covet	Normal	40	100	40

TM/HM

TM/HM#	Name	Type	Power	ACC	PP
TM01	Focus Punch	Fighting	150	100	20
TM03	Water Pulse	Water	60	100	20
TM06	Toxic	Poison	—	85	10
TM10	Hidden Power	Normal	—	100	15
TM11	Sunny Day	Fire	—	—	5
TM16	Light Screen	Psychic	—	—	30
TM17	Protect	Normal	—	—	10
TM18	Rain Dance	Water	—	—	5
TM19	Giga Drain	Grass	60	100	5
TM21	Frustration	Normal	—	100	20
TM22	Solarbeam	Grass	120	100	10
TM24	Thunderbolt	Electric	95	100	15
TM25	Thunder	Electric	120	70	10
TM27	Return	Normal	—	100	20
TM30	Shadow Ball	Ghost	60	—	20
TM31	Brick Break	Fighting	75	100	15
TM32	Double Team	Normal	—	—	15
TM34	Shock Wave	Electric	60	—	20
TM40	Aerial Ace	Flying	60	—	20
TM42	Facade	Normal	70	100	20
TM43	Secret Power	Normal	70	100	20
TM44	Rest	Psychic	—	—	10
TM45	Attract	Normal	—	100	15
TM46	Thief	Dark	40	100	10
HM05	Flash	Normal	—	70	20

EGG MOVES*

Name	Type	Power	ACC	PP
Baton Pass	Normal	—	—	40
Silver Wind	Bug	60	100	5
Growth	Normal	—	—	40

*Learned Via Breeding

MOVE TUTOR
FireRed/LeafGreen and *Emerald* Only

Body Slam*	Counter*	Double-Edge
Mega Kick*	Mega Punch*	Mimic
Seismic Toss*	Substitute	Thunder Wave*

***Emerald* Only**

Dynamicpunch	Endure*	Ice Punch*
Metronome	Mud-Slap*	Psych Up*
Sleep Talk	Snore*	Swagger
Swift*	Thunderpunch*	

*Battle Frontier tutor move (*Emerald*)

315 Roselia™

GRASS | POISON

GENERAL INFO

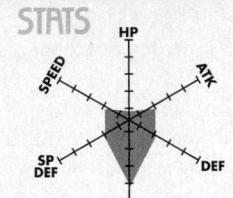

SPECIES: Thorn Pokémon
HEIGHT: 1'00"
WEIGHT: 4 lbs.
ABILITY 1: Natural Cure
Any negative status conditions are automatically healed when you remove Roselia from battle.

ABILITY 2: Poison Point
If an opponent is striking Roselia, it has a 30% chance of being poisoned.

STATS

EVOLUTIONS

DOES NOT EVOLVE

LOCATION(S):

RUBY Rarity: **Common**
Route 117

SAPPHIRE Rarity: **Common**
Route 117

FIRERED Rarity: **None**
Trade from *Ruby/Sapphire*

LEAFGREEN Rarity: **None**
Trade from *Ruby/Sapphire*

COLOSSEUM Rarity: **None**
Trade from *Ruby/Sapphire*

EMERALD Rarity: **None**
Trade from *Ruby/Sapphire*

XD Rarity: **Only One**
Phenac City (Capture from Cipher Peon Fasin)

MOVES

Level	Attack	Type	Power	ACC	PP
—	Absorb	Grass	20	100	20
5	Growth	Normal	—	—	40
9	Poison Sting	Poison	15	100	35
13	Stun Spore	Grass	—	75	30
17	Mega Drain	Grass	40	100	10
21	Leech Seed	Grass	—	90	10
25	Magical Leaf	Grass	60	—	20

Level	Attack	Type	Power	ACC	PP
29	Grasswhistle	Grass	—	55	15
33	Giga Drain	Grass	60	100	5
37	Sweet Scent	Normal	—	100	20
41	Ingrain	Grass	—	100	20
45	Toxic	Poison	—	85	10
49	Petal Dance	Grass	70	100	20
53	Aromatherapy	Grass	—	—	5
57	Synthesis	Grass	—	—	5

TM/HM

TM/HM#	Name	Type	Power	ACC	PP
TM06	Toxic	Poison	—	85	10
TM09	Bullet Seed	Grass	10	100	30
TM10	Hidden Power	Normal	—	100	15
TM11	Sunny Day	Fire	—	—	5
TM17	Protect	Normal	—	—	10
TM19	Giga Drain	Grass	60	100	5
TM21	Frustration	Normal	—	100	20
TM22	Solarbeam	Grass	120	100	10
TM27	Return	Normal	—	100	20

TM/HM#	Name	Type	Power	ACC	PP
TM30	Shadow Ball	Ghost	60	—	20
TM32	Double Team	Normal	—	—	15
TM36	Sludge Bomb	Poison	90	100	10
TM42	Facade	Normal	70	100	20
TM43	Secret Power	Normal	70	100	20
TM44	Rest	Psychic	—	—	10
TM45	Attract	Normal	—	100	15
HM01	Cut	Normal	50	95	30
HM05	Flash	Normal	—	70	20

EGG MOVES*

Name	Type	Power	ACC	PP
Spikes	Ground	—	—	20
Pin Missile	Bug	14	85	20
Cotton Spore	Grass	—	85	40
Synthesis	Grass	—	—	5

*Learned Via Breeding

MOVE TUTOR

FireRed/LeafGreen and Emerald Only

Body Slam	Double-Edge	Mimic
Substitute	Swords Dance	

Emerald Only

Endure*	Mud-Slap*	Psych Up*
Sleep Talk	Snore*	Swagger
Swift*		

*Battle Frontier tutor move (*Emerald*)

---

316 Gulpin™

POISON

GENERAL INFO

SPECIES: Stomach Pokémon
HEIGHT: 1'04"
WEIGHT: 23 lbs.
ABILITY 1: Liquid Ooze
Gulpin inflicts damage on an opponent who uses HP-absorbing moves.

ABILITY 2: Sticky Hold
Protects Gulpin's Held Item from an opponent using Thief.

STATS

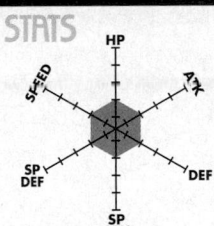

EVOLUTIONS

LV26

LOCATION(S):

RUBY Rarity: **Common**
Route 110

SAPPHIRE Rarity: **Common**
Route 110

FIRERED Rarity: **None**
Trade from *Ruby/Sapphire/Emerald*

LEAFGREEN Rarity: **None**
Trade from *Ruby/Sapphire/Emerald*

COLOSSEUM Rarity: **None**
Trade from *Ruby/Sapphire/Emerald*

EMERALD Rarity: **Rare**
Route 110

XD Rarity: **Only One**
Cipher Lab (Capture from Cipher Peon Purpsix)

MOVES

Level	Attack	Type	Power	ACC	PP
—	Pound	Normal	40	100	35
6	Yawn	Normal	—	100	10
9	Poison Gas	Poison	—	55	40
14	Sludge	Poison	65	100	20
17	Amnesia	Psychic	—	—	20

Level	Attack	Type	Power	ACC	PP
23	Encore	Normal	—	100	5
28	Toxic	Poison	—	85	10
34	Stockpile	Normal	—	—	10
34	Spit Up	Normal	100	100	10
34	Swallow	Normal	—	—	10
39	Sludge Bomb	Poison	90	100	10

TM/HM

TM/HM#	Name	Type	Power	ACC	PP
TM03	Water Pulse	Water	60	100	20
TM06	Toxic	Poison	—	85	10
TM09	Bullet Seed	Grass	10	100	30
TM10	Hidden Power	Normal	—	100	15
TM11	Sunny Day	Fire	—	—	5
TM13	Ice Beam	Ice	95	100	10
TM17	Protect	Normal	—	—	10
TM18	Rain Dance	Water	—	—	5
TM19	Giga Drain	Grass	60	100	5
TM21	Frustration	Normal	—	100	20
TM22	Solarbeam	Grass	120	100	10
TM27	Return	Normal	—	100	20

TM/HM#	Name	Type	Power	ACC	PP
TM30	Shadow Ball	Ghost	60	—	20
TM32	Double Team	Normal	—	—	15
TM34	Shock Wave	Electric	60	—	20
TM36	Sludge Bomb	Poison	90	100	10
TM42	Facade	Normal	70	100	20
TM43	Secret Power	Normal	70	100	20
TM44	Rest	Psychic	—	—	10
TM45	Attract	Normal	—	100	15
TM49	Snatch	Dark	—	—	10
HM04	Strength	Normal	80	100	15
HM06	Rock Smash	Fighting	20	100	15

EGG MOVES*

Name	Type	Power	ACC	PP
Dream Eater	Psychic	100	100	15
Acid Armor	Poison	—	—	40
Smog	Poison	20	70	20
Pain Split	Normal	—	100	20

*Learned Via Breeding

MOVE TUTOR

FireRed/LeafGreen and Emerald Only

Body Slam	Counter*	Double-Edge
Dream Eater*	Explosion	Mimic
Substitute		

Emerald Only

Defense Curl*	Dynamicpunch*	Endure*
Fire Punch*	Mud-Slap*	Rollout
Sleep Talk	Snore*	Swagger
Thunderpunch*		

*Battle Frontier tutor move (*Emerald*)

317 Swalot

POISON

GENERAL INFO
SPECIES: Poison Bag Pokémon
HEIGHT: 5'07"
WEIGHT: 176 lbs.
ABILITY 1: Liquid Ooze
Swalot inflicts damage on an opponent who uses HP-absorbing moves.

ABILITY 2: Sticky Hold
Protects Swalot's Held Item from an opponent using Thief.

STATS

EVOLUTIONS

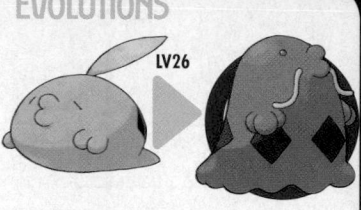

LV26

LOCATION[S]:

RUBY — Rarity: **Evolve**
Evolve Gulpin

SAPPHIRE — Rarity: **Evolve**
Evolve Gulpin

FIRERED — Rarity: **None**
Trade from *Ruby/Sapphire/Emerald*

LEAFGREEN — Rarity: **None**
Trade from *Ruby/Sapphire/Emerald*

COLOSSEUM — Rarity: **None**
Trade from *Ruby/Sapphire/Emerald*

EMERALD — Rarity: **Evolve**
Evolve Gulpin

XD — Rarity: **Evolve**
Evolve Gulpin

MOVES

Level	Attack	Type	Power	ACC	PP	Level	Attack	Type	Power	ACC	PP
—	Pound	Normal	40	100	35	26	Body Slam	Normal	85	100	15
—	Yawn	Normal	—	100	10	31	Toxic	Poison	—	85	10
—	Poison Gas	Poison	—	55	40	40	Stockpile	Normal	—	—	10
—	Sludge	Poison	65	100	20	40	Spit Up	Normal	100	100	10
17	Amnesia	Psychic	—	—	20	40	Swallow	Normal	—	—	10
23	Encore	Normal	—	100	5	48	Sludge Bomb	Poison	90	100	10

TM/HM

TM/HM#	Name	Type	Power	ACC	PP	TM/HM#	Name	Type	Power	ACC	PP
TM03	Water Pulse	Water	60	100	20	TM27	Return	Normal	—	100	20
TM06	Toxic	Poison	—	85	10	TM30	Shadow Ball	Ghost	60	—	20
TM09	Bullet Seed	Grass	10	100	30	TM32	Double Team	Normal	—	—	15
TM10	Hidden Power	Normal	—	100	15	TM34	Shock Wave	Electric	60	—	20
TM11	Sunny Day	Fire	—	—	5	TM36	Sludge Bomb	Poison	90	100	10
TM13	Ice Beam	Ice	95	100	10	TM42	Facade	Normal	70	100	20
TM15	Hyper Beam	Normal	150	90	5	TM43	Secret Power	Normal	70	100	20
TM17	Protect	Normal	—	—	10	TM44	Rest	Psychic	—	—	10
TM18	Rain Dance	Water	—	—	5	TM45	Attract	Normal	—	100	15
TM19	Giga Drain	Grass	60	100	5	TM49	Snatch	Dark	—	100	10
TM21	Frustration	Normal	—	100	20	HM04	Strength	Normal	80	100	15
TM22	Solarbeam	Grass	120	100	10	HM06	Rock Smash	Fighting	20	100	15

MOVE TUTOR
FireRed/LeafGreen and *Emerald* Only

Body Slam*	Counter*	Double-Edge
Dream Eater*	Explosion	Mimic
Substitute		

Emerald Only

Defense Curl*	Dynamicpunch*	Endure*
Fire Punch*	Mud-Slap*	Rollout
Sleep Talk*	Snore*	Swagger
Thunderpunch*		

*Battle Frontier tutor move (*Emerald*)

318 Carvanha

WATER   DARK

GENERAL INFO
SPECIES: Savage Pokémon
HEIGHT: 2'07"
WEIGHT: 46 lbs.
ABILITY: Rough Skin
Recoil hurts the opponent Pokémon when it uses a physical attack.

STATS

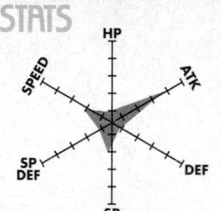

EVOLUTIONS

LV30

LOCATION[S]:

RUBY — Rarity: **Common**
Route 118, Route 119

SAPPHIRE — Rarity: **Common**
Route 118, Route 119

FIRERED — Rarity: **None**
Trade from *Ruby/Sapphire/Emerald*

LEAFGREEN — Rarity: **None**
Trade from *Ruby/Sapphire/Emerald*

COLOSSEUM — Rarity: **None**
Trade from *Ruby/Sapphire/Emerald*

EMERALD — Rarity: **Common**
Route 118, Route 119

XD — Rarity: **Only One**
Cipher Lab (Capture from Cipher Peon Cabol)

MOVES

Level	Attack	Type	Power	ACC	PP	Level	Attack	Type	Power	ACC	PP
—	Leer	Normal	—	100	30	22	Crunch	Dark	80	100	15
—	Bite	Dark	60	100	25	28	Screech	Normal	—	85	40
7	Rage	Normal	20	100	20	31	Take Down	Normal	90	85	20
13	Focus Energy	Normal	—	—	30	37	Swagger	Normal	—	90	15
16	Scary Face	Normal	—	90	10	43	Agility	Psychic	—	—	30

TM/HM

TM/HM#	Name	Type	Power	ACC	PP	TM/HM#	Name	Type	Power	ACC	PP
TM03	Water Pulse	Water	60	100	20	TM32	Double Team	Normal	—	—	15
TM06	Toxic	Poison	—	85	10	TM41	Torment	Dark	—	100	15
TM07	Hail	Ice	—	—	10	TM42	Facade	Normal	70	100	20
TM10	Hidden Power	Normal	—	100	15	TM43	Secret Power	Normal	70	100	20
TM12	Taunt	Dark	—	100	20	TM44	Rest	Psychic	—	—	10
TM13	Ice Beam	Ice	95	100	10	TM45	Attract	Normal	—	100	15
TM14	Blizzard	Ice	120	70	5	TM46	Thief	Dark	40	100	10
TM17	Protect	Normal	—	—	10	HM03	Surf	Water	95	100	15
TM18	Rain Dance	Water	—	—	5	HM07	Waterfall	Water	80	100	15
TM21	Frustration	Normal	—	100	20	HM08	Dive	Water	60	100	10
TM27	Return	Normal	—	100	20						

EGG MOVES*

Name	Type	Power	ACC	PP
Hydro Pump	Water	120	80	5
Double-Edge	Normal	120	100	15
Thrash	Normal	90	100	20

*Learned Via Breeding

MOVE TUTOR
FireRed/LeafGreen and *Emerald* Only

Double-Edge	Mimic	Substitute

Emerald Only

Endure*	Fury Cutter*	Icy Wind*
Mud-Slap*	Sleep Talk*	Snore*
Swagger	Swift*	

*Battle Frontier tutor move (*Emerald*)

319 Sharpedo™

WATER **DARK**

GENERAL INFO
SPECIES: Brutal Pokémon
HEIGHT: 5'11"
WEIGHT: 196 lbs.
ABILITY: Rough Skin
The opponent Pokémon is hurt when it uses a physical attack against Sharpedo.

STATS

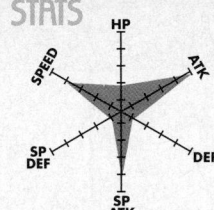

EVOLUTIONS

LV30

LOCATION(S):

RUBY — Rarity: **Rare**
Route 103, Route 118, Route 122

SAPPHIRE — Rarity: **Rare**
Route 103, Route 118, Route 122

FIRERED — Rarity: **None**
Trade from *Ruby/Sapphire/Emerald*

LEAFGREEN — Rarity: **None**
Trade from *Ruby/Sapphire/Emerald*

COLOSSEUM — Rarity: **None**
Trade from *Ruby/Sapphire/Emerald*

EMERALD — Rarity: **Common**
Routes 103, 118, 122, 124–127, 129–134, Mossdeep City, Pacifidlog Town

XD — Rarity: **Evolve**
Evolve Carvanha

MOVES

Level	Attack	Type	Power	ACC	PP	Level	Attack	Type	Power	ACC	PP
—	Leer	Normal	—	100	30	28	Screech	Normal	—	85	40
—	Bite	Dark	60	100	25	33	Slash	Normal	70	100	20
—	Rage	Normal	20	100	20	38	Taunt	Dark	—	100	20
—	Focus Energy	Normal	—	—	30	43	Swagger	Normal	—	90	15
16	Scary Face	Normal	—	90	10	48	Skull Bash	Normal	100	100	15
22	Crunch	Dark	80	100	15	53	Agility	Psychic	—	—	30

TM/HM

TM/HM#	Name	Type	Power	ACC	PP	TM/HM#	Name	Type	Power	ACC	PP
TM03	Water Pulse	Water	60	100	20	TM32	Double Team	Normal	—	—	15
TM05	Roar	Normal	—	100	20	TM39	Rock Tomb	Rock	50	80	10
TM06	Toxic	Poison	—	85	10	TM41	Torment	Dark	—	100	15
TM07	Hail	Ice	—	—	10	TM42	Facade	Normal	70	100	20
TM10	Hidden Power	Normal	—	100	15	TM43	Secret Power	Normal	70	100	20
TM12	Taunt	Dark	—	100	20	TM44	Rest	Psychic	—	—	10
TM13	Ice Beam	Ice	95	100	10	TM45	Attract	Normal	—	100	15
TM14	Blizzard	Ice	120	70	5	TM46	Thief	Dark	40	100	10
TM15	Hyper Beam	Normal	150	90	5	HM03	Surf	Water	95	100	15
TM17	Protect	Normal	—	—	10	HM04	Strength	Normal	80	100	15
TM18	Rain Dance	Water	—	—	5	HM06	Rock Smash	Fighting	20	100	15
TM21	Frustration	Normal	—	100	20	HM07	Waterfall	Water	80	100	15
TM26	Earthquake	Ground	100	100	10	HM08	Dive	Water	60	100	10
TM27	Return	Normal	—	100	20						

MOVE TUTOR

FireRed/LeafGreen and Emerald Only

Double-Edge	Mimic	Substitute

Emerald Only

Endure*	Fury Cutter	Icy Wind*
Mud-Slap*	Sleep Talk	Snore*
Swagger	Swift*	

*Battle Frontier tutor move (Emerald)

---

320 Wailmer™

WATER

GENERAL INFO
SPECIES: Ball Whale Pokémon
HEIGHT: 6'07"
WEIGHT: 287 lbs.
ABILITY 1: Water Veil
Wailmer cannot be burned.
ABILITY 2: Oblivious
The Attract condition does not affect Wailmer.

STATS

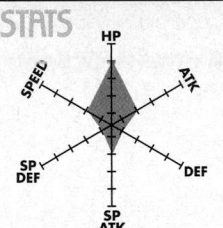

EVOLUTIONS

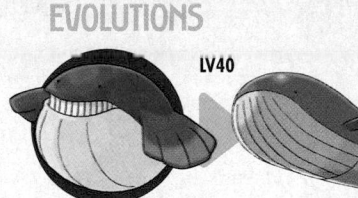

LV40

LOCATION(S):

RUBY — Rarity: **Rare**
Fish in most waters, Route 103, Route 110

SAPPHIRE — Rarity: **Rare**
Fish in most waters, Route 103, Route 110

FIRERED — Rarity: **None**
Trade from *Ruby/Sapphire/Emerald*

LEAFGREEN — Rarity: **None**
Trade from *Ruby/Sapphire/Emerald*

COLOSSEUM — Rarity: **None**
Trade from *Ruby/Sapphire/Emerald*

EMERALD — Rarity: **Common**
Routes 103, 105–110, 115, 121–134, Ever Grande City, Lilycove City, Mossdeep City, Pacifidlog Town, Seafloor Cavern, Shoal Cave

XD — Rarity: **None**
Trade from *Ruby/Sapphire/Emerald*

MOVES

Level	Attack	Type	Power	ACC	PP	Level	Attack	Type	Power	ACC	PP
—	Scratch	Normal	40	100	35	28	Water Pulse	Water	60	100	20
5	Growl	Normal	—	100	40	32	Mist	Ice	—	—	30
10	Water Gun	Water	40	100	25	37	Rest	Psychic	—	—	10
14	Rollout	Rock	30	90	20	41	Water Spout	Water	150	100	5
19	Whirlpool	Water	15	70	15	46	Amnesia	Psychic	—	—	20
23	Astonish	Ghost	30	100	15	50	Hydro Pump	Water	120	80	5

TM/HM

TM/HM#	Name	Type	Power	ACC	PP	TM/HM#	Name	Type	Power	ACC	PP
TM03	Water Pulse	Water	60	100	20	TM32	Double Team	Normal	—	—	15
TM05	Roar	Normal	—	100	20	TM39	Rock Tomb	Rock	50	80	10
TM06	Toxic	Poison	—	85	10	TM42	Facade	Normal	70	100	20
TM07	Hail	Ice	—	—	10	TM43	Secret Power	Normal	70	100	20
TM10	Hidden Power	Normal	—	100	15	TM44	Rest	Psychic	—	—	10
TM13	Ice Beam	Ice	95	100	10	TM45	Attract	Normal	—	100	15
TM14	Blizzard	Ice	120	70	5	HM03	Surf	Water	95	100	15
TM17	Protect	Normal	—	—	10	HM04	Strength	Normal	80	100	15
TM18	Rain Dance	Water	—	—	5	HM06	Rock Smash	Fighting	20	100	15
TM21	Frustration	Normal	—	100	20	HM07	Waterfall	Water	80	100	15
TM26	Earthquake	Ground	100	100	10	HM08	Dive	Water	60	100	10
TM27	Return	Normal	—	100	20						

EGG MOVES*

Name	Type	Power	ACC	PP
Double-Edge	Normal	120	100	15
Thrash	Normal	90	100	20
Swagger	Normal	—	90	15
Snore	Normal	40	100	15
Sleep Talk	Normal	—	—	10
Curse	—	—	—	10
Fissure	Ground	—	30	5
Tickle	Normal	—	100	20

*Learned Via Breeding

MOVE TUTOR

FireRed/LeafGreen and Emerald Only

Body Slam	Double-Edge	Mimic
Substitute		

Emerald Only

Defense Curl*	Dynamicpunch*	Endure*
Icy Wind*	Rollout	Sleep Talk
Snore*	Swagger	

*Battle Frontier tutor move (Emerald)

321 Wailord™

WATER

GENERAL INFO
SPECIES: Float Whale Pokémon
HEIGHT: 47'07"
WEIGHT: 878 lbs.
ABILITY 1: Water Veil
Wailord cannot be burned.
ABILITY 2: Oblivious
The Attract condition does not affect Wailord.

STATS
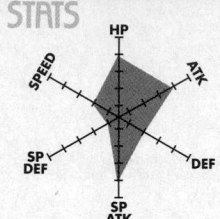

EVOLUTIONS
LV40
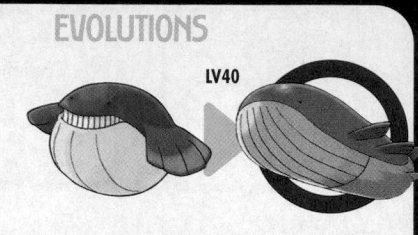

LOCATION[S]:

RUBY   Rarity: **Rare**
Route 129

SAPPHIRE   Rarity: **Rare**
Route 129

FIRERED   Rarity: **None**
Trade from *Ruby/Sapphire/Emerald*

LEAFGREEN   Rarity: **None**
Trade from *Ruby/Sapphire/Emerald*

COLOSSEUM   Rarity: **None**
Trade from *Ruby/Sapphire/Emerald*

EMERALD   Rarity: **Rare**
Route 129

XD   Rarity: **None**
Trade from *Ruby/Sapphire/Emerald*

MOVES
Level	Attack	Type	Power	ACC	PP	Level	Attack	Type	Power	ACC	PP
—	Splash	Normal	—	—	40	28	Water Pulse	Water	60	100	20
—	Growl	Normal	—	100	40	32	Mist	Ice	—	—	30
—	Water Gun	Water	40	100	25	37	Rest	Psychic	—	—	10
—	Rollout	Rock	30	90	20	44	Water Spout	Water	150	100	5
19	Whirlpool	Water	15	70	15	52	Amnesia	Psychic	—	—	20
23	Astonish	Ghost	30	100	15	59	Hydro Pump	Water	120	80	5

TM/HM
TM/HM#	Name	Type	Power	ACC	PP	TM/HM#	Name	Type	Power	ACC	PP
TM03	Water Pulse	Water	60	100	20	TM27	Return	Normal	—	100	20
TM05	Roar	Normal	—	100	20	TM32	Double Team	Normal	—	—	15
TM06	Toxic	Poison	—	85	10	TM39	Rock Tomb	Rock	50	80	10
TM07	Hail	Ice	—	—	10	TM42	Facade	Normal	70	100	20
TM10	Hidden Power	Normal	—	100	15	TM43	Secret Power	Normal	70	100	20
TM13	Ice Beam	Ice	95	100	10	TM44	Rest	Psychic	—	—	10
TM14	Blizzard	Ice	120	70	5	TM45	Attract	Normal	—	100	15
TM15	Hyper Beam	Normal	150	90	5	HM03	Surf	Water	95	100	15
TM17	Protect	Normal	—	—	10	HM04	Strength	Normal	80	100	15
TM18	Rain Dance	Water	—	—	5	HM06	Rock Smash	Fighting	20	100	15
TM21	Frustration	Normal	—	100	20	HM07	Waterfall	Water	80	100	15
TM26	Earthquake	Ground	100	100	10	HM08	Dive	Water	60	100	10

MOVE TUTOR
FireRed/LeafGreen and *Emerald* Only

Body Slam*	Double-Edge	Mimic
Substitute		

Emerald Only

Defense Curl*	Dynamicpunch	Endure*
Icy Wind*	Rollout	Sleep Talk
Snore*	Swagger	

*Battle Frontier tutor move (*Emerald*)

---

322 Numel™

FIRE   GROUND

GENERAL INFO
SPECIES: Numb Pokémon
HEIGHT: 2'04"
WEIGHT: 53 lbs.
ABILITY: Oblivious
Numel is not affected by the Attract condition.

STATS

EVOLUTIONS
LV33

LOCATION[S]:

RUBY   Rarity: **Common**
Route 112

SAPPHIRE   Rarity: **Common**
Route 112

FIRERED   Rarity: **None**
Trade from *Ruby/Sapphire/Emerald*

LEAFGREEN   Rarity: **None**
Trade from *Ruby/Sapphire/Emerald*

COLOSSEUM   Rarity: **None**
Trade from *Ruby/Sapphire/Emerald*

EMERALD   Rarity: **Common**
Route 112, Fiery Path, Jagged Pass

XD   Rarity: **Only One**
Cipher Lab (Capture from Cipher Peon Solox)

MOVES
Level	Attack	Type	Power	ACC	PP	Level	Attack	Type	Power	ACC	PP
—	Growl	Normal	—	100	40	29	Take Down	Normal	90	85	20
—	Tackle	Normal	35	95	35	31	Amnesia	Psychic	—	—	20
11	Ember	Fire	40	100	25	35	Earthquake	Ground	100	100	10
19	Magnitude	Ground	—	100	30	41	Flamethrower	Fire	95	100	15
25	Focus Energy	Normal	—	—	30	49	Double-Edge	Normal	120	100	15

TM/HM
TM/HM#	Name	Type	Power	ACC	PP	TM/HM#	Name	Type	Power	ACC	PP
TM06	Toxic	Poison	—	85	10	TM37	Sandstorm	Rock	—	—	10
TM10	Hidden Power	Normal	—	100	15	TM38	Fire Blast	Fire	120	85	5
TM11	Sunny Day	Fire	—	—	5	TM39	Rock Tomb	Rock	50	80	10
TM17	Protect	Normal	—	—	10	TM42	Facade	Normal	70	100	20
TM21	Frustration	Normal	—	100	20	TM43	Secret Power	Normal	70	100	20
TM26	Earthquake	Ground	100	100	10	TM44	Rest	Psychic	—	—	10
TM27	Return	Normal	—	100	20	TM45	Attract	Normal	—	100	15
TM28	Dig	Ground	60	100	10	TM50	Overheat	Fire	140	90	5
TM32	Double Team	Normal	—	—	15	HM04	Strength	Normal	80	100	15
TM35	Flamethrower	Fire	95	100	15	HM06	Rock Smash	Fighting	20	100	15

EGG MOVES*
Name	Type	Power	ACC	PP
Howl	Normal	—	—	40
Scary Face	Normal	—	90	10
Body Slam	Normal	85	100	15
Rollout	Rock	30	90	20
Defense Curl	Normal	—	—	40
Stomp	Normal	65	100	20

*Learned Via Breeding

MOVE TUTOR
FireRed/LeafGreen and *Emerald* Only

Body Slam*	Double-Edge	Mimic
Rock Slide*	Substitute	

Emerald Only

Defense Curl*	Endure*	Mud-Slap*
Rollout	Sleep Talk	Snore*
Swagger		

*Battle Frontier tutor move (*Emerald*)

323 Camerupt™

FIRE **GROUND**

GENERAL INFO
SPECIES: Eruption Pokémon
HEIGHT: 6'03"
WEIGHT: 485 lbs.
ABILITY: Magma Armor
Camerupt is unaffected by the Freeze condition.

STATS
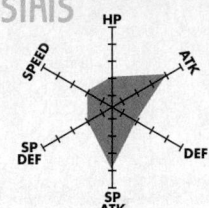

EVOLUTIONS
 LV33

LOCATION[S]:

RUBY	**Rarity: Evolve**
Evolve Numel	
SAPPHIRE	**Rarity: Evolve**
Evolve Numel	
FIRERED	**Rarity: None**
Trade from *Ruby/Sapphire/Emerald*	
LEAFGREEN	**Rarity: None**
Trade from *Ruby/Sapphire/Emerald*	
COLOSSEUM	**Rarity: None**
Trade from *Ruby/Sapphire/Emerald*	
EMERALD	**Rarity: Evolve**
Evolve Numel	
XD	**Rarity: Evolve**
Evolve Numel	

MOVES

Level	Attack	Type	Power	ACC	PP	Level	Attack	Type	Power	ACC	PP
—	Growl	Normal	—	100	40	29	Take Down	Normal	90	85	20
—	Tackle	Normal	35	95	35	31	Amnesia	Psychic	—	—	20
—	Ember	Fire	40	100	25	33	Rock Slide	Rock	75	90	10
—	Magnitude	Ground	—	100	30	37	Earthquake	Ground	100	100	10
25	Focus Energy	Normal	—	—	30	45	Eruption	Fire	150	100	5
						55	Fissure	Ground	—	30	5

TM/HM

TM/HM#	Name	Type	Power	ACC	PP	TM/HM#	Name	Type	Power	ACC	PP
TM05	Roar	Normal	—	100	20	TM35	Flamethrower	Fire	95	100	15
TM06	Toxic	Poison	—	85	10	TM37	Sandstorm	Rock	—	—	10
TM10	Hidden Power	Normal	—	100	15	TM38	Fire Blast	Fire	120	85	5
TM11	Sunny Day	Fire	—	—	5	TM39	Rock Tomb	Rock	50	80	10
TM15	Hyper Beam	Normal	150	90	5	TM42	Facade	Normal	70	100	20
TM17	Protect	Normal	—	—	10	TM43	Secret Power	Normal	70	100	20
TM21	Frustration	Normal	—	100	20	TM44	Rest	Psychic	—	—	10
TM22	Solarbeam	Grass	120	100	10	TM45	Attract	Normal	—	100	15
TM26	Earthquake	Ground	100	100	10	TM50	Overheat	Fire	140	90	5
TM27	Return	Normal	—	100	20	HM04	Strength	Normal	80	100	15
TM28	Dig	Ground	60	100	10	HM06	Rock Smash	Fighting	20	100	15
TM32	Double Team	Normal	—	—	15						

MOVE TUTOR
FireRed/LeafGreen and *Emerald* Only

Body Slam*	Double-Edge	Explosion
Mimic	Rock Slide*	Substitute

Emerald Only

Defense Curl*	Endure*	Mud-Slap*
Rollout	Sleep Talk	Snore*
Swagger		

*Battle Frontier tutor move (*Emerald*)

---

324 Torkoal™

FIRE

GENERAL INFO
SPECIES: Coal Pokémon
HEIGHT: 1'08"
WEIGHT: 177 lbs.
ABILITY: White Smoke
Torkoal is not affected by moves that lower stats.

STATS
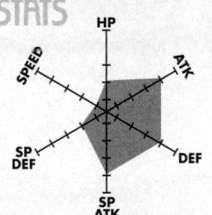

EVOLUTIONS

DOES NOT EVOLVE

LOCATION[S]:

RUBY	**Rarity: Rare**
Fiery Path	
SAPPHIRE	**Rarity: Rare**
Fiery Path	
FIRERED	**Rarity: None**
Trade from *Ruby/Sapphire/Emerald*	
LEAFGREEN	**Rarity: None**
Trade from *Ruby/Sapphire/Emerald*	
COLOSSEUM	**Rarity: None**
Trade from *Ruby/Sapphire/Emerald*	
EMERALD	**Rarity: Rare**
Fiery Path, Magma Hideout	
XD	**Rarity: None**
Trade from *Ruby/Sapphire/Emerald*	

MOVES

Level	Attack	Type	Power	ACC	PP	Level	Attack	Type	Power	ACC	PP
—	Ember	Fire	40	100	25	27	Protect	Normal	—	—	10
4	Smog	Poison	20	70	20	30	Flamethrower	Fire	95	100	15
7	Curse	—	—	—	10	33	Iron Defense	Steel	—	—	15
14	Smokescreen	Normal	—	100	20	40	Amnesia	Psychic	—	—	20
17	Fire Spin	Fire	15	70	15	43	Flail	Normal	—	100	15
20	Body Slam	Normal	85	100	15	46	Heat Wave	Fire	100	90	10

TM/HM

TM/HM#	Name	Type	Power	ACC	PP	TM/HM#	Name	Type	Power	ACC	PP
TM06	Toxic	Poison	—	85	10	TM36	Sludge Bomb	Poison	90	100	10
TM10	Hidden Power	Normal	—	100	15	TM38	Fire Blast	Fire	120	85	5
TM11	Sunny Day	Fire	—	—	5	TM42	Facade	Normal	70	100	20
TM17	Protect	Normal	—	—	10	TM43	Secret Power	Normal	70	100	20
TM21	Frustration	Normal	—	100	20	TM44	Rest	Psychic	—	—	10
TM23	Iron Tail	Steel	100	75	15	TM45	Attract	Normal	—	100	15
TM27	Return	Normal	—	100	20	TM50	Overheat	Fire	140	90	5
TM32	Double Team	Normal	—	—	15	HM04	Strength	Normal	80	100	15
TM35	Flamethrower	Fire	95	100	15	HM06	Rock Smash	Fighting	20	100	15

EGG MOVES*

Name	Type	Power	ACC	PP
Eruption	Fire	150	100	5
Endure	Normal	—	—	10
Sleep Talk	Normal	—	—	10
Yawn	Normal	—	100	10

*Learned Via Breeding

MOVE TUTOR
FireRed/LeafGreen and *Emerald* Only

Body Slam*	Double-Edge	Explosion
Mimic	Rock Slide*	Substitute

Emerald Only

Endure*	Mud-Slap*	Sleep Talk
Snore*	Swagger	

*Battle Frontier tutor move (*Emerald*)

325 Spoink™

PSYCHIC

GENERAL INFO

SPECIES: Bounce Pokémon
HEIGHT: 2'04"
WEIGHT: 67 lbs.
ABILITY 1: Thick Fat
Fire- and Ice-type moves inflict only 50% of the damage.
ABILITY 2: Own Tempo
Spoink cannot become confused.

STATS

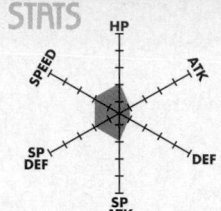

EVOLUTIONS

LV32

LOCATION[s]:

RUBY Rarity: **Rare**
Jagged Pass

SAPPHIRE Rarity: **Rare**
Jagged Pass

FIRERED Rarity: **None**
Trade from *Ruby/Sapphire/Emerald*

LEAFGREEN Rarity: **None**
Trade from *Ruby/Sapphire/Emerald*

COLOSSEUM Rarity: **None**
Trade from *Ruby/Sapphire/Emerald*

EMERALD Rarity: **Rare**
Jagged Pass

XD Rarity: **None**
Trade from *Ruby/Sapphire/Emerald*

MOVES

Level	Attack	Type	Power	ACC	PP	Level	Attack	Type	Power	ACC	PP
—	Splash	Normal	—	—	40	25	Confuse Ray	Ghost	—	100	10
7	Psywave	Psychic	—	80	15	28	Magic Coat	Psychic	—	100	15
10	Odor Sleuth	Normal	—	100	40	34	Psychic	Psychic	90	100	10
16	Psybeam	Psychic	65	100	20	37	Rest	Psychic	—	—	10
19	Psych Up	Normal	—	—	10	37	Snore	Normal	40	100	15
						43	Bounce	Flying	85	85	5

TM/HM

TM/HM#	Name	Type	Power	ACC	PP	TM/HM#	Name	Type	Power	ACC	PP
TM04	Calm Mind	Psychic	—	—	20	TM32	Double Team	Normal	—	—	15
TM06	Toxic	Poison	—	85	10	TM33	Reflect	Psychic	—	—	20
TM10	Hidden Power	Normal	—	100	15	TM34	Shock Wave	Electric	60	—	20
TM11	Sunny Day	Fire	—	—	5	TM41	Torment	Dark	—	100	15
TM12	Taunt	Dark	—	100	20	TM42	Facade	Normal	70	100	20
TM16	Light Screen	Psychic	—	—	30	TM43	Secret Power	Normal	70	100	20
TM17	Protect	Normal	—	—	10	TM44	Rest	Psychic	—	—	10
TM18	Rain Dance	Water	—	—	5	TM45	Attract	Normal	—	100	15
TM21	Frustration	Normal	—	100	20	TM46	Thief	Dark	40	100	10
TM23	Iron Tail	Steel	100	75	15	TM48	Skill Swap	Psychic	—	100	10
TM27	Return	Normal	—	100	20	TM49	Snatch	Dark	—	100	10
TM29	Psychic	Psychic	90	100	10	HM05	Flash	Normal	—	70	20
TM30	Shadow Ball	Ghost	60	—	20						

EGG MOVES*

Name	Type	Power	ACC	PP
Future Sight	Psychic	80	90	15
Extrasensory	Psychic	80	100	30
Substitute	Normal	—	—	10
Trick	Psychic	—	100	10

*Learned Via Breeding

MOVE TUTOR

FireRed/LeafGreen and **Emerald** Only

Body Slam*	Double-Edge*	Dream Eater*
Mimic	Rock Slide*	Substitute

Emerald Only

Endure*	Icy Wind*	Psych Up*
Sleep Talk	Snore*	Swagger
Swift*		

*Battle Frontier tutor move (*Emerald*)

326 Grumpig™

PSYCHIC

GENERAL INFO

SPECIES: Manipulate Pokémon
HEIGHT: 2'11"
WEIGHT: 158 lbs.
ABILITY 1: Thick Fat
Fire- and Ice-type moves inflict only 50% of the damage.
ABILITY 2: Own Tempo
Grumpig cannot become confused.

STATS

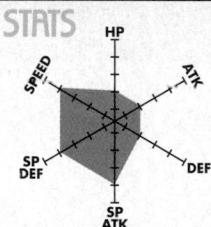

EVOLUTIONS

LV32

LOCATION[s]:

RUBY Rarity: **Evolve**
Evolve Spoink

SAPPHIRE Rarity: **Evolve**
Evolve Spoink

FIRERED Rarity: **None**
Trade from *Ruby/Sapphire/Emerald*

LEAFGREEN Rarity: **None**
Trade from *Ruby/Sapphire/Emerald*

COLOSSEUM Rarity: **None**
Trade from *Ruby/Sapphire/Emerald*

EMERALD Rarity: **Evolve**
Evolve Spoink

XD Rarity: **None**
Trade from *Ruby/Sapphire/Emerald*

MOVES

Level	Attack	Type	Power	ACC	PP	Level	Attack	Type	Power	ACC	PP
—	Splash	Normal	—	—	40	25	Confuse Ray	Ghost	—	100	10
—	Psywave	Psychic	—	80	15	28	Magic Coat	Psychic	—	100	15
—	Odor Sleuth	Normal	—	100	40	37	Psychic	Psychic	90	100	10
—	Psybeam	Psychic	65	100	20	43	Rest	Psychic	—	—	10
19	Psych Up	Normal	—	—	10	43	Snore	Normal	40	100	15
						55	Bounce	Flying	85	85	5

TM/HM

TM/HM#	Name	Type	Power	ACC	PP	TM/HM#	Name	Type	Power	ACC	PP
TM01	Focus Punch	Fighting	150	100	20	TM30	Shadow Ball	Ghost	60	—	20
TM04	Calm Mind	Psychic	—	—	20	TM32	Double Team	Normal	—	—	15
TM06	Toxic	Poison	—	85	10	TM33	Reflect	Psychic	—	—	20
TM10	Hidden Power	Normal	—	100	15	TM34	Shock Wave	Electric	60	—	20
TM11	Sunny Day	Fire	—	—	5	TM41	Torment	Dark	—	100	15
TM12	Taunt	Dark	—	100	20	TM42	Facade	Normal	70	100	20
TM15	Hyper Beam	Normal	150	90	5	TM43	Secret Power	Normal	70	100	20
TM16	Light Screen	Psychic	—	—	30	TM44	Rest	Psychic	—	—	10
TM17	Protect	Normal	—	—	10	TM45	Attract	Normal	—	100	15
TM18	Rain Dance	Water	—	—	5	TM46	Thief	Dark	40	100	10
TM21	Frustration	Normal	—	100	20	TM48	Skill Swap	Psychic	—	100	10
TM23	Iron Tail	Steel	100	75	15	TM49	Snatch	Dark	—	100	10
TM27	Return	Normal	—	100	20	HM05	Flash	Normal	—	70	20
TM29	Psychic	Psychic	90	100	10						

MOVE TUTOR

FireRed/LeafGreen and **Emerald** Only

Body Slam*	Counter*	Double-Edge
Dream Eater*	Mega Kick*	Mega Punch*
Mimic	Seismic Toss*	Substitute

Emerald Only

Dynamicpunch*	Endure*	Fire Punch*
Ice Punch*	Icy Wind*	Metronome
Mud-Slap*	Psych Up*	Sleep Talk
Snore*	Swagger	Swift*
Thunderpunch*		

*Battle Frontier tutor move (*Emerald*)

327 Spinda™

NORMAL

GENERAL INFO
SPECIES: Spot Panda Pokémon
HEIGHT: 3'07"
WEIGHT: 11 lbs.
ABILITY: Own Tempo
Spinda cannot become confused.

STATS
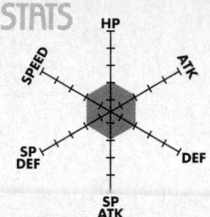

EVOLUTIONS

DOES NOT EVOLVE

LOCATION(S):

RUBY — Rarity: **Rare**
Route 113

SAPPHIRE — Rarity: **Rare**
Route 113

FIRERED — Rarity: **None**
Trade from *Ruby/Sapphire/Emerald*

LEAFGREEN — Rarity: **None**
Trade from *Ruby/Sapphire/Emerald*

COLOSSEUM — Rarity: **None**
Trade from *Ruby/Sapphire/Emerald*

EMERALD — Rarity: **Common**
Route 113

XD — Rarity: **None**
Trade from *Ruby/Sapphire/Emerald*

MOVES

Level	Attack	Type	Power	ACC	PP	Level	Attack	Type	Power	ACC	PP
—	Tackle	Normal	35	95	35	27	Dizzy Punch	Normal	70	100	10
5	Uproar	Normal	50	100	10	34	Teeter Dance	Normal	—	100	20
12	Faint Attack	Dark	60	—	20	38	Psych Up	Normal	—	—	10
16	Psybeam	Psychic	65	100	20	45	Double-Edge	Normal	120	100	15
23	Hypnosis	Psychic	—	60	20	49	Flail	Normal	—	100	15
						56	Thrash	Normal	90	100	20

TM/HM

TM/HM#	Name	Type	Power	ACC	PP	TM/HM#	Name	Type	Power	ACC	PP
TM01	Focus Punch	Fighting	150	100	20	TM31	Brick Break	Fighting	75	100	15
TM03	Water Pulse	Water	60	100	20	TM32	Double Team	Normal	—	—	15
TM04	Calm Mind	Psychic	—	—	20	TM34	Shock Wave	Electric	60	—	20
TM06	Toxic	Poison	—	85	10	TM39	Rock Tomb	Rock	50	80	10
TM10	Hidden Power	Normal	—	100	15	TM42	Facade	Normal	70	100	20
TM11	Sunny Day	Fire	—	—	5	TM43	Secret Power	Normal	70	100	20
TM17	Protect	Normal	—	—	10	TM44	Rest	Psychic	—	—	10
TM18	Rain Dance	Water	—	—	5	TM45	Attract	Normal	—	100	15
TM20	Safeguard	Normal	—	—	25	TM46	Thief	Dark	40	100	10
TM21	Frustration	Normal	—	100	20	TM48	Skill Swap	Psychic	—	100	10
TM27	Return	Normal	—	100	20	TM49	Snatch	Dark	—	100	10
TM28	Dig	Ground	60	100	10	HM04	Strength	Normal	80	100	15
TM29	Psychic	Psychic	90	100	10	HM05	Flash	Normal	—	70	20
TM30	Shadow Ball	Ghost	60	—	20	HM06	Rock Smash	Fighting	20	100	15

EGG MOVES*

Name	Type	Power	ACC	PP
Encore	Normal	—	100	5
Rock Slide	Rock	75	90	10
Assist	Normal	—	100	20
Disable	Normal	—	55	20
Baton Pass	Normal	—	—	40
Trick	Psychic	—	100	10
Smellingsalt	Normal	60	100	10
Wish	Normal	—	—	10

*Learned Via Breeding

MOVE TUTOR
FireRed/LeafGreen and *Emerald* Only

Body Slam*	Counter*	Double-Edge*
Dream Eater*	Mega Kick*	Mega Punch*
Metronome	Mimic	Rock Slide*
Seismic Toss*	Substitute	

Emerald Only

Defense Curl*	Dynamicpunch*	Endure*
Fire Punch*	Ice Punch*	Icy Wind*
Metronome	Mud-Slap*	Psych Up*
Rollout	Sleep Talk	Snore*
Swagger	Swift*	Thunderpunch*

*Battle Frontier tutor move (*Emerald*)

---

328 Trapinch™

GROUND

GENERAL INFO
SPECIES: Ant Pit Pokémon
HEIGHT: 2'04"
WEIGHT: 33 lbs.
ABILITY 1: Hyper Cutter
Trapinch's attack power cannot be lowered.

ABILITY 2: Arena Trap
Prevents the opponent Pokémon from fleeing or switching out of battle. Does not affect Flying-type Pokémon or Pokémon with the Levitate Ability.

STATS
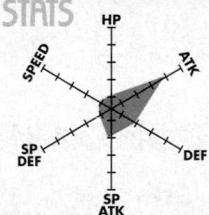

EVOLUTIONS

LV35   LV45

LOCATION(S):

RUBY — Rarity: **Rare**
Route 111

SAPPHIRE — Rarity: **Rare**
Route 111

FIRERED — Rarity: **None**
Trade from *Ruby/Sapphire*

LEAFGREEN — Rarity: **None**
Trade from *Ruby/Sapphire*

COLOSSEUM — Rarity: **None**
Trade from *Ruby/Sapphire*

EMERALD — Rarity: **Common**
Route 111, Mirage Tower

XD — Rarity: **Rare**
Rock Poké Spot

MOVES

Level	Attack	Type	Power	ACC	PP	Level	Attack	Type	Power	ACC	PP
—	Bite	Dark	60	100	25	33	Crunch	Dark	80	100	15
9	Sand-Attack	Ground	—	100	15	41	Dig	Ground	60	100	10
17	Faint Attack	Dark	60	—	20	49	Sandstorm	Rock	—	—	10
25	Sand Tomb	Ground	15	70	15	57	Hyper Beam	Normal	150	90	5

TM/HM

TM/HM#	Name	Type	Power	ACC	PP	TM/HM#	Name	Type	Power	ACC	PP
TM06	Toxic	Poison	—	85	10	TM28	Dig	Ground	60	100	10
TM10	Hidden Power	Normal	—	100	15	TM32	Double Team	Normal	—	—	15
TM11	Sunny Day	Fire	—	—	5	TM37	Sandstorm	Normal	—	—	10
TM15	Hyper Beam	Normal	150	90	5	TM39	Rock Tomb	Rock	50	80	10
TM17	Protect	Normal	—	—	10	TM42	Facade	Normal	70	100	20
TM19	Giga Drain	Grass	60	100	5	TM43	Secret Power	Normal	70	100	20
TM21	Frustration	Normal	—	100	20	TM44	Rest	Psychic	—	—	10
TM22	Solarbeam	Grass	120	100	10	TM45	Attract	Normal	—	100	15
TM26	Earthquake	Ground	100	100	10	HM04	Strength	Normal	80	100	15
TM27	Return	Normal	—	100	20	HM06	Rock Smash	Fighting	20	100	15

EGG MOVES*

Name	Type	Power	ACC	PP
Focus Energy	Normal	—	—	30
Quick Attack	Normal	40	100	30
Whirlwind	Normal	—	100	20

*Learned Via Breeding

MOVE TUTOR
FireRed/LeafGreen and *Emerald* Only

Body Slam*	Double-Edge*	Mimic
Rock Slide*	Substitute	

Emerald Only

Endure*	Mud-Slap*	Sleep Talk
Snore*	Swagger	

*Battle Frontier tutor move (*Emerald*)

329 Vibrava™

GROUND **DRAGON**

GENERAL INFO
SPECIES: Vibration Pokémon
HEIGHT: 3'07"
WEIGHT: 34 lbs.
ABILITY: Levitate
Vibrava is not affected by Ground-type moves.

STATS

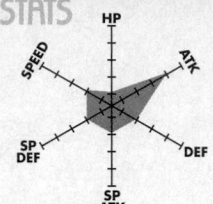

EVOLUTIONS

LV35 LV45

LOCATION[S]:

RUBY   Rarity: **Evolve**
Evolve Trapinch

SAPPHIRE   Rarity: **Evolve**
Evolve Trapinch

FIRERED   Rarity: **None**
Trade from Ruby/Sapphire/Emerald/Colosseum

LEAFGREEN   Rarity: **None**
Trade from Ruby/Sapphire/Emerald/Colosseum

COLOSSEUM   Rarity: **Only One**
Shadow Pokémon Lab

EMERALD   Rarity: **Evolve**
Evolve Trapinch

XD   Rarity: **Evolve**
Evolve Trapinch

MOVES

Level	Attack	Type	Power	ACC	PP	Level	Attack	Type	Power	ACC	PP
—	Bite	Dark	60	100	25	33	Crunch	Dark	80	100	15
—	Sand-Attack	Ground		100	15	35	Dragonbreath	Dragon	60	100	20
—	Faint Attack	Dark	60		20	41	Screech	Normal		85	40
—	Sand Tomb	Ground	15	70	15	49	Sandstorm	Rock	—		10
						57	Hyper Beam	Normal	150	90	5

TM/HM

TM/HM#	Name	Type	Power	ACC	PP	TM/HM#	Name	Type	Power	ACC	PP
TM06	Toxic	Poison	—	85	10	TM32	Double Team	Normal	—	—	15
TM10	Hidden Power	Normal	—	100	15	TM37	Sandstorm	Rock	—		10
TM11	Sunny Day	Fire	—	—	5	TM39	Rock Tomb	Rock	50	80	10
TM15	Hyper Beam	Normal	150	90	5	TM42	Facade	Normal	70	100	20
TM17	Protect	Normal	—	—	10	TM43	Secret Power	Normal	70	100	20
TM19	Giga Drain	Grass	60	100	5	TM44	Rest	Psychic	—	—	10
TM21	Frustration	Normal	—	100	20	TM45	Attract	Normal	—	100	15
TM22	Solarbeam	Grass	120	100	10	TM47	Steel Wing	Steel	70	90	25
TM26	Earthquake	Ground	100	100	10	HM02	Fly	Flying	70	95	15
TM27	Return	Normal	—	100	20	HM04	Strength	Normal	80	100	15
TM28	Dig	Ground	60	100	10	HM06	Rock Smash	Fighting	20	100	15

MOVE TUTOR
FireRed/LeafGreen and Emerald Only

Body Slam*	Double-Edge	Mimic
Rock Slide*	Substitute	

Emerald Only

Endure*	Mud-Slap*	Sleep Talk
Snore*	Swagger	Swift*

*Battle Frontier tutor move (*Emerald*)

---

330 Flygon™

GROUND **DRAGON**

GENERAL INFO
SPECIES: Mystic Pokémon
HEIGHT: 6'07"
WEIGHT: 181 lbs.
ABILITY: Levitate
Flygon is not affected by Ground-type moves.

STATS

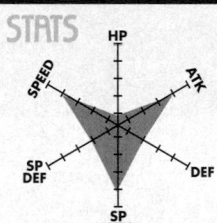

EVOLUTIONS

LV35 LV45

LOCATION[S]:

RUBY   Rarity: **Evolve**
Evolve Vibrava

SAPPHIRE   Rarity: **Evolve**
Evolve Vibrava

FIRERED   Rarity: **None**
Trade from Ruby/Sapphire/Emerald/Colosseum

LEAFGREEN   Rarity: **None**
Trade from Ruby/Sapphire/Emerald/Colosseum

COLOSSEUM   Rarity: **Evolve**
Evolve Vibrava

EMERALD   Rarity: **Evolve**
Evolve Vibrava

XD   Rarity: **Evolve**
Evolve Vibrava

MOVES

Level	Attack	Type	Power	ACC	PP	Level	Attack	Type	Power	ACC	PP
—	Bite	Dark	60	100	25	33	Crunch	Dark	80	100	15
—	Sand-Attack	Ground		100	15	35	Dragonbreath	Dragon	60	100	20
—	Faint Attack	Dark	60		20	41	Screech	Normal		85	40
—	Sand Tomb	Ground	15	70	15	53	Sandstorm	Rock	—		10
						65	Hyper Beam	Normal	150	90	5

TM/HM

TM/HM#	Name	Type	Power	ACC	PP	TM/HM#	Name	Type	Power	ACC	PP
TM02	Dragon Claw	Dragon	80	100	15	TM32	Double Team	Normal	—	—	15
TM06	Toxic	Poison	—	85	10	TM35	Flamethrower	Fire	95	100	15
TM10	Hidden Power	Normal	—	100	15	TM37	Sandstorm	Rock	—		10
TM11	Sunny Day	Fire	—	—	5	TM38	Fire Blast	Fire	120	85	5
TM15	Hyper Beam	Normal	150	90	5	TM39	Rock Tomb	Rock	50	80	10
TM17	Protect	Normal	—	—	10	TM42	Facade	Normal	70	100	20
TM19	Giga Drain	Grass	60	100	5	TM43	Secret Power	Normal	70	100	20
TM21	Frustration	Normal	—	100	20	TM44	Rest	Psychic	—	—	10
TM22	Solarbeam	Grass	120	100	10	TM45	Attract	Normal	—	100	15
TM23	Iron Tail	Steel	100	75	15	TM47	Steel Wing	Steel	70	90	25
TM26	Earthquake	Ground	100	100	10	HM02	Fly	Flying	70	95	15
TM27	Return	Normal	—	100	20	HM04	Strength	Normal	80	100	15
TM28	Dig	Ground	60	100	10	HM06	Rock Smash	Fighting	20	100	15

MOVE TUTOR
FireRed/LeafGreen and Emerald Only

Body Slam*	Double-Edge	Mimic
Rock Slide*	Substitute	

Emerald Only

Endure*	Fire Punch*	Fury Cutter
Mud-Slap*	Sleep Talk	Snore*
Swagger	Swift*	

*Battle Frontier tutor move (*Emerald*)

331 Cacnea™

GRASS

GENERAL INFO
SPECIES: Cactus Pokémon
HEIGHT: 1'04"
WEIGHT: 113 lbs.
ABILITY: Sand Veil

Cacnea's evasion stat rises when a sandstorm blows.

STATS
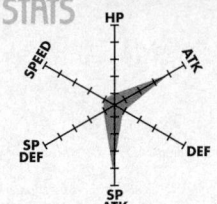

EVOLUTIONS
 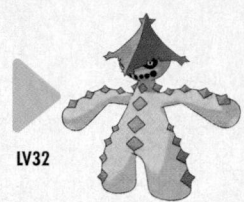
LV32

LOCATION(S):

RUBY	Rarity: **Rare**
Route 111	
SAPPHIRE	Rarity: **Rare**
Route 111	
FIRERED	Rarity: **None**
Trade from *Ruby/Sapphire/Emerald*	
LEAFGREEN	Rarity: **None**
Trade from *Ruby/Sapphire/Emerald*	
COLOSSEUM	Rarity: **None**
Trade from *Ruby/Sapphire/Emerald*	
EMERALD	Rarity: **Rare**
Route 111	
XD	Rarity: **None**
Trade from *Ruby/Sapphire/Emerald*	

MOVES

Level	Attack	Type	Power	ACC	PP
—	Poison Sting	Poison	15	100	35
—	Leer	Normal	—	100	30
5	Absorb	Grass	20	100	20
9	Growth	Normal	—	—	40
13	Leech Seed	Grass	—	90	10
17	Sand-Attack	Ground	—	100	15
21	Pin Missile	Bug	14	85	20

Level	Attack	Type	Power	ACC	PP
25	Ingrain	Grass	—	100	20
29	Faint Attack	Dark	60	—	20
33	Spikes	Ground	—	—	20
37	Needle Arm	Grass	60	100	15
41	Cotton Spore	Grass	—	85	40
45	Sandstorm	Rock	—	—	10
49	Destiny Bond*	Ghost	—	—	5

* Not Available in *Emerald*

TM/HM

TM/HM#	Name	Type	Power	ACC	PP
TM01	Focus Punch	Fighting	150	100	20
TM06	Toxic	Poison	—	85	10
TM09	Bullet Seed	Grass	10	100	30
TM10	Hidden Power	Normal	—	100	15
TM11	Sunny Day	Fire	—	—	5
TM17	Protect	Normal	—	—	10
TM19	Giga Drain	Grass	60	100	5
TM21	Frustration	Normal	—	100	20
TM22	Solarbeam	Grass	120	100	10

TM/HM#	Name	Type	Power	ACC	PP
TM27	Return	Normal	—	100	20
TM32	Double Team	Normal	—	—	15
TM37	Sandstorm	Rock	—	—	10
TM42	Facade	Normal	70	100	20
TM43	Secret Power	Normal	70	100	20
TM44	Rest	Psychic	—	—	10
TM45	Attract	Normal	—	100	15
HM01	Cut	Normal	50	95	30
HM05	Flash	Normal	—	70	20

EGG MOVES*

Name	Type	Power	ACC	PP
Grasswhistle	Grass	—	55	15
Acid	Poison	40	100	30
Teeter Dance	Normal	—	100	20
Dynamicpunch	Fighting	100	50	5
Counter	Fighting	—	100	20

*Learned Via Breeding

MOVE TUTOR

FireRed/LeafGreen and Emerald Only

Body Slam*	Counter*	Double-Edge
Mega Punch*	Mimic	Seismic Toss*
Substitute	Swords Dance*	

Emerald Only

Dynamicpunch	Endure*	Fury Cutter
Mud-Slap*	Sleep Talk	Snore
Swagger	Thunderpunch*	

*Battle Frontier tutor move (*Emerald*)

---

332 Cacturne™

GRASS DARK

GENERAL INFO
SPECIES: Scarecrow Pokémon
HEIGHT: 4'03"
WEIGHT: 171 lbs.
ABILITY: Sand Veil

Cacturne's evasion stat rises when a sandstorm blows.

STATS
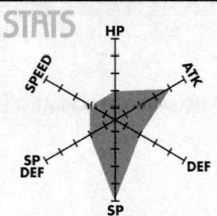

EVOLUTIONS

LV32

LOCATION(S):

RUBY	Rarity: **Evolve**
Evolve Cacnea	
SAPPHIRE	Rarity: **Evolve**
Evolve Cacnea	
FIRERED	Rarity: **None**
Trade from *Ruby/Sapphire/Emerald*	
LEAFGREEN	Rarity: **None**
Trade from *Ruby/Sapphire/Emerald*	
COLOSSEUM	Rarity: **None**
Trade from *Ruby/Sapphire/Emerald*	
EMERALD	Rarity: **Evolve**
Evolve Cacnea	
XD	Rarity: **None**
Trade from *Ruby/Sapphire/Emerald*	

MOVES

Level	Attack	Type	Power	ACC	PP
—	Revenge	Fighting	60	100	10
—	Poison Sting	Poison	15	100	35
—	Leer	Normal	—	100	30
—	Absorb	Grass	20	100	20
—	Growth	Normal	—	—	40
13	Leech Seed	Grass	—	90	10
17	Sand-Attack	Ground	—	100	15
21	Pin Missile	Bug	14	85	20

Level	Attack	Type	Power	ACC	PP
25	Ingrain	Grass	—	100	20
29	Faint Attack	Dark	60	—	20
35	Spikes	Ground	—	—	20
41	Needle Arm	Grass	60	100	15
47	Cotton Spore	Grass	—	85	40
53	Sandstorm	Rock	—	—	10
59	Destiny Bond*	Ghost	—	—	5

* Not Available in *Emerald*

TM/HM

TM/HM#	Name	Type	Power	ACC	PP
TM01	Focus Punch	Fighting	150	100	20
TM06	Toxic	Poison	—	85	10
TM09	Bullet Seed	Grass	10	100	30
TM10	Hidden Power	Normal	—	100	15
TM11	Sunny Day	Fire	—	—	5
TM15	Hyper Beam	Normal	150	90	5
TM17	Protect	Normal	—	—	10
TM19	Giga Drain	Grass	60	100	5
TM21	Frustration	Normal	—	100	20
TM22	Solarbeam	Grass	120	100	10

TM/HM#	Name	Type	Power	ACC	PP
TM27	Return	Normal	—	100	20
TM32	Double Team	Normal	—	—	15
TM37	Sandstorm	Rock	—	—	10
TM42	Facade	Normal	70	100	20
TM43	Secret Power	Normal	70	100	20
TM44	Rest	Psychic	—	—	10
TM45	Attract	Normal	—	100	15
HM01	Cut	Normal	50	95	30
HM04	Strength	Normal	80	100	15
HM05	Flash	Normal	—	70	20

MOVE TUTOR

FireRed/LeafGreen and Emerald Only

Body Slam*	Counter*	Double-Edge
Mega Kick*	Mega Punch*	Mimic
Seismic Toss*	Substitute	Swords Dance*

Emerald Only

Dynamicpunch	Endure*	Fury Cutter
Mud-Slap*	Sleep Talk	Snore
Swagger	Thunderpunch*	

*Battle Frontier tutor move (*Emerald*)

333 Swablu™

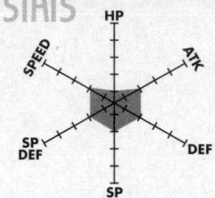  

NORMAL · FLYING

GENERAL INFO

SPECIES: Cotton Bird Pokémon
HEIGHT: 1'04"
WEIGHT: 3 lbs.
ABILITY: Natural Cure

Any negative status conditions are healed when Swablu is removed from battle.

STATS

EVOLUTIONS

LV35

LOCATION(S):

RUBY	Rarity: **Rare**

Route 114, Route 115

SAPPHIRE	Rarity: **Rare**

Route 114, Route 115

FIRERED	Rarity: **None**

Trade from *Ruby/Sapphire/Colosseum/Emerald*

LEAFGREEN	Rarity: **None**

Trade from *Ruby/Sapphire/Colosseum/Emerald*

COLOSSEUM	Rarity: **Only One**

Pyrite Cave

EMERALD	Rarity: **Common**

Route 114, Route 115

XD	Rarity: **None**

Trade from *Ruby/Sapphire/Colosseum/Emerald*

MOVES

Level	Attack	Type	Power	ACC	PP	Level	Attack	Type	Power	ACC	PP
—	Peck	Flying	35	100	35	21	Safeguard	Normal	—	—	25
—	Growl	Normal	—	100	40	28	Mist	Ice	—	—	30
8	Astonish	Ghost	30	100	15	31	Take Down	Normal	90	85	20
11	Sing	Normal	—	55	15	38	Mirror Move	Flying	—	—	20
18	Fury Attack	Normal	15	85	20	41	Refresh	Normal	—	100	20
						48	Perish Song	Normal	—	—	5

TM/HM

TM/HM#	Name	Type	Power	ACC	PP	TM/HM#	Name	Type	Power	ACC	PP
TM06	Toxic	Poison	—	85	10	TM32	Double Team	Normal	—	—	15
TM10	Hidden Power	Normal	—	100	15	TM40	Aerial Ace	Flying	60	—	20
TM11	Sunny Day	Fire	—	—	5	TM42	Facade	Normal	70	100	20
TM13	Ice Beam	Ice	95	100	10	TM43	Secret Power	Normal	70	100	20
TM17	Protect	Normal	—	—	10	TM44	Rest	Psychic	—	—	10
TM18	Rain Dance	Water	—	—	5	TM45	Attract	Normal	—	100	15
TM20	Safeguard	Normal	—	—	25	TM46	Thief	Dark	40	100	10
TM21	Frustration	Normal	—	100	20	TM47	Steel Wing	Steel	70	90	25
TM22	Solarbeam	Grass	120	100	10	HM02	Fly	Flying	70	95	15
TM27	Return	Normal	—	100	20						

EGG MOVES*

Name	Type	Power	ACC	PP
Agility	Psychic	—	—	30
Haze	Ice	—	—	30
Pursuit	Dark	40	100	20
Rage	Normal	20	100	20

*Learned Via Breeding

MOVE TUTOR

FireRed/LeafGreen and *Emerald* Only

Body Slam*	Double-Edge	Dream Eater*
Mimic	Substitute	

Emerald Only

Endure*	Mud-Slap*	Psych Up*
Sleep Talk	Snore*	Swagger
Swift*		

*Battle Frontier tutor move (*Emerald*)

---

334 Altaria™

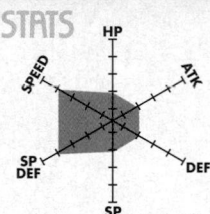  

DRAGON · FLYING

GENERAL INFO

SPECIES: Humming Pokémon
HEIGHT: 3'07"
WEIGHT: 45 lbs.
ABILITY: Natural Cure

Any negative status conditions are healed when Altaria is removed from battle.

STATS

EVOLUTIONS

LV35

LOCATION(S):

RUBY	Rarity: **Rare**

Sky Pillar

SAPPHIRE	Rarity: **Rare**

Sky Pillar

FIRERED	Rarity: **None**

Trade from *Ruby/Sapphire/Colosseum/Emerald*

LEAFGREEN	Rarity: **None**

Trade from *Ruby/Sapphire/Colosseum/Emerald*

COLOSSEUM	Rarity: **Evolve**

Evolve Swablu

EMERALD	Rarity: **Rare**

Evolve Swablu, Sky Pillar

XD	Rarity: **Only One**

Citadark Island (Capture from Admin Lovrina)

MOVES

Level	Attack	Type	Power	ACC	PP	Level	Attack	Type	Power	ACC	PP
—	Peck	Flying	35	100	35	28	Mist	Ice	—	—	30
—	Growl	Normal	—	100	40	31	Take Down	Normal	90	85	20
—	Sing	Normal	—	55	15	35	Dragonbreath	Dragon	60	100	20
—	Astonish	Ghost	30	100	15	40	Dragon Dance	Dragon	—	—	20
18	Fury Attack	Normal	15	85	20	45	Refresh	Normal	—	100	20
21	Safeguard	Normal	—	—	25	54	Perish Song	Normal	—	—	5
						59	Sky Attack	Flying	140	90	5

TM/HM

TM/HM#	Name	Type	Power	ACC	PP	TM/HM#	Name	Type	Power	ACC	PP
TM02	Dragon Claw	Dragon	80	100	15	TM27	Return	Normal	—	100	20
TM05	Roar	Normal	—	100	20	TM32	Double Team	Normal	—	—	15
TM06	Toxic	Poison	—	85	10	TM35	Flamethrower	Fire	95	100	15
TM10	Hidden Power	Normal	—	100	15	TM38	Fire Blast	Fire	120	85	5
TM11	Sunny Day	Fire	—	—	5	TM40	Aerial Ace	Flying	60	—	20
TM13	Ice Beam	Ice	95	100	10	TM42	Facade	Normal	70	100	20
TM15	Hyper Beam	Normal	150	90	5	TM43	Secret Power	Normal	70	100	20
TM17	Protect	Normal	—	—	10	TM44	Rest	Psychic	—	—	10
TM18	Rain Dance	Water	—	—	5	TM45	Attract	Normal	—	100	15
TM20	Safeguard	Normal	—	—	25	TM46	Thief	Dark	40	100	10
TM21	Frustration	Normal	—	100	20	TM47	Steel Wing	Steel	70	90	25
TM22	Solarbeam	Grass	120	100	10	HM02	Fly	Flying	70	95	15
TM23	Iron Tail	Steel	100	75	15	HM06	Rock Smash	Fighting	20	100	15
TM26	Earthquake	Ground	100	100	10						

MOVE TUTOR

FireRed/LeafGreen and *Emerald* Only

Body Slam*	Double-Edge	Dream Eater*
Mimic	Substitute	

Emerald Only

Endure*	Mud-Slap*	Psych Up*
Sleep Talk	Snore*	Swagger
Swift*		

*Battle Frontier tutor move (*Emerald*)

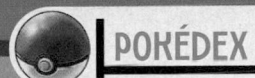

335 Zangoose

NORMAL

GENERAL INFO
SPECIES: Cat Ferret Pokémon
HEIGHT: 4'03"
WEIGHT: 89 lbs.
ABILITY: Immunity
Zangoose cannot be poisoned.

STATS

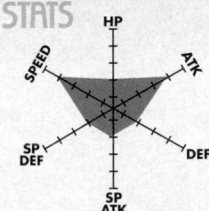

EVOLUTIONS

DOES NOT EVOLVE

LOCATION[S]:

RUBY   Rarity: **Rare**
Route 114

SAPPHIRE   Rarity: **None**
Trade from *Ruby*

FIRERED   Rarity: **None**
Trade from *Ruby*

LEAFGREEN   Rarity: **None**
Trade from *Ruby*

COLOSSEUM   Rarity: **None**
Trade from *Ruby*

EMERALD   Rarity: **None**
Trade from *Ruby*

XD   Rarity: **Only One**
Cipher Key Lair (Capture from Bodybuilder Zook)

MOVES

Level	Attack	Type	Power	ACC	PP	Level	Attack	Type	Power	ACC	PP
—	Scratch	Normal	40	100	35	19	Slash	Normal	70	100	20
4	Leer	Normal	—	100	30	25	Pursuit	Dark	40	100	20
7	Quick Attack	Normal	40	100	30	31	Crush Claw	Normal	75	95	10
10	Swords Dance	Normal	—	—	30	37	Taunt	Dark	—	100	20
13	Fury Cutter	Bug	10	95	20	46	Detect	Fighting	—	—	5
						55	False Swipe	Normal	40	100	40

TM/HM

TM/HM#	Name	Type	Power	ACC	PP	TM/HM#	Name	Type	Power	ACC	PP
TM01	Focus Punch	Fighting	150	100	20	TM27	Return	Normal	—	100	20
TM03	Water Pulse	Water	60	100	20	TM28	Dig	Ground	60	100	10
TM05	Roar	Normal	—	100	20	TM30	Shadow Ball	Ghost	60	—	20
TM06	Toxic	Poison	—	85	10	TM31	Brick Break	Fighting	75	100	15
TM10	Hidden Power	Normal	—	100	15	TM32	Double Team	Normal	—	—	15
TM11	Sunny Day	Fire	—	—	5	TM34	Shock Wave	Electric	60	—	20
TM12	Taunt	Dark	—	100	20	TM35	Flamethrower	Fire	95	100	15
TM13	Ice Beam	Ice	95	100	10	TM38	Fire Blast	Fire	120	85	5
TM14	Blizzard	Ice	120	70	5	TM40	Aerial Ace	Flying	60	—	20
TM17	Protect	Normal	—	—	10	TM42	Facade	Normal	70	100	20
TM18	Rain Dance	Water	—	—	5	TM43	Secret Power	Normal	70	100	20
TM19	Giga Drain	Grass	60	100	5	TM44	Rest	Psychic	—	—	10
TM21	Frustration	Normal	—	100	20	TM45	Attract	Normal	—	100	15
TM22	Solarbeam	Grass	120	100	10	TM46	Thief	Dark	40	100	10
TM23	Iron Tail	Steel	100	75	15	HM04	Strength	Normal	80	100	15
TM24	Thunderbolt	Electric	95	100	15	HM06	Rock Smash	Fighting	20	100	15
TM25	Thunder	Electric	120	70	10						

EGG MOVES*

Name	Type	Power	ACC	PP
Flail	Normal	—	100	15
Double Kick	Fighting	30	100	30
Razor Wind	Normal	80	100	10
Counter	Fighting	—	100	20
Roar	Normal	—	100	20
Curse	—	—	—	10

*Learned Via Breeding

MOVE TUTOR
FireRed/LeafGreen and *Emerald* Only

Body Slam*	Counter*	Double-Edge
Mega Kick*	Mega Punch*	Mimic
Rock Slide*	Seismic Toss*	Substitute
Swords Dance*	Thunder Wave*	

Emerald Only

Defense Curl*	Dynamicpunch*	Endure*
Fire Punch*	Fury Cutter	Ice Punch*
Icy Wind*	Mud-Slap*	Rollout
Sleep Talk	Snore*	Swagger
Swift*	Thunderpunch*	

*Battle Frontier tutor move (*Emerald*)

---

336 Seviper

POISON

GENERAL INFO
SPECIES: Fang Snake Pokémon
HEIGHT: 8'10"
WEIGHT: 116 lbs.
ABILITY: Shed Skin
Every turn, Seviper has a 1/3 chance of recovering from a status condition.

STATS

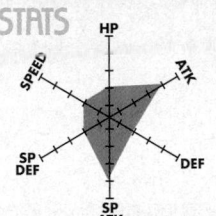

EVOLUTIONS

DOES NOT EVOLVE

LOCATION[S]:

RUBY   Rarity: **None**
Trade from *Sapphire/Emerald*

SAPPHIRE   Rarity: **Rare**
Route 114

FIRERED   Rarity: **None**
Trade from *Sapphire/Emerald*

LEAFGREEN   Rarity: **None**
Trade from *Sapphire/Emerald*

COLOSSEUM   Rarity: **None**
Trade from *Sapphire/Emerald*

EMERALD   Rarity: **Rare**
Route 114

XD   Rarity: **None**
Trade from *Sapphire/Emerald*

MOVES

Level	Attack	Type	Power	ACC	PP	Level	Attack	Type	Power	ACC	PP
—	Wrap	Normal	15	85	20	25	Glare	Normal	—	75	30
7	Lick	Ghost	20	100	30	28	Crunch	Dark	80	100	15
10	Bite	Dark	60	100	25	34	Poison Fang	Poison	50	100	15
16	Poison Tail	Poison	50	100	25	37	Swagger	Normal	—	90	15
19	Screech	Normal	—	85	40	43	Haze	Ice	—	—	30

TM/HM

TM/HM#	Name	Type	Power	ACC	PP	TM/HM#	Name	Type	Power	ACC	PP
TM06	Toxic	Poison	—	85	10	TM32	Double Team	Normal	—	—	15
TM10	Hidden Power	Normal	—	100	15	TM35	Flamethrower	Fire	95	100	15
TM11	Sunny Day	Fire	—	—	5	TM36	Sludge Bomb	Poison	90	100	10
TM12	Taunt	Dark	—	100	20	TM42	Facade	Normal	70	100	20
TM17	Protect	Normal	—	—	10	TM43	Secret Power	Normal	70	100	20
TM18	Rain Dance	Water	—	—	5	TM44	Rest	Psychic	—	—	10
TM19	Giga Drain	Grass	60	100	5	TM45	Attract	Normal	—	100	15
TM21	Frustration	Normal	—	100	20	TM46	Thief	Dark	40	100	10
TM23	Iron Tail	Steel	100	75	15	TM49	Snatch	Dark	—	100	10
TM26	Earthquake	Ground	100	100	10	HM04	Strength	Normal	80	100	15
TM27	Return	Normal	—	100	20	HM06	Rock Smash	Fighting	20	100	15
TM28	Dig	Ground	60	100	10						

EGG MOVES*

Name	Type	Power	ACC	PP
Stockpile	Normal	—	—	10
Swallow	Normal	—	—	10
Spit Up	Normal	100	100	10
Body Slam	Normal	85	100	15

*Learned Via Breeding

MOVE TUTOR
FireRed/LeafGreen and *Emerald* Only

Body Slam*	Double-Edge	Mimic
Substitute		

Emerald Only

Endure*	Fury Cutter	Mud-Slap*
Sleep Talk	Snore*	Swagger
Swift*		

*Battle Frontier tutor move (*Emerald*)

337 Lunatone™

ROCK | PSYCHIC

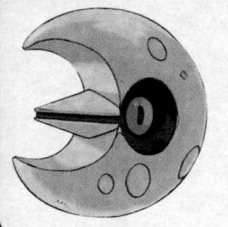

GENERAL INFO
SPECIES: Meteorite Pokémon
HEIGHT: 3'03"
WEIGHT: 370 lbs.
ABILITY: Levitate
Lunatone is not affected by Ground-type moves.

STATS
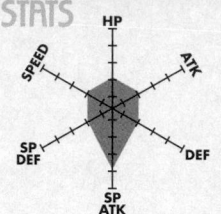

EVOLUTIONS
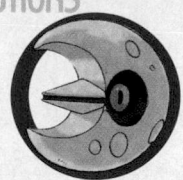

DOES NOT EVOLVE

LOCATION[S]:

RUBY — Rarity: **None**
Trade from *Sapphire*

SAPPHIRE — Rarity: **Common**
Meteor Falls

FIRERED — Rarity: **None**
Trade from *Sapphire*

LEAFGREEN — Rarity: **None**
Trade from *Sapphire*

COLOSSEUM — Rarity: **None**
Trade from *Sapphire*

EMERALD — Rarity: **None**
Trade from *Sapphire*

XD — Rarity: **Only One**
Phenac City (Capture from Cipher Admin Snattle)

MOVES

Level	Attack	Type	Power	ACC	PP	Level	Attack	Type	Power	ACC	PP
—	Tackle	Normal	35	95	35	25	Psywave	Psychic	—	80	15
—	Harden	Normal	—	—	30	31	Cosmic Power	Normal	—	—	20
7	Confusion	Psychic	50	100	25	37	Psychic	Psychic	90	100	10
13	Rock Throw	Rock	50	90	15	43	Future Sight	Psychic	80	90	15
19	Hypnosis	Psychic	—	60	20	49	Explosion	Normal	250	100	5

TM/HM

TM/HM#	Name	Type	Power	ACC	PP	TM/HM#	Name	Type	Power	ACC	PP
TM04	Calm Mind	Psychic	—	—	20	TM29	Psychic	Psychic	90	100	10
TM06	Toxic	Poison	—	85	10	TM30	Shadow Ball	Ghost	60	—	20
TM10	Hidden Power	Normal	—	100	15	TM32	Double Team	Normal	—	—	15
TM13	Ice Beam	Ice	95	100	10	TM33	Reflect	Psychic	—	—	20
TM15	Hyper Beam	Normal	150	90	5	TM37	Sandstorm	Rock	—	—	10
TM16	Light Screen	Psychic	—	—	30	TM39	Rock Tomb	Rock	50	80	10
TM17	Protect	Normal	—	—	10	TM42	Facade	Normal	70	100	20
TM18	Rain Dance	Water	—	—	5	TM43	Secret Power	Normal	70	100	20
TM20	Safeguard	Normal	—	—	25	TM44	Rest	Psychic	—	—	10
TM21	Frustration	Normal	—	100	20	TM48	Skill Swap	Psychic	—	100	10
TM26	Earthquake	Ground	100	100	10	HM05	Flash	Normal	—	70	20
TM27	Return	Normal	—	100	20						

MOVE TUTOR
FireRed/LeafGreen and *Emerald* Only

Body Slam*	Double-Edge	Dream Eater*
Explosion	Mimic	Rock Slide*
Substitute		

Emerald Only

Defense Curl*	Endure*	Psych Up*
Rollout	Sleep Talk	Snore*
Swagger	Swift*	

*Battle Frontier tutor move (*Emerald*)

---

338 Solrock™

ROCK | PSYCHIC

GENERAL INFO
SPECIES: Meteorite Pokémon
HEIGHT: 3'11"
WEIGHT: 340 lbs.
ABILITY: Levitate
Solrock is not affected by Ground-type moves.

STATS
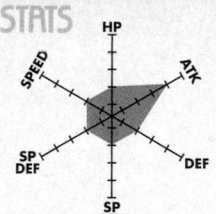

EVOLUTIONS

DOES NOT EVOLVE

LOCATION[S]:

RUBY — Rarity: **Common**
Meteor Falls

SAPPHIRE — Rarity: **None**
Trade from *Ruby/Emerald*

FIRERED — Rarity: **None**
Trade from *Ruby/Emerald*

LEAFGREEN — Rarity: **None**
Trade from *Ruby/Emerald*

COLOSSEUM — Rarity: **None**
Trade from *Ruby/Emerald*

EMERALD — Rarity: **Common**
Meteor Falls

XD — Rarity: **Only One**
Citadark Island (Capture from Cipher Admin Snattle)

MOVES

Level	Attack	Type	Power	ACC	PP	Level	Attack	Type	Power	ACC	PP
—	Harden	Normal	—	—	30	25	Psywave	Psychic	—	80	15
—	Tackle	Normal	35	95	35	31	Cosmic Power	Normal	—	—	20
7	Confusion	Psychic	50	100	25	37	Rock Slide	Rock	75	90	10
13	Rock Throw	Rock	50	90	15	43	Solarbeam	Grass	120	100	10
19	Fire Spin	Fire	15	70	15	49	Explosion	Normal	250	100	5

TM/HM

TM/HM#	Name	Type	Power	ACC	PP	TM/HM#	Name	Type	Power	ACC	PP
TM04	Calm Mind	Psychic	—	—	20	TM30	Shadow Ball	Ghost	60	—	20
TM06	Toxic	Poison	—	85	10	TM32	Double Team	Normal	—	—	15
TM10	Hidden Power	Normal	—	100	15	TM33	Reflect	Psychic	—	—	20
TM11	Sunny Day	Normal	—	—	30	TM35	Flamethrower	Fire	95	100	15
TM15	Hyper Beam	Normal	150	90	5	TM37	Sandstorm	Rock	—	—	10
TM16	Light Screen	Psychic	—	—	30	TM38	Fire Blast	Fire	120	85	5
TM17	Protect	Normal	—	—	10	TM39	Rock Tomb	Rock	50	80	10
TM20	Safeguard	Normal	—	—	25	TM42	Facade	Normal	70	100	20
TM21	Frustration	Normal	—	100	20	TM43	Secret Power	Normal	70	100	20
TM22	Solarbeam	Grass	120	100	10	TM44	Rest	Psychic	—	—	10
TM26	Earthquake	Ground	100	100	10	TM48	Skill Swap	Psychic	—	100	10
TM27	Return	Normal	—	100	20	TM50	Overheat	Fire	140	90	5
TM29	Psychic	Psychic	90	100	10	HM05	Flash	Normal	—	70	20

MOVE TUTOR
FireRed/LeafGreen and *Emerald* Only

Body Slam*	Double-Edge	Dream Eater*
Explosion	Mimic	Rock Slide*
Substitute		

Emerald Only

Defense Curl*	Endure*	Psych Up*
Rollout	Sleep Talk	Snore*
Swagger	Swift*	

*Battle Frontier tutor move (*Emerald*)

339 Barboach™

GENERAL INFO
SPECIES: Whiskers Pokémon
HEIGHT: 1'04"
WEIGHT: 4 lbs.
ABILITY: Oblivious
Barboach is not affected by the Attract condition.

STATS
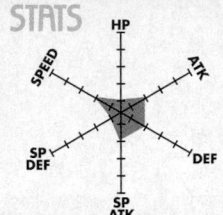

EVOLUTIONS

LV30

LOCATION(S):

RUBY — Rarity: **Rare**
Victory Road, Routes 111, 114, 120

SAPPHIRE — Rarity: **Rare**
Victory Road, Routes 111, 114, 120

FIRERED — Rarity: **None**
Trade from *Ruby/Sapphire/Emerald*

LEAFGREEN — Rarity: **None**
Trade from *Ruby/Sapphire/Emerald*

COLOSSEUM — Rarity: **None**
Trade from *Ruby/Sapphire/Emerald*

EMERALD — Rarity: **Common**
Routes 111, 114, 120, Meteor Falls, Victory Road

XD — Rarity: **None**
Trade from *Ruby/Sapphire/Emerald*

MOVES

Level	Attack	Type	Power	ACC	PP	Level	Attack	Type	Power	ACC	PP
—	Mud-Slap	Ground	20	100	10	21	Amnesia	Psychic	—	—	20
—	Mud Sport	Ground	—	100	15	26	Rest	Psychic	—	—	10
—	Water Sport	Water	—	100	15	26	Snore	Normal	40	100	15
11	Water Gun	Water	40	100	25	31	Earthquake	Ground	100	100	10
16	Magnitude	Ground	—	100	30	36	Future Sight	Psychic	80	90	15
						41	Fissure	Ground	—	30	5

TM/HM

TM/HM#	Name	Type	Power	ACC	PP	TM/HM#	Name	Type	Power	ACC	PP
TM03	Water Pulse	Water	60	100	20	TM32	Double Team	Normal	—	—	15
TM06	Toxic	Poison	—	85	10	TM37	Sandstorm	Rock	—	—	10
TM07	Hail	Ice	—	—	10	TM39	Rock Tomb	Rock	50	80	10
TM10	Hidden Power	Normal	—	100	15	TM42	Facade	Normal	70	100	20
TM13	Ice Beam	Ice	95	100	10	TM43	Secret Power	Normal	70	100	20
TM14	Blizzard	Ice	120	70	5	TM44	Rest	Psychic	—	—	10
TM17	Protect	Normal	—	—	10	TM45	Attract	Normal	—	100	15
TM18	Rain Dance	Water	—	—	5	HM03	Surf	Water	95	100	15
TM21	Frustration	Normal	—	100	20	HM07	Waterfall	Water	80	100	15
TM26	Earthquake	Ground	100	100	10	HM08	Dive	Water	60	100	10
TM27	Return	Normal	—	100	20						

EGG MOVES*

Name	Type	Power	ACC	PP
Thrash	Normal	90	100	20
Whirlpool	Water	15	70	15
Spark	Electric	65	100	20

*Learned Via Breeding

MOVE TUTOR
FireRed/LeafGreen and *Emerald* Only

Double-Edge	Mimic	Substitute

Emerald Only

Endure*	Icy Wind*	Mud-Slap*
Sleep Talk	Snore*	Swagger

*Battle Frontier tutor move (*Emerald*)

---

340 Whiscash™

GENERAL INFO
SPECIES: Whiskers Pokémon
HEIGHT: 2'11"
WEIGHT: 52 lbs.
ABILITY: Oblivious
Whiscash is not affected by the Attract condition.

STATS
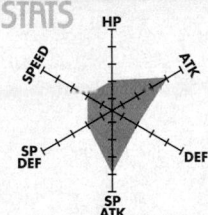

EVOLUTIONS

LV30

LOCATION(S):

RUBY — Rarity: **Rare**
Victory Road, Meteor Falls

SAPPHIRE — Rarity: **Rare**
Victory Road, Meteor Falls

FIRERED — Rarity: **None**
Trade from *Ruby/Sapphire/Emerald*

LEAFGREEN — Rarity: **None**
Trade from *Ruby/Sapphire/Emerald*

COLOSSEUM — Rarity: **None**
Trade from *Ruby/Sapphire/Emerald*

EMERALD — Rarity: **Common**
Evolve Barboach, Meteor Falls, Victory Road

XD — Rarity: **None**
Trade from *Ruby/Sapphire*

MOVES

Level	Attack	Type	Power	ACC	PP	Level	Attack	Type	Power	ACC	PP
—	Tickle	Normal	—	100	20	21	Amnesia	Psychic	—	—	20
—	Mud-Slap	Ground	20	100	10	26	Rest	Psychic	—	—	10
—	Mud Sport	Ground	—	100	15	26	Snore	Normal	40	100	15
—	Water Sport	Water	—	100	15	36	Earthquake	Ground	100	100	10
11	Water Gun	Water	40	100	25	46	Future Sight	Psychic	80	90	15
16	Magnitude	Ground	—	100	30	56	Fissure	Ground	—	30	5

TM/HM

TM/HM#	Name	Type	Power	ACC	PP	TM/HM#	Name	Type	Power	ACC	PP
TM03	Water Pulse	Water	60	100	20	TM32	Double Team	Normal	—	—	15
TM06	Toxic	Poison	—	85	10	TM37	Sandstorm	Rock	—	—	10
TM07	Hail	Ice	—	—	10	TM39	Rock Tomb	Rock	50	80	10
TM10	Hidden Power	Normal	—	100	15	TM42	Facade	Normal	70	100	20
TM13	Ice Beam	Ice	95	100	10	TM43	Secret Power	Normal	70	100	20
TM14	Blizzard	Ice	120	70	5	TM44	Rest	Psychic	—	—	10
TM15	Hyper Beam	Normal	150	90	5	TM45	Attract	Normal	—	100	15
TM17	Protect	Normal	—	—	10	HM03	Surf	Water	95	100	15
TM18	Rain Dance	Water	—	—	5	HM04	Strength	Normal	80	100	15
TM21	Frustration	Normal	—	100	20	HM06	Rock Smash	Fighting	20	100	15
TM26	Earthquake	Ground	100	100	10	HM07	Waterfall	Water	80	100	15
TM27	Return	Normal	—	100	20	HM08	Dive	Water	60	100	10

MOVE TUTOR
FireRed/LeafGreen and *Emerald* Only

Double-Edge	Mimic	Rock Slide*
Substitute		

Emerald Only

Endure*	Icy Wind*	Mud-Slap*
Sleep Talk	Snore*	Swagger

*Battle Frontier tutor move (*Emerald*)

341 Corphish™

WATER

GENERAL INFO
SPECIES: Ruffian Pokémon
HEIGHT: 2'00"
WEIGHT: 25 lbs.
ABILITY 1: Shell Armor
Prevents the opponent Pokémon from scoring a critical hit.
ABILITY 2: Hyper Cutter
Corphish's attack power cannot be lowered.

STATS
HP · ATK · DEF · SP ATK · SP DEF · SPEED

EVOLUTIONS
  LV30

LOCATION(S):

RUBY Rarity: **Common**
Route 102, Route 117, Petalburg City

SAPPHIRE Rarity: **Common**
Route 102, Route 117, Petalburg City

FIRERED Rarity: **None**
Trade from *Ruby/Sapphire/Emerald*

LEAFGREEN Rarity: **None**
Trade from *Ruby/Sapphire/Emerald*

COLOSSEUM Rarity: **None**
Trade from *Ruby/Sapphire/Emerald*

EMERALD Rarity: **Common**
Route 102, Route 117

XD Rarity: **None**
Trade from *Ruby/Sapphire/Emerald*

MOVES

Level	Attack	Type	Power	ACC	PP	Level	Attack	Type	Power	ACC	PP
—	Bubble	Water	20	100	30	25	Knock Off	Dark	20	100	20
7	Harden	Normal	—	—	30	31	Taunt	Dark	—	100	20
10	Vicegrip	Normal	55	100	30	34	Crabhammer	Water	90	85	10
13	Leer	Normal	—	100	30	37	Swords Dance	Normal	—	—	30
19	Bubblebeam	Water	65	100	20	43	Crunch*	Dark	80	100	15
22	Protect	Normal	—	—	10	46	Guillotine	Normal	—	30	5

* Not Available in *Emerald*

TM/HM

TM/HM#	Name	Type	Power	ACC	PP	TM/HM#	Name	Type	Power	ACC	PP
TM03	Water Pulse	Water	60	100	20	TM32	Double Team	Normal	—	—	15
TM06	Toxic	Poison	—	85	10	TM36	Sludge Bomb	Poison	90	100	10
TM07	Hail	Ice	—	—	10	TM39	Rock Tomb	Rock	50	80	10
TM10	Hidden Power	Normal	—	100	15	TM40	Aerial Ace	Flying	60	—	20
TM12	Taunt	Dark	—	100	20	TM42	Facade	Normal	70	100	20
TM13	Ice Beam	Ice	95	100	10	TM43	Secret Power	Normal	70	100	20
TM14	Blizzard	Ice	120	70	5	TM44	Rest	Psychic	—	—	10
TM17	Protect	Normal	—	—	10	TM45	Attract	Normal	—	100	15
TM18	Rain Dance	Water	—	—	5	HM01	Cut	Normal	50	95	30
TM21	Frustration	Normal	—	100	20	HM03	Surf	Water	95	100	15
TM27	Return	Normal	—	100	20	HM04	Strength	Normal	80	100	15
TM28	Dig	Ground	60	100	10	HM06	Rock Smash	Fighting	20	100	15
TM31	Brick Break	Fighting	75	100	15	HM07	Waterfall	Water	80	100	15

EGG MOVES*

Name	Type	Power	ACC	PP
Mud Sport	Ground	—	100	15
Endeavor	Normal	—	100	5
Body Slam	Normal	85	100	15
Ancientpower	Rock	60	100	5

*Learned Via Breeding

MOVE TUTOR
FireRed/LeafGreen and Emerald Only

Body Slam*	Counter*	Double-Edge
Mimic	Substitute	Swords Dance*

Emerald Only

Endure*	Fury Cutter	Icy Wind*
Mud-Slap*	Sleep Talk	Snore*
Swagger		

*Battle Frontier tutor move (*Emerald*)

342 Crawdaunt™

WATER   DARK

GENERAL INFO
SPECIES: Rogue Pokémon
HEIGHT: 3'07"
WEIGHT: 72 lbs.
ABILITY 1: Shell Armor
Prevents the opponent Pokémon from scoring a critical hit.
ABILITY 2: Hyper Cutter
Crawdaunt's attack power cannot be lowered.

STATS
HP · ATK · DEF · SP ATK · SP DEF · SPEED

EVOLUTIONS
  LV30

LOCATION(S):

RUBY Rarity: **Evolve**
Evolve Corphish

SAPPHIRE Rarity: **Evolve**
Evolve Corphish

FIRERED Rarity: **None**
Trade from *Ruby/Sapphire/Emerald*

LEAFGREEN Rarity: **None**
Trade from *Ruby/Sapphire/Emerald*

COLOSSEUM Rarity: **None**
Trade from *Ruby/Sapphire/Emerald*

EMERALD Rarity: **Evolve**
Evolve Corphish

XD Rarity: **None**
Trade from *Ruby/Sapphire/Emerald*

MOVES

Level	Attack	Type	Power	ACC	PP	Level	Attack	Type	Power	ACC	PP
—	Bubble	Water	20	100	30	25	Knock Off	Dark	20	100	20
—	Harden	Normal	—	—	30	33	Taunt	Dark	—	100	20
—	Vicegrip	Normal	55	100	30	38	Crabhammer	Water	90	85	10
—	Leer	Normal	—	100	30	43	Swords Dance	Normal	—	—	30
19	Bubblebeam	Water	65	100	20	51	Crunch	Dark	80	100	15
22	Protect	Normal	—	—	10	56	Guillotine	Normal	—	30	5

TM/HM

TM/HM#	Name	Type	Power	ACC	PP	TM/HM#	Name	Type	Power	ACC	PP
TM03	Water Pulse	Water	60	100	20	TM32	Double Team	Normal	—	—	15
TM06	Toxic	Poison	—	85	10	TM36	Sludge Bomb	Poison	90	100	10
TM07	Hail	Ice	—	—	10	TM39	Rock Tomb	Rock	50	80	10
TM10	Hidden Power	Normal	—	100	15	TM40	Aerial Ace	Flying	60	—	20
TM12	Taunt	Dark	—	100	20	TM42	Facade	Normal	70	100	20
TM13	Ice Beam	Ice	95	100	10	TM43	Secret Power	Normal	70	100	20
TM14	Blizzard	Ice	120	70	5	TM44	Rest	Psychic	—	—	10
TM15	Hyper Beam	Normal	150	90	5	TM45	Attract	Normal	—	100	15
TM17	Protect	Normal	—	—	10	HM01	Cut	Normal	50	95	30
TM18	Rain Dance	Water	—	—	5	HM03	Surf	Water	95	100	15
TM21	Frustration	Normal	—	100	20	HM04	Strength	Normal	80	100	15
TM27	Return	Normal	—	100	20	HM06	Rock Smash	Fighting	20	100	15
TM28	Dig	Ground	60	100	10	HM07	Waterfall	Water	80	100	15
TM31	Brick Break	Fighting	75	100	15	HM08	Dive	Water	60	100	10

MOVE TUTOR
FireRed/LeafGreen and Emerald Only

Body Slam*	Counter*	Double-Edge
Mimic	Substitute	Swords Dance*

Emerald Only

Endure*	Fury Cutter	Icy Wind*
Mud-Slap*	Sleep Talk	Snore*
Swagger	Swift*	

*Battle Frontier tutor move (*Emerald*)

343 Baltoy™

GROUND **PSYCHIC**

GENERAL INFO
SPECIES: Clay Doll Pokémon
HEIGHT: 1'08"
WEIGHT: 47 lbs.
ABILITY: Levitate
Baltoy is not affected by Ground-type moves.

STATS
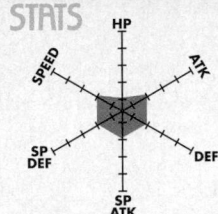

EVOLUTIONS
 LV36

LOCATION[S]:

RUBY	Rarity: **Rare**
Route 111	
SAPPHIRE	Rarity: **Rare**
Route 111	
FIRERED	Rarity: **None**
Trade from *Ruby/Sapphire/Emerald*	
LEAFGREEN	Rarity: **None**
Trade from *Ruby/Sapphire/Emerald*	
COLOSSEUM	Rarity: **None**
Trade from *Ruby/Sapphire/Emerald*	
EMERALD	Rarity: **Rare**
Route 111	
XD	Rarity: **Only One**
Cipher Lab (Capture from Cipher Peon Browsix)	

MOVES

Level	Attack	Type	Power	ACC	PP	Level	Attack	Type	Power	ACC	PP
—	Confusion	Psychic	50	100	25	15	Rock Tomb	Rock	50	80	10
3	Harden	Normal	—	—	30	19	Selfdestruct	Normal	200	100	5
5	Rapid Spin	Normal	20	100	40	25	Ancientpower	Rock	60	100	5
7	Mud-Slap	Ground	20	100	10	31	Sandstorm	Rock	—	—	10
11	Psybeam	Psychic	65	100	20	37	Cosmic Power	Normal	—	—	20
						45	Explosion	Normal	250	100	5

TM/HM

TM/HM#	Name	Type	Power	ACC	PP	TM/HM#	Name	Type	Power	ACC	PP
TM06	Toxic	Poison	—	85	10	TM29	Psychic	Psychic	90	100	10
TM10	Hidden Power	Normal	—	100	15	TM30	Shadow Ball	Ghost	60	—	20
TM11	Sunny Day	Fire	—	—	5	TM32	Double Team	Normal	—	—	15
TM13	Ice Beam	Ice	95	100	10	TM33	Reflect	Psychic	—	—	20
TM16	Light Screen	Psychic	—	—	30	TM37	Sandstorm	Rock	—	—	10
TM17	Protect	Normal	—	—	10	TM39	Rock Tomb	Rock	50	80	10
TM18	Rain Dance	Water	—	—	5	TM42	Facade	Normal	70	100	20
TM21	Frustration	Normal	—	100	20	TM43	Secret Power	Normal	70	100	20
TM22	Solarbeam	Grass	120	100	10	TM44	Rest	Psychic	—	—	10
TM26	Earthquake	Ground	100	100	10	TM48	Skill Swap	Psychic	—	100	10
TM27	Return	Normal	—	100	20	HM05	Flash	Normal	—	70	20
TM28	Dig	Ground	60	100	10						

MOVE TUTOR
FireRed/LeafGreen and *Emerald* Only

Double-Edge	Dream Eater*	Explosion
Mimic	Rock Slide*	Substitute

Emerald Only

Endure*	Mud-Slap*	Psych Up*
Sleep Talk	Snore*	Swagger
Swift*		

*Battle Frontier tutor move (*Emerald*)

---

344 Claydol™

GROUND **PSYCHIC**

GENERAL INFO
SPECIES: Clay Doll Pokémon
HEIGHT: 4'11"
WEIGHT: 238 lbs.
ABILITY: Levitate
Claydol is not affected by Ground-type moves.

STATS
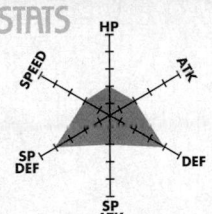

EVOLUTIONS
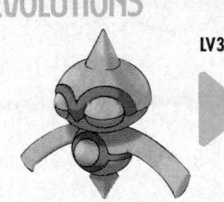  LV36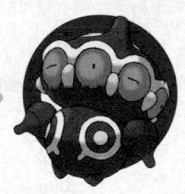

LOCATION[S]:

RUBY	Rarity: **Common**
Evolve Baltoy, Sky Pillar	
SAPPHIRE	Rarity: **Common**
Evolve Baltoy, Sky Pillar	
FIRERED	Rarity: **None**
Trade from *Ruby/Sapphire/Emerald*	
LEAFGREEN	Rarity: **None**
Trade from *Ruby/Sapphire/Emerald*	
COLOSSEUM	Rarity: **None**
Trade from *Ruby/Sapphire/Emerald*	
EMERALD	Rarity: **Rare**
Evolve Baltoy, Sky Pillar	
XD	Rarity: **Evolve**
Evolve Baltoy	

MOVES

Level	Attack	Type	Power	ACC	PP	Level	Attack	Type	Power	ACC	PP
—	Teleport	Psychic	—	—	20	15	Rock Tomb	Rock	50	80	10
—	Confusion	Psychic	50	100	25	19	Selfdestruct	Normal	200	100	5
—	Harden	Normal	—	—	30	25	Ancientpower	Rock	60	100	5
—	Rapid Spin	Normal	20	100	40	31	Sandstorm	Rock	—	—	10
7	Mud-Slap	Ground	20	100	10	36	Hyper Beam	Normal	150	90	5
11	Psybeam	Psychic	65	100	20	42	Cosmic Power	Normal	—	—	20
						55	Explosion	Normal	250	100	5

TM/HM

TM/HM#	Name	Type	Power	ACC	PP	TM/HM#	Name	Type	Power	ACC	PP
TM06	Toxic	Poison	—	85	10	TM29	Psychic	Psychic	90	100	10
TM10	Hidden Power	Normal	—	100	15	TM30	Shadow Ball	Ghost	60	—	20
TM11	Sunny Day	Fire	—	—	5	TM32	Double Team	Normal	—	—	15
TM13	Ice Beam	Ice	95	100	10	TM33	Reflect	Psychic	—	—	20
TM15	Hyper Beam	Normal	150	90	5	TM37	Sandstorm	Rock	—	—	10
TM16	Light Screen	Psychic	—	—	30	TM39	Rock Tomb	Rock	50	80	10
TM17	Protect	Normal	—	—	10	TM42	Facade	Normal	70	100	20
TM18	Rain Dance	Water	—	—	5	TM43	Secret Power	Normal	70	100	20
TM21	Frustration	Normal	—	100	20	TM44	Rest	Psychic	—	—	10
TM22	Solarbeam	Grass	120	100	10	TM48	Skill Swap	Psychic	—	100	10
TM26	Earthquake	Ground	100	100	10	HM04	Strength	Normal	80	100	15
TM27	Return	Normal	—	100	20	HM05	Flash	Normal	—	70	20
TM28	Dig	Ground	60	100	10	HM06	Rock Smash	Fighting	20	100	15

MOVE TUTOR
FireRed/LeafGreen and *Emerald* Only

Double-Edge	Dream Eater*	Explosion
Mimic	Rock Slide*	Substitute

Emerald Only

Endure*	Mud-Slap*	Psych Up*
Sleep Talk	Snore*	Swagger

*Battle Frontier tutor move (*Emerald*)

345 Lileep

ROCK | GRASS

GENERAL INFO
SPECIES: Sea Lily Pokémon
HEIGHT: 3'03"
WEIGHT: 52 lbs.
ABILITY: Suction Cups

Lileep cannot be switched out of the battle by the Roar or Whirlwind moves.

STATS
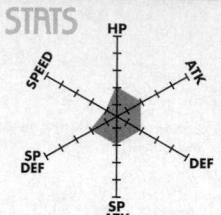

EVOLUTIONS
 LV40

LOCATION(S):

RUBY   Rarity: **Only One**
Obtained on Route 111

SAPPHIRE   Rarity: **Only One**
Obtained on Route 111

FIRERED   Rarity: **None**
Trade from *Ruby/Sapphire/Emerald*

LEAFGREEN   Rarity: **None**
Trade from *Ruby/Sapphire/Emerald*

COLOSSEUM   Rarity: **None**
Trade from *Ruby/Sapphire/Emerald*

EMERALD   Rarity: **Only One**
Route 111 (Root Fossil — bring to Devon Corp. in Rustboro)

XD   Rarity: **None**
Trade from *Ruby/Sapphire/Emerald*

MOVES

Level	Attack	Type	Power	ACC	PP	Level	Attack	Type	Power	ACC	PP
—	Astonish	Ghost	30	100	15	36	Amnesia	Psychic	—	—	20
8	Constrict	Normal	10	100	35	43	Ancientpower	Rock	60	100	5
15	Acid	Poison	40	100	30	50	Stockpile	Normal	—	—	10
22	Ingrain	Grass	—	100	20	50	Spit Up	Normal	100	100	10
29	Confuse Ray	Ghost	—	100	10	50	Swallow	Normal	—	—	10

TM/HM

TM/HM#	Name	Type	Power	ACC	PP	TM/HM#	Name	Type	Power	ACC	PP
TM06	Toxic	Poison	—	85	10	TM27	Return	Normal	—	100	20
TM09	Bullet Seed	Grass	10	100	30	TM32	Double Team	Normal	—	—	15
TM10	Hidden Power	Normal	—	100	15	TM36	Sludge Bomb	Poison	90	100	10
TM11	Sunny Day	Fire	—	—	5	TM37	Sandstorm	Rock	—	—	10
TM17	Protect	Normal	—	—	10	TM42	Facade	Normal	70	100	20
TM19	Giga Drain	Grass	60	100	5	TM43	Secret Power	Normal	70	100	20
TM21	Frustration	Normal	—	100	20	TM44	Rest	Psychic	—	—	10
TM22	Solarbeam	Grass	120	100	10	TM45	Attract	Normal	—	100	15

EGG MOVES*

Name	Type	Power	ACC	PP
Barrier	Psychic	—	—	30
Recover	Normal	—	—	20
Mirror Coat	Psychic	—	100	20
Rock Slide	Rock	75	90	10

*Learned Via Breeding

MOVE TUTOR
FireRed/LeafGreen and *Emerald* Only

Body Slam*	Double-Edge	Mimic
Rock Slide*	Substitute	

Emerald Only

Endure*	Mud-Slap*	Psych Up*
Sleep Talk	Snore*	Swagger

*Battle Frontier tutor move (*Emerald*)

---

346 Cradily

ROCK | GRASS

GENERAL INFO
SPECIES: Barnacle Pokémon
HEIGHT: 4'11"
WEIGHT: 133 lbs.
ABILITY: Suction Cups

Cradily cannot be switched out of the battle by the Roar or Whirlwind moves.

STATS
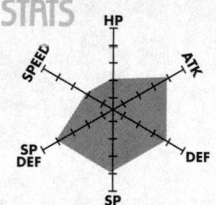

EVOLUTIONS
 LV40

LOCATION(S):

RUBY   Rarity: **None**
Evolve Lileep

SAPPHIRE   Rarity: **None**
Evolve Lileep

FIRERED   Rarity: **None**
Trade from *Ruby/Sapphire/Emerald*

LEAFGREEN   Rarity: **None**
Trade from *Ruby/Sapphire/Emerald*

COLOSSEUM   Rarity: **None**
Trade from *Ruby/Sapphire/Emerald*

EMERALD   Rarity: **Evolve**
Evolve Lileep

XD   Rarity: **None**
Trade from *Ruby/Sapphire/Emerald*

MOVES

Level	Attack	Type	Power	ACC	PP	Level	Attack	Type	Power	ACC	PP
—	Astonish	Ghost	30	100	15	36	Amnesia	Psychic	—	—	20
—	Constrict	Normal	10	100	35	48	Ancientpower	Rock	60	100	5
—	Acid	Poison	40	100	30	60	Stockpile	Normal	—	—	10
—	Ingrain	Grass	—	100	20	60	Spit Up	Normal	100	100	10
29	Confuse Ray	Ghost	—	100	10	60	Swallow	Normal	—	—	10

TM/HM

TM/HM#	Name	Type	Power	ACC	PP	TM/HM#	Name	Type	Power	ACC	PP
TM06	Toxic	Poison	—	85	10	TM32	Double Team	Normal	—	—	15
TM09	Bullet Seed	Grass	10	100	30	TM36	Sludge Bomb	Poison	90	100	10
TM10	Hidden Power	Normal	—	100	15	TM37	Sandstorm	Rock	—	—	10
TM11	Sunny Day	Fire	—	—	5	TM39	Rock Tomb	Rock	50	80	10
TM15	Hyper Beam	Normal	150	90	5	TM42	Facade	Normal	70	100	20
TM17	Protect	Normal	—	—	10	TM43	Secret Power	Normal	70	100	20
TM19	Giga Drain	Grass	60	100	5	TM44	Rest	Psychic	—	—	10
TM21	Frustration	Normal	—	100	20	TM45	Attract	Normal	—	100	15
TM22	Solarbeam	Grass	120	100	10	HM04	Strength	Normal	80	100	15
TM26	Earthquake	Ground	100	100	10	HM06	Rock Smash	Fighting	20	100	15
TM27	Return	Normal	—	100	20						

MOVE TUTOR
FireRed/LeafGreen and *Emerald* Only

Body Slam*	Double-Edge	Mimic
Rock Slide*	Substitute	

Emerald Only

Endure*	Mud-Slap*	Psych Up*
Sleep Talk	Snore*	Swagger

*Battle Frontier tutor move (*Emerald*)

347 Anorith™

ROCK BUG

GENERAL INFO

SPECIES: Old Shrimp Pokémon
HEIGHT: 2'04"
WEIGHT: 28 lbs.
ABILITY: Battle Armor
Prevents the opponent Pokémon from scoring a critical hit.

STATS

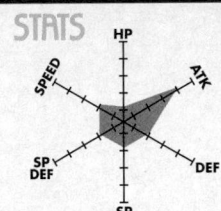

EVOLUTIONS

 LV40

LOCATION(S):

RUBY Rarity: **Only One**
Route 111 (Claw Fossil — bring to Devon Corp. in Rustboro)

SAPPHIRE Rarity: **Only One**
Route 111 (Claw Fossil — bring to Devon Corp. in Rustboro)

FIRERED Rarity: **None**
Trade from *Ruby/Sapphire/Emerald*

LEAFGREEN Rarity: **None**
Trade from *Ruby/Sapphire/Emerald*

COLOSSEUM Rarity: **None**
Trade from *Ruby/Sapphire/Emerald*

EMERALD Rarity: **Only One**
Route 111 (Claw Fossil — bring to Devon Corp. in Rustboro)

XD Rarity: **None**
Trade from *Ruby/Sapphire/Emerald*

MOVES

Level	Attack	Type	Power	ACC	PP
—	Scratch	Normal	40	100	35
7	Harden	Normal	—	—	30
13	Mud Sport	Ground	—	100	15
19	Water Gun	Water	40	100	25
25	Metal Claw	Steel	50	95	35

Level	Attack	Type	Power	ACC	PP
31	Protect	Normal	—	—	10
37	Ancientpower	Rock	60	100	5
43	Fury Cutter	Bug	10	95	20
49	Slash	Normal	70	100	20
55	Rock Blast	Rock	25	80	10

TM/HM

TM/HM#	Name	Type	Power	ACC	PP
TM03	Water Pulse	Water	60	100	20
TM06	Toxic	Poison	—	85	10
TM10	Hidden Power	Normal	—	100	15
TM11	Sunny Day	Fire	—	—	5
TM17	Protect	Normal	—	—	10
TM21	Frustration	Normal	—	100	20
TM27	Return	Normal	—	100	20
TM28	Dig	Ground	60	100	10
TM31	Brick Break	Fighting	75	100	15
TM32	Double Team	Normal	—	—	15

TM/HM#	Name	Type	Power	ACC	PP
TM37	Sandstorm	Rock	—	—	10
TM39	Rock Tomb	Rock	50	80	10
TM40	Aerial Ace	Flying	60	—	20
TM42	Facade	Normal	70	100	20
TM43	Secret Power	Normal	70	100	20
TM44	Rest	Psychic	—	—	10
TM45	Attract	Normal	—	100	15
HM01	Cut	Normal	50	95	30
HM06	Rock Smash	Fighting	20	100	15

EGG MOVES*

Name	Type	Power	ACC	PP
Knock Off	Dark	20	100	20
Rock Slide	Rock	75	90	10
Rapid Spin	Normal	20	100	40
Swords Dance	Normal	—	—	30

*Learned Via Breeding

MOVE TUTOR

FireRed/LeafGreen and *Emerald* Only

Body Slam*	Double-Edge	Mimic
Rock Slide*	Substitute	Swords Dance*

Emerald Only

Endure*	Fury Cutter	Mud-Slap*
Sleep Talk	Snore*	Swagger

*Battle Frontier tutor move (*Emerald*)

---

348 Armaldo™

ROCK BUG

GENERAL INFO

SPECIES: Plate Pokémon
HEIGHT: 4'11"
WEIGHT: 150 lbs.
ABILITY: Battle Armor
Prevents the opponent Pokémon from scoring a critical hit.

STATS

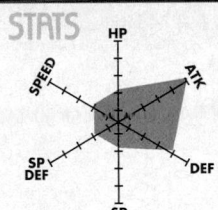

EVOLUTIONS

 LV40

LOCATION(S):

RUBY Rarity: **Evolve**
Evolve Anorith

SAPPHIRE Rarity: **Evolve**
Evolve Anorith

FIRERED Rarity: **None**
Trade from *Ruby/Sapphire/Emerald*

LEAFGREEN Rarity: **None**
Trade from *Ruby/Sapphire/Emerald*

COLOSSEUM Rarity: **None**
Trade from *Ruby/Sapphire/Emerald*

EMERALD Rarity: **Evolve**
Evolve Anorith

XD Rarity: **None**
Trade from *Ruby/Sapphire/Emerald*

MOVES

Level	Attack	Type	Power	ACC	PP
—	Scratch	Normal	40	100	35
—	Harden	Normal	—	—	30
—	Mud Sport	Ground	—	100	15
—	Water Gun	Water	40	100	25
25	Metal Claw	Steel	50	95	35

Level	Attack	Type	Power	ACC	PP
31	Protect	Normal	—	—	10
37	Ancientpower	Rock	60	100	5
46	Fury Cutter	Bug	10	95	20
55	Slash	Normal	70	100	20
64	Rock Blast	Rock	25	80	10

TM/HM

TM/HM#	Name	Type	Power	ACC	PP
TM03	Water Pulse	Water	60	100	20
TM06	Toxic	Poison	—	85	10
TM10	Hidden Power	Normal	—	100	15
TM11	Sunny Day	Fire	—	—	5
TM15	Hyper Beam	Normal	150	90	5
TM17	Protect	Normal	—	—	10
TM21	Frustration	Normal	—	100	20
TM23	Iron Tail	Steel	100	75	15
TM26	Earthquake	Ground	100	100	10
TM27	Return	Normal	—	100	20
TM28	Dig	Ground	60	100	10
TM31	Brick Break	Fighting	75	100	15

TM/HM#	Name	Type	Power	ACC	PP
TM32	Double Team	Normal	—	—	15
TM37	Sandstorm	Rock	—	—	10
TM39	Rock Tomb	Rock	50	80	10
TM40	Aerial Ace	Flying	60	—	20
TM42	Facade	Normal	70	100	20
TM43	Secret Power	Normal	70	100	20
TM44	Rest	Psychic	—	—	10
TM45	Attract	Normal	—	100	15
HM01	Cut	Normal	50	95	30
HM04	Strength	Normal	80	100	15
HM06	Rock Smash	Fighting	20	100	15

MOVE TUTOR

FireRed/LeafGreen and *Emerald* Only

Body Slam*	Double-Edge	Mimic
Rock Slide*	Seismic Toss*	Substitute
Swords Dance*		

Emerald Only

Endure*	Fury Cutter	Mud-Slap*
Sleep Talk	Snore*	Swagger

*Battle Frontier tutor move (*Emerald*)

349 Feebas™

WATER

GENERAL INFO
SPECIES: Fish Pokémon
HEIGHT: 2'00"
WEIGHT: 16 lbs.
ABILITY: Swift Swim
Doubles Feebas's Speed when it's raining.

STATS
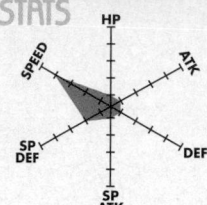

EVOLUTIONS
 MAX BEAUTY

LOCATION[S]:

RUBY   **Rarity: Rare**
Route 119 (Six random spots to fish from, depending on the current Trendy Phrase in Dewford Town)

SAPPHIRE   **Rarity: Rare**
Route 119 (Six random spots to fish from, depending on the current Trendy Phrase in Dewford Town)

FIRERED   **Rarity: None**
Trade from *Ruby/Sapphire/Emerald*

LEAFGREEN   **Rarity: None**
Trade from *Ruby/Sapphire/Emerald*

COLOSSEUM   **Rarity: None**
Trade from *Ruby/Sapphire/Emerald*

EMERALD   **Rarity: Rare**
Route 119 (Six random spots to fish from, depending on the current Trendy Phrase in Dewford Town)

XD   **Rarity: None**
Trade from *Ruby/Sapphire/Emerald*

MOVES
Level	Attack	Type	Power	ACC	PP
—	Splash	Normal	—	—	40
15	Tackle	Normal	35	95	35
30	Flail	Normal	—	100	15

TM/HM
TM/HM#	Name	Type	Power	ACC	PP	TM/HM#	Name	Type	Power	ACC	PP
TM03	Water Pulse	Water	60	100	20	TM27	Return	Normal	—	100	20
TM06	Toxic	Poison	—	85	10	TM32	Double Team	Normal	—	—	15
TM07	Hail	Ice	—	—	10	TM42	Facade	Normal	70	100	20
TM10	Hidden Power	Normal	—	100	15	TM43	Secret Power	Normal	70	100	20
TM13	Ice Beam	Ice	95	100	10	TM44	Rest	Psychic	—	—	10
TM14	Blizzard	Ice	120	70	5	TM45	Attract	Normal	—	100	15
TM17	Protect	Normal	—	—	10	HM03	Surf	Water	95	100	15
TM18	Rain Dance	Water	—	—	5	HM07	Waterfall	Water	80	100	15
TM21	Frustration	Normal	—	100	20	HM08	Dive	Water	60	100	10

EGG MOVES*
Name	Type	Power	ACC	PP
Mirror Coat	Psychic	—	100	20
Dragonbreath	Dragon	60	100	20
Mud Sport	Ground	—	100	15
Hypnosis	Psychic	—	60	20
Light Screen	Psychic	—	—	30
Confuse Ray	Ghost	—	100	10

*Learned Via Breeding

MOVE TUTOR
FireRed/LeafGreen and *Emerald* Only

Body Slam*	Double-Edge	Mimic
Substitute		

Emerald Only

Endure*	Icy Wind*	Mud-Slap*
Sleep Talk	Snore*	Swagger
Swift*		

*Battle Frontier tutor move (*Emerald*)

350 Milotic™

WATER

GENERAL INFO
SPECIES: Tender Pokémon
HEIGHT: 20'04"
WEIGHT: 357 lbs.
ABILITY: Marvel Scale
Marvel Scale multiplies Defense by 1.5 when Milotic has a status condition.

STATS
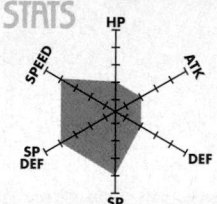

EVOLUTIONS
 MAX BEAUTY

LOCATION[S]:

RUBY   **Rarity: Evolve**
Evolve Feebas

SAPPHIRE   **Rarity: Evolve**
Evolve Feebas

FIRERED   **Rarity: None**
Trade from *Ruby/Sapphire/Emerald*

LEAFGREEN   **Rarity: None**
Trade from *Ruby/Sapphire/Emerald*

COLOSSEUM   **Rarity: None**
Trade from *Ruby/Sapphire/Emerald*

EMERALD   **Rarity: Evolve**
Evolve Feebas

XD   **Rarity: None**
Trade from *Ruby/Sapphire/Emerald*

MOVES
Level	Attack	Type	Power	ACC	PP	Level	Attack	Type	Power	ACC	PP
—	Water Gun	Water	40	100	25	25	Twister	Dragon	40	100	20
—	Wrap	Normal	15	85	20	30	Recover	Normal	—	—	20
10	Water Sport	Water	—	100	15	35	Rain Dance	Water	—	—	5
15	Refresh	Normal	—	100	20	40	Hydro Pump	Water	120	80	5
20	Water Pulse	Water	60	100	20	45	Attract	Normal	—	100	15
						50	Safeguard	Normal	—	—	25

TM/HM
TM/HM#	Name	Type	Power	ACC	PP	TM/HM#	Name	Type	Power	ACC	PP
TM03	Water Pulse	Water	60	100	20	TM23	Iron Tail	Steel	100	75	15
TM06	Toxic	Poison	—	85	10	TM27	Return	Normal	—	100	20
TM07	Hail	Ice	—	—	10	TM32	Double Team	Normal	—	—	15
TM10	Hidden Power	Normal	—	100	15	TM42	Facade	Normal	70	100	20
TM13	Ice Beam	Ice	95	100	10	TM43	Secret Power	Normal	70	100	20
TM14	Blizzard	Ice	120	70	5	TM44	Rest	Psychic	—	—	10
TM15	Hyper Beam	Normal	150	90	5	TM45	Attract	Normal	—	100	15
TM17	Protect	Normal	—	—	10	HM03	Surf	Water	95	100	15
TM18	Rain Dance	Water	—	—	5	HM07	Waterfall	Water	80	100	15
TM20	Safeguard	Normal	—	—	25	HM08	Dive	Water	60	100	10
TM21	Frustration	Normal	—	100	20						

MOVE TUTOR
FireRed/LeafGreen and *Emerald* Only

Body Slam*	Double-Edge	Mimic
Substitute		

Emerald Only

Endure*	Icy Wind*	Mud-Slap*
Psych Up*	Sleep Talk	Snore*
Swagger	Swift*	

*Battle Frontier tutor move (*Emerald*)

351 Castform™

NORMAL

GENERAL INFO
SPECIES: Weather Pokémon
HEIGHT: 1'00"
WEIGHT: 2 lbs.
ABILITY: Forecast
Changes Castform's type and shape depending upon the weather.

STATS
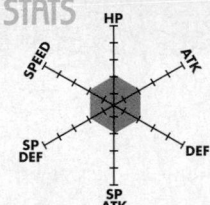

EVOLUTIONS

DOES NOT EVOLVE

LOCATION[S]:

RUBY **Rarity: Only One**
Route 119 (Weather Institute)

SAPPHIRE **Rarity: Only One**
Route 119 (Weather Institute)

FIRERED **Rarity: None**
Trade from *Ruby/Sapphire/Emerald*

LEAFGREEN **Rarity: None**
Trade from *Ruby/Sapphire/Emerald*

COLOSSEUM **Rarity: None**
Trade from *Ruby/Sapphire/Emerald*

EMERALD **Rarity: Only One**
Route 119 (Weather Institute)

XD **Rarity: None**
Trade from *Ruby/Sapphire/Emerald*

MOVES

Level	Attack	Type	Power	ACC	PP	Level	Attack	Type	Power	ACC	PP
—	Tackle	Normal	35	95	35	20	Rain Dance	Water	—	—	5
10	Water Gun	Water	40	100	25	20	Sunny Day	Fire	—	—	5
10	Ember	Fire	40	100	25	20	Hail	Ice	—	—	10
10	Powder Snow	Ice	40	100	25	30	Weather Ball	Normal	50	100	10

TM/HM

TM/HM#	Name	Type	Power	ACC	PP	TM/HM#	Name	Type	Power	ACC	PP
TM03	Water Pulse	Water	60	100	20	TM27	Return	Normal	—	100	20
TM06	Toxic	Poison	—	85	10	TM30	Shadow Ball	Ghost	60	—	20
TM07	Hail	Ice	—	—	10	TM32	Double Team	Normal	—	—	15
TM10	Hidden Power	Normal	—	100	15	TM34	Shock Wave	Electric	60	—	20
TM11	Sunny Day	Fire	—	—	5	TM35	Flamethrower	Fire	95	100	15
TM13	Ice Beam	Ice	95	100	10	TM37	Sandstorm	Rock	—	—	10
TM14	Blizzard	Ice	120	70	5	TM38	Fire Blast	Fire	120	85	5
TM17	Protect	Normal	—	—	10	TM42	Facade	Normal	70	100	20
TM18	Rain Dance	Water	—	—	5	TM43	Secret Power	Normal	70	100	20
TM21	Frustration	Normal	—	100	20	TM44	Rest	Psychic	—	—	10
TM22	Solarbeam	Grass	120	100	10	TM45	Attract	Normal	—	100	15
TM24	Thunderbolt	Electric	95	100	15	TM46	Thief	Dark	40	100	10
TM25	Thunder	Electric	120	70	10	HM05	Flash	Normal	—	70	20

EGG MOVES*

Name	Type	Power	ACC	PP
Future Sight	Psychic	80	90	15
Psych Up	Normal	—	—	10

*Learned Via Breeding

MOVE TUTOR

***FireRed/LeafGreen* and *Emerald* Only**

Body Slam*	Double-Edge	Mimic
Substitute	Thunder Wave*	

***Emerald* Only**

Defense Curl*	Endure*	Icy Wind*
Psych Up*	Sleep Talk	Snore*
Swagger	Swift*	

*Battle Frontier tutor move (*Emerald*)

---

352 Kecleon™

NORMAL

GENERAL INFO
SPECIES: Color Swap Pokémon
HEIGHT: 3'03"
WEIGHT: 49 lbs.
ABILITY: Change Color
Changes Kecleon's type to the type of move that hits it.

STATS
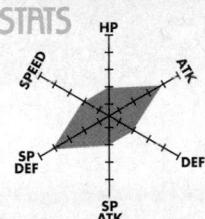

EVOLUTIONS
DOES NOT EVOLVE

LOCATION[S]:

RUBY **Rarity: Rare**
Routes 118, 119, 120, 121, 123 (Devon Scope)

SAPPHIRE **Rarity: Rare**
Routes 118, 119, 120, 121, 123 (Devon Scope)

FIRERED **Rarity: None**
Trade from *Ruby/Sapphire/Emerald*

LEAFGREEN **Rarity: None**
Trade from *Ruby/Sapphire/Emerald*

COLOSSEUM **Rarity: None**
Trade from *Ruby/Sapphire/Emerald*

EMERALD **Rarity: Rare**
Routes 118, 119, 120, 121, 123 (Devon Scope)

XD **Rarity: None**
Trade from *Ruby/Sapphire/Emerald*

MOVES

Level	Attack	Type	Power	ACC	PP	Level	Attack	Type	Power	ACC	PP
—	Thief	Dark	40	100	10	7	Faint Attack	Dark	60	—	20
—	Tail Whip	Normal	—	100	30	12	Fury Swipes	Normal	18	80	15
—	Astonish	Ghost	30	100	15	17	Psybeam	Psychic	65	100	20
—	Lick	Ghost	20	100	30	24	Screech	Normal	—	85	40
—	Scratch	Normal	40	100	35	31	Slash	Normal	70	100	20
4	Bind	Normal	15	75	20	40	Substitute	Normal	—	—	10
						49	Ancientpower	Rock	60	100	5

TM/HM

TM/HM#	Name	Type	Power	ACC	PP	TM/HM#	Name	Type	Power	ACC	PP
TM01	Focus Punch	Fighting	150	100	20	TM32	Double Team	Normal	—	—	15
TM03	Water Pulse	Water	60	100	20	TM34	Shock Wave	Electric	60	—	20
TM06	Toxic	Poison	—	85	10	TM35	Flamethrower	Fire	95	100	15
TM10	Hidden Power	Normal	—	100	15	TM38	Fire Blast	Fire	120	85	5
TM11	Sunny Day	Fire	—	—	5	TM39	Rock Tomb	Rock	50	80	10
TM13	Ice Beam	Ice	95	100	10	TM40	Aerial Ace	Flying	60	—	20
TM14	Blizzard	Ice	120	70	5	TM42	Facade	Normal	70	100	20
TM17	Protect	Normal	—	—	10	TM43	Secret Power	Normal	70	100	20
TM18	Rain Dance	Water	—	—	5	TM44	Rest	Psychic	—	—	10
TM21	Frustration	Normal	—	100	20	TM45	Attract	Normal	—	100	15
TM22	Solarbeam	Grass	120	100	10	TM46	Thief	Dark	40	100	10
TM23	Iron Tail	Steel	100	75	15	TM48	Skill Swap	Psychic	—	100	10
TM24	Thunderbolt	Electric	95	100	15	TM49	Snatch	Dark	—	100	10
TM25	Thunder	Electric	120	70	10	HM01	Cut	Normal	50	95	30
TM27	Return	Normal	—	100	20	HM04	Strength	Normal	80	100	15
TM28	Dig	Ground	60	100	10	HM05	Flash	Normal	—	70	20
TM30	Shadow Ball	Ghost	60	—	20	HM06	Rock Smash	Fighting	20	100	15
TM31	Brick Break	Fighting	75	100	15						

EGG MOVES*

Name	Type	Power	ACC	PP
Disable	Normal	—	55	20
Magic Coat	Psychic	—	100	15
Trick	Psychic	—	100	10

*Learned Via Breeding

MOVE TUTOR

***FireRed/LeafGreen* and *Emerald* Only**

Body Slam*	Counter*	Double-Edge
Mega Kick*	Mega Punch*	Mimic
Rock Slide*	Seismic Toss*	Substitute
Thunder Wave*		

***Emerald* Only**

Defense Curl*	Dynamicpunch*	Endure*
Fire Punch*	Fury Cutter*	Ice Punch*
Icy Wind*	Metronome	Mud-Slap*
Psych Up*	Rollout	Sleep Talk
Snore*	Swagger	Swift*
Thunderpunch*		

*Battle Frontier tutor move (*Emerald*)

353 Shuppet™

GHOST

GENERAL INFO

SPECIES: Puppet Pokémon
HEIGHT: 2'00"
WEIGHT: 5 lbs.
ABILITY: Insomnia
Shuppet cannot be put to sleep.

STATS

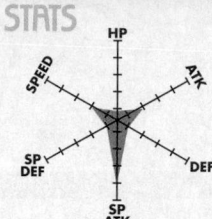

EVOLUTIONS

LV37

LOCATION[S]:

RUBY	Rarity: **Common**
Mt. Pyre	
SAPPHIRE	Rarity: **Common**
Route 121, Mt. Pyre	
FIRERED	Rarity: **None**
Trade from *Ruby/Sapphire/Emerald*	
LEAFGREEN	Rarity: **None**
Trade from *Ruby/Sapphire/Emerald*	
COLOSSEUM	Rarity: **None**
Trade from *Ruby/Sapphire/Emerald*	
EMERALD	Rarity: **Common**
Route 121, Route 123, Mt. Pyre	
XD	Rarity: **None**
Trade from *Ruby/Sapphire/Emerald*	

MOVES

Level	Attack	Type	Power	ACC	PP	Level	Attack	Type	Power	ACC	PP
—	Knock Off	Dark	20	100	20	32	Will-O-Wisp	Fire	—	75	15
8	Screech	Normal	—	85	40	37	Faint Attack	Dark	60	—	20
13	Night Shade	Ghost	—	100	15	44	Shadow Ball	Ghost	80	100	15
20	Curse	—	—	—	10	49	Snatch	Dark	—	100	10
25	Spite	Ghost	—	100	10	56	Grudge	Ghost	—	100	5

TM/HM

TM/HM#	Name	Type	Power	ACC	PP	TM/HM#	Name	Type	Power	ACC	PP
TM04	Calm Mind	Psychic	—	—	20	TM30	Shadow Ball	Ghost	60	—	20
TM06	Toxic	Poison	—	85	10	TM32	Double Team	Normal	—	—	15
TM10	Hidden Power	Normal	—	100	15	TM34	Shock Wave	Electric	60	—	20
TM11	Sunny Day	Fire	—	—	5	TM41	Torment	Dark	—	100	15
TM12	Taunt	Dark	—	100	20	TM42	Facade	Normal	70	100	20
TM17	Protect	Normal	—	—	10	TM43	Secret Power	Normal	70	100	20
TM18	Rain Dance	Water	—	—	5	TM44	Rest	Psychic	—	—	10
TM21	Frustration	Normal	—	100	20	TM45	Attract	Normal	—	100	15
TM24	Thunderbolt	Electric	95	100	15	TM46	Thief	Dark	40	100	10
TM25	Thunder	Electric	120	70	10	TM48	Skill Swap	Psychic	—	—	10
TM27	Return	Normal	—	100	20	TM49	Snatch	Dark	—	100	10
TM29	Psychic	Psychic	90	100	10	HM05	Flash	Normal	—	70	20

EGG MOVES*

Name	Type	Power	ACC	PP
Disable	Normal	—	55	20
Destiny Bond	Ghost	—	—	5
Foresight	Normal	—	100	40
Astonish	Ghost	30	100	15
Imprison	Psychic	—	100	15

*Learned Via Breeding

MOVE TUTOR

FireRed/LeafGreen and *Emerald* Only

Body Slam*	Double-Edge*	Dream Eater*
Mimic	Substitute	Thunder Wave*

Emerald Only

Endure*	Icy Wind*	Mud-Slap*
Sleep Talk	Snore*	Swagger

*Battle Frontier tutor move (*Emerald*)

354 Banette™

GHOST

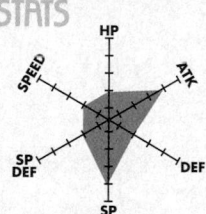

GENERAL INFO

SPECIES: Marionette Pokémon
HEIGHT: 3'07"
WEIGHT: 28 lbs.
ABILITY: Insomnia
Banette cannot be put to sleep.

STATS

EVOLUTIONS

LV37

LOCATION[S]:

RUBY	Rarity: **Evolve**
Evolve Shuppet	
SAPPHIRE	Rarity: **Common**
Sky Pillar	
FIRERED	Rarity: **None**
Trade from *Ruby/Sapphire/Emerald*	
LEAFGREEN	Rarity: **None**
Trade from *Ruby/Sapphire/Emerald*	
COLOSSEUM	Rarity: **None**
Trade from *Ruby/Sapphire/Emerald*	
EMERALD	Rarity: **Rare**
Evolve Shuppet, Sky Pillar	
XD	Rarity: **Only One**
Citadark Island (Capture from Cipher Peon Litnar)	

MOVES

Level	Attack	Type	Power	ACC	PP	Level	Attack	Type	Power	ACC	PP
—	Knock Off	Dark	20	100	20	32	Will-O-Wisp	Fire	—	75	15
—	Screech	Normal	—	85	40	39	Faint Attack	Dark	60	—	20
—	Night Shade	Ghost	—	100	15	48	Shadow Ball	Ghost	80	100	15
—	Curse	—	—	—	10	55	Snatch	Dark	—	100	10
25	Spite	Ghost	—	100	10	64	Grudge	Ghost	—	100	5

TM/HM

TM/HM#	Name	Type	Power	ACC	PP	TM/HM#	Name	Type	Power	ACC	PP
TM04	Calm Mind	Psychic	—	—	20	TM30	Shadow Ball	Ghost	60	—	20
TM06	Toxic	Poison	—	85	10	TM32	Double Team	Normal	—	—	15
TM10	Hidden Power	Normal	—	100	15	TM34	Shock Wave	Electric	60	—	20
TM11	Sunny Day	Fire	—	—	5	TM41	Torment	Dark	—	100	15
TM12	Taunt	Dark	—	100	20	TM42	Facade	Normal	70	100	20
TM15	Hyper Beam	Normal	150	90	5	TM43	Secret Power	Normal	70	100	20
TM17	Protect	Normal	—	—	10	TM44	Rest	Psychic	—	—	10
TM18	Rain Dance	Water	—	—	5	TM45	Attract	Normal	—	100	15
TM21	Frustration	Normal	—	100	20	TM46	Thief	Dark	40	100	10
TM24	Thunderbolt	Electric	95	100	15	TM48	Skill Swap	Psychic	—	—	10
TM25	Thunder	Electric	120	70	10	TM49	Snatch	Dark	—	100	10
TM27	Return	Normal	—	100	20	HM05	Flash	Normal	—	70	20
TM29	Psychic	Psychic	90	100	10						

MOVE TUTOR

FireRed/LeafGreen and *Emerald* Only

Body Slam*	Double-Edge*	Dream Eater*
Metronome	Mimic	Substitute
Thunder Wave*		

Emerald Only

Endure*	Icy Wind*	Mud-Slap*
Psych Up*	Sleep Talk	Snore*
Swagger		

*Battle Frontier tutor move (*Emerald*)

355 Duskull™

GENERAL INFO

SPECIES: Requiem Pokémon
HEIGHT: 2'07"
WEIGHT: 33 lbs.
ABILITY: Levitate

Duskull is not affected by Ground-type moves.

STATS

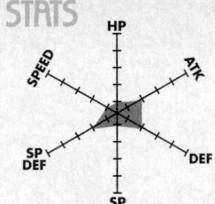

EVOLUTIONS

 LV37

LOCATION(S):

RUBY Rarity: **Common**
Route 121, Mt. Pyre

SAPPHIRE Rarity: **Common**
Mt. Pyre

FIRERED Rarity: **None**
Trade from *Ruby/Sapphire/Emerald*

LEAFGREEN Rarity: **None**
Trade from *Ruby/Sapphire/Emerald*

COLOSSEUM Rarity: **None**
Trade from *Ruby/Sapphire/Emerald*

EMERALD Rarity: **Common**
Mt. Pyre

XD Rarity: **Only One**
Pyrite Town (Capture from Cipher Peon Lobar)

MOVES

Level	Attack	Type	Power	ACC	PP
—	Leer	Normal	—	100	30
—	Night Shade	Ghost	—	100	15
5	Disable	Normal	—	55	20
12	Foresight	Normal	—	100	40
16	Astonish	Ghost	30	100	15

Level	Attack	Type	Power	ACC	PP
23	Confuse Ray	Ghost	—	100	10
27	Pursuit	Dark	40	100	20
34	Curse	—	—	—	10
38	Will-O-Wisp	Fire	—	75	15
45	Mean Look	Normal	—	100	5
49	Future Sight	Psychic	80	90	15

TM/HM

TM/HM#	Name	Type	Power	ACC	PP
TM04	Calm Mind	Psychic	—	—	20
TM06	Toxic	Poison	—	85	10
TM10	Hidden Power	Normal	—	100	15
TM11	Sunny Day	Fire	—	—	5
TM12	Taunt	Dark	—	100	20
TM13	Ice Beam	Ice	95	100	10
TM14	Blizzard	Ice	120	70	5
TM17	Protect	Normal	—	—	10
TM18	Rain Dance	Water	—	—	5
TM21	Frustration	Normal	—	100	20
TM27	Return	Normal	—	100	20
TM29	Psychic	Psychic	90	100	10

TM/HM#	Name	Type	Power	ACC	PP
TM30	Shadow Ball	Ghost	60	—	20
TM32	Double Team	Normal	—	—	15
TM41	Torment	Dark	—	100	15
TM42	Facade	Normal	70	100	20
TM43	Secret Power	Normal	70	100	20
TM44	Rest	Psychic	—	—	10
TM45	Attract	Normal	—	100	15
TM46	Thief	Dark	40	100	10
TM48	Skill Swap	Psychic	—	100	10
TM49	Snatch	Dark	—	100	10
HM05	Flash	Normal	—	70	20

EGG MOVES*

Name	Type	Power	ACC	PP
Imprison	Psychic	—	100	15
Destiny Bond	Ghost	—	—	5
Grudge	Ghost	—	100	5
Memento	Dark	—	100	10
Faint Attack	Dark	60	—	20
Pain Split	Normal	—	100	10

*Learned Via Breeding

MOVE TUTOR

FireRed/LeafGreen and *Emerald* Only

Body Slam*	Double-Edge*	Dream Eater*
Mimic	Substitute	

Emerald Only

Endure*	Icy Wind*	Psych Up*
Sleep Talk	Snore*	Swagger

*Battle Frontier tutor move (*Emerald*)

---

356 Dusclops™

GENERAL INFO

SPECIES: Beckon Pokémon
HEIGHT: 5'03"
WEIGHT: 67 lbs.
ABILITY: Pressure

The opponent spends 2 PP for damage inflicted against Dusclops.

STATS

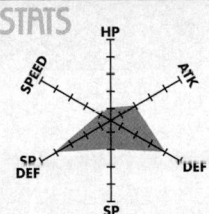

EVOLUTIONS

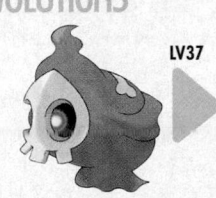 LV37

LOCATION(S):

RUBY Rarity: **Common**
Sky Pillar

SAPPHIRE Rarity: **Evolve**
Evolve Duskull

FIRERED Rarity: **None**
Trade from *Ruby/Sapphire/Emerald*

LEAFGREEN Rarity: **None**
Trade from *Ruby/Sapphire/Emerald*

COLOSSEUM Rarity: **None**
Trade from *Ruby/Sapphire/Emerald*

EMERALD Rarity: **Evolve**
Evolve Duskull

XD Rarity: **Evolve**
Evolve Duskull

MOVES

Level	Attack	Type	Power	ACC	PP
—	Bind	Normal	15	75	20
—	Leer	Normal	—	100	30
—	Night Shade	Ghost	—	100	15
—	Disable	Normal	—	55	20
12	Foresight	Normal	—	100	40
16	Astonish	Ghost	30	100	15

Level	Attack	Type	Power	ACC	PP
23	Confuse Ray	Ghost	—	100	10
27	Pursuit	Dark	40	100	20
34	Curse	—	—	—	10
37	Shadow Punch	Ghost	60	—	20
41	Will-O-Wisp	Fire	—	75	15
51	Mean Look	Normal	—	100	5
58	Future Sight	Psychic	80	90	15

TM/HM

TM/HM#	Name	Type	Power	ACC	PP
TM01	Focus Punch	Fighting	150	100	20
TM04	Calm Mind	Psychic	—	—	20
TM06	Toxic	Poison	—	85	10
TM10	Hidden Power	Normal	—	100	15
TM11	Sunny Day	Fire	—	—	5
TM12	Taunt	Dark	—	100	20
TM13	Ice Beam	Ice	95	100	10
TM14	Blizzard	Ice	120	70	5
TM15	Hyper Beam	Normal	150	90	5
TM17	Protect	Normal	—	—	10
TM18	Rain Dance	Water	—	—	5
TM21	Frustration	Normal	—	100	20
TM26	Earthquake	Ground	100	100	10
TM27	Return	Normal	—	100	20
TM29	Psychic	Psychic	90	100	10

TM/HM#	Name	Type	Power	ACC	PP
TM30	Shadow Ball	Ghost	60	—	20
TM32	Double Team	Normal	—	—	15
TM39	Rock Tomb	Rock	50	80	10
TM41	Torment	Dark	—	100	15
TM42	Facade	Normal	70	100	20
TM43	Secret Power	Normal	70	100	20
TM44	Rest	Psychic	—	—	10
TM45	Attract	Normal	—	100	15
TM46	Thief	Dark	40	100	10
TM48	Skill Swap	Psychic	—	100	10
TM49	Snatch	Dark	—	100	10
HM04	Strength	Normal	80	100	15
HM05	Flash	Normal	—	70	20
HM06	Rock Smash	Fighting	20	100	15

MOVE TUTOR

FireRed/LeafGreen and *Emerald* Only

Body Slam*	Counter*	Double-Edge*
Dream Eater*	Mega Kick*	Mega Punch*
Metronome	Mimic	Rock Slide*
Seismic Toss*	Substitute	

Emerald Only

Dynamicpunch	Endure*	Fire Punch*
Ice Punch*	Icy Wind*	Mud-Slap*
Psych Up*	Sleep Talk	Snore*
Swagger	Thunderpunch*	

*Battle Frontier tutor move (*Emerald*)

357 Tropius™

GRASS | FLYING

GENERAL INFO
SPECIES: Fruit Pokémon
HEIGHT: 6'07"
WEIGHT: 221 lbs.
ABILITY: Chlorophyll
Doubles Tropius's Speed when the sunlight is strong.

STATS

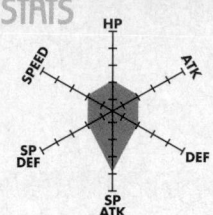

EVOLUTIONS

DOES NOT EVOLVE

LOCATION(S):

RUBY — Rarity: **Rare**
Route 119

SAPPHIRE — Rarity: **Rare**
Route 119

FIRERED — Rarity: **None**
Trade from *Ruby/Sapphire/Colosseum/Emerald*

LEAFGREEN — Rarity: **None**
Trade from *Ruby/Sapphire/Colosseum/Emerald*

COLOSSEUM — Rarity: **Only One**
Realgam Tower

EMERALD — Rarity: **Rare**
Route 119

XD — Rarity: **None**
Trade from *Ruby/Sapphire/Colosseum/Emerald*

MOVES

Level	Attack	Type	Power	ACC	PP
—	Leer	Normal	—	100	30
—	Gust	Flying	40	100	35
7	Growth	Normal	—	—	40
11	Razor Leaf	Grass	55	95	25
17	Stomp	Normal	65	100	20
21	Sweet Scent	Normal	—	100	20
27	Whirlwind	Normal	—	100s	20
31	Magical Leaf	Grass	60	—	20
37	Body Slam	Normal	85	100	15
41	Solarbeam	Grass	120	100	10
47	Synthesis	Grass	—	—	5

TM/HM

TM/HM#	Name	Type	Power	ACC	PP
TM05	Roar	Normal	—	100	20
TM06	Toxic	Poison	—	85	10
TM09	Bullet Seed	Grass	10	100	30
TM10	Hidden Power	Normal	—	100	15
TM11	Sunny Day	Fire	—	—	5
TM15	Hyper Beam	Normal	150	90	5
TM17	Protect	Normal	—	—	10
TM19	Giga Drain	Grass	60	100	5
TM20	Safeguard	Normal	—	—	25
TM21	Frustration	Normal	—	100	20
TM22	Solarbeam	Grass	120	100	10
TM26	Earthquake	Ground	100	100	10
TM27	Return	Normal	—	100	20
TM32	Double Team	Normal	—	—	15
TM40	Aerial Ace	Flying	60	—	20
TM42	Facade	Normal	70	100	20
TM43	Secret Power	Normal	70	100	20
TM44	Rest	Psychic	—	—	10
TM45	Attract	Normal	—	100	15
TM47	Steel Wing	Steel	70	90	25
HM01	Cut	Normal	50	95	30
HM02	Fly	Flying	70	95	15
HM04	Strength	Normal	80	100	15
HM05	Flash	Normal	—	70	20
HM06	Rock Smash	Fighting	20	100	15

EGG MOVES*

Name	Type	Power	ACC	PP
Headbutt	Normal	70	100	15
Slam	Normal	80	75	20
Razor Wind	Normal	80	100	10
Leech Seed	Grass	—	90	10
Nature Power	Normal	—	95	20

*Learned Via Breeding

MOVE TUTOR

FireRed/LeafGreen and Emerald Only

Body Slam*	Double-Edge*	Mimic
Substitute	Swords Dance*	

Emerald Only

Endure*	Fury Cutter*	Mud-Slap*
Sleep Talk	Snore*	Swagger

*Battle Frontier tutor move (*Emerald*)

---

358 Chimecho™

PSYCHIC

GENERAL INFO
SPECIES: Wind Chime Pokémon
HEIGHT: 2'00"
WEIGHT: 2 lbs.
ABILITY: Levitate
Chimecho is not affected by Ground-type moves.

STATS

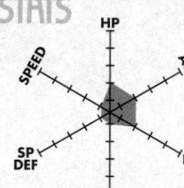

EVOLUTIONS

DOES NOT EVOLVE

LOCATION(S):

RUBY — Rarity: **Rare**
Mt. Pyre

SAPPHIRE — Rarity: **Rare**
Mt. Pyre

FIRERED — Rarity: **None**
Trade from *Ruby/Sapphire/Emerald*

LEAFGREEN — Rarity: **None**
Trade from *Ruby/Sapphire/Emerald*

COLOSSEUM — Rarity: **None**
Trade from *Ruby/Sapphire/Emerald*

EMERALD — Rarity: **Rare**
Mt. Pyre

XD — Rarity: **None**
Trade from *Ruby/Sapphire/Emerald*

MOVES

Level	Attack	Type	Power	ACC	PP
—	Wrap	Normal	15	85	20
6	Growl	Normal	—	100	40
9	Astonish	Ghost	30	100	15
14	Confusion	Psychic	50	100	25
17	Take Down	Normal	90	85	20
22	Uproar	Normal	50	100	10
25	Yawn	Normal	—	100	10
30	Psywave	Psychic	—	80	15
33	Double-Edge	Normal	120	100	15
38	Heal Bell	Normal	—	—	5
41	Safeguard	Normal	—	—	25
46	Psychic	Psychic	90	—	10

TM/HM

TM/HM#	Name	Type	Power	ACC	PP
TM04	Calm Mind	Psychic	—	—	20
TM06	Toxic	Poison	—	85	10
TM10	Hidden Power	Normal	—	100	15
TM11	Sunny Day	Fire	—	—	5
TM12	Taunt	Dark	—	100	20
TM16	Light Screen	Psychic	—	—	30
TM17	Protect	Normal	—	—	10
TM18	Rain Dance	Water	—	—	5
TM20	Safeguard	Normal	—	—	25
TM21	Frustration	Normal	—	100	20
TM27	Return	Normal	—	100	20
TM29	Psychic	Psychic	90	100	10
TM30	Shadow Ball	Ghost	60	—	20
TM32	Double Team	Normal	—	—	15
TM33	Reflect	Psychic	—	—	20
TM34	Shock Wave	Electric	60	—	20
TM41	Torment	Dark	—	100	15
TM42	Facade	Normal	70	100	20
TM43	Secret Power	Normal	70	100	20
TM44	Rest	Psychic	—	—	10
TM45	Attract	Normal	—	100	15
TM48	Skill Swap	Psychic	—	—	10
TM49	Snatch	Dark	—	100	10
HM05	Flash	Normal	—	70	20

EGG MOVES*

Name	Type	Power	ACC	PP
Disable	Normal	—	55	20
Curse	—	—	—	10
Hypnosis	Psychic	—	60	20
Dream Eater	Psychic	100	100	15

*Learned Via Breeding

MOVE TUTOR

FireRed/LeafGreen and Emerald Only

Double-Edge	Dream Eater*	Mimic
Substitute		

Emerald Only

Defense Curl*	Endure*	Icy Wind*
Psych Up*	Rollout	Sleep Talk
Snore*	Swagger	

*Battle Frontier tutor move (*Emerald*)

359 Absol™

DARK

GENERAL INFO
SPECIES: Disaster Pokémon
HEIGHT: 3'11"
WEIGHT: 104 lbs.
ABILITY: Pressure
When hit by a move, the opponent's Pokémon loses 2 PP.

STATS
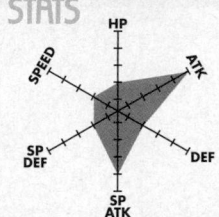

EVOLUTIONS

DOES NOT EVOLVE

LOCATION[S]:

RUBY — Rarity: **Rare**
Route 120

SAPPHIRE — Rarity: **Rare**
Route 120

FIRERED — Rarity: **None**
Route 120

LEAFGREEN — Rarity: **None**
Trade from *Ruby/Sapphire/Colosseum/Emerald*

COLOSSEUM — Rarity: **Only One**
Realgam Tower

EMERALD — Rarity: **Rare**
Route 120

XD — Rarity: **None**
Trade from *Ruby/Sapphire/Colosseum/Emerald*

MOVES

Level	Attack	Type	Power	ACC	PP	Level	Attack	Type	Power	ACC	PP
—	Scratch	Normal	40	100	35	21	Bite	Dark	60	100	25
5	Leer	Normal	—	100	30	26	Swords Dance	Normal	—	—	30
9	Taunt	Dark	—	100	20	31	Double Team	Normal	—	—	15
13	Quick Attack	Normal	40	100	30	36	Slash	Normal	70	100	20
17	Razor Wind	Normal	80	100	10	41	Future Sight	Psychic	80	90	15
						46	Perish Song	Normal	—	—	5

TM/HM

TM/HM#	Name	Type	Power	ACC	PP	TM/HM#	Name	Type	Power	ACC	PP
TM03	Water Pulse	Water	60	100	20	TM32	Double Team	Normal	—	—	15
TM04	Calm Mind	Psychic	—	—	20	TM34	Shock Wave	Electric	60	—	20
TM06	Toxic	Poison	—	85	10	TM35	Flamethrower	Fire	95	100	15
TM07	Hail	Ice	—	—	10	TM37	Sandstorm	Rock	—	—	10
TM10	Hidden Power	Normal	—	100	15	TM38	Fire Blast	Fire	120	85	5
TM11	Sunny Day	Fire	—	—	5	TM40	Aerial Ace	Flying	60	—	20
TM12	Taunt	Dark	—	100	20	TM41	Torment	Dark	—	100	15
TM13	Ice Beam	Ice	95	100	10	TM42	Facade	Normal	70	100	20
TM14	Blizzard	Ice	120	70	5	TM43	Secret Power	Normal	70	100	20
TM15	Hyper Beam	Normal	150	90	5	TM44	Rest	Psychic	—	—	10
TM17	Protect	Normal	—	—	10	TM45	Attract	Normal	—	100	15
TM18	Rain Dance	Water	—	—	5	TM46	Thief	Dark	40	100	10
TM21	Frustration	Normal	—	100	20	TM49	Snatch	Dark	—	100	10
TM23	Iron Tail	Steel	100	75	15	HM01	Cut	Normal	50	95	30
TM24	Thunderbolt	Electric	95	100	15	HM04	Strength	Normal	80	100	15
TM25	Thunder	Electric	120	70	10	HM05	Flash	Normal	—	70	20
TM27	Return	Normal	—	100	20	HM06	Rock Smash	Fighting	20	100	15
TM30	Shadow Ball	Ghost	60	—	20						

EGG MOVES*

Name	Type	Power	ACC	PP
Baton Pass	Normal	—	—	40
Faint Attack	Dark	60	—	20
Double-Edge	Normal	120	100	15
Magic Coat	Psychic	—	100	15
Curse	—	—	—	10
Substitute	Normal	—	—	10

*Learned Via Breeding

MOVE TUTOR
FireRed/LeafGreen and *Emerald* Only

Body Slam*	Counter*	Double-Edge
Dream Eater*	Mimic	Rock Slide*
Substitute	Swords Dance*	Thunder Wave*

Emerald Only

Endure*	Mud-Slap*	Psych Up*
Sleep Talk*	Swagger	Swift*

*Battle Frontier tutor move (*Emerald*)

---

360 Wynaut™

PSYCHIC

GENERAL INFO
SPECIES: Bright Pokémon
HEIGHT: 2'00"
WEIGHT: 31 lbs.
ABILITY: Shadow Tag
The opponent Pokémon cannot run or switch out from the battle.

STATS

EVOLUTIONS
 LV15

LOCATION[S]:

RUBY — Rarity: **Common**
Lavaridge Town (Receive Egg)

SAPPHIRE — Rarity: **Common**
Lavaridge Town (Receive Egg)

FIRERED — Rarity: **Breed**
Must Breed two Wobbuffet; one needs Lax Incense attached

LEAFGREEN — Rarity: **Breed**
Must Breed two Wobbuffet; one needs Lax Incense attached

COLOSSEUM — Rarity: **None**
Trade from *Ruby/Sapphire/Emerald*

EMERALD — Rarity: **Common**
Lavaridge Town (Receive Egg), Mirage Island

XD — Rarity: **None**
Trade from *Ruby/Sapphire/Emerald*

MOVES

Level	Attack	Type	Power	ACC	PP	Level	Attack	Type	Power	ACC	PP
—	Splash	Normal	—	—	40	15	Counter	Fighting	—	100	20
—	Charm	Normal	—	100	20	15	Mirror Coat	Psychic	—	100	20
—	Encore	Normal	—	100	5	15	Safeguard	Normal	—	—	25
						15	Destiny Bond	Ghost	—	—	5

TM/HM

TM/HM#	Name	Type	Power	ACC	PP
None					

EGG MOVES*

Name	Type	Power	ACC	PP
None				

*Learned Via Breeding

MOVE TUTOR
FireRed/LeafGreen and *Emerald* Only

None

361 Snorunt™

ICE

GENERAL INFO
SPECIES: Snow Hat Pokémon
HEIGHT: 2'04"
WEIGHT: 37 lbs.
ABILITY: Inner Focus
Prevents Snorunt from flinching.

STATS
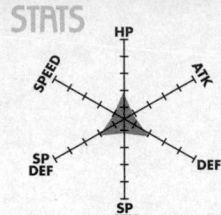

EVOLUTIONS

LV42

LOCATION[S]:

RUBY — Rarity: **Common**
Shoal Cave

SAPPHIRE — Rarity: **Common**
Shoal Cave

FIRERED — Rarity: **None**
Trade from *Ruby/Sapphire/Emerald*

LEAFGREEN — Rarity: **None**
Trade from *Ruby/Sapphire/Emerald*

COLOSSEUM — Rarity: **None**
Trade from *Ruby/Sapphire/Emerald*

EMERALD — Rarity: **Common**
Shoal Cave

XD — Rarity: **Only One**
Phenac City (Capture from Cipher Peon Exinn)

MOVES

Level	Attack	Type	Power	ACC	PP
—	Powder Snow	Ice	40	100	25
—	Leer	Normal	—	100	30
7	Double Team	Normal	—	—	15
10	Bite	Dark	60	100	25
16	Icy Wind	Ice	55	95	15
19	Headbutt	Normal	70	100	15
25	Protect	Normal	—	—	10
28	Crunch	Dark	80	100	15
34	Ice Beam	Ice	95	100	10
37	Hail	Ice	—	—	10
43	Blizzard	Ice	120	70	5

TM/HM

TM/HM#	Name	Type	Power	ACC	PP
TM03	Water Pulse	Water	60	100	20
TM06	Toxic	Poison	—	85	10
TM07	Hail	Ice	—	—	10
TM10	Hidden Power	Normal	—	100	15
TM13	Ice Beam	Ice	95	100	10
TM14	Blizzard	Ice	120	70	5
TM16	Light Screen	Psychic	—	—	30
TM17	Protect	Normal	—	—	10
TM18	Rain Dance	Water	—	—	5
TM20	Safeguard	Normal	—	—	25
TM21	Frustration	Normal	—	100	20
TM27	Return	Normal	—	100	20
TM30	Shadow Ball	Ghost	60	—	20
TM32	Double Team	Normal	—	—	15
TM42	Facade	Normal	70	100	20
TM43	Secret Power	Normal	70	100	20
TM44	Rest	Psychic	—	—	10
TM45	Attract	Normal	—	100	15
HM05	Flash	Normal	—	70	20

EGG MOVES*

Name	Type	Power	ACC	PP
Block	Normal	—	100	5
Spikes	Ground	—	—	20

*Learned Via Breeding

MOVE TUTOR
FireRed/LeafGreen and *Emerald* Only

Body Slam*	Double-Edge	Mimic
Substitute		

Emerald Only

Endure*	Icy Wind*	Sleep Talk
Snore*	Swagger	

*Battle Frontier tutor move (*Emerald*)

---

362 Glalie™

ICE

GENERAL INFO
SPECIES: Face Pokémon
HEIGHT: 4'11"
WEIGHT: 566 lbs.
ABILITY: Inner Focus
Prevents Glalie from flinching.

STATS
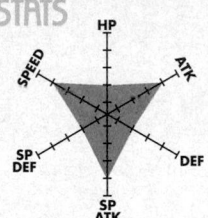

EVOLUTIONS

LV42

LOCATION[S]:

RUBY — Rarity: **Evolve**
Evolve Snorunt

SAPPHIRE — Rarity: **Evolve**
Evolve Snorunt

FIRERED — Rarity: **None**
Trade from *Ruby/Sapphire/Emerald*

LEAFGREEN — Rarity: **None**
Trade from *Ruby/Sapphire/Emerald*

COLOSSEUM — Rarity: **None**
Trade from *Ruby/Sapphire/Emerald*

EMERALD — Rarity: **Evolve**
Evolve Snorunt

XD — Rarity: **Evolve**
Evolve Snorunt

MOVES

Level	Attack	Type	Power	ACC	PP
—	Powder Snow	Ice	40	100	25
—	Leer	Normal	—	100	30
—	Double Team	Normal	—	—	15
—	Bite	Dark	60	100	25
16	Icy Wind	Ice	55	95	15
19	Headbutt	Normal	70	100	15
25	Protect	Normal	—	—	10
28	Crunch	Dark	80	100	15
34	Ice Beam	Ice	95	100	10
42	Hail	Ice	—	—	10
53	Blizzard	Ice	120	70	5
61	Sheer Cold	Ice	—	30	5

TM/HM

TM/HM#	Name	Type	Power	ACC	PP
TM03	Water Pulse	Water	60	100	20
TM06	Toxic	Poison	—	85	10
TM07	Hail	Ice	—	—	10
TM10	Hidden Power	Normal	—	100	15
TM12	Taunt	Dark	—	100	20
TM13	Ice Beam	Ice	95	100	10
TM14	Blizzard	Ice	120	70	5
TM15	Hyper Beam	Normal	150	90	5
TM16	Light Screen	Psychic	—	—	30
TM17	Protect	Normal	—	—	10
TM18	Rain Dance	Water	—	—	5
TM20	Safeguard	Normal	—	—	25
TM21	Frustration	Normal	—	100	20
TM26	Earthquake	Ground	100	100	10
TM27	Return	Normal	—	100	20
TM30	Shadow Ball	Ghost	60	—	20
TM32	Double Team	Normal	—	—	15
TM41	Torment	Dark	—	100	15
TM42	Facade	Normal	70	100	20
TM43	Secret Power	Normal	70	100	20
TM44	Rest	Psychic	—	—	10
TM45	Attract	Normal	—	100	15
HM05	Flash	Normal	—	70	20

MOVE TUTOR
FireRed/LeafGreen and *Emerald* Only

Body Slam*	Double-Edge	Explosion
Mimic	Substitute	

Emerald Only

Defense Curl*	Endure*	Icy Wind*
Rollout	Sleep Talk	Snore*
Thunderpunch*		

*Battle Frontier tutor move (*Emerald*)

363 Spheal™

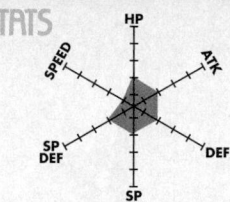

GENERAL INFO
SPECIES: Clap Pokémon
HEIGHT: 2'07"
WEIGHT: 87 lbs.
ABILITY: Thick Fat
Fire- and Ice-type moves inflict only 50% of the damage.

STATS

EVOLUTIONS

LV32   LV44

LOCATION[S]:

RUBY	Rarity: **Common**	
Shoal Cave		
SAPPHIRE	Rarity: **Common**	
Shoal Cave		
FIRERED	Rarity: **None**	
Trade from *Ruby/Sapphire/Emerald*		
LEAFGREEN	Rarity: **None**	
Trade from *Ruby/Sapphire/Emerald*		
COLOSSEUM	Rarity: **None**	
Trade from *Ruby/Sapphire/Emerald*		
EMERALD	Rarity: **Common**	
Shoal Cave		
XD	Rarity: **Only One**	
Cipher Lab (Capture from Cipher Peon Blusix)		

MOVES

Level	Attack	Type	Power	ACC	PP	Level	Attack	Type	Power	ACC	PP
—	Powder Snow	Ice	40	100	25	19	Body Slam	Normal	85	100	15
—	Growl	Normal	—	100	40	25	Aurora Beam	Ice	65	100	20
—	Defense Curl	Normal	—	—	40	31	Hail	Ice	—	—	10
—	Water Gun	Water	40	100	25	37	Rest	Psychic	—	—	10
7	Encore	Normal	—	100	5	37	Snore	Normal	40	100	15
13	Ice Ball	Ice	30	90	20	43	Blizzard	Ice	120	70	5
						49	Sheer Cold	Ice	—	30	5

TM/HM

TM/HM#	Name	Type	Power	ACC	PP	TM/HM#	Name	Type	Power	ACC	PP
TM03	Water Pulse	Water	60	100	20	TM32	Double Team	Normal	—	—	15
TM06	Toxic	Poison	—	85	10	TM39	Rock Tomb	Rock	50	80	10
TM07	Hail	Ice	—	—	10	TM42	Facade	Normal	70	100	20
TM10	Hidden Power	Normal	—	100	15	TM43	Secret Power	Normal	70	100	20
TM13	Ice Beam	Ice	95	100	10	TM44	Rest	Psychic	—	—	10
TM14	Blizzard	Ice	120	70	5	TM45	Attract	Normal	—	100	15
TM17	Protect	Normal	—	—	10	HM03	Surf	Water	95	100	15
TM18	Rain Dance	Water	—	—	5	HM04	Strength	Normal	80	100	15
TM21	Frustration	Normal	—	100	20	HM06	Rock Smash	Fighting	20	100	15
TM23	Iron Tail	Steel	100	75	15	HM07	Waterfall	Water	80	100	15
TM26	Earthquake	Ground	100	100	10	HM08	Dive	Water	60	100	10
TM27	Return	Normal	—	100	20						

EGG MOVES*

Name	Type	Power	ACC	PP
Water Sport	Water	—	100	15
Stockpile	Normal	—	—	10
Swallow	Normal	—	—	10
Spit Up	Normal	100	100	10
Yawn	Normal	—	—	10
Rock Slide	Rock	75	90	10
Curse	—	—	—	10
Fissure	Ground	—	30	5

Learned Via Breeding

MOVE TUTOR
FireRed/LeafGreen and *Emerald* Only

Body Slam*	Double-Edge	Mimic
Rock Slide*	Substitute	

Emerald Only

Defense Curl*	Endure*	Icy Wind*
Mud-Slap*	Rollout	Sleep Talk
Snore*	Swagger	

*Battle Frontier tutor move (*Emerald*)

---

364 Sealeo™

GENERAL INFO
SPECIES: Ball Roll Pokémon
HEIGHT: 3'07"
WEIGHT: 193 lbs.
ABILITY: Thick Fat
Fire- and Ice-type moves inflict only 50% of the damage.

STATS

EVOLUTIONS

LV32   LV44

LOCATION[S]:

RUBY	Rarity: **Evolve**	
Evolve Spheal		
SAPPHIRE	Rarity: **Evolve**	
Evolve Spheal		
FIRERED	Rarity: **None**	
Trade from *Ruby/Sapphire/Emerald*		
LEAFGREEN	Rarity: **None**	
Trade from *Ruby/Sapphire/Emerald*		
COLOSSEUM	Rarity: **None**	
Trade from *Ruby/Sapphire/Emerald*		
EMERALD	Rarity: **Evolve**	
Evolve Spheal		
XD	Rarity: **Evolve**	
Evolve Spheal		

MOVES

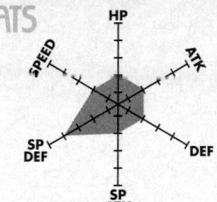

Level	Attack	Type	Power	ACC	PP	Level	Attack	Type	Power	ACC	PP
—	Defense Curl	Normal	—	—	80	25	Aurora Beam	Ice	65	100	20
—	Powder Snow	Ice	40	100	25	31	Hail	Ice	—	—	10
—	Growl	Normal	—	100	40	39	Rest	Psychic	—	—	10
—	Water Gun	Water	40	100	25	39	Snore	Normal	40	100	15
7	Encore	Normal	—	100	5	47	Blizzard	Ice	120	70	5
13	Ice Ball	Ice	30	90	20	55	Sheer Cold	Ice	—	30	5
19	Body Slam	Normal	85	100	15						

TM/HM

TM/HM#	Name	Type	Power	ACC	PP	TM/HM#	Name	Type	Power	ACC	PP
TM03	Water Pulse	Water	60	100	20	TM27	Return	Normal	—	100	20
TM05	Roar	Normal	—	100	20	TM32	Double Team	Normal	—	—	15
TM06	Toxic	Poison	—	85	10	TM39	Rock Tomb	Rock	50	80	10
TM07	Hail	Ice	—	—	10	TM42	Facade	Normal	70	100	20
TM10	Hidden Power	Normal	—	100	15	TM43	Secret Power	Normal	70	100	20
TM13	Ice Beam	Ice	95	100	10	TM44	Rest	Psychic	—	—	10
TM14	Blizzard	Ice	120	70	5	TM45	Attract	Normal	—	100	15
TM17	Protect	Normal	—	—	10	HM03	Surf	Water	95	100	15
TM18	Rain Dance	Water	—	—	5	HM04	Strength	Normal	80	100	15
TM21	Frustration	Normal	—	100	20	HM06	Rock Smash	Fighting	20	100	15
TM23	Iron Tail	Steel	100	75	15	HM07	Waterfall	Water	80	100	15
TM26	Earthquake	Ground	100	100	10	HM08	Dive	Water	60	100	10

MOVE TUTOR
FireRed/LeafGreen and *Emerald* Only

Body Slam*	Double-Edge	Mimic
Rock Slide*	Substitute	

Emerald Only

Defense Curl*	Endure*	Icy Wind*
Mud-Slap*	Rollout	Sleep Talk
Snore*	Swagger	

*Battle Frontier tutor move (*Emerald*)

365 Walrein™

ICE | WATER

GENERAL INFO
SPECIES: Ice Break Pokémon
HEIGHT: 4'07"
WEIGHT: 332 lbs.
ABILITY: Thick Fat
Fire- and Ice-type moves inflict only 50% of the damage.

STATS
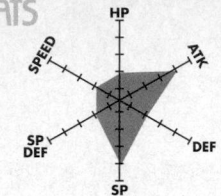

EVOLUTIONS

LV32   LV44

LOCATION[S]:

RUBY   **Rarity:** Evolve
Evolve Sealeo

SAPPHIRE   **Rarity:** Evolve
Evolve Sealeo

FIRERED   **Rarity:** None
Trade from *Ruby/Sapphire/Emerald*

LEAFGREEN   **Rarity:** None
Trade from *Ruby/Sapphire/Emerald*

COLOSSEUM   **Rarity:** None
Trade from *Ruby/Sapphire/Emerald*

EMERALD   **Rarity:** Evolve
Evolve Sealeo

XD   **Rarity:** Evolve
Evolve Sealeo

MOVES

Level	Attack	Type	Power	ACC	PP	Level	Attack	Type	Power	ACC	PP
—	Powder Snow	Ice	40	100	25	25	Aurora Beam	Ice	65	100	20
—	Growl	Normal	—	100	40	31	Hail	Ice	—	—	10
—	Defense Curl	Normal	—	—	40	39	Rest	Psychic	—	—	10
—	Water Gun	Water	40	100	25	39	Snore	Normal	40	100	15
7	Encore	Normal	—	100	5	50	Blizzard	Ice	120	70	5
13	Ice Ball	Ice	30	90	20	61	Sheer Cold	Ice	—	30	5
19	Body Slam	Normal	85	100	15						

TM/HM

TM/HM#	Name	Type	Power	ACC	PP	TM/HM#	Name	Type	Power	ACC	PP
TM03	Water Pulse	Water	60	100	20	TM27	Return	Normal	—	100	20
TM05	Roar	Normal	—	100	20	TM32	Double Team	Normal	—	—	15
TM06	Toxic	Poison	—	85	10	TM39	Rock Tomb	Rock	50	80	10
TM07	Hail	Ice	—	—	10	TM42	Facade	Normal	70	100	20
TM10	Hidden Power	Normal	—	100	15	TM43	Secret Power	Normal	70	100	20
TM13	Ice Beam	Ice	95	100	10	TM44	Rest	Psychic	—	—	10
TM14	Blizzard	Ice	120	70	5	TM45	Attract	Normal	—	100	15
TM15	Hyper Beam	Normal	150	90	5	HM03	Surf	Water	95	100	15
TM17	Protect	Normal	—	—	10	HM04	Strength	Normal	80	100	15
TM18	Rain Dance	Water	—	—	5	HM06	Rock Smash	Fighting	20	100	15
TM21	Frustration	Normal	—	100	20	HM07	Waterfall	Water	80	100	15
TM23	Iron Tail	Steel	100	75	15	HM08	Dive	Water	60	100	10
TM26	Earthquake	Ground	100	100	10						

MOVE TUTOR
FireRed/LeafGreen and *Emerald* Only

Body Slam*	Double-Edge	Mimic
Rock Slide*	Substitute	

Emerald Only

Defense Curl*	Endure*	Icy Wind*
Mud-Slap*	Rollout	Sleep Talk
Snore*	Swagger	

*Battle Frontier tutor move (*Emerald*)

---

366 Clamperl™

WATER

GENERAL INFO
SPECIES: Bivalve Pokémon
HEIGHT: 1'04"
WEIGHT: 116 lbs.
ABILITY: Shell Armor
Prevents the opponent Pokémon from scoring a critical hit.

STATS
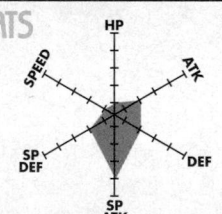

EVOLUTIONS

TRADE WITH DEEPSEATOOTH

TRADE WITH DEEPSEASCALE

LOCATION[S]:

RUBY   **Rarity:** Common
Underwater Route 124, Underwater Route 126

SAPPHIRE   **Rarity:** Common
Underwater Route 124, Underwater Route 126

FIRERED   **Rarity:** None
Trade from *Ruby/Sapphire/Emerald*

LEAFGREEN   **Rarity:** None
Trade from *Ruby/Sapphire/Emerald*

COLOSSEUM   **Rarity:** None
Trade from *Ruby/Sapphire/Emerald*

EMERALD   **Rarity:** Common
Underwater Route 124, Underwater Route 126

XD   **Rarity:** None
Trade from *Ruby/Sapphire/Emerald*

MOVES

Level	Attack	Type	Power	ACC	PP	Level	Attack	Type	Power	ACC	PP
—	Clamp	Water	35	75	10	—	Whirlpool	Water	15	70	15
—	Water Gun	Water	40	100	25	—	Iron Defense	Steel	—	—	15

TM/HM

TM/HM#	Name	Type	Power	ACC	PP	TM/HM#	Name	Type	Power	ACC	PP
TM03	Water Pulse	Water	60	100	20	TM27	Return	Normal	—	100	20
TM06	Toxic	Poison	—	85	10	TM32	Double Team	Normal	—	—	15
TM07	Hail	Ice	—	—	10	TM42	Facade	Normal	70	100	20
TM10	Hidden Power	Normal	—	100	15	TM43	Secret Power	Normal	70	100	20
TM13	Ice Beam	Ice	95	100	10	TM44	Rest	Psychic	—	—	10
TM14	Blizzard	Ice	120	70	5	TM45	Attract	Normal	—	100	15
TM17	Protect	Normal	—	—	10	HM03	Surf	Water	95	100	15
TM18	Rain Dance	Water	—	—	5	HM07	Waterfall	Water	80	100	15
TM21	Frustration	Normal	—	100	20	HM08	Dive	Water	60	100	10

EGG MOVES*

Name	Type	Power	ACC	PP
Refresh	Normal	—	100	20
Mud Sport	Ground	—	100	15
Body Slam	Normal	85	100	15
Supersonic	Normal	—	55	20
Barrier	Psychic	—	—	30
Confuse Ray	Ghost	—	100	10

*Learned Via Breeding

MOVE TUTOR
FireRed/LeafGreen and *Emerald* Only

Body Slam*	Double-Edge	Mimic
Substitute		

Emerald Only

Endure*	Icy Wind*	Sleep Talk
Snore*	Swagger	

*Battle Frontier tutor move (*Emerald*)

367 Huntail™

WATER

GENERAL INFO
SPECIES: Deep Sea Pokémon
HEIGHT: 5'07"
WEIGHT: 60 lbs.
ABILITY: Swift Swim
Doubles Huntail's Speed when it's raining.

STATS

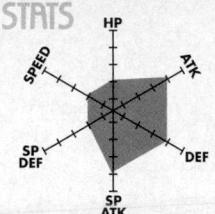

EVOLUTIONS

TRADE WITH DEEPSEATOOTH

LOCATION(S):

RUBY — Rarity: **None**
Evolve Clamperl (Deepseatooth)

SAPPHIRE — Rarity: **None**
Evolve Clamperl (Deepseatooth)

FIRERED — Rarity: **None**
Trade from *Ruby/Sapphire/Emerald*

LEAFGREEN — Rarity: **None**
Trade from *Ruby/Sapphire/Emerald*

COLOSSEUM — Rarity: **None**
Trade from *Ruby/Sapphire/Emerald*

EMERALD — Rarity: **Evolve**
Evolve Clamperl (Deepseatooth)

XD — Rarity: **None**
Trade from *Ruby/Sapphire/Emerald*

MOVES

Level	Attack	Type	Power	ACC	PP	Level	Attack	Type	Power	ACC	PP
—	Whirlpool	Water	15	70	15	29	Scary Face	Normal	—	90	10
8	Bite	Dark	60	100	25	36	Crunch	Dark	80	100	15
15	Screech	Normal	—	85	40	43	Baton Pass	Normal	—	—	40
22	Water Pulse	Water	60	100	20	50	Hydro Pump	Water	120	80	5

TM/HM

TM/HM#	Name	Type	Power	ACC	PP	TM/HM#	Name	Type	Power	ACC	PP
TM03	Water Pulse	Water	60	100	20	TM32	Double Team	Normal	—	—	15
TM06	Toxic	Poison	—	85	10	TM39	Rock Tomb	Rock	50	80	10
TM07	Hail	Ice	—	—	10	TM42	Facade	Normal	70	100	20
TM10	Hidden Power	Normal	—	100	15	TM43	Secret Power	Normal	70	100	20
TM13	Ice Beam	Ice	95	100	10	TM44	Rest	Psychic	—	—	10
TM14	Blizzard	Ice	120	70	5	TM45	Attract	Normal	—	100	15
TM15	Hyper Beam	Normal	150	90	5	TM49	Snatch	Dark	—	100	10
TM17	Protect	Normal	—	—	10	HM03	Surf	Water	95	100	15
TM18	Rain Dance	Water	—	—	5	HM07	Waterfall	Water	80	100	15
TM21	Frustration	Normal	—	100	20	HM08	Dive	Water	60	100	10
TM27	Return	Normal	—	100	20						

MOVE TUTOR
FireRed/LeafGreen and *Emerald* **Only**
Body Slam* — Double-Edge — Mimic
Substitute

Emerald **Only**
Endure* — Icy Wind* — Mud-Slap*
Sleep Talk — Snore* — Swagger
Swift*

*Battle Frontier tutor move (*Emerald*)

---

368 Gorebyss™

WATER

GENERAL INFO
SPECIES: South Sea Pokémon
HEIGHT: 5'11"
WEIGHT: 50 lbs.
ABILITY: Swift Swim
Doubles Gorebyss's Speed when it's raining.

STATS

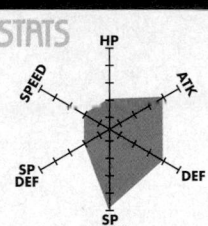

EVOLUTIONS

TRADE WITH DEEPSEASCALE

LOCATION(S):

RUBY — Rarity: **None**
Evolve Clamperl (Deepseascale)

SAPPHIRE — Rarity: **None**
Evolve Clamperl (Deepseascale)

FIRERED — Rarity: **None**
Trade from *Ruby/Sapphire/Emerald*

LEAFGREEN — Rarity: **None**
Trade from *Ruby/Sapphire/Emerald*

COLOSSEUM — Rarity: **None**
Trade from *Ruby/Sapphire/Emerald*

EMERALD — Rarity: **Evolve**
Evolve Clamperl (Deepseascale)

XD — Rarity: **None**
Trade from *Ruby/Sapphire/Emerald*

MOVES

Level	Attack	Type	Power	ACC	PP	Level	Attack	Type	Power	ACC	PP
—	Whirlpool	Water	15	70	15	29	Amnesia	Psychic	—	—	20
8	Confusion	Psychic	50	100	25	36	Psychic	Psychic	90	100	10
15	Agility	Psychic	—	—	30	43	Baton Pass	Normal	—	—	40
22	Water Pulse	Water	60	100	20	50	Hydro Pump	Water	120	80	5

TM/HM

TM/HM#	Name	Type	Power	ACC	PP	TM/HM#	Name	Type	Power	ACC	PP
TM03	Water Pulse	Water	60	100	20	TM27	Return	Normal	—	100	20
TM06	Toxic	Poison	—	85	10	TM29	Psychic	Psychic	90	100	10
TM07	Hail	Ice	—	—	10	TM30	Shadow Ball	Ghost	60	—	20
TM10	Hidden Power	Normal	—	100	15	TM32	Double Team	Normal	—	—	15
TM13	Ice Beam	Ice	95	100	10	TM42	Facade	Normal	70	100	20
TM14	Blizzard	Ice	120	70	5	TM43	Secret Power	Normal	70	100	20
TM15	Hyper Beam	Normal	150	90	5	TM44	Rest	Psychic	—	—	10
TM17	Protect	Normal	—	—	10	TM45	Attract	Normal	—	100	15
TM18	Rain Dance	Water	—	—	5	HM03	Surf	Water	95	100	15
TM20	Safeguard	Normal	—	—	25	HM07	Waterfall	Water	80	100	15
TM21	Frustration	Normal	—	100	20	HM08	Dive	Water	60	100	10

MOVE TUTOR
FireRed/LeafGreen and *Emerald* **Only**
Body Slam* — Double-Edge — Mimic
Substitute

Emerald **Only**
Endure* — Icy Wind* — Mud-Slap*
Sleep Talk — Snore* — Swagger
Swift*

*Battle Frontier tutor move (*Emerald*)

369 Relicanth™

WATER · ROCK

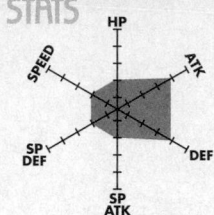

GENERAL INFO

SPECIES: Longevity Pokémon
HEIGHT: 3'03"
WEIGHT: 52 lbs.
ABILITY 1: Swift Swim
Doubles Relicanth's Speed when it's raining.
ABILITY 2: Rock Head
Relicanth does not receive recoil damage from moves such as Double-Edge.

STATS

EVOLUTIONS

DOES NOT EVOLVE

LOCATION[S]:

RUBY — Rarity: **Rare**
Underwater Route 124, Underwater Route 126

SAPPHIRE — Rarity: **Rare**
Underwater Route 124, Underwater Route 126

FIRERED — Rarity: **None**
Trade from *Ruby/Sapphire/Emerald*

LEAFGREEN — Rarity: **None**
Trade from *Ruby/Sapphire/Emerald*

COLOSSEUM — Rarity: **None**
Trade from *Ruby/Sapphire/Emerald*

EMERALD — Rarity: **Rare**
Underwater Routes 124–126

XD — Rarity: **None**
Trade from *Ruby/Sapphire/Emerald*

MOVES

Level	Attack	Type	Power	ACC	PP	Level	Attack	Type	Power	ACC	PP
—	Tackle	Normal	35	95	35	29	Take Down	Normal	90	85	20
—	Harden	Normal	—	—	30	36	Mud Sport	Ground	—	100	15
8	Water Gun	Water	40	100	25	43	Ancientpower	Rock	60	100	5
15	Rock Tomb	Rock	50	80	10	50	Rest	Psychic	—	—	10
22	Yawn	Normal	—	100	10	57	Double-Edge	Normal	120	100	15
						64	Hydro Pump	Water	120	80	5

TM/HM

TM/HM#	Name	Type	Power	ACC	PP	TM/HM#	Name	Type	Power	ACC	PP
TM03	Water Pulse	Water	60	100	20	TM27	Return	Normal	—	100	20
TM04	Calm Mind	Psychic	—	—	20	TM32	Double Team	Normal	—	—	15
TM06	Toxic	Poison	—	85	10	TM37	Sandstorm	Rock	—	—	10
TM07	Hail	Ice	—	—	10	TM39	Rock Tomb	Rock	50	80	10
TM10	Hidden Power	Normal	—	100	15	TM42	Facade	Normal	70	100	20
TM13	Ice Beam	Ice	95	100	10	TM43	Secret Power	Normal	70	100	20
TM14	Blizzard	Ice	120	70	5	TM44	Rest	Psychic	—	—	10
TM15	Hyper Beam	Normal	150	90	5	TM45	Attract	Normal	—	100	15
TM17	Protect	Normal	—	—	10	HM03	Surf	Water	95	100	15
TM18	Rain Dance	Water	—	—	5	HM06	Rock Smash	Fighting	20	100	15
TM20	Safeguard	Normal	—	—	25	HM07	Waterfall	Water	80	100	15
TM21	Frustration	Normal	—	100	20	HM08	Dive	Water	60	100	10
TM26	Earthquake	Ground	100	100	10						

EGG MOVES*

Name	Type	Power	ACC	PP
Magnitude	Ground	—	100	30
Skull Bash	Normal	100	100	15
Water Sport	Water	—	100	15
Amnesia	Psychic	—	—	20
Sleep Talk	Normal	—	—	10
Rock Slide	Rock	75	90	10

*Learned Via Breeding

MOVE TUTOR

FireRed/LeafGreen and Emerald Only

Body Slam*	Double-Edge	Mimic
Rock Slide*	Substitute	

Emerald Only

Endure*	Icy Wind*	Mud-Slap*
Psych Up*	Snore*	Swagger

*Battle Frontier tutor move (*Emerald*)

---

370 Luvdisc™

WATER

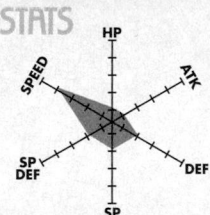

GENERAL INFO

SPECIES: Rendezvous Pokémon
HEIGHT: 2'00"
WEIGHT: 19 lbs.
ABILITY: Swift Swim
Doubles Luvdisc's Speed when it's raining.

STATS

EVOLUTIONS

DOES NOT EVOLVE

LOCATION[S]:

RUBY — Rarity: **Common**
Ever Grande City, Route 128

SAPPHIRE — Rarity: **Common**
Ever Grande City, Route 128

FIRERED — Rarity: **None**
Trade from *Ruby/Sapphire/Emerald*

LEAFGREEN — Rarity: **None**
Trade from *Ruby/Sapphire/Emerald*

COLOSSEUM — Rarity: **None**
Trade from *Ruby/Sapphire/Emerald*

EMERALD — Rarity: **Common**
Ever Grande City, Route 128

XD — Rarity: **None**
Trade from *Ruby/Sapphire/Emerald*

MOVES

Level	Attack	Type	Power	ACC	PP	Level	Attack	Type	Power	ACC	PP
—	Tackle	Normal	35	95	35	24	Take Down	Normal	90	85	20
4	Charm	Normal	—	100	20	28	Attract	Normal	—	100	15
12	Water Gun	Water	40	100	25	36	Sweet Kiss	Normal	—	75	10
16	Agility	Psychic	—	—	30	40	Flail	Normal	—	100	15
						48	Safeguard	Normal	—	—	25

TM/HM

TM/HM#	Name	Type	Power	ACC	PP	TM/HM#	Name	Type	Power	ACC	PP
TM03	Water Pulse	Water	60	100	20	TM27	Return	Normal	—	100	20
TM06	Toxic	Poison	—	85	10	TM32	Double Team	Normal	—	—	15
TM07	Hail	Ice	—	—	10	TM42	Facade	Normal	70	100	20
TM10	Hidden Power	Normal	—	100	15	TM43	Secret Power	Normal	70	100	20
TM13	Ice Beam	Ice	95	100	10	TM44	Rest	Psychic	—	—	10
TM14	Blizzard	Ice	120	70	5	TM45	Attract	Normal	—	100	15
TM17	Protect	Normal	—	—	10	HM03	Surf	Water	95	100	15
TM18	Rain Dance	Water	—	—	5	HM07	Waterfall	Water	80	100	15
TM20	Safeguard	Normal	—	—	25	HM08	Dive	Water	60	100	10
TM21	Frustration	Normal	—	100	20						

EGG MOVES*

Name	Type	Power	ACC	PP
Supersonic	Normal	—	55	20
Water Sport	Water	—	100	15
Mud Sport	Ground	—	100	15
Bounce	Flying	85	85	5

*Learned Via Breeding

MOVE TUTOR

FireRed/LeafGreen and Emerald Only

Double-Edge	Mimic	Substitute

Emerald Only

Endure*	Icy Wind*	Psych Up*
Sleep Talk	Snore*	Swagger
Swift*		

*Battle Frontier tutor move (*Emerald*)

371 Bagon™

DRAGON

GENERAL INFO

SPECIES: Rock Head Pokémon
HEIGHT: 2'00"
WEIGHT: 93 lbs.
ABILITY: Rock Head

Bagon does not receive recoil damage from moves such as Double-Edge.

STATS

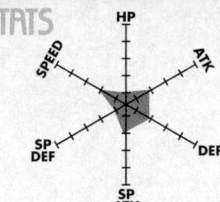

EVOLUTIONS

  LV30  LV50

LOCATION[S]:

RUBY	Rarity: **Common**
Meteor Falls	
SAPPHIRE	Rarity: **Common**
Meteor Falls	
FIRERED	Rarity: **None**
Trade from *Ruby/Sapphire/Emerald*	
LEAFGREEN	Rarity: **None**
Trade from *Ruby/Sapphire/Emerald*	
COLOSSEUM	Rarity: **None**
Trade from *Ruby/Sapphire/Emerald*	
EMERALD	Rarity: **Common**
Meteor Falls	
XD	Rarity: **None**
Trade from *Ruby/Sapphire/Emerald*	

MOVES

Level	Attack	Type	Power	ACC	PP
—	Rage	Normal	20	100	20
5	Bite	Dark	60	100	25
9	Leer	Normal	—	100	30
17	Headbutt	Normal	70	100	15
21	Focus Energy	Normal	—	—	30
25	Ember	Fire	40	100	25
33	Dragonbreath	Dragon	60	100	20
37	Scary Face	Normal	—	90	10
41	Crunch	Dark	80	100	15
49	Dragon Claw	Dragon	80	100	15
53	Double-Edge	Normal	120	100	15

TM/HM

TM/HM#	Name	Type	Power	ACC	PP
TM02	Dragon Claw	Dragon	80	100	15
TM05	Roar	Normal	—	100	20
TM06	Toxic	Poison	—	85	10
TM10	Hidden Power	Normal	—	100	15
TM11	Sunny Day	Fire	—	—	5
TM17	Protect	Normal	—	—	10
TM18	Rain Dance	Water	—	—	5
TM21	Frustration	Normal	—	100	20
TM27	Return	Normal	—	100	20
TM31	Brick Break	Fighting	75	100	15
TM32	Double Team	Normal	—	—	15
TM35	Flamethrower	Fire	95	100	15
TM38	Fire Blast	Fire	120	85	5
TM39	Rock Tomb	Rock	50	80	10
TM40	Aerial Ace	Flying	60	—	20
TM42	Facade	Normal	70	100	20
TM43	Secret Power	Normal	70	100	20
TM44	Rest	Psychic	—	—	10
TM45	Attract	Normal	—	100	15
HM01	Cut	Normal	50	95	30
HM04	Strength	Normal	80	100	15
HM06	Rock Smash	Fighting	20	100	15

EGG MOVES*

Name	Type	Power	ACC	PP
Hydro Pump	Water	120	80	5
Thrash	Normal	90	100	20
Dragon Rage	Dragon	—	100	10
Twister	Dragon	40	100	20
Dragon Dance	Dragon	—	—	20

*Learned Via Breeding

MOVE TUTOR

FireRed/LeafGreen and *Emerald* Only

Body Slam*	Double-Edge	Mimic
Rock Slide*	Substitute	

Emerald Only

Endure*	Fury Cutter	Mud-Slap*
Sleep Talk	Snore*	Swagger

*Battle Frontier tutor move (*Emerald*)

---

372 Shelgon™

DRAGON

GENERAL INFO

SPECIES: Endurance Pokémon
HEIGHT: 3'07"
WEIGHT: 244 lbs.
ABILITY: Rock Head

Shelgon does not receive recoil damage from moves such as Double-Edge.

STATS

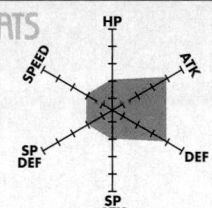

EVOLUTIONS

  LV30  LV50

LOCATION[S]:

RUBY	Rarity: **Evolve**
Evolve Bagon	
SAPPHIRE	Rarity: **Evolve**
Evolve Bagon	
FIRERED	Rarity: **None**
Trade from *Ruby/Sapphire/Emerald*	
LEAFGREEN	Rarity: **None**
Trade from *Ruby/Sapphire/Emerald*	
COLOSSEUM	Rarity: **None**
Trade from *Ruby/Sapphire/Emerald*	
EMERALD	Rarity: **Evolve**
Evolve Bagon	
XD	Rarity: **None**
Trade from *Ruby/Sapphire/Emerald*	

MOVES

Level	Attack	Type	Power	ACC	PP
—	Rage	Normal	20	100	20
—	Bite	Dark	60	100	25
—	Leer	Normal	—	100	30
—	Headbutt	Normal	70	100	15
21	Focus Energy	Normal	—	—	30
25	Ember	Fire	40	100	25
30	Protect	Normal	—	—	10
38	Dragonbreath	Dragon	60	100	20
47	Scary Face	Normal	—	90	10
56	Crunch	Dark	80	100	15
69	Dragon Claw	Dragon	80	100	15
78	Double-Edge	Normal	120	100	15

TM/HM

TM/HM#	Name	Type	Power	ACC	PP
TM02	Dragon Claw	Dragon	80	100	15
TM05	Roar	Normal	—	100	20
TM06	Toxic	Poison	—	85	10
TM10	Hidden Power	Normal	—	100	15
TM11	Sunny Day	Fire	—	—	5
TM17	Protect	Normal	—	—	10
TM18	Rain Dance	Water	—	—	5
TM21	Frustration	Normal	—	100	20
TM27	Return	Normal	—	100	20
TM31	Brick Break	Fighting	75	100	15
TM32	Double Team	Normal	—	—	15
TM35	Flamethrower	Fire	95	100	15
TM38	Fire Blast	Fire	120	85	5
TM39	Rock Tomb	Rock	50	80	10
TM40	Aerial Ace	Flying	60	—	20
TM42	Facade	Normal	70	100	20
TM43	Secret Power	Normal	70	100	20
TM44	Rest	Psychic	—	—	10
TM45	Attract	Normal	—	100	15
HM01	Cut	Normal	50	95	30
HM04	Strength	Normal	80	100	15
HM06	Rock Smash	Fighting	20	100	15

MOVE TUTOR

FireRed/LeafGreen and *Emerald* Only

Body Slam*	Double-Edge	Mimic
Rock Slide*	Substitute	

Emerald Only

Defense Curl*	Endure*	Fury Cutter
Mud-Slap*	Rollout	Sleep Talk
Snore*	Swagger	

*Battle Frontier tutor move (*Emerald*)

373 Salamence™

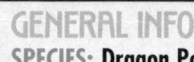

DRAGON   FLYING

GENERAL INFO
SPECIES: Dragon Pokémon
HEIGHT: 4'11"
WEIGHT: 226 lbs.
ABILITY: Intimidate
Lowers the opponent's Attack by one at the battle's start.

STATS
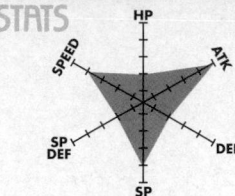

EVOLUTIONS

LV30   LV50

LOCATION[S]:

RUBY   Rarity: **Evolve**
Evolve Shelgon

SAPPHIRE   Rarity: **Evolve**
Evolve Shelgon

FIRERED   Rarity: **None**
Trade from *Ruby/Sapphire/Emerald*

LEAFGREEN   Rarity: **None**
Trade from *Ruby/Sapphire/Emerald*

COLOSSEUM   Rarity: **None**
Trade from *Ruby/Sapphire/Emerald*

EMERALD   Rarity: **Evolve**
Evolve Shelgon

XD   Rarity: **Only One**
Citadark Island (Capture from Cipher Admin Eldes)

MOVES

Level	Attack	Type	Power	ACC	PP	Level	Attack	Type	Power	ACC	PP
—	Rage	Normal	20	100	20	30	Protect	Normal	—	—	10
—	Bite	Dark	60	100	25	38	Dragonbreath	Dragon	60	100	20
—	Leer	Normal	—	100	30	47	Scary Face	Normal	—	90	10
—	Headbutt	Normal	70	100	15	50	Fly	Flying	70	95	15
21	Focus Energy	Normal	—	—	30	61	Crunch	Dark	80	100	15
25	Ember	Fire	40	100	25	79	Dragon Claw	Dragon	80	100	15
						93	Double-Edge	Normal	120	100	15

TM/HM

TM/HM#	Name	Type	Power	ACC	PP	TM/HM#	Name	Type	Power	ACC	PP
TM02	Dragon Claw	Dragon	80	100	15	TM35	Flamethrower	Fire	95	100	15
TM05	Roar	Normal	—	100	20	TM38	Fire Blast	Fire	120	85	5
TM06	Toxic	Poison	—	85	10	TM39	Rock Tomb	Rock	50	80	10
TM10	Hidden Power	Normal	—	100	15	TM40	Aerial Ace	Flying	60	—	20
TM11	Sunny Day	Fire	—	—	5	TM42	Facade	Normal	70	100	20
TM15	Hyper Beam	Normal	150	90	5	TM43	Secret Power	Normal	70	100	20
TM17	Protect	Normal	—	—	10	TM44	Rest	Psychic	—	—	10
TM18	Rain Dance	Water	—	—	5	TM45	Attract	Normal	—	100	15
TM21	Frustration	Normal	—	100	20	TM47	Steel Wing	Steel	70	90	25
TM23	Iron Tail	Steel	100	75	15	HM01	Cut	Normal	50	95	30
TM26	Earthquake	Ground	100	100	10	HM02	Fly	Flying	70	95	15
TM27	Return	Normal	—	100	20	HM04	Strength	Normal	80	100	15
TM31	Brick Break	Fighting	75	100	15	HM06	Rock Smash	Fighting	20	100	15
TM32	Double Team	Normal	—	—	15						

MOVE TUTOR
FireRed/LeafGreen and *Emerald* Only

Body Slam*	Double-Edge	Mimic
Rock Slide*	Substitute	

Emerald Only

Defense Curl*	Endure*	Fury Cutter
Mud-Slap*	Rollout	Sleep Talk
Snore*	Swagger	Swift*

*Battle Frontier tutor move (*Emerald*)

374 Beldum™

STEEL   PSYCHIC

GENERAL INFO
SPECIES: Iron Ball Pokémon
HEIGHT: 2'00"
WEIGHT: 210 lbs.
ABILITY: Clear Body
Moves that lower stats don't affect Beldum.

STATS
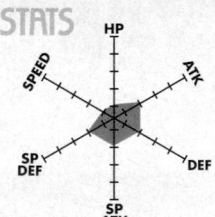

EVOLUTIONS
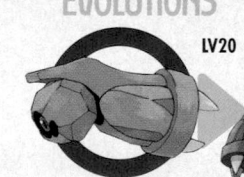 LV20  LV45

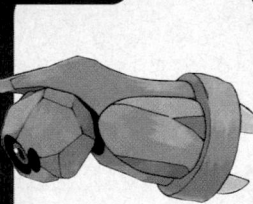

LOCATION[S]:

RUBY   Rarity: **Only One**
Mossdeep City (Steven's House after beating Elite Four)

SAPPHIRE   Rarity: **Only One**
Mossdeep City (Steven's House after beating Elite Four)

FIRERED   Rarity: **None**
Trade from *Ruby/Sapphire/Emerald*

LEAFGREEN   Rarity: **None**
Trade from *Ruby/Sapphire/Emerald*

COLOSSEUM   Rarity: **None**
Trade from *Ruby/Sapphire/Emerald*

EMERALD   Rarity: **Only One**
Mossdeep City (Steven's House after beating Elite Four)

XD   Rarity: **None**
Trade from *Ruby/Sapphire/Emerald*

MOVES

Level	Attack	Type	Power	ACC	PP
—	Take Down	Normal	90	85	20

TM/HM

TM/HM#	Name	Type	Power	ACC	PP
None					

MOVE TUTOR
FireRed/LeafGreen and *Emerald* Only

None

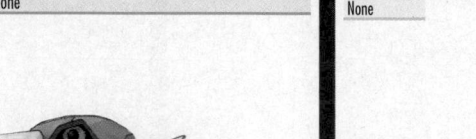

375 Metang™

STEEL | PSYCHIC

GENERAL INFO
SPECIES: Iron Claw Pokémon
HEIGHT: 3'11"
WEIGHT: 447 lbs.
ABILITY: Clear Body
Moves that lower stats don't affect Metang.

STATS

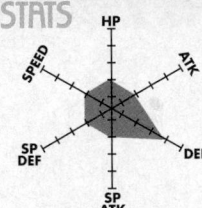

EVOLUTIONS

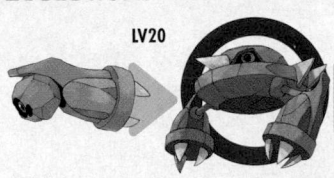

LV20   LV45

LOCATION(S):

RUBY   Rarity: **Evolve**
Evolve Beldum

SAPPHIRE   Rarity: **Evolve**
Evolve Beldum

FIRERED   Rarity: **None**
Trade from *Ruby/Sapphire/Emerald*

LEAFGREEN   Rarity: **None**
Trade from *Ruby/Sapphire/Emerald*

COLOSSEUM   Rarity: **None**
Trade from *Ruby/Sapphire/Emerald*

EMERALD   Rarity: **Evolve**
Evolve Beldum

XD   Rarity: **None**
Trade from *Ruby/Sapphire/Emerald*

MOVES

Level	Attack	Type	Power	ACC	PP
—	Take Down	Normal	90	85	20
20	Confusion	Psychic	50	100	25
20	Metal Claw	Steel	50	95	35
26	Scary Face	Normal	—	90	10
32	Pursuit	Dark	40	100	20

Level	Attack	Type	Power	ACC	PP
38	Psychic	Psychic	90	100	10
44	Iron Defense	Steel	—	—	15
50	Meteor Mash	Steel	100	85	10
56	Agility	Psychic	—	—	30
62	Hyper Beam	Normal	150	90	5

TM/HM

TM/HM#	Name	Type	Power	ACC	PP
TM06	Toxic	Poison	—	85	10
TM10	Hidden Power	Normal	—	100	15
TM11	Sunny Day	Fire	—	—	5
TM15	Hyper Beam	Normal	150	90	5
TM16	Light Screen	Psychic	—	—	30
TM17	Protect	Normal	—	—	10
TM18	Rain Dance	Water	—	—	5
TM21	Frustration	Normal	—	100	20
TM26	Earthquake	Ground	100	100	10
TM27	Return	Normal	—	100	20
TM29	Psychic	Psychic	90	100	10
TM30	Shadow Ball	Ghost	60	—	20
TM31	Brick Break	Fighting	75	100	15

TM/HM#	Name	Type	Power	ACC	PP
TM32	Double Team	Normal	—	—	15
TM33	Reflect	Psychic	—	—	20
TM36	Sludge Bomb	Poison	90	100	10
TM37	Sandstorm	Rock	—	—	10
TM39	Rock Tomb	Rock	50	80	10
TM40	Aerial Ace	Flying	60	—	20
TM42	Facade	Normal	70	100	20
TM43	Secret Power	Normal	70	100	20
TM44	Rest	Psychic	—	—	10
HM01	Cut	Normal	50	95	30
HM04	Strength	Normal	80	100	15
HM05	Flash	Normal	—	70	20
HM06	Rock Smash	Fighting	20	100	15

MOVE TUTOR
FireRed/LeafGreen and *Emerald* Only

Body Slam*	Double-Edge	Explosion
Mimic	Rock Slide*	Substitute

Emerald Only

Defense Curl*	Dynamicpunch*	Endure*
Fury Cutter	Ice Punch*	Icy Wind*
Mud-Slap*	Psych Up*	Rollout
Sleep Talk	Snore*	Swagger
Swift*	Thunderpunch*	

*Battle Frontier tutor move (*Emerald*)

---

376 Metagross™

STEEL | PSYCHIC

GENERAL INFO
SPECIES: Iron Leg Pokémon
HEIGHT: 5'03"
WEIGHT: 1,213 lbs.
ABILITY: Clear Body
Moves that lower stats don't affect Metagross.

STATS

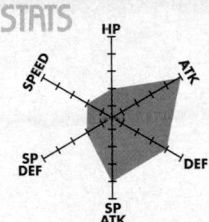

EVOLUTIONS

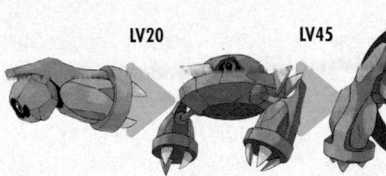

LV20   LV45

LOCATION(S):

RUBY   Rarity: **Evolve**
Evolve Metang

SAPPHIRE   Rarity: **Evolve**
Evolve Metang

FIRERED   Rarity: **None**
Trade from *Ruby/Sapphire/Emerald*

LEAFGREEN   Rarity: **None**
Trade from *Ruby/Sapphire/Emerald*

COLOSSEUM   Rarity: **None**
Trade from *Ruby/Sapphire/Emerald*

EMERALD   Rarity: **Evolve**
Evolve Metang

XD   Rarity: **None**
Trade from *Ruby/Sapphire/Emerald*

MOVES

Level	Attack	Type	Power	ACC	PP
—	Take Down	Normal	90	85	20
—/20	Confusion	Psychic	50	100	25
—/20	Metal Claw	Steel	50	95	35
—/26	Scary Face	Normal	—	90	10
32	Pursuit	Dark	40	100	20

Level	Attack	Type	Power	ACC	PP
38	Psychic	Psychic	90	100	10
44	Iron Defense	Steel	—	—	15
55	Meteor Mash	Steel	100	85	10
66	Agility	Psychic	—	—	30
77	Hyper Beam	Normal	150	90	5

= *Emerald* Only

TM/HM

TM/HM#	Name	Type	Power	ACC	PP
TM06	Toxic	Poison	—	85	10
TM10	Hidden Power	Normal	—	100	15
TM11	Sunny Day	Fire	—	—	5
TM15	Hyper Beam	Normal	150	90	5
TM16	Light Screen	Psychic	—	—	30
TM17	Protect	Normal	—	—	10
TM18	Rain Dance	Water	—	—	5
TM21	Frustration	Normal	—	100	20
TM26	Earthquake	Ground	100	100	10
TM27	Return	Normal	—	100	20
TM29	Psychic	Psychic	90	100	10
TM30	Shadow Ball	Ghost	60	—	20
TM31	Brick Break	Fighting	75	100	15

TM/HM#	Name	Type	Power	ACC	PP
TM32	Double Team	Normal	—	—	15
TM33	Reflect	Psychic	—	—	20
TM36	Sludge Bomb	Poison	90	100	10
TM37	Sandstorm	Rock	—	—	10
TM39	Rock Tomb	Rock	50	80	10
TM40	Aerial Ace	Flying	60	—	20
TM42	Facade	Normal	70	100	20
TM43	Secret Power	Normal	70	100	20
TM44	Rest	Psychic	—	—	10
HM01	Cut	Normal	50	95	30
HM04	Strength	Normal	80	100	15
HM05	Flash	Normal	—	70	20
HM06	Rock Smash	Fighting	20	100	15

MOVE TUTOR
FireRed/LeafGreen and *Emerald* Only

Body Slam*	Double-Edge	Explosion
Mimic	Rock Slide*	Substitute

Emerald Only

Defense Curl*	Dynamicpunch*	Endure*
Fury Cutter	Ice Punch*	Icy Wind*
Mud-Slap*	Psych Up*	Rollout
Sleep Talk	Snore*	Swagger
Swift*	Thunderpunch*	

*Battle Frontier tutor move (*Emerald*)

377 Regirock™

GENERAL INFO
SPECIES: Rock Peak Pokémon
HEIGHT: 5'07"
WEIGHT: 507 lbs.
ABILITY: Clear Body
Moves that lower stats don't affect Regirock.

STATS
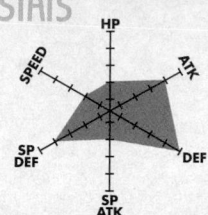

EVOLUTIONS

DOES NOT EVOLVE

LOCATION[S]:

RUBY   Rarity: **Only One**
Route 111 (Inside Desert Ruins)

SAPPHIRE   Rarity: **Only One**
Route 111 (Inside Desert Ruins)

FIRERED   Rarity: **None**
Trade from *Ruby/Sapphire/Emerald*

LEAFGREEN   Rarity: **None**
Trade from *Ruby/Sapphire/Emerald*

COLOSSEUM   Rarity: **None**
Trade from *Ruby/Sapphire/Emerald*

EMERALD   Rarity: **Only One**
Route 111 (Inside Desert Ruins)

XD   Rarity: **None**
Trade from *Ruby/Sapphire/Emerald*

MOVES

Level	Attack	Type	Power	ACC	PP
—	Explosion	Normal	250	100	5
9	Rock Throw	Rock	50	90	15
17	Curse	—	—	—	10
25	Superpower	Fighting	120	100	5
33	Ancientpower	Rock	60	100	5
41	Iron Defense	Steel	—	—	15
49	Zap Cannon	Electric	100	50	5
57	Lock-on	Normal	—	100	5
65	Hyper Beam	Normal	150	90	5

TM/HM

TM/HM#	Name	Type	Power	ACC	PP
TM01	Focus Punch	Fighting	150	100	20
TM06	Toxic	Poison	—	85	10
TM10	Hidden Power	Normal	—	100	15
TM11	Sunny Day	Fire	—	—	5
TM15	Hyper Beam	Normal	150	90	5
TM17	Protect	Normal	—	—	10
TM20	Safeguard	Normal	—	—	25
TM21	Frustration	Normal	—	100	20
TM24	Thunderbolt	Electric	95	100	15
TM25	Thunder	Electric	120	70	10
TM26	Earthquake	Ground	100	100	10
TM27	Return	Normal	—	100	20
TM28	Dig	Ground	60	100	10
TM31	Brick Break	Fighting	75	100	15
TM32	Double Team	Normal	—	—	15
TM34	Shock Wave	Electric	60	—	20
TM37	Sandstorm	Rock	—	—	10
TM39	Rock Tomb	Rock	50	80	10
TM42	Facade	Normal	70	100	20
TM43	Secret Power	Normal	70	100	20
TM44	Rest	Psychic	—	—	10
HM04	Strength	Normal	80	100	15
HM06	Rock Smash	Fighting	20	100	15

MOVE TUTOR
FireRed/LeafGreen and Emerald Only

Body Slam*	Counter*	Double-Edge
Explosion	Mega Kick*	Mega Punch*
Mimic	Rock Slide*	Seismic Toss*
Substitute	Thunder Wave*	

Emerald Only

Defense Curl*	Dynamicpunch*	Endure*
Fire Punch*	Ice Punch*	Icy Wind*
Mud-Slap*	Psych Up*	Rollout
Sleep Talk	Snore*	Swagger
Thunderpunch*		

*Battle Frontier tutor move (*Emerald*)

---

378 Regice™

GENERAL INFO
SPECIES: Iceberg Pokémon
HEIGHT: 5'11"
WEIGHT: 386 lbs.
ABILITY: Clear Body
Moves that lower stats don't affect Regice.

STATS
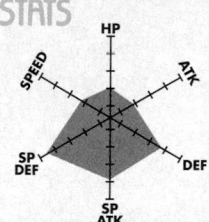

EVOLUTIONS

DOES NOT EVOLVE

LOCATION[S]:

RUBY   Rarity: **Only One**
Route 105 (Inside Island Cave)

SAPPHIRE   Rarity: **Only One**
Route 105 (Inside Island Cave)

FIRERED   Rarity: **None**
Trade from *Ruby/Sapphire/Emerald*

LEAFGREEN   Rarity: **None**
Trade from *Ruby/Sapphire/Emerald*

COLOSSEUM   Rarity: **None**
Trade from *Ruby/Sapphire/Emerald*

EMERALD   Rarity: **Only One**
Route 105 (Inside Island Cave)

XD   Rarity: **None**
Trade from *Ruby/Sapphire/Emerald*

MOVES

Level	Attack	Type	Power	ACC	PP
—	Explosion	Normal	250	100	5
9	Icy Wind	Ice	55	95	15
17	Curse	—	—	—	10
25	Superpower	Fighting	120	100	5
33	Ancientpower	Rock	60	100	5
41	Amnesia	Psychic	—	—	20
49	Zap Cannon	Electric	100	50	5
57	Lock-on	Normal	—	100	5
65	Hyper Beam	Normal	150	90	5

TM/HM

TM/HM#	Name	Type	Power	ACC	PP
TM01	Focus Punch	Fighting	150	100	20
TM06	Toxic	Poison	—	85	10
TM07	Hail	Ice	—	—	10
TM10	Hidden Power	Normal	—	100	15
TM13	Ice Beam	Ice	95	100	10
TM14	Blizzard	Ice	120	70	5
TM15	Hyper Beam	Normal	150	90	5
TM17	Protect	Normal	—	—	10
TM18	Rain Dance	Water	—	—	5
TM20	Safeguard	Normal	—	—	25
TM21	Frustration	Normal	—	100	20
TM24	Thunderbolt	Electric	95	100	15
TM25	Thunder	Electric	120	70	10
TM26	Earthquake	Ground	100	100	10
TM27	Return	Normal	—	100	20
TM31	Brick Break	Fighting	75	100	15
TM32	Double Team	Normal	—	—	15
TM34	Shock Wave	Electric	60	—	20
TM42	Facade	Normal	70	100	20
TM43	Secret Power	Normal	70	100	20
TM44	Rest	Psychic	—	—	10
HM04	Strength	Normal	80	100	15
HM06	Rock Smash	Fighting	20	100	15

MOVE TUTOR
FireRed/LeafGreen and Emerald Only

Body Slam*	Counter*	Double-Edge
Explosion	Mega Kick*	Mega Punch*
Mimic	Rock Slide*	Seismic Toss*
Substitute	Thunder Wave*	

Emerald Only

Defense Curl*	Dynamicpunch*	Endure*
Fire Punch*	Ice Punch*	Mud-Slap*
Psych Up*	Rollout	Sleep Talk
Snore*	Swagger	Thunderpunch*

*Battle Frontier tutor move (*Emerald*)

379 Registeel™

STEEL

GENERAL INFO
SPECIES: Iron Pokémon
HEIGHT: 6'03"
WEIGHT: 452 lbs.
ABILITY: Clear Body
Moves that lower ability values don't affect Registeel.

STATS

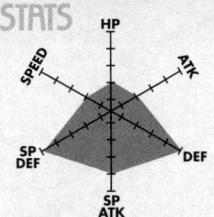

EVOLUTIONS

DOES NOT EVOLVE

LOCATION(S):

RUBY	**Rarity: Only One**
Route 120 (Inside Ancient Tomb)	
SAPPHIRE	**Rarity: Only One**
Route 120 (Inside Ancient Tomb)	
FIRERED	**Rarity: None**
Trade from *Ruby/Sapphire/Emerald*	
LEAFGREEN	**Rarity: None**
Trade from *Ruby/Sapphire/Emerald*	
COLOSSEUM	**Rarity: None**
Trade from *Ruby/Sapphire/Emerald*	
EMERALD	**Rarity: Only One**
Route 120 (Inside Ancient Tomb)	
XD	**Rarity: None**
Trade from *Ruby/Sapphire/Emerald*	

MOVES

Level	Attack	Type	Power	ACC	PP	Level	Attack	Type	Power	ACC	PP
—	Explosion	Normal	250	100	5	41	Iron Defense	Steel	—	—	15
9	Metal Claw	Steel	50	95	35	41	Amnesia	Psychic	—	—	20
17	Curse	—	—	—	10	49	Zap Cannon	Electric	100	50	5
25	Superpower	Fighting	120	100	5	57	Lock-on	Normal	—	100	5
33	Ancientpower	Rock	60	100	5	65	Hyper Beam	Normal	150	90	5

TM/HM

TM/HM#	Name	Type	Power	ACC	PP	TM/HM#	Name	Type	Power	ACC	PP
TM01	Focus Punch	Fighting	150	100	20	TM27	Return	Normal	—	100	20
TM06	Toxic	Poison	—	85	10	TM31	Brick Break	Fighting	75	100	15
TM10	Hidden Power	Normal	—	100	15	TM32	Double Team	Normal	—	—	15
TM11	Sunny Day	Fire	—	—	5	TM34	Shock Wave	Electric	60	—	20
TM15	Hyper Beam	Normal	150	90	5	TM37	Sandstorm	Rock	—	—	10
TM17	Protect	Normal	—	—	10	TM39	Rock Tomb	Rock	50	80	10
TM18	Rain Dance	Water	—	—	5	TM40	Aerial Ace	Flying	60	—	20
TM20	Safeguard	Normal	—	—	25	TM42	Facade	Normal	70	100	20
TM21	Frustration	Normal	—	100	20	TM43	Secret Power	Normal	70	100	20
TM24	Thunderbolt	Electric	95	100	15	TM44	Rest	Psychic	—	—	10
TM25	Thunder	Electric	120	70	10	HM04	Strength	Normal	80	100	15
TM26	Earthquake	Ground	100	100	10	HM06	Rock Smash	Fighting	20	100	15

MOVE TUTOR
FireRed/LeafGreen and *Emerald* Only

Body Slam*	Counter*	Double-Edge
Explosion	Mega Kick*	Mega Punch*
Mimic	Rock Slide*	Seismic Toss*
Substitute	Thunder Wave*	

***Emerald* Only**

Defense Curl*	Dynamicpunch*	Endure*
Ice Punch*	Mud-Slap*	Psych Up*
Rollout	Sleep Talk*	Snore*
Swagger	Thunderpunch*	

*Battle Frontier tutor move (*Emerald*)

---

380 Latias™

DRAGON | PSYCHIC

GENERAL INFO
SPECIES: Eon Pokémon
HEIGHT: 4'07"
WEIGHT: 88 lbs.
ABILITY: Levitate
Latias is not affected by Ground-type moves.

STATS

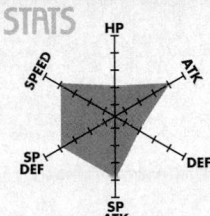

EVOLUTIONS

DOES NOT EVOLVE

LOCATION(S):

RUBY	**Rarity: None**
Trade from *Sapphire/Emerald*	
SAPPHIRE	**Rarity: Only One**
Random event in Hoenn after beating Elite Four	
FIRERED	**Rarity: None**
Trade from *Sapphire/Emerald*	
LEAFGREEN	**Rarity: None**
Trade from *Sapphire/Emerald*	
COLOSSEUM	**Rarity: None**
Trade from *Sapphire/Emerald*	
EMERALD	**Rarity: Only One**
Random event in Hoenn after beating Elite Four	
XD	**Rarity: None**
Trade from *Sapphire/Emerald*	

MOVES

Level	Attack	Type	Power	ACC	PP	Level	Attack	Type	Power	ACC	PP
—	Psywave	Psychic	—	80	15	25	Water Sport	Water	—	100	15
5	Wish	Normal	—	100	10	30	Refresh	Normal	—	100	20
10	Helping Hand	Normal	—	100	20	35	Mist Ball	Psychic	70	100	5
15	Safeguard	Normal	—	—	25	40	Psychic	Psychic	90	100	10
20	Dragonbreath	Dragon	60	100	20	45	Recover	Normal	—	—	20
						50	Charm	Normal	—	100	20

TM/HM

TM/HM#	Name	Type	Power	ACC	PP	TM/HM#	Name	Type	Power	ACC	PP
TM02	Dragon Claw	Dragon	80	100	15	TM29	Psychic	Psychic	90	100	10
TM03	Water Pulse	Water	60	100	20	TM30	Shadow Ball	Ghost	60	—	20
TM04	Calm Mind	Psychic	—	—	20	TM32	Double Team	Normal	—	—	15
TM05	Roar	Normal	—	100	20	TM33	Reflect	Psychic	—	—	20
TM06	Toxic	Poison	—	85	10	TM34	Shock Wave	Electric	60	—	20
TM10	Hidden Power	Normal	—	100	15	TM37	Sandstorm	Rock	—	—	10
TM11	Sunny Day	Fire	—	—	5	TM40	Aerial Ace	Flying	60	—	20
TM13	Ice Beam	Ice	95	100	10	TM42	Facade	Normal	70	100	20
TM15	Hyper Beam	Normal	150	90	5	TM43	Secret Power	Normal	70	100	20
TM16	Light Screen	Psychic	—	—	30	TM44	Rest	Psychic	—	—	10
TM17	Protect	Normal	—	—	10	TM45	Attract	Normal	—	100	15
TM18	Rain Dance	Water	—	—	5	TM47	Steel Wing	Steel	70	90	25
TM20	Safeguard	Normal	—	—	25	HM01	Cut	Normal	50	95	30
TM21	Frustration	Normal	—	100	20	HM02	Fly	Flying	70	95	15
TM22	Solarbeam	Grass	120	100	10	HM03	Surf	Water	95	100	15
TM24	Thunderbolt	Electric	95	100	15	HM05	Flash	Normal	—	70	20
TM25	Thunder	Electric	120	70	10	HM07	Waterfall	Water	80	100	15
TM26	Earthquake	Ground	100	100	10	HM08	Dive	Water	60	100	10
TM27	Return	Normal	—	100	20						

MOVE TUTOR
FireRed/LeafGreen and *Emerald* Only

Body Slam*	Double-Edge	Dream Eater*
Mimic	Substitute	Thunder Wave*

***Emerald* Only**

Endure*	Fury Cutter	Icy Wind*
Mud-Slap*	Psych Up*	Sleep Talk
Snore*	Swagger	Swift*

*Battle Frontier tutor move (*Emerald*)

381 Latios™

| DRAGON | PSYCHIC |

GENERAL INFO
SPECIES: Eon Pokémon
HEIGHT: 6'07"
WEIGHT: 132 lbs.
ABILITY: Levitate

Latios is not affected by Ground-type moves.

STATS
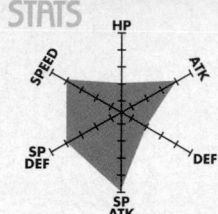

EVOLUTIONS

DOES NOT EVOLVE

LOCATION(S):

RUBY
Rarity: **Only One**
Random event in Hoenn after beating Elite Four

SAPPHIRE
Rarity: **None**
Trade from *Ruby/Emerald*

FIRERED
Rarity: **None**
Trade from *Ruby/Emerald*

LEAFGREEN
Rarity: **None**
Trade from *Ruby/Emerald*

COLOSSEUM
Rarity: **None**
Trade from *Ruby/Emerald*

EMERALD
Rarity: **Only One**
Random event in Hoenn after beating Elite Four

XD
Rarity: **None**
Trade from *Ruby/Emerald*

MOVES

Level	Attack	Type	Power	ACC	PP
—	Psywave	Psychic	—	80	15
5	Memento	Dark	—	100	10
10	Helping Hand	Normal	—	100	20
15	Safeguard	Normal	—	—	25
20	Dragonbreath	Dragon	60	100	20

Level	Attack	Type	Power	ACC	PP
25	Protect	Normal	—	—	10
30	Refresh	Normal	—	100	20
35	Luster Purge	Psychic	70	100	5
40	Psychic	Psychic	90	100	10
45	Recover	Normal	—	—	20
50	Dragon Dance	Dragon	—	—	20

TM/HM

TM/HM#	Name	Type	Power	ACC	PP
TM02	Dragon Claw	Dragon	80	100	15
TM03	Water Pulse	Water	60	100	20
TM04	Calm Mind	Psychic	—	—	20
TM05	Roar	Normal	—	100	20
TM06	Toxic	Poison	—	85	10
TM10	Hidden Power	Normal	—	100	15
TM11	Sunny Day	Fire	—	—	5
TM13	Ice Beam	Ice	95	100	10
TM15	Hyper Beam	Normal	150	90	5
TM16	Light Screen	Psychic	—	—	30
TM17	Protect	Normal	—	—	10
TM18	Rain Dance	Water	—	—	5
TM20	Safeguard	Normal	—	—	25
TM21	Frustration	Normal	—	100	20
TM22	Solarbeam	Grass	120	100	10
TM24	Thunderbolt	Electric	95	100	15
TM25	Thunder	Electric	120	70	10
TM26	Earthquake	Ground	100	100	10
TM27	Return	Normal	—	100	20
TM29	Psychic	Psychic	90	100	10
TM30	Shadow Ball	Ghost	60	—	20
TM32	Double Team	Normal	—	—	15

TM/HM#	Name	Type	Power	ACC	PP
TM33	Reflect	Psychic	—	—	20
TM34	Shock Wave	Electric	60	—	20
TM37	Sandstorm	Rock	—	—	10
TM40	Aerial Ace	Flying	60	—	20
TM42	Facade	Normal	70	100	20
TM43	Secret Power	Normal	70	100	20
TM44	Rest	Psychic	—	—	10
TM45	Attract	Normal	—	100	15
TM47	Steel Wing	Steel	70	90	25
HM01	Cut	Normal	50	95	30
HM02	Fly	Flying	70	95	15
HM03	Surf	Water	95	100	15
HM05	Flash	Normal	—	70	20
HM07	Waterfall	Water	80	100	15
HM08	Dive	Water	60	100	10

MOVE TUTOR
FireRed/LeafGreen and *Emerald* Only

Body Slam*	Double-Edge*	Dream Eater*
Mimic	Substitute	Thunder Wave*

Emerald Only

Endure*	Fury Cutter*	Icy Wind*
Mud-Slap*	Psych Up*	Sleep Talk
Snore*	Swagger	Swift*

*Battle Frontier tutor move (*Emerald*)

---

382 Kyogre™

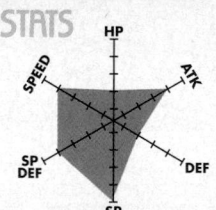

| WATER |

GENERAL INFO
SPECIES: Sea Basin Pokémon
HEIGHT: 14'09"
WEIGHT: 776 lbs.
ABILITY: Drizzle

Rain falls when Kyogre enters battle.

STATS

EVOLUTIONS

DOES NOT EVOLVE

LOCATION(S):

RUBY
Rarity: **None**
Trade from *Sapphire/Emerald*

SAPPHIRE
Rarity: **Only One**
Cave of Origin (After awakening it)

FIRERED
Rarity: **None**
Trade from *Sapphire/Emerald*

LEAFGREEN
Rarity: **None**
Trade from *Sapphire/Emerald*

COLOSSEUM
Rarity: **None**
Trade from *Sapphire/Emerald*

EMERALD
Rarity: **Only One**
Marine Cave

XD
Rarity: **None**
Trade from *Sapphire/Emerald*

MOVES

Level	Attack	Type	Power	ACC	PP
—	Water Pulse	Water	60	100	20
5	Scary Face	Normal	—	90	10
15	Ancientpower	Rock	60	100	5
20	Body Slam	Normal	85	100	15
30	Calm Mind	Psychic	—	—	20

Level	Attack	Type	Power	ACC	PP
35	Ice Beam	Ice	95	100	10
45	Hydro Pump	Water	120	80	5
50	Rest	Psychic	—	—	10
60	Sheer Cold	Ice	—	30	5
65	Double-Edge	Normal	120	100	15
75	Water Spout	Water	150	100	5

TM/HM

TM/HM#	Name	Type	Power	ACC	PP
TM13	Ice Beam	Ice	95	100	10
TM14	Blizzard	Ice	120	70	5
TM15	Hyper Beam	Normal	150	90	5
TM17	Protect	Normal	—	—	10
TM18	Rain Dance	Water	—	—	5
TM20	Safeguard	Normal	—	—	25
TM21	Frustration	Normal	—	100	20
TM24	Thunderbolt	Electric	95	100	15
TM25	Thunder	Electric	120	70	10
TM26	Earthquake	Ground	100	100	10
TM27	Return	Normal	—	100	20
TM31	Brick Break	Fighting	75	100	15

TM/HM#	Name	Type	Power	ACC	PP
TM32	Double Team	Normal	—	—	15
TM34	Shock Wave	Electric	60	—	20
TM39	Rock Tomb	Rock	50	80	10
TM42	Facade	Normal	70	100	20
TM43	Secret Power	Normal	70	100	20
TM44	Rest	Psychic	—	—	10
HM03	Surf	Water	95	100	15
HM04	Strength	Normal	80	100	15
HM06	Rock Smash	Fighting	20	100	15
HM07	Waterfall	Water	80	100	15
HM08	Dive	Water	60	100	10

MOVE TUTOR
FireRed/LeafGreen and *Emerald* Only

Body Slam*	Double-Edge*	Mimic
Rock Slide*	Substitute	Thunder Wave*

Emerald Only

Defense Curl*	Endure*	Icy Wind*
Mud-Slap*	Psych Up*	Sleep Talk
Snore*	Swagger	Swift*

*Battle Frontier tutor move (*Emerald*)

383 Groudon™

GROUND

GENERAL INFO
SPECIES: Continent Pokémon
HEIGHT: 11'06"
WEIGHT: 2,095 lbs.
ABILITY: Drought
The sun shines when Groudon enters battle.

STATS
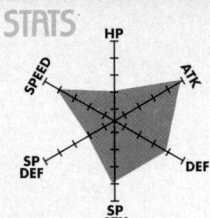

EVOLUTIONS

DOES NOT EVOLVE

LOCATION(S):
RUBY
Rarity: **Only One**
Cave of Origin (After awakening it)

SAPPHIRE
Rarity: **None**
Trade from *Ruby/Emerald*

FIRERED
Rarity: **None**
Trade from *Ruby/Emerald*

LEAFGREEN
Rarity: **None**
Trade from *Ruby/Emerald*

COLOSSEUM
Rarity: **None**
Trade from *Ruby/Emerald*

EMERALD
Rarity: **Only One**
Terra Cave

XD
Rarity: **None**
Trade from *Ruby/Emerald*

MOVES

Level	Attack	Type	Power	ACC	PP
—	Mud Shot	Ground	55	95	15
5	Scary Face	Normal	—	90	10
15	Ancientpower	Rock	60	100	5
20	Slash	Normal	70	100	20
30	Bulk Up	Fighting	—	—	20

Level	Attack	Type	Power	ACC	PP
35	Earthquake	Ground	100	100	10
45	Fire Blast	Fire	120	85	5
50	Rest	Psychic	—	—	10
60	Fissure	Ground	—	30	5
65	Solarbeam	Grass	120	100	10
75	Eruption	Fire	150	100	5

TM/HM#	Name	Type	Power	ACC	PP
TM17	Protect	Normal	—	—	10
TM20	Safeguard	Normal	—	—	25
TM21	Frustration	Normal	—	100	20
TM22	Solarbeam	Grass	120	100	10
TM23	Iron Tail	Steel	100	75	15
TM24	Thunderbolt	Electric	95	100	15
TM25	Thunder	Electric	120	70	10
TM26	Earthquake	Ground	100	100	10
TM27	Return	Normal	—	100	20
TM28	Dig	Ground	60	100	10
TM31	Brick Break	Fighting	75	100	15
TM32	Double Team	Normal	—	—	15
TM34	Shock Wave	Electric	60	—	20

TM/HM#	Name	Type	Power	ACC	PP
TM35	Flamethrower	Fire	95	100	15
TM37	Sandstorm	Rock	—	—	10
TM38	Fire Blast	Fire	120	85	5
TM39	Rock Tomb	Rock	50	80	10
TM40	Aerial Ace	Flying	60	—	20
TM42	Facade	Normal	70	100	20
TM43	Secret Power	Normal	70	100	20
TM44	Rest	Psychic	—	—	10
TM50	Overheat	Fire	140	90	5
HM01	Cut	Normal	50	95	30
HM04	Strength	Normal	80	100	15
HM06	Rock Smash	Fighting	20	100	15

TM/HM

TM/HM#	Name	Type	Power	ACC	PP
TM02	Dragon Claw	Dragon	80	100	15
TM05	Roar	Normal	—	100	20
TM06	Toxic	Poison	—	85	10
TM08	Bulk Up	Fighting	—	—	20
TM10	Hidden Power	Normal	—	100	15
TM11	Sunny Day	Fire	—	—	5
TM15	Hyper Beam	Normal	150	90	5

MOVE TUTOR
FireRed/LeafGreen and *Emerald* Only

Body Slam*	Counter*	Double-Edge
Mega Kick*	Mega Punch*	Mimic
Rock Slide*	Seismic Toss*	Substitute
Swords Dance*	Thunder Wave*	

Emerald Only

Defense Curl*	Dynamicpunch*	Endure*
Fury Cutter*	Fire Punch*	Mud-Slap*
Psych Up*	Rollout*	Sleep Talk*
Snore*	Swagger*	Swift*
Thunderpunch*		

*Battle Frontier tutor move (*Emerald*)

---

384 Rayquaza™

DRAGON | FLYING

GENERAL INFO
SPECIES: Sky High Pokémon
HEIGHT: 23'00"
WEIGHT: 455 lbs.
ABILITY: Air Lock
Makes weather effects disappear.

STATS
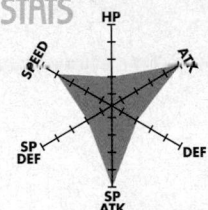

EVOLUTIONS

DOES NOT EVOLVE

LOCATION(S):
RUBY
Rarity: **Only One**
Sky Pillar (After beating Elite Four)

SAPPHIRE
Rarity: **Only One**
Sky Pillar (After beating Elite Four)

FIRERED
Rarity: **None**
Trade from *Ruby/Sapphire/Emerald*

LEAFGREEN
Rarity: **None**
Trade from *Ruby/Sapphire/Emerald*

COLOSSEUM
Rarity: **None**
Trade from *Ruby/Sapphire/Emerald*

EMERALD
Rarity: **Only One**
Sky Pillar (After beating Elite Four)

XD
Rarity: **None**
Trade from *Ruby/Sapphire/Emerald*

MOVES

Level	Attack	Type	Power	ACC	PP
—	Twister	Dragon	40	100	20
5	Scary Face	Normal	—	90	10
15	Ancientpower	Rock	60	100	5
20	Dragon Claw	Dragon	80	100	15
30	Dragon Dance	Dragon	—	—	20

Level	Attack	Type	Power	ACC	PP
35	Crunch	Dark	80	100	15
45	Fly	Flying	70	95	15
50	Rest	Psychic	—	—	10
60	Extremespeed	Normal	80	100	5
65	Outrage	Dragon	90	100	15
75	Hyper Beam	Normal	150	90	5

TM/HM#	Name	Type	Power	ACC	PP
TM14	Blizzard	Ice	120	70	5
TM15	Hyper Beam	Normal	150	90	5
TM17	Protect	Normal	—	—	10
TM18	Rain Dance	Water	—	—	5
TM21	Frustration	Normal	—	100	20
TM22	Solarbeam	Grass	120	100	10
TM23	Iron Tail	Steel	100	75	15
TM24	Thunderbolt	Electric	95	100	15
TM25	Thunder	Electric	120	70	10
TM26	Earthquake	Ground	100	100	10
TM27	Return	Normal	—	100	20
TM31	Brick Break	Fighting	75	100	15
TM32	Double Team	Normal	—	—	15
TM34	Shock Wave	Electric	60	—	20

TM/HM#	Name	Type	Power	ACC	PP
TM35	Flamethrower	Fire	95	100	15
TM37	Sandstorm	Rock	—	—	10
TM38	Fire Blast	Fire	120	85	5
TM40	Aerial Ace	Flying	60	—	20
TM42	Facade	Normal	70	100	20
TM43	Secret Power	Normal	70	100	20
TM44	Rest	Psychic	—	—	10
TM50	Overheat	Fire	140	90	5
HM02	Fly	Flying	70	95	15
HM03	Surf	Water	95	100	15
HM04	Strength	Normal	80	100	15
HM06	Rock Smash	Fighting	20	100	15
HM07	Waterfall	Water	80	100	15
HM08	Dive	Water	60	100	10

TM/HM

TM/HM#	Name	Type	Power	ACC	PP
TM02	Dragon Claw	Dragon	80	100	15
TM03	Water Pulse	Water	60	100	20
TM05	Roar	Normal	—	100	20
TM06	Toxic	Poison	—	85	10
TM08	Bulk Up	Fighting	—	—	20
TM10	Hidden Power	Normal	—	100	15
TM11	Sunny Day	Fire	—	—	5
TM13	Ice Beam	Ice	95	100	10

MOVE TUTOR
FireRed/LeafGreen and *Emerald* Only

Body Slam*	Double-Edge	Mimic
Rock Slide*	Substitute	Thunder Wave*

Emerald Only

Endure*	Fury Cutter*	Icy Wind*
Mud-Slap*	Psych Up*	Sleep Talk*
Snore*	Swagger*	Swift*

*Battle Frontier tutor move (*Emerald*)

POKÉMON
10th Anniversary Pokédex

385 Jirachi™

STEEL	PSYCHIC

GENERAL INFO
SPECIES: Wish Pokémon
HEIGHT: 1'00"
WEIGHT: 2 lbs.
ABILITY: Serene Grace
Moves that have extra effects will occur more frequently when Jirachi attacks.

STATS
HP · ATK · DEF · SP ATK · SP DEF · SPEED

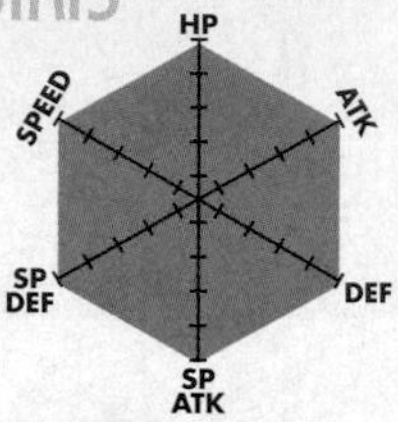

EVOLUTIONS

DOES NOT EVOLVE

LOCATION[S]:

RUBY — Rarity: **None**
Receive from *Colosseum* Bonus Disk

SAPPHIRE — Rarity: **None**
Receive from *Colosseum* Bonus Disk

FIRERED — Rarity: **None**
Only available from *Colosseum* Bonus Disk

LEAFGREEN — Rarity: **None**
Only available from *Colosseum* Bonus Disk

COLOSSEUM — Rarity: **None**
Only available from *Colosseum* Bonus Disk

EMERALD — Rarity: **None**
Only available from *Colosseum* Bonus Disk

XD — Rarity: **None**
Only available from *Colosseum* Bonus Disk

MOVES

Level	Attack	Type	Power	ACC	PP
—	Wish	Normal	—	100	10
—	Confusion	Psychic	50	100	25
5	Rest	Psychic	—	—	10
10	Swift	Normal	60	—	20
15	Helping Hand	Normal	—	100	20
20	Psychic	Psychic	90	100	10
25	Refresh	Normal	—	100	20
30	Rest	Psychic	—	—	10
35	Double-Edge	Normal	120	100	15
40	Future Sight	Psychic	80	90	15
45	Cosmic Power	Normal	—	—	20
50	Doom Desire	Steel	120	85	5

TM/HM

TM/HM#	Name	Type	Power	ACC	PP
TM03	Water Pulse	Water	60	95	20
TM04	Calm Mind	Psychic	—	—	20
TM06	Toxic	Poison	—	85	10
TM10	Hidden Power	Normal	—	100	15
TM11	Sunny Day	Fire	—	—	5
TM15	Hyper Beam	Normal	150	90	5
TM16	Light Screen	Psychic	—	—	30
TM17	Protect	Normal	—	—	10
TM18	Rain Dance	Water	—	—	5
TM20	Safeguard	Normal	—	—	25
TM21	Frustration	Normal	—	100	20
TM24	Thunderbolt	Electric	95	100	15
TM25	Thunder	Electric	120	70	10
TM27	Return	Normal	—	100	20
TM29	Psychic	Psychic	90	100	10
TM30	Shadow Ball	Ghost	80	100	15
TM32	Double Team	Normal	—	—	15
TM33	Reflect	Normal	—	—	20
TM34	Shock Wave	Electric	60	—	20
TM37	Sandstorm	Ground	—	—	10
TM40	Aerial Ace	Flying	60	—	20
TM42	Facade	Normal	70	100	20
TM43	Secret Power	Normal	70	100	20
TM44	Rest	Psychic	—	—	10
TM45	Attract	Normal	—	100	15
TM48	Skill Swap	Psychic	—	100	10
HM05	Flash	Normal	—	70	20

MOVE TUTOR

FireRed/LeafGreen and Emerald Only

Body Slam*	Double-Edge	Dream Eater*
Metronome	Mimic	Substitute
Thunder Wave*		

Emerald Only

Defense Curl*	Dynamicpunch*	Endure*
Fire Punch*	Ice Punch*	Icy Wind*
Mud-Slap*	Psych Up*	Sleep Talk
Snore*	Swagger	Swift*
Thunderpunch*		

*Battle Frontier tutor move (*Emerald*)

note Deoxys comes in three different forms based on which game you Catch it in (in the case of *Ruby/Sapphire*, the form is based on when it's Traded to that game). Each form learns Moves at slightly different speeds, and collecting all three forms can be a difficult task.

386 Deoxys™ (Attack Forme)

PSYCHIC

GENERAL INFO
SPECIES: DNA Pokémon
HEIGHT: 5'05"
WEIGHT: 134 lbs.
ABILITY: Pressure

STATS
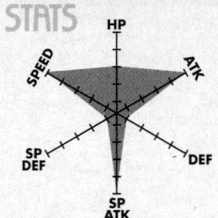

EVOLUTIONS

DOES NOT EVOLVE

LOCATION[S]:

RUBY   Rarity: **None**
Deoxys does not take this form in this game

SAPPHIRE   Rarity: **None**
Deoxys does not take this form in this game

FIRERED   Rarity: **Only One**
Birth Island (Only accessible with the Aurora Ticket gained via special download at live events)

LEAFGREEN   Rarity: **None**
Deoxys does not take this form in this game

COLOSSEUM   Rarity: **None**
Deoxys does not take this form in this game

EMERALD   Rarity: **None**
Deoxys does not take this form in this game

XD   Rarity: **None**
Deoxys does not take this form in this game

MOVES

Level	Attack	Type	Power	ACC	PP
—	Leer	Normal	—	100	30
—	Wrap	Normal	15	85	20
5	Night Shade	Ghost	—	100	15
10	Teleport	Psychic	—	—	20
15	Taunt	Dark	—	100	20
20	Pursuit	Dark	40	100	20

Level	Attack	Type	Power	ACC	PP
25	Psychic	Psychic	90	100	10
30	Super Power	Fighting	120	100	5
35	Cosmic Power	Psychic	—	—	20
40	Zap Cannon	Electric	100	50	5
45	Psycho Boost	Psychic	140	90	5
50	Hyper Beam	Normal	150	90	5

TM/HM

TM/HM#	Name	Type	Power	ACC	PP
TM01	Focus Punch	Fighting	150	100	20
TM03	Water Pulse	Water	60	100	20
TM04	Calm Mind	Psychic	—	—	20
TM06	Toxic	Poison	—	85	10
TM10	Hidden Power	Normal	—	100	15
TM11	Sunny Day	Fire	—	—	5
TM12	Taunt	Dark	—	100	20
TM13	Ice Beam	Ice	95	100	10
TM15	Hyper Beam	Normal	150	90	5
TM16	Light Screen	Psychic	—	—	30
TM17	Protect	Normal	—	—	10
TM18	Rain Dance	Water	—	—	5
TM20	Safeguard	Normal	—	—	25
TM21	Frustration	Normal	—	100	20
TM22	Solarbeam	Grass	120	100	10
TM24	Thunderbolt	Electric	95	100	15
TM25	Thunder	Electric	120	70	10
TM27	Return	Normal	—	100	20

TM/HM#	Name	Type	Power	ACC	PP
TM29	Psychic	Psychic	90	100	10
TM30	Shadow Ball	Ghost	80	100	15
TM31	Brick Break	Fighting	75	100	15
TM32	Double Team	Normal	—	—	15
TM33	Reflect	Psychic	—	—	20
TM34	Shock Wave	Electric	60	—	20
TM39	Rock Tomb	Rock	50	80	10
TM40	Aerial Ace	Flying	60	—	20
TM41	Torment	Dark	—	100	15
TM42	Facade	Normal	70	100	20
TM43	Secret Power	Normal	70	100	20
TM44	Rest	Psychic	—	—	10
TM48	Skill Swap	Psychic	—	100	10
TM49	Snatch	Dark	—	100	10
HM01	Cut	Normal	50	95	30
HM04	Strength	Normal	80	100	15
HM05	Flash	Normal	—	70	20
HM06	Rock Smash	Fighting	20	100	15

MOVE TUTOR
FireRed/LeafGreen and *Emerald* Only

Body Slam*	Counter*	Double-Edge
Dream Eater*	Mega Kick*	Mega Punch*
Mimic	Rock Slide*	Seismic Toss*
Substitute	Thunder Wave*	

*Battle Frontier tutor move (*Emerald*)

386 Deoxys™ (Defense Forme)

PSYCHIC

GENERAL INFO
SPECIES: DNA Pokémon
HEIGHT: 5'05"
WEIGHT: 134 lbs.
ABILITY: Pressure

STATS
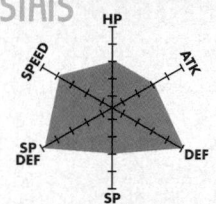

EVOLUTIONS

DOES NOT EVOLVE

LOCATION(S):

RUBY — Rarity: **None**
Deoxys does not take this form in this game

SAPPHIRE — Rarity: **None**
Deoxys does not take this form in this game

FIRERED — Rarity: **None**
Deoxys does not take this form in this game

LEAFGREEN — Rarity: **Only One**
Birth Island (Only accessible with the Aurora Ticket gained via special download at live events)

COLOSSEUM — Rarity: **None**
Deoxys does not take this form in this game

EMERALD — Rarity: **None**
Deoxys does not take this form in this game

XD — Rarity: **None**
Deoxys does not take this form in this game

MOVES

Level	Attack	Type	Power	ACC	PP
—	Leer	Normal	—	100	30
—	Wrap	Normal	15	85	20
5	Night Shade	Ghost	—	100	15
10	Teleport	Psychic	—	—	20
15	Knock Off	Dark	20	100	20
20	Spikes	Ground	—	—	20
25	Psychic	Psychic	90	100	10
30	Snatch	Dark	—	100	10
35	Iron Defense	Steel	—	—	15
35	Amnesia	Psychic	—	—	20
40	Recover	Normal	—	—	20
45	Psycho Boost	Psychic	140	90	5
50	Counter	Fighting	140	100	20
50	Mirror Coat	Psychic	—	100	20

TM/HM

TM/HM#	Name	Type	Power	ACC	PP
TM01	Focus Punch	Fighting	150	100	20
TM03	Water Pulse	Water	60	100	20
TM04	Calm Mind	Psychic	—	—	20
TM06	Toxic	Poison	—	85	10
TM10	Hidden Power	Normal	—	100	15
TM11	Sunny Day	Fire	—	—	5
TM12	Taunt	Dark	—	100	20
TM13	Ice Beam	Ice	95	100	10
TM15	Hyper Beam	Normal	150	90	5
TM16	Light Screen	Psychic	—	—	30
TM17	Protect	Normal	—	—	10
TM18	Rain Dance	Water	—	—	5
TM20	Safeguard	Normal	—	—	25
TM21	Frustration	Normal	—	100	20
TM22	Solarbeam	Grass	120	100	10
TM24	Thunderbolt	Electric	95	100	15
TM25	Thunder	Electric	120	70	10
TM27	Return	Normal	—	100	20
TM29	Psychic	Psychic	90	100	10
TM30	Shadow Ball	Ghost	80	100	15
TM31	Brick Break	Fighting	75	100	15
TM32	Double Team	Normal	—	—	15
TM33	Reflect	Psychic	—	—	20
TM34	Shock Wave	Electric	60	—	20
TM39	Rock Tomb	Rock	50	80	10
TM40	Aerial Ace	Flying	60	—	20
TM41	Torment	Dark	—	100	15
TM42	Facade	Normal	70	100	20
TM43	Secret Power	Normal	70	100	20
TM44	Rest	Psychic	—	—	10
TM48	Skill Swap	Psychic	—	100	10
TM49	Snatch	Dark	—	100	10
HM01	Cut	Normal	50	95	30
HM04	Strength	Normal	80	100	15
HM05	Flash	Normal	—	70	20
HM06	Rock Smash	Fighting	20	100	15

MOVE TUTOR
FireRed/LeafGreen and *Emerald* Only

Body Slam*	Counter*	Double-Edge
Dream Eater*	Mega Kick*	Mega Punch*
Mimic	Rock Slide*	Seismic Toss*
Substitute	Thunder Wave*	

*Battle Frontier tutor move (*Emerald*)

386 Deoxys™ (Normal Forme)

PSYCHIC

GENERAL INFO
SPECIES: **DNA Pokémon**
HEIGHT: **5'05"**
WEIGHT: **134 lbs.**
ABILITY: **Pressure**

STATS

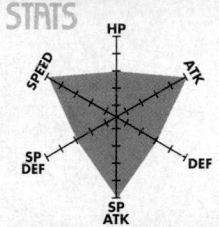

EVOLUTIONS

DOES NOT EVOLVE

LOCATION(S):

RUBY   Rarity: **None**
Must trade from *Pokémon FireRed* or *Pokémon LeafGreen*, and then Deoxys takes Normal Form.

SAPPHIRE   Rarity: **None**
Must trade from *Pokémon FireRed* or *Pokémon LeafGreen*, and then Deoxys takes Normal Form.

FIRERED   Rarity: **Only One**
Birth Island (Only accessible with the Aurora Ticket gained via special download at live events)

LEAFGREEN   Rarity: **None**
Deoxys does not take this form in this game

COLOSSEUM   Rarity: **None**
Must trade from *Pokémon FireRed* or *Pokémon LeafGreen*, and then Deoxys takes Normal Form.

EMERALD   Rarity: **None**
Deoxys does not take this form in this game

XD   Rarity: **None**
Deoxys does not take this form in this game

MOVES

Level	Attack	Type	Power	ACC	PP
—	Leer	Normal	—	100	30
—	Wrap	Normal	15	85	20
5	Night Shade	Ghost	—	100	15
10	Teleport	Psychic	—	—	20
15	Knock Off	Dark	20	100	20
20	Pursuit	Dark	40	100	20
25	Psychic	Psychic	90	100	10
30	Snatch	Dark	—	100	10
35	Cosmic Power	Psychic	—	—	20
40	Recover	Normal	—	—	20
45	Psycho Boost	Psychic	140	90	5
50	Hyper Beam	Normal	150	90	5

TM/HM

TM/HM#	Name	Type	Power	ACC	PP
TM01	Focus Punch	Fighting	150	100	20
TM03	Water Pulse	Water	60	100	20
TM04	Calm Mind	Psychic	—	—	20
TM06	Toxic	Poison	—	85	10
TM10	Hidden Power	Normal	—	100	15
TM11	Sunny Day	Fire	—	—	5
TM12	Taunt	Dark	—	100	20
TM13	Ice Beam	Ice	95	100	10
TM15	Hyper Beam	Normal	150	90	5
TM16	Light Screen	Psychic	—	—	30
TM17	Protect	Normal	—	—	10
TM18	Rain Dance	Water	—	—	5
TM20	Safeguard	Normal	—	—	25
TM21	Frustration	Normal	—	100	20
TM22	Solarbeam	Grass	120	100	10
TM24	Thunderbolt	Electric	95	100	15
TM25	Thunder	Electric	120	70	10
TM27	Return	Normal	—	100	20
TM29	Psychic	Psychic	90	100	10
TM30	Shadow Ball	Ghost	80	100	15
TM31	Brick Break	Fighting	75	100	15
TM32	Double Team	Normal	—	—	15
TM33	Reflect	Psychic	—	—	20
TM34	Shock Wave	Electric	60	—	20
TM39	Rock Tomb	Rock	50	80	10
TM40	Aerial Ace	Flying	60	—	20
TM41	Torment	Dark	—	100	15
TM42	Façade	Normal	70	100	20
TM43	Secret Power	Normal	70	100	20
TM44	Rest	Psychic	—	—	10
TM48	Skill Swap	Psychic	—	100	10
TM49	Snatch	Dark	—	100	10
HM01	Cut	Normal	50	95	30
HM04	Strength	Normal	80	100	15
HM05	Flash	Normal	—	70	20
HM06	Rock Smash	Fighting	20	100	15

MOVE TUTOR
FireRed/LeafGreen and *Emerald* Only

Body Slam*	Counter*	Double-Edge*
Dream Eater*	Mega Kick*	Mega Punch*
Mimic	Rock Slide*	Seismic Toss*
Substitute	Thunder Wave*	

*Battle Frontier tutor move (*Emerald*)

386 Deoxys™ (Speed Forme)

PSYCHIC

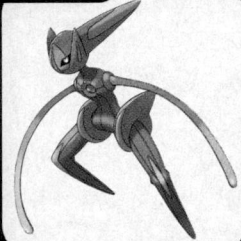

GENERAL INFO

SPECIES: DNA Pokémon
HEIGHT: 5'05"
WEIGHT: 134 lbs.
ABILITY: Pressure

STATS

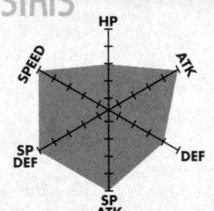

EVOLUTIONS

DOES NOT EVOLVE

LOCATION[S]:

RUBY **Rarity: None**
Deoxys does not take this form in this game

SAPPHIRE **Rarity: None**
Deoxys does not take this form in this game

FIRERED **Rarity: None**
Deoxys does not take this form in this game

LEAFGREEN **Rarity: None**
Deoxys does not take this form in this game

COLOSSEUM **Rarity: None**
Deoxys does not take this form in this game

EMERALD **Rarity: Only One**
Birth Island (Only accessible with the Aurora Ticket gained via special download at live events)

XD **Rarity: None**
Deoxys does not take this form in this game

MOVES

Level	Attack	Type	Power	ACC	PP
5	Night Shade	Ghost	—	100	15
10	Double Team	Normal	—	—	15
15	Knock Off	Dark	20	100	20
20	Pursuit	Dark	40	100	20
25	Psychic	Psychic	90	100	10

Level	Attack	Type	Power	ACC	PP
30	Swift	Normal	60	—	20
35	Agility	Psychic	—	—	30
40	Recover	Normal	—	—	20
45	Psycho Boost	Psychic	140	90	5
50	Extremespeed	Normal	80	100	5

TM/HM

TM/HM#	Name	Type	Power	ACC	PP
HM01	Cut	Normal	50	95	30
HM04	Strength	Normal	80	100	15
HM05	Flash	Normal	—	70	20
HM06	Rock Smash	Fighting	20	100	15
TM01	Focus Punch	Fighting	150	100	20
TM03	Water Pulse	Water	60	100	20
TM04	Calm Mind	Psychic	—	—	20
TM06	Toxic	Poison	—	85	10
TM10	Hidden Power	Normal	—	100	15
TM11	Sunny Day	Fire	—	—	5
TM12	Taunt	Dark	—	100	20
TM13	Ice Beam	Ice	95	100	10
TM15	Hyper Beam	Normal	150	90	5
TM16	Light Screen	Psychic	—	—	30
TM17	Protect	Normal	—	—	10
TM18	Rain Dance	Water	—	—	5
TM20	Safeguard	Normal	—	—	25

TM/HM#	Name	Type	Power	ACC	PP
TM21	Frustration	Normal	—	100	20
TM22	Solarbeam	Grass	120	100	10
TM24	Thunderbolt	Electric	95	100	15
TM25	Thunder	Electric	120	70	10
TM27	Return	Normal	—	100	20
TM29	Psychic	Psychic	90	100	10
TM30	Shadow Ball	Ghost	60	—	20
TM31	Brick Break	Fighting	75	100	15
TM32	Double Team	Normal	—	—	15
TM39	Rock Tomb	Rock	50	80	10
TM40	Aerial Ace	Flying	60	—	20
TM41	Torment	Dark	—	100	15
TM42	Facade	Normal	70	100	20
TM43	Secret Power	Normal	70	100	20
TM44	Rest	Psychic	—	—	10
TM48	Skill Swap	Psychic	—	100	10
TM49	Snatch	Dark	—	100	10

MOVE TUTOR

FireRed/LeafGreen and Emerald Only

Body Slam*	Counter*	Double-Edge
Dream Eater*	Mega Kick*	Mega Punch*
Mimic	Rock Slide*	Seismic Toss*
Substitute	Thunder Wave*	

Emerald Only

Dynamicpunch	Endure*	Fire Punch*
Ice Punch*	Icy Wind*	Mud-Slap*
Sleep Talk	Snore*	Swagger
Swift*	Thunderpunch*	

*Battle Frontier tutor move (*Emerald*)

Extras

Codes

EMERALD

Code	Result
CHALLENGE CONTEST	You will receive a Pamtre Berry
COOL LATIOS	You will receive a Durin Berry
GREAT BATTLE	You will receive a Spelon Berry
OVERWHELMING LATIAS	You will receive a Watmel Berry
SUPER HUSTLE	You will receive a Belue Berry

Item	How to Obtain
Good Rod	Talk to fisherman on Route 118
Old Rod	Talk to fisherman near Dewford Gym
Super Rod	In the house north of the Space Center
Black Flute	Walk 1,000 steps in the ash
Blue Flute	Walk 250 steps in the ash
Pretty Chair	Walk 6,000 steps in the ash
Pretty Desk	Walk 8,000 steps in the ash
Red Flute	Walk 500 steps in the ash
White Flute	Walk 1,000 steps in the ash
Yellow Flute	Walk 500 steps in the ash
Gold Shield (Decoration)	Win 100 battles
Lansat Berry	Obtain all Silver Frontier Symbols
Silver Shield (Decoration)	Win 50 battles
Starf Berry	Obtain all Gold Frontier Symbols

Pokémon	How to Obtain
Beldum	See Steven's house after you beat the Elite Four
Castform	Take out the rival team at the Weather Institute
Chikorita, Cyndaquil, or Totodile	When you complete the 200 Pokemon of Hoenn, Professor Birch will call you on your PokéNav
Deoxys	Get the Aurara Ticket, and go to Birth Island
Groudon	Beat the Elite Four, and go to the land lair
Ho-oh/Lugia	Get the Mystic Ticket, and go to Navel Island
Kyogre	Beat the Elite Four, and go to the Sea Lair
Latios or Latias	After beating the Elite Four, watch the T.V. downstairs in your house
Latios or Latias	Mix records with a Ruby or Sapphire with the Eon ticket, and go to Southern Island
Mew	Get the Old Sea Chart, and go to Faraway Island
Rayquaza	Get Magma and Aqua to get Kyogre and Groudon out of the cave, and go to Sky Pillar
Treeko, Torchic, or Mudkip	Help Proffesor Birch escape the wild Pokémon

Rank	How to Obtain
Bronze Rank	Do one of the tasks mentioned above
Copper Rank	Do two of the tasks mentioned above
Silver Rank	Do three of the tasks mentioned above
Gold Rank	Do all four of the tasks mentioned above

XD

Item	How to Obtain
Amulet Coin	Say "Yes" to every question
Mental Herb	Say "Yes" to 1 question
Quick Claw	Say "No" to every question
White Herb	Say "Yes" to 2 questions

Appendix

TM LIST

#	Name	Type	Power	ACC	PP
TM01	Focus Punch	Fighting	150	100	20
TM02	Dragon Claw	Dragon	80	100	15
TM03	Water Pulse	Water	60	100	20
TM04	Calm Mind	Psychic	—	—	20
TM05	Roar	Normal	—	100	20
TM06	Toxic	Poison	—	85	10
TM07	Hail	Ice	—	—	10
TM08	Bulk Up	Fighting	—	—	20
TM09	Bullet Seed	Grass	10	100	30
TM10	Hidden Power	Normal	—	100	15
TM11	Sunny Day	Fire	—	—	5
TM12	Taunt	Dark	—	100	20
TM13	Ice Beam	Ice	95	100	10
TM14	Blizzard	Ice	120	70	5
TM15	Hyper Beam	Normal	150	90	5
TM16	Light Screen	Psychic	—	—	30
TM17	Protect	Normal	—	—	10
TM18	Rain Dance	Water	—	—	5
TM19	Giga Drain	Grass	60	100	5
TM20	Safeguard	Normal	—	—	25
TM21	Frustration	Normal	—	100	20
TM22	Solarbeam	Grass	120	100	10
TM23	Iron Tail	Steel	75	75	15
TM24	Thunderbolt	Electric	95	100	15
TM25	Thunder	Electric	120	70	10
TM26	Earthquake	Ground	100	100	10
TM27	Return	Normal	—	100	20
TM28	Dig	Ground	60	100	10
TM29	Psychic	Psychic	90	100	10
TM30	Shadow Ball	Ghost	80	100	15
TM31	Brick Break	Fighting	75	100	15
TM32	Double Team	Normal	—	—	15
TM33	Reflect	Psychic	—	—	20
TM34	Shock Wave	Electric	60	—	20
TM35	Flamethrower	Fire	95	100	15
TM36	Sludge Bomb	Poison	90	100	10
TM37	Sandstorm	Ground	—	—	10
TM38	Fire Blast	Fire	120	85	5
TM39	Rock Tomb	Rock	50	80	10
TM40	Aerial Ace	Flying	60	—	20
TM41	Torment	Dark	—	100	15
TM42	Facade	Normal	70	100	20
TM43	Secret Power	Normal	70	100	20
TM44	Rest	Psychic	—	—	10
TM45	Attract	Normal	—	100	15
TM46	Thief	Dark	40	100	10
TM47	Steel Wing	Steel	70	90	25
TM48	Skill Swap	Psychic	—	100	10
TM49	Snatch	Dark	—	100	10
TM50	Overheat	Fire	140	90	5

HM LIST

#	Name	Type	Power	ACC	PP
HM01	Cut	Normal	50	95	30
HM02	Fly	Flying	70	95	15
HM03	Surf	Water	95	100	15
HM04	Strength	Normal	80	100	5
HM05	Flash	Normal	—	70	20
HM06	Rock Smash	Fighting	20	100	15
HM07	Waterfall	Water	80	100	15
HM08	Dive	Water	60	100	10

Berry List

Name	Effect	Flavor	Amount of Powder
Aguav Berry	Eliminates Sleep condition; confuses Pokémon that dislike bitter flavor	Bitter	50
Apicot Berry	When held, raises Sp. Defense stat	Bitter	50
Aspear Berry	Eliminates Ice condition	Sour	20
Belue Berry	Grows into Belue Berry plant	Spicy, Sour	250
Bluk Berry	Grows into Bluk Berry plant	Dry, Sweet	70
Cheri Berry	Eliminates Paralyze condition	Spicy	20
Chesto Berry	Eliminates Sleep condition	Dry	20
Cornn Berry	Grows into Cornn Berry plant	Dry, Sweet	150
Durin Berry	Grows into Durin Berry plant	Sour, Bitter	250
Figy Berry	Restores HPs when it's half or lower; confuses Pokémon that dislike spicy flavor	Spicy	50
Ganlon Berry	When held, raises Defense stat	Dry, Bitter	500
Grepa Berry	Grows into Grepa Berry plant	Dry, Sweet, Sour	100
Hondew Berry	Grows into Hondew Berry plant	Dry, Spicy, Bitter	100
Iapapa Berry	Restores HPs when it's half or lower; confuses Pokémon that dislike sour flavor	Sour	50
Kelpsy Berry	Grows into Kelpsy Berry plant	Dry, Sour, Bitter	100
Leppa Berry	Restores PP when it's zero	Sweet, Spicy, Sour, Bitter	30
Liechi Berry	Raises power of Attacks when HP is low	Sweet, Spicy, Sour	500
Lum Berry	Cures any Status condition	Dry, Sweet, Spicy, Sour, Bitter	30
Mago Berry	Restores HPs when it's half or lower; confuses Pokémon that dislike sweet flavor	Sweet	50
Magost Berry	Grows into Magost Berry plant	Sweet, Bitter	150
Nanab Berry	Grows into Nanab Berry plant	Sweet, Bitter	70
Nomel Berry	Grows into Nomel Berry plant	Spicy, Sour	150
Oran Berry	Restores 10 HPs when it's half or lower	Dry, Sweet, Spicy, Sour, Bitter	30
Pamtre Berry	Grows Pamtre Berry plant	Dry, Sweet	250
Pecha Berry	Eliminates Poison condition	Sweet	20
Persim Berry	Eliminates Confusion condition	Dry, Sweet, Spicy, Sour, Bitter	30
Petaya Berry	When held, raises Sp. Attack stat	Spicy, Bitter	500
Pinap Berry	Grows into Pinap Berry plant	Spicy, Sour	70
Pomeg Berry	Grows into Pomeg Berry plant	Sweet, Spicy, Bitter	100
Qualot Berry	Grows into Qualot Berry plant	Sweet, Spicy, Sour	100
Rabuta Berry	Grows into Rabuta Berry plant	Sour, Bitter	150
Rawst Berry	Eliminates Burn condition	Bitter	20
Razz Berry	Grows into Razz Berry plant	Dry, Spicy	70
Salac Berry	When held, raises Speed stat	Sweet, Sour	500
Sitrus Berry	Restores 30 HPs when it's half or lower	Dry, Sweet, Spicy, Sour, Bitter	30
Spelon Berry	Grows into Spelon Berry plant	Dry, Spicy	250
Tamato Berry	Grows into Tamato Berry plant	Dry, Spicy	150
Watmel Berry	Grows into Watmel Berry plant	Sweet, Bitter	250
Wepear Berry	Grows into Wepear Berry plant	Sour, Bitter	70
Wiki Berry	Restores HPs when it's half or lower; confuses Pokémon that dislike dry flavor	Dry	50

Damage Multiplier Table

Condition	Multiplier
Move is the same type as Pokémon	1.5x
Move is effective against opponent's type	2–4x
Move scores a Critical Hit!	2x
Pokémon has an Item that raises the Move's Strength	1.1x
Rain Dance or Sunny Day Effects (depending on Move)	1.5x or .5x

POKÉMON FACTS

Battling Abra is always an unpredictable affair: sensing it's in grave danger, it attempts to teleport away, making it a difficult Pokémon to catch.

POKÉMON FACTS

Because Farfetch'd is a very rare Pokémon, many Trainers make it a point to Breed them back into prominence—stick and all.

Moves

ST	=	Strength
ACC	=	Accuracy
PP	=	Power Points
Range	=	Who the Move affects in 2-on-2 Battles

The abbreviations used mean:

2E	=	2 Enemies		S/E	=	Self and Enemy
RE	=	Random Enemy		PA?	=	Is the Move a Physical Attack?
1A/2E	=	1 Ally and 2 Enemies (i.e., everyone but the caster)		TM/HM?	=	Does the Move have a TM or HM number?

Name	Type	ST	ACC	PP	Range	PA?	TM/HM?
Absorb	Grass	20	100	20	S/E	N	—
Description: The Pokémon recovers half of the amount of damage that the opponent Pokémon receives from this Attack.							
Acid	Poison	40	100	30	2E	N	—
Description: Has a 10% chance of lowering enemy's Defense by one point.							
Acid Armor	Poison	—	—	40	Self	N	—
Description: Raises the Pokémon's Defense by two points.							
Aerial Ace	Flying	60	—	20	1E	Y	TM40
Description: This Attack is always successful.							
Aeroblast	Flying	100	95	5	1E	Y	
Description: High probability of critical hit.							
Agility	Psychic	—	—	30	Self	N	
Description: Raises the Pokémon's Speed by two.							
Air Cutter	Flying	55	95	25	2E	N	—
Description: Easy to produce a Critical Hit.							
Amnesia	Psychic	—	—	20	Self	N	
Description: Raises the Pokémon's Special Defense by two points.							
Ancientpower	Rock	60	100	5	Self	Y	—
Description: Has a 10% chance of raising all of the Pokémon's abilities by one point.							
Arm Thrust	Fighting	15	100	20	1E	Y	—
Description: Attack 2–5 times in one turn.							
Aromatherapy	Grass	—	—	5	All Allies	N	—
Description: Cures the Status conditions of allied Pokémon.							
Assist	Normal	—	100	20	—	N	—
Description: This Move randomly chooses one of the Moves of a Pokémon not in battle.							
Astonish	Ghost	30	100	15	1E	Y	—
Description: 30% chance of making the opponent Flinch.							

Name	Type	ST	ACC	PP	Range	PA?	TM/HM?
Attract	Normal	—	100	15	1E	N	TM45
Description: Affects only Pokémon of the opposite sex. Prevents the opponent Pokémon from attacking with a 50% probability.							
Aurora Beam	Ice	65	100	20	1E	N	—
Description: Has a 10% chance of lowering the enemy's Attack by one point.							
Barrage	Normal	15	85	20	—	—	—
Description: Attack 2–5 times consecutively in one turn.							
Barrier	Psychic	—	—	30	Self	N	—
Description: Increases the Pokémon's Defense by two points.							
Baton Pass	Normal	—	—	40	Allies	N	—
Description: Changes out the casting Pokémon for one of the other allied Pokémon. The substitute Pokémon inherits any beneficial Effects gained so far. The skill fails if you don't have any Pokémon with which to alternate.							
Beat Up	Dark	10	100	10	—	—	—
Description: Attack opponent a number of times equal to your number of healthy Pokémon.							
Blast Burn	Fire	150	90	5	—	—	—
Description: A high-level Elemental Attack.							
Belly Drum	Normal	—	—	10	Self	N	—
Description: Raises Attack to its maximum level, but in return it decreases the Pokémon's max HPs by half.							
Bide	Normal	—	100	10	S/E	Y	—
Description: Attack continues for 2 turns, and the damage received from the opponent during that time is returned doubled.							
Bind	Normal	15	75	20	1E	Y	—
Description: Consecutive Attacks for 2–5 turns. Enemy can't flee during that time.							

Name	Type	ST	ACC	PP	Range	PA?	TM/HM?
Bite	Dark	60	100	25	1E	Y	—
Description: Causes opponent to Flinch with 30% probability.							
Blaze Kick	Fire	85	90	10	1E	Y	—
Description: 10% chance of Burning the opponent. Easy to score a Critical Hit. Cures Frozen Pokémon.							
Blizzard	Ice	120	70	5	2E	N	TM14
Description: 10% additional chance of Freezing the opponent.							
Block	Normal	—	100	5	1E	N	—
Description: Prevents the opponent from fleeing or being switched out of battle.							
Body Slam	Normal	85	100	15	1E	Y	—
Description: 30% additional Effect of Paralysis.							
Bone Club	Ground	65	85	20	—	—	—
Description: 10% chance of making an opponent back off.							
Bone Rush	Ground	25	80	10	—	—	—
Description: Attack 2–5 times consecutively in one turn.							
Bonemerang	Ground	50	90	10	—	—	—
Description: Attack twice in a row in one turn.							
Bounce	Flying	85	85	5	S/E	Y	—
Description: On the first turn, the Pokémon bounds into the air. On the second turn, the Attack takes place. 30% chance of inflicting Paralysis on the opponent.							
Brick Break	Fighting	75	100	15	1E	Y	TM31
Description: Defeats the Effects of Reflect and Light Screen.							
Bubble	Water	20	100	30	2E	N	—
Description: 10% probability of lowering the opponent Pokémon's Speed.							
Bubblebeam	Water	65	100	20	1E	N	—
Description: 10% additional chance of lowering the opponent Pokémon's Speed.							
Bulk Up	Fighting	—	—	20	Self	N	TM08
Description: Raises your Attack and Defense by one.							
Bullet Seed	Grass	10	100	30	1E	N	TM09
Description: Attack 2–5 times in one turn.							
Calm Mind	Psychic	—	—	20	Self	N	TM04
Description: Raises the Pokémon's Special Attack and Special Defense by one each.							
Camouflage	Normal	—	100	20	Self	N	—
Description: Pokémon's type is changed to a type that corresponds to the battlefield terrain (e.g., on grasslands, Pokémon becomes a Grass-type; sand = Ground-type; on sea or underwater = Water-type).							
Charge	Electric	—	100	20	Self	N	—
Description: The turn after using the Move, Electric-type Moves are doubled in strength.							
Charm	Normal	—	100	20	1E	N	—
Description: Lowers the opponent Pokémon's Attack by two points.							
Clamp	Water	35	75	10	1E	Y	—
Description: Attacks over 2–5 consecutive turns during which the enemy can't flee.							
Comet Punch	Normal	18	85	15	—	Y	—
Description: Attack 2–5 times consecutively in one turn.							
Confuse Ray	Ghost	—	100	10	1E	N	—
Description: Confuses opponent.							
Confusion	Psychic	50	100	25	1E	N	—
Description: 10% additional Effect of Confusion.							
Constrict	Normal	10	100	35	1E	Y	—
Description: Lowers the opponent Pokémon's Speed by one point with a 10% probability.							

Name	Type	ST	ACC	PP	Range	PA?	TM/HM?
Conversion	Normal	—	—	30	—	—	—
Description: Changes your type into one of your Attack types.							
Conversion 2	Normal	—	100	30	—	—	—
Description: Changes your type into one that your opponent's Attack is weak against.							
Cosmic Power	Normal	—	—	20	Self	N	—
Description: Raises your Defense and Special Defense by one each.							
Cotton Spore	Grass	—	85	40	1E	N	—
Description: Lowers the opponent Pokémon's Speed by two points.							
Counter	Fighting	—	100	20	S/E	Y	—
Description: Attacks second in battle and inflicts twice as much damage as the opponent's Physical Attack.							
Covet	Normal	40	100	40	S/E	N	—
Description: Allows you to grab and hold onto the Item the opponent is holding.							
Crabhammer	Water	90	85	10	1E	Y	—
Description: Makes it easy to produce a Critical Hit.							
Cross Chop	Fighting	100	80	5	1E	Y	—
Description: Makes it easier to produce a Critical Hit.							
Crunch	Dark	80	100	15	1E	Y	—
Description: Lowers the opponent Pokémon's Special Defense by one point with a 20% probability.							
Crush Claw	Normal	75	95	10	1E	Y	—
Description: 50% chance of lowering the opponent's Defense.							
Curse	—	—	—	10	S/E	N	—
Description: Raises the Pokémon's Attack and Defense by one point each and lowers the Pokémon's Speed by one point. If cast by a Ghost-type Pokémon, it decreases its own HPs by half and Curses the opponent Pokémon. Each turn a cursed Pokémon loses up to 25% of its HPs.							
Cut	Normal	50	95	30	1E	Y	HM01
Description: Normal Attack. Outside of battle, this cuts down thin trees.							
Defense Curl	Normal	—	—	40	Self	N	—
Description: Raises the Pokémon's Defense by one.							
Destiny Bond	Ghost	—	—	5	S/E	N	—
Description: After using this skill, if your Pokémon faints, the opponent Pokémon does too.							
Detect	Fighting	—	—	5	Self	N	—
Description: Allows you to evade Attack this turn. Success rate decreases with each consecutive use.							
Dig	Ground	60	100	10	1E	Y	TM28
Description: Digs a hole during Turn 1, attacks on Turn 2. Outside of battle, use this skill to escape from caves.							
Disable	Normal	—	55	20	1E	N	—
Description: Disables the skill the opponent Pokémon just used for a number of turns.							
Dive	Water	60	100	10	1E	Y	HM08
Description: On the first turn the Pokémon dives underwater and on the second turn it attacks. Outside of battle, use this to dive underwater and resurface.							
Dizzy Punch	Normal	70	100	10	1E	Y	—
Description: 20% additional chance of Confusing the opponent.							
Doom Desire	Steel	120	85	5	1E	—	—
Description: Waits two turns, then inflicts damage on foe on third turn.							
Double Kick	Fighting	30	100	30	1E	Y	—
Description: Pokémon's Attack hits twice in one turn.							

Name	Type	ST	ACC	PP	Range	PA?	TM/HM?
Double Team	Normal	—	—	15	Self	N	TM32

Description: Raises the Pokémon's Evasiveness by one point.

| **Double-Edge** | Normal | 120 | 100 | 15 | S/E | Y | — |

Description: The casting Pokémon receives 33% of the damage inflicted on the opponent.

| **Doubleslap** | Normal | 15 | 85 | 10 | 1E | Y | — |

Description: Attack 2–5 times in one turn.

| **Dragonbreath** | Dragon | 60 | 100 | 20 | 1E | N | — |

Description: Paralyzes opponent with a 30% probability.

| **Dragon Claw** | Dragon | 80 | 100 | 15 | 1E | Y | TM02 |

Description: Normal Attack.

| **Dragon Dance** | Dragon | — | — | 20 | Self | N | — |

Description: Raises both Speed and Attack.

| **Dragon Rage** | Dragon | — | 100 | 10 | 1E | N | — |

Description: Does 40 points of Damage regardless of the Pokémon's Abilities.

| **Dream Eater** | Psychic | 100 | 100 | 15 | S/E | N | — |

Description: This Effect works only on Sleeping Pokémon. The Pokémon recovers half of the HP damage inflicted.

| **Drill Peck** | Flying | 80 | 100 | 20 | 1E | Y | — |

Description: Normal Attack.

| **Dynamicpunch** | Fighting | 100 | 50 | 5 | 1E | Y | — |

Description: If the skill hits, the opponent becomes Confused.

| **Earthquake** | Ground | 100 | 100 | 10 | 1A/2E | N | TM26 |

Description: Normal Attack. Has no effect against Flying-types, while the strength of the Attack is doubled against Pokémon using the Move Dig.

| **Egg Bomb** | Normal | 100 | 75 | 10 | — | — | — |

Description: Normal Attack.

| **Ember** | Fire | 40 | 100 | 25 | 1E | N | — |

Description: 10% additional chance of Burning the opponent. Cures Frozen Pokémon.

| **Encore** | Normal | — | 100 | 5 | 1E | N | — |

Description: Makes the opponent Pokémon repeat the last skill used for 3–6 turns.

| **Endeavor** | Normal | — | 100 | 5 | 1E | Y | — |

Description: Reduces the opponent's HPs to the same level as yours if its total HPs are higher than yours.

| **Endure** | Normal | — | — | 10 | Self | N | — |

Description: Pokémon always survives with 1 HP regardless of the Attack. The success rate decreases with repeated use.

| **Eruption** | Fire | 150 | 100 | 5 | 2E | N | — |

Description: The lower your HPs, the lesser the Move's power becomes.

| **Explosion** | Normal | 250 | 100 | 5 | All | N | — |

Description: The opponent Pokémon faints after the Attack is finished.

| **Extrasensory** | Psychic | 80 | 100 | 30 | 1E | Y | — |

Description: 10% chance that the opponent will Flinch.

| **Extremespeed** | Normal | 80 | 100 | 5 | 1E | Y | — |

Description: Attack always hits first. If both Pokémon use this, it works for the one with the highest Speed.

| **Facade** | Normal | 70 | 100 | 20 | 1E | Y | TM42 |

Description: The strength of this skill is doubled when you are either Poisoned, Paralyzed, or Burned.

| **Faint Attack** | Dark | 60 | — | 20 | 1E | N | — |

Description: Attack hits opponent without fail.

| **Fake Out** | Normal | 40 | 100 | 10 | 1E | N | — |

Description: Pokémon attacks first and the Attack has a 100% chance of making the opponent Flinch. Can be used during the starting turn only.

| **Fake Tears** | Dark | — | 100 | 20 | 1E | N | — |

Description: Lowers the opponent's Special Defense by 2.

| **False Swipe** | Normal | 40 | 100 | 40 | 1E | Y | — |

Description: Leaves the opponent with 1 HP without fail. (You cannot defeat a Pokémon with this skill.)

| **Featherdance** | Flying | — | 100 | 15 | 1E | N | — |

Description: Lowers the opponent's Attack by two.

| **Fire Blast** | Fire | 120 | 85 | 5 | 1E | N | TM38 |

Description: 10% additional chance of Burning the opponent Pokémon.

| **Fire Punch** | Fire | 75 | 100 | 15 | 1E | N | — |

Description: 10% additional chance of Burning the opponent Pokémon. Cures Frozen Pokémon.

| **Fire Spin** | Fire | 15 | 70 | 15 | 1E | N | — |

Description: Pokémon consecutively attacks for 2–5 turns. During this, the opponent Pokémon can't flee. Cures Frozen Pokémon.

| **Fissure** | Ground | — | 30 | 5 | 1E | N | — |

Description: Defeats the enemy with one Attack. Doesn't work against Flying types.

| **Flail** | Normal | — | 100 | 15 | 1E | Y | — |

Description: Inflicts more damage the lower the Pokémon's HPs are.

| **Flamethrower** | Fire | 95 | 100 | 15 | 1E | N | TM35 |

Description: 10% chance of Burning the opponent. Cures Frozen Pokémon.

| **Flame Wheel** | Fire | 60 | 100 | 25 | 1E | N | — |

Description: 10% chance of Burning opponent; ice is melted if opponent is Frozen.

| **Flash** | Normal | — | 70 | 20 | 1E | N | HM05 |

Description: Lowers opponent's Accuracy by one point. When used outside of battle, this illuminates dark caves.

| **Flatter** | Dark | — | 100 | 15 | 1E | N | — |

Description: Confuses the opponent but raises its Special Attack by one.

| **Fly** | Flying | 70 | 95 | 15 | 1E | Y | HM02 |

Description: Pokémon flies into the air on Turn 1 and attacks on Turn 2. Outside of battle, use this skill to fly to the cities you've visited.

| **Focus Energy** | Normal | — | — | 30 | Self | N | — |

Description: Raises the possibility that your Attack will make a Critical Hit.

| **Focus Punch** | Fighting | 150 | 100 | 20 | S/E | Y | TM01 |

Description: Attack from behind without fail. When you take damage from the enemy, you Flinch and cannot attack.

| **Follow Me** | Normal | — | 100 | 20 | Self | N | — |

Description: You take over the Move the opponent uses in that turn, becoming its teacher.

| **Foresight** | Normal | — | 100 | 40 | 1E | N | — |

Description: Opponent's Evasiveness returns to normal. Fighting-type and Normal-type Attacks become effective against Ghost-type Pokémon.

| **Frenzy Plant** | Grass | 150 | 90 | 5 | | | |

Description: A high-level Elemental Attack.

| **Frustration** | Normal | — | 100 | 20 | 1E | Y | TM21 |

Description: The more the Pokémon hates you, the higher the Move's Attack strength.

| **Fury Attack** | Normal | 15 | 85 | 20 | 1E | N | — |

Description: Attacks 2–5 times consecutively in one turn.

Name	Type	ST	ACC	PP	Range	PA?	TM/HM?
Fury Cutter	Bug	10	95	20	1E	Y	—

Description: The strength of this skill doubles each consecutive turn you successfully use it. It returns to normal when you stop using it or when a hit misses.

Fury Swipes	Normal	18	80	15	1E	Y	—

Description: Attacks 2–5 times consecutively in one turn.

Future Sight	Psychic	80	90	15	1E	N	—

Description: Attacks the opponent Pokémon after two turns.

Giga Drain	Grass	60	100	5	S/E	N	TM19

Description: The Pokémon recovers half of the amount of damage that the opponent Pokémon receives from this Attack.

Glare	Normal	—	75	30	1E	N	—

Description: Paralyzes enemy.

Grasswhistle	Grass	—	55	15	1E	N	—

Description: Puts opponent to Sleep.

Growl	Normal	—	100	40	2E	N	—

Description: Lowers the opponent's Attack by one point.

Growth	Normal	—	—	40	Self	N	—

Description: Raises the Pokémon's Special Attack by one.

Grudge	Ghost	—	100	5	S/E	N	—

Description: Reduces the PP of a Move that causes an opponent to Faint.

Guillotine	Normal	—	30	5	1E	Y	—

Description: In one blow, you Knock Out the opponent. Has no effect if the opponent's level is higher than yours, but it has a higher chance of succeeding if the opponent's level is lower than yours.

Gust	Flying	40	100	35	1E	Y	—

Description: Normal Attack. Damage is doubled when used against a Pokémon using Fly.

Hail	Ice	—	—	10	All	N	TM07

Description: Summons a hail storm that lasts for five turns. At the end of each turn it causes damage to all Pokémon on the battlefield that are not Ice type.

Harden	Normal	—	—	30	Self	N	—

Description: Raises the Pokémon's Defense by one point.

Haze	Ice	—	—	30	All	N	—

Description: Returns all Status conditions (the casting Pokémon's and the opponent Pokémon's) to normal.

Headbutt	Normal	70	100	15	1E	Y	—

Description: 30% chance of causing the opponent to Flinch.

Heal Bell	Normal	—	—	5	All Allies	N	—

Description: Recovers all of an ally's Status conditions.

Heat Wave	Fire	100	90	10	2E	N	—

Description: 10% chance of Burning the opponent. Cures Frozen Pokémon.

Helping Hand	Normal	—	100	20	All Allies	N	—

Description: Move increases the Attack strength of your ally's Move by 1.5.

Hidden Power	Normal	—	100	15	1E	N	TM10

Description: Changes type and power based on the Pokémon using it.

Hi Jump Kick	Fighting	85	100	20	S/E	Y	—

Description: When this Attack fails, you take 25% of the possible damage inflicted.

Horn Attack	Normal	65	100	25	1E	Y	—

Description: Normal Attack.

Horn Drill	Normal	—	30	5	1E	Y	—

Description: In one blow, the opponent is knocked out.

Name	Type	ST	ACC	PP	Range	PA?	TM/HM?
Howl	Normal	—	—	40	Self	N	—

Description: Raises your Attack by one point.

Hydro Pump	Water	120	80	5	1E	N	—

Description: Normal Attack.

Hyper Beam	Normal	150	90	5	1E	N	TM15

Description: Inflicts a large amount of damage, but the Pokémon cannot attack on the next turn.

Hyper Fang	Normal	80	90	15	—	Y	—

Description: 10% chance of making an opponent back off.

Hyper Voice	Normal	90	100	10	2E	N	—

Description: Normal Attack.

Hypnosis	Psychic	—	60	20	1E	N	—

Description: Puts enemy to Sleep.

Ice Ball	Ice	30	90	20	1E	Y	—

Description: Attack lasts more than five turns or until it misses. Damage increases every turn the Attack succeeds.

Ice Beam	Ice	95	100	10	1E	N	TM13

Description: 10% additional Effect of Freezing the opponent Pokémon.

Ice Punch	Ice	75	100	15	1E	Y	—

Description: 10% additional Effect of Freezing the opponent.

Icicle Spear	Ice	10	100	30	—	—	—

Description: High-level Ice Attack for Shellder.

Icy Wind	Ice	55	95	15	2E	N	—

Description: Lowers the opponent Pokémon's Speed by one point.

Imprison	Psychic	—	100	10	S/E	N	—

Description: If you know one of your opponent's Moves, it cannot use that Move in the battle.

Ingrain	Grass	—	100	20	Self	N	—

Description: Each turn you recover a few HPs, but you cannot change out of the battle.

Iron Defense	Steel	—	—	15	Self	N	—

Description: Raises your Defense by two.

Iron Tail	Steel	100	75	15	1E	Y	TM23

Description: 30% probability that it will lower the opponent's Defense one point.

Jump Kick	Fighting	70	95	25	—	Y	—

Description: If an Attack misses, receive 1/8 of the damage that it would have caused.

Karate Chop	Fighting	50	100	25	1E	Y	—

Description: Makes it easier to produce a Critical Hit.

Kinesis	Psychic	—	80	15	1E	N	—

Description: Lowers opponent's Accuracy by one point.

Knock Off	Dark	20	100	20	1E	Y	—

Description: When hit, the opponent drops the Item it is holding, losing its effect. After the battle, the Item is returned.

Leaf Blade	Grass	70	100	15	1E	Y	—

Description: Makes it easy to produce a Critical Hit.

Leech Life	Bug	20	100	15	S/E	Y	—

Description: The Pokémon recovers half of the amount of damage that the opponent Pokémon receives from this Attack.

Leech Seed	Grass	—	90	10	S/E	N	—

Description: Absorbs enemy's HPs with each turn and recovers part of the HPs absorbed. This Effect continues even after the opponent's Pokémon is changed.

Name	Type	ST	ACC	PP	Range	PA?	TM/HM?
Leer	Normal	—	100	30	2E	N	—

Description: Lowers opponent's Defense by one point.

| Lick | Ghost | 20 | 100 | 30 | 1E | Y | — |

Description: Has a 30% chance of causing Paralysis.

| Light Screen | Psychic | — | — | 30 | Self | N | TM16 |

Description: Halves the damage from Special Attacks for five turns. The Effect continues after changing Pokémon.

| Lock-On | Normal | — | 100 | 5 | 1E | N | — |

Description: The Pokémon's Attack hits with certainty on its next turn.

| Lovely Kiss | Normal | — | 75 | 10 | — | — | — |

Description: Makes an opponent Sleep.

| Low Kick | Fighting | — | 100 | 20 | 1E | Y | — |

Description: The heavier the opponent's Pokémon, the stronger the Attack.

| Luster Purge | Psychic | 70 | 100 | 5 | 1E | N | — |

Description: Has a 50% chance of lowering the opponent's Special Defense one point.

| Mach Punch | Fighting | 40 | 100 | 30 | 1E | Y | — |

Description: Makes you able to strike first without fail. (If both Pokémon produce this Attack, the one with the highest Speed rating goes first.)

| Magic Coat | Psychic | — | 100 | 15 | 1E | N | — |

Description: Reflects Leech Seed and Effects such as Poison, Paralyze, Sleep, and Confusion.

| Magical Leaf | Grass | 60 | — | 20 | 1E | N | — |

Description: Move hits the opponent 100% of the time.

| Magnitude | Ground | — | 100 | 30 | 1A/2E | N | — |

Description: Strength of the Attack randomly changes (10, 30, 50, 70, 90, 110, or 150). The strength of the Attack is doubled when used against a Pokémon who has used Dig. Attack affects any ally on the Field except you.

| Mean Look | Normal | — | 100 | 5 | 1E | N | — |

Description: Makes the opponent Pokémon unable to flee from battle or be switched out.

| Meditate | Psychic | — | — | 40 | Self | N | — |

Raises the Pokémon's Attack by one point.

| Mega Drain | Grass | 40 | 100 | 10 | S/E | N | — |

Description: The Pokémon absorbs half of the damage inflicted.

| Mega Kick | Normal | 120 | 75 | 5 | — | Y | — |

Description: Normal Attack.

| Mega Punch | Normal | 80 | 85 | 20 | — | Y | — |

Description: Normal Attack.

| Megahorn | Bug | 120 | 85 | 10 | 1E | Y | — |

Description: Normal Attack.

| Memento | Dark | — | 100 | 10 | S/E | N | — |

Description: Lowers the opponent's Attack and Special Attack by two but makes your Pokémon faint.

| Metal Claw | Steel | 50 | 95 | 35 | 1E | Y | — |

Description: Raises the Pokémon's Defense by one with a 10% probability.

| Metal Sound | Steel | — | 85 | 40 | 1E | N | — |

Description: Lowers opponent's Special Defense by two.

| Meteor Mash | Steel | 100 | 85 | 10 | 1E | Y | — |

Description: 20% chance that it will raise your Attack by one.

| Metronome | Normal | — | — | 10 | — | — | — |

Description: Randomly uses Attack from entire repertoire.

| Milk Drink | Normal | — | — | 10 | — | — | — |

Description: Restores half of HP; splits 1/5 of HP among your other Pokémon.

| Mimic | Normal | — | 100 | 10 | S/E | N | — |

Description: Allows the Pokémon to copy and use the opponent Pokémon's last Attack for the duration of the battle.

| Mind Reader | Normal | — | 100 | 5 | 1E | N | — |

Description: The Pokémon's next Attack always hits.

| Minimize | Normal | — | — | 20 | Self | N | — |

Description: Increases the caster's Evasiveness by one.

| Mirror Coat | Psychic | — | 100 | 20 | S/E | N | — |

Description: Pokémon attacks second in battle (regardless of Pokémon's Speed). Returns double the Special Attacks of the opponent Pokémon.

| Mirror Move | Flying | — | — | 20 | 1E | N | — |

Description: Pokémon counters with the same Attack used by the opponent Pokémon.

| Mist | Ice | — | — | 30 | Self | N | — |

Description: Caster cannot be affected by skills that lower abilities.

| Mist Ball | Psychic | 70 | 100 | 5 | 1E | N | — |

Description: 50% chance of lowering the opponent's Special Attack.

| Moonlight | Normal | — | — | 5 | Self | N | — |

Description: Recovers 50 % of the Pokémon's max HPs. The effectiveness changes based on the time of day.

| Morning Sun | Normal | — | — | 5 | Self | N | — |

Description: Recovers HPs, but the effectiveness changes based on the time of day.

| Mud Shot | Ground | 55 | 95 | 15 | 1E | N | — |

Description: Always lowers the opponent's Speed by one.

| Mud Sport | Ground | — | 100 | 15 | All | N | — |

Description: Halves the strength of all Electric-type Moves.

| Muddy Water | Water | 95 | 85 | 10 | 2E | N | — |

Description: 30% chance of lowering the opponent's Accuracy.

| Mud-Slap | Ground | 20 | 100 | 10 | 1F | N | — |

Description: Lowers opponent's Accuracy by one point.

| Nature Power | Normal | — | 95 | 20 | 1E | N | — |

Description: Changes other Moves to correspond to the battlefield's terrain.

| Needle Arm | Grass | 60 | 100 | 15 | 1E | Y | — |

Description: 30% chance of making the opponent Flinch.

| Night Shade | Ghost | — | 100 | 15 | 1E | N | — |

Description: Inflicts damage equal to the Pokémon's level, regardless of the Pokémon's or the opponent Pokémon's Abilities.

| Nightmare | Ghost | — | 100 | 5 | — | — | — |

Description: Gives an opponent nightmares; works only when opponent is Sleeping.

| Odor Sleuth | Normal | — | 100 | 40 | 1E | N | — |

Description: Opponent's Evasiveness returns to normal. Fighting and Normal Attacks become effective against opponent Pokémon.

| Octazooka | Water | 65 | 85 | 10 | — | — | — |

Description: 50% chance of lowering opponent's Accuracy by one.

| Outrage | Dragon | 90 | 100 | 15 | RE | Y | — |

Description: Consecutive Attacks for 2–3 turns, and inflicts Confusion when the Attack is finished.

| Overheat | Fire | 140 | 90 | 5 | S/E | Y | TM50 |

Description: Lowers the opponent's Special Attack by two. Causes massive damage to the user.

Name	Type	ST	ACC	PP	Range	PA?	TM/HM?
Pain Split	Normal	—	100	20	—	—	—

Description: Combines your HP with your opponent's HP and splits them between both of you.

Name	Type	ST	ACC	PP	Range	PA?	TM/HM?
Pay Day	Normal	40	100	20	—	—	—

Description: After a battle, receive money equal to (your level) x (number of Attacks) x 2.

Name	Type	ST	ACC	PP	Range	PA?	TM/HM?
Peck	Flying	35	100	35	1E	Y	—

Description: Normal Attack.

Name	Type	ST	ACC	PP	Range	PA?	TM/HM?
Perish Song	Normal	—	—	5	All	N	—

Description: Passes a sentence that makes both Pokémon used in battle faint after three turns.

Name	Type	ST	ACC	PP	Range	PA?	TM/HM?
Petal Dance	Grass	70	100	20	RE	Y	—

Description: Attack for 2–3 turns, then when it ends, it Confuses the Pokémon.

Name	Type	ST	ACC	PP	Range	PA?	TM/HM?
Pin Missile	Bug	14	85	20	1E	N	—

Description: Attacks 2–5 times in one turn.

Name	Type	ST	ACC	PP	Range	PA?	TM/HM?
Poison Fang	Poison	50	100	15	1E	Y	—

Description: 30% change of Poisoning the opponent. Poison damage grows greater with each passing turn.

Name	Type	ST	ACC	PP	Range	PA?	TM/HM?
Poison Gas	Poison	—	55	40	1E	N	—

Description: Infects opponent with Poison.

Name	Type	ST	ACC	PP	Range	PA?	TM/HM?
Poisonpowder	Poison	—	75	35	1E	N	—

Description: Infects opponent with Poison. Damage increases with every turn.

Name	Type	ST	ACC	PP	Range	PA?	TM/HM?
Poison Sting	Poison	15	100	35	1E	N	—

Description: 30% additional Effect of Poison.

Name	Type	ST	ACC	PP	Range	PA?	TM/HM?
Poison Tail	Poison	50	100	25	1E	Y	—

Description: Bases damage on random power (10, 30, 50, 70, 90, 110, 150); still has 10% chance of causing Poison Effect.

Name	Type	ST	ACC	PP	Range	PA?	TM/HM?
Pound	Normal	40	100	35	1E	Y	—

Description: Normal Attack.

Name	Type	ST	ACC	PP	Range	PA?	TM/HM?
Powder Snow	Ice	40	100	25	2E	N	—

Description: Freezes the opponent Pokémon with a 10% probability.

Name	Type	ST	ACC	PP	Range	PA?	TM/HM?
Present	Normal	—	90	15	—	—	—

Description: May cause damage of 40, 80, or 120, or may restore HP by 80.

Name	Type	ST	ACC	PP	Range	PA?	TM/HM?
Protect	Normal	—	—	10	Self	N	TM17

Description: Defends against the opponent's current Attack. The success ratio is lowered when consecutively used.

Name	Type	ST	ACC	PP	Range	PA?	TM/HM?
Psybeam	Psychic	65	100	20	1E	N	—

Description: 10% additional chance of Confusion.

Name	Type	ST	ACC	PP	Range	PA?	TM/HM?
Psychic	Psychic	90	100	10	1E	N	TM29

Description: Reduces opponent's Special Defense by one point with a 10% probability.

Name	Type	ST	ACC	PP	Range	PA?	TM/HM?
Psych Up	Normal	—	—	10	S/E	N	—

Description: When the opponent uses Moves that have beneficial side effects, the same Effects benefit your own Pokémon.

Name	Type	ST	ACC	PP	Range	PA?	TM/HM?
Psywave	Psychic	—	80	15	1E	N	—

Description: Randomly causes damage equal to 0.5–1.5 multiplied by the Pokémon's level.

Name	Type	ST	ACC	PP	Range	PA?	TM/HM?
Pursuit	Dark	40	100	20	1E	Y	—

Description: If the opponent changes Pokémon when you use this Move, it inflicts twice the amount of damage as it is changed.

Name	Type	ST	ACC	PP	Range	PA?	TM/HM?
Quick Attack	Normal	40	100	30	1E	Y	—

Description: Get a preemptive Attack without fail. (If both Pokémon use this Attack, the one with the highest Speed lands the Attack first.)

Name	Type	ST	ACC	PP	Range	PA?	TM/HM?
Rage	Normal	20	100	20	1E	Y	—

Description: For one round of battle, the strength of the Attack increases by the amount of damage inflicted by the opponent.

Name	Type	ST	ACC	PP	Range	PA?	TM/HM?
Rain Dance	Water	—	—	5	All	N	TM18

Description: Summons a rain storm that raises the strength of Water-type Attacks for five turns.

Name	Type	ST	ACC	PP	Range	PA?	TM/HM?
Rapid Spin	Normal	20	100	40	S/E	Y	—

Description: Releases the Pokémon from continuous Moves such as Bind, Wrap, Spikes, and Leech Seed.

Name	Type	ST	ACC	PP	Range	PA?	TM/HM?
Razor Leaf	Grass	55	95	25	2E	N	—

Description: Easy to produce a Critical Hit.

Name	Type	ST	ACC	PP	Range	PA?	TM/HM?
Razor Wind	Normal	80	100	10	2E	N	—

Description: Gathers strength during Turn 1 and attacks during Turn 2. Makes it easier to do a Critical Hit.

Name	Type	ST	ACC	PP	Range	PA?	TM/HM?
Recover	Normal	—	—	20	Self	N	—

Description: Recover HPs up to half the maximum points.

Name	Type	ST	ACC	PP	Range	PA?	TM/HM?
Recycle	Normal	—	100	10	Self	N	—

Description: Makes it possible to reuse a Held Item a second time.

Name	Type	ST	ACC	PP	Range	PA?	TM/HM?
Reflect	Psychic	—	—	20	Self	N	TM33

Description: Halves the damage from Physical Attacks for five turns. Effect continues even if you change Pokémon.

Name	Type	ST	ACC	PP	Range	PA?	TM/HM?
Refresh	Normal	—	100	20	Self	N	—

Description: Cures the Status conditions Poison, Paralyze, and Burn.

Name	Type	ST	ACC	PP	Range	PA?	TM/HM?
Rest	Psychic	—	—	10	Self	N	TM44

Description: After the Pokémon recovers all HPs, it lies down to Sleep for two turns.

Name	Type	ST	ACC	PP	Range	PA?	TM/HM?
Return	Normal	—	100	20	1E	Y	TM27

Description: Pokémon you are using becomes stronger the more emotionally attached it is to you.

Name	Type	ST	ACC	PP	Range	PA?	TM/HM?
Revenge	Fighting	60	100	10	1E	Y	—

Description: The Attack's strength doubles when you take damage from the enemy's Attack on that turn.

Name	Type	ST	ACC	PP	Range	PA?	TM/HM?
Reversal	Fighting	—	100	15	1E	Y	—

Description: The less HPs the Pokémon has remaining, the stronger the Attack.

Name	Type	ST	ACC	PP	Range	PA?	TM/HM?
Roar	Normal	—	100	20	1E	N	TM05

Description: Opponent is scared away from battle. In a Trainer Battle, the Pokémon is forcibly changed. Move has no effect if the opponent doesn't have any Pokémon in waiting.

Name	Type	ST	ACC	PP	Range	PA?	TM/HM?
Rock Blast	Rock	25	80	10	1E	N	—

Description: Attacks 2–5 times in one turn.

Name	Type	ST	ACC	PP	Range	PA?	TM/HM?
Rock Slide	Rock	75	90	10	2E	N	—

Description: Causes opponent to Flinch.

Name	Type	ST	ACC	PP	Range	PA?	TM/HM?
Rock Smash	Fighting	20	100	15	1E	Y	HM06

Description: Lowers the opponent's Defense by one point with a 50% probability. Outside of battle, this crushes rocks, possibly releasing a Pokémon.

Name	Type	ST	ACC	PP	Range	PA?	TM/HM?
Rock Throw	Rock	50	90	15	1E	N	—

Description: Normal Attack.

Name	Type	ST	ACC	PP	Range	PA?	TM/HM?
Rock Tomb	Rock	50	80	10	1E	N	TM39

Description: Lowers the opponent's Speed by one.

Name	Type	ST	ACC	PP	Range	PA?	TM/HM?
Role Play	Psychic	—	100	10	Self	N	—

Description: Gives you and the opponent Pokémon the same innate Ability.

Name	Type	ST	ACC	PP	Range	PA?	TM/HM?
Rolling Kick	Fighting	60	85	15	—	Y	—

Description: 30% chance of making an opponent back off.

Name	Type	ST	ACC	PP	Range	PA?	TM/HM?
Rollout	Rock	30	90	20	1E	Y	—

Description: Consecutive Attacks for up to five turns until it misses. Increases damage with each hit. Strength of the Attack is doubled when you use Defense Curl the turn before.

Name	Type	ST	ACC	PP	Range	PA?	TM/HM?
Sacred Fire	Fire	100	95	5	1E	—	—

Description: 50% chance of Burning opponent.

| **Safeguard** | Normal | — | — | 25 | Self | N | TM20 |

Description: Over five turns, this protects against Status conditions. Effect continues when you change Pokémon.

| **Sand-Attack** | Ground | — | 100 | 15 | 1E | N | — |

Description: Lowers opponent's Accuracy by one.

| **Sandstorm** | Rock | — | — | 10 | All | N | TM37 |

Description: For five turns a sandstorm rages, damaging both players each turn. Does not effect Rock, Ground, or Steel types.

| **Sand Tomb** | Ground | 15 | 70 | 15 | 1E | N | — |

Description: Attacks for 2–5 turns. The opponent cannot flee or switch out during the Attack's duration.

| **Scary Face** | Normal | — | 90 | 10 | 1E | N | — |

Description: Lowers opponent's Defense by two.

| **Scratch** | Normal | 40 | 100 | 35 | 1E | Y | — |

Description: Normal Attack.

| **Screech** | Normal | — | 85 | 40 | 1E | N | — |

Description: Lowers the opponent Pokémon's Defense by two.

| **Secret Power** | Normal | 70 | 100 | 20 | 1E | N | TM43 |

Description: 30% chance of giving the opponent a Status condition that corresponds to the battlefield's terrain. Outside of battle, use this to open Secret Bases.

| **Seismic Toss** | Fighting | — | 100 | 20 | 1E | Y | — |

Description: Inflict damage on the opponent equal to the Pokémon's level, regardless of both Pokémon's abilities.

| **Selfdestruct** | Normal | 200 | 100 | 5 | All | N | — |

Description: Pokémon faints after using this Move.

| **Shadow Ball** | Ghost | 80 | 100 | 15 | 1E | N | — |

Description: Lowers opponent's Special Defense by one point with a 20% probability.

| **Shadow Punch** | Ghost | 60 | — | 20 | 1E | Y | TM30 |

Description: Attack that hits without fail.

| **Sheer Cold** | Ice | — | 30 | 5 | 1E | N | — |

Description: In one blow, the opponent is knocked out. Does not affect Pokémon whose level is higher than yours, while the chance of success is greater against Pokémon with a lower level.

| **Shock Wave** | Electric | 60 | — | 20 | 1E | N | TM34 |

Description: This Attack is always successful.

| **Signal Beam** | Bug | 75 | 100 | 15 | 1E | N | — |

Description: 10% chance of Confusing the opponent.

| **Silver Wind** | Bug | 60 | 100 | 5 | Self | N | — |

Description: 10% chance of raising your Attack, Defense, Speed, Special Attack, and Special Defense by one each.

| **Sing** | Normal | — | 55 | 15 | 1E | N | — |

Description: Puts opponent to Sleep.

| **Sketch** | Normal | — | — | 10 | | N | — |

Description: Replaces itself with the opponent's last Attack, Defense, Sp. Attack, Sp. Defense, and Speed by one level.

| **Skill Swap** | Psychic | — | 100 | 10 | S/E | N | TM48 |

Description: Switches innate Abilities with opponent.

Name	Type	ST	ACC	PP	Range	PA?	TM/HM?
Skull Bash	Normal	100	100	15	S/E	Y	—

Description: Raises the Pokémon's Defense by one point during Turn 1 and attacks during Turn 2.

| **Sky Attack** | Flying | 140 | 90 | 5 | 1E | N | — |

Description: Gathers strength during Turn 1, attacks during Turn 2. 30% chance of causing the opponent to Flinch.

| **Sky Uppercut** | Fighting | 85 | 90 | 15 | 1E | Y | — |

Description: More effective against Pokémon using Fly.

| **Slack Off** | Normal | — | 100 | 10 | Self | N | — |

Description: Recover 50% of your max HPs.

| **Slam** | Normal | 80 | 75 | 20 | 1E | Y | — |

Description: Normal Attack.

| **Slash** | Normal | 70 | 100 | 20 | 1E | Y | — |

Description: Easy to produce a Critical Hit.

| **Sleep Powder** | Grass | — | 75 | 15 | 1E | N | — |

Description: Puts opponent to Sleep.

| **Sleep Talk** | Normal | — | — | 10 | | N | — |

Description: Randomly uses one of the skills you possess, but only when you are asleep.

| **Sludge** | Poison | 65 | 100 | 20 | 1E | N | — |

Description: 30% chance of Poisoning the opponent.

| **Sludge Bomb** | Poison | 90 | 100 | 10 | 1E | N | TM36 |

Description: 30% chance of Poisoning the opponent.

| **Smellingsalt** | Normal | 60 | 100 | 10 | 1E | Y | — |

Description: Inflicts twice the damage if the opponent is Paralyzed, but cures that Paralysis.

| **Smog** | Poison | 20 | 70 | 20 | 1E | N | — |

Description: Infects opponent with Poison with 40% probability.

| **Smokescreen** | Normal | — | 100 | 20 | 1E | N | — |

Description: Lowers opponent's Accuracy by one point.

| **Snatch** | Dark | — | 100 | 10 | S/E | N | TM49 |

Description: If your opponent used a Move that recovers HPs or increases its Abilities, this Move steals that effect when used and applies it to you.

| **Snore** | Normal | 40 | 100 | 15 | 1E | N | — |

Description: This is only effective when the Pokémon is asleep. Makes the opponent Pokémon Flinch with a 30% possibility.

| **Softboiled** | Normal | — | 100 | 10 | — | N | — |

Description: Restores half of HP; gives 1/5 of Chansey's HP to another one of your Pokémon.

| **Solarbeam** | Grass | 120 | 100 | 10 | 1E | N | TM22 |

Description: Absorb light on Turn 1 and attack on Turn 2. Move works best during Sunny weather, while the Effect is halved when it is Raining.

| **Sonicboom** | Normal | — | 90 | 20 | 1E | N | — |

Description: Does 20 points of damage regardless of the opponent's Attack or Defense strength.

| **Spark** | Electric | 65 | 100 | 20 | 1E | Y | — |

Description: Paralyzes opponent with a 30% probability.

| **Spider Web** | Bug | — | 100 | 10 | — | N | — |

Description: Prevents escape; prevents substitutions in Trainer battles.

| **Spike Cannon** | Normal | 20 | 100 | 15 | 1E | N | — |

Description: Attacks 2–5 times in one turn.

Name	Type	ST	ACC	PP	Range	PA?	TM/HM?
Spikes	Ground	—	—	20	AE	N	—

Description: Inflicts damage whenever the opponent tries to flee or changes Pokémon. You can use this Move up to three times in a battle and the strength of the Move increases with use.

Name	Type	ST	ACC	PP	Range	PA?	TM/HM?
Spit Up	Normal	100	100	10	1E	N	—

Description: Move's power becomes greater the more the Pokémon uses Stockpile.

Spite	Ghost	—	100	10	1E	N	—

Description: Randomly decreases 2–5 PPs in the skill that the opponent last used.

Splash	Normal	—	—	40	—	N	—

Description: The Pokémon splashes about. Nothing else happens.

Spore	Grass	—	100	15	1E	N	—

Description: Puts the enemy to Sleep.

Steel Wing	Steel	70	90	25	S/E	Y	TM47

Description: Raises the Pokémon's Defense by one point with a 10% probability.

Stockpile	Normal	—	—	10	Self	N	—

Description: Use up to three times to build up the strength of the Moves Swallow and Spit Up.

Stomp	Normal	65	100	20	1E	Y	—

Description: 30% additional chance of causing the opponent to Flinch. Strength of Attack is doubled if opponent used Minimize.

Strength	Normal	80	100	15	1E	Y	HM04

Description: Normal Attack. Outside of battle, use this to move rocks.

String Shot	Bug	—	95	40	2E	N	—

Description: Lowers opponent's Speed one level.

Struggle	Normal	50	100	1	S/E	Y	—

Description: You can use this only after you use up the PPs of all of the Pokémon's other Moves. The Pokémon receives one-quarter recoil damage.

Stun Spore	Grass	—	75	30	1E	N	—

Description: Paralyzes enemy.

Submission	Fighting	80	80	25	S/E	Y	—

Description: The Pokémon takes 1/4 of the damage dealt to the opponent.

Substitute	Normal	—	—	10	Self	N	—

Description: Build the Pokémon's own alter-ego using one-quarter of the Pokémon's max HPs. Pokémon takes no damage while the substitute remains.

Sunny Day	Fire	—	—	5	All	N	TM11

Description: Raises the power of Fire-type Moves for five turns.

Super Fang	Normal	—	90	10	—	Y	—

Description: Knocks opponent's HP to half.

Superpower	Fighting	120	100	5	S/E	Y	—

Description: Lowers your Attack and Defense by one.

Supersonic	Normal	—	55	20	1E	N	—

Description: Confuses enemy.

Surf	Water	95	100	15	2E	N	HM03

Description: Normal Attack. Outside of battle, use this to Surf across the water.

Swagger	Normal	—	90	15	1E	N	—

Description: Makes the opponent Confused, but increases its Attack by two.

Swallow	Normal	—	—	10	Self	N	—

Description: You recover more HPs the more you use Stockpile.

Name	Type	ST	ACC	PP	Range	PA?	TM/HM?
Sweet Kiss	Normal	—	75	10	1E	N	—

Description: Confuses the opponent Pokémon. Also Attracts wild Pokémon.

Sweet Scent	Normal	—	100	20	2E	N	—

Description: Lowers the opponent Pokémon's Evasiveness by one point.

Swift	Normal	60	—	20	2E	N	—

Description: Attack hits without fail.

Swords Dance	Normal	—	—	30	Self	N	—

Description: Raises the Pokémon's Defense by two points.

Synthesis	Grass	—	—	5	Self	N	—

Description: Recovers HPs based on the weather.

Tackle	Normal	35	95	35	1E	Y	—

Description: Normal Attack.

Tail Glow	Bug	—	100	20	Self	N	—

Description: Raises your Special Attack by one.

Tail Whip	Normal	—	100	30	2E	N	—

Description: Lowers opponent's Defense by one point.

Take Down	Normal	90	85	20	S/E	Y	—

Description: Pokémon takes one-quarter of the damage inflicted on the opponent.

Taunt	Dark	—	100	20	1E	N	TM12

Description: In the turn after you use this Move, the opponent can no longer use Defensive Moves.

Teeter Dance	Normal	—	100	20	1A/2E	N	—

Description: Confuses the opponent. It also affects allies when fighting 2-on-2 Battles.

Teleport	Psychic	—	—	20	Self	N	—

Description: Ends the battle. Has no effect in Trainer Battles. Outside of battle, this teleports you to the last Pokémon Center you visited.

Thief	Dark	40	100	10	S/E	Y	TM46

Description: Allows the Pokémon to steal any Item that an opponent has attached to it.

Thrash	Normal	90	100	20	RE	Y	—

Description: Pokémon continues raging for 2–3 turns, then when the Effect ends, a random Pokémon in battle suffers Confusion.

Thunder	Electric	120	70	10	1E	N	TM25

Description: 30% chance of causing the opponent Paralysis. Accuracy becomes 100% when it is Raining, but drops to 50% when Sunny.

Thunderbolt	Electric	95	100	15	1E	N	TM24

Description: 10% additional Effect of Paralysis.

Thunderpunch	Electric	75	100	15	1E	Y	—

Description: 10% additional Effect of Paralysis.

Thundershock	Electric	40	100	30	1E	N	—

Description: 10% additional Effect of Paralysis.

Thunder Wave	Electric	—	100	20	1E	N	—

Description: Paralyzes the opponent Pokémon.

Tickle	Normal	—	100	20	1E	Y	—

Description: Lowers opponent's Attack and Defense by one.

Torment	Dark	—	100	15	1E	N	TM41

Description: Prevents the opponent from using the same Move twice in a row.

Toxic	Poison	—	85	10	1E	N	TM06

Description: Infects opponent with Poison. With each turn the Poison damage increases.

Name	Type	ST	ACC	PP	Range	PA?	TM/HM?
Transform	Normal	80	100	10	—	—	—
Description: Change to same Pokémon as opponent with same Attacks; all PP at 5.							
Tri Attack	Normal	80	100	10	1E	N	—
Description: 20% additional chance of either Paralysis, Burn, or Ice.							
Trick	Psychic	—	100	10	S/E	N	—
Description: The Pokémon and opponent switch the Items they are holding.							
Triple Kick	Fighting	10	90	10	—	Y	—
Description: Attacks three times in a row; damage increases each time.							
Twineedle	Bug	25	100	20	—	—	—
Description: Attacks twice in a row during a turn; 20% chance of Poisoning opponent.							
Twister	Dragon	40	100	20	2E	N	—
Description: 20% chance of causing the opponent Pokémon to Flinch. Attack doubles in strength when used against a Pokémon using Fly.							
Uproar	Normal	50	100	10	All	N	—
Description: For 2–5 turns you and your opponent cannot be affected by Sleep.							
Vicegrip	Normal	55	100	30	1E	Y	—
Description: Normal Attack.							
Vine Whip	Grass	35	100	30	—	Y	—
Description: Normal Attack.							
Vital Throw	Fighting	70	100	10	1E	Y	—
Description: Attacks second in battle; next Attack hits without fail.							
Volt Tackle	Electric	120	100	15	1E	N	—
Description: A high-level Electric attack.							
Waterfall	Water	80	100	15	1E	Y	HM07
Description: Normal Attack. Outside of battle, you can use this to climb waterfalls.							
Water Gun	Water	40	100	25	1E	N	—
Description: Normal Attack.							
Water Pulse	Water	60	100	20	1E	N	TM03
Description: 20% chance of causing the opponent Pokémon to become Confused.							
Water Sport	Water	—	100	15	All	N	—
Description: Halves the strength of Fire-type Moves.							
Water Spout	Water	150	100	5	2E	N	—
Description: The strength of the Attack lessens as your HPs dwindle.							
Weather Ball	Normal	50	100	10	1E	N	—
Description: Changes the type of the Move to correspond with the weather and doubles its power (sunny = Fire; rain = Water; hail = Ice; sandstorm = Rock).							
Whirlpool	Water	15	70	15	1E	N	—
Description: Inflicts damage for 2–5 turns. During this time the opponent Pokémon cannot flee.							
Whirlwind	Normal	—	100	20	1E	N	—
Description: Ends battle by blowing away enemy. In Trainer Battles, the opponent's Pokémon is compulsively changed.							
Will-O-Wisp	Fire	—	75	15	1E	N	—
Description: Burns the opponent.							
Wing Attack	Flying	60	100	35	1E	Y	—
Description: Normal Attack.							
Wish	Normal	—	100	10	Self	N	—
Description: At the end of the turn after using this Move, you recover 50% of your max HPs. Effect continues even if you change Pokémon.							

Name	Type	ST	ACC	PP	Range	PA?	TM/HM?
Withdraw	Water	—	—	40	—	—	—
Description: Raises your defensive power by one level.							
Wrap	Normal	15	85	20	1E	Y	—
Description: Attack for 2–5 consecutive turns. During this, enemy can't flee.							
Yawn	Normal	—	100	10	1E	N	—
Description: Makes the opponent Pokémon fall asleep at the end of the turn after you use this Move.							
Zap Cannon	Electric	100	50	5	1E	N	—
Description: If this Attacks hits, it Paralyzes the opponent Pokémon.							

PRIMA
DOUBLE-SIDED POSTER INSIDE
POKéMON
EMERALD VERSION
GAME BOY ADVANCE
POKéMON
EMERALD VERSION
GAME BOY ADVANCE
The Pokémon Company
Nintendo
PRIMA'S OFFICIAL STRATEGY GUIDE
POKéMON
COLOSSEUM
$9.99
NINTENDO GAMECUBE
POKéMON
COLOSSEUM
The Pokémon Company

PRIMA® OFFICIAL GAME GUIDE

ONLY FOR THE GC!

POSTER INSIDE

Pokémon XD
Gale of Darkness™

Easy-to-navigate maps

Snag and Purify
Shadow Pokémon

Find hidden items

PRIMA
GAMES

BASED ON A GAME
RATED BY THE
ESRB
E

The Pokémon Company

ONLY FOR

NINTENDO
GAMECUBE™

Pokémon XD
Gale of Darkness™

EVERYONE

E
ESRB

The Pokémon Company

Nintendo